Fourth Edition

PERSONAL MONEY MANAGEMENT

THOMAS E. BAILARD

DAVID L. BIEHL

RONALD W. KAISER

SCIENCE RESEARCH ASSOCIATES, INC.
Chicago, Palo Alto, Toronto
Henley-on-Thames, Sydney

A Subsidiary of IBM

Acquisition Editor	Jack Maloney
Project Editor	Gretchen Hargis
Project Designer	Carol Harris
Designer	Naomi Takigawa
Illustrator	Ralph Mapson
Technical Art	House of Graphics
Cover Photograph	Don Shapero
Composition	Computer Typesetting Services, Inc.

We wish to acknowledge the following for permission to reprint or adapt material:

Table 9-3: Copyright 1982 by Consumers Union of United States, Inc., Mount Vernon, NY 10550. Reprinted by permission from *Consumer Reports*, 1982.
Figure 1-2 © 1982 Bailard, Biehl & Kaiser Ventures, Inc., Menlo Park, Calif.
Figure 17-4: *The SRC Blue Book of 3-Trend Cycli-Graphs.* © 1982 by Securities Research Company. Charts courtesy of Securities Research Company, a Division of United Business Services Company.
Figure 18-6: *Standard N.Y.S.E. Stock Reports*, September 2, 1982. Copyright © 1982 Standard & Poor's Corp. All rights reserved.

Library of Congress Cataloging in Publication Data

Bailard, Thomas E.
  Personal money management.

  Includes bibliographical references and index.
  1. Finance, Personal.   2. Insurance.   3. Investments.
  I. Biehl, David L.   II. Kaiser, Ronald W. · III. Title.
HG179.B27   1983   332.024   82-19140
ISBN 0-574-19525-4

Contents

Preface

Because of the continued success of the previous edition of this text and the lack of an expressed need for major changes on the part of users, this fourth edition is in many respects similar to its predecessor. The chapter sequence is the same, and the end-of-chapter material consists of the same elements (vocabulary, questions, case problems, recommended reading, Chuck and Nancy Anderson case), as does also the end-of-text material (consumer agency guide, Social Security addendum, compound interest tables, and glossary). Users will find preserved the approaches and techniques of earlier editions—these prescribe and give direction, as opposed to merely describing.

The apparent similarities notwithstanding, there have been many meaningful changes and improvements in this edition. As today's economic problems continue unsolved, the financial marketplace has become more complex, and we believe that the rate of change has increased over previous periods: new tax laws annually, new insurance products, volatile inflation rates and interest rates, new home financing packages, new IRA eligibility rules, and checking accounts at savings and loans; the list goes on and on. As the financial marketplace becomes more competitive and complex and the rate of change accelerates, the consumer will need more and more objective guidance.

Among the numerous revisions and factual updates that went into the preparation of the fourth edition are the following:

- The 1981 and 1982 tax laws are incorporated, including yearly tax tables for the Economic Recovery Tax Act of 1981.

- New IRA rules and other retirement programs are discussed in Chapters 10 and 21, with investment alternatives covered in Chapter 15. (See the index for all entries on any topic.)
- The new variable mortgages and creative financing techniques are included in Chapter 14 ("Housing").
- New insurance packages are evolving as the insurance companies strive to maintain their share of the consumer/saver's dollar; discussions of these are included where appropriate.
- The development of banking opportunities through savings and loans, credit unions, and money market funds—as alternatives to the services traditionally offered by commercial banks—are discussed in Chapter 11 ("Borrowing and Banking").
- As a result of our continuing research into the consumers' need for financial services, we have put more emphasis on the psychological and life-cycle factors, as you will see particularly in the reorganization of Chapters 1 ("Introduction") and 21 ("Achieving Your Largest Financial Goal: Retirement").
- There are now sample insurance fact sheets in Chapter 3 ("Your Financial Starting Point") for use in the record-keeping systems presented there.
- In Chapter 10 ("Federal Income Taxes on Individuals"), a number of new and old ideas are pulled together under the heading of "Twelve Ways to Reduce Your Income Taxes."

We have kept the text close to its previous length by weeding out material that is obsolete or that is peripheral to the major issues being discussed and by streamlining some discussions.

We believe that this updated version will continue to appeal to instructors who wish to offer in-depth instruction in the methods and philosophy of personal money management. Instructors of undergraduate classes will continue to emphasize the basics of Units I, II, and III (e.g., budgeting, insurance, taxes, housing), whereas instructors of adult night classes will focus more on Units IV and V (investments and retirement and estate planning).

For the first-time user of the text, we shall point out the original features of the book that we believe are unique and, because of their importance to the instructor and student, deserve to be retained:

- The how-to approach is exemplified by topics such as selecting an insurance agent, settling an insurance claim, shopping for a loan, selecting a stockbroker, selecting insurance policies, selecting the best mutual fund, and negotiating a home purchase.
- Step-by-step procedures are presented for such difficult financial decisions as how much life insurance is enough, how to allocate resources to various financial goals, and how large a nest egg you will need for retirement.
- The Chuck and Nancy Anderson case problem series continues throughout the text and shows the interrelationship of all financial decisions; however, to avoid the problem of carrying errors from one chapter's analysis into the next, each case refers back only to the original situation developed in Chapters 1 and 3.
- The glossary of over 600 financial terms has been updated.

We have updated our treatment of inflation and its impact on financial decisions, but we continue to believe it should not be isolated as a major topic on its own. Our study of history indicates that periods of excessive, rising rates of inflation are relatively short-lived and are often followed by periods of deflation. Thus, we counsel a balanced approach. If people were truly to try to profit from inflation, they would borrow as much money as possible (at interest rates lower than the inflation rate) to buy all the real assets they could; yet, if deflation struck, the result would be financial bankruptcy. This is not a book that follows the fads. Instead, this book is based as much as possible on long-term, lasting principles. Although we may have sometimes failed to satisfy proponents on one side or the other of the various issues involved, we believe we have been as financially correct as possible in arriving at our conclusions.

Finally, we have continued to place a rational structure on subject matter that is commonly presented as a random series of topics. Unit I helps you get started: to establish goals, plan or switch careers, determine your present financial position, and set up a budget. Unit II shows how to protect what you have in order to provide for the financial security necessary to proceed confidently to other financial matters. Unit III helps you get more out of your income: to reduce taxes, save interest costs in borrowing, buy autos and major consumer durables, and buy and finance housing efficiently. In short, it helps you to streamline cash flow so that you have money available for your other goals. Unit IV shows how to apply the savings of Unit III to increase your total income through various common investment alternatives. Unit V wraps up with some important issues for retirement planning and estate transfer.

Altogether, we believe that this text offers a directly useful approach to solving the increasingly difficult and very real problems faced by today's family financial manager. We trust that it will serve your needs in this regard.

No text of this breadth would be possible without considerable help from many people. Our reviewers offered direction and assistance in defining the scope of the revision and in polishing the details. Among these, our thanks go to the following for review of the revised text:

Wilson Fraker (College of San Mateo)
Jerry L. Jorgensen (University of Utah)
Michael L. Murray (University of Iowa)

For technical review of certain chapters of the text we thank:

Robert N. Grant and Robert Miller (Attorneys, Ware, Fletcher and Friedenrich, Palo Alto, California)
Thomas R. Rudd and Andrew J. Reid (Ruddco Inc., Insurance Brokers, Palo Alto, California)

Also, much of the work done by reviewers of earlier editions still stands, and we continue to appreciate their help.

Additional thanks go to the helpful staff at SRA, who regularly make the extra effort to work with the time constraints imposed by our commitment to our financial advisory and investment counsel business and its clients. Chief among the SRA staff who contributed to the success of this edition (as well as editions one and three) is

Gretchen Hargis, who continues to edit to her personal high standards for readability, consistency, and accuracy of detail. We also continue to value the enthusiasm and knowledgeable help of our sponsoring editor, Jack Maloney. Unfortunately, we do not always get to see those who work behind the scenes, but among those who worked directly with us, we appreciate the assistance of Arthur A. Micheletti, Katherine Lennihan, John R. Hayes, Therese Z. Jordan, and Rebekah M. Trotter—all of Bailard, Biehl & Kaiser—and Bernice Herkenhoff.

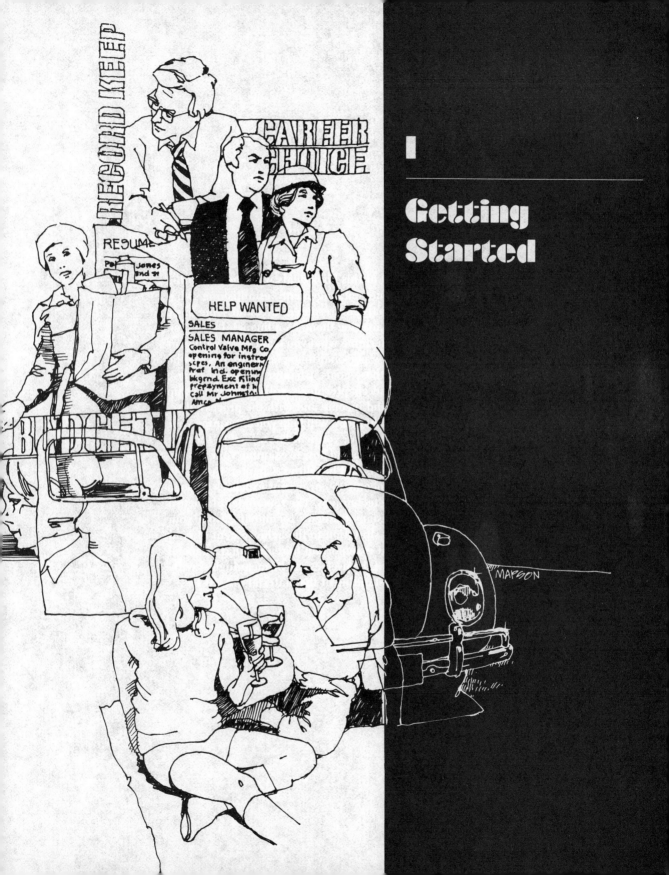

Getting Started

The opening unit of this book deals with the beginning concerns of money management: establishing what one's financial goals and resources are, and some basic techniques for managing them. As a financial manager, you must first determine what you want to do with your resources and how personal financial strategies can be used to achieve these goals. Chapter 1 discusses these issues. The second chapter deals with the relationship between career and income and with the process of selecting a career. Chapter 3 will help you determine your financial starting point; you will learn how to set up a record-keeping system and how to examine your income and expenses, assets and liabilities. Chapter 4 will help you direct your income to cover your expenses through proper budgeting techniques. The remainder of the text will help you design strategies for moving from your present financial situation to the achievement of your goals. However, it is important to realize that financial strategies in and of themselves can be meaningless without a good understanding of the material in Unit I.

1

Introduction

This book is intended to develop your skills in managing your money. How motivated you are to acquire these skills will depend on how important money and the things it can buy are to you. Obviously, their importance varies from person to person. If you are like the great majority of us who must work, two realities will ensure that money and its effective use are of more than just passing interest. First, consider the amount of time you will devote to earning a living if you are a full-time worker. Assuming you work a 40-hour week 48 weeks a year for 40 years, your lifetime commitment is 76,800 hours! For 50 years, it is 96,000 hours. Even the hours spent by a part-time worker—say, 25,000 to 48,000—are still substantial. If you are not the primary breadwinner in your family, your life will still be dramatically influenced by the time commitment that person must make to earning a living.

Second, consider the amount of money you will have to make spending-and-saving decisions about in a lifetime. Again, if you earn an average of $20,000 a year for 40 years, your total earnings are $800,000. Assuming an average annual inflation rate of 5 percent, the amount balloons to $2,400,000! For 50 years, the respective amounts are $1,000,000 and $3,000,000! Thus, no matter how you feel about money, it can seldom be ignored. To gain from the time and effort you commit to earning money, you must be able to manage it skillfully as well as earn it.

This chapter will focus on the two primary elements of the personal money management process: you and the environment in which you must function effectively as a personal money manager.

Let's Begin with You

Initially you should understand where money fits into your life, the objectives of personal money management, some of the forces affecting your decision making, and your role as personal money manager.

WHERE MONEY FITS IN

Everyone has personal assets, financial resources, and goals. Personal assets include natural talents and abilities—such as intelligence, muscle coordination, and creativity—as well as skills and knowledge acquired through education and experience. Financial resources, which result from using personal assets, include both income (e.g., salary, interest, dividends, rents, royalties) and assets (e.g., savings, stocks and bonds, real estate, business interests, mutual funds). Goals are what people want to achieve for themselves and their families. By this definition, a person can have among his or her goals the provision of necessities such as food and shelter. Some goals can be achieved mainly through personal efforts: respect for one's self and for others, a happy family life, job advancement. Other goals require the use of both money and personal efforts: food, shelter, clothing, education, leisure time, certain luxuries. Figure 1-1 shows how personal assets, financial resources, and goals are related to each other.

An individual can use his or her personal assets to achieve personal goals. For example, someone who wants an outlet for her singing ability might join a local singing group. Personal assets can also be used to earn income at a job, thus creating financial resources, which can in turn be used to reach goals. This application of financial resources to goal achievement is known as money management and will be of primary concern in this text. Personal assets and financial resources do not simply end in the fulfillment of goals, however. Out of that fulfillment may come a recycling back to personal assets and financial resources. For example, a person who applies personal assets to win a job promotion will probably increase her or his financial resources through a pay increase. The higher level of skills acquired through the promotion will probably enhance personal assets as well.

An extended example should help make the framework in Figure 1-1 meaningful to you. Gary has excellent muscle coordination and strength, and he enjoys playing football. While in college, he decided to become a professional football quarterback, but he also worked at being a good student. Gary's personal assets would therefore include better than average muscle control and intelligence as well as the acquired skills of a quarterback and a student. Gary signed with a pro team and thus achieved one of his goals. He also went to work as an insurance agent in his spare time, hoping eventually to set up his own agency so that he would have an income long after he

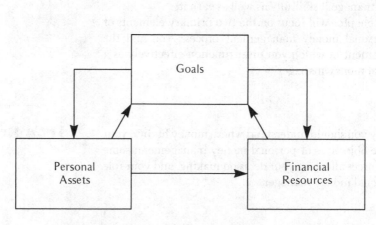

FIGURE 1-1
Relationships between
personal assets, financial
resources, and goals.

retired from professional football. In these ways Gary used his personal assets to create an income and increase his financial resources. When Gary accumulated substantial cash, he had to decide how best to distribute it to achieve his goals. His football goals could be achieved through practice, but many of his other goals (a house, car, insurance, travel, investments) could be achieved only through effective utilization of his financial resources—through money management.

MONEY MANAGEMENT

The objective of money management is to achieve those goals that can best be satisfied with money. If you are to know what you want and how to get it with what you have, you must know how to set financial goals and how to apply money management strategies to achieve them.

Types of Personal Financial Goals

Before we can discuss how to set financial goals, it is helpful to clarify the various types. Goals can be grouped according to the *time* necessary to accomplish them or the time until they will occur. For example, building a college education fund takes several years of saving by parents, and the fund itself is not needed until the child reaches college age. Such a goal is usually long term; others (e.g., buying a new car) may be more immediate.

Goals can also be grouped by *type of purchase.* Purchases such as vacations and entertainment are termed *consumables;* i.e., they retain no lasting economic value, although the lingering memories they provide can greatly enrich one's life. Homes, cars, and appliances are examples of *durables*, as they usually retain some economic value after the owner ceases to use them.

Goals can also be differentiated by the *type of need* satisfied. For example, food, shelter, and clothing are common *tangible* needs; status and peace of mind are much more *intangible* but often of equal importance.

Finally, goals can be categorized by the *frequency* with which they occur, the range being from continuous (bringing home the bacon) to once in a lifetime (college education—one per child, one hopes).

Setting Financial Goals

People work and earn money in order to have food, shelter, and clothing. Because these continuously occurring goals are so ordinary, they may be overlooked in a plan for good money management. Other goals are not easily identified, perhaps because they are bound up in such intangibles as personal values and philosophies that are not easy to explain. Therefore, it is very important that you have a procedure to help you think about using the just discussed categories and put your financial goals in perspective. Personal financial development will probably be aimless and awkward until you decide what your goals are.

Jerry Hennessy resisted everything that smacked of a structured lifestyle. He considered himself a free spirit, a self-image made possible in part by a modest inheritance from his grandfather. Jerry's sister, Jackie, was also named in her grandfather's will. She did not sneer, however, at the virtues of goal setting. She used her inheritance to start a catering business. Five years after their grandfather's death, Jackie had achieved her goal of owning a thriving business and Jerry found himself working for her serving canapes.

The process of personal financial goal setting should best proceed as follows:

1. Consider who should be included in the process. Most good planners will tell you to include anyone who will be substantially involved in the process or affected by achievement of the goals. This description would certainly include your spouse (and his or her own goals) and your children if they are old enough to have goals of their own and to participate meaningfully in setting goals.

2. Simply list your goals and those of other family members, without regard to what the goals are or how they fit together or any other consideration. This nonjudgmental approach will probably cause you to identify about three-quarters of your goals. As you proceed, you will find it easier to list those goals that are often difficult to articulate initially.

3. To refine your master list, begin by placing the goals from that list in the categories shown in Figure 1-2: term (from shortest to longest), frequency (from continuous to once in a lifetime), purchase (from consumable to durable), and purpose (from tangible to intangible). Be sure to observe the sequential nature of each of the categories. For example, a goal to be achieved next year should be placed higher in the term list than one not due until 1990.

   As you proceed, you will notice that certain goals contain both extremes of a category. For example, a home may be tangible as shelter and yet intangible as security or status; therefore, you might best place it midway in the purpose list. Furthermore, certain goals can be included in more than one list. For example, a home is a durable purchase that might be made only two or three times in a lifetime, the first time perhaps five years hence; therefore, "home" would appear in several columns, as shown in Figure 1-2.

   The exercise of figuring out what yours and your family's goals are, plus where and on how many lists each should appear, prepares you for the next step, setting goal priorities.

4. Ranking your goals is an inexact science and your priorities will doubtless change over time. Nevertheless, having some sense of your goal priorities is better than having none at all. The resources you will be bringing to bear to achieve various goals are limited. Therefore, it is very important to ensure that those goals most dear to you are being given the best chance of being realized. You will also want to review your priorities as you proceed through this text, gaining a better insight into which goals are by their nature more readily achievable than others.

5. Once you have developed your goals priority list, the next step is to estimate what it will cost in today's dollars to achieve each goal. This estimate should be placed to the right of each goal in your list.

6. Finally, you are ready to fill out your Financial Goals Achievement Chart, a filled-in sample of which is shown in Figure 1-3.

As a result of this exercise, you will probably become more aware of those things you have long wanted. You may also discover some new goals. With these in mind, you are ready to find out what your financial resources are. In Chapter 3, you will

NAME(S) *Catherine and Robert Snow*

DATE *January 1983*

PERSONAL FINANCIAL GOALS

TERM	FREQUENCY	PURCHASE	PURPOSE
Shortest	Continuous	Consumable	Tangible
Emergency fund $4,000 Car $7,000 Travel $1,000	Emergency fund $4,000 Car $7,000	Travel $1,000	Car $7,000 Jewelry $500
Home $90,000	Home $90,000		Home $90,000
Jewelry $500		Emergency fund $4,000 Car $7,000	Emergency fund $4,000 Travel $1,000
Retirement	Jewelry $500 Retirement	Jewelry $500 Home $90,000	Retirement
Longest	Once in a Lifetime	Durable	Intangible

learn how to assess these resources. This assessment is necessary so that, as you read further in this text, you will see what financial resources can be used (and how) to help you achieve your goals.

FIGURE 1-2
A sample worksheet for analyzing financial goals.

Your Changing Financial Life Cycle

As mentioned earlier, your financial goals and activities will change as your life proceeds. Table 1-1 has been developed to demonstrate some of the financial decisions and actions that occur during certain periods and under certain circumstances of a person's life. It is by no means all-inclusive. Also, activities (e.g., buy or rent living quarters) are shown only in the age bracket (e.g., 18–28) in which they are most likely to occur first. This placement is not meant to imply that these activities can be reasonably expected to occur only once.

NAME(S) *Catherine and Robert Snow*

DATE *January 1983*

FINANCIAL GOALS ACHIEVEMENT CHART

Goals	Projected Expenditures by Year (unadjusted for inflation)							
	19**83**	19**84**	19**85**	19**86**	19**87**	19**88**	19**89**	19**90**
Emergency fund	$2,000	$2,000						
Car		$7,000						
Travel			$1,000					
Jewelry							$500	
Home down payment				$18,000				
Retirement	$500	$1,000	$2,000	$2,000	$2,000	$2,000	$2,000	$2,000
TOTAL	$2,500	$10,000	$3,000	$20,000	$2,000	$2,500	$2,000	$2,000

FIGURE 1-3
Sample financial goals and
projected expenditures
by year.

MOTIVATING FORCES

At least three forces affect how you make your choices concerning the use of money: emotions, values, and advertising. These motivating forces are important for us to discuss at the outset, even though a thorough treatment of each is outside the scope of this book.

Emotions

Observations of many people's behavior toward their financial circumstances indicate that the emotions of fear and greed predominate. Behavior based on fear occurs at three levels: within the individual, between the individual and associates, and between the individual and society. For example, an individual may unconsciously have a feeling of low self-worth; the fear of consciously confronting this attitude may cause the person to buy material goods in order to gain personal esteem. Another individual may have a great fear of being controlled by others (such as family members) and therefore tightly control the family purse strings in order to stave off the feared situation. Finally, during periods of great international economic uncertainty, some people may feel safer having their financial resources in gold.

Examples of how greed affects one's behavior with money also abound. Many people take undue risks on the slim chance of considerable gain. Lotteries, gambling casinos, and race tracks all thrive on this emotion. Many investments, when subjected to close scrutiny, are nothing more than irrational gambles.

TABLE 1-1

Sample Goals and Activities of Personal Financial Life Cycle

Age	Student	Single Childless	Single Parent	Married Childless	Married Parents
			WORKING		
18-28	Get degree. Rent living quarters. Establish credit. Buy car/appliances. Obtain/pay back student loans. Budget.	Start career. Rent/buy living quarters. Establish credit. Buy car/appliances. Budget.	Start career. Rent/buy living quarters. Establish credit. Obtain child care. Buy car/appliances. Budget.	Start career(s). Rent/buy living quarters. Establish credit. Buy car(s)/appliances. Budget.	Start career(s). Rent/buy living quarters. Establish credit. Buy car(s)/appliances. Obtain child care. Budget.
25-45		Refine career. Make decisions re insurance, tax preparation and planning. Write will.	Refine career. Make decisions re insurance, tax preparation and planning. Build up college fund. Write will.	Refine career. Make decisions re insurance, tax preparation and planning. Write wills.	Refine career. Make decisions re insurance, tax preparation and planning. Build up college fund. Write wills.
45-65		Culminate career. Build up retirement fund. Buy second home. Travel more.	Culminate career. Build up retirement fund. Buy second home. Travel more. Buy children car(s).	Culminate career. Build up retirement fund. Buy second home. Travel more.	Culminate career. Build up retirement fund. Buy second home. Travel more. Buy children car(s).
			RETIRED		
55 on		Draft final estate documents. Select retirement benefit options.	Draft final estate documents. Make financial gifts to children. Select retirement benefit options.	Draft final estate documents. Ensure finances of surviving spouse. Select retirement benefit options.	Draft final estate documents. Make financial gifts to children. Ensure finances of surviving spouse. Select retirement benefit options.

Values

Values are fundamental concepts that influence a person's behavior, such as family love, personal success, security, emotional maturity, and personal independence. They usually go deeper than interests (such as hobbies) and attitudes (such as political affiliations).

Each person has a value hierarchy, whereby some values are more important than others. One person may value security, for example, over personal ambition and so choose a career path that produces few anxious moments but also few challenges. Another person may value family association over personal independence, putting off the day for moving out on his or her own.

Unlike emotions, which come from inside a person, values are both internally and externally derived—from the meeting of each person's internal makeup with external reality. It is impossible to identify precisely the sources of one's values. What is important is recognizing that forces from both directions are at work.

Values change over time. What a girl values when she is 10 years old may well be different from what she values 10 years later. As a person grows, peer acceptance is likely to replace family support in importance; then personal achievement may become paramount and, in turn, be superseded by the establishment of varied personal relationships.

The groups an individual identifies with provide the chief external force on the development of personal values. These groups can be classified into three broad categories:

- Demographic—groups based on characteristics such as age, education, family background, income level, occupation, race, and sex
- Geographic—groups based on locale such as city, county, state, and country
- Psychographic—groups based on personality characteristics such as ambition, dependence on others, and social interaction

For example, a man who lives in the South and belongs to a large family that has been in the same town for generations will respond much differently to his company's decision to transfer him to Seattle than would a woman whose father had a career in the military.

There are several important features of identification groups:

1. Identification groups usually establish broad parameters, not exact modes, of approved behavior. For example, college students value travel, but not all of them must travel to Paris to gain peer acceptance.
2. The range of approved behavior varies from one identification group to another. For example, there may be conflict between the values of one's peers and those of one's parents.
3. The groups that one identifies with change over time. A college student may be growing away from heavy reliance on the approval of parents, in need of peer approval, and just beginning to consider the approval of broader social groups such as political parties or communities.

People often make financial choices that are calculated to gain positive feedback and avoid negative feedback from the groups they identify with. For example, a particular college student may choose to spend her money traveling abroad or attending a rock concert because such activities are important to her peer group; her parents, however, may become very upset over such choices, preferring that she spend the time on her studies and the money on academic supplies.

Advertising

Advertising seeks to influence our financial choices by channeling our emotional needs and values toward a particular product or service. For example, the fear of death may cause some people not to write wills, but it sells a lot of life insurance. The need to consume today rather than tomorrow, or to do so at a higher level than one's neighbor, is greatly responsible for the rise in the use of borrowing, occasionally to the detriment of the borrower and frequently to the benefit of the lender. Many people also need to derive entertainment, excitement, or romance from their financial choices. Marketing strategies for personal financial products or services often stress the excitement or the romantic value of these commodities.

The Importance of Self-Knowledge

Consider for a moment a recent financial choice of yours in which the emotional or social motivation was quite apparent to you. Then think of financial choices you have made in which your emotions or values were more hidden. What was the motivation for these choices? Perhaps you thought you bought your coat, for example, because of its functional value as a protection against the cold, but further probing may convince you that you bought it because you perceived it to be more stylish than one owned by a friend of yours. As you watch your motivations with regard to money, you should become adept at recognizing the emotional and social needs you bring to bear on each financial decision.

This self-knowledge is very important. It can enable you to choose financial alternatives that are of real value to you and to avoid buying illusions, perhaps of romance or excitement. You might be motivated, for example, to invest in a played-out mine in Montana just for the thrill of being a part of the Old West when visiting the mine; perhaps this need could be more appropriately fulfilled at a fraction of the cost by spending a week's vacation at a dude ranch. Many such activities are better sources of entertainment than are financial products or services.

Being aware of which groups you identify with can be a first step to greater awareness of your values. Exploration of this type will undoubtedly uncover a subtle but substantial area of conflict: where your internally derived values are at odds with those of various identification groups. Most ill-conceived financial choices are made when the consumer is unaware of a conflict between internal and external values or between the values of several identification groups. Often a financial action is taken in an attempt to ameliorate the conflict. For example, parents may want their teen-age daughter to continue riding a bike to school for economy's sake, but her peer group values fancy cars; if she buys a used compact car, she probably won't be satisfying either group and the conflict will continue.

Emotions and values vary from one person to another, and so developing an awareness of them requires personal investigation. Observing and exploring your actions and motivations is a lifelong process. Do not be discouraged by the potential length of this inquiry. It will be very interesting to see how your emotions and values continually influence your behavior, perceptions, interests, and attitudes.

This text will concentrate on helping you to identify the real financial value to be gained through personal money management. Of course, this is only half the battle, but it is unrealistic to attempt to cover all the variations of emotional behavior that relate to money and impossible to identify which social values are most appropriate. These tasks are best left to you, but don't be misled into thinking that such considerations are less important than the technical and practical ones that follow; they definitely are not.

YOU AS MONEY MANAGER

As a money manager, you should be concerned with the process, functions, and strategies that will enable you to achieve your goals.

The Process

Figure 1-4 illustrates the process of money management: using financial resources to reach goals. Money managers most commonly receive funds from their jobs and investments. They then decide how much of this income should be allocated to normal living expenses, how much to the accumulation of fixed assets, and how much to savings for future goals (investment assets). This last use is simply a tempo-

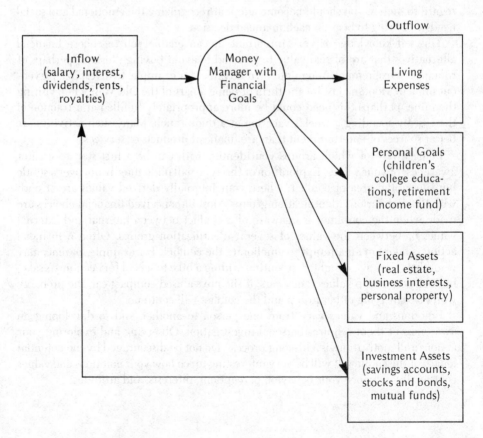

FIGURE 1-4
The money management
process.

rary diversion of some financial resources so that they will increase the total inflow and be available to reach a goal at a later time.

A money manager is distinguished from a money spender by the manner in which goals are reached. The money manager, on the one hand, carefully plans and forecasts goals and then controls both the inflow and the outflow of financial resources to achieve them. In other words, he or she budgets expenses and income needs. A money spender, on the other hand, spends his or her paycheck until it is used up. When faced with a major goal, this person has not planned ahead to achieve it and so must borrow money, probably at high interest rates.

The money spender's philosophy toward spending is "How much can I buy with the income I have?" The money manager's philosophy is "How much income, whether from investments or earnings, do I need to buy what I really want?" This distinction is crucial to personal money management. As a money manager, you control your economic environment rather than being controlled by it.

The Functions

To be an effective money manager, you must be able to plan, direct, and control.

planning   The primary responsibility of money managers is to plan. They vary the size of their financial resources according to their goals rather than varying their goals according to the size of their financial resources. Money managers must first determine their goals, as you have begun to do. To achieve these, they must determine how much of their financial resources should be routed to living expenses, how much to fixed assets, and how much to investments. They can then plan investment strategies and even career choices to provide the proper inflow of financial resources to reach these goals. There are two steps to the planning function: planning the amount and direction of the outflow and planning the source and timing of the inflow.

Planning the outflow of financial resources involves goal setting. You have already begun to think about the types of goals you want to achieve with your financial resources and to list those that are possible. Planning the inflow calls for farsighted money management. To be financially successful over the years, you have to manage your money during the weeks and months. This can best be accomplished through budgeting. By making sure you do not consistently spend all that you earn, you can begin building up your financial resources. No matter how modest they may seem at first, small savings plans can grow into bigger plans. This growth is far more likely when saving is established as a habit early.

The objective of planning is to match your total outflow with your total inflow while protecting the safety of your financial resources and preserving the security of your economic environment. If you carefully follow the strategies outlined in this text, you should be successful in meeting this objective.

directing   There are two aspects of this function. The first involves identifying individuals to assist you in carrying out your financial plans. The second phase involves evaluating how these plans are proceeding and the value of the assistance you are receiving from those individuals. If you are initiating an insurance program,

you must select an insurance agent and company. If you are planning to borrow money, you must seek out the proper lending source. If you are beginning an investment program, you must choose the most appropriate broker, lawyer, or banker. In other words, to direct as a money manager, you must be able to communicate your goals and strategies to the most appropriate individual or organization that will help put them into effect.

The following chapters will help you (1) decide what you want before approaching the people you need, (2) identify which people can help you get what you want, (3) learn the language and the concepts that will help you communicate your needs effectively, and (4) evaluate the performance of the professionals you hire. We will discuss the duties and responsibilities commonly rendered by various business services. We will advise you of the qualities to look for in a stockbroker, insurance agent, lender, creditor, and real estate agent. The basic background you will gain from this book should enable you to evaluate the performance of those selling you their services. Most salespersons know their product or service better than you do. Therefore, it is very important for you to have an independently derived source of expertise that will enable you to look past the sales pitch and judge the proposal on its merits and appropriateness for you.

controlling No one has the foresight to be able to plan his or her entire life's financial future at one sitting. As we stated earlier in this chapter, certain values change over time. Therefore, what is financially important to you now may change as you grow older. The money manager who is in control knows when to rethink old plans and prepare new ones. The control function should link past financial decisions to current desires and ambitions. As a money manager, you should beware of executing plans to achieve goals that no longer exist. For example, the life insurance you bought 15 years ago may have become either unnecessary or inadequate or may have been a poor choice even then. Make it a habit to review and revise your financial programs. Perhaps you should review your insurance program prior to each renewal date and your investment portfolio every month.

Your ability to control depends not only on your current level of knowledge about your emotional needs and value structure, but also on the currentness of your information. Insurance companies are constantly issuing more comprehensive policies and developing more sophisticated rating schemes. Investment yields are always in flux. Federal and local regulations are changing in many areas; this change might signal both good and bad. You must keep on top of a continuous information stream. This course should help you assimilate information in a usable form. You should seek information from the people serving you. Develop relationships of confidence and trust with them and let them know about changes in your financial condition.

The Strategies

The strategies involved in money management may be grouped into three categories: protecting what you have, getting the most out of your income, and increasing your total income. To protect what you have, you must insure against financial calamities such as losing the dollar value of your property, having to pay big medical bills or liability suits, and being unable to provide for your family because of a disability or death. To get the most out of your income, you must direct it to cover your expenses and avoid unnecessary drains. To increase your total income, you must make investments that agree with your goals.

To be successful as a money manager, it is important to have a good understanding of the environment in which you must operate. The remainder of this chapter is devoted to discussing the various participants in this environment, the various services that have been springing up in recent years to help you manage your financial affairs, and inflation—a pervasive economic condition that affects most personal financial decisions.

The Personal Financial Environment

THE PARTICIPANTS

The most obvious participant is you as a consumer and income producer. Earlier in this chapter we addressed the process, functions, and strategies you should follow. Much of the rest of this book will provide you with detailed information to be used in carrying out these activities.

The second category of participants is the business community. Many of the employment opportunities that enable you to become an income producer originate here. Of course, career opportunities also exist in other areas such as government, medicine, and education. The business community is somewhat unique, however, in that it provides most of the products and services you consume. Within the services sector, the financial services have been burgeoning. Nowhere was this more evident than in the merger of several large organizations: Bache and Prudential (securities and insurance), Shearson and American Express (securities and financial services) and Dean Witter and Sears (securities and retailing) in the early 1980s. Their common goal was to offer you as a consumer and income producer as many financial service alternatives through one organization as possible. We will discuss how you should approach these organizations and utilize them in the next section of this chapter.

Finally, there is the government sector. A complete treatment of all its functions is more appropriately handled in other courses. Our purpose here is to identify government's main areas of impact on your personal finances.

1. Federal, state, and local governments currently provide approximately 17 percent of the nation's employment opportunities.
2. Taxes can be levied on you by all three levels. Therefore, when tax laws are changed, as they are frequently, your financial strategies must shift also.
3. Goverments regulate many of the ways the business sector relates to the consumer sector. Sometimes true protection for the consumer from abusive business practices occurs. Other times, we are all burdened with ineffective bureaucratic "red tape" that benefits no one (with the possible exception of attorneys and accountants) and increases the cost of goods and services for everyone.
4. The federal government also attempts to eliminate the extremes of economic

activity: booms and depressions. In the course of this and other government activities, it has become a major cause of inflation, as will be discussed in the last part of this chapter.

It is obvious to most observers that governments have fallen short of our recent expectations for improvements in our national lifestyle, including our personal finances. Indeed, government intervention has changed the rules of the ballgame so frequently and in such complex ways that a whole new service sector, "the financial planning industry," has developed to "help" you through the maze created by government regulations and the array of options created by financial institutions.

WHERE TO TURN FOR HELP

Before discussing your alternatives for assistance in optimizing your personal financial resources, one critical distinction should be understood. This pertains to the motives why any individual or organization is willing to help you with your personal finances. Currently the vast majority of "financial plannners" are merely glorified salespersons of various financial products (e.g., insurance, securities, tax shelters, annuities, trusts). In such circumstances, the salesperson's compensation is derived primarily from commissions paid by the financial organization sponsoring the product. Because this compensation does not come from you, the customer/client, the salesperson's economic self-interest and yours are not necessarily aligned. The stories of ill-advised recommendations to the unwitting are legion under such circumstances.

Your alternative is assistance from individuals or organizations that are compensated solely from fees they charge their clients. Your authors pride themselves on having founded one such organization, Bailard, Biehl & Kaiser, Inc. There is an additional cost for such assistance, however. Because "fee only" professionals do not take commissions for products they might recommend, they must charge fees "over and above" the commissions you will be charged by the financial organizations that are recommended to you by pure advisors. The main justification for paying these additional fees is the assurance that you are receiving a professional's advice about what financial alternatives are most appropriate for your circumstances versus the possibility that the financial products salesperson is advising you to buy certain products merely to line his or her pockets with commissions.

Table 1-2 outlines your alternatives for personal financial assistance. As you can see, your alternatives and considerations are many; therefore, it behooves you to research several alternatives before making your selection.

When doing this research, you should ascertain:

1. What is the prospective advisor's main area of expertise? CPAs tend to focus on tax issues, attorneys on legal and/or tax issues, investment counselors on investments, and so on.
2. What training and amount of experience does he or she have?
3. How will he or she be compensated for the financial planning phase? What will this cost be?
4. Does he or she have the capability to assist you in implementing your plan's recommendations and what will be the additional cost of this service?

TABLE 1-2

Alternatives for Personal Financial Assistance

Aspects	Do It Yourself			Hire Someone Else						
		Courses		Commission Compensated				Fee Compensated		
	Self-Help Books	Publicly Sponsored	Privately Sponsored	Investments only	Insurance only	Tax planning and shelters	Full financial planning	Investments only	Wills, trusts, and tax planning	Full financial planning
Areas Covered	Ranges from specific topics (e.g., real estate investments) to general survey treatments			Investments only	Insurance only	Tax planning and shelters	Full financial planning	Investments only	Wills, trusts, and tax planning	Full financial planning
Who Does It	Private authors	School faculty or local practitioners	Local practitioners	Securities salespersons	Insurance salespersons	Salespersons, some attorneys, and CPAs	Generally securities and insurance salespersons	Investment advisors and counselors	Attorneys and CPAs	Independent individuals and organizations, bankers, and CPAs
What It Costs	$5-$25	$0-$100	$50-$500	Nothing *except* commissions generated from products purchased as a result of financial recommendations made				$100-$2,000	$500-$10,000	$1,000-$10,000
Level of Service	Nil	Typical classroom experience		Depends on amount of commissions generated				Ranges from newsletter or computerized package to 100-page customized analyses and recommendations plus several meetings		
When Is It Appropriate	For people who have the time, inclination, and ability to do it themselves			For people with straightforward, often single-issue circumstances who are not concerned with the potential conflicts of interest				For people with more complex circumstances who need unbiased, broad-perspective counsel		

© 1982 Bailard, Biehl & Kaiser Ventures Inc., Menlo Park, CA

5. What type of clients are typically served?
6. What do local bankers, CPAs, attorneys, and other financial advisers think of this prospective financial planner?
7. Are you comfortable sharing your personal financial circumstances with this individual?
8. What depth of other expertise is represented by any other individuals affiliated with this person? How might they assist you also?

Given the complexity, array of choices, and changing environment that confronts you, obtaining some expertise is well-advised. Deciding from whom to obtain it requires careful analysis.

INFLATION/DEFLATION

One major element of the financial environment with which you will probably have to cope continuously is the changing value of money itself. When it takes more and more money to buy the same good or service, that is *inflation*. For example, if the cost of living increases 25 percent over a five-year period, then it will take $1.25 at the end of this period to buy a widget that sold for $1 at the beginning of the period. Conversely, the purchasing power of the dollar has fallen to 80 percent of its original power ($1.00 \div 1.25$). This means that while $1 bought one widget five years ago, it now buys only 80 percent of a widget.

If the widget manufacturer has developed a method of making widgets more efficiently (therefore, they cost less to produce or sell), then the price of widgets may not rise as fast as the overall cost of living. Alternatively, if the consuming public demands a more sophisticated or complex widget than the original one, the quality improvements may cause the cost of a widget to rise even faster than the cost of living. Neither of these instances involves changes in the value of money. Therefore, when you discover that the price of something has shot up 20 percent since you last purchased it, remember that part of the increase could be because you are now buying an improved good or service that might have cost even more had the manufacturer not developed a more efficient way to produce and sell it.

The opposite of inflation is *deflation*, in which the value of money increases. The widget now costs $.80 instead of $1.00. Because periods of inflation are much more prevalent in our economy, however, the remainder of this discussion will be directed toward the causes of inflation and its measurement. (For a historical perspective on inflation, see the comparisons in Table 1-3.)

Causes of Inflation

Economists have diverse opinions about what causes inflation. Probably there are several different but interrelated causes, some more important than others at any given time. Here are several of the more generally recognized causes of inflation.

too much money in circulation If the economy neither grows nor declines during one year while the supply of money available increases, there will be more money at year-end competing to buy the same level of goods and services. As elementary economics teaches us, when supply (of goods and services) remains fixed

TABLE 1-3

Some Examples of the Effect of Inflation on Food Prices

Commodity and Amount	Average U.S. Retail Price				
	1920	*1950*	*1960*	*1976*	*1982*
White bread (1 lb. loaf)	$ .12	$ .14	$ .20	$ .35	$ .49
Sugar (1 lb.)	.19	.10	.12	.24	.32
Chuck roast (1 lb.)	.26	.62	.62	.97	1.68
Cheese (1 lb.)	.42	.52	.69	.87	1.49
Coffee (1 lb.)	.47	.79	.75	1.87	2.43
Eggs (1 doz.)	.68	.60	.57	.84	.96
Potatoes (15 lb.)	.95	.69	1.08	2.19	2.89

Source: U.S. Department of Labor, *Handbook of Labor Statistics,* 1977 (Bulletin 1966). Latest figures based on West Coast supermarket prices.

while demand (as reflected by having more money to spend) increases, prices must rise, resulting in one form of inflation.

The source of more money is the Federal Reserve System (FRS), which will be discussed further in Chapter 12. One principal responsibility of this federal agency is to monitor the rate of growth in the nation's money supply. When a greater supply of money is deemed advisable by the governors of the Federal Reserve Board, new currency is printed and additional deposits are created for the commercial banking system. If the governors err in their judgment and increase the money supply at a rate faster than the rate of growth in the economy can accommodate, inflation may result.

federal government spending   Because the federal budget represents such a significant portion of our nation's annual economic output, it is possible for the government to increase economic activity by increasing its own level of spending. Given the trauma of high unemployment (almost 25 percent at one point) and economic depression that characterized this country during most of the 1930s, maximum economic growth and a high level of employment have been national priorities since then. Congress and the president have been willing to sacrifice price stability and lower prices to attain these two goals. Many federal spending programs are created, in part, to stimulate economic growth and employment.

Not all nations share our priorities, and indeed ours may currently be undergoing some change. For example, Germany's most significant economic trauma was the galloping inflation that engulfed that country in the early 1920s. Toward the end of that period, literally wheelbarrows of German marks were required to purchase a loaf of bread. You can imagine the attraction of gold as a store of wealth while the value of the German currency plummeted during such skyrocketing inflation. As a consequence, German economic priorities in recent decades have stressed price stability and a strong currency. Given the dramatic increases in inflation that occurred in the United States in the late 1960s and 1970s, some observers have argued that we are now more willing to tolerate a slower rate of economic growth and a higher rate of unemployment in exchange for a more stable price level.

Government spending or deficits to stimulate economic activity, although often very valuable, can produce inflation. When the federal spending or deficit level cannot be entirely covered with the existing money supply, the FRS must create money at a faster rate to cover the difference. Hence, an inflationary syndrome is started.

structural considerations   Certain elements of the business and/or labor sectors of the economy have become so powerful that they dictate wage and price levels without regard for basic market conditions of supply and demand. In some industries, one firm may be so large that all other firms follow that company's pricing policy or risk going out of business. A union that has a monopoly on certain types of workers may be able to win higher wages for its members because the corporations involved do not have the financial strength to survive a shutdown by strike; or the corporations may know that they can pass along the wage increases to their customers in the form of higher prices. If a few corporations dominate an industry, and consumers have few options for shopping elsewhere, the price increases will be accepted, at least until other alternatives become available.

shortages   In the 1970s an old form of inflation was resurrected—inflation caused by shortages. When the supply of cattle was restricted, the price of beef increased significantly. Similarly, when the supply of gas, coffee, sugar, housing, silver, and lumber became tight, their prices also increased.

deterioration in value of currency   In terms of international trade, a deteriorating currency can raise the cost of living for the consumer. For example, if inflation in the United States causes the dollar to deteriorate relative to the yen, then it takes more American dollars to buy an imported Japanese product. Thus, the cost of living is escalated in yet another way.

Projecting the Future

To structure your personal finances to deal with inflation, you will need to make some assumptions about what inflation will be in the future. Prices have been rising for as long as most of us can remember. The temptation is to assume that they will continue to do so.

The assumption that economic events will proceed as they have in the immediate past may well produce some wrong forecasts and, in turn, some wrong strategies. It is true that the past can be a valuable teacher, but we may need to take a longer view of it than just the time within our individual memories.

Figure 1-5 summarizes periods of generally rising and falling consumer prices over the past 175 years in the United States. As you can see, the cycles of rising and falling prices varied in duration from 14 to 35 years. A Russian economist, Nicholas Kondratieff, hypothesized that wholesale prices rise and fall in long-term economic cycles lasting 50 to 55 years. If you accept his theory, the U.S. economy is due for a major break in prices sometime in the 1980s.

Some researchers have found even longer-term cycles of inflation. Using a 700-year price index, David Warch and Lawrence Minard (in the November 15, 1976,

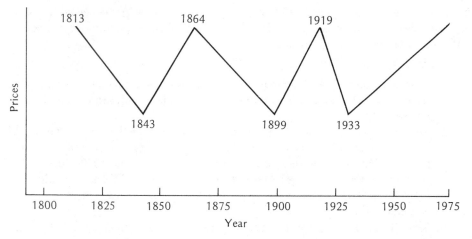

FIGURE 1-5
Cycles of generally rising and falling consumer prices in the United States. (The curve should not be taken as indicating absolute values.)

issue of *Forbes*) suggest that there have been three periods of major price explosions:

950–1350	Commercial Revolution
1520–1640	Capitalist Revolution
1750–1850	Industrial Revolution

They maintain that we are now in the fourth period, which they call the Public Revolution and characterize as a period in which citizens make dramatic new demands for services from their governments.

While it is difficult to assess the validity of such theories, they no doubt have some merit. The important thing to take from this discussion is that it can be sheer folly to assume events will persist as they have in the immediate past, particularly if you happen to be living during a major turning point. You should also bear in mind that no one has yet demonstrated an ability to foretell the future consistently. Therefore, be cautious about relying on any expert's prognostications. Herein lies the greatest argument for diversification in your financial and investment strategies. This subject will be treated in Unit IV of this text.

Measuring the Rate of Inflation

How do you judge what the overall rate of inflation is? The price of movie tickets may have increased 33⅓ percent (from $3 to $4), in your community, but the cost of stereo records may have remained stable at $6.95 for quite a while. How do the price changes in these and all the other goods and services that you purchase fit into some overall scheme called "the cost of living"?

The federal government regularly publishes a myriad of statistics that purport to measure various aspects of the nation's economic activity. Probably the most widely used measure of the cost of living is the consumer price index (CPI). The Bureau of Labor Statistics computes this index to measure "changes in the average price of a representative sample of goods and services purchased by typical wage earners and clerical workers in urban areas of the United States." Prices of 398 goods and

services from approximately 18,000 retail outlets in 56 cities are collected for use in the index. The major categories of items are food, housing, apparel and its upkeep, transportation, and medical care.

This index is less than accurate for several reasons:

1. It is based only on prices found in urban areas. Since many people are emigrating from major urban areas to more rural areas, the index is not as representative as it once was.
2. Although surveys are taken every decade to redetermine the weight that should be given to each category, the period between surveys has averaged more than 10 years. Furthermore, there are delays (four years for the 1970s' survey) between when the surveys are taken and when the uncovered changes are included in the index. The CPI therefore cannot quickly or continuously reflect changes in consumer preferences.
3. The CPI cannot discriminate between price changes caused by inflation and those caused by changes in the quality of goods and services.
4. The expense patterns of most people do not match that of the "typical wage earner or clerical worker."

The next time you hear that the cost of living has gone up, you will probably have some insight into why this rise occurred and also into how this evaluation was made. You can retain a healthy skepticism about the accuracy of the statistics upon which such pronouncements are based. In the words of Commander Holloway H. Frost: "There are three kinds of lies—lies, damnable lies, and statistics."

As you proceed through this text, procedures will be offered for dealing with the effects of inflation on money matters such as life insurance needs, borrowing, investing, and retirement.

USING THIS BOOK

This book is organized into five units. These divisions and the order in which they appear are not accidental. Units II, III, and IV parallel the financial strategies discussed earlier in this chapter. Unit I, called "Getting Started," includes the chapter you have just read; Chapter 2, which covers career and income considerations; Chapter 3, which concerns financial statements and a record-keeping system; and Chapter 4, which will enable you to come to grips with your spending habits. Unit II, "Protecting What You Have," consists of five chapters on personal insurance, including property, auto, health, and life coverages.

Unit III, "Getting the Most Out of Your Income," is intended to help you avoid costly errors in regard to income taxes, loans, banks, credit, and the purchase of automobiles, appliances, and housing. Unit IV is entitled "Increasing Your Income." For younger students the investment areas covered in Chapters 15 through 20 may initially seem remote considerations; however, the best way to hurry the time when investing is a realistic consideration is to begin now to search for ways to increase your savings and reduce your expenses. Investing can be a challenging and interesting talent to develop, as well as personally and financially rewarding when you are successful. As such, it is a much more positive part of personal money management than the tasks of insuring against some unknown calamity or cutting the costs of certain financial services.

Unit V, Chapters 21 and 22, is called "Planning for Retirement and Estate Transfer." Parts of both these topics could have been treated in the earlier units, but because these considerations concern the later years of life, they have been placed in a unit by themselves.

In addition, where appropriate, each chapter will give you step-by-step procedures to help you determine your needs. The various alternatives for satisfying your needs will be treated to make your financial choices easier and more rational. Finally, the text should be retained for future reference. While many of the statistics and numbers cited will change, the principles and procedures of personal money management probably will not.

CONCLUSION

The purpose of this chapter has been to prompt you to begin seriously thinking about your financial goals. As a backdrop for this inquiry, you should consider how important money is to you and where it fits into your financial life cycle. One of the more useful tasks is to start becoming aware of how your emotional needs and cultural values affect your financial choices. You should also have come to appreciate the process, functions, and strategies you will employ as a money manager. By having an appreciation of the participants, opportunities for assistance, and challenges you face, you can develop the ability to control and expand your personal finance environment. The idea of money management need not intimidate and confuse you. It can become a powerful and effective tool in helping you achieve the things you really want and in freeing you from the daily worries and problems of mismanaged money.

VOCABULARY

consumer price index (CPI)	financial life cycle	living expenses
Federal Reserve System (FRS)	financial resources	inflation/deflation
financial goals	money management	investment assets

CASE PROBLEMS

1. Develop lists of your goals, your personal assets, and your financial resources. Identify the goals that can be achieved by financial means. Develop a chart similar to Figure 1-2 showing your major personal financial goals by *term, frequency, purchase,* and *purpose.* Then prioritize and estimate the timing and amount of these goals in a manner similar to Figure 1-3.
2. List the five most recent choices you made concerning personal financial alternatives. Now describe the emotional and social factors that played a part in these decisions. As you become more aware of these considerations, do you find any that surprise you? If so, why? Given this enhanced perspective, how would you approach the same decisions next time?

3. Below is a price list for five goods and services:

	1973	1983
Movie ticket	$1.50	$4.00
Calculator	100.00	10.00
New car	4,000.00	8,000.00
Fancy French meal for two	30.00	75.00
Stereo record album	5.95	6.95

What problems would this list present if used to calculate the consumer price index?
4. List the advantages and disadvantages of seeking personal financial assistance from an individual who is compensated by sales commissions and one who receives only fees. Which one do you prefer? Why?

RECOMMENDED READING

Case, John. *Understanding Inflation*. New York: William Morrow, 1981.
Explains inflation and the interplay with political and economic policies.

Goldberg, Herb, and Lewis, Robert T. *Money Madness: The Psychology of Saving, Spending, Loving and Hating Money*. New York: William Morrow, 1978.
An excellent treatment of the emotional aspects of money, a very important but seldom investigated dimension of personal money management.

Malabre, Alfred L., Jr. *Understanding the Economy: For People Who Can't Stand Economics*. New York: Dodd, Mead, 1976.
An excellent book that accomplishes much of what the title indicates.

Nagdeman, Julian J. "Measure for Measure?" *Barron's*, February 20, 1978, pp. 9–16.
Discusses the construction and weaknesses of the new consumer price indices.

CHUCK AND NANCY ANDERSON

Chuck Anderson is 35 years old and works as a salesman. His wife Nancy, also 35, works as a legal secretary. They were married 12 years ago, shortly after Chuck took his present job. Three years later he received a promotion and was transferred. Soon after the move they bought a $25,000 two-bedroom home six miles from the office. Within a year they had a son named Jim and three years later a daughter named Melissa.

Since their move, the Andersons have bought much of the furniture for their house, some of it on installment. They have also purchased the necessary insurance policies in addition to the life insurance Chuck bought at the time of their marriage. To celebrate Chuck's second promotion last year, they traded in their six-year-old car and took out a $6,000 loan to buy a new "success image" car for Chuck. Nancy still drives a five-year-old compact.

The Andersons would like to have more money for things such as a family vacation abroad and a motorboat. They would also like to begin a savings or investment program so that they will have enough money for a college education for each of their children. Nancy's car should probably be replaced soon. In addition, Chuck and Nancy want to be assured of having a comfortable retirement when that time comes. These are the financial goals the Andersons have set for themselves.

To date, the Andersons have done some things right, but there are many areas of money management in which they could do better, as we shall see.

2

Your Career and Income

The study of personal money management is a useless exercise for someone who has no money to manage. Most of this book deals with *spending* (and investing) money, but only this chapter deals with your primary source of *earning money*—your job. In general, the more you earn, the more flexible and numerous your spending alternatives are.

A comfortable standard of living is not something to be casually assumed. About 30 percent of American families are faced with these alternatives: subsist on an inadequate budget, live with someone else to share expenses, or look to someone else (parents, children) for additional support. As you can see from Figure 2-1, to support a typical American, urban, four-person family at least at an "intermediate" standard of living (as defined by the U.S. government) requires that the family's income rank with those earned by about the top half of all American families. The austere "lower" budget requires an income such as is earned by about the top 64 percent of all American families.

The day of the family's dependence on the husband as the sole breadwinner may be coming to an end. Now women who learn a career are more inclined to pursue it, sometimes out of financial necessity. As the cost of living rises, some families need two incomes in order to maintain their style of life. Two incomes also give greater flexibility for the couple in achieving personal fulfillment: one spouse can go back to school, start a business, or switch careers, while the other spouse continues to provide an adequate living. In many families the woman is the sole provider, whether because of divorce, death or illness of the spouse, or some other circumstance. In fact, more than one out of five Americans lives alone and is, therefore, responsible for his or her own level of support. Often these people receive extra support, either financially or in the form of hand-me-down household goods, from parents, children, other relatives and friends, or government programs.

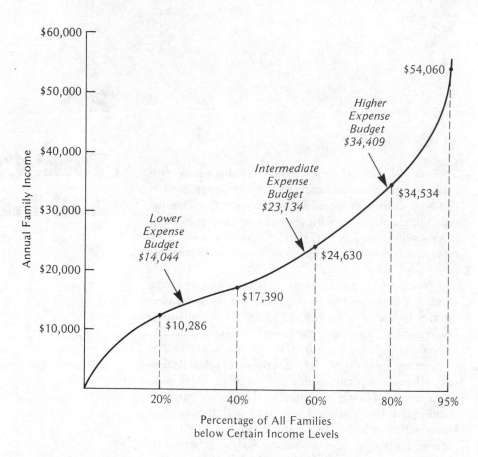

$60,000

$54,060

$50,000

*Higher
Expense
Budget
$34,409*

$40,000

*Intermediate
Expense
Budget
$23,134*

$30,000

$34,534

Annual Family Income

*Lower
Expense
Budget
$14,044*

$24,630

$20,000

$17,390

$10,000

$10,286

20%   40%   60%   80%   95%

Percentage of All Families
below Certain Income Levels

Source: Data on income from U.S. Bureau of the Census, "Money Income in 1980 of Families and Persons in the United States," *Current Population Reports*, Series P-60, No. 127, 1981. Data on expenses
from U.S. Bureau of Labor Statistics, *Autumn 1980 Urban Family Budgets*, No. 81-195, April 22, 1981.

In this chapter we will look first at the factors that affect one's income and then at
the particular processes of choosing a career and getting a job.

WHAT CAUSES DIFFERENCES IN INCOMES?

Many factors influence your level of salary income, including your choice of career,
your educational attainment, your age and experience, as well as your geographic
location, racial background, sex, family heritage, and luck. Perhaps most important
is an individual's skill and perseverance in obtaining a certain income. Some examples of salary differences by career are shown in Table 2-1.

Type of Work

The ranking of occupations by salary varies over time. A shortage of qualified
individuals for a given job category causes the price (salary) to rise, making the

TABLE 2-1
Annual Income for Selected Occupations in 1978

Occupation	Average Starting Salary	Average Salary of Experienced Individuals
Accountant	$12,800	$15,700-27,300
Accountant, chief	n.a.	23,700-39,900
Air traffic controller	12,500	25,400
Bank teller[a]	6,300	7,000-9,400
Bank officer, B.A. trainee	11,400	n.a.
Bank officer, M.B.A.	18,000	n.a.
College placement director	n.a.	18,100
Dental assistant[a]	8,400	10,500
Dental hygienist	9,400	12,000-13,500
Dentist	19,300	50,000
Dietitian, hospital	12,600	15,000-30,000
Electrician[a]	11,700	23,400
Engineer, B.S.	16,800 ⎫	
Engineer, M.S.	18,700 ⎬	30,500+[b]
Engineer, Ph.D.	24,000 ⎭	
Firefighter[a]	12,700	14,200-18,000
Flight attendant[a]	9,000	14,400
Lawyer	18,000	50,000+
Librarian, M.L.S.	11,900	12,900-38,700
Mail carrier[a]	14,600	17,200
Market researcher	14,000	24,000+
Newspaper reporter	12,500	19,200
Nurse, registered	11,800	16,800+
Personnel administrator	12,000	23,600
Physical therapist	13,000	16,000+
Physician	13,500+	65,400
Physicist, M.S.	17,400 ⎫	
Physicist, Ph.D.	23,000 ⎭	30,200[b]
Police officer, state	13,200	17,000-19,000
Programmer, computer	13,000	20,000+
Sales worker, retail[a]	6,000-10,400	14,800
Secretary[a]	n.a.	9,800-13,000
Securities sales worker	10,800-14,400	29,000-57,000
Social worker, public	10,300	17,000
Teacher, secondary school	n.a.	15,500
Teacher, college, university	n.a.	25,100
Telephone operator[a]	9,000	13,000
Truck driver, long distance[a]	n.a.	29,000

Source: U.S. Bureau of Labor Statistics, *Occupational Outlook Handbook*, 1980-81 edition (Bulletin 2075), 1980.

Note: By 1981 inflation probably boosted these figures by 30 percent on the average, although some occupations fared better than average and some worse.

[a]Occupations that generally do not require a college degree.
[b]Educational backgrounds not differentiated in these figures.
"n.a." means that figures were not available in the source publication.

career so attractive that a surplus of job-seekers in the field develops. Because so many people are competing for the same type of job, employers can afford to lower the salaries paid in that area, relative to the salaries paid in the rest of the economy. The supply-demand cycle then swings back to a period of relative shortage.

In the post-Sputnik era, for example, the demand for engineers and scientists increased; salaries soared in the 1960s, producing a boom in the college-degree programs leading to such lucrative careers. By the early 1970s the job market had dried up for new Ph.D. holders in these fields. Employed engineers who did not continue their educations to stay abreast of their fields often found themselves laid off in slow economic times. The cycle was renewed by 1980, when engineers were again in demand. Similarly, teachers' salaries progressed at a rate faster than inflation during the 1960s because of the baby boom (from 2.7 million births in 1945 to 4.2 million in 1960); by the late 1970s teachers faced the threat of layoffs not only because education schools had been effective in increasing their output of teachers, but also because annual births had receded to about 3.5 million by the mid-1960s.

Some jobs may be somewhat sheltered from market supply-demand pressures because of rules instituted by professional societies or the influence of labor unions. Careers in medicine and law tend to consistently offer high pay because of the initial training required and the continuing commitment required of doctors and lawyers to do their jobs well. Of course, the difficult qualification requirements have been set up by the professional societies (via bar exam or residency requirements) ostensibly to set high standards for the profession, but they also serve to protect the jobs of the existing workers from the intense competition that would develop in a freer market.

There are also permanent (noncyclical) differences in salary levels relative to the type of work. These differences reflect the importance of the work to society and the difficulty in obtaining qualified people to do the work. For example, in the large organizations required to run today's highly automated and specialized economy, the manager becomes increasingly important for planning, assembling, and motivating the factors of production—land, labor, and capital. The responsibilities and pressures can be intellectually challenging and emotionally overwhelming. As a result, managers are usually well paid for paying the personal price necessary to achieve society's economic goals.

Education

Education may cost a lot, but you should view it as investing in yourself. As shown in Table 2-2, higher levels of educational attainment correlate directly with higher average levels of income. Perhaps, people with the ability and incentive to earn diplomas and degrees also have greater ability and motivation to earn a living. As Figure 2-2 shows, high school dropouts have the highest unemployment rate while college graduates have the lowest unemployment rate. This has been a consistent pattern for many years and is likely to continue because of the ever-increasing complexity of the working world.

There used to be a distinct demarcation between one's years of formal education and the working years. Once the career was begun, training was generally accom-

TABLE 2-2

Education and Income for Full-Time Workers
25 Years Old and Over

Years of School Completed	Median Income
Fewer than 8	$ 6,381
Completed elementary	8,732
1-3 years high school	11,536
Completed high school	16,211
1-3 years college	18,010
Completed college	21,838
Some graduate school	25,234

Source: U.S. Bureau of the Census, "Money Income and Poverty Status of Families and Persons in the United States, 1980," *Current Population Reports*, Series P-60, No. 127, August 1981, p. 17.

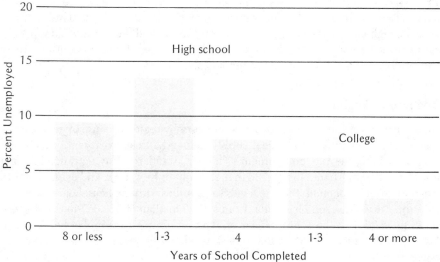

Source: U.S. Bureau of Labor Statistics, *Occupational Outlook Handbook*, 1978-1979 edition (Bulletin 1955), p. 26.

FIGURE 2-2
Unemployment rates for adults by education.

plished on the job. Today, the pace of change is accelerating, and many careers require workers to take continuing education courses to keep their skills from becoming obsolete. Sometimes this training is made available by the employer. Often, it requires the workers to stay abreast on their own, either formally through schooling on weekends or at night or informally through reading, conferences, and interaction with fellow workers at other organizations.

Age and Experience

A trainee in a new job would find it almost impossible to be as productive as an equally motivated worker with 10 years' experience. An experienced worker usually earns more, as a result of either merit or seniority or both. In 1980, starting salaries for the careers shown in Table 2-1 ranged from $6,000 (retail sales worker) to $24,000 (engineer, Ph.D.); the earnings for experienced persons in these careers averaged from $7,000 (bank teller) to $65,400 (physician). As the table also shows, careers that require at least a college degree tend to pay higher salaries both to individuals just starting out and to experienced individuals than do careers with more modest education requirements.

Many women are new participants in the labor force. In 1950, only 33.9 percent of women over age 15 were in the labor force, whereas in 1980 51.2 percent were. Women today are building a longer history of experience by staying with their careers during their child-rearing years. In 1950, only 34 percent of women ages 25 through 34 were in the labor force compared to 63.8 percent in 1980.° (Interestingly, labor force participation rates for men have declined from 86.4 percent in 1950 to 77.2 percent in 1980.)

As shown in Figure 2-3, a person's highest earning years are usually between ages 45 and 54. Younger persons are still gaining the experience necessary to perform at top productivity in their jobs. Older people may be opting for less demanding work once the high-expense years of raising a family are behind them. Some older people earn less, not because they choose to, but because they failed to continue their education or expand their skills throughout their careers.

Geographic Region

Absolute levels of income and costs of living vary by region because of government regulation, taxes, union influence, supply-demand forces, weather, and historic trends. In 1980, the U.S. government's "higher" standard of living ranged from a low of $31,229 in Atlanta to $42,736 in metropolitan New York, and even higher in Anchorage and Honolulu. Income levels for families with the householder working full-time varied in a similar fashion from a 1980 median of $28,357 in the Western states to $24,641 in the South. However, the rate of growth is probably greater in low-cost areas (such as the Sun Belt states), where employers locate new plants and offices in order to obtain labor at relatively low rates.

°U.S. Bureau of Labor Statistics, *Perspectives on Working Women: A Databook, October 1980* (Bulletin 2080).

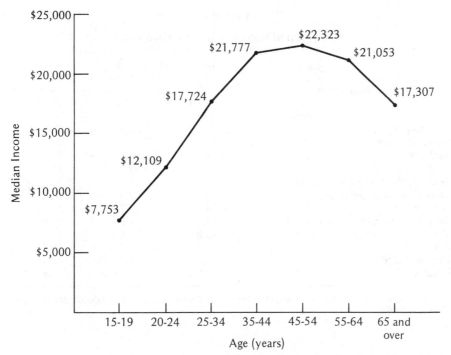

FIGURE 2-3
Comparison of age and
income for year-round
full-time male workers in
1980.

Source: U.S. Bureau of the Census, "Money Income and Poverty Status of Families and Persons in the United States, 1980," *Current Population Reports*, Series P-60, No. 127, August 1981.

Discrimination

Discrimination against various groups of individuals—whether because of age, sex, race, or religious beliefs—sometimes results in barriers to personal financial success. While differences in income due to such characteristics are still substantial, they are lessening as the population's sensitivity and tolerance increase, and as government legislation curbs the more flagrant abuses.

For example, with regard to race, the median family income of blacks and other races was 51.1 percent of white family income in 1947, 55.3 percent in 1960, and 63.2 percent in 1980.° Obviously, there is still much room for improvement.

With regard to sex, 1980 statistics show that full-time female workers in the United States have a median income of $9,350—only 59.4 percent of the male median. As shown in Table 2-3, women have dominated such lower-paying careers as secretarial work and nursing. Historically, society has labeled these careers as being appropriate for women, and the pay scales for them developed accordingly. Recent trends, however, indicate that women have been successfully combating the attitudes that caused such stereotypes and are making significant inroads into such

°U.S. Bureau of the Census, *Money Income and Poverty Status of Families and Persons in the United States, 1980*, August 1981.

TABLE 2-3

Employment of Women in Selected Occupations

Occupation	Women as Percentage of All Workers in Occupation		
	1950	1970	1979
Secretary-typist	94.6%	96.6%	98.6%
Nurse, registered	97.8	97.4	96.8
Bank teller	45.2	86.1	92.9
Bookkeeper	77.7	82.1	91.1
Teacher, elementary, secondary	74.5	70.4	70.8
Teacher, college, university	22.8	28.3	31.6
Accountant	14.9	25.3	32.9
Bank officer/financial manager	11.7	17.6	31.6
Manager-administrator	13.8	16.6	24.6
Physician	6.5	8.9	10.7
Lawyer, judge	4.1	4.7	12.4
Engineer	1.2	1.6	2.9

Source: U.S. Bureau of Labor Statistics, *Perspectives on Working Women: A Databook*, October 1980 (Bulletin 2080).

high-salary jobs as bank officer, physician, and lawyer. These trends will become more pronounced, as indicated by the dramatically increasing enrollment of women in graduate schools and in union apprenticeship programs. In turn, these women will provide a greater variety of role models for women than were available when women had easy access to only a limited range of jobs with limited opportunities for advancement.

Family Heritage

Statistics show that families in the top fifth by income level earn several times that of families in the bottom fifth, whether measured in 1950, 1965, or 1980. (See Table 2-4. The dollar amounts relating to the 1980 percentages are shown in Figure 2-1.) However, do these statistics support the commonly held belief that the same families dominate their respective ends of the spectrum, generation after generation? In other words, do the rich stay rich and the poor stay poor?

The facts indicate that there is considerable mobility from one generation to the next. While families in the top fifth have incomes about 6.5 times that of the lowest fifth, the sons of the top fifth wind up earning only 1.75 times the income of the sons of the lowest fifth.° Furthermore, of the chief executive officers of the 500 largest U.S. corporations in 1975, one-fourth had fathers who were either blue-collar or

---

°Christopher Jencks, *Inequality* (New York: Basic Books, 1972), pp. 213, 215.

TABLE 2-4

Percent Distribution of Aggregate Family Income

Year	Percentage of Total Aggregate Income in Each Rank			
	Lowest Fifth *(1-20%)*	*Middle Fifth* *(40-60%)*	*Highest Fifth* *(80-100%)*	*Top 5%*
1950	4.5%	17.4%	42.7%	17.3%
1965	5.2	17.8	40.9	15.5
1980	5.1	17.5	41.6	15.3

Source: U.S. Bureau of the Census, *Current Population Reports*, Series P-60, Nos. 114, 116, and 127.

clerical workers (vs. 1 in 20 in 1900).° If such a dramatic shift can occur in only a single generation, perhaps America can still claim to be a land of equality of opportunity, even if there is no equality of current income levels.

Luck, Ability, and Drive

Some people *are* in the right place at the right time. Real estate brokers in California in the late 1970s, for example, earned extraordinary incomes compared to individuals with similar skills and dedication in other occupations. (As a result, the number of people taking the California real estate license exam mushroomed from 41,783 in 1970 to 120,186 in 1978.)

However, over time and on the average, we are inclined to agree with the late coach Vince Lombardi that "luck" happens to those who are prepared to take advantage of the opportunity when it comes. If this were not so, we doubt that people would devote such effort to improving their ability to earn an income.

THE PROCESS OF SELECTING A CAREER

The selection of a career is among the very few semipermanent decisions a person makes in life, the others being marriage and parenthood. Unfortunately, most of us have to make such decisions before we have the wisdom gained by experience and maturity. Thus, many people wind up in a career that started with the first job they took, merely because it was the first job they heard about, seemed glamorous, or was an easy job to get.

Long-term planning while still in college, even before choosing a major course of study, is time well spent. Instead of merely following the path of least resistance, only to find yourself in a job someday that doesn't fully meet your needs for income and satisfaction, spend some time today getting to know yourself and the career alternatives.

°Charles G. Burke, "A Group Profile of the Fortune 500 Chief Executives," *Fortune* (May 1976), p. 175.

Step 1: Know Yourself

One very bright recipient of a master's degree in business administration took his first job with a national accounting firm and soon was recognized and promoted to regional consultant on special client projects requiring a high degree of creativity and analytical ability. A few months short of qualifying for his certified public accountant license, he switched to a position as advisor to the senior vice-president of a major bank. Less than a year later, he was still unsatisfied and started job-hunting again. Finally, upon reflecting on his past on the family farm in the Midwest, he remembered the great satisfaction he felt every autumn when they would bring in the harvest, when the job was *completed*. Then he realized that his previous two business jobs were merely consulting or advisory positions, where he was not the one who would take charge of the job that was prescribed by his analysis, and *complete* it. He was missing the satisfaction of the harvest, and so he knew he should look for a manager's job instead of a consultant's job.

Coming to know oneself is probably the most difficult step in the process of selecting a career. No single method of self-evaluation will work for everyone. You will find a number of books in your library offering various questionnaires, checklists, and other schemes. A good example is *What Color Is Your Parachute?* This and other helpful books are listed in the selected readings at the end of this chapter. Vocational counselors can give a variety of aptitude and interest tests.

Essentially, you must make a thorough and honest search of your background, your personal experiences, and your interests and aspirations. Be sure to consider your past jobs, school courses, volunteer activities—the impact (both monetary and nonmonetary) that these experiences had on your lifestyle, including social relationships, personal growth, self-respect, and leisure time. You will need to project the kind of lifestyle you want for yourself in the future in all these areas too. Your career will indeed affect your life in more ways than just influencing your potential income. After all, most jobs require more of our time (usually eight to ten hours out of every weekday) than we can devote to any other single activity (except maybe sleeping!).

Looking at your past

- What have you gotten satisfaction from doing?
- What experiences made you unhappy, frustrated, afraid, or bored?

Fitting your career into your life

- Do you anticipate your work being the center of your life? Would you prefer that your work interfere minimally with your other relationships and interests? Do you look on work primarily as a means of making enough money to enjoy your leisure time as much as possible?
- Do you want a job you can work at part-time for a period of years, perhaps during the early child-rearing years? Is it possible to do this in the career you prefer? Is even 80 to 90 percent of full-time possible? Could a different part-time job keep your options open for the full-time career you really want?

- Do you want to take time out from your career for a period of years, perhaps for family formation, military service, or a Peace Corps job? What problems might you face in maintaining your skills or knowledge in the interim? Is the technology likely to change much during your absence?
- Do you anticipate moving from place to place for personal reasons? Is your chosen career readily transferable?

Looking at your abilities, preferences, needs

- Do you enjoy working with people, perhaps as a salesperson or a manager, or do you prefer to work by yourself?
- Are you better at doing something or at thinking?
- Do you want a very high level of income? Are you willing to take some risks to achieve it, or would you prefer a more modest career that offers much job security?
- Do you want diversity in the people you meet and work with, or would you prefer to work in close cooperation with people in a particular field of interest?
- Could you accept danger, tension, or long hours if they were part of an otherwise attractive career?
- Are you willing to move to different geographic locations from time to time to advance your career? Can you and your family deal with the problems of uprooting: finding new friends, setting up a new home, learning a new city, or interrupting your children's education or your spouse's job?
- Do you need to prove yourself at new challenges and be recognized for extraordinary achievement, or do you derive adequate gratification from doing a more conventional, secure job well?
- Do you want to continue to grow or do you become anxious about a job that requires change? Will you face boredom or job obsolescence if you choose a static job?
- Are you choosing your career because it is what *you* want, or because somebody else (parents, a professor, a friend) thinks you should choose it?

Many people do not adequately answer these personal questions before they embark on a career, and either spend years of unhappiness in one job or jump from job to job looking for the one that feels right. A person should be cautioned, however, against choosing an occupation solely because it promises high earnings. It is most important that we really like what we are doing. If we do, we will probably become very good at it and, as a consequence, command better-than-average pay for the quality and quantity of work we do.

personal growth For many of us, the rate of personal growth would slow dramatically after college were it not for the influence of our working environment. The demands of a job put pressure on an individual to develop new skills; to learn new ways of interacting with, influencing, or managing people; and to adapt to changing technology or methods. Job promotions continue to demand new skills or better mastery of old ones; such challenges can add considerable interest to life.

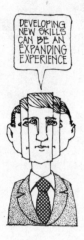

DEVELOPING NEW SKILLS CAN BE AN EXPANDING EXPERIENCE

Many people derive considerable satisfaction from doing something well, completely, creatively, or efficiently. In addition, you can derive much self-respect from the personal growth that makes you a more capable person, or from simply being recognized for the work you do—whatever you make happen in your corner of the economy or of society. Your ego will be involved with the employer you work for or with the product or service you offer, so choose it carefully.

no ideal choice   Getting everything you want out of the same job choice is probably impossible. You may have to compromise your ideal choice in friends, location, or leisure, for example, to get the salary, status, respect, or other personal satisfaction you want. Other people can give you information about careers, but only you know which values are the most important to you. You won't know all the answers before you must decide, and the choice will not be easy, but only *you* can make the decision, because only you know the personal assessments involved.

Step 2: Know the Alternatives

Once you know your specific interest—such as police work, computer programming, selling, accounting, medical work, or financial management—you must sort out the various alternatives for work in your area of interest. Job counselors and career guidebooks can be a help in explaining what jobs are available, but you must be prepared to answer several questions for yourself.

Do you want the relative security and predictability of a job in the nonprofit sector (government, medical, and educational institutions)? Or do you prefer the potentially better paying jobs in the profit-oriented private sector, where there may be less job security, less predictability in your job description, and more emphasis on doing only those things that contribute to the profitability of the enterprise?

Do you want the advantages of a large employer: higher starting salary, extensive training programs, relative job security, diverse opportunities for transferring jobs, better fringe benefits, large staff resources, and carefully thought out and clearly stated policies regarding management practices and job promotions?

On the other hand, maybe you would prefer the advantages of a small firm: a less structured job, possibly meaningful ownership, quicker and more flexible recognition of individual abilities, more control over your area of responsibility and greater influence on the performance of the organization, greater variety in your responsibilities, closer relations with top management but less supervision and support from immediate supervisors.

Do you want to work for yourself? This may mean being a lawyer, doctor, accountant, computer programmer, or nursery school teacher on your own or in a small partnership. Or it may mean opening your own store or business and facing the demands of long hours and low income in the early years and the high failure rate for new enterprises. But if you persist and succeed, it can mean financial success and greater control over your environment (except that dealing with the realities of the marketplace can often be as demanding and frustrating as dealing with one's boss).

not carved in stone   Don't let the importance of the career decision put you in such a panic that you cannot make a decision. The longer you wait to try your hand at some meaningful career for you, the longer you will have to wait for the benefits of the training and experience you will acquire.

Early career job switching is not necessarily harmful. Time well spent in two or three different jobs will give you a breadth of experience to aid you in your working life. On the other hand, if you make a habit of switching employers every year or two, you will soon find employers unwilling to take a chance on hiring you, for fear of seeing you leave again just after you learn the job well enough to be truly productive.

Many people find mid-career changes to be the most satisfying of all. In exchange for the high pay that may come after the 10 or 20 years of experience they have accumulated in the same job or company, they obtain the variety and challenge of new skills, a different lifestyle, or a new enterprise. Teachers have become real estate brokers. Investment counselors have become administrators of charitable institutions. Employees have started their own businesses.

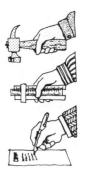

FINDING AND LANDING A JOB

Jobs do not necessarily get filled by the person most qualified to do the work. Instead, they are filled by the person most able to locate the job and sell himself or herself to the employer on their qualifications for the position.

Where Are the Jobs?

The advertised positions are the easiest to locate. Your college placement office should be contacted a year in advance of graduation, because the waiting lists to see job recruiters often fill up early. Want ads in the newspapers, *Wall Street Journal*, or trade magazines in your area of interest are another good source. State employment agencies will list many of the more common job openings. Jobs with special requirements may be listed with a private employment agency; check first to see who pays the agency's fee—you or the employer.

Many good jobs are filled without ever being advertised. Tell your friends, acquaintances, professors, and business contacts what you are looking for. They may have just the right job for you or know of one to refer you to. Also, don't be afraid to prospect a company "cold." The firm may not have a position at the moment, but they may be so impressed with your interest in working in a particular area of their firm that they will keep your name on file and contact you when an opening is available.

Obtaining That First Interview

Signing up for the interview schedule with a major recruiter at the placement office is easy. Beyond that, you will probably be forced to make your first impression on a potential employer via a résumé and cover letter.

Even if a résumé is not required to obtain the interview, it will probably be asked for either before or during a job interview. There are many ways to structure a résumé, but it is essentially a one- or two-page outline of your education, experience, and job qualifications. It should be up-to-date and directed at the particular type of work you are seeking. Condense or eliminate material not related to the job applied for. If you are looking for more than one type of job, perhaps you should write more than one résumé, each tailored to a different career area.

The person reading your résumé has dozens to look at and will probably spend only a minute or two skimming yours. It should therefore be short (one page if you do not have extensive work experience), easy to read, and clearly laid out. You can fill in the details and give explanations in your interview. The résumé should merely be an honest representation of the positive aspects about yourself that will make the reader want to interview you.

Figure 2-4 is one illustration of how the following résumé components could be portrayed. The finished résumé looks best if it is produced by some printing method, usually inexpensive.

- *Heading.*   Include a phone number where you can be reached or a message left. Most employers will call to arrange an interview.
- *Professional objective.*   If you want to make your résumé more flexible, this can be described in your cover letter instead of here.
- *Work experience.*   List in order, most recent job first. If your work experience is not particularly impressive, put the education section above this section. Include names and locations of employers, positions held, and types of work performed.
- *Education.*   Again, list the most recent first. Give the names and locations of schools (or corporate training programs), degrees, major studies, and any honors. Leave out high school if you have a college degree.
- *Interests, background, other activities.*   Here is where you round out your first impression, listing special skills, hobbies, community service, college activities. This will give many interviewers a chance to discuss some area of mutual personal interest, to get to know you better. However, this material is optional and should be eliminated if it may serve to discriminate against you.
- *Personal.*   Also optional (cannot legally be required): age (or birth date), marital status, number of children, health, military status.
- *References.*   These can be on the résumé or supplied separately at or after the first interview. Check with your references first. If they agree, give their names, addresses, and phone numbers.

The *cover letter* that accompanies your résumé should also be brief (perhaps a half-page) and clearly worded. It should be addressed to a named individual (call the receptionist to ask for the name of someone in personnel, if necessary) and be personalized as much as possible and yet be businesslike. State the job you seek and the reasons for wanting that position *with the particular company* you are writing. State also your availability to interview and to begin the job, if it is offered. Type it neatly.

The First Interview

This interview will probably last only a half-hour. Do not expect the job to be offered then and there. The interviewer, especially if the person is a recruiter, is probably trying to reduce the number of applicants to a select group of finalists.

SUSAN A. SAINT
100 River Road
Santa Clara, Calif. 94300

Phone: Work (415) 329-1340
Home (415) 422-1342

PROFESSIONAL OBJECTIVE	Accountant. Ultimately, controller or chief financial officer for a manufacturing firm.
EXPERIENCE	
April 1982 to present	Widgets, Inc., San Jose, California.
	Junior accountant. Prepared monthly closings and monitored inventory control. Designed new reporting systems.
June 1981 to April 1982	Berger's Books, Palo Alto, California.
	Administrative assistant, bookkeeper, general office tasks.
Summer 1980 and 1979	Berger's Books, Palo Alto, California.
	Sales clerk and inventory clerk.
EDUCATION	M.B.A., to be received June 1984
	University of Santa Clara Santa Clara, California
	Major: Accounting and data processing
	B.A. 1981
	California State University at San Jose San Jose, California
	Major: Business, emphasis in finance.
BACKGROUND	Peace Corps work in Indonesia in small business consulting, 1977-79.
INTERESTS AND ACTIVITIES	Treasurer of Business School Association, member of California Society of Accountants. Interests include tennis, skiing, family.
PERSONAL	Married, one child; excellent health; 5'8'', 120 lbs; born 6/23/58

FIGURE 2-4
A sample résumé.

Be yourself, but also show that you want the job. Appropriate dress, a firm handshake, and pleasantly eager responses to questions help make the best first impression, and that is all you have time for in a half-hour. Be prepared for questions like:

• Why do you want to work for us?
• What are your strong points?
• Why did you leave your last job?
• What do you want to know about our company?

Don't be afraid to volunteer your strong points or relevant experiences if the interviewer fails to ask for them. It helps to be alert to opportunities to put the interviewer at ease too; the other person may also be nervous about the interview.

Defer the details on salary, fringe benefits, and vacations to the next interview. Focus this time on learning about the job and selling yourself to the interviewer. You should know something about the company before the interview. Read over the company's annual report or read about it in one of the investment references listed at the end of Chapter 18. If you can, talk to someone who works at the company.

You will be told when to expect a letter or call. To help encourage a positive response to your application, you might send a follow-up letter thanking the interviewer for his or her time and confirming your interest in the position. If you are among the applicants still being considered, you will often be invited to visit the company, perhaps at the employer's expense.

The Second Interview

This interview will be longer, and you will have a chance to meet potential associates and supervisors as well as to ask about any details you want to know. Try to learn as much as possible about the work. If possible, talk to someone already doing the job. How will your performance be reviewed and rewarded? Don't be afraid to ask about the dark side of the job as well. Remember, you may have to decide about whether or not to accept a job there.

Don't forget to continue to sell yourself in a way that is natural for you. Try to be enthusiastic, pleasant, considerate, and a good listener.

The Acceptance Decision

If you need more information from the prospective employer in order to decide whether to take the job, you may request another interview (at your expense) to cover the issues forgotten the last time around. Make sure you find out what you'll be doing, so you won't be disappointed later, if you accept the job.

After you decide, don't burn your bridges at the other firms who interviewed you, especially those that made an offer to you. Send a polite thank-you letter saying you took another position. Leaving a good impression may help you in the future if you decide to leave your first-choice company.

CONCLUSION

Your career will dictate your lifestyle in terms of how much money you earn, your social life, personal growth, self-respect and satisfaction, and leisure time. It is one of the most important decisions you will ever make.

Income differentials exist because of career choice, age and experience, education, region, race, sex, heritage, luck, and personal ability and drive.

To select a career, you must first know yourself, and then select the alternative that best fits your needs. You will have to trade off some pluses against some minuses. If the decision proves to be in error, it can be changed, a few times.

To obtain the right job will require considerable skill and time in screening the alternatives, preparing a résumé, writing letters, interviewing, and following up. Good luck!

VOCABULARY

career
résumé

QUESTIONS

1. What points should one consider in choosing a career?
2. What is important to you in a career?
3. For which careers could you qualify? Which are desirable to you?
4. List four sources that could help you find a job.
5. What is the primary purpose of a résumé?
6. What are the two major issues to be discussed in the first interview for a job?
7. Why is the second interview, usually a visit to the employer, important?

CASE PROBLEMS

1. Irene decided it was time to switch careers from teaching music and some general business courses at the community college to personnel administration. She had taken several evening courses at the business department of a local four-year college. She had prepared a two-page résumé, carefully describing her involvement in school musicals, the band, and the civic chorus. She now planned to send the résumé to about a hundred companies in a local business directory. Is she well prepared to achieve her career change? What would you advise?
2. Dave was in his junior year at college and had not yet decided on a career. He figured that after graduation he might work full-time at his summer job as office clerk at the lumber mill near home while he made up his mind about a career. Why should Dave not delay his decision? What can he do to get help with this process?
3. View yourself in the career selection process. What do you view as important in a job? What special circumstances do you have? What emotional needs should your job fulfill? What would you have to do to qualify for the careers that interest you? What is blocking your way to achieving the career of your choice? Can you—or do you want to—overcome this obstacle?

RECOMMENDED READING

Bolles, Richard Nelson. *What Color Is Your Parachute?* Berkeley, Calif.: Ten Speed Press, 1982.
> A practical manual for job-hunters and career changers, with exercises to help you understand what is important to you in choosing your vocation. Revised and enlarged from previous editions.

College Placement Council. *College Placement Annual 1982.* Annual Editions. Bethlehem, Pa.: College Placement Council, 1982.
> A very useful guide for the college student attempting to select a career and find a job. The 1981 edition was available for $5 from the publisher, P.O. Box 2263, Bethlehem, PA 18001.

Encyclopedia of Careers and Vocational Guidance. 4th ed., 1978. Chicago: J. G. Ferguson Publishing Co., 1978.
> Volume I—*Planning Your Career.* Discussions are organized by industry and include job outlook as well as explanations of how the various jobs within an industry interrelate.

> Volume II—*Careers and Occupations.* Jobs are for both college graduates and non–college graduates. For each job, the following topics are covered: definition, history, nature of work, requirements, opportunities for experience and exploration, methods of entering, advancement, employment outlook, earnings, conditions of work, social and psychological factors, and sources of additional information.

Greco, Ben. *How to Get the Job That's Right for You.* Homewood, Ill.: Dow Jones, Irwin, 1980.
> A generalist's book on career decision strategies and the techniques of job search.

Kennedy, Marilyn M. *Salary Strategies: Everything You Need to Know to Get the Salary You Want.* New York: Rawson Wade, 1982.
> An approach to evaluating the market value of a job, negotiating a salary, and planning a career that maximizes your earning potential.

Kocher, Eric. *International Jobs: Where They Are, How to Get Them; A Handbook for over 500 Career Opportunities around the World.* Reading, Mass.: Addison-Wesley, 1979.
> This book provides a unique focus for persons interested in jobs outside the United States.

Kristol, Irving. "The High Cost of Equality." *Fortune,* November 1975, pp. 199-200.
> An interesting commentary comparing equality of income to equality of opportunity and discussing the costs and benefits of each type of equality.

Mucciolo, Louis, ed. *Small Business: Look Before You Leap.* Dobbs Ferry, N.Y.: Marlu, 1978.
> A catalogue of sources of information, government agencies, franchiser addresses, book outlines, sample forms, and the like to help you start and manage your own business. Can be obtained by writing Marlu, P.O. Box 111, Dobbs Ferry, N.Y. 10522.

Ramirez, Anthony. "Family on the Move: A Manager's Transfers Impose Heavy Burden on His Wife, Children." *Wall Street Journal,* February 28, 1979, p.1.
> A case history of some typical problems resulting from geographical job transfers.

Robbins, Paula I. *Successful Midlife Career Changes.* New York: Amacom (division of American Management Associations), 1978.
> A thorough analysis of the "midlife crisis" provides some insight for self-understanding. Strategies for action include a discussion of job change opportunities and an evaluation of the resources available to career changers.

U.S. Bureau of Labor Statistics. *Occupational Outlook for College Graduates*. 1980–81 edition. Washington, D.C.: U.S. Government Printing Office, 1980. (Bulletin 2076—biennial editions)
> A thorough listing of career possibilities, including brief discussions about the nature of the work; places of employment; training required, other qualifications, and advancement; employment outlook; and earnings and working conditions.

Winter, Dorothy. *Help Yourself to a Job—A Guide for Retirees*. Boston: Beacon Press, 1976.
> Although the Social Security discussions are dated, there is a good discussion of resources and opportunities available to retirees seeking to land a job or start a business.

Wright, John W. *The American Almanac of Jobs and Salaries*. New York: Avon, 1982.
> A survey of hundreds of jobs and their pay scales, with an analysis of the outlook for careers in various fields.

Zimmeth, Mary. *The Women's Guide to Re-Entry Employment*. Mankato, Minn.: Gabriel Books, 1979.
> A very "how-to" book, from the unique standpoint of preparing the re-entering homemaker with the tools and confidence to get the desired job.

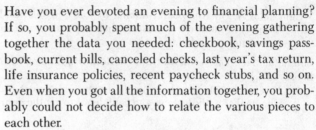

3

Your Financial Starting Point

Have you ever devoted an evening to financial planning? If so, you probably spent much of the evening gathering together the data you needed: checkbook, savings passbook, current bills, canceled checks, last year's tax return, life insurance policies, recent paycheck stubs, and so on. Even when you got all the information together, you probably could not decide how to relate the various pieces to each other.

Financial planning would be a lot easier if you could gather the necessary records together in a few minutes and then review a summary of the important relationships within your entire financial picture. In this chapter we will discuss a simple but adequate system of record keeping and the use of an income statement and a balance sheet.

RECORD KEEPING

The problem of locating your financial records can be solved by keeping them in a series of manila folders in a single box, preferably fireproof. Eventually you may need a file cabinet to store all your records.

As you can see in Table 3-1, the file system is composed of a general file, a budgeting file, a housing file, several insurance files, several investment files, and a tax file as well as files for guarantees and warranties, employment information, personal résumé, and credit records. An appropriate heading should be written on each one, along with a list of the contents and a notation about where the original documents can be found—whether in a safe-deposit box, at an attorney's office, or at a broker's office. Certain documents you will probably want to keep in a safe-deposit box because they are very difficult to replace:

- Birth certificate
- Military-discharge papers
- Wills (copy at home for reference)
- Marriage certificate

TABLE 3-1

Contents and Operational Checklist for Each File of Financial Records

Heading	Contents	Operational Checklist
General	Personal information sheet (Fig. 3-1) List of items in safe-deposit box Letter of last instructions (Chapter 22) Copy of will (Chapter 22) [The original should be kept with attorney or in a safe-deposit box.]	Update personal information sheet to reflect any changes. Update safe-deposit box list as new items are added or old ones eliminated.
Budgeting	Lists of goals Income statement (Chapter 3) Forecasts of income and expenses (Chapter 4) Forecasts for short-term and long-term goals (Chapter 4) Old budget control sheets (Chapter 4)	Review budget planning sheets. Revise goals, if necessary.
Housing	Purchase contract and receipt [deed in safe-deposit box] Mortgage papers Title insurance policy Home improvement receipts (including landscaping expenses) Property tax receipts Termite inspection and policy Copy of lease or rental agreement	Keep records of all permanent home improvements so that you can establish an accurate cost basis if you ever sell your home.
Property Insurance	Details of property insurance coverage [Insurance policies or a data sheet in a safe-deposit box.] Personal property inventory (Chapter 6) [copy in safe-deposit box] Pictures of highly valued items [negatives in safe-deposit box]	Change insurance limits on policy annually to reflect changes in personal property holdings and/or changes in replacement costs of all structures. Update personal property inventory once a year: add new items; revalue old items; eliminate items sold or lost; take more pictures, if necessary. Shop for rates. Get a minimum of three quotes before each renewal date (Fig. 6-2).

- Dissolution papers
- Diplomas
- Passports
- Property deeds

- Stock and bond certificates
- Automobile title papers
- Personal property inventory
- Insurance policies or data

Table 3-1 (continued)

Heading	Contents	Operational Checklist
Auto Insurance	Details of auto insurance coverage Record of traffic violations and accidents Auto registration receipts [ownership certificate in safe-deposit box]	Update fact sheet annually by adding new cars, amending coverages, and raising drivers' ages (Fig. 3-4). Update traffic violation and accident records. Note which violations or accidents occurred over three years ago and stop including them in insurance applications. Shop for rates. Get a minimum of three quotes before each renewal date (Fig. 7-1).
Health Insurance	Insurance policies or details of present health coverage, including employee plans Current medical history for each family member List of drugs to which each family member is allergic	Update health insurance fact sheet to reflect changes in limits, coverage (Fig. 3-4). Update medical histories to reflect new ailments, diseases, and immunizations received. Shop for rates. Get three quotes before each renewal date (Fig. 8-6)
Life Insurance	Details of insurance policies owned, including employee group plans [insurance policies or a data sheet in safe-deposit box] Results of eight-step procedure (Chapter 9) for determining life insurance needs	Recompute insurance needs using eight-step procedure every five years—sooner if new financial assets are acquired, or if family income or expenses change significantly. Update life insurance fact sheet to reflect changes in beneficiaries and coverage increases in employee policies (Fig. 3-4). Shop for at least three rate quotes before each change in policy (Fig. 9-10). Review the need for beneficiary changes.
Investments— General	Goal planning sheet (11-step procedure, Chapter 15) Annual balance sheets (Chapter 3) List of checking/savings accounts	Replan goals using 11-step procedure. Plot your progress using annual balance sheet.
Investments— Stocks and Bonds	Records of purchase and sale [All stock certificates and bonds should be kept either with broker or in safe-deposit box.] Records of stock dividends and bond interest List of stock certificate numbers and dates of issue (if you keep certificates in safe-deposit box rather than with broker) Transaction slips and monthly statements (annual envelopes)	Update records to reflect purchases and sales evidenced by transaction slips. Add new stock numbers and dates of issue to list (if certificates are sent to you). Place each year's transaction and monthly statements in an envelope.

Table 3-1 (continued)

Heading	Contents	Operational Checklist
Investments— Mutual Funds	Records of purchase and sale of mutual funds [Keep mutual fund shares with broker, with the mutual fund transfer agent, or in safe-deposit box.]	Use transaction slips and statements to update records of purchases, sales. Place each year's transaction slips and monthly statements in an envelope.
Tax	Purchase receipts, interest payment records, charitable gift confirmations, medical expense records, and so on. Tax forms, schedules, and supporting data for past 10 years Quarterly estimated tax forms W-2 forms, 1099 forms, and so on All canceled checks for last seven years	File all receipts required to substantiate deductions. After your annual tax form is filed, place all receipts and other substantiating records in an envelope and file either here or in extra storage boxes.
Guarantees and Warranties	All warranties relating to appliances, tires, carpets, and the like. Receipts Repair instructions	Add items to file as soon as purchased. Remove once each year all that have expired.
Employment Information	Employment contract, if any Employee handbook Fringe benefits information	Update file as necessary.
Personal Résumé	Details of previous education: years, major, degree(s), major professors and advisors (with address, phone number) Employment record: job titles, dates responsibilities, supervisors' names and addresses Residence record: dates and addresses	When you switch jobs, put information from employment file in here. Before you leave a school, update file with addresses you may need.
Credit Records	Papers showing resolution of prior debts Credit card numbers, names, and addresses Notification forms for lost or stolen cards	Update file as necessary.

Insurance policies need not be kept in a safe-deposit box; the insurance company has copies that in the event of a disaster can be requested. A list of insurance policy names, numbers, and addresses should be kept in the safe-deposit box, however, so that copies can be requested, if necessary, even by survivors who would not know the existence of all policies.

The appropriate operational checklist should be written on each file. It is a good idea to leave space in which to record the date when each task was last performed. The meaning of the checklists will become clear as you proceed through the text. In all cases, however, useless and outdated information should continually be weeded out, lest the files become unmanageable. Those files that accumulate bulky loads (tax files, for example) may require separate storage boxes. Not only will this file system be convenient; it could also save you money if you regularly update the information.

You will not be able to complete all the forms for the various files at this time since only the personal information sheet (Fig. 3-1), income statement (Fig. 3-2), and balance sheet (Fig. 3-3) will be dealt with in this chapter. For now, simply assemble as much of the file as you can and put important papers in your safe-deposit box.

FINANCIAL STATEMENTS

Locating your financial data is the first step in preparing for your tasks as money manager. The second step is to review your present financial situation and see how your assets and liabilities, income and expenses interrelate. You can do this by periodically drawing up an income statement and a balance sheet. The income statement shows where your money has come from and where it has gone over the past year. The balance sheet lists financial assets and debts and shows the difference between them—financial net worth. This is a distinction you should keep in mind: the income statement describes your recent financial history, whereas the balance sheet describes your financial situation at one point in time.

The Income Statement

The income statement is actually an income and expense statement. It summarizes where your income for the past year came from, where you spent your money, and how much you added to (or subtracted from) your savings and investments by the end of the year. The income statement used in this text does not follow strict accounting rules. Instead, it is an illustration of your cash inflows and outflows.

constructing an income statement To show you how to construct an income statement, we have provided a sample income statement (Fig. 3-2) and a set of instructions. The numbered steps in the instructions correspond to the numbers in the sample. The sample has been filled out for a fictitious couple, George and Sybil Barnes. Sybil has begun her career as a paralegal and is the family's primary source of income until George finishes graduate school. Note how they arrive at the numbers on their income statement, and then construct your own.

NAME(S)_____

DATE_____

Social Security No._____ Military I.D. No._____

PERSONAL INFORMATION SHEET

	ACCOUNT NUMBER	INSTITUTION NAME
Checking accounts	_____	_____
	_____	_____
Savings accounts	_____	_____
	_____	_____
Safe-deposit box (Location of keys)	_____	_____
Brokerage account	_____	_____

Location of stock certificates_____

Location of deeds_____

Location of other securities_____

Location of will_____

Executor's name_____ Phone_____

  Address_____

Attorney's name_____ Phone_____

  Address_____

Broker's name_____ Phone_____

  Address_____

Accountant's name_____ Phone_____

  Address_____

Insurance agent's name_____ Phone_____

  Address_____

(   ) name_____ Phone_____

  Address_____

FIGURE 3-1
Personal information
sheet for general file.
Other members of one's
family should know
where it is kept.

Instructions

1 *Income. List the dollar amounts of income received from all sources during the past year.*

NAME(S) *George and Sybil Barnes*

FOR THE YEAR BEGINNING JAN. 1, *1982* AND ENDING DEC. 31, *1982*

INCOME STATEMENT

1 *Income*

Wages or salary		
Husband *(summer job)*	$ 3,600	
Wife *(full-time job)*	16,000	
Dividends and interest	65	
Capital gains and losses (e.g., from sale of stock)	_____	
Rents, annuities, pensions, and such		
Other *sale of old car*	600	

2 *TOTAL INCOME* — $20,265

3 *Taxes*

Personal income taxes	$ 2,785
Social Security and disability taxes	1,230

4 *TOTAL TAXES* — 4,015

5 *Amount Remaining for Living Expenses and Investment* — 16,250

6 *Living Expenses*

	Fixed	Variable
Housing		
Utilities	700	_____
Repairs	_____	_____
Insurance	_____	_____
Taxes	_____	_____
Rent or mortgage payments	4,200	_____
Other_____		
Food	_____	4,100
Clothing (including laundry, dry cleaning, repair, and personal effects)	_____	900
Transportation		
Gas	_____	700
Repairs	_____	380
Licenses	_____	70
Insurance	400	
Auto payments or purchase	1,800	_____
Recreation, entertainment, and vacations	_____	750
Medical		
Doctor	_____	
Dentist	_____	120
Medicines	_____	60
Insurance		
Personal	1,800	180
Life insurance	100	
Outlays for fixed assets	_____	480
Other expenses_____		200
SUBTOTAL	9,000	7,940

7 *TOTAL ANNUAL LIVING EXPENSES* — $ 16,940

8 *Amount Remaining for Savings and Investment* — $ (690)

Sybil made $16,000 her first year working at a law firm. George made $3,600 working in a bank during the summer. Both of these figures represent gross income—what the employer paid, not the actual take-home salary. (Income taxes and Social Security and disability taxes will be subtracted in step 3.) The Barneses received $15 interest from a savings account at the local savings and loan and $50 from a mutual fund. George also sold his 1971 car for $600. He marked this cash inflow under "other."

2 *Total Income. Add all income items.*

George and Sybil accumulated $20,265 in 1982.

3 *Taxes. Enter the combined total of federal and state income taxes paid last year and the amount paid in Social Security taxes.* If you have a state disability tax, this should also be included here.

George and Sybil paid $2,785 in income taxes and $1,230 in Social Security taxes.

4 *Total Taxes. Add all tax items.*

The total for George and Sybil is $4,015.

5 *Amount Remaining for Living Expenses and Investment. Subtract total taxes (step 4) from total income (step 2).*

George and Sybil arrived at $16,250.

6 *Living Expenses. List those expenses that were reasonably fixed and those over which you had some control (variable).* Only by knowing which outlays you are committed to (that is, fixed expenses) will you be able to decide how much flexibility you will lose by undertaking additional fixed expenses.

To complete these blanks, George and Sybil looked back through their checkbooks and old receipts but had to make some guesses as well. In order of entry, their expenses were $700 for utilities; $4,200 for rent; $4,100 for food; $900 for clothing, repair, and personal effects; $1,150 for gas and car expenses; $400 for auto insurance; $1,800 for monthly payments on their car; $750 for entertainment; $180 for medicine and medical miscellany (Sybil's employer provides health insurance coverage); $1,800 for tuition; $180 for books, newspapers, and magazines; $100 for life insurance premium; $480 for a television; $200 for miscellany such as gifts, charitable donations, and unaccounted-for items.

7 *Total Annual Living Expenses. Add the subtotals of the fixed and variable expenses.*

George and Sybil spent $16,940 in 1982.

8 *Amount Remaining for Savings and Investment. Subtract living expenses (step 7) from the amount remaining for living expenses (step 5).* This amount represents the cash flow surplus realized from financial activities of the past year.

The Barneses lost $690—a loss they were able to cover by increasing the amount of their education loan. Eventually they will have to generate enough net income to repay the loan plus interest; during their college years, however, they expect to have a net cash outflow or to break even at best.

TABLE 3-2

Typical Expenses for a Four-Person Urban U.S. Family
(Annual budget as estimated in autumn 1980)

Category	Lower Budget		Intermediate Budget		Higher Budget	
	Cash Amount	*Percent of Total Budget*	*Cash Amount*	*Percent of Total Budget*	*Cash Amount*	*Percent of Total Budget*
Housing						
Shelter total	$ 1,959	14%	$ 3,998	17%	$ 5,382	16%
Renter	(1,959)		(2,533)		(3,988)	
Homeowner	(n.a.)		(4,486)		(5,628)	
Furnishings and operations	650	5	1,108	5	2,096	6
Food at home	3,717	26	4,664	20	5,558	16
Food away from home	605	4	907	4	1,466	4
Transportation total	1,160	8	2,116	9	2,751	8
Auto owners	(1,555)		(2,225)		(2,751)	
Clothing	907	6	1,292	6	1,888	5
Personal care	352	2	471	2	668	2
Medical care	1,298	9	1,303	6	1,359	4
Other consumption[a]	597	4	1,109	5	1,829	5
Other expenses[b]	583	4	957	4	1,610	5
Social Security and disability insurance taxes	881	6	1,427	6	1,608	5
Income taxes	1,337	10	3,781	16	7,924	23
Total Budget[c]	$14,044	100%	$23,134	100%	$34,409	100%

Source: U.S. Bureau of Labor Statistics, "Autumn 1980 Urban Family Budgets," Release: #81-195, April 22, 1981.

[a] Includes recreation and entertainment, books and magazines, tobacco, alcohol, and education.

[b] Includes gifts, charitable contributions, life insurance, and job-related expenses.

[c] 1981 figures released by the U.S. Department of Labor in April 1982 indicate these yearly incomes to maintain a lower-level, middle-level, and higher-level standard of living: $15,323, $25,407, $38,060.

"n.a." means "not applicable" since lower-budget households could not afford to buy a home.

Parentheses around numbers indicate that these are the expense figures for a subgroup in that expense category.

statistics on income and expenses Now that you have completed your income statement, you may want to get a perspective on it. Let's review a typical American family's income and expenses. Table 3-2 illustrates typical expense patterns for urban American families of four—parents in their thirties, one family breadwinner, two grade-school children—with incomes ranging from $14,000 to $35,000. As you can see from Table 3-3, roughly half of *all* American households were within that income range. For four-person households, this figure would be higher if, as is likely, smaller households include a higher proportion of sub-$10,000 earners. It should also be noted that families in certain high-cost Northeastern or Western metropolitan areas had to spend about 5 to 15 percent more than the figures in Table 3-2 to achieve the standard of living shown, whereas lower-cost Southern cities allowed budgets about 10 percent lower.

TABLE 3-3

Percent Distribution of Family Income

Income Level Constant (1979 dollars)	1955	1970	1979
Under $5,000	16.2%	7.4%	7.0%
$ 5,000-$ 9,999	22.7	13.9	13.6
$10,000-$14,999	27.4	16.1	15.6
$15,000-$19,999	18.7	22.2	15.0
$20,000-$24,999	7.0	11.6	14.4
$25,000-$34,999	4.9	18.1	19.2
$35,000-$49,999	2.0	6.9	10.3
Over $50,000	1.1	3.7	5.2
Median	$11,976	$18,444	$19,661

Source: U.S. Department of Commerce, *Statistical Abstract of the United States*, 1981, 102d edition, December 1981, pp. 435-36.

The figures in these two tables and the research behind them show the following differences in spending and income between lower- and higher-income families:

1. Lower-income families tend to rent housing while higher-income families tend to own their housing.
2. A higher proportion of lower-income families travel on mass transit systems rather than own their own cars.
3. Actual dollars spent for medical care (including insurance) are about the same for both lower- and higher-income families.
4. Discretionary "other consumption" (largely recreation) tends to rise relatively rapidly as income increases.
5. The percentage of the total budget spent on food decreases as income increases.

review your income statement   How does your income statement look? Are you spending money where you really want to? Are your fixed expenses too high to allow variable expense flexibility? Is your total housing expense less than 25 to 35 percent of your cash income? If it's over 35 percent, and especially if it's over 40 percent, you may have overextended yourself in this area. Look at your installment loans. If they're under 10 percent of your total income, you're probably being realistic about your financial commitments; over 20 percent and you may be getting yourself into financial trouble.

comparison of income statement and budget   How does an income statement differ from a budget? An income statement is a report on the *past*; a budget is a plan for the *future*. Before you can construct a budget, you must have some idea of how you have spent your money in the past. When you budget, you can assign priorities to various expense categories. Further discussion of the budget will be deferred to Chapter 4.

The Balance Sheet

The balance sheet lets you know your present financial position, which is the result of your past financial activities. The balance sheet is composed of assets and liabilities, balanced against each other. An asset is something you own, something you have acquired; in filling out your balance sheet, use the fair market value of your assets. A liability is money that you owe. The mathematical difference between assets and liabilities is *net worth*. Another way to look at a balance sheet is to say that your assets are the sum of what you have contributed (net worth) and what lenders have contributed (liabilities).

constructing a balance sheet   Fill out a balance sheet for yourself by completing steps 1 through 18 as in the sample (Fig. 3-3) for George and Sybil Barnes.

Instructions

1 *Cash. List total cash by noting cash on hand, checking account balance, and money in savings accounts, savings certificates, and money market funds.*

George and Sybil have on hand $15 cash. Their checking account balance reads $150 and they have $300 in a savings account at the local savings and loan. Therefore, their total cash is $465.

2 *Money Loaned. Estimate the return you can reasonably expect on money loaned.*

The Barneses loaned Sybil's brother $100 a year ago and as yet have not been repaid. They decide that there is a 25-percent chance of being repaid, and so they put $25 (25 percent of $100) on their balance sheet.

3 *Investments. List total investments by noting the values of savings bonds, stocks and bonds, mutual funds, life insurance, annuities, and retirement funds (put IRA and Keogh accounts here, as well as your employer's plan).* If you have savings bonds or bank bonds, determine how many years you have had them and read the current cash value off the table on each bond. To find the total value of your stock market investments, use the values in stock and bond and mutual fund tables in today's newspaper. Call your broker if a stock is not listed. Use the bid price, not the asked price, for over-the-counter stocks and mutual funds. If a fund is not listed in your local newspaper, check the *Wall Street Journal* at your library.

To find the current guaranteed cash value of a life insurance policy, turn to the table printed in the policy itself. Figures in the table are for each $1,000 of the face amount (total amount of insurance) for each year of the policy's age. The cash value of annuities can be determined in the same way. However, if you have started taking payments from your annuity policy, deduct the total payments received to date from the total amount you invested.

The cash value of a retirement fund should include only the amount you could withdraw in an emergency. Amounts that can be withdrawn only at retirement should be shown under fixed assets.

NAME(S) *George and Sybil Barnes*
DATE *January 10, 1983*

BALANCE SHEET

	ASSETS		LIABILITIES	
MONETARY ASSETS			12 *Unpaid Bills*	
1 *Cash*	$		Taxes	
On hand	15		Insurance	$
Checking account	150		premiums	210
Savings account	300		Rent	
TOTAL CASH		465	Utilities	32
			Charge accounts	323
2 *Money loaned to others*			Other	
(repayment expected)		25	TOTAL UNPAID BILLS	565
3 *Investments*				
Savings bonds	—		13 *Installment Loans* (balance due)	
Stocks and bonds			Automobile	3,580
Mutual funds	950		Other *television*	150
Cash value of			TOTAL	3,630
life insurance	50			
Cash value of				
annuities	—		14 *Loans* (balance)	
Cash value of			Bank	
retirement fund	—		Education	6,200
TOTAL INVESTMENTS		1,000	Other	—
4 TOTAL MONETARY ASSETS		$ 1,490	TOTAL	6,200
FIXED ASSETS			15 *Mortgage Loans* (balance due)	
5 *Home and property*	—		Home	—
6 *Investments*			Other	—
Other real estate	—		TOTAL	—
Retirement fund	—			
7 *Automobiles*	5,200		16 TOTAL LIABILITIES	$ 10,395
8 *Ownership interests*				
in small businesses	—			
9 *Personal property*	3,200		17 NET WORTH	(505)
10 TOTAL FIXED ASSETS		$ 8,400		$
11 TOTAL ASSETS OF FAMILY		$ 9,890	18 LIABILITIES AND NET WORTH	9,890

George inherited $900 worth of a mutual fund two years ago. Checking the stock market quotations, he finds that his investment is now worth $950. The Barneses' only other investment is a $10,000 life insurance policy that is three years old. Sybil looks down the "years" column on the table to 3 and reads across the "cash values" column to $5. Since the stated cash value applies to each $1,000 of coverage, she has a current cash value of $50 ($5 per $1,000 × 10 thousands). She has no accumulated dividends or interest, and so she puts $50 on

FIGURE 3-3
Sample balance sheet.

her balance sheet under "cash value." George and Sybil have a total of $1,000 in investments.

4 *Total Monetary Assets. Add total cash (step 1), money loaned (step 2), and investment assets (step 3). These assets can be quickly converted to cash if necessary.*
George and Sybil have $1,490 in monetary assets.

5 *Home and Property. Estimate what your house and land would sell for if you were to sell them today.* Check the newspaper listings, call a local realtor, or compare the price that a similar house on your block sold for recently.
The Barneses are renting and so enter nothing here.

MEASURING
YOUR NET
WORTH

6 *Investments. For "other real estate" compute the current market value as you did in step 5.* If you are in a partnership or syndicate, enter the current value of your proportionate share. Also include here the current cash value of any benefits that are available to you only at retirement or upon disability.
The Barneses own no real estate and so enter nothing here.

7 *Automobiles. Compare the blue book value of your car with the prices in the classified ads for similar cars and estimate the car's worth.*
George and Sybil bought a car a year ago for $6,200. They put down $1,400 and borrowed the rest at 14 percent interest per year. They estimate the car's present worth at $5,200.

8 *Small Business Interests. Use the current book value (total assets minus total liabilities) to determine your ownership interest in a small business.*
The Barneses have no such investments.

9 *Personal Property. Estimate the market value of salable possessions.*
The Barneses have some dishes, books, clothing, a new color television, and a diamond wedding ring. They estimate that if they were to sell these, they would get $3,200.

10 *Total Fixed Assets. Add the figures in steps 5, 6, 7, 8, and 9.*
George and Sybil have total fixed assets of $8,400.

11 *Total Assets of the Family. Add the figures in steps 4 and 10.*
The Barneses have total assets valued at $9,890.

12 *Unpaid Bills. Add the total amounts of bills that you have received but have not yet paid.* Bills that you know you will have to pay several months from now but have not yet come due should not be included.
George and Sybil have a $210 insurance premium, $32 utility bill, and $323 credit card balance—a total of $565 in unpaid bills.

13 *Installment Loans. Add the balance due (both principal and interest) on installment loans.*
George and Sybil have a total balance of $3,580 due on their automobile (a total loan of $4,800 minus total repayments to date of $1,220) and a balance of

$150 due on their television—a total installment loan balance of $3,630.

14 *Loans. Add the balance due (both principal and interest) on loans from bank, government, or other sources.*

George and Sybil owe $6,200 on loans they have taken out over the years to finance their educations. They have not yet started to repay these loans.

15 *Mortgage Loans. Enter only the principal balance due.*

The Barneses do not own a home and therefore have no mortgage.

16 *Total Liabilities. Add unpaid bills (step 12) and balance due on installment loans (step 13), loans (step 14), and mortgage loans (step 15).*

The Barneses have $10,395 in debts.

17 *Net Worth. Subtract liabilities (step 16) from assets (step 11).*

The Barneses have a negative net worth of $505. They do not have enough assets to cover all their debts. Although this is not a healthy financial position, it is fairly typical among college students today. One very important asset that does not appear on the Barneses' balance sheet is their educational attainment. This education may have little monetary value now, but probably represents hundred of thousands of dollars in future income.

18 *Liabilities and Net Worth. Add liabilities (step 16) and net worth (step 17).* This sum serves as a check on the math in each column. The sum of steps 16 and 17 should equal the total in step 11. This equality is essential to a balance sheet.

The Barneses' assets of $9,890 equal the sum of their liabilities and net worth.

evaluating your financial position   Now that you have computed your balance sheet, look at the figures. Are there any surprises? What questions do the figures raise? Why is your money used the way it is?

Consider your assets. Where have you put most of your money—into fixed assets or monetary assets? A good guideline is to try to have at least 30 to 50 percent of your net worth (the higher percentage as you approach retirement) in monetary assets. Your monetary assets are your emergency reserve and your source of funds to take advantage of unusual investment opportunities. Have you been accumulating monetary assets in anticipation of investment income or large purchases? What purpose does each of your assets serve? Do you have too much in any one asset? With the exception of your home, you are probably taking too much risk if you have any single asset (such as a single stock) worth more than 10 to 20 percent of your net worth.

Look at your liabilities. Compare your total amount of cash with your total bills due and with your monthly fixed expenses. Is your emergency cash reserve large enough to carry you for a few months if you were unable to work? Look at the loan liabilities you have incurred. If your non-mortgage loans total more than 50 percent of your non-real estate assets, you should be concerned about taking on any more debt. Such a high figure indicates that you tend to acquire assets by borrowing money and maybe that you are unable to save money or to pay off these debts. Which assets did these loans finance? Or did you use them to cover ordinary living

YOUR FINANCIAL
CONDITION ?

expenses? In general, how healthy is your financial condition? These are some of the questions we will help you answer in the following chapters.

How the Income Statement Affects the Balance Sheet

There are three basic changes that can occur in your balance sheet from one year to the next.

1. Funds can shift from one area to another, as when you sell an asset and buy another.
2. Your assets can increase or decrease, as when their market value changes.
3. Your liabilities can increase, as when you borrow money, or decrease, as when you pay off an installment loan.

Changes in your surplus or deficit (the "bottom line") on your income statement will affect the net worth that shows up on your balance sheet. For example, a surplus of $1,000 on your income statement might show up on your balance sheet as follows:

	Before	*After*
Assets	$20,000	$21,000
Liabilities	3,000	3,000
Net worth	$17,000	$18,000

If you had used the $1,000 surplus to pay off some of the liabilities, your net worth would still show a $1,000 increase. Similarly, a deficit or loss of $1,000 would wind up as either $1,000 less in assets or $1,000 more in liabilities.

In conclusion, you can increase your net worth by showing a surplus on your income statement (which has the effect of increasing assets), by making payments on your installment loans (which has the effect of reducing liabilities), or by having your assets increase in market value (a matter of luck, perhaps).

USING FINANCIAL STATEMENTS

Financial statements are often very helpful for such uses as filling out forms to borrow money, determining your insurance needs, making out a will, settling a divorce or an estate, and preparing your income tax forms.

Financial statements are also quite useful in helping you with your budget. Once you have constructed your income statement and balance sheet, you need not refer directly to the original data. With the income statement, you can plan next year's budget. You can see what you must spend, and you can allocate the remainder according to the goals you set in Chapter 1, whether for current consumption or for savings. With the balance sheet, you can reallocate assets according to your investment strategy (which will be discussed in Chapter 15). Or you can consider which debts to pay off first (generally those with the highest interest costs, as we shall see in Chapters 11 and 12).

In your directing function as money manager, you will probably rely more on personal judgment than on financial statements to help you select the best people or proper financial instruments. There are times, however, when you will need these statements even in this function. For example, when you apply for a loan or your children apply for college financial aid, you will have to present your financial statements.

To control your financial resources, you will again rely on these financial statements. With the income statement you know where your money went and can therefore make adjustments in the future. The balance sheet helps you see how well you have achieved your objectives. Only by creating a new balance sheet each year (more often if you prefer) can you monitor your progress.

Your Emergency Assets: Insurance Fact Sheets

Your insurance constitutes your emergency assets. These emergency assets are also part of your current financial condition, even though there is no traditional place for them on the balance sheet. However, they do represent cash assets in the case of certain emergencies. Therefore, you should summarize your emergency assets.

To help you organize this process, you can prepare fact sheets as in Figure 3-4 to insert in each insurance file you prepare (Figure 3-1). If you do not understand now all of the entries, you will once you study Chapters 6 through 9.

How Not to Do It

In 1973, a 40-year-old executive became senior vice-president of a major corporation; he felt on top of the world. He was drawing a $90,000 salary, hoped to receive at least $30,000 as an annual bonus (the average bonus received by his predecessor), and had accumulated $50,000 worth of his company's common stock.

In keeping with his new role, and to reward himself for his years of hard work, he bought a $25,000 Mercedes-Benz car (on a three-year loan) and moved into a big house with a sauna (and mortgage and property tax payments of $2,200 a month). He also felt he should own more of his company's stock, and so he used his existing stock as collateral for a bank loan and bought stock worth another $25,000.

After income taxes, his annual take-home pay was about $60,000, but his annual living expenses now ran close to $70,000. He figured that the $15,000 take-home pay on a $30,000 bonus would easily cover the deficit.

Unfortunately, 1974 and 1975 were not good years for the economy, and the corporation's profits fell, as did also the price of the stock. His bonus was only $5,000 ($2,500 take-home), and so his living expense debts continued unpaid—those on his credit cards at 18 percent interest. When the value of his $75,000 stock investment plummeted to $35,000, his banker firmly reminded him of the conditions of the $25,000 loan: collateral in stock equal to twice the amount of the loan.

The aggressive approach of this executive to spending and borrowing cost him much. He had to modify his lifestyle so that he could bring down his debts, and it was 1978 before his balance sheet got back to where it had been nearly five years earlier. A big income was no assurance of financial security. He had failed to apply to himself the very principles of balance sheet and income statement management that he used in his job!

PROPERTY INSURANCE FACT SHEET

Policy type _____

Company _____ Renewal date _____

	Limits		*Yes*	*No*
Home	$ _____	Endorsements		
Detached buildings	$ _____	Extended theft	____	____
Trees, shrubs, plants	$ _____	Inflation protection	____	____
Personal property on premises	$ _____	Replacement cost	____	____
		Full measure plus	____	____
Personal property off premises	$ _____	Other (e.g., earthquake, flood)	____	____
Additional living expenses	$ _____			
Comprehensive personal liability	$ _____			
Medical expense payments	$ _____	Deductible	$ _____	
Scheduled items	$ _____	Total annual premium $ _____		

AUTO INSURANCE FACT SHEET

	Car _____	Car _____
Company	_____	_____
Renewal date	_____	_____
Driver's age(s)	____ ____	____ ____
Public liability	*Limits*	*Limits*
Bodily injury	$ _____	$ _____
Property damage	$ _____	$ _____
Medical expenses (no fault)	$ _____	$ _____
Uninsured motorist protection	$ _____	$ _____
Physical damage		
Comprehensive	$ _____	$ _____
Deductible	$ _____	$ _____
Collision	$ _____	$ _____
Deductible	$ _____	$ _____
Annual premium	$ _____	$ _____

Total annual premium $ _____

LIABILITY INSURANCE FACT SHEET

Underlying Coverage	*Overriding Coverage*
Automobile $ _____	Company _____
Homeowners $ _____	Renewal date _____
	Amount $ _____
	Annual premium $ _____

FIGURE 3-4
Your emergency assets:
insurance fact sheets.

DISABILITY INCOME FACT SHEET

	Policy 1	*Policy 2*
Company	_____	_____
Renewal date	_____	_____
Monthly benefits		
For total disability	$ _____	$ _____
For partial disability	$ _____	$ _____
Maximum benefits		
Accident	$ _____	$ _____
Illness	$ _____	$ _____
Waiting period		
Accident	_____	_____
Illness	_____	_____
Total disability means	_____	_____
	_____	_____
	_____	_____
Annual premium	$ _____	$ _____

MEDICAL EXPENSE FACT SHEET

Base Coverage

Company _____ Renewal date _____

Benefits

  Room and board $ _____ for _____ days (maximum) _____

  Surgical maximum $ _____

  Hospital extras $ _____

  Physician care $ _____

Exclusions _____

Deductible $ _____ (per _____)

Annual premium $ _____

Major Medical Coverage

Company _____ Renewal date _____

Major medical maximum $ _____ (per _____)

Benefits _____ % of expenses in excess of deductible

Deductible $ _____ (per _____)

Reinstatement provisions _____ % or $ _____ per year per person

  whenever claims of more than this amount are not made in the year.

Exclusions _____

Annual premium $ _____

FIGURE 3-4
(continued)

LIFE INSURANCE FACT SHEET

On life of _____

	Policy 1	Policy 2
Company	_____	_____
Policy type	_____	_____
Face amount	$ _____	$ _____
Current coverage amount[a]	$ _____	$ _____
Issue date	_____	_____
Policy owner	_____	_____
Beneficiary	_____	_____
Dividend option[b]	_____	_____
Disability waiver	_____	_____
Accidental death and dismemberment	_____	_____
Net annual premium	$ _____	$ _____

On life of _____

	Policy 1	Policy 2
Company	_____	_____
Policy type	_____	_____
Face amount	$ _____	$ _____
Current coverage amount[a]	$ _____	$ _____
Issue date	_____	_____
Policy owner	_____	_____
Beneficiary	_____	_____
Dividend option[a]	_____	_____
Disability waiver	_____	_____
Accidental death and dismemberment	_____	_____
Net annual premium	$ _____	$ _____

[a]The actual amount of coverage may be different from the face amount if you have borrowed from the policy or if the policy (e.g., reducing term) has certain special features.

[b]Dividend code: (1) reduces premium, (2) accumulates with interest, (3) purchases paid-up additions, (4) purchases one-year term insurance, (5) paid in cash, (6) no dividend.

FIGURE 3-4
(continued)

CONCLUSION

In the first chapter you learned about setting financial goals and about the functions of a money manager. This chapter offers the tools necessary to begin managing. Only by first getting your financial records in order and by using your financial statements to know your present financial position can you establish a starting point from which to begin implementing the three primary strategies that will be discussed in the next three units.

VOCABULARY

balance sheet
fixed assets
fixed expenses
income statement

liabilities
monetary assets
net worth
variable expenses

CASE PROBLEM

Richard is just finishing his senior year in college. He carried a heavy course load that allowed him no time for a job during the school year. Last summer he went to a science camp, and so he has earned no money in the past 12 months. His only support for the year was $5,000 that his parents gave him and $1,600 that he borrowed through the college loan program. He will have to begin repaying this loan when he finishes school. His expenses for the year were $1,200 for tuition, $2,150 for room and board, $300 for books and supplies, $950 for gas and maintenance of his car, $500 for car insurance, and $1,500 for miscellaneous.

Richard's assets consist of his five-year-old car ($4,500 new, $1,400 after five years' use), his checking account ($180), and his personal belongings ($2,400). Liabilities include his college loan, a bookstore bill of $40, and the auto insurance annual premium that will come due next month.

Draw up Richard's income statement and compute his net income or loss for the past 12 months. Also, draw up his balance sheet as of today and compute his net worth.

RECOMMENDED READING

Curtin, Richard T. (ed.). *Surveys of Consumers 1974–75: Contributions to Behavioral Economics*. Ann Arbor: University of Michigan, Institute for Social Research, 1976.

    Articles describing many aspects of families as consumers, including income, expenses, assets, liabilities, and attitudes.

CHUCK AND NANCY ANDERSON

Their Balance Sheet and Income Statement

As you try to help Chuck and Nancy reach their financial goals in some of the next chapters, you will need to use their balance sheet and income statement.

As you can see from their income statement (Fig. 3-5), Chuck and Nancy together have a good income. They did incur a capital loss, however, on the sale of some common stock. Fixed expense items include auto payments of $133 a month ($1,600 a year) and furniture financing payments of $92 a month ($1,100 a year).

The balances outstanding on these loans show up on their balance sheet (Fig. 3-6) as liabilities. The balance due on the $4,000 automobile loan is $3,192 (24 monthly payments remaining). This loan could be repaid with a single $2,850 cash payment against the principal. The additional $342 is the 12 percent interest that is due over the remainder of the loan period. The balance due on the $4,000 furniture loan is $2,600. This five-year loan is two years old and carries a 15 percent annual interest cost.

Other loans on which they owe money are a $1,500 margin loan and a $45,000 first mortgage (10 percent interest for 30 years—$395 a month). The margin loan is money that Chuck's broker loaned him, at variable interest-only payments, to help him purchase stock. (As we shall see in Chapter 18, buying on margin is one example of an inappropriate financial strategy for the Andersons.) Without this loan, Chuck's common stock value would total $5,600. The principal balance due on the home mortgage is $43,500. This mortgage was a refinance of an earlier mortgage, which existed at the time of the sale.

On the assets side of their balance sheet, their house shows up as worth $85,000. It has appreciated in value almost $60,000 since they bought it nine years ago.

Questions

1. Judging by their income statement, what general financial concerns do you think the Andersons probably have? How important is each? What recent purchases helped to create a problem? Are all of the problems you see recurring ones?
2. With regard to the balance sheet, what factors appear to have contributed most to their positive financial position?

NAME(S) *Chuck and Nancy Anderson*

FOR THE YEAR BEGINNING JAN. 1, *1982* AND ENDING DEC. 31, *1982*

INCOME STATEMENT

1 *Income*

Wages or salary		
Husband	$26,000	
Wife (*half-time teacher*)	18,000	
Dividends and interest	430	
Capital gains and losses (e.g., from sale of stock)	(1,100)	
Rents, annuities, pensions, and such	————	
Other _____	————	

2 *TOTAL INCOME* — $43,330

3 *Taxes*

Personal income taxes	9,060	
Social Security and disability taxes	3,050	

4 *TOTAL TAXES* — $ 12,110

5 *Amount Remaining for Living Expenses and Investment* — $ 31,220

6 *Living Expenses*

	Fixed	Variable
Housing		
Utilities		2,400
Repairs		450
Insurance	320	
Taxes	1,100	
Rent or mortgage payments	4,740	
Other _*gardening*_		180
Food		5,260
Clothing (including laundry, dry cleaning, repair, and personal effects)		2,900
Transportation		
Gas		960
Repairs	151	1,050
Licenses	100	
Insurance	743	
Auto payments or purchase	1,600	
Recreation, entertainment, and vacations		2,860
Medical		
Doctor		194
Dentist		250
Medicines		25
Insurance	481	
Personal		950
Life insurance	570	
Outlays for fixed assets (*furniture*)	550	70
Other expenses *allowances for children*		110
SUBTOTAL	10,355	17,659

7 *TOTAL ANNUAL LIVING EXPENSES* — $ 28,014

8 *Amount Remaining for Savings and Investment* — $ 3,206

FIGURE 3-5
The Andersons' income statement.

NAME(S) *Chuck and Nancy Anderson*
DATE *January 16, 1983*

BALANCE SHEET

	ASSETS		LIABILITIES

MONETARY ASSETS

1 *Cash*
On hand — $ 50
Checking account — 350
Savings account — 1,200
TOTAL CASH — $1,600

2 *Money loaned to others*
(repayment expected) — 200

3 *Investments*
Savings bonds — 1,500
Stocks and bonds — 7,100
Mutual funds — 1,400
Cash value of
life insurance — 4,800
Cash value of
annuities — ———
Cash value of
retirement fund — ———
TOTAL INVESTMENTS — 14,800

4 TOTAL MONETARY ASSETS — $16,600

FIXED ASSETS

5 *Home and property* — 85,000

6 *Investments*
Other real estate — ———
Retirement fund — ———

7 *Automobiles* — 4,600

8 *Ownership interests
in small businesses* — ———

9 *Personal property* — 15,000

10 TOTAL FIXED ASSETS — $104,600

11 TOTAL ASSETS OF FAMILY — $121,200

12 *Unpaid Bills*
Taxes — ———
Insurance
premiums — ———
Rent — ———
Utilities — ———
Charge accounts — $ 620
Other — ———
TOTAL UNPAID BILLS — $620

13 *Installment Loans* (balance due)
Automobile — 3,192
Other *furniture* — 2,600
TOTAL — 5,792

14 *Loans* (balance)
Bank — ———
Education — ———
Other *margin account* — 1,500
TOTAL — 1,500

15 *Mortgage Loans* (balance due)
Home — 43,500
Other — ———
TOTAL — 43,500

16 TOTAL LIABILITIES — $51,412

17 NET WORTH — $69,788

18 LIABILITIES AND NET WORTH — $121,200

FIGURE 3-6
The Andersons' balance sheet.

4

Budgeting

Budgeting is simply allocating one's income to cover one's expenses. Some people realize that they need to budget when they cannot write a check to cover the price of something they want or need. For example, if you find a $300 dishwasher you want, but you have only $100 in the bank, you are forced either not to buy it or to buy it on credit and pay an interest cost of 18 percent or more a year. Some people do not realize that they need to budget until their lack of financial management has more serious consequences: they often run out of money before the next paycheck comes, they cannot pay their bills but keep incurring new ones, or they are unable to save any money.

Budgeting requires that you set goals. When a budget provides a means for you to improve or maintain your lifestyle in the ways you and your family select, it is worthwhile. In general, budgeting will help you *achieve your goals* by allowing you to consider all your spending alternatives within a single framework. Specifically, budgeting will help you do the following:

1. Save for the things you want (reducing the need for consumer credit).
2. Live within your income by planning ahead.
3. Provide a means for resolving family financial arguments.
4. Keep an annual record of all tax deductions for income tax purposes, since budgeting involves a system of record keeping.

If you recognize far enough in advance that you will need something, you can save money each month so that you can buy it when the time comes. People who dread trying to save should realize that when they buy something on credit they are, in effect, enrolling in a forced savings plan. Each month, instead of investing the amount of their payment and *earning* interest on it, they are giving that money to the creditor and *paying* interest. The price of buying on credit is the monetary difference between the interest you would receive from a savings account and the interest you must pay for using credit.

You probably think a lot about vacations because you are forced to plan for them. Your school tells you months in advance when vacations begin and end. When you begin a full-time job, you probably are required to schedule your vacation months ahead. By planning for a vacation, you prepare to get the most out of it so that when it finally comes, you are ready for it. This technique of planning for things in advance can make you financially prepared to enjoy them. It gives you something to look forward to, some reason for saving money or waiting until you can get the best.

Budgeting can mean a lot to couples who frequently accuse each other of spending too much money. It enables you to spend money without guilt. By deciding jointly how much money to spend on what before the money is spent, you can make planned purchases knowing that other family members agree with your spending. Budgeting, then, can be a means of keeping peace in the family by uniting family members to achieve goals that have been planned for and selected in advance. This is all the reason most families need to give budgeting a try.

Budgeting, as described in this chapter, is meant to be a tool for you to use to get what you want with money. It can help you plan expenditures, control them, and record them. If it becomes merely tedious bookkeeping, then it is not serving its purpose.

HOW NOT TO DO IT

Phil Whitney believed he was on his way to being a successful architect, but business debts and rising overhead were keeping his income from rising as quickly as the family's aspirations. Last year he made $27,000 but the family spent $28,200. At least that's what Phil estimated from the fact that there wasn't money in the checkbook in recent months to pay off the credit card balance of about $1,200.

Now the family was building the dream home that Phil and Ellie had been designing for several years. They hadn't stopped to figure out how much they could spend. Ellie was busy raising the children and completing her college education on a part-time basis. Phil felt guilty about his long hours at work away from the family and was too embarrassed to admit that he wasn't earning enough.

A year later, the debts and expenses weighed even more heavily. The credit cards were all at the limit allowed. The bank would lend no more than the $5,000 already extended because Phil couldn't show how he could pay it off out of his then $31,000 income. The new house cost more to operate than he had expected, the kids were costing more, and Ellie was still a year away from earning her degree.

Phil couldn't postpone facing the problem any longer. He spent a whole weekend locked in his study preparing a budget to get them out of debt within five years. At last he was finished. His four-point plan was as follows:

1. All charge cards would be locked in the safe-deposit box until the debts were paid.
2. No member of the family could spend more than $5 a week without getting authorization from Phil.

3. Ellie would get a part-time job right away, then a full-time job after graduation, and deposit her entire paycheck in the checking account that Phil would manage.
4. There would be no entertainment expenses except for one movie a month that the whole family would decide on.

There was an immediate revolt. Over the next few months, Phil and Ellie fought constantly about money. Divorce threatened. These problems distracted Phil from his work; his productivity fell off.

Fortunately, Phil and Ellie saw a marriage counselor, who helped them learn to communicate about money. Then a credit counselor worked out a plan, with the consent of Phil and Ellie, that resulted in getting their debts paid off over the next four years; but money remained an unpleasant topic of conversation in the family.

HOW TO SET UP A SUCCESSFUL BUDGET: THE PLANNING STAGE

It is not enough merely to decide to try budgeting. To develop a good, workable budget requires careful planning.

The Objectives of Budgeting

Budgeting has two objectives, both of which must be accomplished if a budget is to be successful. The first objective is to *implement a system of disciplined spending.* Instead of spending money each month until the checkbook balance reads zero, you and your family must learn to spend each month only as much as is allotted for various expense categories. For example, if the money allotted for entertainment has been used up, none of the extra $100 in the checkbook can be spent on entertainment since that money has been allotted for something else (perhaps, the insurance premium that is due next month).

The second objective is to *reduce the amount of money wasted through needless expenditures* in each budgeted expense category. One way is to save on interest payments by properly spacing out your major purchases. Another way is to get family agreement on how money should be spent. Much money is wasted when family members try to get their "fair share" after one member's impulse purchase.

Step 1: Becoming Aware of Expenditure Patterns

The first step in planning a successful budget is to become aware of how your money has been spent in the past and how it is being spent now. Check your income statement (Chapter 3) for past expenditures. To get an up-to-date, detailed breakdown of current expenditures, keep a trial budget. We suggest that you decide on a manageable budget period (perhaps a month) during which to study your family's spending habits. Then, for one period simply record what you and your family are doing with the money you receive. Keep a pad of paper and a pencil in a place where it will be convenient for every member of the family to jot down daily how much he or she spent that day and what was purchased. Round the amounts to the nearest dollar and keep a running total for each day. Of course, if you spend small amounts daily (such as 50¢ for coffee), add these together on a weekly basis and round the total amount.

Step 2: The Planning Session

During the planning session you and your family will meet to decide what you want to spend your money on and set priorities for your goals. Each family member should be involved in giving direction to your family's life. If all have a say in the goals represented by the budget, everyone will probably try to help make the system work.

Before the actual meeting, you must find out what your average income will be for the next year and decide on appropriate expense categories for your budget. Then the family members can make known their goals and determine the monthly cost of reaching them.

sources of income for the coming year Let us assume that you have chosen to use a month as the budget period. To help yourself forecast your average income over the next year, design a worksheet like that shown in Figure 4-1, which has been filled out for a fictitious young couple, Alexander and Karen. Karen is 18 months from completing her education and training in physical therapy. They have a two-year-old son.

1. Estimate your annual after-tax income in each category other than salary.
2. Enter the amount of your after-tax paycheck (your take-home pay) in the appropriate salary category for each month in the next year. You may also use gross pay if you show taxes and other payroll deductions in the appropriate budget expense category.
3. Divide the annual total for each category by 12 to get the average estimated income per month.
4. Total the monthly figures to get the amount that is to be distributed for monthly expenditures (your total average monthly expenditures allowed), and enter that figure in the box at the bottom of the "average per month" column.
5. At the end of the year, total the year's actual income in the last column.

From your income you will need to set aside a minimum cash reserve of probably between $300 and $600. This checkbook (or savings account) working capital can be used to allow for intermediate fluctuations in expenses such as will occur with large lump-sum fixed expenses that come due before enough money has been accumulated to cover them.

grouping expenses It is easier to budget and plan your expenditures if you group expenses. Break down your recorded expenditures for the past budget period into several general categories such as food, clothing care, personal grooming, entertainment, transportation, and shelter. Examples of expense groupings compiled from several successful budgets are given in Figure 4-2. You may want to make some changes such as having a separate category for vacations, or putting all clothing-

NAME(S) Alexander and Karen

DATE December 1982

FORECASTING INCOME

Source	Jan.	Feb.	Mar.	Apr.	May	June	July	Aug.	Sept.	Oct.	Nov.	Dec.	Estimated 12-Month Total	Average Per Month	Actual Year's Income
Husband's take-home wages or salary	1,200	1,200	1,300	1,300	1,300	1,300	1,300	1,300	1,300	1,300	1,300	1,300	$15,400	$1,283⅓	
Wife's take-home wages or salary															
Bonuses or commissions												1,000	1,000	83⅓	
Interest	10			10			10			10			40	3⅓	
Dividends			40			40			40			40	160	13⅓	
Rents															
Annuities, pensions															
Other															
TOTAL	1,210	1,200	1,340	1,310	1,300	1,340	1,310	1,300	1,340	1,310	1,300	2,340	$16,600	$1,383	

FIGURE 4-1
Sample worksheet for estimating next year's income.

Housing (20-35%)
 Rent
 Mortgage payments
 Repairs and improvements
 Property insurance
 Property taxes

Utilities (4-7%)
 Gas and electricity
 Waste disposal
 Water
 Telephone

Food (15-30%)
 All food items
 Meals taken out
 Pet food

Family Necessities (2-4%)
 Laundry and dry cleaning
 Toiletries and cosmetics
 Barber and hairdresser
 Postage and stationery
 Minor home furnishings

Medical (2-8%)
 Insurance
 Drugs and medicines
 Hospital bills
 Doctor bills
 Dentist bills

Clothing (3-10%)
 All clothing purchases
 Alterations
 Repairs (shoes and so on)

Automobile and Transportation (6-20%)
 Purchase or installment payments
 Gas and oil
 Insurance and license fees
 Repairs, parking, and tolls
 Rental, taxi, and bus fare

Recreation and Entertainment (2-6%)
 Admissions
 Games and hobbies
 Club dues
 Alcoholic beverages
 Tobacco
 Photographic supplies
 Musical supplies
 Sporting goods

Personal Improvement*
 Books
 Magazines and newspapers
 Tuition and course fees

Short-Term Goal Fund*
 Vacations
 Other special purchases

Savings and Investment (5-9%)
 Long-term goals

Outlays for Fixed Assets (2-8%)
 Major purchases or installment
  payments on appliances, garden
  equipment, and furniture
 Repairs (appliance and television)

Mad Money (1-4%)

Gifts*

Church and Charity*

Life Insurance*

Taxes*

Contingency*
 Legal services
 Unspecified debt repayments
 Union/professional dues

FIGURE 4-2
Suggested budget and
expense classifications
and expense guidelines.

(Figures in parentheses are suggested budget limits for each category, in percentages of total budget remaining after taxes. Variations are due to income levels, family size, and—primarily—personal choice.)

*These categories have no suggested limits since such expenditures vary greatly from person to person.

related expenses into one classification that includes laundry and dry cleaning expenses. Of course, some categories may not pertain to you at all. Tax, for example, should be included only if you usually pay more than is withheld from your paycheck. This category will then help you plan for the excess amount. However, if you budget your gross pay, you should put your withholding tax here and your other payroll deductions in the appropriate expense category.

Note that the suggested classifications also include a savings and investment category. If you do not budget for savings and actually deposit the amounts budgeted, you probably will find it difficult to save for things you want such as a new rug or your children's college educations. Instead, you may have to do without or borrow the money at 18 percent and make interest payments that cut into what you can spend on other things.

Note also the "mad money" category. This is designed to keep your family from resenting the budget scheme. It minimizes the chances that the budget will become too restrictive. Every member of the family should have a certain amount of money to spend on impulse or save for something special without having to account for it. It also would help to have a separate clothing budget for each member of the family.

No matter how you classify your expenses, you should observe a few logical rules:

1. Keep similar expenses in the same category.
2. Set up enough different categories so that you have a meaningful record of your expenses. Do not lump too many different expenses into catchall categories.
3. Keep the number of categories small enough to make bookkeeping simple.

emotional insights into budgeting   It is extremely important that each family member understand that in setting up family budgets, holding planning meetings, or operating a budget, certain emotional problems may arise. Being aware of these potential problems is part of the solution; if each family member is willing to discuss sensitive issues before they flare up and threaten to get out of hand, then you are a long way toward a complete solution.

Have each family member review this list of attitudes and emotions that often impair a family's ability to set up and operate a successful budget.

- *Spending for status*. Spending money in the same way as your identification group (see Chapter 1) is one way of achieving acceptance by your peers. Ask yourself whether it is really *your* values that make you want to buy dancing lessons for your daughter, put a pool in your backyard, or buy a luxury car.
- *Use of money to control*. Does one member of the family write all the checks, withhold information about family finances, belittle other family members' spending wishes, or require everyone else to ask the "controller" for money? Such a situation would definitely lead to lack of cooperation or even rebellion by the other members of the family with regard to a budget.
- *Retaliatory spending*. To get her fair share out of a husband's promotion and a transfer that requires her to give up her home and move to another town, the wife might go out and buy a fur coat. Then, to get his share as well, the husband might decide that he needs a new car to go along with his new status and then buy one without consulting his wife. Acting on these emotional urges can cause a budget to get out of balance quickly.
- *First claim to money earned*. In a two-income family, are the salaries considered "hers" and "his"? There is a common tendency for wage earners to spend the

money on themselves first. After all, they earned it, right? This problem can also initiate a cycle of retaliatory spending.

- *Lack of self-esteem.* Many people spend more on their family than they can afford in an effort to win affection within the family. Others spend lavishly on gifts for friends or coworkers to gain social acceptance in their identification groups.

FIGURE 4-3
Sample forecast for
short-term goals.

family meeting The first order of business should be to inform your family what they are currently spending their money on. Identify the areas and the totals. Do not be critical of how money was spent or chastise any member of the family for seemingly spendthrift ways. Simply inform. The second order of business should be to discuss goals—the areas in which each member would like to see money spent. Ask each person to number his or her goals in order of importance (see Chapter 1 for goal planning) and transcribe these goals onto a goal forecasting sheet. Use the short-term goal sheet (Fig. 4-3) for goals that can be reached during the next 12 months. You can call this your short-term goals fund. Some people like to put unexpected or surplus income into this category as well, to allow for budget flexibility. If unneeded here, it can be added to savings later. For long-term goals, use the long-term goal sheet (Fig. 4-4), and set aside funds in the savings and investment category to achieve them. In Chapter 15 we will see how to use investment planning and monthly investment commitments to reach these goals.

NAME(S) *Alexander and Karen*

DATE *December 1982*

FORECASTING SHORT-TERM GOALS

Goals	Jan.	Feb.	Mar.	Apr.	May	June	July	Aug.	Sept.	Oct.	Nov.	Dec.	Total	Average by Month
New rug										240			240	20
Ski trips	150	150											300	25
Build barbecue					84								84	7
Vacation								600					600	50
Visit family												108	108	9
TOTAL	150	150			84			600		240		108	1,332	111

NAME(S) *Alexander and Karen*

DATE *December 1982*

FORECASTING LONG-TERM GOALS

Goals	Years from Now					Beyond Five Years
	1	2	3	4	5	
European vacation					3,300	
Summer home						10,000 (uncertain)
Replace car			4,140			
Son's education						10,000 (yr. 16)
TOTAL			4,140		3,300	20,000

FIGURE 4-4
Sample forecast for long-term goals.

goals   Divide the cost of each goal that can be reached within five years by the number of months you have in which to achieve it, and place the total monthly figure in your savings and investment category. (We are not yet ready to consider goals that will be reached after more than five years. For these we must take into account inflation, taxes, and investment yield, which will be dealt with in Chapter 15.) For shorter-term goals it is probably adequate to assume that the interest earned will roughly offset the inflation in the price of the goal. Karen and Alex had to allocate $115 a month ($4,140 × 36) for replacing their used car three years from now and $55 a month ($3,300 × 60) for the European trip they expect to take in five years.

expenses   Forecast the rest of your expenses by using your month-long expense record and your checkbook.

First, determine the cost of fixed expenses such as rent or mortgage, insurance premiums, and installment payments. Enter these amounts under the months when the expenses will be incurred. (See Figure 4-5 for an example.) This breakdown will let you know when your major bills are due and will enable you to plan to pay them without having to borrow. Take careful note of the fixed expenses that will come due within the next few months. If you do not have a large enough cash reserve, temporarily cut back your spending in other categories to make sure you can meet these early obligations without borrowing.

NAME(S) *Alexander and Karen*

DATE *December 1982*

FORECASTING

Expense Category	Fixed and Variable Subcategories	Jan.	Feb.
Housing	Rent, mortgage payments, insurance, and taxes	$320	$320
	Repairs and improvements		
Utilities		46	46
Food		220	220
Family necessities		45	45
Medical	Insurance		
	Doctor, dentist, drugs, and hospital	20	20
Clothing		80	80
Automobile	Purchase payments, insurance, and license fees	192	36
	Gas, oil, repairs, parking, tolls, and so on	80	80
Recreation and entertainment	General	45	45
Personal improvement	Magazines and newspapers	12	12
	Books and tuition	120	
Short-term goal fund		150	150
Savings and investment	For long-term goals	170	170
Outlays for fixed assets	Repairs	10	10
	Purchases and installments	20	20
Mad money		40	40
Gifts		20	20
Church and charity		25	25
Life insurance			
Taxes			
Contingency	Legal services, debt repayments, union dues	16	16
TOTAL BY MONTH		1,631	1,355

FIGURE 4-5
Sample forecast of
expenses.

EXPENSES

Mar.	Apr.	May	June	July	Aug.	Sept.	Oct.	Nov.	Dec.	12-Month Total	Average by Month
$320	$320	$320	$320	$320	$320	$320	$320	$320	$320	$3,840	$320
43	40	40	39	35	35	35	38	40	43	480	40
220	220	220	220	220	220	220	220	220	220	2,640	220
45	45	45	45	45	45	45	45	45	45	540	45
				paid by employer							
20	20	20	20	20	20	20	20	20	20	240	20
80	80	80	80	80	80	80	80	80	80	960	80
			192							420	35
80	80	80	80	80	80	80	80	80	80	960	80
45	45	45	45	25	45	45	45	45	65	540	45
12	12	12	12	12	12	12	12	12	12	144	12
	120					120				360	30
		84			600		240		108	1,332	111
170	170	170	170	170	170	170	170	170	170	2,040	170
10	10	10	10	10	10	10	10	10	10	120	10
20	20	20	20	20	20	20	20	20	20	240	20
40	40	40	40	40	40	40	40	40	40	480	40
20	20	20	20	20	20	20	20	20	260	480	40
25	25	25	25	25	25	25	25	25	25	300	25
					240					240	20
				covered by withholding							
16	16	16	16	16	16	16	16	16	16	192	16
1,166	1,283	1,247	1,162	1,330	1,998	1,278	1,401	1,163	1,534	16,548	1,379

FIGURE 4-5
(continued)

Second, estimate amounts for the remaining expense and investment categories. If you wish to keep the same lifestyle as in previous months (at least in some categories), look back over your past expenditures. From them you can estimate what amounts to enter in your budget plan. Do not become too involved in deciding exactly how many dollars to allocate to each category. After you use your budget for a couple of months, you can revise the amounts (especially for regular expenses such as food, laundry, and commuting) to reflect more closely your actual expenses.

The following tables and figure may give you some idea of whether your estimates are grossly over or under what might be expected under certain conditions:

- Table 3-2 (p. 52) shows approximately what portion of the total living expenses a typical urban U.S. family of four is likely to spend on major expense categories.
- Figure 4-2 suggests some guidelines for certain expense categories.
- Table 4-1 shows broad expense allocations for Americans as a group. Note that durable goods (such as autos and appliances) consume about 10 percent of total income, nondurable goods (such as clothing and food) take 31 percent, services (such as health and meals out) and interest take 37 percent, and the balance of around 5 percent is saved.
- Table 4-2 shows variations in living expenses based on family size.
- Table 4-3 shows variations in living expenses for selected urban areas. Persons who live in rural areas may need to spend less than do these city-dwellers.

Consider these norms in light of your own circumstances and experience.

Total each category for the 12-month projection and divide by 12 to arrive at monthly allowable expense limits. Now total the monthly averages.

priorities   Can the total monthly average be accommodated by your average monthly income? If not, start making some priority decisions. Where can you make changes? What goals can be postponed? Let the family set some priorities. Do they want several magazines each month or more steak dinners? Do they want a camping trailer or more clothes? A long summer trip or weekend activities? An expensive new car or a compact? Because your income is limited, your family cannot have everything they want all at once. They must learn to use money to buy only those things they really want. The planning process will require sacrifices and compromises, but it is best to resolve these issues before the money is spent.

HOW TO SET UP A SUCCESSFUL BUDGET: RECORDING EXPENDITURES

The success of a budget depends partly on how often family members record their expenditures. Expenditures should be recorded often enough that none is forgotten, but not so often that the procedure becomes a nuisance. Perhaps recording expenditures could be done when the entire family is together. If each member sees other family members trying to make the budget work, everyone will be motivated to participate. Or, you may wish to make a habit of recording expenses as soon as you get home from shopping, work, or school, before you forget what you spent that day. If the family tends to congregate in the kitchen, you might keep the budget book there. The idea is to make the recording function as automatic as possible.

TABLE 4-1
Use of Personal Income in the United States
(Figures in billions of dollars)

Year	Personal Income	Personal Taxes	Disposable Personal Income (DPI)	Consumption Expenses			Personal Saving	
				Durable Goods	Nondurable Goods	Services	Amount	% of DPI
1967	$ 629	$ 83	$ 546	$ 73	$215	$205	$ 41	7.5%
1970	801	115	686	85	265	269	51	7.4
1973	1,052	151	902	124	334	352	70	7.8
1974	1,155	170	985	122	376	391	72	7.3
1975	1,256	169	1,087	133	409	438	84	7.7
1976	1,381	196	1,184	157	443	491	68	5.7
1977	1,538	226	1,312	179	479	548	74	5.6
1978	1,722	259	1,463	199	530	620	76	5.2
1979	1,944	302	1,642	212	602	696	86	5.2
1980	2,160	338	1,822	212	676	785	101	5.6
1981	2,404	388	2,016	232	743	883	107	5.3
1967-81 Increase	+282%	+367%	+269%	+218%	+246%	+331%	+161%	—

Source: Council of Economic Advisors, *Economic Indicators* Washington, D.C.: Government Printing Office, February 1982), pp. 4, 6. 1967 data are from pre-1975 issues.

Note: The figures in this table relate to each other as follows: personal income minus personal taxes equals DPI; DPI minus consumption expenses equals personal saving. For a perspective on how personal income relates to other components of national income, see Figure 17-2.

TABLE 4-2

Consumption Budgets for Different Family Types—Autumn 1980
(Annual figures for average urban U.S. family)

Family Type	Average Living Expenses (excluding income and Social Security taxes)		
	Lower Budget	*Intermediate Budget*	*Higher Budget*
Single person, under 35	$ 3,940	$ 5,940	$ 8,140
Married couple, under 35			
No children	5,510	8,310	11,400
Two children, under 6	8,090	12,220	16,750
Married couple, 35-54			
One child, 6-15	9,220	13,910	19,080
Two children, 6-15	11,243	16,969	23,266
Three children, up to 15	13,040	19,680	26,990
Married couple, over 65	5,730	8,650	11,870

Source: U.S. Department of Labor, Bureau of Labor Statistics. "Autumn 1980 Urban Family Budgets."
Note: For a breakdown of living expenses by category for a typical four-person family, see Table 3-2.

TABLE 4-3

Cost of Living in Selected Urban Areas—Autumn 1980
(Annual figures for a four-person family)

Metropolitan Area	Average Living Expenses (including income and Social Security taxes)		
	Lower Budget	*Intermediate Budget*	*Higher Budget*
Anchorage	$20,987	$29,682	$42,125
Honolulu	18,480	28,488	44,396
Boston	15,076	27,029	41,306
New York-New Jersey	14,393	26,749	42,736
San Francisco-Oakland	15,735	24,704	36,817
Washington, D.C.	15,392	25,203	37,398
Detroit	13,939	23,168	34,268
Chicago	14,303	23,387	34,198
Seattle-Everett	15,684	23,392	33,524
Los Angeles-Long Beach	15,172	22,500	34,124
Denver	13,821	22,813	33,607
Houston	13,519	21,572	31,519
Atlanta	13,082	21,131	31,229

Source: U.S. Department of Labor, Bureau of Labor Statistics.

A Recommended System

To make it easy to record expenses, the record-keeping system should be simple—with the budget categories easy to find and the arithmetic easy. Yet it should allow you to keep close watch on how much is being spent. Here is one system that meets these specifications.

1. Keep budget category sheets in a loose-leaf binder. Set aside plenty of pages for each category and mark each category section with a paper clip, tab, or colored sheet of paper to make it easy to find.
2. For a while, you may wish to use a bankbook type of entry system for each category, as shown in Figure 4-6. For example, if you spend $30 of the monthly $240 food allotment, enter the date of the expenditure, the item purchased, and the amount spent; then subtract the amount ($30) from the previous balance ($240). Subtract the next food expenditure from the remaining balance ($210). This system lets you see how much money you have left in a category at any time.
3. In the last column put a check by expenses that qualify as tax deductions and therefore might help you determine your taxable income. If, for example, you bought the $30 worth of groceries for a Boy Scout picnic, you can deduct the expense as a charitable gift. In fact, you might well have chosen to record this item in the "charitable contributions" category instead of in "food." (Chapter 10 will cover the expense categories that might have tax ramifications.)
4. To make the arithmetic quick and easy, round each expense entry to the nearest dollar.

For those who do not need to know exactly what the current balance is in each category during the month, it would be much simpler to record the description and amount of each item, to be totaled at the end of each month. Keep each category on a separate page.

Recording Transactions and Monthly Statements

If you make purchases on a charge account or with a credit card, it is better to record each transaction as you make it than to wait until the monthly statement arrives and enter all the purchases at one time. Although the latter method is easier, it may let

Date	Item	Amount	Balance	Tax Check (✓)
1/2/83			$240	
1/5/83	groceries	$30	210	✓ Boy Scout picnic
1/8/83	lunch	5	205	

FIGURE 4-6
Sample system for recording expenses.

you run over your budget, whereas the former method lets you keep track of your expenses and control them before you have spent too much. Only for regular expenses such as gasoline, perhaps, can you safely use the monthly statement method.

When accounting for a cash loan or installment purchase-loan in your budget, enter the loan repayments as an expense each month. Do not enter either the loan amount or the initial purchase. In other words, you fit the monthly loan repayments (including interest)—not the actual purchase—into the budget category that you spent the loan money on.

HOW TO SET UP A SUCCESSFUL BUDGET: CONTROLLING EXPENDITURES

At the end of the month when you try to see how well the budget has worked, remember that you want to make your family comfortable with the budget system. Remind yourself not to get upset if the money spent that month bears no resemblance to the amount you budgeted. Nothing will damage a budget's chances for success more than a premature indictment of the family's spending habits. Also, do not try to account for every dollar. Some small amount of money will always be unaccounted for, and will have disappeared as surely as if the family cat had eaten it.

If you have kept your budget up to date, the control function can be accomplished in three steps.

1. Add all the expenditures for the budget period, category by category, and enter these figures on the budget control sheet (Fig. 4-7) under "actual."
2. Subtract the actual expenses in each category from the budgeted expenses and enter these figures on your control sheet under "plus or minus." You will then be able to see how much you have left over or how much you overspent in each category. For example, in January Alex and Karen overspent on food by $5 but spent only $25 of their $40 gift allotment (Fig. 4-7).

   The +$170 in the savings category is not a good sign, but, due to heavy expenses in other categories, they were unable to put $170 into savings in January; however, they got back on track in their savings program by March.

   In later months you will be subtracting actual expenses from the figure in the balance forward column to get the amount of money you have overspent or underspent. The balance forward equals the plus or minus amount added to the monthly budgeted amount.
3. Consider those expense categories that exceeded the budget limits and those that fell short. Was too little money budgeted for the former categories and too much for the latter? Or did you simply overspend in some categories because of carelessness or unusual circumstances?

A budget must be realistic before a family can feel comfortable with it and be concerned about reducing expenditures in various categories. Every few months carefully analyze which categories were so far underestimated that they carried forward large deficits and which ones were so liberally funded that they carried

BUDGET CONTROL SHEET

NAME(S) *Alexander and Karen*

DATE *January – April 1983*

Expense Category	Budgeted Monthly Average	Month: Jan.		Month: February			Revised Monthly Average	Month: March			Month: April		
		Actual	Plus or Minus	Balance Forward	Actual	Plus or Minus		Balance Forward	Actual	Plus or Minus	Balance Forward	Actual	Plus or Minus
Housing	$320	$320		$320	$320			$320	$320		$320	$320	
Utilities	40	48	-8	32	46	-14		26	42	-16	24	41	
Food	220	225	-5	215	222	-7		213	226	-13	207	221	
Family necessities	45	40	+5	50	32	+18	40	58	38	+20	60	44	
Medical	20	25	-5	15	17	-2		18	13	+5	25	31	
Clothing	80	170	-90	-10	5	-15		65	50	+15	95	65	
Automobile	115	222	-107	8	88	-80		35	127	-92	23	87	
Recreation and entertainment	45	40	+5	50	46	+4		49	42	+7	52	51	
Personal improvement	42	92	-50	-8	17	-25		17	29	-12	30	102	
Short-term goal fund	111	151	-40	71	156	-85	116	31	0	31	147	63	
Savings and investment	170	0	+170	340	100	+240		410	410	0	170	170	
Outlays for fixed assets	30	70	-40	-10	10	-20		10	0	+10	40	20	
Mad money	40	40		40	40			40	20	+20	60	30	
Gifts	40	25	+15	55	20	+35		75	16	+59	99	21	
Church and charity	25	20	+5	30	20	+10		35	20	+15	40	38	
Life insurance	20	0	+20	40	0	+40		60	0	+60	80	0	
Taxes													
Contingency	16		+16	32	22	+10		26		+26	42	17	
TOTAL	1,379	1,488	-109	1,270	1,161	+109		1,488	1,353	+135	1,514	1,321	

FIGURE 4-7
Sample budget control sheet.

forward large surpluses. Once you have determined why there were deficits and surpluses, you can control your budget either by decreasing spending or by re-allocating your income to allow for smaller or larger expenses.

As you go over your budget and update it, remember that categories such as insurance premiums and taxes may develop large plus balances, since they are built up during the year to provide enough money for a lump-sum payment. For example, Karen and Alex have a March surplus in gifts because they plan to use most of the allotment to buy Christmas presents later (Fig. 4-7).

There are two methods that can help you control expenses: the fail-safe budget and the flexible budget.

Control Method I: The Fail-Safe Budget

The fail-safe budget is designed to make sure that you meet your budgeted goals. With this method you should try never to spend more than the current amount in any budget classification, but do be sure that your classification limits are realistic. There should not be any negative numbers in the plus or minus columns of the budget control sheet, except for categories involving disbursements that are made only once a year (e.g., insurance premiums).

You may, however, have a surplus in certain budget categories. For example, you may budget $80 a month for clothes and spend $50 the first month so that you will have $110 to spend in that category the next month. If you do this for several consecutive months, you will have saved enough to make a major purchase. Other-wise, you would have had either to cut back in some other category, to use some of your savings, or to buy it on credit. By using the fail-safe budget, you have forced yourself to save for a major purchase.

You should observe two cautions, however, in using the fail-safe budget. First, do not let this method rule with too tight a fist! It may put an unnecessary strain on you or some member of your family (for example, if it prevented getting a new vacuum cleaner when it was really needed). Second, do not pay for such things as life insurance on a monthly basis just to keep the "plus or minus" figure from being negative or you will be paying unnecessary service charges. If you pay $360 a year for such an item, simply budget $30 a month. If the premium is due next month and you have to pay it out of your cash reserve, the budget category will go minus, but it will come out even in the long run. In such cases, negative numbers are compatible with the fail-safe budget.

Control Method II: The Flexible Budget

The flexible budget is designed to allow for natural variations in month-to-month expenditures. Negative or positive accumulations may occur within categories. For example, as we can see in Figure 4-7, in January Alex and Karen spent $90 more than their monthly allotment of $80 for clothing. In February the balance forward was reduced to minus $10 because of the $80 budgeted monthly average. Recogniz-ing that the clothing category was already minus $10, Alex and Karen spent only $5 on clothing in February, making their "plus or minus" figure minus $15. In March the $80 budgeted monthly average combined with the minus $15 carried forward to create a balance forward of plus $65. Anytime a budget category has a negative balance forward, purchases of items in that category should be held back as much as possible until the balance is positive again. Otherwise, you will overspend your budget.

Look at the monthly totals along the bottom of the budget control sheet (Fig. 4-7). Karen and Alex's budget allows spending and investment of $1,379 a month. In January they spent $1,488, leaving them minus $109. So in February they had to keep their total expenditures under control. To do this, they cut back everywhere they could and spent only $1,270, including a $100 deposit to savings. You can see that going into April they have built up a surplus of $135. Of course, they would not spend $135 on something frivolous, because this surplus has been built up for future outlays. Look back again at their forecast in Figure 4-5 and you can see that they have a heavy expense month of $1,998 coming up in August. One of the strengths of a successful budget scheme is that it helps prevent you from spending the extra money you have today if you know you will need it in the future.

There are two cautions that should be observed if you choose to use the flexible budget control method. First, your family should have enough self-restraint to avoid overspending in a category that has gone into the red. You must refrain from saying, "Oh well, it won't hurt if I let that category go a little more minus for one more month." Otherwise, your budget is no longer a control device. It only tells you where the money went. Budgeting does take a certain amount of personal discipline in order to make it work! Second, do not let too many of the categories go negative at the same time. You may far overspend your income for one month and have either to borrow at high interest rates to cover the expenditures or to draw down your investments. Your budget will have failed in its control function if this happens.

If you observe these two cautions, the flexible budget can provide for successful control without the continuous feeling of a straitjacket.

RETHINKING THE BUDGET PROCESS

After you have been on a budget system for a couple of months, you will be able to predict pretty accurately what size each budget category should be. At this time you should begin to consider whether you are getting full satisfaction out of the money you are spending. Even though your family may be spending precisely the amount available in each category, they may not be happy with what they are achieving. A budget must be continually updated to reflect the changing needs and wants of the family.

Short-Term Changes

Perhaps every three months your family should reconsider what they want from money. Going to a movie every weekend may have been an important family goal three months ago, but now they might want to spend more money on new clothes. Once you have rethought your goals, you can adjust your spending categories accordingly.

Family Cycle Changes

Over time, the family will go through some significant changes. On the income side, it may go from having one earned income to having two. This second income will add considerable flexibility to the family budget. However, if there is a reasonable chance of reverting to one income for a period of time, the family should keep its basic living expenses within the means of one income. If this is not done, family members may find it very difficult to accept the "downgrading" of their "upgraded" lifestyle when the second income is no longer coming in; it is hard enough to give up the "extras" or the savings that a temporary second income can provide.

On the expense side, the acquisition of a home or the addition of children can make dramatic demands on the budget. Note the differences due to family size and age in Table 4-2. As children become adolescents, their expenses are as high as those of adults. When the children are in college, it often seems almost impossible to make ends meet. However, the apparently desperate situation ends when the children go off on their own. Then the parents can expand their lifestyle somewhat and still put money into savings. If they move to less expensive housing, their savings should grow even faster.

The Budget and Inflation

It may well be necessary to rethink the budget process if the rate of inflation increases or decreases. You may be tempted to think, "Well, the consumer price index rose 8 percent last year, so I'd better adjust my budget up by 8 percent in every category." Your gross income, however, may not have risen by 8 percent, or, if it did, taxes may have taken away part of that increase. (See Table 4-4 for the trend of per capita disposable income vs. inflation.) Even if your income did rise enough, not all expenses would have risen uniformly. Your electricity bill might have gone up by 20 percent, while your life insurance premium remained level. Table 4-5 illustrates this point for six typical expense items. Revise your budget based on how inflation *actually* affects your expense categories, not on how you think it *might* affect them.

ALTERNATIVE BUDGETING SYSTEMS

By now, some of you may have had certain reactions to the budgeting approach just presented. These could probably fit into one of four groups:

1. "That's exactly what I need!"
2. "Why do I need a budget? I always seem to have enough money for everything I need."
3. "I need a budget, but I'm already on a different system that works for me. Should I switch to this one?"
4. "I sure do need a budget, but every one I've ever tried has been a pain in the neck, and this one looks no different. I'm just not the type to keep all those detailed records."

For those of you in group 1, why not get started right now?

TABLE 4-4

Disposable Personal Income vs. the Cost of Living

Year	Per Capita Disposable Personal Income[a]		Consumer Price Index		Per Capita Disposable Income (1967 dollars)
	Amount	Change (%)	Index	Change (%)	
1967	$2,740	—	100.0	—	$2,740
1975	5,075	+ 86%	161.2	+ 61.2%	3,148
1976	5,477	+ 8	170.5	+ 5.8	3,212
1977	5,954	+ 9	181.5	+ 6.4	3,280
1978	6,571	+ 10	195.4	+ 7.6	3,363
1979	7,293	+ 11	217.4	+ 11.3	3,255
1980	8,002	+ 10	246.8	+ 13.5	3,242
1981	8,769	+ 10	272.4	+ 10.4	3,219
1967-81		+220%		+172.4%	+17.5%

Source: Council of Economic Advisors, *Economic Indicators* (Washington, D.C.: Government Printing Office, February 1982). 1967 data are from pre-1975 issues.

[a]Equals disposable personal income in Table 4-1 divided by the total U.S. population.

TABLE 4-5

Variations in the Movement of Consumer Prices

Year	Consumer Price Index	Index for Selected Groups of Products and Services					
		Food	Rent	Autos (new)	Medical Care	Gasoline	Clothing
1967	100.0	100.0	100.0	100.0	100.0	100.0	100.0
1970	116.3	114.9	110.1	107.6	120.6	105.6	116.5
1975	161.2	175.4	137.3	127.6	168.6	170.8	141.2
1976	170.5	180.8	144.7	135.7	184.7	177.9	145.8
1977	181.5	192.2	153.5	142.9	202.4	188.2	151.6
1978	195.4	211.4	164.0	153.8	219.4	196.3	155.7
1979	217.4	234.5	176.0	166.0	239.7	265.6	161.1
1980	246.8	254.6	191.6	179.3	265.9	369.1	171.1
1981 (May)	269.0	272.5	205.9	190.9	289.0	416.5	177.2

Source: U.S. Department of Commerce, *Statistical Abstract of the United States*, 1981, p. 468. Of the dozens of categories shown in this source, only a few have been selected for this table.

Those people in group 2 are very lucky indeed. Some people have a "sixth sense" that keeps them from spending more than they earn. They keep the due dates of major cash outlays, such as insurance or property taxes, in their heads and are able to accumulate the money needed for these items, so that they never need to borrow at expensive consumer credit interest rates.

Persons in group 3 should also be glad. The purpose of this chapter is not to espouse the *only* workable budget system, but to illustrate one that has worked for others and that can easily be adapted to individual needs and circumstances. Numerous other budgeting systems are available—as forms sold at stationery or variety stores, as a free service at a bank, or in other personal finance texts. Regardless of the system you select, many of the ideas involving planning, family involvement, and flexibility that are covered in this chapter should be given careful consideration.

Those in group 4 have a real problem, but one with at least a minimal solution. First of all, look back through your checkbook and list all those items that gave you trouble finding enough cash to pay them. These are likely to show up in any of three ways:

- Owing on two or more charge account or credit card bills that came due simultaneously, any one of which you could have paid, but which were simply too large in the aggregate for you to pay at one time.
- Buying items over $100 via the installment method, thereby reducing the amount of money you had available for other expenses because of the interest costs you were bearing.
- Paying for insurance via monthly premiums instead of annually or semiannually, either of which costs less.

The first problem can probably only be solved either by adopting a budgeting system such as the fail-safe system or by closing out your charge accounts and tearing up your credit cards. Then it's sure not to happen again.

The second problem will probably not be solved unless you summon the determination to plan ahead and regularly put money in your savings account to pay cash for the items you want to purchase. The dollar savings can be substantial, as you will see in Chapter 11.

The third problem is probably the easiest to solve. Simply total all the unusually large expenses that occur infrequently throughout the year and always catch you short of cash. These might include insurance premiums, vacations, holiday gifts, or property taxes. Deposit one-twelfth of this sum in your savings account each month before you can spend it elsewhere. Better yet, have your bank or credit union automatically make the withdrawal from your checking account or your paycheck. Then, when one of the large expense items that you listed comes up, you make a withdrawal from the savings account to cover that outlay. The key to the success of this budgeting method is that you must never dip into that savings account for anything other than the items for which the monthly deposits were made. (Other savings techniques will be discussed in Chapter 15.)

CONCLUSION

Some people feel that budgeting takes the fun out of spending money; yet spending too much money can take the fun out of life by creating needless worry. Budgeting need not be a straitjacket if done as described in this chapter.

Budgeting lets you plan where the money goes, allowing you to eliminate unnecessary spending and get what you really want. Also, the budgeting process will help you see how the spending and saving ideas in the next two units of the text all relate to each other.

VOCABULARY

after-tax income
budget
budget period

disposable personal income (DPI)
fail-safe budget
flexible budget

QUESTIONS

1. Using the information on Karen and Alex's budget control sheet (Fig. 4-7), compute their April plus or minus and May balance forward.
2. At the end of June, Karen and Alex will make their six-month review of their budget. In light of their experience to date, which expense categories, if any, should probably be revised upward (have greater expense limits)? Which categories, if any, could be revised downward to allow for the upward revision of other budget categories? Why?
3. Describe at least three distinct advantages to being on a budget.
4. What is probably the best method for recording charge account purchases? Why?
5. Under what circumstances can an expense category be given a little flexibility in the fail-safe budget?
6. What alternatives are available to the person who cannot stick to a budget system?

CASE PROBLEMS

1. Janet is a freshman at State University. She has several sources of income to provide for her education and living expenses. Her parents will give her $200 a month during the nine months she goes to school and also pay her basic living expenses during the summer when she lives at home. The state provides a $1,500 annual scholarship, one-third at the beginning of each term. Janet expects to earn $1,500 (net) on a summer job and $100 a month during the school year.

   Janet's expenses fluctuate widely. Tuition of $240 is due at the beginning of each of the three terms, as are room and board fees of $750. Books will probably cost $240 for the year. Transportation and personal expenses are expected to total $160 a month during the school year and $250 a month for the three-month summer vacation because of a trip she plans to take.

   Janet thinks that, because of this irregular pattern of income and expenses, a monthly budget would be useless, and so she plans just to keep a tight watch on her expenses.

   Do you agree with Janet that a monthly budget would not work for her? Why or why not? If she were to use a monthly budget, what should her budgeted monthly average income be? Compute her monthly average expense total. Is there any discrepancy between this and her average income? What probably will happen if Janet does not set up a budget and stick to it—provided that her monthly income and expenses do not change?

2. Dale found himself chronically short of money. His auto license of $75 surprised him each January. His insurance bills totaled $740 a year because he paid them monthly, rather than paying the single annual premium total of $680. At Christmas he usually borrowed $500 on a six-month loan that cost him $550 in payments, and for his summer vacation, he borrowed another $500 on the same terms. He rebelled at the thought of

going on a budget, but he also was tired of operating as he had. What would you suggest? How should he implement your suggestion? What is the minimum he would save each year by following your suggestion?

3. Review the Phil and Ellie Whitney case in this chapter. How was Phil able to recognize the need for a budget? How would you critique the weekend of planning that went into preparing the Whitney budget? How would you improve on Phil's four-point program?

RECOMMENDED READING

"How to Manage All That Money." *Changing Times*, March 1981, pp. 29–33.
    When two working singles become a two-income couple, there's more need to plan, not less: an overview of changes that take place in insurance, investments, and taxes.

"Kids and Money: What They Need to Know, When They Need to Know It." *Changing Times*, June 1981, pp. 17–20.
    Too many kids are uninformed about money issues, even at college age. This article offers points about allowances, savings, earning money, and teaching reality.

Priest, A. "How to Set up a Budget Your Family Can Live With," *McCalls*, September 1978.
    An approach for families who rebel against more rigorous budgeting techniques.

U.S. Department of Agriculture. *A Guide to Budgeting for the Family.* Home and Garden Bulletin No. 108. Washington, D.C.: U.S. Government Printing Office, 1976.
    More suggestions for making a budget work.

Changing Times and *Money* magazines have articles in almost every issue that provide insights into the expenditure patterns of typical American families, ways to stretch budgets and beat inflation, and the like.

CHUCK AND NANCY ANDERSON

Setting Up a Budget

Chuck and Nancy do not have a budget. As a result, their income seems to be slipping away without their getting the most out of it. In preparing to set up a budget, they looked at their balance sheet (Fig. 3-6) and income statement (Fig. 3-5) to find out how much money they have and where it is likely to be spent.

Questions

1. What is the average income per month, after taxes and Social Security, that the Andersons should use in setting up their budget? (Do not include in your computations their capital loss on the sale of stock.)
2. If they spend money this year as they did last year, will there be a budgeted deficit for the year?
3. If they want to eliminate a deficit and/or expand the surplus for savings and investment, what categories of income and/or expenses should they reevaluate?
4. How should Chuck and Nancy structure their budget to avert quarrels over the amounts each of them spends on personal expenses?

II

Protecting What You Have

In Chapter 5 we present an overall view of insurance, including the various methods of insuring one's assets. In Chapters 6 through 9 we devote a chapter to each type of insurance available to the individual: property insurance, comprehensive liability and automobile insurance, health insurance, and life insurance. Each chapter covers the purpose of the particular type of insurance under discussion, ways of determining one's insurance needs, the various policy alternatives available as well as other alternatives for fulfilling these needs, and the costs of fulfilling them.

5

Insurance Principles

The purpose of insurance is to restore financial well-being after a financial calamity. It can take the form of an insurance policy or a self-established reserve. Insurance does not promise to return your $4,000 automobile if it is destroyed in an accident; it simply promises to return $4,000. In short, insurance is money.

WHAT RISKS ARE INSURABLE?

Every day you encounter many risks, or possibilities of loss. In the morning you run the risk that you will oversleep. On your way to class or to work you risk having an accident. Every step of your life can involve some sort of risk.

Insurance, however, is concerned only with *fortuitous risks that result in financial loss and are personal in origin*. A person is said to have an *insurable interest* in assets that are vulnerable to insurable risks. The risk of a significant financial loss may seem remote to you if you have not yet accumulated many assets. Several years from now, however, if you own a home and are making a good salary, the potential financial loss may appear very large.

Fortuitous Risks

Fortuitous risks occur because of chance, not because of deliberate action on the part of the insured. The chance that lightning may start a fire at your summer cabin is a fortuitous risk, but the possibility that you may intentionally set fire to the cabin is not. Insurance companies spend much time and money determining causes of financial losses before settling claims.

Risks Involving Financial Loss

To qualify as an insurable risk, a risk must produce a reduction in monetary value. The theft of your car would constitute a financial loss. To restore your financial well-

93

being, if your car were stolen, you would probably need money not only to buy a new car but also to replace property left in the stolen car and to provide transportation until you buy a new car or the old one is recovered.

In contrast, if you do not prepare for a class and therefore are unable to answer a professor's question properly, your grade and self-esteem may go down, but there will probably be no immediate monetary effect: such a situation would not qualify as an insurable risk. Nor are wagers, bets, or investment risks insurable, since they carry with them the chance for profit. Some people think that insurance, like gambling, is an opportunity for gain as well as for loss. On the contrary, insurance is a way of restoring value, not enhancing it. You cannot profit from insurance.

Risks Personal in Origin

The last qualification for an insurable risk is that it be personal in origin; that is, the risk should not be so large that it imperils large numbers of people all at once (e.g., war). Rather, an insurable risk affects individuals randomly (e.g., tonsilectomy). An auto accident, for example, is an isolated loss affecting only a few people.

HOW TO DEAL WITH INSURABLE RISKS

There are three ways to deal with an insurable risk: take preventive measures to reduce or eliminate the risk, retain the risk and assume financial responsibility for absorbing the loss yourself, or transfer the risk and potential financial burden to someone else. Sound insurance planning utilizes all three methods of dealing with insurable risks.

Minimizing Risks

You can minimize risks by not engaging in activities likely to cause accidents or loss. For example, the risk of accidental injury or death is increased if you ride motorcycles, fly small private aircraft, or engage in certain hazardous occupations. In other words, you can reduce risks by being cautious.

Insurance rates are set partly according to the magnitude of risk. The greater the risk, the higher the premium you must pay to obtain coverage for that risk. Conversely, the smaller the risk, the lower the premium. By watching your behavior patterns and tempering your more dangerous inclinations, you will not only reduce risk but also minimize the price you would pay for insurance coverage if you decided to transfer the risk.

Government at all levels is active in reducing risk and preventing financial loss. Police departments and fire departments, for example, are loss-preventive agencies. They contribute much to the reduction of the risks we face and the premiums we have to pay for insurance. National, state, and local health and safety agencies have printed hundreds of brochures and booklets describing precautionary measures you can take around the home, in your car, and concerning your health. A list of these agencies and their addresses is given at the end of this chapter. Since the cheapest insurance is careful behavior, you would do well to read some of the pamphlets and follow the advice given.

Retaining Risks

Along with trying to prevent financial loss by reducing risk, you must decide whether to retain the risk of financial burden or transfer it to an insurance company. Since this decision will be made in favor of the more financially attractive alternative, you must use your personal loss experience and your financial statements to help you decide.

Your *personal loss experience* is a record of how much money or monetary value you have lost because of insurable risks. If you have never had any loss, then you have a good loss record. If you have had three accidents in the last three years costing you a total of $5,000, then you have a poor loss record. Your personal loss record can be used in all areas of insurance underwriting to determine whether you are a good risk. The better risk you are, the lower will be your insurance costs, whether you decide to retain the risk yourself or to transfer the risk to an insurance company.

Your balance sheet and income statement can be used to determine where the risks are, the size of the financial burden to be assumed, and whether you have the financial strength to assume all the risk of a financial burden. Your asset of greatest value constitutes your largest exposure to financial loss and therefore probably also your greatest insurance problem.

- What would happen if your assets were reduced? If your liabilities increased? If your income were reduced? If your expenses increased?
- Would you need $2,000 or $7,000 to replace your car if it were stolen?
- Would your family need $1,800 or $2,500 a month to live on if you died or became disabled?
- Where is the most value on your balance sheet and income statement? Car? Home? Income?
- How great is your financial capacity to assume risk? Do you have enough in your savings account, for example, to replace your car if it were damaged beyond repair?

If you have enough monetary assets to equal the fixed assets subject to financial risks, then you can afford to *self-insure* those assets—to set aside adequate funds to protect yourself against possible losses.

To determine whether it is financially sound for you to self-insure, do the following:

1. Find out the annual premium you would have to pay if you were to obtain coverage from an insurance company.
2. Using your loss history, arrive at an average dollar loss per year by dividing the total amount of dollars lost by the number of years in which the financial burden has been assumed. Is your average annual loss less than the annual premium?
3. Consider whether your loss experience is unlikely to change for the worse.
4. Consider whether your monetary assets could cover the loss if your experience did worsen.

If the average loss per year is less than the required annual premium *and* if you can reasonably expect that your loss experience will not worsen *and* if you have enough monetary assets to cover the total loss in case your experience does worsen, *then* consider retaining the risk.

Transferring Risks

The third method of dealing with financial risks is to transfer the responsibility for the potential financial burden to someone else, usually an insurance company. Such a company pools risks and uses statistics to calculate probabilities of loss. Because an insurable risk affects only a few people at a time, the financial consequences of such a loss can be spread over a number of exposures.

insurance premiums A fee called a *premium* is charged on the basis of the risk involved, the size of the financial loss the company might be required to absorb, and the number of individual risks the company can gather together. In addition, the premium must be large enough to cover policy administration costs, a commission to the insurance salesperson, and advertising costs, while still providing a profit to the insurance company.

To arrive at a fee that will both cover the expected loss and render a profit, the company follows generally the same procedure as you would to determine whether to self-insure. Instead of using data on just one individual, however, the company pools information about the loss experience of thousands of policyholders throughout the country. Mathematicians, called actuaries, use probability theory to calculate the degree of risk in each potential loss situation. For each type of risk, they divide the total expected loss by the number of loss exposures and arrive at a base premium (the price insurers may charge their customers in exchange for insurance coverage). Insurers then add a sum to cover administration costs and profit to the base premium to arrive at the premium charged the policyholder.

For example, if you wanted to determine the base premium for fire damage coverage in an area of 10,000 homes, you would first determine the total expected loss due to fire based on the history of fire damage in that area. If this figure turned out to be $320,000, the base charge to each homeowner would be $32 ($320,000 expected loss ÷ 10,000 exposures) to cover the risk of fire. The cost of insurance will rise if the expected loss due to bad loss experience increases or if the number of good risks over which to spread the total expected loss decreases.

Now that you know how premiums are set, you can see that if your loss experience is better than the average experience of the group to which you are assigned by an insurance company, self-insurance may be more economical, provided you have assets sufficient to cover your largest potential loss. If your experience is worse than the average of the group to which you are assigned, consider yourself lucky to be able to transfer the financial responsibility for your actions to someone else.

probability of loss There is another aspect you should consider before you decide whether to transfer an insurable risk. If there is a great probability that a loss will occur to nearly all potential policyholders, it is useless to insure against it: the price you pay will equal or exceed the loss itself. For example, many people have a physical examination from a doctor once a year; so if you plan to have a physical each year, the price you pay the doctor will probably be less than the price you pay the insurance company for a general medical policy (see Chapter 8), which includes administrative costs, commissions, and profit.

It is generally best to retain those risks that involve relatively small financial losses and have a high probability of occurrence. The risks that are best transferred involve relatively large financial losses and have a low probability of occurrence.

THE BUYING PROCESS

Once you have decided to transfer the risks of a financial calamity to an insurance company, you have to determine exactly what your needs for insurance are and how to fulfill those needs with the least cost and effort. There are five major questions you should answer.

- What should I insure?
- What perils should I insure against?
- How much should I insure for?
- How long should I keep the insurance in force?
- How should I buy the policy?

These five questions are applicable to all types of insurance policies and represent the only variables about which you as a policyholder need be concerned. Having decided what you want to insure, what you want to insure against, and what insurance benefits you need, you have automatically determined the type of insurance policy you need. All policies are simply combinations of these three variables.

Each of these five questions will be dealt with in more detail in the next four chapters when the particular types of insurance are discussed: property insurance, comprehensive liability and automobile insurance, health insurance, and life insurance.

What to Insure

What you need to insure is not always easy to determine. Since insurance protects the pocketbook, you will want to insure only those things that, if lost or destroyed, would cause you or someone dependent upon you a monetary loss. Therefore, your first task is to identify the various assets you own and their respective values. Your income, home, and personal property, if lost, might cause financial hardship. Determine priorities. Which assets are most important to you? Given that the cost of protection may be a constraint, separate your assets into those that must be insured, those that should be insured, and those that might be insured. Table 5-1 gives you an idea of what you can protect.

As you determine your insurance needs, make sure you are using insurance properly. Ask yourself whether you are truly guarding against a financial calamity or merely making a prepayment for an anticipated loss that is likely to occur. If you buy insurance to cover small expenses that have a high probability of occurrence, you may be paying a cost for that coverage almost equal to the expected loss. In such a situation, it would be more prudent to invest an amount of money equal to the probable expense.

TABLE 5-1

What You Can Insure, against What Perils, and with What Type of Policy

What You Can Insure	Type of Perils	Type of Policy
Your net worth and future income stream	Bad health	Medical expense policy, disability income policy
	Premature death	Accident policy, life policy
	Lawsuit	Comprehensive liability policy, catastrophic liability policy
Your assets		
Home	Most perils	Homeowners policy, dwelling building policy, fire policy
Personal property	Most perils	Homeowners policy, dwelling contents policy, floater policy
Automobile	Most perils	Auto policy
Real property	Most perils	Dwelling building policy, fire and extended theft policy

What Perils to Insure Against

Once you have decided what assets you want to insure, you must decide what hazards and perils pose a threat to their safety. This is a difficult decision because it is impossible to foresee all the calamities that might occur. As a student, the major perils you face are probably poor health and loss of personal property. If you marry and have others dependent upon you, loss of life becomes a major peril.

Most insurance companies separate perils into groups according to their probability of occurrence. To determine this, they look at past experience. Since as many cases of vandalism have occurred as theft, for example, vandalism and theft are considered to be of equal risk and are therefore grouped in the same peril category. Because of this practice of grouping perils, you often must buy policies that offer protection against events unlikely to occur in your circumstances. For example, you may live on a farm and need insurance against windstorms or hail, but your policy might also cover damage due to riot or civil commotion. Naturally, the more perils you insure against, the greater will be the premium cost. Some policies offer all-risk coverage. These policies cover virtually all perils or hazards that might jeopardize what you are insuring. Because these policies offer the broadest coverage, they are the most expensive.

How Much to Insure For

In order to answer this question, you must be able to determine the value of what you are insuring. The value of personal property may not be difficult to determine. Determining the financial effect of your death, however, is a weighty task. In Chapter 9 you will learn an effective way to do this.

You may not be able to retain the entire risk of financial loss, but you can retain a portion of it through the use of deductibles. The *deductible clause* in an insurance policy provides that you pay all expenses incurred in a loss up to a specified limit. The company will pay losses above that amount up to the maximum coverage of the policy. Naturally, the higher the limit you set on the deductible, the less risk and financial burden the insurance company has to assume. Your premiums are small because the insurance company reduces its operating costs by not having to settle many small claims and by reducing the payout on larger claims.

If you use deductibles, you should establish an *emergency fund* from which deductibles can be paid. Normally, this fund should be large enough to cover not only all deductibles but also the replacement cost of items you are self-insuring as well as items that are not insurable. The financial consequences of losing one's job, however, probably pose the largest potential emergency cash drain, and your emergency fund should be large enough to withstand this drain for probably at least six months.

To determine the appropriate amount to handle a six-month job loss (and therefore the maximum size of your emergency reserve), you should take into account how much the family could cut back expenses in an emergency; sources of support you could count on (unemployment insurance, food stamps, sick pay allowances if ill, and so on); how much you could extend your credit on current credit cards and accounts; and other sources of support (investments not earmarked for important goals, family help, and so on). An easier, though sometimes less precise, method is to create a fund equal to two to three times your monthly pay minus income and Social Security taxes and amounts put into payroll investment plans. If your take-home pay is $1,000 a month, an appropriate emergency fund would be $2,000 to $3,000, depending on your current debts. This amount—combined with severance pay, unemployment insurance benefits (which are free of income tax in most states), and frugality—would probably be enough to carry you through six months of unemployment. You should plan that after that time you would either have a new job or begin liquidating investments. Such an emergency fund would probably be large enough to pay any insurance deductible you might have as well.

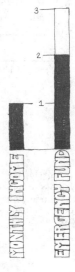

property insurance Figure 5-1 demonstrates how you determine the size of deductible to select on a homeowners policy, given your loss experience and the size of your emergency reserve. Graphing the size of the deductible along the vertical axis and the size of the annual premium on the horizontal axis, you can plot the premiums for each level of deductible you might choose. For example, the premium for a homeowners policy with a $500 deductible is $202. Assuming that your emergency reserve is $650 and your average annual loss experience is $300, which policy should you select? The columns to the right of the graph indicate the annual premiums, your expected cash flow requirement (the amount of either the deductible or your loss experience, whichever is smaller), and your total expected cash flow burden (adding the two together).

Premium + Lesser of deductible or loss experience = Expected annual cost

Since the potential loss should never be larger than your emergency reserve ($650),

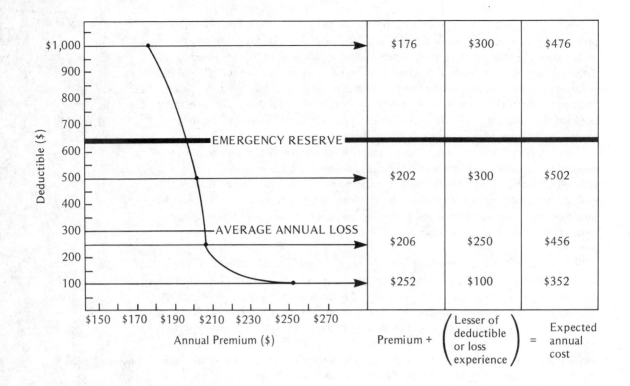

Deductible	Premium +	Lesser of deductible or loss experience	= Expected annual cost
$1,000	$176	$300	$476
$500	$202	$300	$502
$250	$206	$250	$456
$100	$252	$100	$352

EMERGENCY RESERVE

AVERAGE ANNUAL LOSS

Deductible ($) — y-axis: $1,000, 900, 800, 700, 600, 500, 400, 300, 200, 100

Annual Premium ($) — x-axis: $150, $170, $190, $210, $230, $250, $270

FIGURE 5-1
An example of self-insuring to reduce your insurance costs: $70,000 homeowners policy.

the $1,000 deductible alternative must be disregarded. Of the remaining options for deductibles, the $100 deductible offers the lowest expected annual cost ($352). Therefore, as a smart insurance shopper, you would select the policy with the $100 deductible.

auto insurance   Suppose you have a car worth $500. Your insurance agent says it will cost you $100 a year to insure it against collision damage. Suppose as well that you have incurred $250 in damage costs over the last five years because of collisions. This would mean that your average annual loss has been $50—half the annual premium. If you can expect that your loss experience will not worsen, the financially sound alternative would be to put $500 (an amount equal to the value of the car) into a reserve savings account and not purchase collision insurance. You thereby have enough money to cover a total loss. You also have interest income on the $500, and you have saved the $100 annual premium. In addition, any loss above $100 is deductible from your taxable income. Therefore, if your car were stolen, you could deduct $400 ($500 − $100) from your taxable income and save $120 in taxes if you were in the 30 percent marginal tax bracket ($400 × 30% = $120).

health insurance   Regarding health risks, you use the same self-insurance procedure to determine the size of the deductible you can afford, not the maximum potential loss. For example, you may have been spending $1,200 a year to buy a health insurance policy with no deductible, although your total annual medical bills have averaged only \$320. For \$300 you might purchase a health insurance policy with a \$500 deductible (i.e., the insurance company would assume any loss over \$500) and save an average of \$580 a year since you would be paying only a \$300 premium and an average of \$320 in medical bills rather than a \$1,200 premium.

life insurance When determining the financial effects of your premature death, examine the financial statements of your beneficiaries and their potential earning capacities. These may or may not be the same as your own. You need to know both how much money they will need to support themselves after your death and how many of your financial assets can be used to satisfy their needs. Previous loss experience, of course, plays no part in life insurance planning. Building a life insurance reserve on your own rather than transferring the risk to an insurance company could save you tens of thousands of dollars in your lifetime.

How Long to Keep the Insurance in Force

Most property insurance is issued for either six-month or one-year terms. Life insurance is issued for as long or as short a period as you want. Health and property policies are normally written for one-year terms. Auto policies, however, are normally written for periods of six months. Consider the length of time appropriate for you. Keep insurance in force only as long as you have a need for it. If a policy has a *guaranteed renewable provision,* it is automatically continued until you give instructions to the contrary. Since your insurance needs are constantly changing, you should make certain that your protection period is neither too short nor too long nor too inflexible to allow you to make adjustments as your needs change.

How to Buy the Policy

Buying the insurance policy is important because the success of your plans depends largely on the people you choose to carry them out. Your buying decision involves selecting the agent to sell you the policy, obtaining the best price for the coverage involved, and choosing the best insurance company among those offering the least expensive coverage. You will be evaluating primarily service and price.

One way to begin the selection process is to ask friends, attorneys, bankers, or accountants to recommend agents who have proven satisfactory. Another way is to check the Yellow Pages of your local telephone directory. You may want to call the largest independent agencies in town. Chances are that most insurance companies will want to license agents who can give their products the broadest market exposure and these agents will be found in the largest agencies.

Once you have gathered the names of recommended agents or of agents you wish to call from the phone directory, it is time to get rate quotes and find out where you can obtain coverage at the lowest cost. You start the process of selecting the best policy with agent selection because a good agent should give you exposure to the best companies with the best rates; the best rates along with a broad exposure to available coverages and customer service are what you are looking for. Each insurance chapter in this book (Chapters 6 through 9) contains a form to help you shop for and compare coverage alternatives.

Become aware of general trends in insurance rates in the type of insurance you are shopping for. If rates are on the rise, and Company A has just instituted a rate increase, its low rate is more significant than Company B's rate if Company B has not yet raised its rates. A good premium rate must be viewed in light of the pattern of rates throughout the industry.

After you have obtained several rate quotes and found which agents seem to offer the best coverage at the lowest cost, look at the insurance company itself. If the insurance company offering the lowest rate is represented by a large agency with a good reputation, you can feel fairly confident that the company is a good one. If you have any doubts, write the nearest department of insurance for information about the company's financial strength, length of registration to do business within the state, and so on. Or you may wish to check the company's background and rating in *Best's Insurance Guide* at your local library.

The only way to know whether you have the best insurance deal is to shop for rates both when you first buy the policy and when you renew. Be sure you read your policies so that you know exactly what you are paying for and the true cost of each increment of coverage you select. Compare costs before making a final choice. The cost savings will probably more than make up for the time and effort you spend.

Of course, cost is not everything. It is important that an agent be willing and able to help you determine your needs and select the right policy for your needs. These attributes in an agent can truly make your insurance policy cost-effective.

THE INSURANCE AGENT

Agents can be classified according to the type of insurance they sell. *Property/casualty agents* handle auto insurance, home insurance, personal property floaters, and such. These agents make the sales for an insurance company and do some of the underwriting as well. That is, they sometimes determine whether the applicant is a good risk and how much should be charged. They often have the power to bind an insurance company to the desired coverage before the policy is issued by the company. In this way a potential policyholder can become insured immediately. Since the property/casualty agent owns the policyholder's records, this person has the power to transfer a policyholder's coverage from one insurance company to another. A release need not be obtained first from the present insurer. All in all, the property/casualty agent has much more underwriting and service responsibility than does the life/health agent. The *life/health agent* determines which insurance company offers the required coverage and then submits a potential policyholder's application to that insurance company. The decision to accept or reject the application is up to the company itself.

Agents can also be classified according to their relation to insurance companies. Exclusive agents sell policies for just one company. They are salaried sales personnel, usually employed by very large insurance companies. Independent agents sell policies for several companies. Brokers are similar to independent agents in that they are licensed by more than one company; but, unlike agents, they can sell many lines of insurance, not simply one or two.

Insurance agents are usually compensated by commissions from the insurance companies for the policies they sell for them. The size of the commission depends on the type of insurance and the size of the premium. Some types of policies make more money for the agent than do other types.

THE INSURANCE POLICY

An insurance policy is a legal contract. It spells out what the insurance company will or will not do in certain loss situations. There are basically two types of provisions in an insurance policy: jacket provisions and coverage provisions. *Jacket provisions* set forth the insurance company's commitment to the policyholder. There are usually five such provisions:

1. General insuring agreement, whereby the company agrees to pay any sum of money that the contract directs as settlement against a coverage claim.
2. Supplementary payments, whereby the company outlines the expenses, if any, it will pay in addition to the settlement expense (provision 1).
3. Definitions, whereby the company defines some common terms relating to the conditions of its coverage.
4. Conditions, whereby the company details those conditions under which the contract will be considered valid.
5. Declarations, whereby the company identifies who is to be covered against what (as determined by the coverage provisions that the policyholder selects).

The *coverage provisions* are the policyholder's instructions to the insurance company. By choosing one or more coverage provisions, the policyholder tells the insurance company who is to be covered, what injury or property damage is to be covered, and what is not to be covered.

Policies are required to conform to state insurance statutes. Therefore, policies written by the same company in different states may cover the same insurable risks in different ways, depending on the state in which they are written. *Endorsements* (amendments) are often added to policies to restrict or expand coverage. Some endorsements may be required by state law or by the insurance company. Others may be automatically included unless specifically excluded by the policyholder. Still others may be added only if the policyholder so requests.

Policies can be paid for in various ways. Paying premiums more frequently than upon the policy's anniversary date is likely to result in a larger total premium because more administrative work is required. Premiums may be upgraded so that smaller-than-ordinary amounts are paid in earlier years and larger-than-ordinary amounts are paid in later years.

If a policy is canceled by the insured before the end of a policy term, the policyholder may be able to receive a refund according to the company's short rate table and refund policy.

THE INSURANCE COMPANY

The insurance company offers financial responsibility through pooling risks and providing for losses out of its reserves. You contract for this service by paying a premium. You thereby absorb a small but certain loss (the premium) to avoid the burden of a much larger potential loss (theft of your car, for example).

The insurance company normally makes a profit through underwriting (assuming a risk by means of insurance) and investing. An insurance company earns an *underwriting profit* when actual losses stay below expected losses. Such a profit indicates that the company is either attracting more good risks than bad, performing efficiently, or charging too high a premium. An insurance company earns an *investment profit* when its invested reserves earn a yield in excess of investment costs. This profit indicates that the company is selecting good investment instruments.

There are five types of insurers: stock insurance companies, mutual insurance companies, health expense associations, Lloyds of London, and reciprocals. Reciprocals are formed only in rare business insurance situations and so will not be discussed here. All insurance companies, whatever the type, are regulated by the states in which they operate. Laws governing the types of policies that may be sold and the business practices of each licensed insurer differ from state to state. Historically, New York and California have been the most progressive in championing better insurance protection. State departments of insurance enforce the laws and regulate the insurance industry. Offices of the state department of insurance are usually located in major cities throughout the state and serve to test and license insurance sales representatives, investigate policyholder complaints, disburse financial information on all insurers licensed to do business in the state, and much more. Sometimes the federal government steps in to deal with insurance problems that are too big for each state to handle. National crime insurance, flood insurance, and Medicare have resulted from such intervention.

Stock Insurance Companies

Stock insurance companies are owned by the stockholders. All profits belong to the stockholders in the form of dividends or retained earnings. Stock companies offer two types of policies. The first is called a *participating policy* (par policy). It returns a portion of the premium to the policyholder at the end of the policy period. This portion is called a *dividend*; but it is actually a refund of premium, not a payment of earnings. The other type of policy is called a *nonparticipating policy* (nonpar policy). It does not refund any portion of the premium at the end of the policy period. Be sure to compare the costs of these two types of policies. Many times, the difference in price between the two is the amount of the proposed premium refund or dividend, the size of which cannot be guaranteed. Most property and casualty policies are written by stock companies.

Mutual Insurance Companies

Mutual insurance companies are owned by the policyholders, not by stockholders. In other words, the policyholders share in the profit of the company. As in the participating policies issued by stock companies, the profits are distributed through dividends attached to the policies. Theoretically, the greater the profits, the greater the dividends received by each policyholder. Most life and health policies are written by mutual companies.

There has long been controversy as to whether stock insurance companies or mutual insurance companies offer the least expensive product. Proponents of the former maintain that, because of the profit motive, stock companies have to be efficient and offer products at the best rate. Proponents of the latter argue that, because mutual companies do not have to pay their shareholders a dividend, they can offer the least expensive coverage and pass on any gains to the policyholders as premium refunds. In reality, nothing conclusive can be proven one way or the other. The potential policyholder must shop both stock and mutual companies to determine which offers the best policy at the cheapest rate for a specific situation.

Health Expense Associations

Health expense associations are insurance organizations formed by hospitals and physicians' groups to disburse medical services. Unlike stock or mutual insurance companies that pay to injured parties whatever money is required, health expense associations pay physicians according to a specific fee structure. The associations make money by offering medical services at the lowest cost. In contrast, corporate insurers have no control over cost and make money by selecting good risks.

There are two types of plans offered by these associations: *closed-end plans*, which stipulate that services must be rendered only at certain contracted hospitals, and *open-end plans*, which enable the insured to obtain medical care from any hospital. The two largest health expense associations are Blue Cross and Blue Shield.

Lloyd's of London

Lloyd's of London is an insurance group composed of many subgroups or syndicates. Each syndicate is made up of from 10 to 100 individuals who invest in insurance risks. Unlike other insurers, who specialize in certain risks and pool only similar exposures, Lloyd's gathers different types of risk exposures together in the same syndicate, thereby balancing certain risk exposures against the experiences of other risks. Normally these syndicates insure very large risks to which there may be only one or two exposures. Insuring a concert pianist's fingers or the overland shipment of millions of dollars by armored car are examples of such risks. Lloyd's of London, however, is licensed to sell their services in only a few states in this country.

CONCLUSION

Insurance is a way of protecting what you have by eliminating or easing the financial hardships resulting from a calamity. You can either minimize risk by taking precautionary measures to reduce the likelihood that a calamity will occur, retain the risk by providing a cash reserve, or transfer the risk to an insurance company by buying an insurance policy. Most likely you will use a combination of all three measures.

Through insurance policies, insurance companies offer a means of transferring the risk of calamity and the resulting financial losses to them. To select the policy most appropriate to your needs, you must decide what you want to insure, what perils you want to insure against, how much you want to insure for, how long you want to insure, and whom you want to insure with. You will pay a premium for this service based on the insurance company's past experience with similar insurance arrangements. Know how much each policy will cost before you buy and take time to select a knowledgeable and helpful agent.

VOCABULARY

coverage provisions
deductible clause
emergency fund
endorsement
guaranteed renewable provision
health expense association
insurable interest
insurable risk
investment profit
jacket provisions

life/health agent
Lloyd's of London
mutual insurance company
personal loss experience
premium
property/casualty agent
reciprocal
self-insure
stock insurance company
underwriting profit

QUESTIONS

1. What are the major differences between investment risks and insurable risks?
2. Discuss the three ways insurable risks can be treated. How might you use all three ways to deal with the risk of fire damage to your personal property?
3. You pay $100 a year for collision coverage on your automobile. Since you began driving five years ago, you have wrecked your car once and had to pay damage repairs of $400. You anticipate that your driving record will remain the same. Under what circumstances should you self-insure? Under what circumstances should you not?
4. You pay $55 a month for medical expense insurance that covers every dollar of medical expense you might incur. An insurance agent has offered you a medical expense policy covering all your costs above the first $100 for only $35 a month. Your medical expenses over the last five years have been $50, $75, $175, $100, and $0, respectively. Assuming both policies are of the same quality, which one would you buy? Why?
5. Which risks listed below might reasonably be retained? Which risks might reasonably be transferred? Why?

Your home might burn down.
Your bicycle might be stolen.
You might die, leaving no dependents.
You might have a heart attack and need to be hospitalized.
You might have to receive a shot of penicillin.
A tree might fall on your car, crushing it.
You might die, leaving a spouse and two children.

6. What would the base premium be for auto theft insurance in the following situation? Auto thefts of a certain make of car in Detroit next year are expected to result in $50,000 worth of losses. There are 2,500 owners of this make of car in Detroit.

CASE PROBLEM

Bob and Julie Phillips are both 31 years old and have been married for eight years. They have decided to review their insurance programs for their house, car, and personal property in order to find out what assets they should insure, how much of the financial burden they should retain, and how much of it they should transfer. In the five years that they have owned their home, with a current market value of $65,000, they have incurred only $300 in losses due to natural perils. Their present home insurance policy costs them $280 a year. During the 15 years that Bob and Julie have each been driving, they have incurred a total of $450 in car damages from collisions that were their fault. They now pay $85 a year for collision coverage on their car, which is worth $500. Since they have been married, Bob and Julie have lost $160 in stolen personal property. Their present property insurance costs them $15 a year to cover $15,000 worth of personal property.

What is the Phillipses' greatest financial risk? Their second greatest? Their third greatest? Which of these risks can be transferred to an insurance company? Which risk should be entirely transferred?

In trying to determine whether they would be able to self-insure, the Phillipses compare their assets and liabilities. They find that they have $4,360 in monetary assets (cash, savings account, mutual funds, and savings bonds) and $80,500 in fixed assets (home, car, and personal property) for a total of $84,860. Their liabilities consist of $150 in unpaid bills, $4,000 for an education loan, and $20,000 for a home mortgage, making their net worth $25,710.

Which risks might the Phillipses absorb either in part or in the entirety? Which might they retain? Use the information in Table 5-2 to determine how much money all your insurance recommendations would save the Phillipses each year.

TABLE 5-2

Insurance Rates for the Phillipses' Existing Policies

Home ($35,000)		Automobile (Collision)		Personal Property ($15,000)	
Deductible	Annual Premium	Deductible	Annual Premium	Deductible	Annual Premium
$ 100	$126	$100	$71	$100	$135
250	113	200	61	250	122
500	101			500	108
1,000	88				

RECOMMENDED READING

Vaughan, Emmett J. *Fundamentals of Risk and Insurance*. 3d ed. New York: John Wiley & Sons, 1982.

> The author discusses the theory of risk management and differences in dealing with property, personal, and liability risks. Part 1 is especially relevant to this chapter. Parts 2 and 3 relate more to our Chapters 6 through 9.

Organizations offering materials on preventive measures in dealing with risks:

> Aetna Life and Casualty
> Public Relations and Advertising Dept.
> 151 Farmington Avenue
> Hartford, CT 06156
> Free loan films (safety)

> American Insurance Association
> Engineering and Safety Dept.
> 110 William Street
> New York, NY 10038
> Leaflets, pamphlets, film catalog

> Insurance Institute for Highway Safety
> 600 New Hampshire Avenue
> Suite 300
> Washington, DC 20037

Detailed source list of companies and organizations that issue laymen's publications on traffic safety:

> Kemper Insurance
> Public Relations Dept.
> 120 S. La Salle Street
> Chicago, IL 60603
> Pamphlets

> Liberty Mutual Insurance Company
> Public Relations Dept.
> 175 Berkeley Street
> Boston, MA 02117
> Pamphlets

> National Safety Council
> Director of Public Information
> 444 N. Michigan Avenue
> Chicago, IL 60611
> Films, pamphlets, posters

> Public Health Service
> Inquiries Branch
> U.S. Dept. of Health and Human Services
> Washington, DC 20201
> Leaflets on farm and home safety, poisons, and so on

> The Travelers Insurance Companies
> Public Information and Advertising
> One Tower Square
> Hartford, CT 06115
> Posters and booklets containing street and highway accident data

CHUCK AND NANCY ANDERSON

Computing the Size of Their Emergency Fund

The Andersons' emergency fund should cover deductibles on insurance policies, items not covered by insurance (such as unusual dental costs), and items for which they choose to self-insure (such as collision coverage on their five-year-old compact). However, all of these expenses are of limited consequence when compared with the possibility, no matter how remote, that Chuck might lose his job, even temporarily. Therefore, if Chuck's possible loss of job is the one item he provides for, he would also have sufficient funds to cover the family's other emergency needs.

Questions

1. If the Andersons' annual take-home pay is almost $32,000, what is an appropriate amount for their emergency fund? (Keep in mind that Chuck has financial assets he can call on in emergencies.)
2. How will the Andersons' balance sheet and income statement be affected if they decide to place their emergency fund in a passbook savings account?

6

Property Insurance

For insurance purposes, the term *property* refers to two categories: personal property (one's belongings) and physical structures (most commonly a house). Land is not considered insurable by the insurance industry. Therefore, when we refer in this text to property, we exclude land holdings.

Property probably represents your largest investment. Look at the assets side of your balance sheet, which you constructed in Chapter 3. Are the figures representing your home and personal property greater than the figure representing your total monetary assets? Do you have enough monetary assets to replace all of your property if it were lost, stolen, or destroyed?

Look at the liabilities side of your balance sheet. What percentage of your total property asset value is represented by items that are still being financed? If you were to lose some of your property that is not completely paid for, could you convert enough monetary assets not only to replace what you have lost but also to complete the payments on them?

Such questions may make you anxious about both the safety and the relative importance of your fixed property assets. Property insurance is designed to relieve your anxieties by reimbursing you for property that is destroyed or damaged through fire or some other calamity. To appraise your property insurance needs, consider the following questions. What property can I insure? How do I value my property for insurance purposes? How do I choose the insurance coverage I need—at the lowest cost?

WHAT PROPERTY CAN YOU INSURE?

You can insure anything that belongs to you and has a determinable value except land. Insurance companies insure only property that, if damaged, will cause financial loss to the person actually holding the insurance policy. No matter how much you like your neighbor's home, for example, you are not permitted to buy property insurance on it, since your neighbor has the only true monetary interest in the property.

Even though your right to ownership may be unquestioned, the property itself may still be uninsurable by most insurance companies because of the difficulty involved in determining its value. Any items that are difficult to value, or appear to have value only to you—manuscripts, rare book collections, or family heirlooms—may be covered, but the company will charge you a much higher premium to insure these articles and may pay you only a fraction of their value if they are damaged.

In addition, items of personal property may be considered uninsurable by an insurance company because of too great a risk of loss. Insurance coverage for personal property belonging to college students while attending school was long avoided by most insurance companies, because the incidence of theft was too great. Only recently have holders of standard homeowners policies been able to include theft coverage for a student's belongings while away at college.

Specifically, you can insure your home and attached structures (e.g., garage); detached structures (e.g., tool shed, separate garage); trees, plants, and shrubs around the house; personal property when on the premises; personal property when away from the premises; other people's property while on the premises; and additional living expenses, if you are forced to vacate your home.

The manner in which you value your property is extremely important. Let us look at the proper methods of evaluating your home and personal property so that you can tell how much insurance you really need.

VALUING YOUR PERSONAL PROPERTY FOR INSURANCE PURPOSES

What do you own? Larger items may be easy to identify—house, refrigerator, color television. You would readily remember items you use every day if they were destroyed or stolen. But what about things such as the wedding silver that may be packed away or gold jewelry? These may receive little use but may be of great value. You may own dishes, clothing, garden tools, furniture, and books that you wish to protect. In order to know what you do own, you must inventory your personal property.

You may be thinking that you would not want to replace some articles if they were lost or destroyed. Consider, however, what the insurance company would pay you if you lost only those items that really matter to you—probably nowhere near the amount of money you would need to buy them new today. The only way to have enough money available for items you care about is to insure everything. In practice, it may be wise to insure all of your personal property.

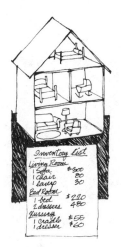

Personal Property Inventory

If a fire were to start in a closet of your house and completely destroy that closet and the adjoining room, how easy would it be for you to identify all the items of personal property that were destroyed in those two places? If your estimate of loss appeared to be abnormally high because of a mink coat in the closet where the fire began, would your insurance company demand documented proof of the alleged contents of the closet? A room-by-room inventory of your personal property can be used not only to let you know what has been lost but also to substantiate your claim.

A personal property inventory—which is easy to update as personal property is acquired, given away, or moved from one room to another—facilitates matching the value of your insurance coverage with that of the property you have accumulated year by year. The inventory will also tell you how you have distributed value throughout your home. Many people have most items of value in one or two rooms. To reduce the magnitude of loss through any one incident, you might distribute them more evenly throughout the house. Ask your insurance agent to provide the forms for taking your own personal property inventory. Keep a copy of the completed inventory away from the premises (in a safe-deposit box, for example) so that it cannot be destroyed along with your property.

how not to do it   When Pat and Leonard moved to Chicago, they felt the move presented them with an excellent opportunity to make out a personal property inventory. As the moving van was unloaded, Pat stood outside the front door with a clipboard marking down every item that the movers brought in, by category. At the end of the day, they'd accounted for 15 chairs, 2 sofas, 4 beds, 6 tables, . . ., and, finally, 9 boxes of junk. That night Leonard put the inventory in the nightstand by the bed and Pat and Leonard settled down for a much deserved night's sleep.

In the middle of the night, Pat was awakened by the smell of smoke. Grabbing Leonard's hand, she dragged him to the bedroom door and they stumbled down the stairs and out of the house. The firefighters arrived very soon and put out the fire that had begun in the guest bedroom, but only after it had destroyed most of the upstairs. The next morning, as Pat and Leonard sadly sifted through the debris, Leonard uncovered the half charred personal property inventory. Unfortunately, their efforts of the day before had been for naught because they had made three mistakes:

1. They had not taken inventory room by room, and so they didn't know what property was where.
2. They had not included everything (such as the contents of the boxes of "junk") so that they could make the largest justifiable claim.
3. They had not kept the inventory in a safe place away from their home.

Don't make the same mistakes Pat and Leonard made.

Market Value

As you take inventory room by room, you may have difficulty setting a value on certain items. How much is that green sofa really worth? Even though you may have spent a lot for it when it was new, you probably would receive only a fraction of that amount if you were to sell it today. What about your wardrobe? What value do you put on a four-year-old suit that is worn at the elbows? Insurance companies have an answer to this dilemma, and you should be aware of their solution and apply it to your personal property. Too many families have learned, only after fire has destroyed their belongings, that their insurance coverage is scarcely enough to replace many of them.

The *market value* of an item is the dollar value that you could realize if you were to sell that item. This value is considered by the insurance industry as the appropriate value to assign to personal property, since it best reflects the amount of money necessary to restore your financial position after a loss. Unlike the purchase price, market value reflects any changes in value. For example, the value of automobiles, furniture, and clothing normally declines with use. These items are said to *depreciate*. Homes, antiques, and real estate, however, will probably be worth more today than when they were purchased. These assets are said to *appreciate*. Because most insurable items depreciate, an old item's market value may bear no relation to the cost of replacing that item with a new one at current prices. The policy itself may use the term "actual cash value" to reflect current market value. These two values would differ from each other only if abnormal economic conditions caused the demand for a piece of property to exceed its replacement cost less depreciation (i.e., its actual cash value).

Insurance adjusters use depreciation schedules to determine the market value of goods lost or stolen. A sample depreciation schedule is provided in Table 6-1. The articles with the largest annual depreciation percentages lose their value the fastest. Which types of articles are these? Which articles retain their value? This depreciation schedule will help you determine the amount of insurance you need; by using these figures, you can approximate the amount you could collect on a claim.

Taking Inventory

A sample personal property inventory is provided in Figure 6-1. The following instructions tell you how to apply the personal property depreciation schedule (Table 6-1) to determine your property's market value. The first step in the instructions corresponds to the first column in the sample inventory and so on for all nine columns. You may want to round your figures to the nearest 10, as has been done in the sample.

Instructions

1 *Within each room separate the articles of personal property into categories.*

2 *Indicate the number of articles in each category.*

3 *Write the original cost for the entire group of articles in each category.* This figure is often useful in claims adjustment. If you do not know the original cost of an article, estimate what you think it might have been.

4 *Estimate the collective age of the various articles in each category and write down the average number of years of age.* In Figure 6-1, for example, even though books may have been accumulated over several years, the average age is two years.

5 *Using the depreciation schedule (Table 6-1), record the appropriate annual depreciation percentage for each category of articles.* The annual depreciation factor for wooden tables, for example, is 7 percent.

TABLE 6-1

Personal Property Depreciation Schedule

Article or Class of Articles	Annual Depreciation	Article or Class of Articles	Annual Depreciation
Appliances		Women's blouses, shoes, nightclothes	33
Phonograph	10%	Women's hats, fabric handbags	50
Tape recorder	10	Women's fur coats, jackets	7
Refrigerator	7	Dishes and Glassware	Use 90% of replacement cost
Television	10		
Automatic washer	12	Draperies and Curtains	
Automatic dryer	8	Drapes	10
Stove or range	7	Curtains	20
Minor appliances	10	Shades	10
Bedding		Venetian blinds	7
Blankets (cotton)	10	Foodstuffs	Use replacement cost
Blankets (wool)	5	Furniture	
Box springs	5	Upholstered, chrome or plastic	10
Mattresses	5	Wood	7
Sheets, pillowcases	20	Other	20
Bedspreads	10	Lamps	
Books		Table or floor	7
Reference	Use 60% of replacement cost	Shades	20
Fiction or nonfiction	4	Linens	20
Paperbacks	Use 75% of replacement cost	Silverware	
Carpets and Rugs		Plated	4
Under $5/yd.	20	Sterling	Use 90% of replacement cost
$5-$10/yd.	10	Toys	10
Over $10/yd.	7	Yard Equipment	20
Clothes		Miscellaneous	
Men's sport coats, suits, slacks, sweaters, and such	20	Luggage	5
Men's shirts, underwear, hose, shoes, and such	33	Mirrors	5
Men's topcoats, raincoats	10	Picture frames	5
Women's dresses, suits, skirts, leather handbags, evening gowns	20	Tools (power or hand)	5
		Ornaments, decorations	Use 75% of replacement cost

Source: Aetna Life & Casualty Company's Scheduled Guide, 1979.

PERSONAL PROPERTY INVENTORY

1 Article Category	2 Number of Articles	3 Total Original Cost	4 Average Age (Years)	5 Annual Depreciation	6 Total Depreciation	7 Today's Cost	8 Accumulated Dollar Depreciation	9 Market Value
Carpets	1	$250	4	10%	40%	$300	$120	$180
Chairs	2	100	2	10	20	150	30	120
Tables (wooden)	2	50	2	7	14	70	10	60
Couch	1	85	4	10	40	100	40	60
Record player	1	60	6	10	60	100	60	40
Television	1	250	2	10	20	300	60	240
Mirrors	1	50	4	5	20	75	15	60
Lamps	3	60	2	7	14	70	10	60
Drapes	2	100	4	10	40	150	60	90
Window shades	2	10	4	10	40	16	6	10
Picture frames	2	25	2	5	10	33	3	30
Decorations	15	30	2	Use 75% of replacement cost	25	40	10	30
Bookcases	1	25	2	7	14	35	5	30
Books (fiction)	30	100	2	Use 60% of replacement cost	40	100	40	60
TOTAL	48	$1,235				$1,589	$499	$1,090

FIGURE 6-1
Sample personal property inventory for living room.

6 *Determine the total depreciation to date by multiplying the annual depreciation percentage (column 5) by the age (column 4).* For the two tables in Figure 6-1 that are two years old, the total depreciation to date is 14 percent (2 × 7%).

7 *Estimate what it would cost today to replace the old items with new ones.* Newspaper ads should give a good idea of current prices. According to Figure 6-1, new end tables would cost about $35 each.

8 *Multiply the total depreciation percentage (column 6) by today's cost (column 7) to get the accumulated dollar depreciation.*

9 *Subtract the accumulated dollar depreciation (column 8) from today's cost (column 7) to compute the present market value.* This is the amount you could probably collect on a claim to the insurance company. For example, the total dollar depreciation to date for the two tables in Figure 6-1 is $9.80 (14% × $70). Therefore, the tables' present market value is $60.20 ($70.00 − 9.80), or simply $60.

In addition to taking your personal property inventory, take pictures of the various rooms in your home to use as evidence. Snapshots taken from opposite corners of a room should encompass most of what you have and give you bargaining power in adjusting your claim. Or, use a movie camera to better demonstrate what and where your furnishings are, especially in relation to each other. Pictures help the claims adjuster determine not only the value but also the quantity of personal property in each room. Once again, do not keep the pictures in your home.

Replacement Cost

Some insurance policies now allow you to purchase coverage for your personal property's replacement cost, not market value. For an additional premium, normally 5 to 15 percent of the policy's total premium, you can disregard any depreciation of your property's value and receive money from the insurance company sufficient to purchase a new item exactly like the one that was destroyed or stolen. If your personal property is several years old, this replacement coverage for personal property—normally in the form of an endorsement to your policy's personal property coverage—can be quite valuable. Items of personal property destroyed but not replaced, however, will be valued at their actual cash value (depreciated value).

In judging how much insurance coverage you should carry if you select the replacement cost coverage for your belongings, look at the figures you arrived at in column 7 of Figure 6-1.

VALUING YOUR HOME FOR INSURANCE PURPOSES

Most insurance companies require the policyholder to insure the home and other building structures for their replacement cost rather than their market value. To understand the difference, consider the case of a wood frame garage constructed three years ago at a total cost of $25,000. Because of damage from weathering, a heavy hailstorm, and daily use, the garage has an estimated current market value of only $15,000. The garage can be said to have depreciated by $10,000 or 40 percent. If inflation and other factors have raised the cost of new construction at an annual rate of about 8 percent for the past three years, then the cost of building a new garage just like the one constructed three years ago is $31,000 ($25,000 + 24% of $25,000). The garage's replacement cost is $16,000 higher than its market value.

In insuring your home for replacement cost, you must not only determine its replacement value but also keep up with inflation's effect on construction costs.

Determining Your Home's Replacement Cost

The standard way of determining replacement cost for a house or any other structure (such as a garage) is to multiply the local construction costs per square foot by the number of square feet in the house. As a rule of thumb, multiply the square footage of your home by $40 to $80, depending upon your regional costs and the construction quality of your home. The resulting figure represents the replacement cost of your home today according to current construction cost indices. For example, if you have a 2,000-square-foot home of standard frame construction in an average cost area, multiply the 2,000 square feet by $60 per square foot. The current replacement cost of the home is $120,000.

how not to do it   Tina and Garcia just bought their first home for $50,000 on a quarter acre lot in a suburb. When they called an insurance agent to buy property insurance, Garcia told the agent their home was worth $50,000 and therefore purchased a homeowners policy for $50,000 worth of coverage.

Unfortunately, $50,000 may have no bearing on their home's replacement cost, which is the value they should use in setting property insurance limits. First of all, the $50,000 purchase price for their home includes a value attributable to the land. As a rule of thumb, roughly 20 percent of the purchase price of a home can be applied to the land. Therefore, for Tina and Garcia, approximately $10,000 (20% × $50,000) of the $50,000 is the price of the lot. Second, the market value (or the purchase price) will rarely equal the replacement cost for a home. Garcia's home had 2,000 square feet of livable space and would cost $50 per square foot to replace, or $100,000. Because the home is 30 years old, its market value is less than what it would cost to replace.

Don't be like Tina and Garcia—insure your home for its replacement cost.

The Coinsurance Clause

According to the coinsurance clause, when insurance equal to 80 percent of the replacement cost of the home is carried, the insurance company will reimburse the policyholder for the entire loss, not to exceed the amount of the policy. The penalty for not accurately gauging your home's replacement cost and insuring for at least 80 percent of that amount may be a reduction in the benefits available to you under your insurance contract. This penalty is spelled out in the policy's coinsurance clause.

If insurance less than 80 percent of the home's replacement cost is carried, the insurance company applies the following formula to determine the amount to be paid in the event of a loss:

$$\frac{\text{Amount of insurance in force}}{80\% \text{ of replacement cost of structure at time of loss}} \times \text{Total loss}$$

However, when the loss equals or exceeds 80 percent of the structure's replacement cost, the insurance company pays 100 percent of the loss up to, but not to exceed, the amount of the policy, no matter what percentage of the replacement cost the policy represents.

As Table 6-2 shows, the penalty stipulated by the coinsurance clause comes into effect only when *both* the amount of insurance carried *and* the amount of the loss fall *below* 80 percent of the replacement cost.

Most homeowners policies today offer an *inflation-protection endorsement,* which eliminates the coinsurance clause and therefore the problem of having to gauge accurately your home's replacement cost each year. As you can see from the preceding paragraphs, eliminating the coinsurance clause would certainly be desirable; so check with your agent about the availability of such an endorsement.

Keeping Up with Inflation

Many insurance companies offer *inflation guard policies* that automatically adjust policy limits upward approximately 8 to 10 percent every year. However, some of these policies base their adjustments on changes in the consumer price index (CPI), although historically construction costs have risen twice as fast as the CPI. Other policies use nationwide construction indices, which may not reflect local variations.

You should compute your home's replacement cost annually on the basis of local construction cost information, rather than purchase a policy that automatically determines replacement cost. If your construction costs are rising more slowly than

DEPRECIATION

INFLATION

TABLE 6-2

Comparison of Insurance Paid, by Amount of Insurance in Force and Amount of Loss, on Home with $50,000 Replacement Cost

Insurance in Force	Amount of Loss	What Insurance Pays
$40,000[a]	$50,000	$40,000
40,000[a]	40,000	40,000
40,000[a]	30,000	30,000
35,000[b]	40,000	35,000
35,000[b]	30,000	26,250[c]
30,000[b]	30,000	22,500[c]
25,000[b]	30,000	18,750[c]

[a] Equals 80 percent of the home's replacement cost.

[b] Less than 80 percent of the home's replacement cost.

[c] Insurance coverage divided by 80 percent of the home's replacement cost ($40,000) times amount of loss ($30,000).

national averages, computing the replacement cost yourself or with the help of your insurance agent will be more accurate and may save you money in insurance premiums. Conversely, if rates in your area are rising faster, you can keep from being underinsured by computing the replacement cost yourself.

Some insurance companies offer a homeowners replacement cost and inflation protection endorsement, which puts the burden of accurately determining your home's replacement cost on the insurance company. Under this endorsement, the insurance company can raise or lower your home insurance limits. If they make an error in judgment and affix a coverage limit that, at the time of a loss, is determined to be under 80 percent of the replacement cost of the structure destroyed, the insurance company must pay the total amount of the loss, up to the policy's limits. Thereby, the insured can avoid any unwitting violation of the coinsurance requirements. However, make sure your insurance company accepts the consequences of underestimating your home's replacement cost, or you may not receive the total amount of money you need to rebuild if your home is completely destroyed. In other words, even though the insurance company has set limits that satisfy the coinsurance requirements (80 percent of replacement cost), the additional 20 percent of replacement cost may have to be borne by you. Therefore, accept the responsibility for determining replacement cost yourself or choose a company that will stand behind its responsibility of determining replacement cost for you.

One way in which an insurance company assumes the burden of a loss greater than what was anticipated is with a "full measure plus" endorsement. Such an endorsement says that the amount of coverage on the dwelling, detached buildings, unscheduled personal property, and additional living expenses shall apply as a blanket limit of liability for all the property mentioned, thereby negating their individual limits. For example, assume that the following are the coverages at the beginning of the policy period on a particular homeowners policy:

Dwelling	$100,000
Detached buildings	10,000
Unscheduled personal property	70,000
Additional living expenses	20,000
Total	$200,000

This $200,000 becomes the blanket limit of liability for this policy. If a detached garage were destroyed by fire and cost $15,000 to rebuild, the full $15,000 replacement cost (since it is less than the $200,000 blanket limit) would be covered. Similarly, if the dwelling burned down and cost $130,000 to replace, it would be replaced for $130,000 as long as all other losses (i.e., personal property, detached buildings, and additional living expenses) did not exceed $70,000.

In addition, the full measure plus endorsement provides for an increase in replacement cost to be added to the blanket limit of coverage up to 1 percent of the total blanket limit of liability for each month after the effective date of the current policy period. For example, if the full blanket amount of liability were $200,000, and the policy had been in effect five months, up to 5 percent more coverage (five months at 1 percent per month) or $10,000 would be added to the blanket limit if the actual replacement cost warranted this addition.

TYPES OF INSURANCE COVERAGE AVAILABLE

Now that you have decided what property you want protected, you must decide what you want to protect that property against. There are many possibilities, as shown in the key to perils in Tables 6-3 and 6-4. Using this list of perils commonly covered by property insurance contracts, decide which are dangerous to you because of the nature of the property you wish to insure, the area in which you live, or both.

Those risks that are seldom, if ever, covered include excessive heat or scorching (no flame), self-inflicted hazards (such as pouring gasoline around your home and lighting it), and war. With your insurance needs in mind, you are ready to consider the kinds of property coverage available.

There are five groups of policies that cover your home or your personal property, or both:

- *Standard fire policies* cover your home and other physical structures against damage due to fire. Because they cover only one peril, they are to be used cautiously.
- *Dwelling building(s) and contents forms* offer coverage for physical damage done by a burglar but do not cover the actual property stolen.
- *Homeowners forms* are the most popular contracts and are specifically designed to meet the needs of homeowners and renters. *Package policies* combine all of your property and casualty insurance needs (including auto insurance) in one policy.
- *Floaters* cover personal property (not physical structures) anywhere in the world. They are used to cover highly valued items such as furs and jewelry.

Tables 6-3 and 6-4 show the various types of coverage these policies offer. We will discuss only the latter three types in more detail here.

Homeowners Policy

The homeowners policy is a package policy or multiple-line insurance program. In other words, this policy contains a number of types of coverage (home, personal property, and personal liability). Homeowners policies normally have the following features.

1. They cover the dwelling; any detached structures located on the premises; unscheduled personal property (property not specifically defined on the face of the policy) on and off the premises; trees, plants, and shrubs; and additional living expenses.
2. They cover all personal property while in transit (up to 10 percent of the total insured value of all your property), and while at a new location for a maximum of 30 days (up to 50 percent of the total insured value of all your property).
3. They cover the cost of removing debris caused by a loss or damage covered by the policies.
4. They provide for the payment (up to $250) of any fire department service charge incurred.

TABLE 6-3
Coverage of Various Policies for Home ($100,000) or Personal Property ($50,000)

Coverage	Home ($100,000)		Personal Property ($50,000)		
	Standard Fire Contract	Dwelling Building(s) Special Form	Personal Articles Floater	Personal Property Floater	Homeowners Form 4
Perils[a]	1-3	All risks[b]	All risks[b]	All risks[b]	1-11, 13-19
Home	Insured value of home		No coverage		
Detached buildings	10% of insured value of home		No coverage		
Trees, shrubs, plants	No coverage	5% of insured value of home	No coverage		
Personal property on premises	No coverage		Insured value of scheduled property	Insured value of any property	Face value of policy[c]
Personal property off premises	No coverage				10% of insured value of property
Additional living expenses	No coverage	10% of insured value of home	No coverage		20% of insured value of property
Annual cost[d]	$131	$213	$515	$271	$278

[a]Key to Perils
1. Fire and lightning
2. Damage to property removed from house (for a period of time not to exceed five days) if endangered by fire
3. Damage from water and chemicals used to extinguish fire
4. Windstorm and hail
5. Explosion
6. Riots and civil commotion
7. Damage by aircraft
8. Damage by vehicles other than those owned and operated by people covered in policy
9. Damage from smoke
10. Vandalism and malicious mischief
11. Theft
12. Window breakage
13. Damage from falling objects.
14. Weight of snow, ice, sleet
15. Collapse of part or all of building
16. Damage from steam heating system or appliance for heating water
17. Water or steam leakage or overflow
18. Freezing of plumbing, heating, air conditioning
19. Short circuit injury to appliances and such

[b]All-risks coverage protects against all perils except those specifically excluded (e.g., war, vermin). Therefore, perils 1 through 19 plus other imaginable perils are insured under all risks.

[c]If personal property is normally located at another residence of the insured, then a limit of 10 percent of the usual value of property on the premises applies.

[d]Sample costs are for Santa Clara County, California, 1982. Northern California, Class 3, $100 deductible, 1982. HO4 includes a $250 deductible for theft, $100 for all the rest.

5. They impose certain per occurrence limits on the following stolen valuables: money, bank notes, and bullion ($100 limit); securities, bills, deeds, letters of credit, passports, tickets, stamps, watches, precious and semiprecious stones, jewelry, and furs ($500 limit); manuscripts ($1,000 limit). Some companies also include silverware in this list.
6. They include personal liability and medical expense coverage arising out of

TABLE 6-4
Coverage of Various Policies for Home ($100,000) and Personal Property ($50,000)

Coverage	Home ($100,000) and Personal Property ($50,000)						Home ($100,000) and Personal Property ($50,000) and Autos and Other Homes
	Dwelling Building(s) and Contents Form	Dwelling Building(s) and Contents Broad Form	Home-owners Form 1	Home-owners Form 2	Home-owners Form 3	Home-owners Form 5	Package Policies
Perils[a]	1-10	1-10, 12-19	1-11	1-19	All risks[b]	All risks[c]	All risks[c]
Home	Insured value of home						$1,000,000 or more for all dwellings or detached buildings and other liability claims (i.e., auto)
Detached buildings	10% of insured value of home						
Trees, shrubs, plants	No coverage	5% of insured value of home ($250 maximum per item)					$250 per item up to $1,000 per loss
Personal property on premises	Insured value of property		50% (may be reduced or increased) of insured value of home			50% (may not be reduced but may be increased) of insured value of home	$1,000,000 or more for all property anywhere in the world (includes autos)
Personal property off premises	10% of insured value of property on premises						
Additional living expenses	10% of insured value of home			20% of insured value of home			$1,000,000 or more including losses to home and personal property
Annual cost[d]	$267	$352	$260	$309	$326	$489	$435

[a] Key to Perils
1. Fire and lightning
2. Damage to property removed from house (for a period of time not to exceed five days) if endangered by fire
3. Damage from water and chemicals used to extinguish fire
4. Windstorm and hail
5. Explosion
6. Riots and civil commotion
7. Damage by aircraft
8. Damage by vehicles other than those owned and operated by people covered in policy
9. Damage from smoke
10. Vandalism and malicious mischief
11. Theft
12. Window breakage
13. Damage from falling objects
14. Weight of snow, ice, sleet
15. Collapse of part or all of building
16. Damage from steam heating system or appliance for heating water
17. Water or steam leakage or overflow
18. Freezing of plumbing, heating, air conditioning
19. Short circuit injury to appliances and such

[b] Applies only to home. Personal property covered only against perils 1-19.

[c] All-risks coverage protects against all perils except those specifically excluded (e.g., war, vermin). Therefore, perils 1 through 19 plus other imaginable perils are insured under all risks.

[d] Sample costs are for Santa Clara County, California, 1982. Northern California, Class 3, $100 deductible, 1982. Package policies come only with a $250 deductible.

personal liability suits. (These will be discussed in Chapter 7 as part of general liability coverage.) The basic maximum limits are $25,000 liability per occurrence, $500 in medical expenses per person, and $250 in property damages per occurrence. Any of these limits can, of course, be raised by paying an additional premium.

7. They offer a choice of two deductible clauses. One clause provides a $100 deductible for damages done by a windstorm or hail. If the damage is between $100 and $500, the insurance company will pay 125 percent of those damages in excess of $100. In other words, if you incur $200 worth of damage because of a severe windstorm or hail, your insurance company will pay you $125 (125 percent of $100) and you will have to pay only $75. When the damage exceeds $500, there is no deductible, and the insurance company pays for everything. Such a deductible arrangement is called a *declining deductible* because the deductible, or what you must pay, decreases as the amount of damage or loss increases. The other clause merely provides a choice of deductible of from $100 to $500 to be applied to all perils.

8. The theft coverage extension endorsement provides coverage for personal property stolen from an automobile or water craft regardless of whether there are signs of forcible entry or all windows are closed or all doors locked. Because of the sophistication of thieves, signs of forcible entry may not accompany thefts. This endorsement may therefore be well worth the extra cost.

There are six types of homeowners policies. They differ in the range and nature of perils covered, the maximum benefit allowed under each type of coverage (i.e., home, personal property, personal liability), and minimum coverages. Homeowners forms 1, 2, 3, and 6 limit minimum coverage to $8,000. Homeowners form 5 has a minimum coverage of $15,000 and homeowners form 4 has a $5,000 minimum.

homeowners form 1 (HO-1) (homeowners basic form)   HO-1 covers only a limited range and nature of perils. For example, the fire coverage excludes loss resulting from sudden and accidental injury to or disturbance of electrical appliances, fixtures, or wiring, if that loss was caused by anything other than lightning. The smoke coverage excludes any damage from smoke escaping from a fireplace; and the explosion coverage excludes damage due to sonic booms, leakage from steam boilers and pipes, and bursting of water pipes. The breakage of glass coverage excludes any loss above $50 and is void if the residence is vacant for more than 30 days. The accidental collapse of a building is not covered.

homeowners form 2 (HO-2) (homeowners broad form)   HO-2 covers a wide range of perils, including all kinds of fire, smoke, and explosion damage. Unlike HO-1, HO-2 imposes no $50 ceiling for glass damage. Whereas HO-1 defines theft as any act of stealing or attempt to steal, HO-2 broadens the meaning to include mysterious disappearance—that is, loss of property from a known place under circumstances when a probability of theft exists. The vehicle coverage is also broadened in HO-2. HO-1 excludes loss caused by any vehicle damaging fences, driveways, or walks, whereas HO-2 excludes only damage caused by vehicles owned or operated by any occupant of the premises.

homeowners form 3 (HO-3) (homeowners special form)   HO-3 combines broad form peril coverage for unscheduled personal property (as in HO-2) with all-risk coverage for the dwelling and detached structures. With regard to personal property, falling objects coverage is expanded to cover objects other than those falling from aircraft. Also, under HO-3, vehicle damage is unqualified. That is, any loss will be covered no matter who drives a vehicle into your house or other property.

HO-3 covers any loss or damage to television antennas, awnings, and outdoor equipment, whereas HO-2 specifically excludes these items from coverage. Because of its diversified coverage, HO-3 is now the most popular homeowners package, and many consider it the broadest coverage for the least cost.

homeowners form 4 (HO-4) (contents broad form)   HO-4 is a policy for renters. It covers unscheduled personal property on or away from the premises plus additional living expenses. As a broad form, it covers the same range of perils as HO-2. The only difference in the nature of the perils covered occurs under vandalism and malicious mischief. Unlike HO-2, all losses are covered against vandalism and malicious mischief even if the apartment is vacated for 30 days or longer. If you build any additions to or make alterations in your apartment at your expense, these additions can be covered for an amount not exceeding 10 percent of the face amount of the policy, even though they are actually a permanent part of the building. If you are a student and are not covered under your parents' policy, you should consider purchasing this policy.

homeowners form 5 (HO-5) (homeowners comprehensive form)   HO-5 offers comprehensive coverage for your home and unscheduled personal property. It is the broadest coverage available under either the dwellings or the homeowners programs. Basically HO-5 extends all-risk coverage to your personal property as well as your home and detached structures. For example, your personal property is covered against earthquake damage, and glass breakage coverage is expanded to cover mirrors. However, in return for this all-risk coverage, you may have to pay twice as much in premiums as you would for any other policy.

homeowners form 6 (HO-6) (condominium-unit owner's coverage)   HO-6 covers unscheduled personal property, including additions and alterations made by the unit owner, and additional living expenses against loss by the same perils as provided in HO-4. In addition, you can cover your unscheduled property if you rent the condominium to others and any loss assessment for which you, the condominium owner, may be liable through optional endorsements added to HO-6.

Package Policies

In recent years, a number of package policies that include more than one residence and one or more automobiles all on the same policy have been created. Continental and St. Paul Insurance Company were two of the first insurers to offer such policies.

The key to these policies is the offering of one single liability limit (normally $1,000,000) to cover each and all liability situations, regardless of where they occur.

Such a single limit eliminates any gaps in coverage that might exist if a person had a separate homeowners policy and a separate auto policy. In addition, these package policies offer higher limits on scheduled high-value property. Where the normal homeowners policy covers high-value property for $500 in the aggregate on a per occurrence basis, these package policies offer limits of $500 to $15,000 for each category of high-value property (e.g., antiques, jewelry, furs). As in an HO-5 policy, all-risk coverage is extended from the dwelling to all unscheduled personal property. The actual replacement cost of the house is guaranteed even if it is more than the face amount of the policy.

These package policies represent the wave of the future as insurance companies in the property/casualty field seek to cover families against risk rather than cover separate items of property.

Floater Policies

Floater policies are basically personal property policies. They cover property not just in your home but wherever you might transport it. Such policies may also be called by their original name, *inland marine*. There are two types of general property floater policies, both of which protect your property against all perils except war, radioactive contamination, insects or vermin, and normal wear.

personal articles floater This policy provides all-risk protection for specified classes of personal property. It is called a schedule floater because each article or class of articles to be insured must be listed on the face of the policy along with the conditions under which it is insured. For example, you might want to insure your golf clubs against theft when they are in your car. To keep the premiums low, the policy might state that the clubs are covered only if the car or compartment of the car from which they were stolen was locked at the time of theft and if there is clear physical evidence of forced entry.

The more articles you wish to insure and the more conditions you wish to guard against, the higher the premiums you will have to pay. Once you have recorded a class of articles such as golf clubs on your policy, you do not have to change your policy until you renew it even if you acquire new items in the same categories as those you have already insured. Coverage is applicable in Canada and the United States and all of its territories.

Details of sample floaters are provided in Table 6-5. The personal effects floater, for example, is basically an all-risk policy, but its use is quite limited. It covers only personal property worn or carried by travelers away from the insured premises. Because it offers such specialized coverage, it is usually attached to other property floater policies for periods often no longer than three months. The amount of coverage for jewelry, watches, and furs is limited to the lesser of 10 percent of the total coverage amount or $100 for each article lost or stolen.

personal property floater Unlike the personal articles floater, this policy offers protection on *all* articles (not just high-value items), scheduled or not, on a world-wide basis. You have a choice of three types of policies, each with varying levels of coverage on high-value items.

1. Limits coverage on jewelry, watches, and furs ($250 per occurrence of damage); money ($100 per occurrence); and securities ($500 per occurrence).
2. Allows jewelry, watches, furs, and other property of extraordinary value to be

TABLE 6-5
Personal Articles Floaters

Article or Class of Articles	Deductible or Special Conditions	Exclusions	Cost
Personal effects	$25 deductible (sometimes)	Money, passports, auto licenses, tickets, securities, baggage	$15 plus 1% of total insured value
Bicycle	$5 deductible	Damage from rust or mechanical breakdown	$10 per $100 of coverage
Camera			$1.65 per $100 of coverage
Fine arts		Damage from restoration or breakage of fragile objects	18¢ per $100 of coverage 15¢ per $100 if breakage coverage applies
Furs		Damage caused by moths or vermin	50¢ per $100 of coverage
Jewelry			$1.92 to $3.24 per $100 depending on city and state
Musical instruments			Nonprofessional: 65¢ per $100 of coverage Professional: $3.50 per $100 of coverage
Silverware		Pencils, pens, articles of personal adornment, smoking implements	50¢ per $100 of coverage
Sports equipment		Loss due to failure of people to return equipment you loaned to them	$1.40 per $100 of coverage
Stamp and coin collections	$250 limit on any one stamp or coin		Stamps: 60¢ per $100 of coverage Coins: $1.75 per $100 of coverage
Wedding presents	Covered before wedding and 90 days afterward	Damage from breakage of fragile objects	13¢ per $100 of coverage 25¢ per $100 if breakage coverage applies
Food freezer	Food in family freezer covered if power goes off		$1 per $100 of food

Source: Insurance Services Office, August 1981, for California.

scheduled on the face of the policy and insured separately for whatever price the policyholder wants.

3. Similar to the first type of coverage except that jewelry, watches, and furs may be insured for an additional amount beyond the $250 limit against the perils of fire and lightning only.

Because personal property floaters are expensive, they are seldom used. However, if you are a student, this policy or your parents' homeowners policy may be the only way to cover your property.

Flood Insurance

In 1969 a program jointly sponsored by private insurance companies and the federal government made flood insurance available, at rates far below expected losses, to homeowners living in qualified communities. In effect, taxpayers nationwide subsidize insurance for flood-prone communities that qualify with the U.S. Department of Housing and Urban Development by enacting land use control measures to reduce the potential damage from future flooding. At present, over 2,800 communities nationwide qualify for this federally subsidized flood insurance. In some areas, lenders may require home buyers to carry flood insurance as a condition of the mortgage.

Earthquake Insurance

Earthquake insurance is normally written as an addition to a fire or homeowners insurance policy. In some states, minimum premiums are as low as 3¢ per $100. The standard deductible is 5 percent of the replacement cost of the home—probably large enough to cover the damage resulting from most minor earthquakes. As with flood insurance, lenders in some areas may require home buyers to purchase earthquake insurance as a condition of the mortgage.

Californians account for about two-thirds of all earthquake insurance in force in the United States. Undoubtedly, that is because in this century earthquakes have generally struck most often and most severely along the Pacific Coast.

Clauses to Be Aware Of

There are four clauses that may be appended to the dwelling building(s), dwelling contents, or homeowners policies: the other insurance clause, the mortgagee clause, the leasehold clause, and the apportionment clause.

other insurance clause   This clause protects insurance companies against having to pay, collectively, an amount more than the damaged property is worth when the insured has similar policies with more than one company. With this clause, an insurance company limits its liability to that portion of the loss that is equal to the company's portion of the total insurance coverage. In other words, if you were to hold three policies with equal coverage benefits on your home, each insurance company would pay only one-third of the damages.

mortgagee clause This clause covers the rights of the mortgagee (the issuer of the mortgage—usually a bank or savings and loan). Since the mortgagee, by virtue of the mortgage, can be said to have an insurable interest in your home, this person or organization may require that your property insurance policy contain a mortgage clause that promises to pay the mortgagee an amount equal to the mortgage debt outstanding at the time your home is destroyed. As the debt is paid off, the mortgagee's interest in the property decreases. Once the mortgage is paid off, the clause becomes ineffective.

leasehold clause This clause covers renters for damages to any leasehold improvements they may have made. For example, if you have just repainted at your own expense the apartment you are renting, you can be reimbursed for that expense in the event that fire or some other peril stipulated in the policy destroys the apartment.

apportionment clause This clause states that the maximum extended coverage for any peril covered by a fire insurance policy equals the ratio of that policy's fire coverage to the total amount of fire coverage on the property. For example, suppose you have two policies: a $25,000 fire policy and a $25,000 fire policy with extended coverage endorsement for your $50,000 home. If an airplane crashed into your home and caused damages of $10,000, your fire plus extended coverage policy would pay you only $5,000, since that policy's fire protection is only 50 percent of the total fire protection on the home, even though the face amount of falling object protection is $25,000.

In addition, the apportionment clause states that the maximum extended coverage for any peril covered by a fire insurance policy equals the ratio of that policy's extended coverage to the total amount of extended coverage insurance covering the property. In other words, if you have two basic fire policies, each with an extended coverage endorsement, each would pay 50 percent of the damage caused by a covered peril. However, the apportionment clause applies only to policies with extended coverage riders.

REDUCING YOUR COSTS OF PROPERTY INSURANCE

Property insurance premiums are based on two separate sets of data: the number of fires and extent of fire damage in any one specific area and the number of thefts and extent of theft loss in any one specific area. In addition to these data, the prevalence of civil disorder in the area and the probability of perils other than fire and theft may be taken into account in your premium rate, depending upon the policy purchased.

You may be paying a higher premium for identical coverage from the same insurance company than someone else living in the same part of town. This happens because property insurance rate-making takes into consideration the relative vulnerability of many types of property to many types of perils. For example, one person may live in a brick house while another lives in a frame house. One person may have fire extinguishers in the kitchen and garage, while another does not.

Although both people will receive the same benefit payments if calamity strikes, the person who lives in a brick house equipped with fire extinguishers may be paying 20 percent less each year in premiums.

Here are ways that you can lower the cost of your property insurance.

1. Pay premiums computed on a three-year basis (if available), rather than on a one-year basis.
2. Increase the deductible.
3. Buy a house that is constructed of fire-resistant materials.
4. Put fire extinguishers throughout your home.
5. Live in an area where theft activity and civil disorder are low.
6. Purchase package policies rather than separate policies for different perils.

There are also conditions that may raise the cost of your property insurance: if you live over five miles from a fire department; if you live over 1,000 feet from a fire hydrant; if your home is a wood structure; if the building is not satisfactorily maintained (broken plaster, broken windows); if there is an unsafe arrangement of cooking devices, heating devices, or wiring; if there is a hazardous accumulation of rubbish in the attic or basement; if your home is within several feet (usually 10 feet) of another building; if the premises are occupied by three or more families; if the building is under construction. Check with your insurance agent to see how any of these factors might affect your policy.

You may want to use Figure 6-2 to help you organize the information you obtain when you shop for rates.

CONCLUSION

Several questions must be answered by the potential property insurance policyholder.

1. What property can I insure? What property do I want to insure? (Be sure you keep a personal property inventory.)
2. Am I going to value my personal property at market value or replacement cost?
3. What is the replacement cost of my home and other structures?
4. Which policy covers my property against the most threatening perils at a cost I can afford?

If you can satisfactorily answer these questions, you are ready to deal intelligently with an insurance agent.

SHOPPING FOR PROPERTY INSURANCE

	Insurer 1	Insurer 2	Insurer 3
Policy type			
Company			
Renewal date			

	Limits	Premiums	
Home			
Detached buildings			
Trees, shrubs, plants			
Personal property on premises			
Personal property off premises			
Additional living expenses			
Comprehensive personal liability[a]			
Medical expense payments[a]			
Scheduled items			
Endorsements			
Extended theft			
Inflation protection			
Replacement cost			
Full measure plus			
Other (e.g., earthquake, flood)			
Deductible			
Total annual premium			

[a]For explanation of these categories, see Chapter 7.

FIGURE 6-2
Data sheet for use in shopping for property insurance.

VOCABULARY

coinsurance clause
floater policies
flood and earthquake coverage
full measure plus endorsement
homeowners forms
inflation guard policies
inflation protection endorsement

insurable interest
package policies
market value
personal property inventory
replacement cost
scheduled property coverage

QUESTIONS

1. Can you insure your neighbor's home? Why or why not?
2. Tim has two insurance policies on his $40,000 bungalow: a fire policy for $40,000 and a homeowners form 2 for $20,000. How much would each policy pay if Tim's bungalow were totally destroyed by fire?
3. What are the major reasons why you should prepare a personal property inventory?
4. Use the personal property depreciation schedule (Table 6-1) to determine the market value for the following items: a four-year-old sofa that would cost $800 new today; a two-year-old wooden dinette set that would cost $300 new today; and a three-year-old television that would cost $400 new today.
5. What is the best way to take inflation into account when insuring your home?
6. The expected fire loss next year to the 5,000 single-family residences in Middletown is $200,000. What would insurance companies have to charge each homeowner as a base premium to cover their expected losses?
7. Harry's home has a replacement cost of $60,000. Harry insures it for $30,000 with a homeowners form 3 policy. If his home suffers a fire loss of $10,000, how much will his insurance policy pay?
8. Which homeowners form offers the broadest coverage at the least cost for home and personal property? Why?
9. Which property insurance policies are best suited to apartment dwellers? Why?
10. What are the primary differences between floater policies and homeowners policies?

CASE PROBLEMS

1. Jim and Janet Lewis were married in their last year of college and moved into a one-bedroom apartment near school. Items of furniture they purchased and their respective market values are a new queen-sized bed ($250), a two-year-old dinette set ($150), two 10-year-old chairs ($50), a new bookcase ($20), a 15-year-old desk ($25), a new stereo ($200), and a four-year-old bureau ($80). In addition to these furnishings, they each have approximately $500 worth of clothes.

   How large is the Lewises' risk exposure, assuming they can only afford coverage equal to their property's market value? How much of the potential loss could be covered by insurance? What type of property insurance (basic fire, dwelling building(s) and contents, homeowners, package policies, or floater) would you recommend for them? If you chose either of the last three types, specify also the kind of policy. What policy limits would you recommend?

2. Harry and Melinda Lee bought their first home a year ago for $40,000. They had it insured with a homeowners form 3 policy at that time for $30,000. The replacement cost on their home today is 10 percent higher than the purchase price. How much insurance

should the Lees have on their home? What's the minimum amount they should have if they want to be able to receive 100 percent of any claim up to the insured amount? How much would their existing coverage pay if there were a $10,000 loss?

RECOMMENDED READING

Eastman Kodak. *Photos Help You When Disaster Strikes*. Rochester, New York: Eastman Kodak, Consumer Market Division.
   Available from Eastman Kodak, Rochester, NY 14630.

"Filing a Home Insurance Claim? You May Be In for a Shock." *U.S. News and World Report*, February 21, 1977.

Insurance Information Institute. *A Family Guide to Property and Liability Insurance*. New York, 1973.
   Describes coverages available but does not render advice.

CHUCK AND NANCY ANDERSON

Insuring Their Home against Financial Calamity

The Andersons bought a $25,000 standard fire insurance policy and a $10,000 homeowners form 1 policy on their 1,250-square-foot home when they bought it for $26,000 ($21,000 for the house and $5,000 for the land) nine years ago. They wanted the full replacement value of their home covered against fire because that seemed to be the peril most likely to destroy it, and so they bought the basic fire policy. The homeowners policy provides coverage against fire damage, too, but it also covers damage due to perils such as windstorm and hail, which are less likely to occur. The Andersons pay $42 a year for the basic fire policy and $80 a year for the homeowners form 1 policy.

   The Andersons recently took a personal property inventory and found that their personal property has a current market value of $14,986 and a replacement cost of $18,340. They also had an estimate made on the house and found out that it would cost $55 per square foot to replace it.

Questions

1. Do the Andersons have too little, too much, or just enough insurance coverage on their house?
2. Which of the following policies would you recommend: dwelling building(s) and contents form ($260 a year), homeowners form 3 ($460 a year), homeowners form 5 ($750 a year), or would you advise them to retain their present coverage? Why? What dollar limit would you suggest for the policies you are recommending?
3. What effect would your recommendations have on the Andersons' balance sheet and/or income statement?

7

Comprehensive Liability and Auto Insurance

If you were sued, taken to court, and found to be financially liable for damages against someone's person or property, you could lose everything you own and be forced into bankruptcy. Even an out-of-court settlement of a large claim against you could result in your paying as much as half of your income for several years. Liability insurance protects the policyholder against claims arising from bodily injury and property damage to others.

The two kinds of liability insurance discussed in this chapter are *comprehensive*, which covers a wide range of potential liability situations, and *automobile*, which covers only one or two areas of exposure. Auto liability insurance is probably more important to you than comprehensive liability insurance because you are more exposed to liability risks when you are driving a car than at any other time. Two-thirds of the civil liability suits clogging our courts today involve bodily injury and property damage claims arising out of automobile accidents. Also, auto liability claims tend to be larger than other liability claims. Auto insurance may cover property damage to your own car and its contents as well as the liability claims of others against you. In this chapter we shall discuss fully both of these types of auto insurance.

Unlike property insurance, liability insurance pays money to others, not to you. However, your liability insurance premiums also cover the cost of services such as investigating and settling claims against you, interviewing witnesses, and defending you in court. The insurance company performs these services whether the claim against you is just or fraudulent.

LIABILITY AND THE LAW

There are three types of liability with which you should be familiar: negligence, absolute liability, and vicarious liability.

Negligence

One potential source of liability is negligence. Negligence laws require each of us, at all times, to take reasonable care to avoid injury to others and their possessions. Courts define a breach of that duty as the failure to exercise the same degree of care as would a prudent person in the same or similar circumstances. A lawsuit based on negligence can result from either an act or a failure to act that is the direct cause of a predictable injury to a person or property.

By legal definition, the person who is negligent could have exercised a proper degree of care, but failed to do so, causing foreseeable consequences. Thus the legal definition of negligence suggests that there is a norm of human behavior and of moral standards that a prudent person would follow. In a suit based on negligence the injured party must prove that the injuries resulted directly from the defendant's failure to live up to that norm.

The degree of care owed to persons coming onto your property varies. For example, your invited guests are owed a higher degree of care than are trespassers.

Absolute Liability

The second type of liability occurs when a person is responsible for the existence of abnormally dangerous conditions or activities that lead to injury or loss. For example, you may have a dangerous dog that bites the mail carrier. Anyone who owns a dangerous animal, domestic or wild, and who is or should be aware of its nature is absolutely liable for injuries it causes. Statutes and ordinances may impose liability on the owner of a dog regardless of knowledge of its dangerous propensity. Other activities that are generally considered to be abnormally dangerous include fumigation with poison and blasting with explosives. When liability is absolute, the injured party is not required to prove negligence on the part of the defendant.

Vicarious Liability

The third type of liability is vicarious liability. You may be liable for actions of people in your employ, particularly when you direct the manner and method of work they do. For example, if you direct the gardener to mow especially close to trees and the mower blade strikes a root and sends a splinter into a neighbor's eye, you may be sued for bodily injury.

Defenses against Liability

To lessen your exposure to liability suits, be aware of the following types of defenses:

1. You exercised a proper degree of care.
2. The injured person was aware of the risk or voluntarily exposed himself or herself to that risk.
3. The injured person was to some degree responsible for the injury incurred. If you have taken proper precautions, contributory negligence may be fairly easy to prove.

It used to be that injured persons lost their entire claim if their own negligence contributed to the accident in *any* way. However, courts in a number of states have rewritten the rule of contributory negligence, substituting a doctrine of "comparative negligence." This doctrine maintains that even if an injured person was *somewhat* at fault, the person should recover something through the claim. Needless to say, this treatment of negligence spurs more court cases and more judgments against defendants and consequently higher liability premiums.

LIABILITY AND YOU

Could any of the following situations happen to you?

- An elderly woman takes a shortcut across your yard, trips over a surfaced root from a large elm tree, and breaks her elbow. She sues you for negligence.
- Your dog bites a visitor, and the visitor sues for damages.
- As you approach an intersection, the traffic signal turns yellow. You gun the engine to beat the red light and you hit a car that is pulling out from the cross-street. The driver sues you for carelessness.

Anyone can be sued. Reports of lawsuits are common in newspapers. As we have seen, however, in the discussion of types of liability and defenses against them, a suit does not necessarily mean that the defendant is liable for the actions that prompted the suit. One thing you can do to reduce your liability is to look around your home for hazards and nuisances and check to see that you have taken appropriate precautions.

Determining Your Liability Exposure

Before you buy coverage for your liability exposure, you should know what that exposure is—the total amount of money or property for which someone might sue and attempt to collect damages. As we have seen in Chapter 6, property coverage needs are rather easy to determine: you simply total the value of your personal property and insure the total amount against whatever perils you choose. Liability coverage, however, is not so easy to determine.

Selecting the proper amount of liability insurance depends on both the nature of the liability exposures you and your family face and the relative visibility of your family's wealth. The first factor requires an assessment of your family's activities. Do you or does any of your family members engage in activities that involve physical interaction with other people? Contact sports, for example, pose more opportunities for bodily injury or property damage caused by carelessness or negligence than does bird-watching or card-playing. Do you own property that contains attractive nuisances such as a swimming pool or a fruit tree? These offer opportunities for injuries to children, who might decide to take a swim or to steal some fruit. Do you own or operate any motor vehicles? Automobiles, snowmobiles, motorcycles, dune buggies, or motorboats can cause much damage and probably represent your greatest liability exposure. Do you own any pets? Dogs and cats, if unleashed or not fenced in, can easily provoke a lawsuit. In short, consider all your activities.

The second factor to consider in analyzing your liability exposure is your financial position and its visibility. Certain professions, for example, are known to offer high salaries. If you or your family are known or believed to have achieved relative financial wealth, your liability exposure is increased considerably. Therefore, even though the number of situations that might provoke a lawsuit may be limited, your potential loss per exposure might be great. Consider both factors—the number of exposures and visible wealth—when planning your liability insurance.

You will probably go through three or four phases of liability exposure in your lifetime. The first phase occurs when you are under 21 and are still covered by your parents' policy. The second phase stretches from the time you leave home to the time you either buy a house or accumulate a net worth of approximately $25,000 or both. Phase three occurs when you are making a good salary and your net worth is from $25,000 to $100,000. Phase four begins when your net worth exceeds $100,000. At this point, your salary may be quite high (over $40,000), and you would have become financially visible.

Maybe none of these phases exactly reflects your situation; but you and your family will probably confront several phases of liability exposure, and you should analyze your needs in light of these changes.

Determining the Amount of Coverage You Need

You can put your liability insurance limits at whatever level you desire. Naturally, the limits you select will be determined, in part, by the number and nature of the liability exposures you have.

There are several methods for computing how much liability insurance to buy. We will discuss three of them:

1. *Life value method*: Purchase enough comprehensive liability insurance to equal your present net worth (assets minus liabilities) plus the aggregate value of your future earnings. For example, if your net worth is $50,000 and you can expect to earn an average of $20,000 a year for 45 years, according to this method you should purchase $950,000 ($50,000 + (45 × $20,000)) of liability coverage. This is perhaps the most conservative approach to determining your liability needs, because you can never be successfully sued for more than what you have now and will have in the future.
2. *Net worth method*: Purchase enough insurance to cover your present net worth. This method assumes that future income will not be attached to fulfill a claim.
3. *Jury awards method*: Purchase enough insurance to equal the maximum jury awards being assessed by your local courts. For example, if a local court recently awarded $300,000 in a bodily injury suit and this is the largest amount to be awarded for such a suit, according to this method you should insure yourself for $300,000.

Actually, the time and effort involved in assessing your coverage needs precisely may be incommensurate with the potential cost savings. For example, $25,000 of liability coverage automatically attached to section II of a homeowners policy adds only $7 to the policy's annual premium; $50,000 of coverage would cost only $3 more than that. Raising your auto insurance liability limits from $50,000 to $100,000 per person might cost an extra 10 percent a year. As you can see from these examples, the cost of personal liability insurance is relatively low; this is because the likelihood of a lawsuit is not great. Nevertheless, the question of how much liability insurance to buy should not be avoided.

TYPES OF COMPREHENSIVE LIABILITY INSURANCE

There are two types of comprehensive liability insurance: general and umbrella.

General Liability Policies

General liability policies offer coverage over a variety of potential liability situations. Section II of the homeowners policy is such a policy. It covers activities in and around the home as well as away from the home. Some of the exposures it does not cover are situations involving slander or libel and activities involving motor vehicles. The first exception, however, may be covered by an umbrella policy and the second by an auto liability policy, both of which will be discussed later in this chapter.

All general liability policies have jacket provisions, which define the insurance company's commitments to the policyholder, and coverage provisions, which state who is covered, what is covered, and what is not covered.

jacket provisions Under these provisions, the insurance company will make supplementary payments on your behalf if you are sued. These payments usually include all expenses incurred while investigating claims and defending the insured; court bonds; bail bond expenses up to $250; expenses incurred by the insured; and other reasonable expenses (including up to $25 a day for missed salary while the insured attends legal hearings). The jacket provisions also state the following:

1. The insurance company reserves the right to inspect the insured's property at any time. The insurance company, however, is not obligated to make inspections and therefore cannot be held legally liable for an accident occurring on the property.
2. The insured must notify the company in writing of any occurrence that has led or might lead to a damage claim.
3. If two or more policies for the same coverage exist, each insurance company pays only its share of the total coverage.

coverage provisions Your comprehensive liability policy covers you and your spouse, any relatives living with you, and anyone under 21 years of age living in your care. Therefore, you need only one policy for your entire household.

Comprehensive policies cover bodily injury and property damage under the following circumstances:

• If incurred on or around your premises by guests, visitors, resident employees, or delivery people.

- If incurred from the acts of members of your household; from the acts of animals; from the use of sport or recreational equipment (including owned or rented power boats under 50 horsepower or sailboats under 26 feet in length); or from fire, smoke, explosion, or smudge caused by household members to property not owned but in control of the insured.
- If incurred at hotels or other temporary residences, at cemetery plots, at owned vacant land, or at rented dwellings.

Medical expenses due to accidents are covered and paid, regardless of who is at fault. The usual amount of protection is $500 per person but more can be purchased.

Supplementary coverage can be purchased to cover minor damages up to $250 per accident, regardless of fault. Even intentional damage caused by children under the age of 13 is covered under this supplementary coverage. Otherwise, these policies do not cover intentional injury or damage; any business activities (these must be covered in a separate comprehensive business policy); the operation of automobiles, aircraft, and boats above the prescribed size limits; and injury to employees covered by workers' compensation (Chapter 8).

Umbrella Liability Policies

Umbrella liability policies (otherwise known as personal catastrophe insurance) were originally available only to doctors, lawyers, and other professionals, but in the last several years have been made available to everyone. These policies not only extend your liability coverages but also broaden the definition of liability exposure to include more situations. Umbrella policies cover personal injury claims (i.e., slander, libel) as well as the standard comprehensive liability situations.

In order to purchase an umbrella policy, you must maintain underlying liability limits on your auto insurance of $250,000 per person, $500,000 per accident, $25,000 property damage liability (or $300,000 single-limit coverage), and $50,000 to $100,000 of comprehensive coverage on your homeowners policy. (These underlying limit requirements may vary from state to state.) You can purchase from $1,000,000 to $5,000,000 of umbrella liability insurance.

The annual cost for $1,000,000 of coverage (if you don't have rental income property) ranges from $100 to $150 in most states. This is not much to pay in exchange for the potential coverage and service you might receive.

Relating These Coverages to Your Needs

Table 7-1 shows the four phases of liability exposure and the relative costs of purchasing the necessary coverage. The comprehensive policy attached as section II of the homeowners form automatically gives $25,000 worth of liability coverage per occurrence, $250 for property damage, and medical expense limits of $500 per person. During phase two of your liability exposure, you can probably cover your comprehensive liability exposures adequately by maintaining this $25,000 coverage. During phase three you would do well to raise this coverage to $100,000. The best coverage if you are in phase four would probably be a $1,000,000 umbrella

TABLE 7-1

Policy Limits and Cost for Each Phase of Liability Exposure

| Phase | Policy Limits | | Annual Cost[a] |
	Comprehensive Liability	Umbrella	
1	[Parents' policy]		
2	$ 25,000 (as part of a homeowners policy)		$ 7
3	$100,000		$10
4	$ 50,000[b]	$1,000,000	$120

[a]Sample costs are for Santa Clara County, California, 1981, assuming $500 medical payments.

[b]Plus the underlying limits required on auto liability insurance: $250,000 per person, $500,000 per accident, and $25,000 property damage (or $300,000 single-limit coverage).

liability policy to supplement the liability coverage provided by section II of the homeowners and by auto liability insurance. If you purchase a package policy, $1,000,000 of castastrophic liability coverage is automatically provided.

TYPES OF AUTOMOBILE INSURANCE

Automobile insurance consists of liability coverage and physical damage coverage. The former includes bodily injury and property damage liability, uninsured motorist, and medical expenses. The latter includes comprehensive and collision. Like general liability policies, auto insurance policies have jacket and coverage provisions.

Jacket Provisions

Auto insurance has the same basic jacket provisions as other liability policies we have discussed. One important difference, however, is that auto insurance policies contain a *cancellation clause*. This clause gives the insurance company the right to cancel a policy for any reason during the first 60 days of the policy term. After 60 days, a policy can be canceled only with 30 days' notice, and if the insured or any member of the insured's household has his or her driver's license suspended; becomes subject to heart attacks or epilepsy; has three traffic violations within an 18-month period; or is convicted of a felony, criminal negligence with regard to the operation of a motor vehicle, or drunken driving.

Insurance companies use the cancellation clause at their discretion. Some companies seek only preferred risks and therefore enforce the cancellation clause quite stringently. Other companies raise their rates, and the risk of cancellation with these companies is low.

Coverage Provisions

Like comprehensive liability policies, auto policies may be written to include bodily injury and property damage liability, and medical expense payments. Unlike other liability coverage, auto policies offer physical damage coverages that act in the same way as property insurance coverage. Some auto policies offer only property damage coverage and no liability coverage, while others offer only liability coverage. In addition, auto coverage protects the policyholder against bodily injury caused by a driver who carries no insurance. Table 7-2 compares these various types of coverage.

bodily injury and property damage liability coverage   This coverage protects you, your spouse, and anyone who claims your home as primary residence against claims for bodily injury and property damage while driving your car and occasionally driving cars belonging to others. In addition, it covers anyone driving your car with your permission.

Bodily injury limits are normally stated on a per individual and per occurrence basis. You have a choice of liability limits. If you choose bodily injury liability limits of \$15,000/\$30,000 (15/30), as is common, your insurance company will make \$30,000 available to pay bodily injury claims arising from an accident in which you are at fault. However, only \$15,000 of the \$30,000 can be used for any one person. Some policies offer single-limit liability coverage, by which a maximum amount of money can be allocated to meet the injured parties' expenses in whatever manner necessary.

Liability limits vary from state to state. They may run up to 100/300 or higher. Most states have financial responsibility laws, which require the driver of a vehicle involved in an accident that was his or her fault and that involved bodily injury or property damage claims of more than \$50 to \$250 (depending on the state in which the accident occurs) to show proof of *financial responsibility*. Financial responsibility may be demonstrated by posting a bond, by depositing cash or securities with the

TABLE 7-2

Types of Auto Insurance and Their Coverage

Type of Auto Insurance	Coverage Applying To:					
	Those in Your Car			Those in Car You Hit		
	Car and Property	Driver	Others in Car	Car and Property	Driver	Others in Car
Bodily injury liability		X[a]	X		X	X
Property damage liability				X		
Uninsured motorist		X	X			
Medical expense		X	X			
Comprehensive damage	X					
Collision damage	X					

[a]Only in states with no-fault insurance laws.

state treasurer, or by purchasing an auto liability insurance policy for a specified amount (normally 10/20 or 15/30). This proof is required immediately after an accident and may be required for one year following the accident. If a driver fails to show financial responsibility, his or her driver's license is suspended until the person's financial responsibility can be proven.

Property damage liability (injuries to the other party's car and personal property) is normally written in limits of $5,000, $10,000, or $25,000 per accident.

uninsured motorist coverage   If you sustain bodily injury from a motorist who has no auto liability insurance or who is underinsured relative to the claim filed against him or her or whose auto insurance company has become insolvent within a year from the date of the accident, this coverage pays you the amount of money you would have been legally entitled to recover if the motorist had enough insurance. Uninsured motorist coverage offers payments in excess of what you may collect either from medical expense coverage or from the uninsured motorist up to the amount to which you are legally entitled. This coverage also protects you from bodily injury loss incurred because of an unapprehended hit-and-run driver.

The maximum limits you may purchase (normally 10/20 or 15/30) are governed by the state. Some insurance policies, however, allow you to buy whatever limits you choose in excess of those recommended by the states; e.g., the package policies discussed in Chapter 6 allow higher limits. In other words, for an extra premium, you can raise your uninsured motorist limits from 15/30 to 100/300, for example. Remember that in most states damage to your automobile is not covered under uninsured motorist coverage; only bodily injury claims are.

medical expense coverage   This coverage promises to pay any reasonable medical expenses incurred within one year from the date of an accident by any person riding in your car who sustained bodily injury as a direct result of that accident, regardless of fault. Benefits are also paid if you or a member of your family is a pedestrian injured by a motor vehicle or a passenger injured while riding in another person's vehicle. The expenses covered include medical supplies, surgery, X rays, hospital expenses, dental care, ambulance costs, professional nursing care, and funeral expenses. People not riding in your car are reimbursed through your bodily injury liability coverage, provided you were at fault.

The normal medical expense limits are $1,000, $2,000, or $5,000 per person.

physical damage coverage   This coverage provides payments for the repair and replacement of your automobile, its equipment, and its material contents. There are two major coverage options available: comprehensive coverage and collision coverage.

Comprehensive coverage insures your car against loss caused by theft and larceny, explosions, earthquakes, windstorm and hail, falling missiles, water and flood, vandalism and malicious mischief, and riot and civil commotion. It also insures your car's contents (and, in most states, the car) against loss caused by fire and lightning. To be eligible for this coverage, the contents of the car—often referred to as robes, wearing apparel, and other personal effects—must be owned by the insured or by

HELLO, AJAX INSURANCE?
I HAVE A QUESTION ABOUT
MY COMPREHENSIVE
COVERAGE...

residents in his or her household. (If your car burns with your neighbor's golf clubs in the trunk, for example, your auto insurance comprehensive coverage does not cover these golf clubs. Your property insurance will cover losses to property in the car for up to 5 percent of the insured value of your home.) Comprehensive does not cover your car against collision damage.

Collision coverage for the automobile you are driving is separate from comprehensive coverage because of the greater probability that an auto accident will happen. Collision insurance covers impact with an object, another vehicle, or the earth (a turnover), regardless of who was at fault.

The amount of the physical damage insurance benefits available to you after your car has been damaged depends on the market value of your car at the time the damage occurred.

Relating These Coverages to Your Needs

bodily injury and property damage Bodily injury coverage is the most important coverage to have because it protects you where you are most vulnerable to very large losses through court judgments against you. If you now carry only minimal coverage, you may want to consider raising your liability limits. As we have already mentioned, there is a greater chance for large medical bills and liability claims when automobiles are involved than in general home accidents. Furthermore, the people you injure on the highway will probably be strangers, whereas the people you injure in your home or at school are likely to be acquaintances. Persons who do not know you and do not expect to have to face you again may try to get all they can in a claim against you. One last consideration is that higher limits may help you get better service from the insurance company since the company would probably lose a lot of money by not vigorously defending you in a lawsuit. If, however, you maintain low liability limits, the insurance company stands to lose much less and may not be able to justify the costs of a good defense.

It may be wise also with property damage coverage to keep your limits high. The destruction of just one power pole with three or four different users (electric company, telephone company, cable television, for example) could cost you over $10,000. Since you can be charged for damages by the state department of highways, by municipal governments, and by private businesses who own property you destroy as well as by the owner of the automobile you run into, it is not hard to imagine $25,000 worth of claims arising out of one accident.

uninsured motorist coverage Collision damage caused by an uninsured motorist will probably have to be paid out of your own pocket, since this is not covered by uninsured motorist coverage and since drivers who do not have auto insurance may not be able to afford the cost of repairing your car if it is damaged in an accident that is their fault.

medical expense coverage If you and everyone who rides in your car has adequate health and disability coverage, then medical expense coverage is superfluous. (Also, if your state laws allow your passengers to sue you for their injuries when you are at fault, they would be covered by your bodily injury coverage even if they do not own a health and disability policy.) However, some insurance companies make medical expense coverage mandatory. And you cannot always know who will be at fault in an accident or whether your passengers have adequate health and disability coverage. It may therefore be wise to include a couple of thousand dollars of medical expense coverage in your auto policy.

physical damage coverage   Since most physical damage claims arise from accidents involving collisions, the basic premiums for this type of coverage are as much as six times the premium for the same amount of comprehensive coverage. The high cost of collision coverage, however, can be reduced 20 percent or more through the use of a $100 or $200 deductible.

To determine whether to carry physical damage coverage, you must compare the out-of-pocket cost if your car were destroyed and you did not carry insurance with the cost of the premium if you did. You can estimate the current market value of your car by applying the following percentage depreciation factors to the car's original cost: first year, 25 percent; second year, 18 percent; third year, 14 percent; fourth year, 11 percent; and for every year after that until the car reaches a minimum value of $250, 9 percent. Subtract from your car's original cost the dollar depreciation figure for each year of your car's present age, and you have its current market value.

For example, Jill has a four-year-old car that originally cost her $5,000. Its market value over the last four years is indicated in Table 7-3. Jill carries $100 deductible collision insurance on her car. The premium is $106. If she carried collision insurance and she had an accident in which her car was destroyed, her out-of-pocket cost would be $206 ($106 premium + $100 deductible). Theoretically, if her car is worth $1,600 and its value is declining by 9 percent of its original cost each year, she will be better off not buying collision coverage even if she wrecks her car every two and one-half years (see Table 7-4).

In Jill's situation it may be wise to self-insure. This option is appropriate if (1) Jill has enough money in a ready cash reserve to replace her car this year if she has an

TABLE 7-3

Market Value of Jill's Car over Last Four Years

Age (years)	Depreciation Factor [a]	Dollar Depreciation (depreciation factor X original cost)	Market Value
New	0%	$ 0	$5,000
1	25	1,250	3,750
2	18	900	2,850
3	14	700	2,150
4	11	550	1,600

[a] *Journal of American Insurance*, American Mutual Insurance Alliance.

TABLE 7-4

Jill's Potential Loss and Insurance Outlays over Next Four Years

Time	Market Value	Annual Premium[a]	Cumulative Premium Plus $100 Deductible	Difference in Potential Loss and Accumulated Insurance Outlay
Today	$1,600	$106	$206	$1,394
One year from now	1,150	106	312	838
Two years from now	700	106	418	282
Three years from now	250	106	524	(274)
Four years from now	250	106	630	(380)

[a]Assumed to stay level to simplify the calculations. In reality, the premium will rise each year as rates in general rise.

accident and (2) her loss record indicates that she will probably not accumulate damage repair bills totaling more than the accumulated insurance premiums over the next one and one-half years.

This computation does not take into consideration the potential tax savings if Jill itemizes her deductions on her annual income tax. Since the nonreimbursable loss of an asset above 10 percent of your adjusted gross income is deductible from your income, you can save taxes because your taxable income becomes less. The amount of taxes you save depends on your marginal tax bracket and the size of the loss relative to your income. If Jill makes $25,000 a year and is in the 30 percent marginal tax bracket, her tax deduction will be zero ($1,150 market value − $2,500, or 10 percent of $25,000). Obviously, this potential tax benefit would be attractive only if Jill had a very small income or a very large loss. Before the Tax Equity Act of 1982, all losses above $100 were deductible, and so the tax savings used to make self-insurance more attractive. (Tax deductions will be fully explained in Chapter 10.)

This procedure for determining what physical damage coverage you need is more applicable to collision insurance than to comprehensive insurance. To some extent you can control collisions that are your fault (the main type of collisions your insurance will cover). By driving safely, you can avoid these accidents and, there-fore, reduce the need for collision coverage. Accidents covered by comprehensive insurance (i.e., damage caused by vandals, windstorm, and so on) are normally beyond your control. Your loss record in this respect is largely a function of luck. Therefore, comprehensive coverage is a worthwhile coverage to buy in most situa-tions whereas collision coverage may not be.

Coverage for Leisure Vehicles

With the advent of recreational vehicles such as motor homes, dune buggies, golf carts, trail bikes, camper trailers, tent trailers, snowmobiles, and all-terrain vehicles, a new type of insurance policy has been created. This policy provides not only the standard liability and physical damage coverages provided in auto policies, but also coverage for additional living expenses (if you're forced to live in a motel while your motor home is being repaired) and miscellaneous personal property (such as canvas awnings, television and antenna, clothing, bedding, tools, housewares, gas cans, and cushions). They are rated in the same way as on an auto policy and allow single-limit or separate-limit liability coverages.

The liability premium costs will be higher than for an automobile if the use is more hazardous (as for dune buggies and snowmobiles). The comprehensive and collision damage premiums will, of course, rise with the value of the vehicle insured. All your leisure vehicles, however, can be covered under one insurance policy.

AUTO INSURANCE RATES

Auto insurance rate-making is based on the past driving experience of motorists in a given locality and the total dollar amount of claims paid out by insurance companies. Standard premium rates are established by a few national rating bureaus for each "rating territory." A rating territory may be a city, a part of a city, a suburb, or a rural area. These rates serve as a basis for each company's insurance policy pricing. Drivers (called preferred risks) who, according to past experience, are less likely to have an accident may pay less than the standard rate. Drivers with a higher accident experience may pay more than the standard rate. Although each insurance company has its own formula for setting premium rates, they all rely on certain factors. The classification system used by the national rating bureaus for liability/medical and collision classes is outlined in Table 7-5.

Insurance companies consult the various classification systems, apply the appropriate discounts, and then set a premium rate. This rate is a composite of individual rates for liability, medical expense, uninsured motorist, and physical damage coverage. For example, Bill Morris is 40 years old, married, and has no children of driving age. He owns a four-year-old car worth $3,750 and he has a good driving record. His annual premium of $335 is composed of the following rates:

bodily injury liability ($50,000 per person, $100,000 per accident)	$108
property damage liability ($25,000 per accident)	$50
medical expense coverage ($5,000 per person)	$18
uninsured motorist coverage (15/30/5)	$16
comprehensive physical damage coverage ($50 deductible)	$38
collision physical damage coverage ($100 deductible)	$105

Safe Driver Plans

Safe driver plans involve a point system whereby points are allocated to certain types of automobile traffic violations. The total number of points a motorist accumulates (usually over two or three years) determines the amount of reduction or increase to be applied to the person's premium rate as determined from his or her liability and collision classification (Table 7-5). In a family with more than one

TABLE 7-5

Liability and Collision Classification System for Determining Premium Rates

Major Factors Determining Classification	Liability Class[a]			Collision Class[b]	
If insured is male driver over 25, or female driver	1A	1B (10% higher rates than 1A)	1C (45% higher rates than 1A)		
If male under 25 lives in insured's household	2A (90% higher rates than 1A)		2C (3 times higher rates than 1A)	2A (45% higher rates than 1)	2C (90% higher rates than 1)
If insured's auto is used for business purposes	3 (1½ times higher rates than 1A)			3 (25% higher rates than 1)	

[a]Liability Classes

1A The insured auto is owned by an individual and is used for personal reasons; there is no male operator under 25 living in the insured's household.

1B As in class 1A, but auto is used to drive to or from place of business, and the one-way mileage to or from work is less than 10 miles. (Cars used in car pools or driven to and from the railroad station as part of commuter travel are included in class 1B, not 1C, no matter how many miles are driven.)

1C Same as class 1B, but mileage to or from work is 10 miles or more.

2A The insured auto is owned by an individual with one or more male operators younger than 25 residing in the household. No under-25-year-old, however, is the owner of the car or its principal operator. (It makes no difference whether the car is used for business or pleasure.) Underage (24 years or less) males who are married and owners or principal operators fall into this class.

2C The owner or principal operator is unmarried and under 25.

3 The insured's auto is used in business or owned by a corporation.

[b]Collision Classes

1 The insured car is owned by an individual, not customarily used in business, and not used by any underage male operator residing in the household. It makes no difference whether the car is driven to or from work.

2A Same as class 1, but there is a male operator under 25 residing in the household. If this male operator is the principal operator or owner, he must be married to qualify for this classification.

2C Same as class 2A, but the male owner or principal operator under 25 is unmarried.

3 Same as class 3 liability rating.

motorist the points accumulated by each driver are added together to determine the rate adjustment. Rate decreases or increases may be applied to bodily injury and property damage liability coverage, medical expense coverage, and collision coverage.

Safe driver plans were first introduced in 1959 in California, but have since been instituted in almost every state. Now insurance rate-makers consider a motorist's driving record in addition to general information about the individual that may or

TABLE 7-6

Points for Each Violation under California Safe Driver Plan

Violation	Number of Points
Driving while intoxicated	3
Failure to stop and report an accident when involved	3
Manslaughter	3
Driving while your license has been suspended or revoked	3
Reckless driving	3
Any moving vehicle violation	1
Any accident resulting in property damage of more than $200	1
Illegal parking	0
If you are in an accident for which someone other than you is convicted	0
If your auto is damaged by a hit-and-run	0
If payments for an injury are handled by you, not your insurance company	0

TABLE 7-7

Effect of Point Accumulation on Insurance
Premiums in California

Total Number of Points	Premium Reduction or Increase
0	No change
1	40% increase
2	90% increase
3	150% increase
4	220% increase
5 or more	Assigned risk

may not indicate driving expertise. Safe driver plans tend to differ from state to state in the length of the experience period required, the number of points assigned to each violation, and the allowable credit for insureds with no points or only one point. Table 7-6 shows how many points are assigned by the California safe driver plan to each violation. Table 7-7 shows the effect various accumulations of points will have on a driver's premium rates in California. To be certain of your state's point system, check with the state department of motor vehicles.

State Auto Insurance Plans

Sometimes insurance companies do not insure drivers who have poor driving records. Such drivers can still buy minimum insurance through state-regulated assigned-risk pools. When they apply for insurance, they are assigned to insurance companies who must then cover them for three years for the state-designated

liability limits. Every insurance company licensed to sell insurance within the state must accept a certain percentage of the drivers in the assigned-risk pool. These drivers have no choice about which insurance company underwrites their specific risk, nor do the insurance companies have a choice about which assigned risks they receive.

Keeping Your Rates Low

With insurance premiums doubling every 10 years because of rising medical care costs, more expensive automobile repairs, and more generous lawsuit settlements, you should consider ways to keep your rates low.

driver experience   In general, liability rates will be lower for the driver who has a good driving record over the two- to three-year period before the policy begins. If you have no points in the safe driver point system, you may be eligible for the lowest basic rate (Table 7-7). If an underage driver (younger than 25) has taken an accredited driver education course, class 2 rates may be reduced by 10 percent.

type and use of car   It is usually cheaper to insure a compact car than an expensive car. In addition, most insurance companies charge higher premiums for higher horsepower engines. Such a "hot car" surcharge may run as much as 50 percent higher. Auto depreciation is another factor to remember in trying to lower your collision and liability rates.

If you drive 6,500 miles or less each year, you may be able to reduce your premiums by 10 percent. If you are a farmer or use your car primarily on a farm or ranch, both liability and collision rates may be reduced by 30 percent.

other factors   If you are an underage driver and are away at school or in the armed services, or if you are a student whose grades average B or better, you may be eligible for a discount. If you are employed, perhaps your company offers a special group insurance plan with automatic deductions from your paycheck, which can save you 15 percent or more.

If more than one car is insured under the same policy, both liability and collision rates may be reduced by 25 percent on each additional car.

how not to do it   Jeremy loved cars. "Cars are my life," as he used to say. He lived at home with his parents to save money. Finally he had enough money for a down payment on a sports car and borrowed the rest. His monthly payments on a four-year loan were $320. When he went to buy auto insurance, he was flabbergasted to find that his premium came to $1,200 a year, or $100 a month. With another $40 a month for gas and $20 a month for projected maintenance, his monthly auto expenses totaled $480 (320 + 100 + 40 + 20)—$200 more than he could afford. Soon he had to sell his car and go back to riding the bus.

If you like cars but finances are a problem, buy a car whose initial and ongoing costs you can afford. A compact car would cost Jeremy only $160 a month in loan payments and $50 a month for gas and maintenance together. By not buying a "hot car" he could save 50 percent on his insurance premium. By putting the car on his parents' policy he could save another 25 percent. Therefore, 75 percent of the $1,200 premium could be eliminated, producing a premium for the compact car of only $300 a year, or $25 a month. His total monthly costs would then be $235, less than half of the total cost of caring for and "feeding" the sports car Jeremy started with.

shopping around   Auto insurance rates vary from company to company depending upon both individual company loss experience with various types of drivers and the company's intended market. Since different companies hold different conditions important in their rate-making, it will be important for you to shop for rates whenever you renew your insurance policy. The company that thinks you are an excellent risk today, as a young married man or woman, may consider you a bad risk when you have a child of driving age.

Table 7-8 shows how rates for the same risk vary among six insurance companies. Notice that the company with the least expensive policy changes as conditions change. Not all of the examples of potential policyholders would be acceptable as new business to the companies used in this comparison. These examples are used for information only.

TABLE 7-8

Variations in Annual Premiums (1982) among Six Insurance Companies

Potential Policy-holder[a]	Zurich (Guarantee)	St. Paul (Easy Auto)[b]	Fireman's Fund (Economy Plus)[b]	United Pacific	Aetna Casualty (Auto-Rite I)[b]
1	$392	$441	$405	$409	$448
2	524	568	473	528	534
3	575	678	713	765	837
4	707	812	779	883	923
5	342	373	353	389	405
6	475	527	423	508	491

[a] Key to potential policyholder.

1. Man and wife, age 45, clean driving record (San Mateo County, California). Vehicle is a three-year-old, two-door sedan, small engine.
2. Same as 1 except for one chargeable accident.
3. Same as 1 except for one occasional male operator, age 20, with driver training but without good student discount.
4. Same as 3 except for one chargeable accident.
5. Over-65 driver in good physical condition as noted on recent physician's report, pleasure use only, clean driving record.
6. Same as 5 except for one chargeable accident.

[b] Rates are based on 50/100 bodily injury liability or $100,000 single-limit liability (depending on company format), $5,000 property damage (or company minimum), $2,000 medical payments, full comprehensive, $100 deductible collision, and coverage for uninsured motorist (included in single-limit liability in some cases).

You may want to use Figure 7-1 to help you organize the information you obtain when you shop for auto insurance.

AFTER AN AUTO ACCIDENT

FIGURE 7-1
Fact sheet for use in
shopping for auto
insurance.

Regardless of who is at fault in an auto accident, there are certain things you should do. First, ask to see the police report of the accident and obtain a copy if possible. Having this information may avoid problems of establishing who was at fault later on. Second, obtain the names, drivers' license numbers, license plate numbers,

SHOPPING FOR AUTO INSURANCE

		Insurer 1	Insurer 2	Insurer 3
Company				
Renewal date				

	Limits Car 1 | Car 2	Premium[a]		
Public liability				
Bodily injury				
Property damage				
Medical expenses (no fault)				
Uninsured motorist protection				
Physical damage				
Comprehensive				
Deductible				
Collision				
Deductible				
Total annual premium				

[a] Total premium for coverage area, regardless of number of cars.

insurance agents' names, and make, model, and year of cars of the other parties involved in the accident. Remember not to volunteer information, either to the other parties involved in the accident or to their insurance agents, until after you've discussed the accident with your insurance agent.

In general, as soon as possible after you are in an accident, you should write down all the details you remember about it. You should also get the names and addresses of witnesses; but do not harass them or try to force them to see the accident your way.

Most important, always notify your insurance agent of any accident, whether or not you were at fault and even if you decide to pay for the damage yourself. If you do not report an accident to the insurance agent within a reasonable amount of time following the accident (normally 48 hours), your insurance company can refuse to honor any claim that may be lodged against you. Remember that a person has up to one year from the date an injury was incurred to file such a claim. Reporting an accident will not cause your premiums to be raised, and it is the best means of ensuring that the coverage you have paid for will be there when you need it.

How Not to Do It

Heidi was hurrying to work one morning in a light fog when she accidentally bumped into the car in front of her at a stop sign. Both drivers got out of their cars but found no significant damage to either car. Since both were in a hurry to get to work, Heidi and the driver of the car she hit assessed the damage to his bumper at $50 and she hastily wrote him a check. Getting back into her car, Heidi sped away from the scene of the accident, never expecting to see the other car or its driver again.

Since it was such a small accident and she didn't want her auto insurance premiums to go up, she didn't report the accident to her insurance agent. She soon forgot about the whole episode.

One day nine months later, she received a letter from someone who identified himself as the person whose car she had hit. He wrote that since the accident he had experienced recurring neck pains and that repeated doctor visits and hospital treatments had failed to correct the situation. In short, he was demanding payment of $10,000 for medical bills and "pain and suffering"! Well, you can imagine how happy Heidi was at that moment to have an auto insurance policy. At last she would be able to get some of her premium money back in a claims settlement. Quickly she called her agent to inform him of her misfortune.

Everything seemed to be going fine as Heidi told her understanding agent of the "minor" accident she had experienced. However, when the agent asked when the accident occurred and Heidi responded "nine months ago," the agent's helpful voice suddenly turned concerned. Heidi then suffered through an embarrassing explanation of how she should have reported the accident to the agent within 72 hours in order for the insurance company to make good on the claim. The agent ended the conversation by saying that he would "see what he could do" but advised her "not to get her hopes up."

A week later, Heidi received a form letter from her insurance company informing her that because she had not reported the accident to her insurance company within a "reasonable amount of time" from the date of the accident, her claim was now void.

Regardless of whether or not you want the insurance company to pay for a loss incurred in an accident, *always* report the accident to your agent.

What Happens If an Accident Is Not Your Fault

If you are involved in an automobile accident that is another person's fault, your own insurance policy may be of little value in covering your own expenses. Instead, you will be testing the strength and resources of the other person's policy. It is important that you know how to file a claim so that you can reach a satisfactory settlement with the insurance company.

The claims adjuster is the link between you and the other driver's insurance company. This person performs three tasks:

1. Determines what kind of person you are, the extent of your injury, your eagerness to get well, the extent of damage to your car, and so on.
2. Estimates the amount of money that the insurance company will probably have to pay to come to a satisfactory settlement. This estimate is the *reserve limit*, the amount required to fulfill the insurance company's obligation under its insurance contract.
3. Settles the claim as quickly as possible by delivering a check to you, the claimant. Your acceptance of this check releases the insurance company from any future liability.

Now that you know what the claims adjuster does, you should consider what you will do during each stage in the process.

meeting the claims adjuster Normally, the claims adjuster is one of the first people who will visit you while you are recuperating after an accident that is clearly someone else's fault. The adjuster may be a salaried employee of the insurance company used by the person responsible for the accident, but is more likely to be an independent adjuster hired by the company to settle the claim. Usually, this person will discuss the accident and ask questions about how it happened and who was at fault; discuss your medical condition and ask questions about your injury, your doctor, and your probable length of stay in the hospital; and ask questions about your background such as who you work for, your age, and your medical history.

In general, it is all right to talk to the claims adjuster as long as you do not say anything that might prejudice your case. Specifically, do not discuss your medical background. If the insurance company finds that you have had a similar injury before, they may claim that your present injury is merely a recurrence of an old medical problem. Do not discuss the accident. The insurance company may try to prove that you contributed to the accident by being careless or negligent. Instead of saying "I don't remember" to questions involving the accident, merely respond with "I do not care to answer that." Do not sign any statement or allow any tape recording of the discussion. In short, be pleasant and thank the adjuster for showing interest in your health and welfare, but be very uninformative. Remember that this person represents the insurance company of the driver at fault in the accident.

estimating the claim   After visiting you, the adjuster will estimate the size of your claim by estimating the following:

- Your total medical expenses including hospital or convalescent room and board, doctor visits, X rays, lab tests, drugs, physical therapy, wheelchair and other special apparatus, and nursing care.
- Amount of income lost because of your medical condition and inability to return to work—taking into consideration both overtime you might normally have received and your base wage.
- Miscellaneous expenses that you or your family incurred because of the accident—mileage expenses to and from the hospital or doctor's office, babysitting fees, damage to your clothes or other personal property, and the like.

To the total of medical expenses, loss of income, and miscellaneous bills the adjuster will apply the pain and suffering multiplier. Normally this multiplier is three. For example, if all other expenses are estimated at $2,000, the amount of the claim that the adjuster figures will be made for pain and suffering will be $6,000 (3 × $2,000). In this instance then, the total claim would be projected at $8,000 ($2,000 expenses + $6,000 pain and suffering).

This estimate of expenses expected to be incurred by you, the claimant, serves as the reserve limit that the insurance company allocates to your case. In other words, by notifying the insurance company that your case should have a reserve limit of $8,000, the adjuster is saying, "I think we can settle this claim for $8,000 or less."

By duplicating the process the claims adjuster uses, you can project what a reasonable claim might be. If your claim is above the reserve limit, you will have more trouble settling with the insurance company. Since the skill of claims adjusters is measured by how often they settle within the reserve limit they stipulate, they will fight to keep claims within the limits.

settling the claim   Since each dollar of medical expense can raise the eventual claim by $4 (through the pain and suffering multiplier), it is easy to understand why insurance companies want to settle quickly. Usually, they will make an initial settlement offer as soon after the accident as possible. You might think this offer is quite generous. Remember, however, that once you endorse an insurance settlement check, you are most likely releasing the insurance company from any future liability. Therefore, wait to file a claim until you know what all your expenses are going to be. Depending on the state, you have one to two years from the date of the accident to file a valid claim. To substantiate future claims, take photographs of your injuries. File your claim with the insurance company of the person responsible for the accident before your statute of limitations runs out (normally one year from the date of the accident). If your injury is a serious and expensive one, such as a back injury, it is wise to hire a good attorney. Too much money may be at stake for an amateur prosecutor such as yourself to deal with.

If you have filed a claim and have been waiting weeks or even months to receive compensation, often the mere threat of involving an attorney will bring a quick settlement. Insurance companies do not like to see attorneys involved because the attorney's fee (normally one-third of the eventual settlement) will automatically raise the claim settlement. For example, if an insurance company is balking at paying a $1,000 claim and an attorney becomes involved and the company loses the case, the company may have to pay $1,500 to the claimant—$1,000 for the claim and $500 for the attorney. In addition, insurance companies do not like to go to court because of the expense of defending their client and the long court delays often involved. They realize that the longer they have to wait to get a court date, the higher the claim against them will be. Time, they feel, is never on their side, since time may bring more medical bills, more miscellaneous expenses, and more pain and suffering. Therefore, if you are at an impasse with an insurance company, it may help to tell the company that you will turn the case over to an attorney if just compensation is not received within a certain time.

No-Fault Insurance

Insurance companies are losing money on their auto insurance underwriting. Rates are steadily increasing. Policyholders are dissatisfied that only 42¢ of every $1 paid in premiums is paid out in claims. Both insurers and insureds admit that there are inadequacies in the system. These inadequacies are basically that few people involved in auto accidents are fully reimbursed for their losses; settlements are often uneven and the settlement process long and expensive; and insurance protection itself is expensive. Some find fault with the tort liability structure of the law, which gives an injured party the right to sue the negligent party for damages. Others find fault with trial lawyers who win huge jury awards for their clients. Many people feel that, if injured parties can be compensated without first having to determine who was at fault, a number of the problems within the current system would be solved.

No-fault insurance reimburses injured parties for their economic losses from auto accidents (i.e., medical expenses and loss of income) without regard to fault. It enables you to receive payments from your own insurance company without going through the settlement process. No-fault also makes pain and suffering claims available only to people who have suffered permanent impairments. Its proponents are the insurance commissioners and most insurance companies who are looking for a way to reduce their costs and improve their service. Those who disagree with the concept feel that no-fault insurance would deny people their constitutional right to receive just compensation for their losses from the person responsible. They are also afraid that the power to determine just compensation would lie with the insurance industry instead of with the insured through the aid of an attorney.

Forms of no-fault insurance have existed in Saskatchewan, Canada, since 1946 and have proven reasonably successful in reducing insurance costs. It has also been reasonably successful since its inception in Puerto Rico in 1969. The battle over no-fault still rages, however, because states are unwilling to throw out the tort liability system. Massachusetts was the first state to adopt a no-fault auto insurance law, effective January 1, 1971. Since that time, many states (Delaware and Illinois, for example) have adopted no-fault laws, but these vary from state to state in the way they treat the following:

- Amount to be paid an insured person for medical expenses or, in case of death, for funeral expenses
- Amount of loss of income to be paid an injured breadwinner

- Amount to be paid to a person hired to perform essential services that an injured nonincome producer, such as a homemaker, is unable to perform because of injuries
- Conditions allowing the right to sue (which usually include death, permanent injury, or disfigurement) and the arbitrarily stipulated amount of medical expenses above which a lawsuit may be permitted
- Inclusion or exclusion of property damage coverage

If you live in a state that now has a no-fault law, you should understand how your insurance coverage will respond to the issues listed above. As time goes on, more and more states will likely have some form of no-fault law to govern people, no matter where they may wish to drive.

CONCLUSION

Comprehensive liability policies cover all liability exposures other than those surrounding the operation of motor vehicles and those involving slander and libel. They are inexpensive and should be purchased with limits that correspond to both your liability exposures and your visible wealth.

Auto liability represents probably your greatest liability exposure. Bodily injury and property damage liability, medical expense payments, uninsured motorist protection, and comprehensive physical damage coverage are all valuable coverages to have. The need for collision coverage depends upon the value of your car. The lower the value of the car, the less the need for this type of insurance.

Shop for auto insurance rates. Different companies favor different driver characteristics. If you have forgotten how to shop for rates, refer to Chapter 5. The best way to minimize your costs is to keep your driving record clean.

Know how to get just compensation from a claim if you are involved in an accident that is not your fault and therefore may not involve your insurance company. Remember always to notify your insurance company of any accident you are involved in.

VOCABULARY

absolute liability
claims adjuster
comparative negligence
contributory negligence
coverage provisions
financial responsibility
general liability policy
jacket provisions
liability
negligence

no-fault insurance
pain and suffering multiplier
preferred risk
reserve limit
safe driver plan
state auto insurance plans
tort
umbrella liability policy
uninsured motorist coverage
vicarious liability

QUESTIONS

1. What are three ways to defend against a liability claim without using a liability policy?
2. Larry has a current net worth of $10,000 and expects to earn $15,000 a year for the next 40 years. Under the life value approach to determining comprehensive liability limits, how much comprehensive liability insurance should Larry purchase?
3. What coverage does an umbrella liability policy offer that a normal comprehensive liability policy does not?
4. How is an auto insurance policy different from a comprehensive liability policy?
5. Tom has auto bodily injury liability limits of 50/100. If three people sustain injuries because of Tom's careless driving and each injured person files a claim for the same dollar amount, what is the maximum amount of money Tom's insurance policy can pay each of them?
6. Under what conditions should a person self-insure rather than buy collision coverage for his or her car?
7. A claims adjuster estimates that your medical expenses will be $500, your loss of income $1,000, and your miscellaneous expenses $100. How large a reserve limit will probably be set for your case?
8. What types of auto coverages are normally denied insureds under state insurance plans?
9. Ron paid $200 a year for auto insurance before he was convicted of reckless driving. Under the California safe driver plan, how much will Ron's auto insurance rates increase?
10. What problems do proponents of no-fault auto insurance claim it will solve? What problems do its opponents feel it will create?

CASE PROBLEMS

1. Sally Bond is a junior in college. Last year she bought a six-year-old compact car for $600, so that she would be able to drive to classes and to a part-time job. Sally has few assets besides the car, which she has driven approximately 20,000 miles. She had a perfect driving record until this year when she was given three tickets for speeding.

    Should Sally purchase auto insurance? If so, which types and what limits might be appropriate? Why? How much greater will her rates be because of her three speeding tickets than if she qualified for reduced rates under the safe driver plan? (Assume that she is a licensed California driver.) What can she do to reduce her rates?
2. Larry Hanson has a family of four and is earning $25,000 a year. In addition, the Hansons' net worth is $70,000. How much comprehensive liability insurance should the Hansons own and why?

RECOMMENDED READING

"Auto Insurance Companies Offer Cost-Cutting Advice to Motorists." *Consumer Newsweek*, November 15, 1976.

   A discussion of areas of premium saving for the insurance buyer.

Vaughan, Emmett J. *Fundamentals of Risk and Insurance*. 3d ed. New York: John Wiley & Sons, 1982.

   Chapter 24 covers the concepts of liability and negligence.

"How to Cut Your Insurance Costs and Still Be Safe." *Better Homes and Gardens*, April 1977.

Recommendations for reducing premiums through judicious use of deductibles.

Insurance Information Institute. *A Family Guide to Property and Liability Insurance*. New York: Insurance Information Institute, 1973.

Describes coverages available but does not render advice.

No-Fault Automobile Insurance. Pueblo, Colo.: Consumer Information Center.

A six-page brochure on how no-fault insurance works and which states have it. Available free by writing Consumer Information Catalog 510g, Consumer Information Center, Dept. 29, Pueblo, Colorado 81009.

CHUCK AND NANCY ANDERSON

Insuring against the Financial Calamity of a General Liability Suit

For $7 a year, Chuck and Nancy's homeowners policy provides $25,000 personal liability coverage, $500 for medical expenses, and $250 for damage to others' property. They can either retain this coverage, raise the liability limit to $100,000 for an extra $10 a year, or buy an umbrella liability policy with $1,000,000 worth of coverage for an extra $100 a year.

Questions

1. Which of the three alternatives would you recommend that they select? Why?
2. What effect would this recommendation have on the Andersons' balance sheet and/or income statement?

Insuring against the Financial Calamity of an Auto Liability Claim

Chuck holds separate policies on his two cars for bodily injury and property damage liability (15/30/5), medical expense coverage ($1,000), and physical damage coverage—comprehensive (full value) and collision ($50 deductible). The annual premiums are shown in Table 7-9.

TABLE 7-9

Annual Premiums Paid by the Andersons for Auto Insurance

Coverage	High Horsepower Car	Compact Car
Liability (15/30/5)	$156	$124
Medical expenses ($1,000)	15	12
Comprehensive ($50 deductible)	49	38
Collision ($100 deductible)	137	105
TOTAL	$357	$279
"Hot car" surcharge (30%)	107	
Annual premium	$464	$279
TOTAL PREMIUM	$743	

While shopping for better coverage at reduced rates, Chuck and Nancy learned what various coverages would cost on an annual basis for several limits (Table 7-10). In addition, they learned that if they put both cars on the same policy, they would save 25 percent of the total premium on the cheaper car.

Questions

1. Which coverage limits would you raise? Which would you reduce or eliminate? Why?
2. How much would the coverage you recommend cost? (Assume that their driving records improve.)
3. What effect would your recommendations have on the Andersons' balance sheet and/or income statement?

TABLE 7-10

Rate Alternatives for the Andersons for Auto Insurance

Coverage	High Horsepower Car	Compact Car
Liability		
15/30/5	$156	$124
50/100/15	203	162
100/300/25	240	196
Medical expenses		
$1,000	15	12
$3,000	17	17
$5,000	21	21
Comprehensive		
$50 deductible	49	38
Collision		
$100 deductible	137	105
Uninsured motorist (15/30)	14	14

8

Health Insurance

If you can afford only one type of insurance, health insurance is the most important to have. As long as you are able to work and earn an income, you can replace personal property, rebuild an estate, or build a new home. If, however, you were sick for a long time or became totally disabled, you would face big medical bills at a time when you have lost your income-producing capability. Health insurance is designed to minimize the effect of these drains.

DETERMINING YOUR MEDICAL EXPENSE INSURANCE NEEDS

As with every type of insurance, you must plan for peril protection before the peril strikes. Even though you may rarely be sick, you should consider buying health insurance. If you became ill or disabled when you were uninsured, you would probably be ineligible for health insurance and, therefore, unprotected when you and your family most needed protection. Furthermore, as you get older you will probably become more susceptible to sickness and poor health—and less able to meet the rising costs of medical care. Figure 8-1 indicates how fast medical care costs have risen in the United States relative to the consumer price index, especially since 1965.

It is difficult to determine medical expense insurance needs. Unlike planning for property insurance coverage, you cannot determine the extent of your potential loss. In other words, it is nearly impossible to establish with accuracy the economic value of your family's health or the potential costs of medical care or disability should their health become impaired.

Even though you cannot put a maximum value on the medical costs that you might face, you can identify the types of expenses that could occur. Because the people who serve you medically are highly trained and use sophisticated equipment, their services tend to be expensive. Also, because precision and accuracy are a must, there are

159

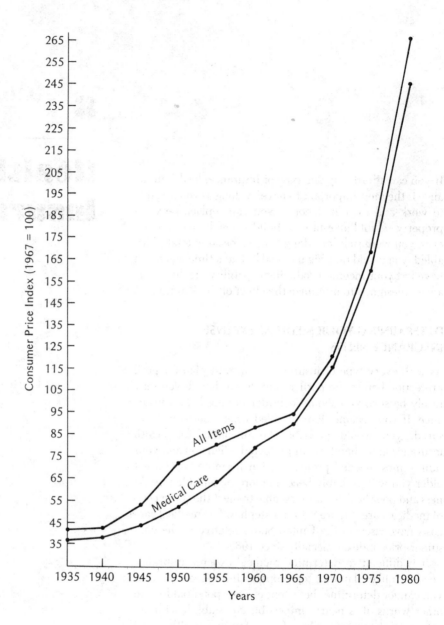

FIGURE 8-1
Rising medical care costs
in the United States
(relative to consumer
price index).

normally many checks and counterchecks (such as lab tests, consultations with specialists, and round-the-clock nursing care) to ensure that the quality of service is high. These checks are also expensive. Generally, the cost of medical treatment varies with the skill, the time, and the nature of the medicines and machines required to administer treatment—as well as where you live. The average daily hospital expense, listed by state, is provided in Table 8-1.

TABLE 8-1

Average Hospital Costs—1980

State	Average Cost to Hospital per Patient Day	Average Cost to Hospital per Patient Stay[a]	State	Average Cost to Hospital per Patient Day	Average Cost to Hospital per Patient Stay[a]
Alabama	$210	$1,471	Nebraska	$195	$1,538
Alaska	409	2,290	Nevada	344	2,201
Arizona	291	2,034	New Hampshire	203	1,443
Arkansas	186	1,169	New Jersey	213	1,850
California	363	2,393	New Mexico	264	1,556
Colorado	248	1,757	New York	257	2,471
Connecticut	272	2,038	North Carolina	187	1,402
Delaware	238	1,953	North Dakota	177	1,541
D.C.	358	3,189	Ohio	241	1,907
Florida	247	1,805	Oklahoma	240	1,535
Georgia	218	1,371	Oregon	277	1,664
Hawaii	246	1,844	Pennsylvania	235	1,950
Idaho	209	1,253	Rhode Island	261	2,162
Illinois	278	2,193	South Carolina	187	1,362
Indiana	214	1,629	South Dakota	190	1,270
Iowa	199	1,475	Tennessee	204	1,429
Kansas	207	1,596	Texas	227	1,498
Kentucky	189	1,269	Utah	272	1,467
Louisiana	233	1,492	Vermont	183	1,467
Maine	217	1,715	Virginia	210	1,634
Maryland	251	2,135	Washington	263	1,523
Massachusetts	294	2,591	West Virginia	195	1,405
Michigan	267	2,083	Wisconsin	218	1,767
Minnesota	203	1,828	Wyoming	243	1,190
Mississippi	175	1,171			
Missouri	230	1,843	United States	246	1,867
Montana	160	1,330			

Source: Data from American Hospital Association, *Hospital Statistics, 1981*, and Health Insurance Association of America.
Note: Costs are for community hospitals, which do not include hospitals funded by county, state, or federal governments.
[a] Average length of hospital stay ranges from almost 5 days (Wyoming) to almost 10 days (New York).

PLANNING TO ABSORB MEDICAL COSTS

Look at your balance sheet. How much could you reasonably afford to spend on medical expenses before incurring a financial hardship? Which types of medical expenses (such as doctor bills for periodic family checkups) occur with relative certainty and regularity? Which types of expenses are impossible to predict? The larger the financial burden you are able to assume, the smaller the burden you have to pass on and the smaller the premium you have to pay.

Self-Insuring through Deductibles

The key to using deductibles in purchasing medical expense policies is to self-insure as much as you can afford (i.e., eliminate "first-dollar" coverage) and buy higher coverage maximums with the premium dollars saved.

Because annual premiums decrease as the deductibles increase on a major medical expense policy, this self-insurance strategy allows you to buy much more insurance coverage, as shown in Figure 8-2.

Determine the extent to which you can use deductibles by evaluating your financial capacity to assume risk. Often you will find it wise to use your cash reserves to raise your deductibles; this will lower your health insurance premiums and/or increase the maximum benefits you can buy. Of course, the decrease in premium caused by raising the deductible must justify taking on a greater risk.

Because of the great uncertainties surrounding a potential financial calamity caused by poor health, you will need to transfer much of the risk to the insurance industry.

Transferring Health Risk to the Insurance Industry

When looking at health insurance policies, be sure to distinguish between those types of protection that are truly insurance plans and those that are merely prepayment plans. True insurance protection requires the payment of a small premium for possible benefits exceeding the total amount of the premiums paid. By paying a premium, you are accepting a small loss today to prevent a potentially large loss in the future.

Prepayment insurance gives you coverage for an event that is almost certain to occur (such as an annual physical). In this case, the insurance company requires you to pay enough money to cover such an occurrence. Such a plan has two major disadvantages. First, you must assume the cost of commissions, claim servicing, and so on. As a consequence, your total premiums will probably be higher than the actual cost of the certain-to-occur event. You do not have this extra expense if you pay for your own medical services. Second, if you do not buy the insurance to cover these almost certain-to-occur events, you can regularly invest the amount of the

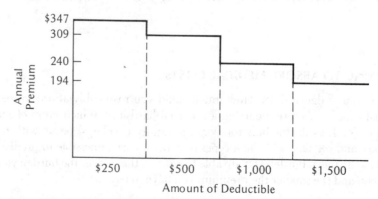

FIGURE 8-2
Decrease in premiums as deductibles increase (major medical expense policy for a male, age 21, $1 million maximum, semiprivate room).

Note: Rates from Blue Shield, 1982.

premiums saved and have even more money when the bills come. A possible advantage, however, is that prepayment insurance plans motivate you to save.

You should also beware of indemnity plans. The most common type of indemnity plan is the hospital indemnity plan, which is often advertised in a supplement to the Sunday newspaper. These ads promise "$100 per day for every day you're hospitalized, regardless of any other health coverage you may have in force." In other words, indemnity plans provide a fixed number of dollars for each day of hospitalization. Such plans ignore medical expenses that do not require hospitalization; they also ignore the actual cost of being hospitalized. You should seek a policy that reimburses you for actual expenses, regardless of where they are incurred or how large they may be. Since there is no way to know this in advance, it's not wise to guess through the purchase of a hospital indemnity plan. In addition, indemnity plans have hidden coverage restrictions, pay a smaller portion of their premium dollars out in benefits, and may cover only one health problem (e.g., cancer).

Types of Medical Expense Coverage

Planning to meet your needs for medical expense coverage is really a matter of understanding what is available and then purchasing the maximum limits you can afford. Basically, there are five types of medical plans: hospital expense, surgical expense, general medical expense, major medical, and comprehensive medical expense. Table 8-2 outlines the major features of each type of coverage. However, most of you will be covered under employer group insurance plans and will not need to purchase individual policies; your group plan will more than likely contain comprehensive medical expense coverage.

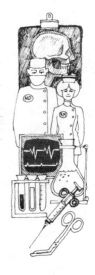

hospital expense insurance Most individual policies are guaranteed to be renewed each year until the insured reaches age 65. Premium rates, however, may change from year to year depending upon the insured's age and health. It has become popular to include a deductible clause of $100 or more in the policy to reduce high premiums caused by the costs of small claims.

The policy may be written to cover your dependents including your spouse; unmarried children under 18 (sometimes under 21); children under 23 who are full-time students; and (under certain group policies) adopted children, foster children, and stepchildren living in your home. There are four basic benefit provisions under hospital coverage: room and board charges, hospital extra-service charges, maternity charges, and nursing charges.

Room and board charges include the housing and feeding of a hospital inpatient. The insurance company may handle these charges on a valued basis or a reimbursement basis. The valued basis pays a set sum (such as $100) for each day, no matter what expenses have been incurred. The more popular reimbursement basis pays the actual costs incurred by the patient (less any deductible) as long as those costs are "usual, customary, and reasonable." These policies usually stipulate that you must accept a double room or ward unless a contagious disease requires a private room. Most policies cover room and board expenses for a maximum period of 70 to 120 days per hospitalization. Some policies cover periods as short as 30 days or as long as two years. Obviously the longer the covered period, the more expensive the policy.

TABLE 8-2

Medical Expense Coverage

Type of Coverage	Items Covered[a]	Items Not Covered[a]	Range of Benefits (per occurence)		Deductible	Remarks
			Time	Money		
Hospital expense	1-10	23-29	30 days to 2 years	$10 and up per day room and board; $10,000 expenses	$25 to $1,000	Most popular plan
Surgical expense	11	Anything not stated on schedule of operations		$300 to unlimited per operation	At discretion of insured	Usually attached to hospital expense coverage as rider
General medical expense	12-14	23-24	50 to 100 days	$5 to unlimited per day; total limit $250 to $500	At discretion of insured	Little more than a prepayment plan
Major medical	1-22	23-33	1 to 3 years	$10,000 to unlimited	$100 to $1,000	10 to 25% of all expenses to be paid by the insured in addition to deductible of his or her choice
Comprehensive medical (group plan)	All expenses	23-28	1 to 3 years	$25,000 to unlimited	$100 to $500	10 to 20% of all expenses to be paid by the insured in addition to a deductible

[a]Key to Expense Coverage

1. Hospital room and board
2. X rays
3. Drugs
4. Laboratory examinations
5. Dressings
6. Physiotherapy
7. Maternity (including complications)
8. Mental disorders
9. Nursing expenses, in hospital
10. Nursing expenses, outside hospital
11. Operations
12. Doctor's home visits
13. Doctor's office visits
14. Doctor's hospital visits
15. Crutches
16. Splints
17. Blood and blood plasma
18. Braces
19. Prosthetics
20. Oxygen
21. Radiology
22. Rental of oxygen equipment, wheel chairs, hospital beds, and iron lungs
23. Anything not recommended or approved by a legally qualified physician
24. Injury sustained before the initial date of policy
25. Injury or illness due to war, declared or undeclared
26. Injury sustained while on active duty
27. Self-inflicted injury
28. Dental work
29. Eye examinations
30. Cosmetic surgery
31. Illness due to narcotic addiction
32. Illness due to alcoholism
33. Health examinations
34. Travel expenses (not ambulance)

To be eligible for benefits, the patient must be admitted to a hospital (not a nursing home or convalescent center) upon the recommendation of a medical doctor licensed to practice in the state.

Hospital extra-service charges include such costs as X rays, drugs, laboratory examinations, dressings, and physical therapy. Instead of instituting a maximum expense limit for each service, most insurance companies apply a blanket limit (usually 5 to 20 times the daily room and board benefit) to all types of charges. However, some companies reimburse the patient for the full amount of the extra-service expense up to a certain dollar limit and then pay only a percentage of the remaining expenses.

Maternity charges are now covered as any other medical expense. Maternity benefits usually begin after the policyholder has been covered for 9 to 12 months. Single women can get maternity policies as a part of their medical insurance coverage.

Nursing charges vary from policy to policy. Some policies cover nursing expenses only while the patient is in the hospital; others cover them outside the hospital as well. Normally there is a separate coverage limit for each type of disease or accident. Such limits may be as short as 5 days or as long as 180 days.

surgical expense insurance   This is the second most popular type of health insurance coverage. Most policies contain a schedule of operations that specifically indicates what operations are covered by the policy and what the dollar limits are for each operation. The most serious operations normally have a maximum dollar limit of $300 to $2,500, depending on the policy. The better policies reimburse you for usual, customary, and reasonable (UCR) expenses instead of using a relative value table. All operations must be performed by a legally qualified surgeon. In most policies, a portion of the dollar limit for an operation may be applied to the cost of services rendered by either a second surgeon or an anesthesiologist. Maternity benefits are provided only after the policy has been in effect for 9 to 12 months. Individual health insurance policies normally contain surgical expense coverage in the form of a rider attached to the basic hospital coverage.

general medical expense insurance   This type of insurance covers little more than the expense of a doctor's visit. It usually provides a benefit of $5 for each day of hospitalization for in-hospital medical coverage, more than $5 a day for home visits, and less than $5 a day for office visits. Group general expense policies normally impose an aggregate dollar limit that cannot be exceeded. For example, if the daily rate is $5 a day and you are hospitalized for 100 days, the benefit payable will be $500. However, if the insurance company imposes an aggregate limit of $300 for the same time period, you can collect only $300. Coverage exclusions under this type of policy include pregnancy, childbirth, miscarriage, dental work, eye examinations, X rays, drugs, dressings, medicines, and equipment. Since this type of policy covers only the doctor's hourly visiting fee plus routine items involved in such a visit (such as blood tests) up to the maximum specified limit, its limits are small in relation to the premium charged. You should consider the advantages and disadvantages to see whether this type of plan is financially appropriate for you.

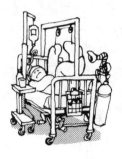

major medical insurance   This insurance covers expenditures on nearly all types of medical care and equipment: hospital room and board; treatment by physicians and surgeons; psychiatric care for mental disorders; administration of anesthesia; radiology, physiotherapy, nursing care, and laboratory examinations; maternity expenses; drugs, medicines, and blood and plasma; casts, splints, braces, crutches, and artificial limbs; and rental of oxygen and oxygen equipment, wheelchairs, hospital beds, and iron lungs.

Rather than having a schedule of limits for each of these expenses, major medical covers a fixed percentage of all expenses. Some limits are imposed for room and board, extended care, private nursing, and outpatient psychiatric treatment. Group contracts normally contain a single lifetime maximum covering all types of injuries. Upper limits for most individual contracts range from $10,000 to unlimited. These limits normally restore themselves by $1,000 to $5,000 per year if no benefits are required during the year; this benefit is stipulated in what is called the *automatic restoration clause*. Some insurance companies also impose time limits within which expenses must be incurred. In other words, if your leg is broken in a motorcycle accident, the insurance company will probably cover only those medical expenses accumulated within one to three years from the date of injury.

Deductibles are an important way to reduce the costs of major medical coverage. They should be used not only to eliminate costs of small claim handling but also to eliminate duplication of coverage. The most popular form of deductible is the initial deductible, whereby the insured pays an initial specified amount. The most common deductibles are $500, $750, and $1,000, although they can be as low as $100.

In addition to deductibles, insurance companies usually require the insured to pay from 10 to 25 percent of all the eligible expenses in excess of the chosen deductible amounts. For example, if a person who is covered by a policy that pays 80 percent of all costs above a $500 initial deductible incurs medical costs of $1,000, the person pays 20 percent ($100) of the expense above the $500 deductible (or a total of $600). The purpose of this percentage participation procedure is to encourage the insured to keep costs to a minimum. This procedure is called a *coinsurance feature*. Many group major medical plans limit coinsurance to the first $2,500 to $10,000 of covered expenses. Above this level the plan pays 100 percent. For example, if the coinsurance feature requires you to pay "20 percent up to a total of $2,000," once the total covered costs exceed $10,000 (20% × $10,000 = $2,000), the plan pays everything. This limitation of the policyholder's liability for medical expenses is often referred to as a *stop-loss limit*.

Major medical is the most important coverage you can buy. Raise your limits as high as you can afford ($100,000 or more) while trying to reduce annual premiums by raising the deductible.

comprehensive medical expense insurance   There are two types of comprehensive insurance. A pure comprehensive insurance policy is merely an extension downward of major medical insurance. By lowering the deductible and thereby raising the percentage of the total medical expenses the insurance company must pay, comprehensive insurance eliminates almost all of the financial headaches of

Policy Benefits	Expenses	Base Insurance Pays
Base Insurance		
Hospital Benefits		
Room and board in semiprivate room for up to 365 days	$4,500 ($250/day x 18 days)	$4,500
X rays, lab, medicines, and such up to $500	$2,000	$ 500
Surgical Expense (according to schedule, $2,500 maximum)	$3,500	$2,500
Physician's Expense ($15/day for 50 weeks)	$2,000 ($40/visit x 50 visits)	$ 750
TOTAL	$12,000	$8,250

		Major Medical Pays	You Pay
Major Medical			
80% of first $10,000 of covered expenses	(same expenses as above)	$2,920 (80% x $3,650[a])	$730 (20% x $3,650[a])
100% of all expenses above $10,000			
$100/calendar year deductible			$100
TOTAL	$12,000	$2,920	$830

[a]Expenses not covered by base insurance ($12,000 − $8,250 = $3,750) minus deductible ($100) equals amount covered by major medical ($3,650).

illness and injury. Most comprehensive plans are written for a group, rather than on an individual basis. An example of the coverage provided by a typical group comprehensive plan is shown in Figure 8-3.

FIGURE 8-3 Example of coverage provided by comprehensive medical expense insurance policy.

Modified comprehensive insurance is a further extension of major medical insurance in that it covers 100 percent of all medical costs. No deductibles are permitted. Naturally, this first-dollar coverage costs much more than any other type of health insurance.

DETERMINING YOUR DISABILITY INCOME NEEDS

In addition to the costs of medical services, health insurance can cover loss of income caused by *disability* due to accident or illness. Although your medical expense needs can be estimated only roughly, you can determine how much disability income you might need by using the following procedure. Of course, this procedure will have to be repeated whenever your needs or your assets substantially increase or decrease.

To illustrate the procedure, we will use the example of a fictitious couple, Judy and Art, who are schoolteachers. Their statement of disability income needs as calculated for Art is shown in Figure 8-4. The same procedure would be used to determine how much disability insurance Judy would need if she were disabled.

Instructions

1 *Annual Living Expenses. Determine your current annual living expenses,* based on the figures you computed for your income statement in Chapter 2. Judy and Art's living expenses amount to $12,000.

2 *Adjusted Annual Living Expenses. Make adjustments in categories that would be affected if you were to become disabled.* Since disability income payments are not taxed, you need not allocate money for income taxes on disability income payments. However, if you have investment income or the spouse works and thereby generates earned income, these types of income would still be taxed. Take into account also that some expense categories such as transportation and entertainment may be reduced if you become disabled. Furthermore, if your insurance policies have waiver of premium clauses that enable you to retain insurance coverage without paying premiums while disabled, subtract the amount of the annual premiums from your living expense needs.

FIGURE 8-4
Sample statement of
income disability needs.

NAME *Art*

DATE *January 1983*

STATEMENT OF INCOME DISABILITY NEEDS

1 *Annual Living Expenses*		$12,000
2 *Adjusted Annual Living Expenses*		
Tax savings	$ 2,000	
Insurance premiums waived	1,000	
Other_____	_____	
3 *Spouse's Income*	3,100	
4 *Investment Income*	500	
5 *Social Security Benefits*	4,400	
6 *TOTAL ADJUSTMENTS*	$11,000	
7 *Net Annual Disability Income Needs*		$ 1,000

Taxes for Judy and Art average $2,000 annually. Their health and life insurance policies have waiver of premium clauses and together cost $1,000 in annual premiums.

3 *Spouse's Income. Determine how much income your spouse would earn if you became disabled and he or she continued working or returned to work.*

Since Judy is working as a substitute teacher and probably would continue to do so if Art were disabled, she would have an annual income of $3,100.

4 *Investment Income. Determine how much investment income you can expect to receive.* Investment income is the return you receive on your investments, such as the interest on your savings accounts, dividends on stock, or rental income from real estate.

Judy and Art have $7,500 of investable assets in savings and mutual funds. The average annual current yield on their investment is about $500. They assumed that this yield would keep pace with inflation if invested prudently.

5 *Social Security Benefits. Check the Social Security addendum in the appendix to determine the level of benefits you would be entitled to if you have worked long enough to qualify for Social Security.* Social Security benefits are paid, however, only if you are unable to perform any gainful employment and the disability is expected to last at least 12 months. They will begin after you have been disabled 5 months. (Social Security benefits will be discussed in more detail later in this chapter.)

State Disability Insurance is available in several states (California, Hawaii, New Jersey, New York, and Rhode Island). California, for example, pays approximately $105 per week after you have been disabled just 7 days and continues payments for 9 months. If you are eligible for State Disability payments, add these to your Social Security benefits.

Art figures that his annual benefits from Social Security would be approximately $4,400. He does not live in a state offering State Disability Insurance.

6 *Total Adjustments. Add the items (steps 2, 3, 4, and 5) that may reduce your living expense needs if you became disabled.*

The total adjustments for Judy and Art are $11,000.

7 *Net Annual Disability Income Needs. Subtract the amount found in step 6 from the amount found in step 1 to arrive at your net annual disability income needs.* These are the needs that must be met with income from other sources.

Judy and Art have net annual disability income needs amounting to $1,000.

Unfortunately, your needs may rise, but your disability insurance benefits will probably stay the same. Herein lies the greatest coverage problem. To solve it, there are three things you might do:

• Cut your living expenses. Judy and Art would have to reduce their living expenses by $1,000 a year (in today's dollars).
• Buy a policy that provides an automatic benefit increase for each year benefits are paid. While this policy may not match inflationary increases in your standard of living, it will come closer than any other type of coverage.

• Estimate inflation's effect over your remaining life expectancy and buy a policy for this increased amount. However, be aware of policy maximum benefit limitations: normally you are limited to purchasing 66⅔ percent of your current monthly income. For example, Judy and Art can expect to live 60 years longer (predicted age of death 85—their present age 25). Assuming an annual inflation rate of 5 percent, their average annual need would be $3,325, not the $1,000 they determined. As long as Art's income exceeds $5,000 ($5,000 × 66⅔% = $3,325), he can buy the needed $3,325 of coverage.

In fact, most of us will find that we need to buy the maximum amount of coverage possible until our investable assets build to such a degree that they can carry the bulk of our disability income needs.

PLANNING TO ABSORB LOSS OF INCOME

As we have seen in the procedure for determining disability income needs, it is a little easier to plan for these needs than for medical expense needs because you can make some assumptions about your future lifestyle based upon your present lifestyle. Of course, as your standard of living increases and inflation causes prices to rise, satisfying your monthly needs will cost more.

Self-Insuring through Waiting Periods

How long could you support yourself with your present assets? If you need $600 a month and you have saved $1,200 in an emergency fund, you could theoretically support yourself for two months. Hence, an appropriate policy would begin to pay you $600 a month after 60 days. This *waiting period* serves as a deductible in time rather than in money. It forestalls income payments until they are required. Other things being equal, the longer the waiting period you can afford, the lower your premium will be. This relationship between waiting period and premium is expressed in Figure 8-5. Sick leave benefits may help you determine how long your waiting period should be since they can be used to bridge the gap between the time when you are disabled and the time when your employer's long-term disability benefits begin.

Income Loss Coverage

Under the broadest definition of disability, income loss coverage (sometimes called "salary continuation insurance") provides payments to the policyholder as long as the person is unable to perform any or all functions of his or her occupation. Under a strict definition of disability, income loss coverage provides payments only if the insured can perform no gainful employment whatsoever.

In 1976, the insurance industry began to redefine their approach to disability income coverage. Instead of insuring the occupation, many companies began to insure the income stream. In other words, instead of providing insurance benefits only if the insured could not perform the duties of his or her occupation, insurance

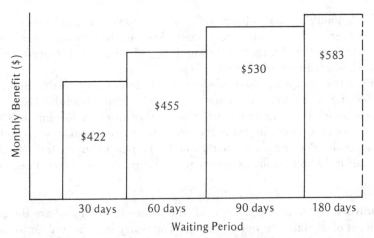

Note: Rates and monthly benefits from Paul Revere Life Insurance Company, preferred 35 disability income policy, with benefits for life if disabled by accident, to age 65 if by illness, 1982.

FIGURE 8-5
Amount of disability
income that can be
purchased for a $100
annual premium for a
male, age 21.

companies have now become more concerned with motivating the insured to embark upon some gainful employment without missing out on valued insurance benefits. The result is the *residual policy*, which enables the insured to receive benefits even if he or she goes back to work.

Let's assume a man was earning $2,000 a month before his disability and has a policy with benefits of $1,000 a month. After his disability, the insured can only get a job paying $1,000 a month. His insurance policy pays him 50 percent of his stated monthly benefit ($1,000) or $500, because his current salary represents 50 percent of his salary prior to the disability. Therefore, the insured receives insurance benefits even though he has returned to work. This new approach to compensation is an important step for the insurance industry because it focuses attention away from the disability and toward the rehabilitation of the insured.

If a disability occurs because of accidental injury, payments may be made for life; in the case of a disabling illness, payments may be made only to age 65. The maximum possible limits on payments are $6,000 a month or, normally, 50 percent of the disabled person's salary, whichever is smaller. Also, there can be a waiting period of up to one year before payments begin. You should consider your own needs in relation to these limits.

Several disability insurance companies now provide a cost-of-living adjustment (7 percent) to their policy benefits for either a specific period of years, or for life, depending on the policy. If your monthly benefit is $1,000 in year 1, the benefit would automatically be increased to $1,070 (7 percent of initial benefit) for year 2, $1,140 (14 percent of initial benefit) for year 3, $1,210 (21 percent of initial benefit) for year 4, and so on. Some policies grow at a compound rate just like inflation. This type of policy at least addresses and partially solves the biggest problem in disability income protection: providing a benefit that, once payment begins, keeps pace with rising living expenses.

Women used to be discriminated against in health insurance underwriting, especially in disability income policies. Today, most women can purchase disability income coverage in the same amounts as men. However, the rates for women 45 or younger are higher than for men of the same age, whereas those for women older than 45 are lower than for men over 45.

Recently, a few companies have made disability insurance available to homemakers. Because of the difficulty in applying a dollar figure to all that the homemaker does, insurance companies have chosen rather arbitrary, low limits ($200–$400 per month maximum). In reality, the disability of a homemaker with children may cost a family $600 or more a month. You should think of buying this coverage, however, only if the breadwinner's income would be insufficient to carry these extra costs.

basic contract   Basic contracts (also called commercial contracts) are the most popular form of disability income coverage. The policy may be written to cover total or partial disability due to accident or illness. It may provide income benefits if you become totally disabled and unable to perform either your regular job or any other job. The most common contracts cover you for two years if you are unable to perform your previous job. Then, if you cannot perform your own job, but can perform another one, benefits stop even if the income from the new job is insufficient to cover your needs. The most liberal policies cover you until age 65 if you are unable to work at your own job, and then revert to the strict definition of disability. If you are totally disabled because of an accident, income benefits may last for your lifetime. However, if you are totally disabled because of disease, few policies pay benefits beyond age 65.

OK, SO I'M NOW AN ENGINEER AND MAKE A PRETTY GOOD LIVING... BUT GADS, I USED TO BE A PLUMBER!

Three types of clauses may be part of basic contracts: presumptive disability, double indemnity, and prorating. *Presumptive disability* clauses, contained in many basic contracts, define the conditions under which the insured will be deemed disabled.

Double indemnity clauses provide that you will receive twice the normal benefit payment if you suffer certain kinds of losses in specified kinds of accidents. For example, if you lose both legs in an auto accident, you might receive double the amount of benefits. However, if you lose both legs in some sort of accident not specified in this clause, you would receive only the normal benefit amount. This type of clause often receives a lot of attention, particularly from insurance salespeople; but it is nothing more than a sales gimmick. The rationale that you would need more money (double benefits) because of the nature of the accident rather than the nature of the injury, seems illogical.

Prorating clauses are provisions for altering the cost of your insurance. For example, if you change your occupation, your rate may change; if your new job is in any way more hazardous than your old one, your rate will go up. In addition, the insurance policies covering the insured will never pay—either individually or collectively—monthly benefits totaling more than the current monthly salary of the insured or the average monthly salary of the insured over the past few years, whichever is greater.

life insurance riders   A disability income rider can be attached to your life insurance policy if you choose. This extra-cost rider generally offers a disability income benefit of $10 a month for each $1,000 of the face amount of your life insurance policy. Approximately one-third of the insurance companies offer such an option.

limited contracts   Limited disability income contracts impose restrictions and exclusions beyond those in basic contract policies. The most common limitation concerns the type of accident or disease covered and the length of the coverage period. Aviation ticket policies are the most popular type of limited contract. These policies are sold through coin-operated machines in airport terminals. Coverage includes injuries sustained as a result of accidents while one is a passenger on a scheduled U.S. common carrier airline, in transit to the airport on an airport bus or limousine (not taxi), or on the airport premises waiting for a flight. Benefits from $20,000 to $100,000 may be purchased for 25¢ per $10,000 of insurance benefit. You will be paid the full value of the face amount if you suffer loss of sight, double dismemberment (i.e., loss of one arm and one leg), or death; one-half of the face amount for single dismemberment; and one-fourth of the amount for loss of one eye. If you really believe, however, that you and your family need $100,000 to live on in case you are totally disabled, you would do better to insure yourself for this amount against all accidents.

industrial policies   Industrial policies are similar in coverage to basic contracts except in the amount and duration of the benefits provided. These policies, which have nothing to do with company-sponsored group plans, are sold and issued individually. The amount of protection is generally less than basic contract coverage, and the premiums are paid weekly or monthly to an agent who calls at the home of the insured. To keep costs down, a minimum waiting period of five weeks is usually imposed and there are few extras. The benefits, typically $10 to $20 a week, are paid in cash sums daily or weekly.

The major advantage of such a policy is that it provides a means for a person of low income and/or poor savings habits to obtain a minimum amount of short-term disability protection at a cost within his or her weekly budget. No physical examination is required. Since the insured is billed weekly, the person need make only a small commitment each time. For these reasons, industrial insurance may be the only type of health insurance available to homemakers, the unemployed, students, or welfare recipients. The major disadvantage is long-term cost. The carrying, collection, and commission costs are so high that the benefits are smaller per premium dollar than for most other types of policies. It is a very high price to pay for convenience and the lack of a good budgeting habit.

WHAT YOU MAY ALREADY BE PROVIDED WITH

If you work now or have ever worked, you may be entitled to medical and disability benefits under the federal Social Security system (or a similar retirement system) and your state's workers' compensation program. These benefits can form a base on which to build the coverage limits you desire, but rarely will they satisfy your needs for health insurance. In addition to federally supported medical coverage, some states have medical care programs for individuals earning what each state considers to be a "poverty level" income.

Social Security Health Benefits

Social Security provides disability income benefits and health expense benefits. In order to qualify for disability income payments, you must have a severe mental or physical condition that prevents you from doing not only your present job but also any other substantial work. This condition must be expected to last at least 12 months or until death. After you have been disabled for five months, Social Security benefits can begin if you are under 24 years of age and have Social Security credit for one and one-half of the three years preceding disability; if you are between 24 and 31 years old, have worked at least half the time between your twenty-first birthday and the date of disablement, and have earned a minimum of $340 a quarter per year since you were age 21; or if you are over 31 years of age and have worked five of the 10 years prior to disablement. The size of the benefit payments you receive is a percentage of your earnings over a period of years. To see what the monthly payment might be if you were to qualify, look at the Social Security addendum in the appendix.

In order to qualify under Social Security for medical expense coverage (Medicare), you have to be age 65 or over and have accumulated 40 quarters of credits (discussed in the Social Security addendum). In addition, if you have received disability income payments from Social Security for two consecutive years, you qualify for medical expense coverage. The benefits available include coverage for hospitalization and medical expenses. Hospitalization benefits (Table 8-3)—often referred to as Medicare Part A—are automatic and free. Medical expense benefits—referred to as Medicare Part B—are optional and must be applied for within three months before or after your sixty-fifth birthday or during the first three months of any calendar year thereafter.

Medical benefits under the optional medical expense portion of Medicare include physician's and surgeon's services, no matter where you receive them (at home, hospital, doctor's office); home health care (such as nursing care)—even if you have not visited a hospital—up to 100 home visits per calendar year; diagnostic tests, surgical dressings and splints, and rental or purchase of medical equipment; outpatient physical therapy service, and the like. Because the federal government matches your premium payment, dollar for dollar, under this plan, the medical expense portion of Medicare is probably the least expensive insurance available for persons over age 65.

Workers' Compensation Benefits

Workers' compensation covers accidental (not self-inflicted) injuries and illness arising from one's employment. Unlike Social Security, workers' compensation programs are mostly state controlled and funds are provided by employer contributions.

The majority of states allow full coverage of any accident or illness arising from one's job. One-third of the states, however, list diseases that are occupational in origin and therefore should be covered. In either situation, the burden of showing that a disease or accident resulted from the occupation rests with the employee. If

TABLE 8-3

Hospitalization Benefits under Medicare

Place	Limits within Benefit Period[a]		Lifetime Reserve		Home Health Visits	Remarks
	Time	*Money*	*Time*	*Money*		
Hospital	90 days	Total expenses over $260 (first 60 days); expenses over $65/day (next 30 days)	60 days	Expenses over $130/day		Lifetime limit of 190 days of care in mental hospital
Nursing home	100 days	All covered expenses (first 20 days); expenses over $22.50/day (last 80 days)				Coverage applicable only if hospitalized for at least 3 days and then admitted to extended care facility within 14 days
Outpatient care		80% of reasonable charges above $60 deductible				Called "Part B" coverage. Must pay monthly fee for this protection.
Home					Up to 100 (by health workers, such as nurses, therapists, and aides, from participating agency)	Must be within 365 days following at least a 3-day hospital stay or release from extended care facility

Source: U.S. Department of Health, Education, and Welfare, *Your Medicare Handbook* (Washington, D.C.: Government Printing Office, 1982).

[a] A benefit period begins the first time you enter a hospital after your hospital insurance starts. It ends after you have not been an inpatient for 60 continuous days in any hospital or facility that mainly provides skilled nursing care.

you are now employed, check with your employer to find out what workers' compensation offers in your state. Some states (as mentioned in step 5 of the procedure for calculating income disability needs) offer state disability indemnity insurance to cover monthly needs for up to nine months (when Social Security begins) on non–work-oriented disabilities.

Group Insurance Plans

In addition to fulfilling their obligations under the workers' compensation laws, employers may provide group health insurance coverage for their employees. Normally, such health coverage is made available to both the employee and the employee's family. The employer may pay the complete cost of the insurance, a portion of that cost, or none at all. If you are married and both spouses work, evaluate each spouse's group plan and try to have just one plan in effect so that the cost savings to the company can be passed on to one of you in the form of more salary compensation.

If you leave your job, you usually have 30 days in which to switch your group coverage to an individual policy with the same company. If you fail to do so within 30 days, you must show proof of insurability (i.e., pass a physical examination) before a new policy will be issued. Normally, once you're eligible, you can enroll in your group plan and need not prove insurability for a limited period of time, beyond which you must pass a physical examination to be insured.

Five types of group insurance may be offered: group health expense coverage, short-term disability benefits, long-term disability benefits, accidental death and dismemberment, and dental insurance.

group health expense coverage   This coverage is usually made available in equal amounts to all members of a general class of employees (e.g., managers, clerks, supervisors). There may be a short waiting period before a new employee is eligible to join the plan. If you have such coverage at work, you should know both the major medical maximum to which you are entitled under your plan and the amount of any deductible required.

short-term disability benefits   Sick leave is the time an employer allots an employee for absence from work because of sickness or accident. If it can be proven satisfactorily that the absence occurred for legitimate reasons, the employee will be paid his or her normal salary. Sick leave credits are usually allocated according to length of employment—the longer a person has worked, the more days of sick leave the person is allotted. Sick leave benefits are important because they bridge the gap between the time a person becomes disabled and the time the employer's long-term disability benefits begin. The longer the sick leave, the less the employee has to worry about financing his or her disablement needs.

long-term disability plans   These plans are coordinated with Social Security and workers' compensation payments. They generally offer monthly benefits proportionate to the employee's salary (often 66⅔ percent). Benefits begin after waiting periods of from one to 24 months, depending on the plan, and continue paying benefits to age 65 or 70. As an employee, you should find out from your employer what the maximum benefits are, when they start, and when they end. When benefits end depends on the plan's definition of disability. Many plans stop benefit payments after two years if it can be proven that you are capable of working at any gainful employment, not merely the job you held prior to the disability.

accidental death and dismemberment   This coverage is normally offered on a voluntary basis and is paid in a lump sum if the employee dies or loses a bodily member in an accident. The shortcomings of this double indemnity type of coverage were discussed earlier in this chapter. You should buy enough coverage to insure you properly, no matter how you become disabled or die.

dental insurance   Many group plans offer dental insurance, which covers such expenses as examinations, fillings, and extractions. There are three types of general dental insurance: basic, comprehensive, and combination. *Basic* covers most expenses except for orthodontics to a maximum of $500 within a certain period. *Comprehensive* requires a $25 to $50 deductible per family each year. For a single individual, a $25 deductible is required the first year and a $10 deductible in the successive years. The maximum benefits per family are $500 for the first year, $750 the second, and $1,000 thereafter. The maximum benefits for an individual are $200, $300, and $400, respectively. The insured is also required to pay 20 percent of the cost of examinations, for any care in excess of his or her limit, and 40 to 50 percent of the cost of denture replacement and orthodontics. *Combination* coverage offers full reimbursement for basic expenses such as examinations and fillings, and partial reimbursement for more expensive or voluntary treatment such as oral surgery or orthodontics. These policies may contain a schedule of benefits for each procedure, a lifetime maximum or other variations of deductible and coinsurance features.

Analyze the cost versus benefits of the individual policies carefully. The individual plan may be nothing more than a prepayment plan.

Avoiding Duplication of Coverages

Bill and Sherry recently graduated from college, got married, and found good jobs at two different companies. As part of their job orientations, each learned about the company's fringe benefits, which included a group health expense policy, long-term disability insurance, and life insurance.

Sherry learned that she contributed $30 per month for her group health plan and $5.60 per month for her long-term disability plan. Life insurance (which was only $5,000) was automatically included on her group health policy. Bill didn't have to pay anything for his group health expense policy unless he wanted dependent coverage (which would cost $12 per month); he paid $20 per month for long-term disability but paid nothing for $5,000 worth of life insurance. All insurance payments were automatically taken out of their paychecks.

When Bill went to his life insurance agent to buy additional life insurance, his agent noted that Bill and Sherry were wasting money on their health expense policies. Since both policies offered identical coverage and yet Sherry had to pay $30 a month for hers, the agent suggested that Sherry drop her group health policy and be included as a dependent on Bill's policy, thereby saving $18 a month.

When both spouses work for different firms, look closely at both employers' benefits and select the best, most cost-effective coverages from both.

Participation Limits

Dan worked for XYZ Company and earned an annual salary of $32,000. Under his company's long-term disability (L-T-D) income policy, Dan would receive up to 50 percent of his annual salary ($16,000) in benefits (including any applicable payments from Social Security or workers' compensation) if he were to become totally and permanently disabled. However, when Dan determined his needs for disability insurance, he figured he would need an average of $3,200 a month ($38,400 a year) in benefits, taking into account the effects of inflation over his 50-year life expectancy. Therefore, he purchased an individual disability income policy that would pay him, after a 180-day waiting period, $1,800 a month, or $21,600 a year if disabled. His total annual benefits from all sources would therefore be $37,600 and would just about meet his disability income needs.

Unfortunately, Dan neglected to tell his agent about the group's L-T-D policy at work and, as a result, his agent neglected to point out the *participation limits* in the policy Dan bought. These limits stated that if Dan had other disability income coverages already in force, the maximum he could receive from all sources— including Social Security and workers' compensation—would be 80 percent of his salary at the time the disability occurred. With an annual salary of $32,000, all Dan could receive from his combined sources would be $25,600. Each disability income policy would pay only its pro rata share of the benefits.

Therefore, be aware of participation limits when buying new disability income contracts. You may be paying for benefits you could never collect.

WHERE TO OBTAIN ADDITIONAL INSURANCE COVERAGE

There are three types of organizations from which health insurance is available: Blue Cross and Blue Shield, health maintenance organizations (HMOs), and commercial insurance companies. In the future, a national health insurance plan may replace some or all of these organizations.

Blue Cross and Blue Shield

Blue Cross (founded in 1929) and Blue Shield (founded in 1946) are the largest single health expense plans in the nation. Blue Cross offers primarily hospitalization coverage, whereas Blue Shield provides surgical and general medical insurance. Often these nonprofit associations cooperate in issuing joint plans for comprehensive medical care. To receive medical treatment, you go to any doctor's office or any hospital (except an independent association) and show proof of membership in the plan.

Health Maintenance Organizations (HMOs or Independent Associations)

There are many independent medical service groups, sometimes called health maintenance organizations (HMOs), that render treatment in return for monthly or annual dues. These associations are composed of doctors and medical service personnel. They own their own facilities and provide medical care at a reasonable cost. The monthly dues are kept low so that people will seek out medical care before major treatment is required. Normally, there is no limit to the amount of care provided, and only nominal charges are made for laboratory work and medicines. The primary disadvantage of such a plan is that it is often difficult to see a particular doctor on a regular basis.

The Kaiser Foundation Health Plan in California is one of the most successful independent association plans in the country. It even served as a model when the federal government in 1973 provided millions of tax dollars toward the establishment of privately operated health maintenance organizations. The purpose of this federal system is to offer efficient and effective health care rather than reimbursement for that care, as do normal insurance policies. Individuals become members of an HMO by enrolling and paying a fee that entitles them to full use of the health care services provided by the HMO. This prepaid health care delivery system bases its economic survival on the value of preventive care—that it costs less to prevent disease than to cure it.

The advantage of belonging to an HMO is that needless health care services (such as duplication of tests) can be avoided; the physicians are financially motivated to work efficiently and have easy access to all of a patient's health records. Critics of HMOs say that since the physicians at an HMO know the maximum amount of revenue they will be receiving from each patient (his or her annual fee), they will provide the least amount of care necessary to keep the patient enrolled in the program. These critics feel that the question of controls and safeguards must be raised when such a premium for speed and "doing only what's necessary" exists.

However, HMOs are controlled by their members who, in turn, determine the level of benefits and fees and who hire the physicians. It is therefore unlikely that members would let themselves be treated in an unsatisfactory manner. The economic problems the HMOs have had can best be traced to certain government requirements for funding that have left their membership rolls filled with the chronically ill (such as open membership for at least 30 days a year, allowing anyone to enroll, regardless of health).

Commercial Insurance Companies

Commercial insurance companies specialize in policies that conform to individual needs and desires. A policyholder can receive medical care wherever he or she chooses and does not have to be admitted to certain member hospitals or doctors' offices. For those who wish to have a specific private doctor rather than select from those that belong to a certain clinic, individually issued health policies (with a commercial insurance company, Blue Cross, or Blue Shield) may be the best answer.

However, the costs are generally higher than similar coverage provided in group plans or through HMOs, and few insurance companies offer individual health policies.

National Health Insurance

Several bills have been put before Congress for providing health care and health insurance on a nationwide basis to persons under age 65. Already over $100 billion is being spent by the federal government on health care, and so the plans that have been proposed call not for the creation of a system of socialized medicine, but for an extension of it. One version would pay 100 percent of all health care except nursing home care, drugs and medical appliances, some dental care, and the treatment of mental illness. It also calls for major revamping of the nation's entire health care delivery system before the insurance program would become effective.

The advantages of a national health insurance plan (as opposed to a national health care program as in England) center on the fact that the doctors would still compete for patients, therefore keeping the quality of health care high. The disadvantages are based on the fact that the already overloaded health care delivery systems would be even more overloaded, for a national health insurance plan would definitely encourage people to seek medical care. Whether or not a national health insurance plan can succeed where private plans as well as public plans (HMOs) have failed—in the delivery of high-quality, fast, economical health care—remains to be seen.

COST CONSIDERATIONS

The four major factors, other than age and health, that determine the cost of premiums for health insurance are size of deductible, length of policy term, type and amount of coverage (major medical, for example), and provisions covering renewal of the policy. The cost relationships between premiums and deductibles or policy terms are fairly simple. The bigger the deductible, the smaller the premium. The shorter the term, the smaller the premium.

You may want to use Figure 8-6 to help you organize and compare the information you obtain when shopping for health insurance.

Type of Coverage

The type and amount of coverage you purchase is the major determinant of policy costs. For medical expense coverage, modified comprehensive and independent association plans are the most expensive. Regular comprehensive is next most expensive. Hospital and surgical policies are the least expensive but offer the least coverage. General medical is really a prepayment plan. Major medical protects against catastrophic risks at a cost below most hospital expense policies. Under such a plan, however, you must normally pay 10 to 25 percent of expenses. If you anticipate using your health insurance coverage because you have a large family or because you are accident-prone, HMOs represent the greatest value. If you seldom go to the

SHOPPING FOR HEALTH INSURANCE

	Insurer 1	Insurer 2	Insurer 3
Medical Expense Coverage			
Company	_____	_____	_____
Limits	_____	_____	_____
Room and board	$_____	$_____	$_____
Surgical maximum	$_____	$_____	$_____
Hospital extras	$_____	$_____	$_____
Physician care	$_____	$_____	$_____
Major medical maximum	$_____	$_____	$_____
Deductible	$_____	$_____	$_____
Reinstatement provisions	_____	_____	_____
Annual premium	$_____	$_____	$_____
Exclusions			
Disability Income Coverage			
Company	_____	_____	_____
Monthly benefits			
Total disability	$_____	$_____	$_____
Partial disability	$_____	$_____	$_____
Maximum age			
Accident	_____	_____	_____
Illness	_____	_____	_____
Waiting period	_____	_____	_____
Annual premium	$_____	$_____	$_____

FIGURE 8-6
Data sheet for use in shopping for health insurance.

doctor and yet want to be covered in case of a major illness or accident, major medical probably represents the greatest value.

For income coverage, industrial policies are the most expensive. Limited contract policies cost the least. Basic contract policies have the best combination of cost and breadth of benefit coverage. In general, group policies offer the best coverage for the premium dollar, since operating costs are minimized. Moreover, if the policy is for an employee group, the employer may shoulder part of the cost.

Renewability Provisions

Renewability provisions determine who has the right to cancel your coverage once the policy terms are completed—you or the insurance company. Such provisions affect the premium rate.

Optionally renewable policies can be renewed only at the option of the company. If your health deteriorates during the policy term, you may be unable to renew your policy except at much higher rates. *Guaranteed renewable* policies must be renewed by the company at their expiration, if you so request. The premiums may be changed only if they are altered for your whole classification group, as they may be if medical costs rise or risk experience changes. The guaranteed renewable policy costs more than an optionally renewable one but less than the noncancellable policy. *Noncancellable guaranteed renewable* policies must be renewed, with no change in premium, at the end of the policy term if you so request. For this privilege you pay a higher premium from the beginning, but the security may be worth the extra cost. Find out the difference in premiums before you decide.

CONCLUSION

Many people carefully protect their physical assets but not their most important possessions—the lives and health of themselves and their families. If you were to become sick or disabled, you and your family might lose a significant portion of the income that produced the material assets you enjoy. In addition, a prolonged illness could severely drain the financial resources your family has built up.

Gauge your needs carefully. If you can purchase only one type of health insurance, consider major medical. This policy prevents sizable losses due to the expense of serious illness or accident. Social Security would provide a minimum income if you were totally disabled. Be sure you understand where you are protected and where you are not. Avoid excess premium costs by eliminating duplication of coverage and by setting your deductibles as high as your emergency financial resources allow.

VOCABULARY

coinsurance feature
disability
double indemnity
health maintenance organization (HMO)
Medicare
participation limits
prepayment plan

presumptive disability
prorating
residual policy
restoration clause
stop-loss limit
waiting period

QUESTIONS

1. Why is it difficult to determine medical expense insurance needs?
2. What purpose do deductibles serve in purchasing a health insurance policy?
3. For $350 a year Lucy can buy a hospital and surgical expense policy that would cover her medical bills in their entirety up to $10,000. For $225 a year she can also purchase a $10,000 major medical policy with a $200 deductible. Over the last 10 years, Lucy has had medical expenses totaling $800. Which policy would you recommend that Lucy purchase and why?
4. What is the difference between a true insurance plan and a prepayment plan?
5. Jerry contracted hepatitis and ran up the following medical expenses: $800 for hospital room and board, $400 for X rays and lab work, $500 for physician's fees, and $150 for medicines. How much of these expenses will Jerry have to pay if he carries a major medical policy with a $100 deductible and an 80 percent coinsurance feature?
6. What factors should govern your decision concerning the length of the waiting period to select when purchasing a disability income policy?
7. An employee earned $600 a month before he was disabled. Under his employee plan, his long-term disability coverage pays 50 percent of his former monthly salary. How much would the employee receive in total benefits each month?
8. Which renewability provision offers the most safety to the policyholder? Why?
9. What is the major difference between a health insurance medical expense policy and an independent association plan?
10. Define *double indemnity*. What value does it have? Why?

CASE PROBLEMS

1. Jeff Mapson graduated from college last June and began earning $1,700 a month as an auto salesman. He uses only $1,300 of his monthly earnings to live on since he pays $300 a month in income taxes and adds $100 each month to his money market fund, which now amounts to $3,000. Jeff's company provides him with a long-term disability policy that would pay, after three months, benefits equal to 50 percent of his salary at the time of the disability.

   How much would Jeff's company pay him if he were to be disabled now? Does Jeff need more disability income insurance? If he were to buy a policy on his own, what benefits and how long a waiting period would you recommend? Disregard any potential Social Security or workers' compensation.
2. Shortly after graduating from college last June, Mary Ann Sims began working in a summer light opera company that offers no medical insurance benefits. Mary is unmarried and earns a sporadic salary that averages $1,000 a month, which is sufficient to meet her living expense needs. In addition, she has a savings account that totals $1,200. In shopping for medical expense coverage she found the following three coverages:

1. Combination hospital/surgical expense policy that pays up to $70 per day for room and board and up to $2,500 per surgery. The policy has a $100 per cause deductible and costs $200 a year.

2. A major medical policy that covers all expenses up to $100,000 and has a $200 deductible. After the first $200, the insurance company pays 80 percent of the next $2,500 of expenses and then 100 percent of expenses up to $100,000. The policy costs $200 a year.

3. A general medical policy that covers doctors' visits (at home, office, or hospital) for up to $20 per day and up to $500 per illness. The policy has no deductible and costs $200 a year.

Which policy would you recommend that Mary Ann select? Why?

RECOMMENDED READING

Boronson, Warren. "Diagnosing Your Health Insurance." *Money Magazine*, September 1974, pp. 39–52.

>   Discusses policy provisions and compares coverage provided by private companies with that provided by nonprofit organizations.

"Insurance That Covers the Dentist Bills." *Changing Times*, May 1977, pp. 43–44.

>   A discussion of available dental insurance coverage.

"National Health Insurance: Which Way to Go." *Consumer Reports*, February 1975, pp. 118–24.

>   An insightful look at the problems of one health care delivery system and suggested solutions.

"Prevention or Cure? Behind the Shift in Health Care." *U.S. News and World Report*, April 4, 1977, p. 62.

>   A discussion of the shift from curing people who are sick to preventing the sicknesses from occurring in the first place.

"Your Health Insurance. Be Sure You Have What You Need." *Changing Times*, June 1977, pp. 45–47.

>   A guide to selecting the insurance coverage you need.

CHUCK AND NANCY ANDERSON

Insuring against a Financial Calamity due to Loss of Income

If Chuck were disabled, his company's long-term disability plan would pay him 60 percent of his salary, or $1,300 a month, beginning six months after the date of disability. This plan costs him $300 a year. Chuck figures that, if he were disabled, Nancy would continue earning her same salary and he would receive Social Security benefits (based on $20,855 of average annual earnings) as well as the benefits from his company's disability plan. He also plans to annuitize $15,000 of investable assets at 7 percent, and he can take advantage of waiver of premium clauses on his health and life insurance policies.

Question

How much extra disability income insurance should Chuck buy? (Consider the benefits from his company's disability plan only after you have inflated the Andersons' annual needs.)

9

Life Insurance

Life insurance is really death insurance, for it takes on the financial responsibilities of the family's breadwinner at his or her death. If people (such as your spouse, children, or parents) are dependent upon you, you must consider how they will be cared for after you die. Perhaps, those who are in good health and have a marketable skill can get a job and provide for themselves. Perhaps, they can turn to an alternate source of income, such as Social Security combined with dividends or interest from investments. In most cases, however, the only way a breadwinner can provide for dependents after his or her death is through life insurance. By paying a relatively small sum each year (an annual insurance premium), you ensure that your family will be paid a larger sum if you die prematurely.

If you are thinking of buying life insurance, you should ask yourself several questions:

- What purpose does life insurance serve for you?
- Is there anyone you want to protect after you die? If so, who? If not, do you really need life insurance?
- Assuming you are married, if you were to die now, would your widow or widower be likely to remarry or live with parents or other family? If so, do you really need life insurance?
- How much of the responsibility for her or his support (and that of any dependents) would your spouse be willing or able to shoulder after your death? Could the person continue to work or get a job or adjust to a lower standard of living? If so, how should this affect your life insurance needs?

By answering these questions, you are to some extent envisioning your family's lifestyle without you. Look at the ramifications of your death with candor and honesty. Talk over the alternatives with your family. The premiums you now pay will, to a degree, influence your family's current lifestyle. The death benefit you plan for will determine their lifestyle after you die.

185

Determining whether you need life insurance is not as difficult as deciding how much life insurance you should have.

DETERMINING THE RIGHT AMOUNT OF LIFE INSURANCE

Before buying life insurance, it is important to identify what your needs are and when they will arise. Since death may come at any time, consider what your dependents' needs would be if you were to die now, not 10 or 20 years from now.

How Not to Do It

Joe's wife, Mindy, recently gave birth to their first child, Mortimer. Both Joe and Mindy feel it's a good time to review their life insurance program. They have a $25,000 policy on Joe's life—enough to bury Joe and give Mindy about a year to find a job. When they bought the policy three years ago, Mindy felt that, since she has a nurse's credential, she would have no problem getting a job as a registered nurse and earning enough money to live comfortably. But now Mortimer has changed things. Mindy wants to be home with her son, at least until he enters high school. And there are things like a college education and a higher cost of living now that there are three in the family.

Joe and his life insurance agent have just sat down to review Joe's life insurance needs. The agent looks at the family budget, then takes out those expenses that would be eliminated were Joe to die. The agent figures that Mort and Mindy's living expenses over the next 13 years, until Mort enters high school, will average $18,000 a year in today's dollars. Applying an inflation factor of 8 percent, the agent then multiplies the average yearly sum of $18,000 by the compound interest factor for 13 years at 8 percent (21.5, Table B in the appendix), resulting in a gross need of $387,000 ($18,000 × 21.5). Adding $3,000 for Joe's funeral, the agent recommends a $390,000 life insurance policy on Joe's life.

The procedure just described is not a bad way to determine your life insurance needs, but it does ignore one essential point: not all $390,000 is needed the day Joe dies, but over a 13-year period. Joe should buy enough insurance to provide $390,-000 over the 13-year period assuming that the amount is invested to earn some yield over that period of time. For example, if Mindy could earn 6 percent on her money (2 percent less than the assumed 8 percent inflation rate), all she would need would be $267,000 at Joe's death, not $390,000. If Mindy could earn a yield equal to inflation, all she would need would be $237,000.

In determining your needs for life insurance, look at how the proceeds will be invested as well as your projected standard of living. The eight-step procedure next does just that.

An Eight-Step Procedure for Determining Life Insurance Needs

To compute your life insurance needs, use the following eight-step procedure. With this procedure, you can determine your family's financial needs after your death and the sources of income to meet those needs. You can then plan to use insurance to make up the difference between the two. While the procedure makes some assumptions, which may seem arbitrary, it will nonetheless give you a close enough approximation of your insurance needs that you can make an intelligent decision about the amount of life insurance you need to buy.

To illustrate the procedure, we will use the example of a fictitious family, Leroy and Thelma Jackson (each 22) and their two-year-old son Jerry. Figure 9-1 shows the needs and income that the Jacksons predicted for themselves if Leroy were to die now.

FIGURE 9-1
Sample eight-step procedure.

NAME(S) *Leroy and Thelma Jackson*

DATE *January 1983*

EIGHT-STEP PROCEDURE

1 *Funeral, Administrative, and Estate Tax Expenses* $ 2,200

2 *Debt Resolution* (excluding home mortgage) $ 1,075

3 *Contingency Fund* (twice your monthly take-home pay) $ 2,000

4 *College Fund* $ 28,000

5 *NET ANNUAL LIVING EXPENSES*

   A. Average annual living expenses $ 12,000

   B. Spouse's average annual income $ 5,440

   C. Average annual Social Security $ 4,000

   D. Net annual income needs (A − B − C) $ 2,560

   E. Number of years in period   68

   F. Average annual investment rate factor (Table 9-1)   35

   G. TOTAL NET INCOME NEEDS (D x F) $ 89,600

6 *TOTAL MONETARY NEEDS* (1 + 2 + 3 + 4 + 5G) $ 122,875

7 *TOTAL INVESTMENT ASSETS* $ 900

8 *Your Life Insurance Needs* (6 − 7) $ 121,975

Instructions

1 *Funeral, Administrative, and Estate Tax Expenses*
If your gross estate (net worth on your balance sheet plus any life insurance proceeds) is less than $20,000, put $2,200 in the blank. If your gross estate is between $20,000 and $200,000, use $5,000; if it is over $200,000, put $10,000 in the blank.

The Jacksons' gross estate is $5,000, and so they estimate their expenses to be $2,200.

2 *Debt Resolution*
Look at your current debts as indicated by the liabilities on your balance sheet. All of these debts except your home mortgage should be resolved at death; put your total debt figure in this blank.

Leroy and Thelma Jackson have $1,075 in nonmortgage debts.

3 *Contingency Fund*
With all the other worries your family will have upon your death, you do not want them to worry unnecessarily about having enough money for immediate living expenses. A good rule of thumb is to put aside an amount twice your monthly take-home wage. Multiply your monthly salary by two and place that figure in this blank.

Leroy earns $1,000 (take-home wage) each month, and so their contingency fund should be $2,000.

4 *College Fund*
Estimate how much it would cost to send your children to college. At a state-supported college, the annual cost for tuition, room and board, and books would be $7,000. A private college might cost almost twice as much. Multiply the number of years of college your children will need by $7,000 or $12,000 (state or private), and place that figure in this blank.

The Jacksons want to send their son to a state college for four years. Therefore, they put $28,000 ($7,000 × 4) in the blank.

5 *Net Annual Living Expenses*

A. *Average Annual Living Expenses*   From your present living expenses, determine how much money your family would need to maintain their current standard of living if you died today. Since all families go through various stages (as indicated in Figure 9-2), estimate an average level of expenditure over the remaining life of your spouse. Put this estimate of family living expenses in blank A.

The Jacksons thought it would take an average of $12,000 a year to provide for the family over Thelma's remaining years.

B. *Spouse's Average Annual Income*   If your spouse will work after your death, estimate the level of take-home earnings and put that figure in blank B.

Thelma thought she would like to get a job once Jerry finished high school, 16 years from now. With her previous sales experience, she felt she could make $10,000 a year (in today's dollars) and work until she could retire at age 65. Over this 37-year period (present age plus years until work minus age at retirement) she would make $370,000 (37 × $10,000). To get an average earning figure over her entire lifetime, not just her working years, they decided to assume that she would live exceptionally long—to age 90, or another 68 years (age at death minus present age). Her average earnings over this 68-year period would be approximately $5,440 ($370,000 ÷ 68). This $5,440 figure is what Leroy put in blank B.

C. *Average Annual Social Security*   If you qualify for Social Security and have two or more minor children, put $5,000 in blank C; if you have one child, put $4,000 in blank C; if you have no children, put $3,000 in blank C, to account for the retirement benefit to your beneficiary.

The Jacksons have one child, and so they put $4,000 in blank C.

D. *Net Annual Income Needs*   Subtract the figures in blanks B and C from the figure in blank A, and put the result in blank D. This figure represents the family's net annual living expenses.

The Jacksons subtracted the $5,440 of spousal earnings and $4,000 of Social Security from the $12,000 of projected need and arrived at a net need of $2,560 a year.

E. *Number of Years in Period*   Assume that your beneficiary will die by age 90. Subtract your beneficiary's present age from 90 and put that figure in blank E.

Thelma's age is 22, which, when subtracted from 90, leaves 68 years.

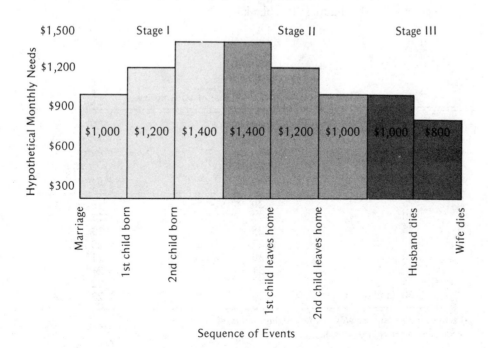

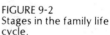

FIGURE 9-2
Stages in the family life cycle.

F. *Average Annual Investment Rate Factor* In column 1 of Table 9-1 find the number of years that is closest to the figure you put in blank E. Select the corresponding factor from either column 2 or column 3, depending on which type of investments you feel more comfortable with. Put that figure in blank F.

The Jacksons prefer the safer type of investments, and so the appropriate factor for them is 35.

G. *Total Net Income Needs* Multiply your family's net annual living expense need (blank D) by the factor in blank F to arrive at the total aggregate living expense needs if you were to die today. Put this figure in blank G.

Multiplying the Jacksons' $2,560 of annual income needs times their investment factor, 35, gives an aggregate need of $89,600.

6 *Total Monetary Needs*

Add the figures in steps 1 through 5 to determine how much money your family will need to cover initial expenses and provide for themselves after your death. Put that figure in this blank.

The Jacksons' total monetary needs are $122,875.

7 *Total Investment Assets*

Look at your balance sheet to see what investment assets your family would have available to cover their expenses. Put that figure in the blank.

The Jacksons have $900 in a savings account.

8 *Your Life Insurance Needs*

Subtract your family's monetary assets (step 7) from your family's aggregate needs (step 6). This result indicates the amount of insurance protection you should buy. Put that figure in this blank.

TABLE 9-1

Factors for the Present Value of an Annuity

(1) Years	(2) Annuities, Savings Accounts, Bonds[a]	(3) Bonds, Securities, Real Estate[b]
25	20	16
30	22	17
35	25	19
40	27	20
45	30	21
50	31	21
55	33	22
60 (and over)	35	23

[a] Factors for 2 percent real growth after inflation and taxes.
[b] Factors for 4 percent real growth after inflation and taxes.

Subtracting the $900 savings from the $122,875 total monetary needs leaves an insurance requirement for the Jacksons of $121,975.

Decreasing Needs and Increasing Assets

In designing an insurance program, it is helpful to understand how needs change during one's lifetime. If you marry and have a family, your needs may increase as your family grows in size. With time, your total insurance needs decrease, largely because your beneficiary has an increasingly shorter life expectancy (living expenses being by far the largest needs). When your spouse dies or your dependents reach adulthood, their living expense needs end.

Although, in the aggregate, needs seem to decrease in a uniform manner, individual needs do not. Funeral and administrative expenses as well as federal and state estate taxes increase as your estate grows larger. Liabilities (large purchases involving debts) usually come at the middle of one's life and can be expected to decrease. The need for a contingency fund remains constant because it is a need that occurs at death. However, the size of the fund needed may increase slightly as your standard of living increases. College education funds represent needs that have a fixed lifetime. A child's education fund will be needed only when the person goes to college. Such a need tends to remain constant for a fixed period of time and then disappears entirely. Of course, providing a college education may not be among your goals, or your child may help provide it through his or her own earnings.

Whereas, over all, needs decrease, assets increase (Fig. 9-3). If your monetary assets are invested in money market funds, mutual funds, real estate, or common stock, they should grow. If you add to these investments in order to meet specific goals, your total investments should become larger.

The total Social Security benefits you can expect decline as the years pass. The earlier you die, the greater the total amount your family will receive from Social Security. However, once your youngest child is 16, your spouse receives nothing from Social Security until age 60—an interim known as the blackout period (Fig. 9-4a). Although your aggregate living needs decrease over time, the resources available to fulfill them (i.e., assets and Social Security) eventually become large enough to cover them and should continue to grow after that (Fig. 9-4b).

Life insurance is most important while your needs exceed your assets. The pattern of the difference between these two factors over the years shows the need for life insurance first increasing and then decreasing (Fig. 9-4c).

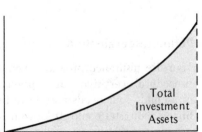

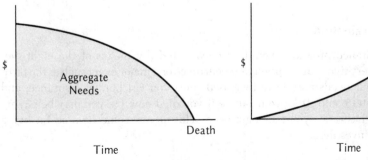

FIGURE 9-3
Over one's lifespan, needs tend to decrease and assets tend to increase.

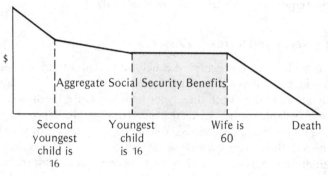

(a) Social Security Payments

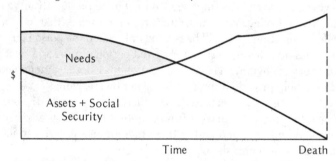

(b) Decreasing Needs Plotted against
Increasing Assets Plus Social Security

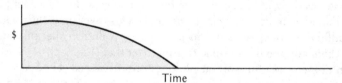

(c) Life Insurance Needs
(until intersection with assets)

FIGURE 9-4
One's life insurance
needs tend to rise and fall
with the pattern of one's
needs, assets, and Social
Security.

Periodic Reevaluation

Your life insurance program should be reevaluated (by means of the eight-step procedure) every five years or upon the occurrence of a major event such as the birth of a child. Your needs may have increased since you last bought insurance, and financial disaster could strike your family if you died now. Or, you may be paying premiums on insurance you no longer need. This money could be used for living expenses and investments.

keeping up with your living expenses   What may be adequate to meet your needs today may well be inadequate five years from now. If inflation were to persist at a compound rate of 5 percent annually, the dollar's purchasing power would be reduced by over 25 percent in five years. Furthermore, the younger you are, the more difficult it is to predict accurately what your needs will be. New goals arise to replace old ones. You may not have children for a couple of years, and yet 20 years from now you may be faced with the expenses of providing a college education for your children.

time to self-insure   When your increasing resources and Social Security benefits exceed your decreasing needs, you are basically "self-insured." That is, you have sufficient resources on your own to meet your family's survivorship income requirements plus your death expenses without having to rely on insurance benefits. Most people will reach this self-insured position by the time they retire at age 65. After all, if you can afford to retire and support both yourself and your spouse, there will be sufficient assets or income to support one of you, should the other one die. So as you plan your insurance program, realize that you will more than likely outlive your need for life insurance once you retire or reach a point of financial independence.

life insurance to pay estate settlement costs?   Suppose that 32 years ago you bought a cash value policy with a face amount of $100,000. You reach retirement age and you realize that, from a survivorship income point of view, you don't need insurance. But the insurance agent says, "Keep your policy because the cheapest way to pay estate taxes is with life insurance." The argument is that by continuing to pay the premiums, you're going to have more money available to pay estate taxes from the proceeds payable by the insurance policy.

Actually, if you keep the policy, no matter when you die, you will receive the face amount of the policy—no more, no less. As an alternative, you could invest, at 5 percent after tax for the rest of your life, the policy's cash value (now $57,000) and the money you would otherwise spend on annual premiums. If you lived to age 85, you would have $197,415 available from the reinvested cash value and annual premiums—almost twice as much as you would have from the face amount of the policy itself had you kept it in force. If you were to graph the level amount of insurance against the increasing amount of this fund that you would be developing after you cashed in the policy, you would find that the amounts of money available from these two sources would equal each other in about eight years. In other words, to break even, regardless of which alternative you select, you have to live eight years. This is roughly 60 percent of your life expectancy at age 65.

What you are doing by maintaining a policy after it is no longer serving to replace the decedent's income stream is engaging in "actuarial gambling." If you think you're going to die prematurely, keep the life insurance policy. On the other hand, if you don't have inside knowledge that you will die earlier than normal, why bet against the best actuaries in the world and also against yourself? (If these actuaries were wrong too many times, the life insurance companies could not remain in business.)

Actually, when you read Chapter 22 on estate transfer, you will learn that there is no reason to pay estate taxes at the death of one spouse or, in most cases, at the death of the other spouse. The estate should not need to pay taxes at all.

Reducing Your Need for Life Insurance

Life insurance needs can be reduced in three ways:

1. If you reduce your family's expected standard of living, your life insurance requirements are lowered.
2. If you devote more money to investments, your assets should become larger and come closer to covering your needs.
3. If you can make your investments earn a higher yield, your assets rise more sharply.

FIVE BASIC VARIABLES IN LIFE INSURANCE POLICIES

There are hundreds of different life insurance policies. But they vary primarily in only five areas: protection, savings, face amount, policy period, and premium. Table 9-2 shows how these variables change depending on the type of policy.

Protection

Protection is the primary purpose for which life insurance is designed—protection of the people who would be without a means of support if the insured were to die. Depending on the type of policy, the amount of this protection may increase, decrease, or remain constant.

Savings

Unlike term insurance, which provides only protection, cash value insurance provides also *savings*—the cash from the premium that is stored by the insurance company as a reserve. In a cash value policy, the savings pattern is the reciprocal of the protection pattern (Fig. 9-5). Assuming the face amount of the policy remains

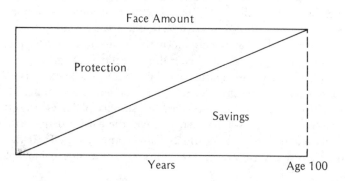

FIGURE 9-5
Protection and savings in
a cash value policy.

TABLE 9-2

Comparison of Policy Types for $50,000 of Life Insurance

Type of Policy	Period	Annual Premiums at Age				Protection and Savings	Remarks
		25	35	45	55		
Level term	Any number of years but seldom past age 70	$110.00[a]	$ 122.50[a]	$ 224.00[a]	$ 488.00[a]	All protection	True insurance; premiums increase at renewal
Decreasing term	Any number of years but seldom past age 70	$146.00[b]	$ 203.50	$ 332.00[b]	$ 531.50	All protection	Level of insurance decreases; premiums remain level
Whole life	Whole life	$565.50	$ 798.50	$1184.00	$1832.50	Protection and savings	Half investment, half insurance; cash value buildup; premiums remain level
20-payment life	Whole life	$950.00[c]	$1212.50	$1543.50	$2133.00	Medium protection and high savings	Premiums paid within 20 years; cash value rises rapidly; premiums remain level
Life-paid-up-at-65	Whole life	$705.50	$ 983.50	$1543.50	$3355.50	Medium protection and medium savings	Premiums paid before retirement; cash value rises rapidly; premiums remain level

Note: Rates quoted from New England Life Insurance Co. and Jackson National Life Insurance Co. of Michigan.

[a] Rates are for five-year term insurance. Such policies are usually guaranteed renewable to age 65 or 100.

[b] Rates are for 20-year term insurance. Minimum premium is usually $100 a year.

[c] A participating policy. Dividends have been subtracted from the annual premiums to make the policy comparable.

constant, the protection element decreases as the savings element increases. When premiums are first paid on cash value policies, most of the money is used to provide protection (the death benefits). As the years go by, more and more of the annual premium goes to building up a reserve (the savings element).

Face Amount

Over the life of the policy, the *face amount* payable at death may increase, decrease, or remain constant.

Policy Period

The *policy period* may be for a specified number of years or for the rest of your life. If you choose a policy period other than lifetime, you should consider renewability provisions. For example, if you purchase a five-year renewable term insurance policy, you can renew the policy at the end of five years without showing proof of insurability. Although this feature costs a few dollars in premiums over each five-year period, it assures you that, if you suffer some accident or illness that renders you uninsurable, you can still protect your family.

Premium

Premiums may be paid for the duration of the policy or for shorter periods. They may be paid annually in equal amounts (level premiums) or in decreasing or increasing amounts. They may or may not be guaranteed to remain at certain levels throughout the policy period. If not guaranteed, they may be altered in future years to reflect changes in underwriting practices or mortality data. The size of the premium depends on the other four policy variables (protection, savings, face amount, and policy period) and on your age and health.

Life insurance premiums are based on mortality tables—sets of statistics showing how many people die at various ages. Insurance companies use these tables to determine how much total insurance coverage will be needed and how much money they have to charge each policyholder in order to have enough income to cover their needs.

For example, according to mortality tables, at age 40 there will be 353 deaths for every 100,000 people. If each of these 353 people carried $20,000 life insurance coverage, the insurance companies would need $7,060,000 to meet all the required payments. In order to collect $7,060,000, the companies must charge each of the 100,000 people a premium of $70.60 plus charges for administrative cost, commissions, and profit (or dividends). If the policyholder is over 40, the probability of death increases and the total amount of money needed increases. If the policyholder is younger, the opposite is true.

TERM INSURANCE

Term insurance is pure insurance issued for a set period of time. You can purchase term insurance to cover yourself through age 100. Because term insurance has no savings element or cash value, it requires the smallest cash premiums. The insurance company will pay money only if you die, and then that money is received by your beneficiary. Since relatively few people die before most term policies terminate (age 65), the insurance company will experience a very low level of losses. Term insurance follows the same principle as auto, property, and health insurance and pays only if there is a loss.

Renewable Term Insurance

There are two types of renewable term insurance. One can be renewed every year; the other can be renewed every 5, 10, 15, or 20 years.

Annual renewable term insurance offers pure protection for periods of one year. Its prime advantages are that it requires a small cash outlay and that it is flexible. At each renewal date you can lower the level of coverage or keep it the same. You cannot raise it, however, without demonstrating to the insurance company that you are insurable. The premium per $1,000 of coverage increases with the age of the insured. If you reduce your total coverage level, the premium may be the same or less, even though the cost per $1,000 has risen. Normally the annual premium rises very slowly in the early years and then quite rapidly as you near age 65 (see Figure 9-6). Most term policies stop coverage at age 65 or 70, but some go on even to age 100. If you purchase an annual term policy with a guaranteed renewable feature, you may renew the policy each year, even though your health may have rendered you uninsurable. Guaranteed renewable may be a little more expensive, but it saves having to requalify with a physical every year in order to keep the insurance in force.

Five, 10-, 15-, and 20-year renewable term resembles annual renewable term except that the coverage stays level for longer periods between renewal dates. The premiums stay level during these periods as well, but this feature usually represents no real advantage. The level premium on a five-year renewable policy, for instance, is simply the average of the five separate annual renewable rates for that five-year

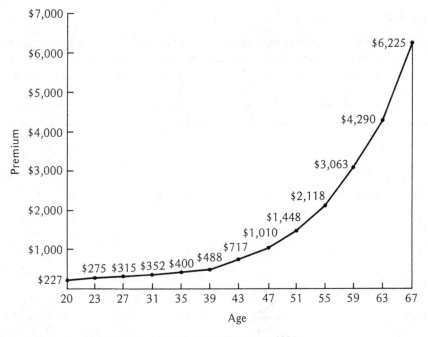

Note: Rates from Jackson National Life Insurance Company, 1981.

FIGURE 9-6
Sample rates, by age, for $50,000 of annual renewable term coverage.

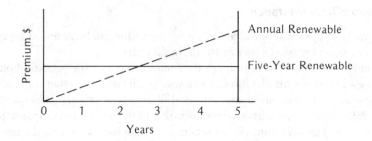

FIGURE 9-7
Comparison of premiums
for two types of term
insurance.

period. Therefore, in the first half you would be paying more for five-year renewable term than you would for annual renewable term, and in the last half you would be paying less (see Figure 9-7). If you might cancel a term policy before the term period is over, it is better to buy annual renewable term.

Level Term to Age 65

This type of insurance offers protection at the same premium year in and year out. It provides the longest term of unrenewed protection of any term policy. The premiums are higher than those of renewable term policies in the early years, but lower in the later years. Most corporation group life insurance plans utilize this form of insurance.

Decreasing Term Insurance

Uniform decreasing term insurance provides coverage that decreases by the same dollar amount each year the policy is in force (Fig. 9-8a). Therefore, if you purchase a $20,000 decreasing term policy for 20 years, the coverage level would drop $1,000 a year (20,000 ÷ 20).

Mortgage term insurance decreases in uneven dollar amounts, which keep pace with the reduction of the principal balance due on a mortgage loan (Fig. 9-8b).

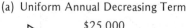

FIGURE 9-8
Comparison of death
benefits for two types of
term insurance.

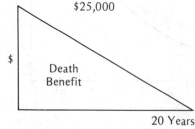

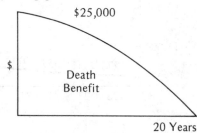

Since in the early years of a home mortgage a large portion of each mortgage payment goes to pay interest, reduction in the amount of principal due on the loan is slight, and the reduction in coverage of your mortgage term insurance is correspondingly slight. In the later years, the principal balance is reduced quickly because most of the interest has been paid; your mortgage term insurance coverage decreases equally quickly. (Chapter 14 will explain the home mortgage in greater detail.) If you expect your needs to decrease less in the early years of the term (perhaps while your family is growing up) than in the later years (after your children leave home), decreasing mortgage term might make sense.

CASH VALUE INSURANCE

This type of insurance has a savings element and is issued for a set period of time or for life. This savings element, or cash value, is not refunded when you die; instead only the face amount benefits are payable to your beneficiary. He or she receives only the face amount of the policy, no matter what the level of cash value is.

A cash value policy is nothing more than a decreasing term policy and a savings plan put together. As your investment increases, your protection decreases (Fig. 9-5). Both the savings element gain and protection loss, however, are so timed that the face amount remains the same.

In recent years, most life insurance companies have tended to deemphasize cash value insurance and to stress term coverage or some form of hybrid policy (such as universal life). These hybrid policies either combine term and cash value insurance or offer a variable, higher guaranteed cash value feature. We will discuss some of these hybrids as well.

Ordinary and Whole Life

Ordinary and whole life are different names for the same policy. Premiums are the same each year and continue for life, or until you cash in the policy. It has the smallest cash value accumulation for your premium dollar (Fig. 9-9a) and is the least expensive form of cash value insurance.

Limited Payment Life

This type of insurance is like whole life, except that it becomes paid up within 10 to 20 years or by age 65 and no more premium payments are required to keep it in force. The shorter the premium period, the greater each premium payment is. However, the shorter the period over which premiums need be paid, the faster the cash value buildup. For younger people, 20-payment life yields a guaranteed cash value at age 65 that exceeds total premiums paid. This type of policy enables the policyholder to meet the cost of the insurance during his or her income-producing years. Life-paid-up-at-65 is another example of this type of insurance. These policies have declined so much in popularity that many companies do not write them anymore.

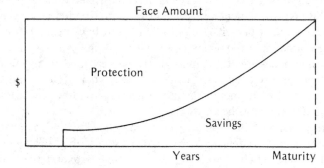

(a) Whole Life Policy

Face Amount

Protection

$

Savings

Years   Age 65

(b) Endowment Policy

Face Amount

Protection

$

Savings

Years   Maturity

FIGURE 9-9
Comparison of savings
and protection for two
types of cash value
insurance.

Endowment

This type of life insurance is generally designed for people who wish to build up a significant investment, while obtaining a certain amount of insurance protection. Endowment policies build up cash value at such a rate that at maturity there is no term insurance protection left (Fig. 9-9b). The death benefit is entirely covered by the cash paid in.

The maturity term of the policy is equal to the premium paying period. Policies are written to mature in 10, 20, or 30 years, or at age 60, 65, 70, and so on. Your guaranteed cash value will exceed your total paid-in premiums if you purchase the policy at a young enough age. Since these policies are written for terms as short as 10 years, you can use them to accumulate funds for fairly short-term goals, provided you can meet the higher annual premiums.

Retirement endowment policies are designed to accumulate funds for retirement income. They are a special form of endowment policy in that you continue to pay premiums until age 65—beyond the point at which the cash value reaches the face amount, which is usually at 55. As with limited payment life, few insurance companies sell endowment policies today.

Hybrid Policies

The most recent example of an insurance policy that combines features of both term and cash value insurance is called *universal life*. Although this new insurance policy is really nothing more than term insurance plus a variable investment fund, it was widely acclaimed when it appeared in early 1981. It seeks to remedy the deficiencies of whole life and make combining protection with a savings element more attractive.

To initiate a universal life policy, the policy buyer voluntarily "contributes" to a fund a sum of money, which may vary within certain limits. From this fund the insurance company withdraws an amount of money necessary to pay the pure protection costs (essentially term insurance) and an amount to cover expenses and profit. (Unlike cash value policies, hybrid policies identify and disclose to the policyholder the costs for the insurance and overhead.) Whatever moneys are left in this fund are invested to earn an interest rate that has been determined by the company but reflects current money market and interest rate conditions. Unlike cash value policies (whose cash value grows at perhaps 6 percent a year if held for 20 years or more), universal life's cash value earns an advertised 11 or 12 percent a year. However, the actual yield is much lower. To find it, we must subtract the front-end load of 5 to 10 percent on each contribution and weigh the effect of being able to earn only 4 percent on the first $1000 of cash value; then the actual yield is more in the neighborhood of 2 to 6 percent, depending on the amount of contribution and how long the cash value is left to grow.

Other interesting features of this policy include cost-of-living increases to the face amount of the policy, the ability to add more insurance to the same policy (although only with evidence of insurability), and the capability of varying (or neglecting completely) the amount of the annual contribution. Table 9-3 compares some existing universal life policies. In summary, universal life is clearly better than cash value insurance in terms of growth of cash value available, but probably not as good as buying term insurance and investing the difference on your own. Also, the attractiveness of a universal life policy could be reduced by the discontinuance of the tax deferral available on its cash buildup.

Other hybrid policies, with odd names like "Termanent Protection," provide annual renewable term protection for, perhaps, five years and then automatic conversion to whole life. The premiums on these types of policies typically go up every year for the first 10 to 20 years, then level off. Once converted to whole life, they can be converted back to annual renewable term at a later date.

Hybrids are interesting for their novelty, yet rarely offer any better insurance buy than term insurance or whole life or, if you like, a little of both.

CHOOSING THE RIGHT POLICY FOR YOU

The essential question in choosing a suitable policy centers around term insurance versus cash value insurance. Since cash value insurance contains an investment feature and term insurance does not, it is hard to make a valid comparison of the two alternatives unless you assume that you will take the difference in the term premium

Table 9-3

Some Universal-Life Policies

(Fall 1981 data)

Company (and Policy)	Minimum Face Amount	First-Year Fee for $100,000 Policy	Recurring Fee[a]	Interest Based On	Recent Rate[b]	Guaranteed Rate[b]
Hartford Life (The Solution)	$100,000	$575	5%	Company decision	12%[c]	4%
E.F. Hutton Life (CompleteLife)	25,000[d]	360	7.5	Company decision	11.75[c]	4
Life Ins. Co. of Virginia (The Challenger)	100,000	708	9	Index of 20-year Treasury bonds	12.36[c]	4
Transamerica Occidental Life (T Plan Life)	75,000[e]	None	10	Index of 13-week Treasury bills	13.6	3

Source. "Universal-Life Insurance," *Consumer Reports* (January 1982), p. 44.

[a] Percentage of each premium payment.

[b] Gross rate.

[c] But 4% on first $1000 of cash value.

[d] Smaller at ages 55 and up.

[e] Varies by age; amount shown is minimum for ages 30-49.

and the cash value premium and create your own "cash value" investment feature. Then the decision becomes whether to buy a cash value policy or buy term and reinvest the difference. You must look at both alternatives for their investment as well as insurance protection merits. To see how this comparison might work, let's look at an example.

An Example

Jenny, a single woman of 37, has a well-paying career and finds herself in the 30 percent marginal tax bracket. Her 58-year-old mother lives with her and depends on her for living expenses and therefore creates a need for Jenny to have life insurance. A life insurance agent has suggested that, for an annual premium of $716, Jenny could buy a $50,000 life-paid-up-at-65 policy to cover her retirement needs and protect her mother. Although Jenny can afford this policy, she wants to examine a few alternatives before deciding what to do. During her investigation she finds that she can also purchase $50,000 of 20-year mortgage (decreasing) term insurance for $202 annually. This policy offers an average of $1,000 less in death benefits each year until it reaches zero in 20 years, when Jenny's mother would be 78 years old. Jenny thinks that during those 20 years she could build up enough cash in another investment to make up for the decreasing amount of protection. The annual amount that she would have to invest by taking the term rather than the cash value insurance would be $514 ($716 − $202).

According to projections of cash values and dividend accumulations made by Jenny's insurance agent, the life-paid-up-at-65 policy would probably yield about $18,909 in 20 years. If she buys term insurance and invests the difference ($514 a year) in an insured deposit yielding 6 percent after tax, her total investment would be worth about $18,908 in 20 years. The total yield from both would be the same; however, she feels that she would be more likely to pay life insurance premiums since she would be billed for them.

Another alternative would be to purchase term insurance and invest the difference in a mutual fund (see Chapter 19) recommended by a broker. The fund she is considering has achieved an average annual compound rate of growth of 8 percent after tax since its founding 15 years ago. This rate yields a total investment of approximately $23,522 and represents a larger possible investment value than either of the other two alternatives. As we shall see in succeeding chapters, this investment alternative carries significant risks (short-term price fluctuations) when compared to the guaranteed investments offered by the first two alternatives. However, Jenny is willing to live with these interim risks since she views this investment over a long period of time.

Jenny is still worried, however, that she might not make her investments on a regular basis, although she has generally been able to budget her money well for similar commitments or purchases. Her broker tells her that, if she enrolls in a voluntary savings accumulation plan (Chapter 19), the mutual fund will prod her with regular monthly statements. Jenny feels this would be all the encouragement she would need and she chooses the last alternative.

Jenny's three alternatives are compared in Table 9-4. The effect of the age of the investor upon these three alternatives is shown in Table 9-5. To make computations to fit your own situation and alternatives, refer to compound interest Tables A and B (appendix).

How Not to Do It

Four months after Paul graduated from college, he received a telephone call from a member of that year's championship football team—a fellow graduate but someone Paul had known only by reputation. He told Paul that he had joined a life insurance agency after graduation and would like to sit down with his "old school pal" to discuss Paul's life insurance needs. Paul was, of course, flattered that the ex-football hero would know his name from among the 500 students who graduated that year, and so he agreed to meet with him that evening.

When the life insurance salesman arrived at Paul's apartment, he immediately proceeded to tell Paul why everyone needed life insurance. Even though Paul was not married and had no one dependent upon him for support, he was told that everyone must plan for the future and build an estate either to rely on at retirement or to pass on to one's heirs. The salesman used a number of computer printouts to show that the policy really wouldn't cost Paul anything if he held it for 20 years or

TABLE 9-4

$25,000 of Life-Paid-up-at-65 versus

$25,000 of 20-Year Decreasing Term and Investing the Difference in Premiums

Alternative	Annual Cash Outlay			Possible Value in 20 Years	Investment Risk	Saving Discipline Required
	Premium	Cash Investment	Total			
Life-paid-up-at-65 (protection only)	$615		$615	$18,909[a]	Very little	Premium notice forces her to save
20-year decreasing term and savings account (yielding 6% annual after-tax return)	101	$514	615	18,908	None, if insured by federal government	Requires considerable self-discipline
20-year decreasing term and mutual fund (yielding 8% annual after-tax return)	101	514	615	23,522	Significant	Monthly statement will remind her, but there is no obligation

Source: New York Life Insurance Company premium rates, cash values, and dividends for 35-year-old male (approximately those for 37-year-old female), 1979; Occidental Life, 1978, rates current in 1979.

[a] Includes guaranteed cash value and projected dividend accumulations.

TABLE 9-5

**$25,000 of Life-Paid-up-at-65 versus
$25,000 of Decreasing Term and Investing the Difference in Premiums**

Alternative	Age at Policy Purchase		Annual Cash Outlay			Possible Value in 10 Years	Possible Value in 20 Years
	F^a	M	Premium	Cash Investment	Total		
Life-paid-up-at-65 (protection only)	27	25	$ 396		$ 396	$ 4,038[b]	$11,962[b]
	37	35	615		615	6,453[b]	18,909[b]
	48	45	1,010		1,010	10,893[b]	29,890[b]
20-year decreasing term and savings account (yielding 6% annual after-tax return)	27	25	91	$305	396	4,020	11,220
	37	35	101	514	615	6,775	18,908
	48	45	160	896	1,010	11,810	32,960
20-year decreasing term and mutual fund (yielding 8% annual after-tax return)	27	25	91	305	396	4,418	13,957
	37	35	101	514	615	7,446	23,522
	48	45	160	896	1,010	12,979	41,002

Source: New York Life Insurance Company premium rates, cash values, and dividends for females, 1979; Occidental Life, 1978 rates, current in 1979.
[a] Results for female approximate those for male two to three years younger.
[b] Includes guaranteed cash value and projected dividend accumulations.

more. Paul was told that the "net cost" for the policy would actually be a minus $1,500. In other words, as the ex-football hero said, Paul would be ahead $1,500 after 20 years, plus he would have had all the life insurance over that period of time.

Paul was impressed. Then the salesman told him about all the other football players on his team who had already purchased policies just like the one outlined. As the salesman took out the application, he dropped his pen at Paul's feet. Paul reached to pick up the pen, the salesman quickly handed Paul the contract to sign, and Paul suddenly became the proud owner of a life insurance policy.

Needless to say, don't buy life insurance unless you have dependents who would need it were you to die; and only buy from a reputable agent who knows his business, not just how to close a sale.

THE LIFE INSURANCE CONTRACT

Most life insurance contracts contain eight clauses. Each of them involves decisions that determine the effectiveness of your policy in accomplishing your goals. You must decide not only how much insurance you need but also who is to receive the benefits upon your death; how the benefits are to be paid (lump-sum, installments, and so on); whether to borrow on your policy; whether to pay your premiums annually, semiannually, or monthly; how to receive dividends (if any) from your policy; how to provide for cancellation of your policy and still receive your cash value; how to provide for reinstatement of your policy's five variables—protection, savings (if any), face amount, period, and premium—if you fail to pay the premium and policy coverage lapses; and how to change your policy from cash value to term or vice versa.

Beneficiary Clause

There are two classes of beneficiaries: the primary beneficiary and the contingent beneficiaries. The *primary beneficiary* is the person designated by the insured to receive the policy death benefits. If the primary beneficiary dies before the benefits have been completely distributed, the remainder of the policy's benefits go to the *contingent beneficiaries* named in the policy. For example, you may choose your spouse as your primary beneficiary and, in the event of her or his death, your children as contingent beneficiaries.

Settlement Options

The insurance company allows you, as the policyholder, to choose how the policy's death benefits will be distributed to your beneficiaries or how the policy's cash value will be distributed to yourself. If you surrender the cash value of your policy, you also have your choice of nonforfeiture options (to be discussed later in this chapter). There are four ways in which the proceeds can be received:

1. The benefits can be withdrawn in installments of any fixed amounts you choose until all the benefits are distributed or in equal installments over a specified period of time (installment option).

2. The beneficiary may leave the proceeds with the company and receive the interest on them annually, semiannually, quarterly, or monthly (interest option).
3. The benefits may be paid to the beneficiary for as long as he or she lives (life annuity option).
4. The benefits can be withdrawn in one lump sum (lump-sum option).

The settlement options can be changed at will by the policy owner. However, if an option other than lump-sum withdrawal is chosen by the insured before death, it cannot be changed by the beneficiary, unless an option was signed by the insured leaving complete discretion to the beneficiary.

installment payments   The installment payments option provides monthly income, consisting of both interest and principal, until the funds are exhausted. You may select either the fixed period or fixed amount option. With the *fixed period* option, the payee designates the number of years over which monthly payments will be received (usually from one to 30), and the company declares the size of the payment, based on the amount of interest earned. With the *fixed amount* option, the payee chooses the monthly amount of benefits he or she wishes to receive, and the company makes payments of that amount until the money runs out—with interest credited to the principal at the current year's rate. (The rate is usually guaranteed at a certain minimum, often 2.5 percent.) In either case, if you die before the funds are exhausted, the remaining payments will be made to your beneficiary.

The advantage of the installment payments option over the lump-sum option is that you spread the taxable gain (ordinary income) on your insurance investment over a period of years and, by not having to declare it all in one year, avoid the possibility of placing yourself in an unnecessarily high tax bracket. This advantage would not apply if payment were being made to a beneficiary since life proceeds are not subject to income tax.

interest income   You may choose to receive interest income only. The size of the payment depends on your policy's cash value and the company's current rate of interest (usually guaranteed at a minimum rate, such as 2.5 percent). You retain ownership of the cash value of your policy and it will eventually become part of your estate, payable to the beneficiary of your choice. If you decide that the interest provides you with insufficient income, you may change your option and withdraw the cash as a lump sum.

annuity   There are four standard annuity options available with most life insurance policies. All of them guarantee monthly benefits for life. As Tables 9-6 and 9-7 show, the size of the monthly payment varies depending on the amounts left over for contingent beneficiaries.

Straight life annuity (also known as the life-income-without-refund annuity) offers monthly payments for life, regardless of how long the payee lives. If the payee dies young, the company keeps the remaining funds; if the payee's life is unusually long, he or she collects not only more than was put in but also interest as well. The payment rate depends upon the interest the company earns on the money the payee

TABLE 9-6

Typical Monthly Payments for Three Annuity Options
($10,000 lump-sum annuity value)

Age of Payee on First Payment Date		Straight Life Annuity	Refund Annuity	Certain and Continuous Annuity[a]	
M	F			10 Years	20 Years
20	25	$29	$28	$29	$29
30	35	33	31	31	31
40	45	37	35	36	35
50	55	45	41	43	41
60	64	57	51	54	43
65	69	66	58	63	51
70	73	79	67	72	53

[a] Refund guaranteed to beneficiary if death occurs before 10 years or 20 years, depending on option chosen.

TABLE 9-7

Typical Monthly Payments for Joint-and-Survivorship
Annuity with Two-Thirds to Survivor
($10,000 lump-sum annuity value)

Age at Start of Payments Female	Age at Start of Payments Male			
	55	60	65	70
55	$42	$44	$46	$47
60	47	50	53	57
65	50	54	58	63
70	54	59	64	70

Note: Here is an example that shows how to read this table. If at the start of benefits the man is age 65 and the woman is age 60, the monthly benefit will be $53 while they are both alive. When one of them dies, the monthly benefit to the survivor will be two-thirds of that amount, or $35.50.

invests; but it is guaranteed at the rate set in the table of the policy. Generally, under this option you must outlive the normal life expectancy by as much as 10 to 25 years to recoup your original investment plus interest.

Refund annuity offers income payments for the rest of the payee's life; if any funds remain upon the payee's death, they are paid to the payee's beneficiaries. The minimum guaranteed payment rate set by the company for this type of annuity is somewhat lower than for the straight life annuity since the insurance company must ultimately pay back the entire investment. The only conditions under which you would wish to choose a refund annuity would be if you wished to leave an estate to your heirs and did not mind taking a lower monthly income for yourself, or if your family had a history of early deaths and you felt that you would not otherwise collect your full investment.

Certain and continuous annuity also offers income for life; if the payee dies within a specified period (usually 5, 10, or 20 years), payments are made to the beneficiaries for the remainder of that period. Again, the monthly payments are lower than with the straight life annuity.

Joint-and-survivorship annuity offers a lifetime income for two persons, even if one outlives the other. The two recipients need not be related. If one of the payees dies, payments continue to the second payee at a specified rate—usually the same as, two-thirds of, or half of the amount of the payment made to both persons. The smaller the rate of payment chosen for the second payee alone, the larger the monthly payment will be for the two together. Again, the payment rate is set at a guaranteed minimum and may rise above that rate if a better interest return is earned by the insurance company on its investments.

Be sure to determine what your company is actually paying as retirement income before reaching a decision regarding any of these annuity options.

lump sum   This last option offers the most flexibility because it enables the beneficiary to consider settlement option alternatives not offered by the policy. The beneficiary might put the benefits into an investment medium that earns a higher return (interest rate) than is offered by insurance companies. Used this way, the option also offers the greatest opportunity to reduce insurance costs because the initial amount of benefits needed, or the policy's face amount, can be lowered. For example, a $100,000 policy might earn $3,000 interest a year at 3 percent. However, that same $3,000 can be gained from only a $30,000 investment in a savings certificate at 10 percent.

There is one serious disadvantage to the lump-sum settlement option. Persons who receive large sums of money are often easily tempted to overspend and dissipate the funds within a few years. This reaction defeats a primary purpose of life insurance—to provide financial security for one's family long after one's death. To avoid this problem, you may want to arrange with your banker and lawyer, before your death, to set up a trust to protect the funds from your life insurance and invest them at a reasonably high yield. (Chapter 22 gives more information on trusts.)

Loan Clause

This clause details the provisions under which you can borrow from your cash value policy, in which you have built up an equity. Your loan limit at any one time is the amount of cash value plus dividends and interest that your policy has accumulated up to that time. When you borrow, the face amount of the policy (your death benefit) is reduced by the amount of the loan during the period for which the money is borrowed unless you apply a portion of the policy's dividend to buy a one-year term addition to restore the full amount of your policy's face value. When the money is repaid, your policy returns to full force.

There are advantages to borrowing from your policy if you need to borrow: the interest rates are often lower than those available from financial institutions; no fees or carrying charges are imposed; and you may repay the loan in full whenever you can. If you choose not to, the loan never has to be repaid.

Premium Payment Clause

Premium payments can be made on an annual, semiannual, or some other basis. The insurance company charges an additional administration fee if the premium is paid other than annually. This fee may be as much as 18 percent of the annual premium. If you pay your premiums annually rather than monthly or quarterly, you can obtain significant cost savings on your insurance.

Dividend Clause

Dividends are the monetary rewards paid to an insurance policyholder at the end of the year. Holders of "participating" life insurance policies typically receive annual "dividends" that are, in effect, rebates of premium overcharges. They mean different things depending on whether they are issued by mutual companies or stock companies. Mutual companies are nonprofit organizations established for the benefit of the policyholders, who are the owners. Any time a mutual company anticipates more deaths than actually occur and consequently charges a higher premium than necessary, it passes this saving on to the policyholders as a dividend. A mutual company dividend, then, is a refund of premium.

A stock company pays dividends to its shareholders (not policyholders) as a return on their investments. The shareholders are the owners of the company; they may or may not be policyholders. In recent years, stock companies have begun to offer participating policies (par policies), which compete with mutual policies by offering a dividend to their policyholders. This dividend, like a mutual company's dividend, is a refund of premium. However, these stock company par policy dividends are made available by intentionally charging a higher premium than necessary so that there will be something left at the end of the year to return to the policyholders. In addition to this premium refund, stock companies continue to pay true dividends to their stockholders.

There are six dividend options from which you must choose if you decide to buy a participating policy from a mutual or stock company.

1. You can take the dividends in the form of a check to do with as you please.
2. You can apply the dividends to premium payments (i.e., partially pay your premiums with your dividends).
3. You can leave the dividend with the insurance company, as you leave money in a bank, to accumulate interest at 3 to 5½ percent, or possibly a little more if you are fortunate.
4. You can buy *paid-up additions*, which are nothing more than prepaid cash-value insurance. In other words, each dividend can be used to purchase additional coverage. The face amount of a paid-up addition depends on the age of the policyholder, the duration of the additional coverage, and the cost charged by the company. The higher the cost, the lower the amount of protection one dividend can buy. The main advantage of paid-up additions is that they are

issued without evidence of insurability. The main disadvantage is that, since they are single-premium policies (paid before coverage starts), they are the most expensive form of life insurance.

5. You can buy term additions, which provide additional term insurance coverage, with your dividends. Unlike paid-up additions, term additions have no cash value, and therefore each dividend dollar buys protection only, not savings. You can get much more protection for your dividend dollar through term additions than through paid-up additions.

6. You can use some of your dividend dollars to buy term insurance and leave the rest to accumulate interest with the insurance company.

Nonforfeiture Clause

This clause declares what the insurance company must do if you default on your policy. Only cash value policies contain such a clause. There are three nonforfeiture options for you to consider.

1. You can withdraw the cash value of your policy (the *cash surrender value*).
2. You can trade your policy's cash surrender value for a fully paid-up policy of the same duration as your previous policy. However, because its cash value in no way equals the sum of the annual premiums you would have to pay to keep the policy in force for the rest of your life, the face amount of the policy will be less than that of your previous policy. The face amount will be further reduced because the company will charge you the current rate, not the rate at which you purchased your first policy.
3. You can trade your policy's cash surrender value for a fully paid-up term policy with a shorter duration than your previous policy but with the same face amount.

If you do not choose a specific nonforfeiture option, your policy, if discontinued, will automatically be transferred to a term policy (third option). The details and current status of these options are printed in tables on the policy.

Reinstatement Clause

This clause gives policyholders who have discontinued their policies the opportunity to put them in force again. They may do this if they have not already redeemed the policy's cash surrender value; if they pay all unpaid premiums, plus accumulated interest, in cash; if they still qualify for insurance protection; and if they request reinstatement within a specified time after their policies have been discontinued.

Change of Policy Clause

This clause may be provided in both cash value and term policies. It enables policyholders to change their policies after buying them. For example, if you have a whole life policy and wish to change it to a 20-payment life policy, you are moving to a coverage that has a higher annual price since the total premium payments are spread over only 20 years instead of your whole life, which may be very much longer. In this case the insurance company would charge you either the difference in cash values between the two policies plus a carrying charge or the difference in back premiums plus interest.

Suicide Provision Clause

If the policyholder commits suicide within two years of the purchase date of the policy, the beneficiary will receive no benefits.

SHOPPING FOR RATES

Always shop for rates before buying a life insurance policy. The rate for a given type of policy can vary as much as 100 percent between the highest and lowest premium. In addition, rates have been coming down dramatically in recent years due to increased life expectancy and competition among insurance companies. Check with the agents of several major companies, as well as with several independent agents, before making your decision. Sometimes a company will offer an unusually low rate on a certain type of policy in the hope of selling you a different policy or obtaining further business from you. You may want to use Figure 9-10 to help you organize and compare the information you obtain while shopping for rates.

FIGURE 9-10
Data sheet for use in
shopping for life
insurance.

SHOPPING FOR LIFE INSURANCE

	Insurer 1	Insurer 2	Insurer 3
Policy type	_____	_____	_____
Company	_____	_____	_____
Face amount	$_____	$_____	$_____
Net annual premium	$_____	$_____	$_____
Disability waiver of premium	$_____	$_____	$_____
Accidental death and dismemberment rider	$_____	$_____	$_____
Policy owner	_____	_____	_____
Beneficiary	_____	_____	_____
Dividend option[a]	_____	_____	_____

[a]Dividend code: (1) reduces premium, (2) accumulates with interest, (3) purchases paid-up additions, (4) purchases one-year term insurance, (5) paid in cash, (6) no dividend.

Discounts

Most companies realize that some of their expenses do not vary in direct proportion to the amount of benefits carried. As their coverages increase, their costs do not. Therefore, they have started to pass these savings on to the policyholder by way of quantity discounts (i.e., the more you buy, the less the cost per $1,000 of insurance). Discounts can also be realized through the purchase of group policies because in this situation insurance companies save on administrative expenses and can better predict their risk exposure. In addition, many insurers now have preferred rates for nonsmokers.

Determining the Cost of a Policy

Cost is important when buying life insurance. It is based on (1) the length of time the policy will be in force, (2) the policy's cash surrender value (if any) at the end of that time, and (3) the costs of maintaining the policy during that time. Since we cannot know in advance how long we will live, these factors must be estimated.

The method traditionally used by the life insurance industry to determine a policy's cost is called the "net cost" or "average payment" approach. Under this method, the annual dividend (if any) and annual increase in the policy's cash surrender value (if any) are deducted from the annual premium. However, this method disregards the timing of premium, dividend, and cash value payments. It ignores, for example, the fact that money not spent on a premium today can earn interest or that a dividend received in a policy's first year can be more valuable to the policyholder than a dividend received in the policy's fifteenth year. A $100 dividend invested at 5 percent a year for 15 years, for example, would be worth $210, or twice as much as the same $100 dividend received in the fifteenth year.

To overcome the inadequacies of the traditional method, a new and more accurate cost determination method has been developed by a special committee appointed by the life insurance industry. This new method, known as the *interest-adjusted method*, considers the time various payments are made by applying an interest adjustment to the annual premiums, dividends, and cash value. The special industry committee recommended that all insurance companies provide the insurance buyer with detailed information about (1) premiums charged, (2) cash value at the end of various periods from one to 20 years, (3) illustrative dividends at these same points, and (4) special policy benefits and provisions. They also recommended that cost information include both a 10- and 20-year cost index by the interest-adjusted method based on an interest rate of 4 percent a year. The committee felt that the 4 percent interest rate was reasonably close to the after-tax rate of return readily obtainable on personal investments of security and stability comparable to life insurance cash values. When you compare insurance policies, be sure to ask for interest-adjusted cost comparisons.

CONCLUSION

Many people buy life insurance because they think it is the thing to do. They feel they must have life insurance, even though there may be no one to protect. Many purchase life insurance in response to their emotional needs—not the financial needs of the individuals who will receive the actual benefits. Remember that your plans should include only those who will be financially disadvantaged when you die. Often the opposite approach is taken: "Why should I leave any money behind, if it is not going to do me any good?" This attitude is selfish and inappropriate when determining one's life insurance needs.

It is important to realize that, no matter what financial hardship results from your death, you are not going to be the one to experience it. Unlike property, liability, and health insurance, life insurance provides financial protection solely for someone other than yourself.

If you are now in the market for life insurance or think you may be soon, you should proceed carefully through these five steps.

1. Keep your emotions under control.
2. Buy the right amount of insurance. If you buy too much, you will limit your family's current purchasing power. If you buy too little, you will leave them inadequately protected. Use the eight-step procedure to determine your needs.
3. Tailor the protection, savings, face amount, policy period, and premium pattern to fit your needs.
4. Be sure you understand all clauses and options. This understanding will enable you to choose what is right for you.
5. Consider choosing the lump-sum settlement option. You can set up a trust to receive the amount and have it invested at a higher rate of return than the insurance policy will provide, thus reducing the face amount you have to purchase.

VOCABULARY

annuity	paid-up addition
cash surrender value	policy period
cash value insurance	primary beneficiary
contingent beneficiary	protection
endowment policy	savings
face amount	settlement option
limited payment policy	term insurance
nonforfeiture option	

QUESTIONS

1. Discuss the methods by which you can reduce your needs for life insurance coverage. Given your situation, which methods make the most sense?
2. Bill has a life insurance policy for a stated face amount of $10,000. Currently, it has $3,000 in accumulated cash value. How much can Bill borrow from his policy? If Bill borrows the maximum from his policy, how much insurance will remain in force?
3. Jim and Louise (both age 30) determined that, if Jim died today, Louise and their daughter would need $6,000 a year to live on in addition to what Louise would receive from Social Security until her expected death at age 85. If Louise could achieve a 2

percent rate of growth after taxes and inflation, by investing the benefits from Jim's life insurance in a portfolio of savings and bonds, how much life insurance would the family need to buy today? (Assume that their present investments are sufficient to pay funeral, administrative, and estate expenses; to resolve all debts; to provide a contingency fund; and to send their daughter to college.)

4. Which type of term insurance is the most flexible? Why?
5. What are the major advantages of the lump-sum settlement option? What are the disadvantages?
6. Everyone needs life insurance. From what you have learned in this chapter, do you agree or disagree? Why?
7. "Life insurance is love." Does this advertising slogan help the buyer determine how much life insurance he or she needs?

CASE PROBLEMS

1. Jason and Heather Bell were married during their senior year in college. Soon after they graduated, a life insurance salesman talked with them about buying a life insurance policy. He emphasized their need for permanent protection. He said that if Jason bought a $10,000 whole life policy and paid $200 in level premiums every year for 40 years, he could then cash in his policy for $8,000 (40 × $200). The salesman said that the policy would actually cost Jason nothing.

   A friend of the Bells, who was also in the life insurance business, told them they could buy $10,000 worth of term coverage for $20 the first year. The premium would increase each year they held the policy, and 40 years from now the premium would be $100. The average premium over the 40 years would be $60. Jason figured that if each year he invested at 5 percent the $140 difference between the average term premium and the limited payment premium, over the 40 years his investment would grow to $16,800.

   Under what circumstances might it be more appropriate for Jason to buy the limited payment policy? Under what circumstances might it be more advantageous to buy the term insurance? Why is there such a difference in the return from these two investment alternatives?

2. Frank Hall was in the process of determining his life insurance needs through the eight-step procedure. He had figured that his net annual income need (line 5D) was $4,000 a year for 40 years.

   If Frank chose to have his family's money managed by a bank trust department at his death, in a pooled fund of common stocks which he thought would earn an average of 4 percent a year after taxes and inflation, how much life insurance would he need? (Assume Frank has no investment assets.)

RECOMMENDED READING

"A Guide to Life Insurance." *Consumer Reports*, January, February, and March 1974, Parts I, II, and III.
   A comparison of rates for both term and whole life policies for 125 companies.

Belth, Joseph M. *Life Insurance: A Consumer's Handbook*. Bloomington, Ind.: Indiana University Press, 1973.
   A guide to policies and options available to the life insurance purchaser.

Denenberg, Herbert S. *A Shopper's Guide to Life Insurance*. Harrisburg: Pennsylvania Insurance Department, April 1972.
   A discussion of policies and companies available to the insurance consumer.

"Insurance Salesmen Admit Unethical Practices on Campuses." *Consumer Newsweekly,* March 21, 1977.

> An exposé of seamy practices on the part of life insurance agents to sell policies to college-age students.

Tarrant, Marguerite. "Life Insurance for the Uninsurable." *Money Magazine,* March 1976, pp. 49–50.

> A discussion of insurance alternatives for those who do not medically qualify for standard life insurance ratings.

"Universal Life Insurance," *Consumer Reports,* January 1982, pp. 42–44.

> A discussion of this hybrid form of insurance and comparison with traditional whole life.

"What's Happening to Life Insurance Dividends?" *Consumer Reports,* November 1976, pp. 659–662.

> A discussion of the practice, on the part of some life insurance companies, of reducing the size of dividends for older policyholders.

CHUCK AND NANCY ANDERSON

Insuring Chuck's Life

Chuck and Nancy have a whole life policy with a face amount of $20,000 payable to Nancy upon Chuck's death. The dividends from the whole life policy are applied to the purchase of paid-up additions. The Andersons also have a mortgage term policy to cover the amount of the mortgage payments due on their home if Chuck dies before the mortgage is paid off. The face amount of this term policy decreases each year by the amount that the total balance due on their mortgage has decreased.

The Andersons have total benefits of $34,500 that could be received now. The whole life policy costs them $360 a year in premiums; the mortgage term costs $65 a year; and the paid-up additions cost $145 in dividends from the whole life policy. The annual total amount the Andersons are paying for life insurance is $570.

Now that his children are growing up, Chuck feels that he needs more life insurance. He figures that, if he dies, his family will need an average of $26,000 a year until Nancy dies, approximately 50 years from now. Chuck's average earnings (credited for Social Security purposes) have been $20,855 a year. He also wishes to provide for a four-year state college education for each of his children. Since Chuck is considering buying annual renewable term insurance, he found out that for a male age 35 such a policy costs $2 per $1,000 of coverage for the first year, whereas whole life costs $18 per $1,000.

Questions

1. How much life insurance does Chuck need? Use the eight-step procedure and the balance sheet for Chuck and Nancy (Chapter 3). Assume that Chuck has no present coverage and that Nancy would invest the proceeds from his life insurance in a 10 percent money market fund.
2. If Chuck buys term insurance, how much will it cost him the first year to cover his family's needs? How much will it cost him the first year if he buys whole life? Under what circumstances would term be more appropriate than whole life? Under what circumstances would whole life be more appropriate than term? Under what circumstances might Chuck want to surrender his present whole life policy and buy only term insurance?

III

Getting the Most Out of Your Income

In Chapters 5 through 9 you learned how to protect your home, property, health, income-producing ability, and life from many common perils. You learned how to do this with minimum cost and without duplicating you insurance coverage.

The strategy for getting the most out of your income will be dealt with in Chapters 10 through 14. This strategy is to avoid such unnecessary drains on your income as overpaid income taxes, excessive consumer credit costs, an improperly made decision to rent or buy a place to live, or an improperly purchased car, major appliance, or home. Chapters 10 through 14 discuss these and similar problems. You will learn how to minimize your income taxes; how to analyze the costs, dangers, and benefits of credit; and when and how to buy a car, major appliances, and a home. This strategy for getting the most out of your income should enable you to free more money for use in increasing your total income, the strategy discussed in Unit IV.

10

Federal Income Taxes on Individuals

Federal taxation of personal income is ever changing. There have been four recent major changes in federal income tax laws—1976, 1978, 1981, and 1982. It probably represents one of the most complex bodies of laws, rules, and regulations in history. There are three reasons for this.

1. The sources and nature of personal income are so complex that any attempt to tax that income is bound to become complex itself.
2. Income taxation is used not only to raise revenues for the federal government, but also to benefit certain forms of economic activity. For example, certain economic sectors that Congress deems to be of vital interest to the nation (e.g., home ownership) enjoy preferential tax treatment to attract home buyers.
3. There is a large and divergent group of special interests that lobby to have personal and corporate income tax laws written more favorably or to have the more stringent applications of tax laws softened for them.

The end result of all this is the quagmire of a tax system we now find ourselves in. This was acknowledged by the Commissioner of the Internal Revenue Service in a 1976 speech: ". . . we had a choice this year of putting out a form that was comprehensible but illegal, or legal but incomprehensible, and naturally we opted for the latter."° Since 1976, tax law compliance has become so complex and expensive that there is a rising public outcry for a simplified, one-page, flat-rate income tax system.

What can you reasonably expect to learn about such a complex and ambiguous subject in just one chapter? This chapter will focus on the basic elements of our income tax system—gross income, deductions, and exemptions. It is beyond the scope of this chapter to give you the tools to prepare a tax return of even average complexity. Instead, we will focus on the planning and professional help aspects.

°*The Journal of Taxation*, May 1976, p. 319.

In addition, this chapter offers some common methods of tax reduction and tax planning that should enable you to assess the tax effects of various financial actions, thus helping you make financial decisions and pay no more tax than is reasonable. There are few significant tax reduction strategies that are of real value to your net worth, even if you are wealthy. Subsequent chapters will treat the tax aspects of particular subjects as part of the general discussion of those subjects.

Tax reductions are not as possible with other forms of personal taxation. Social Security is the same for all. Property taxes vary with the value of property. Sales taxes represent a fixed percentage of the value of items purchased. The only other taxes that warrant some effort at tax savings are gift and estate taxes, which will be discussed in Chapter 22.

GROSS INCOME

Gross income serves as the starting point for all income tax computations. As defined by the Internal Revenue Service (IRS), it includes all income in the form of money, property, and services that is not, by law, expressly exempt from tax. Income that must be included consists of wages, salary, tips, rent, royalties, interest, dividends, alimony, bonuses, commissions, gambling winnings, and even buried treasure.

Exclusions are items *not* considered income for income tax purposes. Among these items, the main category is various forms of insurance proceeds.

- Accident, health, and term life insurance premiums paid by an employer (Premiums for over $50,000 of group life insurance are included as taxable income.)
- Accident and health insurance proceeds
- Annuity payments that are a return of an original investment
- Damage payments received for injury or illness
- Death payments to survivors of Armed Forces personnel who died on active duty
- Disability pensions (including workers' compensation)
- Employee death proceeds up to $5,000
- Life insurance proceeds
- Portion of certain pension or annuity payments attributable to a taxpayer's contributions
- Railroad Unemployment Insurance Act benefits
- Self-insured medical reimbursement payments from qualified plans
- Social Security benefits (both disability and retirement)
- Veterans' disability compensation benefits
- Veterans' insurance proceeds and dividends paid either to veterans or to their beneficiaries
- Veterans' pensions paid either to veterans or to their families

Other exclusions are not easily categorized in a large group or groups.

- Armed Forces trailer-moving allowance
- Amounts received for expenses incident to education
- Benefit payments from a general welfare fund in the interest of the general public
- Bequests
- Campaign contributions received by candidates
- Car-pool receipts by automobile owner

- Child-care reimbursement payments to foster parents
- Child-support payments received from a divorced spouse
- Clergy member's rental allowance
- Combat service pay
- Dividends from U.S. corporations (up to $100 tax-free annually on separate return, $200 on joint return)
- $125,000 of the gain on sale of residence for individuals 55 and over
- Gifts and inheritances
- Federal income tax refunds
- Interest on debt obligations (bonds and notes) of states and municipalities
- Peace Corps travel and living allowances
- Pulitzer Prize
- Scholarships and fellowship grants
- School board allowance for transporting children to and from school
- Stock rights and stock dividends
- Strike benefits in the form of food or rent
- Unemployment compensation benefits, unless total taxpayer income exceeds $12,000 ($18,000 for a joint return)
- Veterans' allowance benefits for education, subsistence, training

This list of tax-exempt income is partial and does not indicate qualifications or limitations that may accompany certain items. Therefore, when considering items that you may be able to exclude from gross income, be sure to check a more extensive list, which may be found in Publication 17, *Your Federal Income Tax—for Individuals*. (This publication is revised annually by the Internal Revenue Service and published by the Government Printing Office.) None of the exclusions from gross income need be listed on your tax return.

DEDUCTIONS

Deductions are expenses that may be subtracted from one's gross income or adjusted gross income. No item may be considered a deduction unless a specific provision in the tax law or regulations makes it one, and even then it may be qualified or limited in some way. Deductions show up in two places on your tax return. Some deductions are subtracted from gross income to arrive at *adjusted gross income*. The IRS calls these "adjustments to income." These deductions are generally derived from business expenses that arise for probably less than half of all individual taxpayers. These deductions must always be itemized—that is, listed on the tax return. Here is a partial list.

- Alimony payments
- Business expenses from operating a business—depreciation, employee benefits, entertainment, gifts, loan interest, property rents and repairs, salaries, travel and transportation
- Capital losses
- Convention expenses
- Education travel expenses required by employer
- Expenses of traveling salesperson
- Lobbying expenses

- Moving expenses due to job transfers (for moves over 35 miles)
- Payments by an employee to an individual retirement account (IRA)
- Payments by self-employed persons to a retirement fund (Keogh)
- Travel expenses ordinary and necessary for the performance of employment (not commuting)

A second category of deductions applies to all individual taxpayers. These are subtracted from adjusted gross income to give *income before exemptions.*

In the Tax Tables or Tax Rate Schedules each taxpayer is automatically granted a deduction against adjusted gross income (the *zero bracket amount*) equal to $3,400 if you file a joint return ($2,300 if you file a single or head-of-household return). In addition, if you have itemized deductions that are allowed to be subtracted from adjusted gross income, you may take these to the extent that they *exceed* the zero bracket amount. There are certain requirements you must adhere to if you and your spouse decide to file separate returns. IRS Publication 17 can assist you here.

How will you know whether you have *excess itemized deductions* which you should take in addition to the zero bracket amount?

1. Know the major categories of deductions against adjusted gross income that can be itemized:
    - Contributions to qualified charities
    - Interest on indebtedness
    - Nonfederal taxes
    - Dental, hospital, and medical expenses
    - Net losses because of casualties or theft
    - Ordinary and necessary expenses incurred for employer's benefit
    - Expenses of earning nonbusiness income

2. Keep records throughout the year of expenditures that qualify as these types of deductions. Certain expenditures (most commonly sales taxes) can be estimated at the end of the year from tables in the tax booklet in which Form 1040 comes. However, keep your sales receipts for expensive items such as cars, furniture, and building materials. The sales tax on these purchases can be deducted in addition to the amounts shown in the tables.

3. If your itemized deductions exceed the zero bracket amount, take the excess as a deduction from adjusted gross income to determine income before exemptions.

Here is a partial list of itemized deductions, set out in major categories.

Medical, dental, and hospital expenses

- Medical, dental, and hospital expenses (including prescription drugs and insurance premiums) in excess of 5 percent of adjusted gross income

Taxes

- General sales tax (state and local)
- Personal property tax (state and local), including auto registration fees above a certain figure (varies by state)

- Real property taxes (state, local, and foreign)
- State and local income taxes (those actually paid or withheld during the tax year)

Interest

- Finance charge on installment payments, charge account credit, and small loans
- Interest on home mortgage, including *points* (Chapter 14) to buyer
- Margin account interest or other interest on money borrowed for investment (subject to certain maximum limits)

Charitable contribution

- Certain automobile expenses (e.g., use of car for charitable work)
- Contributions of cash or property to qualified charitable and nonprofit organizations

Casualty losses

- Personal and property casualty losses in excess of 10 percent of adjusted gross income (and not reimbursed by insurance)

Miscellaneous

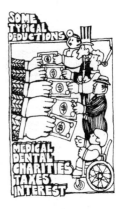

- Fees for tax consultation and preparation of your return
- Fees for bond interest collection
- Gambling losses to the extent of gambling winnings
- Investment advisory fees, expenses for investment publications, and the like
- Obtaining employment (fees paid)
- Personal nonbusiness bad debts (reported as a short-term capital loss)
- Professional publications used by employees
- Professional societies' dues paid by employees
- Safe-deposit box fees (for boxes used to hold documents related to the production of income, such as stocks and bonds)
- Union dues paid by employees

Some expenses cannot be used as deductions. Among these are:

- Adoption fees
- Commuting costs
- Estate taxes
- Food
- FICA employee taxes
- Funeral expenses
- Gift taxes
- Life insurance premiums
- Passport fees
- Rent
- Self-employment tax
- Social Security tax paid for domestic help
- Tax penalty payments
- Traffic tickets or fines
- Uniforms for military personnel
- Upkeep on pleasure car

The Economic Recovery Tax Act of 1981 provided a tax incentive for charitable giving by taxpayers whose total deductions do not exceed the zero bracket amount. The amount of the charitable deduction for those who do not itemize is limited as follows:

Year	Maximum Allowed Deduction
1983	25% of the first $100 of contributions
1984	25% of the first $300 of contributions
1985	50% of all contributions
1986	100% of all contributions

As you can see, the biggest benefit is in 1985 and 1986. From a tax point of view, you might consider deferring 1984 contributions until 1985 and 1986. This tax law provision is scheduled to terminate after 1986.

EXEMPTIONS

Exemptions represent specific, stated amounts that, under certain circumstances, can be deducted from *income before exemptions* to arrive at *taxable income*. The amount allowed for each exemption is $1,000.

The most commonly applied exemptions are for oneself, for a spouse when filing a joint return, and for each dependent. To qualify as an exemption, the dependent must be recognized as a dependent by law (as are most close relatives and adopted or foster children), have over 50 percent of his or her support furnished by the taxpayer who wants to take this additional exemption, and have a gross annual income that is lower than the level at which he or she would be required to file a return ($1,000 for

TABLE 10-1

Changes in Federal Tax Rates
by the Economic Recovery Tax Act of 1981

Income Bracket for Selected Taxable Incomes	Tax on Low End of Income Bracket Range, Plus Rate on Income in the Bracket							
	1980		1982		1983		1984	
	Tax	Rate	Tax	Rate	Tax	Rate	Tax	Rate
For Joint Returns								
$11,900-16,000	$ 1,404	21%	$ 1,234	19%	$ 1,149	17%	$ 1,085	16%
16,000-20,200	2,265	24	2,013	22	1,846	19	1,741	18
20,200-24,600	3,273	28	2,937	25	2,644	23	2,497	22
24,600-29,900	4,505	32	4,037	29	3,656	26	3,465	25
29,900-35,200	6,201	37	5,574	33	5,034	30	4,790	28
35,200-45,800	8,162	43	7,323	39	6,624	35	6,274	33
45,800-60,000	12,720	49	11,457	44	10,334	40	9,772	38
60,000-85,600	19,678	54	17,705	49	16,014	44	15,168	42
For Single Returns								
$ 8,500-10,800	$ 1,072	21%	$ 948	19%	$ 866	17%	$ 835	16%
10,800-12,900	1,555	24	1,385	22	1,257	19	1,203	18
12,900-15,000	2,059	26	1,847	23	1,656	21	1,581	20
15,000-18,200	2,605	30	2,330	27	2,097	24	2,001	23
18,200-23,500	3,565	34	3,194	31	2,865	28	2,737	26
23,500-28,800	5,367	39	4,837	35	4,349	32	4,115	30
28,800-34,100	7,434	44	6,692	40	6,045	36	5,705	34
34,100-41,500	9,766	49	8,812	44	7,953	40	7,507	38
41,500-55,300	13,392	55	12,068	50	10,913	45	10,319	42

taxable year 1980). A child under 19 or a full-time student (no age limit) may be claimed as an exemption, no matter what the person's gross income, as long as the support condition is met and he or she is your child.

You qualify for an extra exemption if you are 65 or older, if your spouse is 65 or older (when filing a joint return), if you are blind at the end of the taxable year, or if your spouse is blind at the end of the taxable year (when filing a joint return). Other blind dependents do not qualify as exemptions.

CREDITS

Some expenses may be taken as credits against taxes due. For example, 20 percent of child-care expenses for working parents is allowed as a tax credit. There is a limit of $480 for one child and $960 for two or more children. For taxpayers with incomes under $30,000, the percentage may be as high as 30 percent and the tax credit limits are correspondingly as high as $720 and $1,440. Other credits for such things as political donations and energy conservation are explained in Publication 17.

TAX COMPUTATION

The income, deductions, and exemptions of most taxpayers entitle them to compute their taxes using one of the four Tax Tables; these tables have been constructed by the IRS to take the zero bracket amount and personal exemptions into account. For certain taxpayers, generally those with high adjusted gross incomes and/or excess itemized deductions, the Tax Rate Schedules will apply. The Tax Rate Schedules also have the zero bracket amount built in. Portions of two Tax Rate Schedules are shown in Table 10-1, with the appropriate taxes and rates for 1980, 1982, 1983, and 1984. To determine which is appropriate for you, consult Publication 17.

Who Must File a Return

All U.S. citizens, including minors, and all aliens residing in this country must file tax returns on either Form 1040 or 1040A (short form) by April fifteenth each year if their gross income for the previous year exceeded certain limits (see Table 10-2).

TABLE 10-2
Selected Filing Requirements for Taxpayers

Characteristics of Taxpayers	If Gross Income Exceeds
Single person, including head of household	
Under 65	$3,300
65 or older	4,300
Surviving spouse	4,400
Married persons filing joint return	5,400
One spouse 65 or older	6,400
Both spouses 65 or older	7,400
Married persons filing separate returns	1,000

(You may apply on Form 4068 for two months' automatic extension of time for filing your return.) U.S. citizens living abroad and nonresident aliens who have earned money in the United States are required to file returns by June fifteenth each year if their incomes for the preceding year exceeded these limits.

Joint and Separate Returns

If you are married, you and your spouse may elect to file either a joint return or separate returns. (A married individual may not be entitled to file a joint return if either spouse uses a different taxable year or at any time of the year is a nonresident alien.) In most instances, especially those in which one spouse has little or no income, filing a joint return results in a lower tax. Surviving spouses may elect to file either a joint or a separate return for the year in which their spouse died. Since this decision may be closely related to the settlement of the deceased's estate, you should consult your attorney and the executor of the estate before deciding how to file.

Prior to 1982 two unmarried people who each had taxable income were discouraged from getting married by the nature of the federal income tax. For example, if each had $20,000 of taxable income, as single people in 1981 they would each pay $4,170, for a total of $8,340 in taxes. If they were married, they would pay $10,202 tax on their joint return!

The Economic Recovery Tax Act of 1981 reduced this problem somewhat by allowing for a deduction from taxable income of an amount equal to 10 percent of the lower-earning spouse's "qualified income," up to a maximum deduction of $3,000 beginning in 1983. Thus, in our example above, the couple, if married, would pay a joint return tax of $9,352 (the tax on $38,000, or $40,000 minus 10 percent of $20,000).

TABLE 10-3'

Contents of Tax Schedules

Schedule	Contents
A	Itemized deductions against adjusted gross income
B	Dividend and interest income that cannot be included directly on Form 1040
C	Profits or losses from one's business
D	Gains and losses on sales or exchanges of property
E	Income from pensions, annuities, rents, royalties, partnerships, estates, trusts, small business corporations, and miscellaneous sources
F	Farm income and expenses
G	Income averaging computations
R	Retirement income credit
SE	Self-employment tax
TC	Tax computation for taxpayers who cannot use the Tax Tables or itemize deductions

Form 1040, Schedules, and Other Forms

All individual taxpayers file their tax returns on Form 1040 or Form 1040A.

Some taxpayers may have to include certain schedules to give details about the year's financial transactions. Most of these schedules are included in the tax booklet in which Form 1040 comes. Schedules not included in the booklet can be obtained from an IRS office, or often at a bank or savings and loan association. The information asked for in these schedules is shown in Table 10-3. If you need to include one or more of them with your next return, you may want to consult either the local IRS office or a private tax consulting firm for advice.

From time to time you may have other contacts with the Internal Revenue Service. Table 10-4 shows the various forms that may be used. All of these forms except the W-2 and the 1099 are for individual use.

TABLE 10-4

Purpose of IRS Forms

Form	Purpose
SS-5	To obtain a Social Security number, replace a lost card, or obtain a Federal Taxpayer Identification number
W-2	To indicate total wages subject to withholding, the amount of income tax withheld by an employer, and the total amount withheld for Social Security taxes (FICA)
W-4	To file with an employer the number of dependent exemptions
W-4E	To obtain an exemption from withholding if no tax liability is foreseen (primarily for students and retired individuals)
843	To apply for a refund of excess FICA taxes
935	To grant power of attorney to another individual for a tax return
1040A	To file a return when deductions are not itemized and gross income consists only of wages and of dividends and interest under $400 each
1040ES	To declare an estimated tax
1040X	To amend an already filed return
1099	To inform the IRS how much income was made on accounts (filed by banks, savings and loan associations, brokerage houses, and similar institutions)
2119	To declare the sale or exchange of a residence
2333	To request blank income tax forms
2441	To claim child-care credit
4070	To report tips
4506	To request a copy of a previously filed return
2688/4868	To apply for an extension of time in which to file a return
5695	To claim energy conservation credit

An Example

An analysis of the tax computations for the Martinezes' 1981 income may be helpful. Their combined gross income includes $32,000 salary ($20,000 for Jose and $12,000 for Dolores Martinez for part-time work), $300 (interest from their savings account), and $100 (raffle prize). The $500 they received in health insurance proceeds is not included in the total gross income of $32,400. Jose changed jobs, and so the Martinez family moved in early 1981. The deductible expenses related to moving were $800, which they deduct from their gross income ($32,400). Their adjusted gross income is $31,600. Jose and Dolores plan to file a joint return and they have no excess itemized deductions. Therefore, their adjusted gross income ($31,600) becomes their income before exemptions. From this amount three $1,000 exemptions (for Jose, Dolores, and their son) are subtracted to arrive at the taxable income. On this final amount of $28,600 the Martinezes compute their tax, using the Tax Rate Schedules. (They could also have used the Tax Tables by looking up their adjusted gross income.)

Mr. and Mrs. Martinez decide to compare what their tax would be if they filed separate returns with what it would be if they filed a joint return. Table 10-5 gives the figures they arrived at. As you can see, filing separate returns (in a noncommunity property state) would result in a $5,913 tax, whereas the tax on a joint return would be $5,721.

WITHHOLDING

One of the most common ways of paying the federal income tax (as well as the Social Security tax) is for an employer to withhold a portion of each employee's income

TABLE 10-5

Comparison of Tax Computation for Separate Returns and Joint Return

Elements of Tax Computation	Separate Returns		Joint Return
	Jose	Dolores	
Gross income[a]	$20,400	$12,000	$32,400
Deductions from gross income	800	—	800
Adjusted gross income	19,600	12,000	31,600
Excess itemized deductions	0	0	0
Income before exemptions	19,600	12,000	31,600
Exemptions[b]	2,000	1,000	3,000
Taxable income	17,600	11,000	28,600
Tax[c]	4,041	1,872	5,721

[a] In community property states, one-half of all community property income would be claimed by each spouse on his or her separate return.

[b] Because he has the larger income and is, therefore, in a higher tax bracket, Jose takes both himself and his son as exemptions in this example.

[c] Tax computed from 1981 rate tables.

and send it to the IRS within three business days (or up to three months, for firms with small payrolls). For income tax, the portion withheld depends on the level of job income and the number of withholding exemptions claimed.

As of July 1, 1983, payers of interest (in excess of $150 per year to each payee) and of dividends must withhold 10 percent of the amount and pay it to the IRS. Certain low-income or exempt taxpayers may file certificates with the payer claiming exemption from withholding. This 1982 law (Tax Equity Act) will greatly add to the private sector's expense and nuisance. It might have been simpler and more straightforward to raise the tax rate.

For example, Jose Martinez will make $20,000 this year from his job as a hospital administrator. His income tax on that amount will be withheld by his employer and sent to the federal government; at the end of the year Jose should have paid all the necessary tax on his income from that job. The hospital will summarize Jose's tax record for the year and send the summary to him on a W-2 form sometime in January. This form gives Jose figures to use in filling out his tax return. The hospital also sends a copy to the IRS to use in checking his tax return. Similarly, beginning in July 1983, Jose will have $30 withheld from the interest on his savings account.

ESTIMATED TAX

In spite of withholding, many taxpayers with sources of income other than wages would incur a large tax liability on their annual income tax return were they not required to estimate their tax ahead of time and make quarterly payments. The estimated tax gives the federal government a means of quickly collecting taxes on income not subject to withholding. If it were not for the estimated tax and withholding, the Treasury would have to wait until April 15 of each year to collect taxes on income made during the previous taxable year. Because of its revenue needs, the U.S. government is compelled to collect income taxes as quickly as possible after income is earned.

Filing Requirements

Estimated tax is filed on Form 1040ES. This form is composed of instructions for filing, a worksheet for your computations, four vouchers (one to accompany each of your installment payments), and four addressed envelopes in which your vouchers and payments are to be sent. In general, you must submit 1040ES by April 15 of the current taxable year if you can reasonably expect that your total income tax (including self-employment tax) will be $100 or more greater than the amount to be withheld by your employer. Specifically, a declaration must be filed if your gross income can reasonably be expected to consist of wages subject to withholding exceeding (1) $20,000 and you are an unmarried individual, a surviving spouse entitled to special tax rates, a head-of-household, or a married individual whose spouse has no earned income; (2) $10,000 and you are a married individual whose spouse has an earned income; (3) $5,000 and you are a married individual not entitled to file a joint declaration. The last condition under which you must file a declaration is if you can reasonably expect that more than $500 income will come from sources other than wage earnings.

Computation Procedure

The estimated tax is computed on Form 1040ES as follows:

1. Estimate your income, deductions, and exemptions for the current taxable year.
2. Compute your tax on this amount from the table that suits your circumstances and comes with the form.
3. Add any self-employment tax (to be discussed later in this chapter) to this amount.
4. Deduct the amount expected to be withheld by your employer (ask for an estimate) plus any tax credits (credits against future taxes because of past over-payments) from the amount derived in step 3.
5. The remaining amount is your estimated tax. If it is less than $100, you are not required to file Form 1040ES. If it is $100 or over, your estimated tax should be divided into four equal amounts and paid in installments on April 15, June 15, and September 15 of the current year and on January 15 of the following year. The IRS will not bill you for each installment; you will have to remember to make your payments on time.

Avoiding underpayments is important because an interest charge is assessed against delinquent amounts. The interest rate is set each January 1 and July 1 at the average bank prime rate in effect from three to nine months earlier. Delinquent amounts are computed by the IRS as the difference between 80 percent of the amount that should have been paid and the amount, if any, actually paid. This penalty will not be applied, however, even in the case of an underpayment if, for example, the combination of estimated tax and withholding tax paid is equal to or more than the combined income and self-employment taxes paid for the previous taxable year.

TAXES ON CAPITAL GAINS

Taxes are levied against income received from the sale of a capital asset such as real estate, stocks and bonds, jewelry, and furs. A *capital gain* is the gain, after commissions and brokerage fees, resulting from the sale or exchange of a capital asset. Of course, a *capital loss*, rather than a capital gain, may result from such a sale. A long-term capital gain or loss occurs when an asset was owned for more than one year. A short-term capital gain or loss occurs when an asset was held for a shorter period prior to the sale. A tax advantage applies to long-term capital gains in that only 40 percent of the realized gain must be included in taxable income.

In general, long-term capital gains income can be viewed as the cumulation of one or more years' ordinary income, received in one lump sum. Let us assume that you bought a piece of real estate for $30,000 and sold it 10 years later, realizing $60,000—a taxable gain of $30,000. Theoretically, this is equivalent to $3,000 income for each of the 10 years you held the property. However, you could not pay income tax on that $3,000 each year because the capital appreciation did not occur regularly or in easily determined amounts. If the gain were to be taxed at the progressive rates that apply to ordinary income for the year during which you sold the property, the $30,000 added to your regular income for the year would place you in a much higher tax bracket and the resulting tax bill would be more than if taxes had been paid on an extra $3,000 each year.

The capital gains tax was created to protect people against unnecessarily high tax rates where capital appreciation has occurred over an extended period of time. Another reason for a capital gains tax is to encourage people to invest in capital assets since the profits they make because of long-term appreciation will be taxed at rates that are lower than for regular income.

Before the Tax Reform Act of 1978, 50 percent of capital gains was included in taxable income. With the inclusion of a special preference tax as well, capital gains were taxed at a rate as high as 49 percent. After 1978, the maximum rate was 28 percent. A Treasury Department study done under the Carter administration showed that this cut in rates did indeed encourage taxpayers to take more capital gains income. In 1979, the reduced tax rates cost the government $2.6 billion, but the dramatic increase in reported capital gains income resulted in $2.5 billion, and so there was only a $100 million net loss to the U.S. Treasury. Beginning with the 1980 Tax Act, the maximum capital gains rate is only 20 percent (40 percent of the gain included in income and taxed at the reduced maximum tax bracket of 50 percent.)

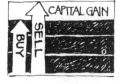

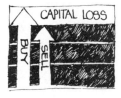

Computation Procedure

Computing your capital gains tax can seem rather complicated since there may be many gains and losses, both long-term and short-term, in any one year. We recommend that you use the five-step procedure below and the five guidelines that follow it to ensure that you accomplish this task correctly. The first three steps must be done for each gain and loss, whether long-term or short-term, so that in steps 4 and 5 you can determine your net short- and long-term gains or losses. The guidelines tell how to use these net gains and losses in determining your gross income and thus your capital gains tax.

1. Determine whether the gain or loss qualifies for tax treatment. All gains from the sale or exchange of capital assets must be included in gross income. All capital losses, except those due to the sale of your house or personal effects, may be deducted from gross income. (Depending on the amount, this deduction may have to be taken over a period of years.)
2. Determine the amount of the gain or loss by first calculating the original value or purchase price of the capital asset involved. (Remember to include any expenses you incurred in acquiring this asset, the cost of any capital improvements you made to it, and any expenses incurred in selling or exchanging it.) Then subtract the adjusted original value or purchase price from the final exchange value or sale price.
3. Determine whether the transaction qualifies as a short-term or long-term gain or loss.
4. Determine the net short-term capital gain or loss by subtracting your short-term

capital losses from your short-term capital gains. For example, if your short-term capital gains for the taxable year are $1,500 and your short-term capital losses are $1,000, then your net short-term capital gain is $500.

5. Determine the net long-term capital gain or loss by using the same procedure as in step 4.

Five Guidelines

1. When a net short-term gain is greater than a net long-term loss, all of the excess should be included in gross income on your tax return.
2. When there is a net short-term gain and no net long-term loss, the entire gain is included in gross income.
3. When a net short-term loss is greater than a net long-term gain (or there is no net long-term gain), the excess (up to $3,000) is deducted from gross income. Any remaining excess is carried forward to the next year when it is offset first against net short-term gains, then against net long-term gains, then against $3,000 of gross income. This offsetting is done each year until the excess is exhausted. (The excesses carried forward each year must be shown on Schedule D, which you use to compute your capital gains.)
4. When a net long-term gain is greater than a net short-term loss (or there is no net short-term loss), only 40 percent of the excess is included in gross income.
5. When there is a net long-term loss greater than a net short-term gain, 50 percent of this excess up to $3,000 is deducted from gross income. Any remaining portion of the excess is carried forward to the next year when it is offset against first net long-term gains, then net short-term gains, then up to $3,000 of gross income, and so on for the remaining years until it is exhausted.

This ability to deduct capital losses results in the popular practice of selling the stocks or bonds that are losers just before year-end in order to generate the realized capital losses. We do not recommend this practice *except when you are taking short-term losses to offset short-term gains*. If you take your long-term losses, switch to another depressed-value investment, and are eventually successful, you will have an equally large capital gain then as the one you offset now. In the process, you would merely have reduced your investment gains by the amount of the transaction costs to make the switch—and enriched your broker.

Capital Gains Taxes and Selling a Home

Capital gains taxes on the sale of your home receive special consideration. If you sell your principal place of residence at a profit, you do not have to pay a capital gains tax if you buy or start to build another home with the proceeds within the four-year period extending from 24 months before to 24 months after the sale. If you do not buy or build a home of at least the same value, whether or not you actually reinvest all the sale proceeds, you will be taxed on the difference in cost (but no more than the total amount of the realized capital gain). Take, for example, a $100,000 house sale on which you get $50,000 cash. If you buy a house for $100,000 or more, even if you use less than the $50,000 cash by virtue of taking out a bigger mortgage, taxes will be deferred on that sale. But if you buy a house for $90,000, then because your new house is $10,000 lower in price than the old house, you will have to pay taxes on the $10,000 capital gain.

If you sell your home and do not reinvest the proceeds in another house, you will want to minimize the capital gains tax you might owe. To do this, you want your purchase cost of the house you are selling to be as high as can be legally justified. All money that you spent to *improve* the long-term value of the property can likely be added to your purchase cost. For example, you should keep receipts for landscaping purchases, expenses for home remodeling, or outlays for the installation of a sprinkler system. You will want to report these on Form 2119 as an addition to your carried-forward basis each time you sell or exchange your residence, so that if you eventually do pay a tax, it will be as small as possible.

THE FEDERAL INCOME TAX AS A PROGRESSIVE TAX

Probably the most important feature of the federal income tax system is that it is *progressive* as opposed to *regressive*. The more income you make, the higher the percentage that is taken from it in taxes. The progressive structure of our tax system is illustrated in Figure 10-1. Increasing amounts of income are taxed at increasing rates.

For example, on $24,600 of taxable income the 1983 tax for a married couple filing a joint return is $3,656, or approximately 15 percent. For every $1 of the next $5,300 of taxable income, 26¢ must be paid to the federal government. This $24,600–$29,900 range is an example of a *tax bracket*—the spread of income that is

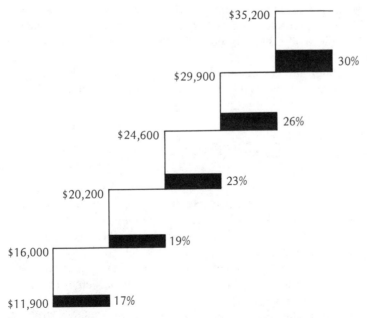

Note: Percentages are marginal tax rates for married persons filing a joint return in 1983.

FIGURE 10-1
Progressive structure of
federal income tax
system.

PROGRESSIVE TAX

subject to a certain percentage of taxation, or tax rate. The fact that the total tax of $3,656 is equal to 15 percent of the income is a result of averaging together the taxes from brackets ranging from 0 percent to 26 percent.

This tax system is unlike the Social Security tax, which is *proportional;* that is, the tax rate is the same for all people. Because the Social Security tax is levied only up to a fixed amount of income ($32,400 in 1982), it has a regressive effect. In other words, people with earnings of $32,400 or less pay a larger percentage of their total earnings in Social Security taxes than do people who earn more than $32,400.

Two dangers arise when progressive tax structures are taken to the extreme. One, capital investment (our primary means of creating jobs and generating income) is discouraged. Investors are not willing to put up capital to form new enterprises if their after-tax return does not justify the assumption of such investment risks. Two, the individual's incentive to work is thwarted. When the federal income tax is added to state income taxes, Social Security taxes, and sales and property taxes, many people find that they must work three to six months each year just to pay all their various taxes.

Marginal Tax Rates

When making certain financial decisions, it is important to take into account the tax effect of various alternatives. One of the simplest ways to determine the tax effect of additional income or deductible expense items is to use the *marginal tax rate*—the highest tax rate at which, given a particular level of income, any additional income is taxed.

Your marginal tax rate is different from your *aggregate income tax rate*—the average of the rates for all the preceding levels of income. For example, in 1984 on amounts over $15,000 of taxable income, for a single person the marginal tax rate is 23 percent. The aggregate income tax rate is derived by dividing the total taxes paid ($2,001) by the total taxable income ($15,000); the result is approximately 13.3 percent.

To understand how the marginal tax rate works, let us take as an example the difference in tax on 1984 taxable income between $15,000 and $18,200.

Taxable Income	Tax	Marginal Tax Rate
$18,200	$2,737	
−15,000	−2,001	$\dfrac{736}{3,200} = 23$ percent
$ 3,200	$ 736	

This marginal tax rate means that 23¢ of every $1 of taxable income between $15,000 and $18,200 goes to the federal government in income tax. Conversely, every $1 of deductible expense that reduces one's taxable income between $15,000 and $18,200 represents 23¢ in taxes saved. With our progressive tax structure, in lower income brackets the percentage rate is less than 23 percent and in higher income brackets it is more. This variation can readily be seen by examining the IRS Tax Rate Schedules (Table 10-1).

As mentioned earlier, the Tax Reform Act of 1978 created four Tax Tables for the use of most taxpayers. The objective was to make tax determination easier by integrating the zero bracket amount and exemptions into the tables. One disadvantage now is that if you use the Tax Tables, you cannot readily determine what your top marginal tax rate is. To find your top marginal rate, take your Tax Table income and subtract $1000 times your number of exemptions. This calculation will give you the taxable income to look up in the Tax Rate Schedules, where your marginal rate is the percentage figure given for your income bracket.

Assume that Jose Martinez receives a $400 bonus from his employer. If he knows that his taxable income places him in a bracket with a marginal tax rate of 25 percent, he can determine that the additional tax he owes as a result of the bonus will be $100 (25 percent of $400). As a further example, assume that the Martinezes are planning to itemize their deductions. If they buy a home, property taxes and the interest on the mortgage ($1,500 in sum) will qualify as deductions in excess of the zero bracket amount. Provided that these deductions do not change the tax bracket the Martinezes are in, the taxes saved as a result of the additional deductions would be $375 (25 percent of $1,500).

The Effect of Inflation

Inflation has an adverse effect on after-tax income because of the progressive nature of our income tax system. Congress attempted to deal with this problem by increasing the personal exemption from $750 to $1,000 and widening the tax brackets in the Tax Reform Act of 1978. Unfortunately, inflation since 1978 continued to hurt taxpayers. For example, in 1979 through 1981, inflation could have pushed a $20,000 salary up 35 percent to $27,000. In 1978, after $3,829 in federal tax for a single individual with no itemized deductions, a $20,000 salary offered $16,171 in spendable income. In 1981, the new $27,000 salary would have netted only $20,268. (The salary increase was taxed in the 34 percent and 39 percent tax brackets.) Taxes rose 76 percent (from $3,829 to $6,732), while take-home salary rose only 25 percent. In short, the U.S. Treasury profited from inflation, while the taxpayer fell behind in purchasing power.

The Economic Recovery Tax Act of 1981 did a better job of recognizing this problem by enacting a 23 percent gradual reduction in tax rates by 1984 and, beginning in 1985, by automatically indexing tax brackets, the $1,000 personal exemption, and the zero bracket amount to reflect annual changes in the consumer price index. The problem with that solution is that the CPI does not always accurately reflect changes in the true cost of consumer spending.

TWELVE COMMON METHODS OF TAX REDUCTION*

Taxpayers cannot legally evade payment of taxes, but they can avoid paying too much. *Evasion* means an unlawful escape from taxation, whereas *avoidance* refers to legal reduction of the amount of tax that must be paid.

To lower the amount of tax you must pay, you must primarily reduce the amount of your taxable income. Secondarily, you may also increase your tax credits, via certain kinds of equipment and real estate investments.

---

* ©Bailard, Biehl & Kaiser, Inc., 1982, by permission.

Because of the complexity of the tax laws, many people find ways to reduce their income tax, often to the point of paying no tax at all. Sometimes this reduction is the result of the taxpayer's peculiar circumstances at the time. Often it is the result of an individual's focusing only on tax reduction and investing his or her money in a way that yields subpar returns over the long term when compared with other strategies.

The following discussion is not intended to cover all the peculiarities of the tax law. Instead, we will briefly describe a dozen of the most common methods by which taxpayers can wisely reduce their federal income tax.

One: Keep Good Records

There are no studies showing how much tax is unnecessarily paid due to sloppiness, but in our experience too many taxpayers do not take all the itemized deductions they have coming. There are certain relatively easy things to do, at a minimum:

- Keep all canceled checks, and review them for possible deductions at tax time each year.
- Keep receipts for all cash charitable donations, or write them on a slip of paper and put them in your annual tax envelope.
- Keep receipts, in your tax envelope, for all large purchases (furniture, cars, etc.) showing the amount of sales tax paid.
- Keep all year-end charge card or charge account statements. This is where your interest charges for the year are summarized.
- Put any other receipts that might qualify as deductions in the tax envelope that you keep in a convenient place.

Two: Sales Tax as New Homeowners

The IRS provides tables of average sales tax deductions in the tax booklet it sends each year. However, during those years when you're filling up the house and yard, you will probably spend more than the average on sales tax. If you keep *all* receipts showing sales tax during the year, you might well total $100 to $500 more in deductions than allowed by the tables.

Three: Bunch Deductions into Every Other Year

To get maximum value from itemized deductions, you may want either to prepay some of them or to postpone your payment of them so that as many as possible occur in one year and thus exceed the zero bracket amount in aggregate value. In the preceding or succeeding year in which you have minimal itemized deductions, you can use solely the zero bracket amount.

For example, let us assume that if you were to itemize your deductions in each of two years, you would be able to subtract $2,600 from your adjusted gross income each time—$800 less than the zero bracket amount if you file a joint return. Obviously, it would reduce your taxable income more to take the zero bracket amount both years. A more profitable method, however, would be to prepay as much of the second year's $2,600 in the first year as possible (prepay property taxes, for example) so that your itemized deductions would be greater than $3,400. Then you could also deduct your excess itemized deductions the first year and take only the zero bracket amount the second year. (Since 1976, interest can be deducted only in the year in which it is due.)

Four: Tax Money for Your Retirement—
IRA, Keogh, or Salary Reduction

This is one of the biggest tax breaks available to most Americans. In effect, you can get Uncle Sam to help contribute to your possible early retirement. How much can this be worth? If you are in a 30 percent tax bracket and earmark $2,000 of your salary for retirement savings, you have only $1,400 to set aside each year after taxes (30% × $2,000 = $600 income tax on that amount of salary). If you invested that at an average 10 percent yield, you could net 7 percent per year after tax; $1,400 per year at 7 percent return would compound to a nice nest egg of $61,600 after 20 years.

If you put $2,000 into an IRA or Keogh account (at a bank, savings and loan, brokerage house, or mutual fund company), you do not have to pay income tax on that amount of salary; in effect, you would contribute $1,400 and Uncle Sam would match your contribution with the $600 you would otherwise have to pay in income taxes. Further, all earnings within the IRA or Keogh account accumulate tax-free. (When you retire and withdraw funds, of course, all such withdrawals would be included in your taxable income, which would likely be in a lower tax bracket because of your reduced level of income.) The $2,000 invested each year at 10 percent for 20 years would build to a retirement account of $114,600, nearly double what the sum would be without the tax benefits of an IRA or Keogh account! Over 30 years the comparisons are even more dramatic: $132,300 vs. $328,000. Table 10-6 presents these and other comparisons.

To set up and participate in an IRA program, you must earn a salary or wage. You are entitled to contribute up to 100 percent of your compensation, with a limit of $2,000 per year. You may set up your own IRA even if your employer also has a retirement program for its employees. For couples filing a joint return where one spouse has no earned income, the limit is $2,250 per year.

Self-employed persons may contribute to a Keogh plan 15 percent of earnings up to a limit of $15,000 per year. If you have any employees, you must contribute to their retirement as well in your Keogh plan.

The drawback to IRA or Keogh plans is that you cannot withdraw any funds before disability or reaching age 59½ without including the amounts in your taxable income for the year and also paying a 10 percent penalty tax. Thus, you should view these programs as a long-term strategy, and not rely on these assets for anything other than disability, retirement, or an extraordinary emergency.

A similar alternative, which may be offered by your employer, is a salary reduction plan authorized under Secton 401(k) of the Internal Revenue Code. Such a plan may be better than an IRA in several ways: (1) you may contribute up to 10 percent of your salary even if that percentage exceeds $2,000; (2) saving is easier because you use regular payroll reductions; (3) the payroll reductions mean that you save Social Security taxes, provided you are under the $32,000 maximum for that tax; (4)

TABLE 10-6
The Value of a Tax-Sheltered Retirement Program
(IRA or Keogh)

If your marginal tax rate averages	You would have this amount left out of $2,000 of salary to invest	In an IRA/Keogh Uncle Sam would match this much	Investment accumulated at 10% pretax in an IRA/Keogh vs. 10% less tax elsewhere					
			10 years		20 years		30 years	
			IRA/Keogh	Elsewhere	IRA/Keogh	Elsewhere	IRA/Keogh	Elsewhere
20%	$1,600	$ 400	$31,800	$23,200	$114,600	$73,300	$328,000	$180,800
30%	1,400	600	31,800	19,300	114,600	61,600	328,000	132,300
40%	1,200	800	31,800	15,800	114,600	44,200	328,000	94,800
50%	1,000	1,000	31,800	12,600	114,600	33,100	328,000	66,400

you may make hardship withdrawals without paying a 10 percent penalty tax; and (5) there may be more favorable tax treatment of withdrawals in retirement. One disadvantage of such plans is that you generally must accept the investment results of whatever plan is made available by your employer, whereas the choice of investments is completely up to you in an IRA. (See Chapter 15 for more on the types of investments recommended for an IRA.)

Five: Tax-Free Dividends

The law allows each individual taxpayer to receive up to $100 of dividends from common stock or preferred stock ($200 on a joint return). Thus, instead of having all your money earning fully taxable interest, you might buy shares of some large, secure company, say 100 shares costing $15 each where the dividend is $1 per year. In your savings account, $100 of interest results in your paying $20, $30, or $40 of tax, depending on your marginal rate, whereas the first $100 of dividends is tax-free.

Six: Tax-Free Interest

Interest received on municipal bonds (see Chapter 17) is free of federal income tax. If you have a 10 percent savings account and are in a 40 percent tax bracket, you keep only 6 percent per year. You would be better off investing in a good municipal bond yielding 7 percent, and you'd feel a lot better paying no tax on the income.

Table 10-7 indicates the equivalent taxable interest yield you would have to earn in order to equal various municipal bond yields at certain tax brackets. If the figure in the table (for your tax bracket) is higher than the yield on the taxable account you are considering, then you would be better off investing in the corresponding municipal bond. Your after-tax return would be higher even though the stated interest rate is lower.

Seven: Income Averaging

Taxpayers who have significant fluctuations in their incomes from year to year are at a disadvantage because of the progressive structure of income tax rates. In high income years, they pay a larger tax than they would pay on an average of their

TABLE 10-7

Equivalent Taxable Interest Yields

Tax Bracket	Municipal Bond Yield				
	6%	8%	10%	12%	14%
20%	7.5%	10.0%	12.5%	15.0%	17.5%
30%	8.6	11.4	14.3	17.1	20.0
40%	10.0	13.3	16.7	20.0	23.3
50%	12.0	16.0	20.0	24.0	28.0

incomes for each year. Income averaging gives these taxpayers a way to spread their income evenly over a period of five years and thus avoid these problems.

It is up to you to use the averaging procedure if it applies; otherwise you will pay more tax than you should. Even though the computational procedure for income averaging has been simplified somewhat, it is still too extensive to allow full treatment here. The following formula, however, will serve as a quick guide in helping you determine, once you have computed your taxable income for the current year, whether income averaging could save you tax dollars.

1. Take the sum of your taxable incomes for the previous four years, not including the current year.
2. Multiply this sum by 30 percent (0.3).
3. Add $3,000 to this amount.

If your current year's taxable income is larger than the amount computed using the formula, then it may be worth your time to fill out the income averaging form and compare the total tax with the regular tax.

Eight: Income Splitting

This technique involves shifting income from an individual in a high tax bracket to one in a lower tax bracket. For example, if you build up a college fund for your daughter, you may set it up so that the income from the fund goes to her. She will probably pay tax at a lower rate than you do (or maybe no taxes), thus saving tax dollars and making it easier to increase the eventual size of the investment. Custodial gifts can often be used to accomplish such an end.

Let us assume that your current year's taxable income is projected to be $20,200. As a married person filing a joint return, your projected 1984 federal tax should be $2,497. Let us also assume that $800 of your taxable income represents interest earned on an 8 percent savings certificate of $10,000. You have earmarked this investment to provide funds to put your eight-year-old child through college. It is possible to make a gift to your child of the $10,000 savings certificate without incurring federal gift taxes because of available exemptions. By doing this, you will effect two tax savings. First, your projected taxable income will be reduced to $19,400 ($20,200 − $800) and your recomputed tax will be $2,353—a tax savings of $144. Over the 10-year period before your child enters college, your savings could be $1,444 or more. Second, assuming that your child does not have more than $3,300 income in any one year, the interest earned on the certificate should go untaxed each year. Because of compounding, by the tenth year this investment should have grown to $22,000, tax-free. If you had not made the custodial gift, the after-tax value would be $19,000. By this technique of income splitting, your tax savings have caused your child's college fund to increase by an additional $3,000 over a 10-year period.

Nine: Don't Overpay or Underpay the Required Tax

Some people intentionally overwithhold on their income tax so that they can enjoy the delight of a tax refund check. If this is the only way you can force yourself to save money, fine, but remember that Uncle Sam pays no interest while acting as your bank. If you overwithhold by $100 a month, you have lost, say, 8 percent interest on an average balance of $600 at the IRS—$48 in lost interest. That would buy a nice dinner out.

If you underpay the amount required by the estimated tax procedure described earlier, Uncle Sam will charge you interest equal to the prime rate. (Doesn't sound fair, does it?)

Ten: Charitable Gifts of Stocks vs. Cash

Taxpayers who make large charitable gifts are becoming more sophisticated about having Uncle Sam help support their favorite cause. Instead of giving cash, they give certificates of stock whose market price has appreciated above what they paid for it.

Let's look at an example. Ms. Browning put a $10 check in the church offering plate each week for 50 weeks. Ms. Gray simply gave 10 shares of stock at one time during the year, and the market price quoted in the paper for that stock the day of the gift was $50 per share. Both women gave $500 of value (the church probably sold Ms. Gray's stock as soon as possible after receiving it and maybe actually netted $485 after commission costs, depending on the price at the time of sale); and since each was in a 30 percent tax bracket, each saved $150 in taxes as a result of including this charitable gift in her itemized deductions.

But what if Ms. Gray had sold the stock first to raise the $500 cash so that she could put $10 each week in the plate? If the stock had cost her $10 per share to buy over a year ago, she would have to report a long-term capital gain of $40 per share, or $400. Of this, 40 percent, or $160, would be included in her taxable income, and on this she would have to pay a tax of $48 ($160 × her 30 percent tax bracket). Thus, Ms. Gray would not have $500 to give the church, but only $452. (The church does not pay any capital gains tax on the sale because it is a tax-exempt organization.) By giving stock, she in effect gave $452, and the IRS gave $48 (the tax they would otherwise have had). By taking the $500 value as a tax deduction for charity, she saved $150 in taxes, and so the total contribution from Uncle Sam to her church was $198 ($150 + $48). In effect, it cost Ms. Gray only $302 to give $500 of value to her church.

Eleven: Invest in Real Estate

Even if you have only $5,000 to invest in one of the real estate limited partnerships discussed in Chapter 20, you can take advantage of the depreciation deductions allowed by law. Although some of the details are complicated and should be handled by a tax return specialist if you own your own property, the effect is that you can deduct the cost of a building (not the land) and any capital improvements over a 15-year period as a deduction from gross income, whether or not you itemize. If you sell the property, you must report the total of these deductions as a long-term capital gain (as long as you sell the property for at least as much as you paid for it).

Thus, you have taken deductions against ordinary income and report only 40 percent of them as income *if you sell*. The other 60 percent is never reported. You have converted ordinary income to capital gains income. Thus, real estate invest-

ments can result in a profit even if they do not go up in price. This tax incentive can add to the attractiveness of real estate as an investment.

Twelve: Make Your Pleasure Your Business

Many people figure out how to make a profit out of things they enjoy doing, thereby enabling them to deduct as business expenses items that would otherwise be non-deductible personal expenses. This business may be either a spare-time activity or a full-time occupation, depending on its financial possibilities. If you like pets, raise dogs for profit and write off your dog food and vet bills. If you like to travel, become a travel agent, tour guide, or travel writer. If you like tinkering with cars, charge your friend enough labor fees so you can write off the cost of your tools and costs of transportation to the auto parts store and car shows. These kinds of things can be complicated, and so it can pay to get the advice of a tax expert to stay clean with the IRS.

TAXES AND THE RICH

When President John Kennedy proposed reducing the maximum tax rate from 91 percent to 70 percent in the early 1960s, the pundits charged favoritism of the rich at the expense of the economically disadvantaged, assuming that government tax receipts would drop. Actually, the opposite occurred. In 1961 (four years before the top rate went down to 70 percent) total tax collections from individuals with adjusted gross incomes of $100,000 or more amounted to approximately $2.6 billion. In 1966, the second year at the 70 percent top rate, approximately $4.2 billion was collected from this same group. This 62 percent increase in tax revenues cannot be completely explained by having more dollars in circulation (inflation) or general economic growth.

Nevertheless, the great preponderance of personal income taxes is paid by middle-class taxpayers because of their sheer numbers. "Soak the rich" strategies do not significantly increase tax revenues. High tax rates produce real economic disincentives and, proportionately, there just aren't enough rich people to soak to make a big difference. After all, Howard Hughes's entire estate, if turned over to the federal government, would not pay for one day's expenditures.

True, the top 10 percent of all taxpayers in 1978 paid half of all U.S. income taxes that year. However, those nine million taxpayers can scarcely be called "rich" since they include all persons with incomes over $29,414. The top 50 percent of all taxpayers in 1978, those with incomes over $10,960, paid 93.5 percent of the tax bill, up from 91.6 percent in 1973. °

Tax Shelters

Faced with high tax rates, many economically fortunate individuals attempt to gain some relief from their tax burdens. One legal approach is through so-called "tax

---

°*Wall Street Journal*, July 16, 1980, p. 1.

shelters." This term applies to a variety of investment opportunities that allow an investor to derive deductions that can be offset against the investor's income.

There are only three real *tax shelters*—investments that allow the taxes on them to be avoided *permanently:* (1) the conversion of ordinary income to long-term capital gains income through depreciation; (2) the depletion allowance for mineral oil and gas investments; and (3) the investment tax credit. Space considerations do not allow for a fuller explanation of these strategies here. In a reasonably prudent investment portfolio, these factors can save an investor a small percentage of his or her tax bill.

Most other shelters offer merely a *deferral* of taxes from the current year to some time in the future. Thus, only the after-tax return on the taxes deferred is gained. Given the considerable economic risk in tax shelter investments that one may lose all of one's investment, the small return gained here often cannot justify the assumption of such risk.

Contrary to popular opinion, extreme tax sheltering is generally not worth the investment. In general, it is not possible to regain in tax savings all that was put into a tax shelter investment. Thus, while the economic risk of these investments can be minimized, it cannot be avoided. For tax savings to equal the amount invested, the tax shelter must be 100 percent and the tax rate must also be 100 percent.

Don't be misled that somehow the rich are successfully avoiding more than a small portion of their taxes at your expense. Because of their dislike for 50 percent tax rates, they may be avoiding taxes temporarily, but at the potential expense of incurring significant real after-tax investment losses.

The Alternative Minimum Tax

The concept of a minimum income tax was created by the Tax Act of 1969 to prevent wealthy individuals and corporations from escaping taxation by investing in situations that enjoy special tax treatment. Later tax acts amended this to create two different schemes—a minimum tax on preference income and an alternative minimum tax. The Tax Equity Act of 1982 changed this again to a single alternative minimum tax.

The basic concept of this complex provision is that the taxpayer must pay the *greater* of two different methods of calculating his or her tax: (1) the regular method described in this chapter or (2) the alternative minimum tax (AMT). The AMT is equal to 20 percent of the alternative minimum taxable income (AMTI) above $30,000 ($40,000 for a joint return). AMTI is essentially equal to your adjusted gross income plus tax preference items minus a more restricted list of itemized deductions than the normal tax method allows. The most significant tax preference item is the 60 percent excluded portion of a capital gain. Others include the profits in employee stock options, the accelerated portion of depreciation taken on real or leased personal property, and certain deductions on oil drilling programs. Finally, most tax credits, such as the investment tax credit, are not allowed to be used against the AMT.

The end result is that few taxpayers with large incomes (except for municipal bond income) and/or large capital gains will be able to avoid paying some significant amount of tax. If you think that the AMT applies to you, seek the advice of a professional tax return preparer.

ALTERNATIVES FOR TAX RETURN PREPARATION

Not only are U.S. income tax laws complex and incomprehensible to many; they are also subject to differing interpretation from one tax authority to the next. As a result, it has become very difficult to file an error-free return. When the General Accounting Office checked certain returns being audited in 1974, approximately 60 percent contained at least one error as originally prepared. The irony here is that the returns sampled had all been prepared with the assistance of professionals such as CPAs and commercial tax preparers.

Given this perspective on tax return preparation, who or what can you rely on to get this annual task accomplished? Unfortunately, there is no simple, straightforward answer; however, there are several alternatives.

Do It Yourself

Are your financial circumstances simple? In other words, do you not have multiple income sources or deductible expenses? Do you keep good records on a regular basis? Do you enjoy the challenge of form preparation? If you can honestly answer yes to these questions, then you should consider preparing your own tax return.

As mentioned earlier, you will want to have the latest copy of the IRS Publication 17, *Your Federal Income Tax*, on hand. Remember, however, that the IRS is primarily concerned with collecting the nation's tax revenues, whereas the tax courts are charged with the duty of ruling on the correctness of tax interpretations. Therefore, the IRS should not be viewed as an impartial source of information. You might also obtain a privately published guide to get a non-IRS perspective on important tax matters that concern you.

You can have the IRS assist you by phone or at a local IRS office while you prepare your return. When requesting help, you should diplomatically try to determine how much training and experience the individual has. Remember the following points: the IRS does not have an untarnished record in error-free return preparation; it tends to give assistance from its revenue-gathering bias; and the courts have ruled that IRS advice is not binding if your return is subsequently audited.

You will give yourself the best opportunity to file a correct return if you do not wait until the evening of April 14 to begin preparing your return.

IRS Assistance

The IRS will prepare your return for you if you meet all of the following qualifications:

1. Your adjusted gross income is $20,000 or less ($40,000 or less if you are married and filing a joint return).
2. Your income consists only of wages, salaries, tips, pensions, annuities, dividends, and/or interest.

3. You do not itemize your deductions against adjusted gross income.
4. You do not use income averaging.
5. You file by April 15.

Private Assistance

It is a common joke that, each time "comprehensive" tax legislation is passed, the bill should be labeled "Professional Tax Preparers' Relief Act" because the increased tax complexities drive more taxpayers to seek professional advice. The Tax Equity Act of 1982 is probably most equitable for paid tax return preparers. Almost everyone with investments and a moderately large income must not only pay his or her taxes but also pay a tax accountant.

A vast array of individuals is available to prepare your return. Determining the level of expertise you need and the competence of the individuals offering their services is difficult.

CPAs and tax attorneys have the most extensive training and experience in tax matters. Generally, because of the level of their fees, they are best used for complex tax situations only. CPAs prepare the bulk of the returns at this level. Attorneys primarily give tax advice on specific matters, although in some instances they prepare returns also. Both professions are legally qualified to represent clients before the IRS. Finding good "high-powered" tax assistance is like any other personnel search. Get referrals from parties whose judgment you respect and then interview several before making your choice. Make sure you understand their fee schedules and ascertain their familiarity with your type of circumstances before committing yourself.

Public accountants, not to be confused with CPAs (who have to pass extensive qualification exams), generally cater to small businesses and individuals with simple accounting needs. Because qualifications to practice are rarely stringent if they exist at all, you should use utmost care in selecting such a professional to assist you in tax preparation. If the accountant has passed the nine-hour examination administered by the U.S. Treasury, which allows him or her to represent clients before the IRS, you can have some assurance of competency. To determine which public accountants (or other individuals in your area) have passed this exam, contact your nearest district IRS office.

National tax services are probably best suited to prepare returns too complex for the uninitiated taxpayers but too simple to justify the expense of a CPA or attorney. If your return has any complexity, then you probably should seek assistance. The national tax services prepare returns primarily for individuals with simple income sources who itemize their deductions.

Local tax services also exist. Because they may lack the motivation of a national tax service to maintain a good reputation, your chances of stumbling onto a dishonest practitioner are greater here. The level of competency will also vary greatly. Therefore, use utmost caution and scrutiny if you consider selecting such an individual or organization to prepare your return.

The Tax Reform Act of 1976 specified certain requirements that professional tax preparers must fulfill for each client.

1. The preparer must sign and include his or her Social Security number or employer's tax ID number on each return prepared.
2. The taxpayer must be given a copy of the return no later than the time the original return is presented for signature.
3. The professional preparer must retain a copy of all returns prepared for three years, for purposes of government inspection.
4. Tax preparers must notify the IRS regularly of their activities.
5. Professional preparers cannot generally negotiate refund checks for taxpayers to be used for paying their fees, settling a loan to the taxpayer, or the like.

There are various penalties imposed on the preparer for not complying with these requirements as well as for intentionally understating a taxpayer's liability.

In recent years, computer packages have been developed to prepare returns, but most of these programs only calculate returns. The computer buzzword "GIGO" (garbage in, garbage out) applies here. If the program is given faulty or inaccurate information, the results will be faulty or inaccurate, too. The use of a computer package should not release you or any preparer you engage from diligently assuring the accuracy of all figures used.

How Not to Do It

Rodney Jennisen had very strong feelings against paying income taxes. Therefore, he deducted many questionable expenses when preparing his return. After several years of this practice the IRS became suspicious and audited Rodney's most recently filed tax return. Because Rodney did not bother to keep records of his expenses and because many of the expenses claimed as deductions were clearly not allowable, the IRS disallowed all of the excess itemized deductions on his return. The agent then audited Rodney's returns for the previous two years, found similar errors, and initiated proceedings to collect the unpaid taxes on those returns too. By failing to keep good records and prepare his returns within the general guidelines of tax law, Rodney ended up paying more taxes, plus interest and penalties, than if he had behaved more responsibly.

Summary

You have the primary responsibility for determining your lawful tax. Do it yourself if you are so inclined and your circumstances are simple. Use public accountants and tax services if you are not inclined to prepare your own return but it does not present any unusual problems or complexities. CPAs and tax attorneys are best engaged in complex circumstances. No matter whom you engage, be sure to do the following:

1. Satisfy yourself as to the adequacy of his or her training and experience.
2. Proof his or her work thoroughly. You are the one who is ultimately responsible for the completeness and correctness of your return.
3. Make sure the person figured your taxable income by every method available and considered all possible tax credits to ensure you are paying the lowest tax you could under the circumstances.

4. Have the person sign the return along with you so that he or she shares some of the responsibility for the accuracy of the return.

YOUR RELATIONS WITH THE IRS

Depending on your circumstances, you are obliged to observe certain dates in each taxable year. To the extent that you meet these deadlines and other filing requirements, your relations with the tax authorities should remain on good terms. Here are some of the more important dates.

- *January 15*. Final day to pay remaining estimated tax for the previous year's income.
- *January 31*. Final day for employer to mail W-2 forms to employees.
- *April 15*. Income tax returns for the previous year are required of individuals (self-employed or otherwise) and partnerships, and for decedents who died in the previous year. If necessary, individuals must also file estimated tax Form 1040ES for the current year and pay the first installment of estimated tax due.
- *June 15*. Income tax returns for the previous year are required of nonresident aliens and citizens living abroad. Second installment of estimated tax must be filed by individuals.
- *September 15*. Third installment of estimated tax due.

Penalties

Penalties may be levied against you if you fail to comply with these due dates or other filing requirements. For late filing of the return itself, the penalty is 5 percent of the tax due for each month that your return is outstanding, up to a maximum of 25 percent of the unpaid tax. For underpaying your tax, the penalty is an interest charge on the late payment, much as you pay interest on late charge card payments. The rate that is charged during each calendar year is set at the bank prime rate in effect on January 1 of that year—the same as would be charged if you file your estimated tax and underpay it. (Conversely, if you overpay your tax, the government will pay you interest at the same annual rate for each day they hold your money past the April 15 tax return due date.) For negligence, or intentional disregard of rules and regulations but without intent to defraud, the penalty is 5 percent of the tax due. Frivolous tax returns now also incur an additional $500 penalty. For fraud, the penalty is 50 percent of the tax deficiency and possible criminal proceedings against you by the IRS.

Auditing of Returns

The IRS audits, or carefully checks, many tax returns each year, and it is possible that you and the IRS may not agree on certain issues. The IRS may view as unlawful evasion what you honestly regard as lawful avoidance of paying unnecessary taxes.

Your chances of being audited can be as low as one in 50. If your income is substantial, or you belong to a particular profession or invest in tax shelters, however, your probability of being audited is much higher. In 1978, 2.63 percent of personal tax returns with adjusted gross incomes between $10,000 and $50,000 were audited.

Of those over $50,000, the percentage audited was 10.4 percent. Returns are now monitored via computers. They are programmed to spot various anomalies among the relationships of income to deductions to credits and so on. When anomalies are noted, audits often follow.

If your tax return is audited and some questions are raised by the IRS, an agent will contact you. You should attempt to resolve the disputed issues informally with this agent. You may wish to compromise on one point if the agent gives in on another, in the interest of a speedy and inexpensive resolution of the differences. It is important to keep in mind, however, that not all agents are of equal ability and that this one may have made a mistake. Agents also have a bias; their job is to collect taxes, not to rule on the legality of certain tax strategies. If you are unable to negotiate a satisfactory settlement with the agent and you genuinely believe you are right, ask for a hearing with other IRS personnel. The individuals at the hearing might have views different from your agent's on the matter under contention. If you are still unsuccessful at this level, you can take your case to the IRS appellate division.

Small tax cases involve disputes between you and the IRS for amounts up to $5,000 (either income or estate taxes). Tax commissioners handle these cases under the supervision of the chief judge of the Tax Court. These commissioners are in various cities at certain times of the year to hear cases. To petition the IRS Small Case Tax Court for a hearing before the commissioners, write the U.S. Tax Court (Box 70, Washington, D.C. 20044) and ask for its Form A–S. Answer the five questions on this form and submit it according to the instructions thereon. You will be notified when your case is to be heard. You have the option of seeking legal assistance if desired, but because of the size of these claims, the hearing procedures have been set up so that you may represent yourself. Decisions of the court for small tax cases may not be appealed.

If you want a hearing before an independent body, you must turn to the federal courts. Before you venture into these courts, engage a good tax attorney. He or she should be willing to give you, in advance, an opinion on your chances of winning your case and an estimate of the fee for representing you. It probably would be best to solicit opinions and fee estimates from several tax attorneys before deciding on one. Consider this alternative only if the amount under contention is quite large in relation to the potential fee costs, as it may be necessary to follow the appeals process all the way to the Supreme Court.

Table 10-8 shows how taxpayers fared against the IRS in disputes in 1977. Similar results occurred in appellate court tax cases.

SOCIAL SECURITY TAXES

There are essentially three Social Security taxes that are of interest to the individual. These taxes are not deductible for federal income tax purposes.

Federal Insurance Contributions Act

The Federal Insurance Contributions Act (FICA) combined all old-age, survivors, disability, and hospital insurance taxes into a single tax. The rate is the same for both

TABLE 10-8

Resolution of Tax Cases in 1977

Court	IRS Won	Taxpayer Won	Partial Victories for Each Party	Number of Opinions
Tax Court	54.8%	10.5%	34.7%	988[a]
Federal District Court	66.3	22.7	11.0	359
Court of Claims	68.2	27.3	4.5	44

Source: IRS Commissioner's 1977 Annual Report.
[a]Of these, 468 were small tax cases.

you and your employer. In other words, you each pay half of the amount that goes toward this federal insurance program. The tax is applied to your annual income and is deducted from your paycheck up to a certain income limit each year as determined by federal law. For 1982 the rate is set at 6.7 percent of one's earnings, up to a maximum salary of $32,400. Thus, for workers earning that much, or more, the FICA tax is $2,171 on the worker plus another $2,171 paid by the employer.

If you change jobs in the middle of the year, each employer will take the total FICA tax out of your paycheck as each has been instructed to. This may result in your paying the tax on more income than is required for that year. If you consult the IRS and find out that you have paid too much FICA tax, you can use the excess taxes paid as a credit against your personal income taxes. For example, if you paid $43 too much FICA tax in a year, you could pay $43 less on your federal income tax. Or you may use Form 843 to apply for a refund. However, you must take the initiative within three years to establish the overpayment and keep all your records of taxes paid (paycheck stubs and W-2 forms). Otherwise, the extra taxes paid are lost. (Note that the IRS does not refund the extra taxes paid by the second employer.)

The standard age at which you may begin to receive retirement benefits from this tax is 65. (See Chapters 8, 9, and 21 and the Social Security addendum for a more complete discussion of Social Security benefits.)

Federal Unemployment Tax Act

The Federal Unemployment Tax Act (FUTA) created the unemployment insurance tax. This tax is imposed on employers only. Up to a certain limit and at rates specified by federal law, employers must pay taxes on the wages they pay each year. The proceeds from this tax are used to finance federal-state unemployment compensation programs that are administered by the state. When you receive unemployment benefit payments, they are paid by your state. Some states levy additional unemployment taxes on employers.

Self-Employment Tax Act

The Self-Employment Tax Act (SETA) created the self-employment and hospital insurance tax. This tax is levied against self-employed individuals whose income from their work is $400 or more a year (with certain exceptions for religious ac-

TABLE 10-9

All Those Other Taxes

Tax	By Whom	On Whom	On What
Income tax	Federal government, most state governments, some local governments	Individuals, corporations, estates and trusts	Income
Social Security and self-employment tax	Federal government	Employees and employers	Income
Excise tax	Federal, most state, and some local governments	End users	Alcohol, tobacco, gasoline, telephones
Unemployment tax	Federal government, most state governments	Employers	Income
General sales tax	Most state and local governments	Final retail purchaser	Spending
Real property tax	Some state and local governments	Property owners	Assets
Use tax	Most state and local governments	Final retail purchaser	Spending
Personal property and inventory tax	Some state and local governments	Property owners	Assets
Business licenses	Most state and local governments	Businesses	Right to do business
Registration fees	Most state governments	Motor vehicle and boat owners primarily	Assets
Estate tax	Federal and state governments	Estates	Assets
Inheritance tax	Most state governments	Inheritors	Assets
Gift tax	Federal and most state governments	Donors	Assets

tivities). It is computed as a fixed percentage of a certain amount of earnings above $400 and is paid along with the regular income tax. This tax provides the same benefits for self-employed individuals as the FICA tax provides for employed persons.

ALL THOSE OTHER TAXES

This chapter has focused primarily on the federal income tax, with brief treatment of the FICA, unemployment, and self-employment taxes. In addition, you are probably exposed to a greater range of taxes than you might think. Table 10-9 lists these taxes and indicates which taxing authority levies them and who pays them.

This last consideration, who pays the tax, has raised considerable controversy, primarily in regard to the corporate income tax, the real property tax, and Social Security taxes. It is often argued either that the first two taxes are passed along to the buyer through higher prices or that the rate of return to the corporation or the real estate seller is lowered by the amount of the tax. There is no conclusive evidence to support either of these extreme interpretations. Probably both considerations apply in varying degrees. That is, corporate income taxes and property taxes are both passed on to the purchaser through higher prices and shared by the seller in terms of a reduced return on investment.

The FICA tax is probably borne by three different entities, again in varying and indeterminable degrees: the consumer in terms of higher prices, the employer in terms of a lower return on investment, and the employee in terms of lower earnings. In addition, the employee may be affected by this tax in terms of unemployment. This effect would occur if Social Security taxes were viewed as burdensome by the employer because they increase total payroll costs. Therefore the employer either gets by with less labor or replaces employees with labor-saving machinery.

CONCLUSION

Rather than merely show you how to fill out the forms, we have presented a framework for many of the considerations about the federal income tax. This discussion has focused on how income, deductions, and exemptions relate to each other in order to give you the information and perspective that will enable you to make financial decisions for the best tax advantage and to avoid paying unnecessary taxes. We have taken a brief look at the many other taxes that are levied. We also hope we have dispelled some of the myths about tax shelters.

VOCABULARY

adjusted gross income
alternative minimum tax
avoidance of tax
capital gain
capital loss
deduction
estimated tax
evasion of tax
exclusion
exemption
Federal Insurance Contributions Act (FICA)
Federal Unemployment Tax Act (FUTA)
Form 1040
gross income
income averaging

income splitting
marginal tax rate
progressive tax
public accountant
regressive tax
Self-Employment Tax Act (SETA)
taxable income
tax bracket
tax credit
tax exempt
Tax Rate Schedules
tax shelter
Tax Tables
withholding
zero bracket amount

QUESTIONS

1. Your current taxable income is $13,000, and your marginal tax rate is 21 percent. You are informed that unexpected dividends will increase your income by $800. What will be the tax effect?
2. Your current taxable income is $15,500, on which your marginal tax rate is 23 percent. The bank informs you that you owe $2,600 in interest on your newly written home mortgage. How will your taxes be affected by this added deductible expense, and in what amount?
3. Under what circumstances might too much be paid in Social Security taxes? How could you correct this overpayment?
4. List five sources of income that can be excluded from gross income for tax purposes.
5. What is the primary purpose of tax planning and how does it differ from tax preparation?
6. What is the most common tax break available to all gainfully employed taxpayers? How much tax could this save in the first year for a salaried worker in the 30 percent tax bracket?
7. Give two reasons why the IRS cannot be completely relied upon for tax advice.
8. What alternative is available to you if you and the IRS cannot settle a disputed tax return?
9. What are the three possible entities to bear the Social Security tax? How is this tax cost reflected in each case?

CASE PROBLEMS

1. John and Marsha Howard's taxable income for the current year is $18,500. Their taxable incomes for the four previous years were $8,000, $12,000, $6,000, and $15,000. Do the Howards qualify for income averaging this year? Would they qualify if their current taxable income were to drop to $15,000?

   The Howards derive $2,500 of their $18,500 income from an investment with John's three married brothers. The total income from this investment is $10,000, which is split evenly among the four brothers. If each of the other brothers has a taxable income of approximately $18,000, what is each brother's marginal tax rate in 1982? What will be the total amount of tax paid on the $10,000 of investment income? How much would be saved in taxes on each of the brothers' returns if this investment provided $200 of depreciation deductions for each of them?

2. What questions should you ask a professional tax preparer you are considering hiring?
3. Compute the loss in after-tax purchasing power from the following facts.

- Taxable income in year 1: $16,000 with a tax of $2,300 due.
- Taxable income in year 5: $24,000 with a tax of $4,500 due.
- Inflation for the period is 48 percent.

RECOMMENDED READING

MAGAZINE AND NEWSPAPER ARTICLES

"Don't Let the IRS Scare You." *Changing Times*, March 1980, pp. 29–32.
What to realistically expect when dealing with the IRS.

Ehrbar, A. F. "Manifesto for a Tax Revolution." *Fortune*. April 1977.
A thoughtful discussion of alternatives for reforming our income tax system.

Eisenberg, Richard. "Taxes, Now What Do I Do?" *Money*, September 1981, pp. 56–63.
A good review of the differences brought on for most taxpayers by the Economic Recovery Tax Act of 1981.

Evans, Michael K. "Taxes, Inflation and the Rich." *Wall Street Journal*. August 7, 1978.
A surprising bit of research into the results of high taxation.

"How to Find A . . . ." *Money*, February 1981, pp. 70–72.
Tips on picking a good tax preparer.

BOOKS

Commerce Clearing House. *Federal Tax Course*. Published annually.
A complete and accurate overview of federal taxation.

Internal Revenue Service. *Your Federal Income Tax—for Individuals*. Washington, D.C.: Government Printing Office. Published annually.
An authoritative source of information on filing your tax return. It may be bought at post offices for a small charge.

Lasser, S.J. *Everyone's Income Tax Guide*. New York: Hilltop Publications, 1982.
This useful book has been published annually for 28 years to keep the taxpayer up to date.

Price, J.R., and Putney, Valerie F. *In This Corner, the IRS*. New York: Dell, 1982.
A former IRS agent explains how the IRS system works and how to avoid getting into trouble with it.

CHUCK AND NANCY ANDERSON

Computing Their Income Taxes

Chuck and Nancy have asked you to help them fill out their Form 1040. The Andersons give you the following list of items that they say represents their tax lives for the past year.

charitable contributions	$ 130
Widget Salesman subscription fee	5
salaries	44,000
two auto licenses	100
nonreimbursed auto expenses related to employment	125
interest paid	
furniture loan	182
car loan	645
home mortgage	3,540
margin loan	55
dividends received	310
health insurance premiums	150
interest received	120
medical and dental expenses	
doctor	194
dentist	250
medicines	25
employee tools (briefcase)	55
long-term capital loss	1,100
taxes	
previous year's state income taxes actually paid or withheld	1,275
sales taxes (table value from IRS tax booklet)	453
property taxes	1,100
health insurance settlement proceeds	675

Your first task is to make some order out of this list. After perusing the IRS tax booklet, you find the following regulations that seem to apply.

Only medical expenses in excess of 5 percent of adjusted gross income may be used as a deduction against adjusted gross income. The sales tax deduction is the value allowed in the IRS tax booklet for a family of four with the Andersons' gross income. The first $11 paid on each auto license is not deductible.

Questions

1. What item on the Andersons' list should not be included in gross income?
2. How should the Andersons' dividends be treated for federal tax purposes?
3. What are the two deductions against gross income on the Andersons' list?
4. How much of their long-term capital loss can be offset against their gross income?
5. What are their total itemized deductions?
6. What is the current exemption level allowed by the IRS per person? What is the total amount of the Andersons' exemptions?
7. Does their medical expense qualify as a deduction against adjusted gross income?
8. What is the Andersons' taxable income?
9. What would be the tax due on a 1982 joint return?

11

Borrowing and Banking

Chapters 11 and 12 deal with borrowing money. The principal reason for treating this subject in two chapters is that we felt there was too much information to cover in one chapter. Chapter 11 deals with basic considerations about borrowing and consumer loans plus a discussion of some of the other services available from commercial banks. Chapter 12 covers consumer credit transactions. The distinction between consumer loans and consumer credit is subtle. A borrower who takes out a consumer loan goes to one party (the lender) to obtain funds that he or she then gives to a second party (the seller) to purchase something from that party. When a borrower uses consumer credit, however, the lender and the seller are the same.

THE CONCEPT OF BORROWING

When you borrow money, you obtain the use of someone else's money for a certain period of time in order to expand your immediate purchasing power. In exchange for the use of this money, you pay a fee, often called a *finance charge*. This fee is composed of two elements: *interest*, the amount you pay for the opportunity to borrow money, and *carrying costs*, the costs (as for bookkeeping, collection, and insurance) the lender incurs by loaning you money. Interest rates have legal ceilings that are established by state usury laws.

Finance charges can be either added to the principal or deducted from it; in the latter case, they are paid in advance. For example, lender A is willing to lend you $2,000 at a finance charge of $200 that would be added to the principal: you would get $2,000 and pay back $2,200. If you are to pay back the loan in one year, the charge would be 10 percent. Lender B, who uses discounted interest, will also charge $200 to loan you $2,000 but will deduct the $200 in advance. You actually have use of only $1,800 and will pay back $2,000; the charge is slightly in excess of 11 percent.

In the above examples, the *principal* part of the loan is the money actually borrowed, $2,000 and $1,800 respectively. As portions of the principal are paid off with each monthly payment, the amount remaining is termed the *balance outstanding*.

An Example

Assume that you want to build a patio but cannot pay cash for it. In shopping for a loan that would enable you to purchase the patio materials, you obtain quotes from five different lenders (see Table 11-1). From these five quotes, it is apparent that *the longer the payback period, the more the finance charge*. Also, *the higher the rate charged, the more the finance charge will be*.

You decide to accept the terms offered by lender 1. Once the necessary documentation is completed, the lender gives you $400, which you are free to use to buy the materials necessary to build the patio. He also gives you a loan book that consists of a cover page and twelve other pages, one for each payment you will make on the loan. Each page states the amount of the payment and the date on which it is due. Every month you will tear out the appropriate page, enclose it in an envelope with your payment, and mail it to the lender. On the stub remaining in the booklet, you record the amount paid and the date the payment was made. When there are no more payment pages in your loan book, your loan, plus the finance charge, will be paid off. By borrowing against your future income, you have gained the immediate use of a new patio.

Amortization

Prior to the 1930s many loans were written so that only interest was due for a specified term, and then the entire principal of the loan was due upon maturity. It takes a special kind of savings discipline to put money away voluntarily toward the lump-sum payment of a loan's principal. Many borrowers did not have this disci-

TABLE 11-1

Sample Quotes for a $400 Loan

Lender	Amount of Loan	Repayment Period (months)	Monthly Payments	Finance Charge	Annual Percentage Rate	Total ($)
1	$400	12	$35.00	$20	10%[a]	$420
2	400	12	35.83	30	15[a]	430
3	400	24	18.34	40	10[a]	440
4	400	36	13.29	78[b]	12	478
5	400	48	10.34	96[b]	11	496

[a] Effective cost of borrowing (to be discussed later in this chapter).
[b] Derived by using an amortization table.

pline. When their loans matured or, because of the Great Depression, the loans were called prematurely by anxious lenders, many borrowers were forced to default.

Since this traumatic period, one of the improvements in lending practices has been amortization—gradual payback of both principal and interest, presumably at a level well within a borrower's ability to pay. Thus, the prospect of having to pay off all the principal of a loan on short notice during bad economic times has been virtually eliminated.

The great majority of loans nowadays are amortized. Table 11-2 shows how this process works. In effect, you make regular payments to retire your debt rather than paying it off in just one payment. Generally, these will be payments of equal amounts in which the portions of principal and interest vary or, less commonly, equal principal payments with declining amounts of interest due. Note that in the fixed total payment example used in Table 11-2 the total interest cost is $68 more than in the fixed principal payment example. This is because the principal portion of the loan is retired more slowly.

Debt Obligations

When lenders evaluate a prospective borrower, they look for some assurance that the money they lend will in fact be repaid. One method of gaining this assurance is

TABLE 11-2

Payment Schedule for Loans Amortized over Four Years

	Fixed Principal Payment		Fixed Total Payment	
Annual Interest Rate	12%		12%	
Amount Borrowed	$4,000		$4,000	
End of Year 1				
Principal due	1,000		837	
Interest due	480		480	
Total payment	1,480		1,317	
Amount remaining		3,000		3,163
End of Year 2				
Principal due	1,000		938	
Interest due	360		379	
Total payment	1,360		1,317	
Amount remaining		2,000		2,225
End of Year 3				
Principal due	1,000		1,050	
Interest due	240		267	
Total payment	1,240		1,317	
Amount remaining		1,000		1,175
End of Year 4				
Principal due	1,000		1,175	
Interest due	120		142	
Total payment	1,120		1,317	
TOTAL	5,200		5,268	

to ask the prospective borrower for *collateral*, or security, which can come in either of two forms. The first requires that the borrower pledge an asset (chattel)—most likely the one to be purchased with the borrowed funds. If the borrower defaults on the loan, the lender can take possession of the asset to compensate for the money loaned. The second form of security is called a *loan endorsement* or guarantee. The prospective borrower has someone (called the cosigner) whose credit worthiness is stronger than his or her own promise to make the loan good (i.e., to repay it) if the borrower defaults on the payments. A *secured loan* has one of these two forms of security. An *unsecured loan* does not.

Lenders often discourage the borrower from paying off a loan in advance. The borrower who does this denies the lender the interest income that would have been received had the loan been paid off on schedule. Admittedly, the lender can take the amount paid off in advance and lend it to someone else but probably not without losing interest while looking for another borrower. Therefore, the lender requires some compensation in the form of a *prepayment penalty*, usually a sliding percentage of the debt outstanding at the time of prepayment.

Lenders also levy a penalty, usually 5 percent of the delinquent amount, for loan payments that are late; this penalty is intended to motivate the borrower to make the payments on time.

TO BORROW
OR NOT TO BORROW

People often choose not to borrow. When this decision is based on emotional reactions to borrowing, it is less sound than when based on financial considerations.

A common reason for not borrowing is fear of personal insolvency, of not being able to honor debt obligations because of inadequate income. Application of the financial principles discussed in this text should help eliminate this danger.

Another reason often given is lack of confidence in the government's ability to keep the economy relatively stable and to prevent another Great Depression. In our opinion an economic debacle of that magnitude is unlikely. We believe that government regulation of the securities markets and supervision of other sectors of our economy can forestall the speculative excesses that led to the crash of 1929 and the ensuing economic difficulties. We believe, however, that serious economic recessions and unemployment will occur from time to time. You must form your own opinions about the stability of our economy and your own ways of dealing with its ups and downs.

The primary advantage of borrowing is that *it permits people who lack the discipline or time to save money for cash purchases to acquire consumer goods*. Therefore, borrowing forces a person to save after the fact, so to speak—the person has spent money before saving it. The principal disadvantage of borrowing is that, because it involves finance charges ranging from 8 to 35 percent a year, you will be paying more for the merchandise over the long run than if you had paid cash initially. Also, *when borrowing money, you pay interest to the lender; when saving money, the interest is paid to you*.

PROPER USE OF DEBT

If you have decided to accept borrowing in principle, you are ready to begin thinking about how much you should borrow and for what.

When to Borrow?

You should borrow only if a loan is needed to finance an asset (home, car, education) or as part of an investment program. Consumer loans are generally used to buy expensive, fairly durable items such as a car or home furnishings. A mortgage loan to buy a house is not considered a consumer loan. Consumables (food, clothing, travel, entertainment) should come entirely out of your income. These quickly used-up items should be a regular part of your budget. We advise that you *limit the times you borrow money to major durable purchases, but maximize the amounts borrowed.*

Some people use loans to help consolidate many small debts into one lending arrangement. This consolidation often involves a longer repayment period so that the monthly payment can be brought down to an acceptable level. People are likely to find such consolidation attractive, because the resulting monthly payment is smaller than the sum of the payments of the debts outstanding before consolidation. The ultimate effect, however, of borrowing enough money over an extended period of time to cover one's small debts is a higher total finance charge (including perhaps consolidation fees also) paid out. Therefore, if you can meet your current payments, it is almost always better to let them stand rather than consolidate.

Setting Debt Limits

There is no one formula you can use in all instances to calculate debt limits for yourself. Generally, your debt limit at any one time is a product of two factors. The first factor is your need for borrowed money, which depends on both the stage of your financial life cycle and your income level. For example, if you buy a home and raise children during the early years of marriage, the financial requirements will probably be great, relative to your income. As you grow older, these requirements will probably subside and your income will probably increase.

The second factor involves the lender's estimation of your ability to repay a debt. For example, you may feel that you need $50,000 to meet your current financial needs, whereas the lender may feel that you are able to repay only $15,000 at most. In this case, the lender would probably be unwilling to lend more than the latter amount. At any one time, your debt limit will be determined by both your need to borrow money and your ability to do so, which is based on your ability to repay.

Each time you consider borrowing money, ask yourself several questions:

- Do I want or need what I am going to buy with this borrowed money enough right now to justify remaining in debt for the loan period?
- Can another liability (a loan) be realistically added to my financial obligations without jeopardizing the soundness of my financial resources?

• Will I be able to repay this loan without taking money away from necessary expenditures (such as living expenses)?

Your responses to these questions should indicate whether you are near your debt limit.

debt/equity ratio   Commercial lenders generally agree that it is time to stop lending a firm money when its debts (liabilities) become equal to or greater than its equity (net worth). You might also use this debt/equity ratio as an upper limit on your borrowing. In your computation of the ratio, do not include the value of your home (an asset) and its mortgage (a liability). Therefore, if you find that all your other interest-bearing debt is as great as or greater than your net worth (minus your home and its financing), you should probably not take on more debt obligations.

This is just one possible measure and will not apply in all instances. As we indicated in Chapter 3, the student who is heavily laden with education loans may have a negative net worth, but he or she possesses income-earning potential that may offset this otherwise weak economic position.

no more than 20 percent of disposable income   Another way to measure your debt limit is to consider your ability to cover your debt payments out of your disposable income. If no more than 20 percent of your disposable income is used to make installment debt payments and other interest-bearing debt payments *(exclusive of home mortgages)*, you probably will avoid misuse of debt.

You should not, however, try to keep your debt payments (not including mortgage payments) below 20 percent of your take-home pay by borrowing for longer periods. If you extend the maturities (time periods) of your debt arrangements, you reduce your monthly payments, but you also increase your total borrowing costs. If you rely on this tactic to keep your loan repayments manageable, you are probably misusing debt.

resolving debts every three years   As a final way to set debt limits, you might try to resolve all your debt obligations, exclusive of home mortgages and education loans, every three years. If you add new obligations to banks or lending companies before you pay off old ones or if you are frequently delinquent on payments, you are probably making too liberal and continuous use of debt.

THE EFFECTIVE COST OF BORROWING

You ask to borrow $500 from a lender. This person informs you that the simple interest rate is 6 percent. Is the cost of borrowing the money then $30 a year?

Assume that you are to pay off this loan in 12 equal monthly installments beginning in 30 days. Therefore, you actually have use of the full $500 for only the first month of the lending period. If the balance outstanding at the end of the 12-month period is zero, the average balance for the entire period is approximately $250. A $30 interest charge on an average outstanding balance of $250 is in reality costing you 12 percent a year. In this case, the effective cost of borrowing is twice as large as the stated rate.

Unfortunately, the terminology used for different types of interest treatment (such as simple interest and add-on interest) is not straightforward. Therefore, it is best to compare all loan proposals by their effective cost since the method for calculating this was standardized by the Truth-in-Lending Act. Although most lending sources are required to let the borrower know the effective cost of borrowing before a borrowing contract is completed, you should make this determination on your own. With this knowledge, you will be able not only to check the lender's honesty but also to provide this information for yourself when you are not protected by legislation—in leasing arrangements, for example.

In deciding whether the immediate use of an item or service is worth the additional expense, you must compare the dollar credit cost with the interest you would receive on the money if you put it in a savings account instead; you must also consider the effect of inflation and income taxes on these figures.

Determining the Cost of Borrowing

The following formula (constant ratio formula) can be used to determine the approximate effective *annual percentage rate* of interest (APR). This formula approximates the effective cost for short-term loans only.

$$\frac{200 \, (C) \, \times \, n}{a \, \times \, (P \, + \, 1)} \, = \, APR$$

where

$\quad\quad C \, = \,$ dollar credit cost
$\quad\quad n \, = \,$ number of payments per year
$\quad\quad a \, = \,$ amount borrowed
$\quad\quad P \, = \,$ total number of payments

To demonstrate the use of this formula, let us assume that you make a $25 down payment on a $250 dishwasher and borrow $225 to pay off the rest. The dollar cost of credit as specified in the purchase agreement is $26.25. You are to pay off this debt in 18 equal monthly installments. The number of yearly payments is 12, and the total number of payments plus one is 19. These figures can be inserted in the formula as follows:

$$\frac{200 \, (\$26.25) \, \times \, 12}{225 \, \times \, 19} \, = \, \frac{63,000}{4,275} \, = \, 14.7\% \, APR$$

This method should be used when the payment schedule calls for regularly occurring payments of equal amounts. Computations involving deferred or irregular payments are more difficult, and you should seek professional help for determinations of this type.

Determining the Dollar Drain Due to Borrowing

Suppose you were trying to decide whether to use credit to purchase a $2,000 living room set or to wait for two years until you have saved the money to pay for it. The following procedure will help you determine the actual dollars you would lose if you bought the furniture on credit rather than saved for it by putting your money in a savings account.

1. *Determine the dollar credit cost* by using the following formula to check the information supplied by the lender or to determine it for yourself if he or she is not required to supply it.

$$\frac{APR \times a \times (P + 1)}{200 \times n} = \text{dollar credit cost}$$

Assume that you could pay back the $2,000 in monthly payments over a two-year period at a rate of 15 percent. Your dollar credit cost would be as follows:

$$\frac{15 \times \$2,000 \times 25}{200 \times 12} = \frac{\$750,000}{2,400} = \$312.50 \text{ credit cost}$$

Notice that in the formula you use the APR (15 percent) as a whole number, not as a decimal since the constant (200) is used.

2. *Determine how much interest you would receive in a savings account if you made regular deposits.* In the furniture example, assume that the savings account yields 8 percent and that you put in $83.30 each month for a total of $1,000 per year. During the first year you receive interest on an average balance of $500 and during the second year the average balance is $1,500. The interest received for the first year is 8 percent of $500 or $40, and for the second year is 8 percent of $1,500 or $120. The total interest is $160.

3. *Add the amounts computed in steps 1 and 2 to arrive at the total dollar drain due to credit buying.* In our example, you would lose $472.50 of potential purchasing power if you bought the furniture on credit. Not only would you have to pay $312.50 in finance charges, but also you would lose $160 in earnings from a savings account. This total of $472.50 is the cost of borrowing before the effect of inflation and income taxes is taken into account.

Now we need also to consider the effect of inflation and income taxes on the effective cost of borrowing.

Effect of Inflation

As we saw in Chapter 1, inflation reduces the purchasing power of money. Let us apply this concept to the borrowing process in which a lump sum is obtained from a lender and installment payments are made until the debt is resolved. If the amount borrowed is spent immediately (perhaps for a car, home, or appliance), you have gained the current purchasing power of the dollars borrowed. Assume that inflation persists during the payback period. With each payment, you relinquish dollars of less and less purchasing power. The purchasing power you must give up (loan payments) to obtain immediate purchasing power (the loan) is less than if inflation did not exist. Remember, however, since lenders are aware of the effect of inflation on the value of money paid back, they adjust their rates as inflation grows or diminishes.

Effect of Income Taxes

Income taxes also reduce the cost of borrowing because interest may be taken as an excess itemized deduction against adjusted gross income (Chapter 10). For example, assume that your taxable income without a deduction for loan interest is $18,000. If you are married and file a joint return, your tax is $2,226. Now let us assume that you have excess itemized deductions to take against adjusted gross income and that you have interest charges of $500. This deductible expense reduces your taxable income to $17,500 and your tax liability to $2,131, a tax savings of $95. You can also arrive at this figure by using the marginal tax rate of 19 percent (Chapter 10). Hence, your after-tax cost of borrowing would be $405 ($500 interest cost − $95 tax savings).

An Example of the Effect of Inflation and Income Taxes

Table 11-3 shows how a 5 percent annual rate of inflation and a 25 percent marginal tax rate affect the cost of borrowing $3,000 at 10 percent to be paid back over a period of three years. The annual payment is $1,000 plus interest on the outstanding balance. As you can see, in the third year the combined effect of tax savings and inflation (total cost savings) is so significant that the total repayment for that year (including interest) represents giving up less purchasing power than was received ($1,000) when the money was borrowed. Although inflation and tax savings can substantially reduce the cost of borrowing, it would still cost $100 in today's after-tax dollars to borrow $3,000 for three years.

To calculate the effective annual percentage rate *after tax*, the following expanded computation should be made.

$$\text{APR} \times \left[1 - \left(\frac{\text{MTR}}{100} \right) \right] = \text{APR after tax}$$

where   MTR = marginal tax rate

TABLE 11-3
Effect of Inflation and Tax Savings on Cost of $3,000 Loan

Year	Amount Paid Back			Tax Savings[a]	Reduction in Purchasing Power[b]	Total Cost Savings	Net Cost of Borrowing	
	Prin-cipal	Inter-est	Total					
1	$1,000	$300	$1,300	$75	$ 65	$140	$160	5.3%
2	1,000	200	1,200	50	120	170	30	1.5
3	1,000	100	1,100	25	165	190	(90)	

[a]interest x 25%   [b]5% annual inflation of repayment

To calculate the effective annual percentage rate *after tax and inflation,* the following formula applies.

$$\text{APR} \times \left[1 - \left(\frac{\text{MTR}}{100}\right)\right] - \text{ARI} = \text{APR after tax and inflation}$$

where   ARI = annual rate of inflation

As an example, if the APR is 12 percent and your tax bracket is 25 percent and inflation is at a 6 percent annual rate, your APR after tax and inflation is:

$$12\% \times .75 = 9\% - 6\% = 3\%$$

Returning to our previous example of the *dollar* drain due to credit buying, let us assume that the tax savings relative to interest cost were $78 (25% marginal tax rate = $312.50 interest cost). The reduction in purchasing power (5% annual inflation) would be computed in the following way. Your monthly payments each year would amount to $1,156.25 (($2,000 + $312.50) ÷ 2). The average inflation rate in year one would be 2½ percent (0% on the first day of the year and 5% by the end of the year). In the first year of the payback period, the reduction due to inflation would be $17.34 (2.5% × $1,156.25), and in the second year it would be $34.69 (7.5% × $1,156.25) for a total of $52.03 ($52 rounded). As a result, the after-tax-and-inflation effective cost of borrowing the $2,000 for a living room set is $182.50 ($312.50 — $78 — $52). When the $160 lost in interest is added to this amount, your cost of immediate enjoyment is really $342.50. If, by waiting two years to buy the $2,000 living room set through savings, the cost of the furniture has increased 10 percent due to inflation, it will now cost $200 more than if you had purchased it at the beginning of the period. As you can see, because of inflationary price increases, the cost of immediate enjoyment has been reduced to $142.50 ($342.50 — $200).

TRUTH IN LENDING

The Consumer Credit Protection Act of 1968 has four main sections dealing with (1) the establishment of a consumer interest agency, (2) limitations on the activities of organized crime in the area of consumer credit, (3) wage garnishment, and (4) truth in lending. It is truth in lending that is of most interest here.

The act, which went into effect July 1, 1969, covers credit up to $25,000 extended to individuals for personal, family, household, and agricultural uses. However, all real estate credit extended to individuals is covered no matter what the amount. Compliance is required of any person or business that regularly extends or arranges for credit to individuals for personal, family, household, agricultural, or real estate purposes. Most commonly this includes banks, savings and loan associations, department and retail stores, credit card companies, automobile dealers, credit unions, consumer finance companies, mortgage bankers, hospitals, doctors, home building and repair contractors, and the like. Credit exempted by the act includes business and commercial credit and securities and commodities credit as well as consumer credit in excess of $25,000 (real estate credit excepted).

The most significant requirement of this section of the act is that the terms of various credit transactions between lender and consumer be fully disclosed before the transaction is completed. The lender must identify the cash price, all other charges, the down payment, and the amount to be financed. This last amount must be equal to the cash price plus all other charges minus the down payment. The total cost of credit must also be expressed in terms of an annual percentage rate (APR) or an annual dollar amount. Whichever way it is expressed, this cost must be identified as the finance charge. This charge is not considered by this law as synonymous with interest rates. It is considered to include interest, investigation and finder's fees, service and carrying charges, and insurance and loan guarantee costs.

The repayment schedule must be set out according to number of payments, amount of each payment, and either the final due date for all payments or the total length of time over which the payments must be made. Any items to be used as collateral for the transaction must be described. According to the Consumer Credit Protection Act, when a consumer loan is secured by a second mortgage on one's home, the consumer has the right to cancel the transaction within three days after signing the credit agreement if he or she decides not to take the loan or not to use the mortgage as security. Any default, delinquency, and late payment penalties must also be disclosed.

Your signature on the documents of the purchase agreement is considered proof that the lenders or creditors have fulfilled their disclosure responsibilities. Therefore, you should make sure that they have complied with the disclosure requirements and that you understand what you are signing.

Enforcement responsibilities rest primarily with the Federal Trade Commission, although other federal agencies such as the Federal Reserve Board and Federal Home Loan Bank Board may also have jurisdiction. Because there are no severe financial penalties (the maximum fine is $1,000) and the individual consumer may prove weak against a major creditor, more effective forms of enforcement and legal redress may yet have to be developed.

PREPARING TO SHOP FOR A LOAN

Before you contact a lending source, you should do several things.

1. Decide on the exact amount of money you need. This will make it easier for you to identify the most appropriate loan source. A consumer finance company, for example, would be able to make loans only up to a certain amount. Furthermore, lenders often look more favorably on loan applicants who have a firm idea of how much money they need.
2. List the reasons why you want to take out a loan in this amount. Most likely one of your reasons will be that you do not have the cash you need for a particular purchase.
3. Note the use or uses to which the borrowed money will be put. You may, for example, want to use the money to buy new carpeting for your living room.
4. Locate your balance sheet and income statement so that you will be able to tell the lender about your financial resources—net worth, sources and amounts of income, and existing debts.

5. Be sure you can tell the lender about your financial responsibilities—number of dependents, amount and timing of existing debt repayments, and monthly living expenses (check your budget sheets).
6. Review your employment record so that you can describe any jobs you have had in the last five to ten years in addition to your present job. Be able to state how long you have been both in your current occupation and with your current employer.
7. Review your credit record so that you can accurately describe your borrowing experiences and the installment loans you have paid off on time. List your credit references such as credit cards, charge accounts, and banks.

SHOPPING FOR A LOAN

Investigate the loan possibilities at several sources such as banks, savings and loan associations, credit unions, and consumer finance companies. Collect the following information.

1. What is the exact amount of money that will be given to you?
2. How will the finance charges be treated? Will they be added to the principal, or will they be deducted from the principal and paid in advance?
3. What will be your effective annual rate of interest? The lender is required to provide you with this information, but you can check its accuracy by using the formula for APR.
4. What is the repayment schedule?
5. Will there be a penalty if you decide to pay back the loan before it is due or if a payment is late?
6. What collateral will be required? Lenders with whom you now have or have had successful borrowing relationships may require less collateral than other lenders.

Once you have collected this information from several sources, you should be able to identify which one offers you the best conditions and why.

Meeting the Lender

A lender usually evaluates three characteristics when deciding whether to extend credit: ability to repay, willingness to honor debt obligations, and the availability of collateral in the event of failure to repay. In particular he or she will want to know how much of your income is being used to repay other debts in order to estimate whether you will be able to take on more debt. The lender will also want to know how regularly and faithfully you have paid off previous credit arrangements and what can legally be confiscated if you fail to repay the loan. If you have done your homework as we suggested, you will have all the necessary information ready to answer all questions and will probably make a favorable impression.

A personal information form is commonly used by lenders to get an initial picture of your financial situation. On this form you will be asked to list credit accounts and references (including your bank) and either your annual or monthly income. If you are a minor, an adult (usually your parent) may be asked to provide a guardian's guarantee. In accordance with the Equal Credit Opportunity Act, no questions about the sex or marital status of the prospective borrower may be asked.

An interview with the lender is often the second step. He or she will use this session to obtain information in addition to that found on the form you completed. Answer all questions truthfully. If you do not and the lender finds out the truth through a routine credit check, your credit rating will be very low.

A credit investigation will be conducted to check the accuracy of the information you gave on the form and during the interview. This investigation will cover your credit record with the local credit bureau or existing creditors, your employment history, and your character. If you pass all these checks, you qualify for a loan.

Disreputable Money Sources

When you look for an appropriate lending source, beware of individuals or organizations known as loan sharks. You may often be tipped off to their unreliability if they do not display an official state lender's license, do not require you to qualify for a loan, attempt to predate a loan, urge you to sign loan papers before they are completely filled out, or refuse to give you a receipt or copies of the loan agreement.

Reputable lenders comply with the truth-in-lending provisions of the Consumer Credit Protection Act. These provisions are for your protection. If a lender refuses to comply with them, do not deal with him or her. Under no circumstances is dealing with disreputable lenders worth the cost and anxiety.

SOURCES OF CONSUMER LOANS

Sources of consumer loans include family and friends, life insurance policies, credit unions, consumer finance companies, commercial banks, savings and loan associations, and pawnbrokers. Even second mortgages are in some ways similar to consumer loans. A second mortgage is a loan specifically secured by your equity (market value minus first mortgage balance) in your home. Admittedly, lenders of second mortgage money do not fall strictly in the category of sources of consumer loans. Nevertheless, because these cash loans are advertised and made for many of the same reasons as consumer loans, they deserve some treatment in this chapter. The specifics of first and second mortgages will be deferred until Chapter 14. Table 11-4 gives a general comparison of these sources, aside from family and friends.

Family and Friends

When they need to borrow funds, many people turn first to family and friends rather than to professional, impersonal sources of loans. The main advantages of borrowing from family or friends are that it's private, the funds are readily available (assuming a willing lender), and there is a minimum of technical paperwork. Furthermore, because of personal interest in you or a more creative approach to lending, family and friends may be willing to lend funds to you for purposes that aren't generally viewed with enthusiasm by professional lenders, such as investment programs or starting a business—projects where a successful outcome is in doubt.

TABLE 11-4

Comparison of Sources of Consumer Loans

	Life Insurance Policies	Credit Unions	Consumer Finance Companies	Commercial Banks	Savings and Loan Associations	Pawnbrokers	Second Mortgage Lenders
Types of loans available	Single and partial payment loans	Single or installment cash and automatic overdraft loans	Secured and unsecured loans	Single or installment cash, automatic overdraft, savings passbook, second mortgage, and credit card loans	Personal cash, automatic overdraft, savings passbook, second mortgage, and credit card loans	Personal cash loans	Single or installment cash loans
Who is eligible	Policyholders	Members	Anyone meeting credit qualifications	Anyone meeting credit qualifications	Anyone meeting credit qualifications	Anyone with personal property	Anyone with equity in a home
Effective annual cost	5 to 8 percent	10 to 15 percent	12 to 36 percent	12 to 24 percent	12 to 24 percent	24 to 120 percent	12 percent and up
Maximum maturity	Unlimited	5 years for unsecured loans; 10 years for secured loans	18 months to 5 years	Varies with circumstances of the loan	Varies with circumstances of the loan	1 year	3 to 15 years
Maximum loan amount	Insurance policy's cash value	$1,000 to $5,000 on unsecured loans; $10,000 on secured loans	$1,000 to $10,000	Varies with circumstances of the loan	Varies with circumstances of the loan	50 to 60 percent of appraised value of personal property	50 percent of home's equity
Collateral required	Insurance policy's cash value	On secured loans only—cosigner or chattel mortgage	On secured loans only	On secured loans only	On secured loans only	Personal property	Home
Credit investigation	No	No	Yes	Yes	Yes	No	Yes

Whatever the purpose of the loan, always conduct borrowing transactions involving family and friends in a businesslike manner. Signing a note with stated interest rate and repayment schedule will reduce any fears that you might take advantage of your personal relationship with the lender.

In most cases, it is inappropriate to borrow from a relative or friend if the professional lenders have refused you because of your inability to repay the loan. If their judgment is correct, you can imagine the strain that will be put on your personal relationship when the time comes to repay a relative or friend and you are unable to do so.

Vicky Harris "borrowed" $4,000 from her adoring grandfather to buy a car to take to college. At the time she asked Gramps for the loan, she told him of her plans to get a part-time job while at school to pay him back within two years. Gramps was so happy to help that he refused to charge interest on the loan. Once at school, Vicky became preoccupied with other matters and never got a job. She also never mentioned the loan to Gramps when she was home on vacation. As the months passed, Gramps became increasingly cool toward his granddaughter.

If you know you will be unable to repay such a loan, but you have an unavoidable need for a certain amount of money, then perhaps you would do better to ask for a gift or financial assistance of some sort. A relative or friend may be very willing to offer this type of support. This approach avoids upsetting the lender who learns after the fact that in reality he or she has been your benefactor.

Life Insurance Policies

The maximum loan amount available to you on a cash value life insurance policy is usually limited to its accumulated cash value, plus dividends and interest. Loans on term life insurance policies are not available because such policies have no cash values.

There are several advantages to borrowing on the cash value of your policy.

1. The interest rate is fixed and generally stated in the policy. In periods when interest rates are high, a policy written when rates were lower may offer a much lower loan charge.
2. Interest is usually charged only on the balance of the loan outstanding, and it may be paid with your regularly scheduled premium payments.
3. Principal repayment schedules and periods are usually flexible and may not be specified at all. Although you may not be required to pay back the principal, the interest payments will probably continue as long as the debt is outstanding.
4. These loans can be obtained by simply writing the company for appropriate forms, filling them out, and returning them. Rarely does the life insurance company want to know your reasons for requesting a loan or ask for information such as your employment history. Within a month you should have the amount you requested.

There are two disadvantages to using this type of borrowing despite its inherent attractiveness. First, the face value of your policy (its death benefit) is decreased by the amount borrowed. For example, if you had a $20,000 life insurance policy with an accumulated cash value of $6,250 and you borrowed $5,000 on the policy, the benefits your beneficiary would receive, if you died, would be only $15,000 ($20,000 face value minus $5,000 loan outstanding). As you repaid the principal of this loan, however, the face value of the policy would increase. One way to avoid this reduction in death protection is to buy term insurance for the duration of the loan. Second, if the repayment schedule and period are not specified, you may put off resolving the debt and consequently continue to pay interest year after year. This disadvantage can be offset if you are disciplined enough to set your own schedule and stick to it.

Credit Unions

Sometimes a group of people with a common interest or activity join together to form credit unions that extend consumer loans to their members at rates lower than those they could obtain from commercial lenders. These rates are possible because credit unions do not seek a profit and because they generally have low-cost operations, often using some volunteer labor offered by the members.

They provide financial services (emergency loans, credit counseling, insurance benefits, and the like) only for their members. The primary requirement for membership usually is that a certain amount of savings be invested in the credit union. This limit is often expressed as a dollar amount. Some credit unions require as little as $5 or $10. This nominal entrance amount gives you a vote. Subsequent deposits, however, do not give you more votes. Generally, maximum loan limits are determined by the policies of each credit union within the guidelines set down by appropriate government agencies.

Borrowing from a credit union can be quite attractive.

1. Interest costs are comparatively low—the lowest available for many people.
2. Security and endorsements are not required on small loans (up to $1,000 for some of the larger credit unions).
3. As a borrower, you can have confidence in the integrity of the lending organization because it consists of your associates. This last circumstance may also result in particularly sympathetic services.
4. Credit unions often have programs that encourage systematic savings, thus reducing your need to borrow in the first place.

One disadvantage is that if you are not a member of a credit union, you cannot borrow from one. In other words, availability is limited. Another is that as a borrower, you may hesitate to divulge your need for a loan to your associates. While they may employ a professionally trained person to handle the lending duties, he or she will probably be overseen by a committee composed of credit union members, who may or may not know you (as through contact at work).

Consumer Finance (Small Loan) Companies

Consumer finance companies specialize in small loans. The maximum loan limit for unsecured loans is set by some state governments and ranges from $1,000 to $5,000.

The maximum maturity is also set by some state governments and ranges from 18 months to five years. In other states, small loan companies are allowed the discretion of setting their own maximums for maturities and loan amounts.

Both the advantages and the disadvantages of borrowing from consumer finance companies derive from their specializing in small loans with short and intermediate terms. These organizations are generally willing to write loans in smaller amounts than most other loan sources. However, a disadvantage is that they are limited in the amount they may lend and in the length of time over which the loan may be repaid. Qualification and security requirements are not as stringent as with some other sources. If you have a poor credit rating, finance companies may be your only loan source, but the disadvantage in this is that the interest charged is often higher than what other sources would charge if you qualified for a loan. (The higher rate is necessary to encourage consumer finance companies to grant these higher risk loans.) One last advantage is that interest is often charged only on the outstanding balance, not on the initial amount borrowed. Many people overlook the disadvantages of borrowing from small loan companies because they see these organizations as less formidable and imposing than banks. For this reason, the prospective borrower may feel more at ease at a consumer finance company.

Before the Consumer Credit Protection Act, only some states had guidelines regulating consumer finance companies. Regulation was often haphazard and inconsistent and provided insufficient protection for the consumer. In some instances, unscrupulous lending practices flourished. This legislation, combined with increasingly rigorous small loan state laws plus a better-educated consumer population, has done much to repair the reputation of this basically sound source of consumer loans.

Commercial Banks

The term *commercial banks* includes all institutions, except mutual savings banks, commonly referred to as banks. In general, commercial banks require that their customers have better credit records than consumer finance companies require. Because the risk of default is less for banks, their interest charges are lower than those levied by finance companies.

Banks offer consumer loan customers more extensive services than do most other lending institutions. Regarding installment loans, unsecured loans require only the borrower's signed promise to repay and are written generally for shorter periods and higher interest charges than are secured loans. Unsecured loans include regular loans, loans against a bank credit card, and loans that are automatically extended whenever a check is written for more money than is in a checking account. You must fulfill certain qualifications, however, before banks will allow you to use these unsecured loans, and the costs of using them are relatively high. Therefore, if you need to borrow money, be sure to consider getting it more cheaply with a secured loan.

Secured loans usually require some form of collateral. For automobile or home furnishing loans, the purchased item(s) can serve as security. A savings passbook loan uses your savings account as collateral; such a loan may cost less for the short term than drawing down your savings just before interest is due—if interest is paid only on amounts held in the account for the full quarter. Real estate mortgage loans may be written for either home improvements or the purchase of a home, though only the former are, by definition, consumer loans. The maturity on these ranges from five to 25 years, and security is provided by the property itself.

Special payment or automatic transfer plans can direct the bank to deduct money from checking accounts to pay consumer loan and consumer credit repayments, and certain bills such as utilities and insurance premiums. The authority to do this is granted in a written agreement.

There are definite advantages to borrowing from a commercial bank.

1. Because of strict federal regulations, the integrity of most banking institutions is rarely violated.
2. Because of their credit requirements for applicants, borrowing costs are comparatively low.
3. Successful borrowing and punctual repayment on your part will result in the establishment of a good credit rating that will make future loans less expensive and easier to obtain. This may be an advantage of dealing with any lender, but a good bank credit rating is of particular benefit.

The disadvantages are that it is difficult to obtain loans in small amounts and the qualification and payback requirements are quite rigid.

Savings and Loan Associations

Until the 1980s savings and loan associations served a dual purpose. As savings institutions they offered returns slightly higher than those offered by commercial banks. As lending institutions they served mainly the home mortgage market. In addition to mortgage loans, many savings and loan associations offered FHA-insured home repair and modernization loans as well as consumer loans. In 1972 the federal government authorized a more extensive consumer lending program for savings and loan associations. As a result, these associations could make loans for such things as vacation and mobile homes as well as house improvements and household equipment (such as air conditioning systems).

These consumer loans are still available. They are usually made solely against the value of savings held by a member (or depositor) of the institution granting the loan. The maximum loan limit is usually 90 percent of one's savings investment for state chartered associations and 100 percent for federally chartered associations. With this type of loan no credit investigation is required. Over the very short term, such a loan may cost less than drawing down your savings account just before interest or dividends are paid, if interest is paid only on accounts held for the full quarter. Of course, such loans are available only to savings account holders. The finance charge is generally 1 to 2.5 percent above the return represented by one's investments in savings and loan associations.

In the late 1970s interest rates rose dramatically in the United States. The old 5¼ percent time deposit savings would not allow savings and loan associations to compete effectively for funds with other financial institutions, mainly commercial banks and money market funds. To attract funds, savings and loans found it necessary to offer a new range of savings opportunities (to be discussed in Chapter 16). Furthermore, legislation enacted in the late 1970s and early 1980s enabled savings and loan associations to offer a wider array of lending opportunities—including automatic overdraft accounts, credit card loans, education loans, second mortgages, and personal cash loans.

Pawnbrokers

Pawnbrokers most commonly serve as a lending source either in emergencies or when the applicant's credit is not accepted by other lenders. There is no need for a signed note because the personal property brought by the borrower serves as security. The pawnbroker rarely offers a loan exceeding 50 to 60 percent of the appraised market value of the property.

You may generally redeem your property within a year by paying a lump sum of principal plus interest, which may range from 24 to 120 percent annually. Installment payments are not used. If you fail to make the required payment, the pawnbroker has the right to auction your property, either publicly or privately, in order to retrieve his or her investment. Amounts in excess of the investment gained from the auction are rightfully yours. Instances of such surplus amounts are rare, however.

The chief advantages of pawnbrokers as a lending source are that transactions are quick and may be kept secret. Disadvantages are that interest rates are exceptionally high, and there is insufficient protection for the consumer because government regulations are often lax and vary from state to state.

Second Mortgages

The true costs of second mortgages are often obscured by their small monthly payments. In reality, the effective annual cost can be 20 percent or more because of a 15 to 80 percent annual interest charge plus fees that are attached at the beginning of the loan. The small monthly payments frequently represent little more than interest payments, with the amount of the loan itself coming due in one large payment at the end of the mortgage maturity. The danger in this form of borrowing is that you may be unable to make this large last payment and therefore have to refinance the loan at the continued high interest cost.

EDUCATION LOANS

Education loans are available in varying amounts and for varying terms through either government or private sources.

Government Sources

The Middle-Income Student Assistance Act passed by Congress in late 1978 greatly expanded the government aid available to college students. The Basic Educational Opportunity Grant (BEOG) involves direct federal grants of from $200 to $1,800 for students from families with incomes up to approximately $30,000. (Previously the upper limit was $15,000.) The actual size of the grant is dictated by the family's financial circumstances.

The National Defense Education Act enables students at most colleges to borrow $1,000 a year up to a total of $5,000 while they are undergraduates. Repayment begins nine months after leaving school. The payback period is 10 years and the annual interest rate on the outstanding balance is 5 percent. Interest does not begin to be charged until the individual is no longer a full-time student. Service with the Peace Corps, Vista, or the military; attendance at a graduate school; or employment as a teacher can result in the deferment of the payback period (interest is not charged during deferral) or in reduction or cancellation of the amount owed. If the loan is cancelled, the IRS treats the amount of debt forgiven as income that year to the borrower. Eligibility requirements and applications for such loans are handled by the colleges themselves.

The Guaranteed Student Loan Program offers loans from private sources (banks, individuals, credit unions, and the like) that are guaranteed by the federal government. In some instances they may be guaranteed by the United Students Aid Fund, which derives part of its reserves from contributions by participating educational institutions. In 1982, eligibility standards were tightened so that families with annual adjusted gross incomes in excess of $30,000 must meet certain new need requirements. Up to $2,500 is available each year for undergraduates, not to exceed a total of $12,500; for graduate students the maximum per year is $5,000, and $25,000 overall. A 5 percent loan origination fee is required to be paid up front. Unlike the NDEA, interest must be paid while the student is attending college. Above the "below market" interest rate set for borrowers, up to 12 percent additional interest can be paid by the federal government. The payback period, which begins nine months after graduation, varies from five to 10 years; as with NDEA, repayment may be postponed for certain types of national service. Maximum interest rates are set currently at 14 percent for the former student. The government will continue to pay any interest above 14 percent that was necessary originally to encourage the lender to write the loan.

Pell grants, named after Senator Claiborne Pell, have an annual maximum of approximately $1,700. They are limited to families with adjusted gross incomes of $26,000 or less.

Private Sources

Private organizations, churches, colleges, unions, and service organizations occasionally have their own loan programs. Eligibility is more limited than with government loans, but terms are often quite favorable. Commercial lenders often grant installment loans, at market terms, to cover education expenses. Generally, the best place to get up-to-date information about education loans is from the student aid office at your college or university.

PREPAYMENT

Assume you enter into an installment loan agreement in which you receive $1,100 initially and are to repay the principal ($1,100) and finance charge ($100) in monthly installments of $100 each. After making six monthly payments, you decide to repay the loan fully. How much do you still owe? $600? But a portion of the remaining payments is for the finance charge. Since the loan is being repaid ahead of schedule, you should not be liable for the future finance charge on the principal that you are now prepaying.

Rule of 78

The most common method of determining what rebate on finance charges is due you is known as the rule of 78. The name comes from the fact that the sum of the digits 1 through 12 equals 78. The calculation is made as follows:

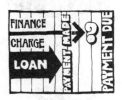

1. Determine what would be the inverse of the numerical notation of the months yet to be paid off. For this procedure, the numerical notation for each month is the inverse of the usual sequence; for example, month 3 in a 12-month loan is notated as 10, month 8 as 5. In our example with the $1,100 installment loan, the numbers for the remaining months would be 1, 2, 3, 4, 5, and 6.
2. Add the numbers found in step 1. In our example, the sum is 21.
3. Divide the sum found in step 2 by 78. In our example, the result is 26.92 percent.
4. Multiply the percentage found in step 3 by the original finance charge. The result is the amount of the rebate. In our example, $26.92 of the original finance charge of $100 ($1,200 due less $1,100 borrowed times .2692) is to be rebated.
5. Subtract the amount of the rebate (as found in step 4) from the amount still due on the loan if all the remaining payments were made. The result is the amount due on the loan if it is paid off now. In our example, $573.08 ($600 minus $26.92) is the amount you would pay to pay off the loan now.

You may ask why only 26.92 percent of the finance charge remained on the loan when it was already halfway to its maturity. As the example of amortization in Table 11-2 showed, the largest portion of finance charges applies to the earliest stages of an installment loan. That is when the greatest amount of principal (upon which the finance charges are made) is outstanding. Thus, 73.08 percent of the finance charge was paid during the first six months of the loan. This payment can be determined by adding $12 + 11 + 10 + 9 + 8 + 7$ to obtain 57 and then dividing that sum by 78.

The inverse of the numerical notation of the months involved is a practical way of determining what portion of finance charges is to be rebated. The procedure can be applied to any set of circumstances. For example, on a 13-month payment plan, paid off after six months of payments, the calculation of the percentage to multiply times the finance charge is as follows.

$$\frac{1 + 2 + 3 + 4 + 5 + 6 + 7 \text{ (months remaining)}}{1 + 2 + 3 + 4 + 5 + 6 + 7 + 8 + 9 + 10 + 11 + 12 + 13 \text{ (total months)}}$$

$$= \frac{28}{91} = 30.77\%$$

The rule of 78 results in a slightly lower rebate than if it were calculated by the APR method discussed earlier in this chapter.

Prepayment Penalty

Some loans may contain prepayment penalties to compensate the lender for the time and interest lost on loans that are prematurely paid off, necessitating the origination of a new loan with a new borrower. When determining (by the rule of 78) the cost savings of early payment of a loan, check to see whether there is also a prepayment penalty. It could reduce or eliminate the benefit of finance charges saved by early repayment.

BANKRUPTCY

Sometimes people use debt improperly and ignore the guidelines on limiting indebtedness that we discussed earlier. Sometimes the market value of a person's assets can diminish to the point where it is less than the person's debts. At this point the person may be entitled to declare bankruptcy, whereby he or she gives up certain assets in return for being legally released from certain debts.

Not all assets are subject to bankruptcy proceedings, nor can all debts be discharged through bankruptcy. Social Security benefits, alimony, child support, disability benefits, retirement benefits, and veterans' benefits are among the assets exempted. Certain portions of home equity, an economical car, and a family's personal effects, such as clothing, are also exempted. Debts such as alimony, unpaid income taxes from the last three years, child support, and those incurred under false or fraudulent pretenses cannot be discharged through bankruptcy.

If you find yourself financially bankrupt, you should seek legal assistance. Official declaration of bankruptcy entails (a) preparing and filing a petition, (b) meeting your creditors in Bankruptcy Court to resolve their claims as much as possible, and (c) having a court-appointed trustee collect and sell your assets and distribute the proceeds to your creditors as appropriate. Congress passed a law in 1978 revising bankruptcy laws and upgrading the Bankruptcy Court and judges. The basic thrust of the old laws, however—to balance a debtor's right to a new beginning against the creditor's right to minimize his or her losses—has been retained.

If you are at or near bankruptcy but would rather be given the opportunity to resolve your indebtedness in full, then perhaps you should consider the "Chapter 13" repayment plan (called "wage-earner plan" under the old law). Under this arrangement you would draw up a plan, with the help of a financial counselor, to fully resolve your debts over a specific period of up to three years (up to five years with special court approval). If you can get the court and enough of your creditors to agree to accept this regular pattern of debt resolution, then you will begin making payments as specified to the court. The court in turn will pay your creditors. During this period, interest and late payment penalties are generally waived. As long as you adhere to the plan, you retain the right to all of your assets. "Chapter 13" also covers self-employed persons and people who cosigned notes with you before your financial difficulties became apparent.

Declaring bankruptcy is not a matter to be taken lightly. You should fully explore its limited benefits and considerable disadvantages with legal counsel before you proceed. Having filed for bankruptcy, you must wait six years before being allowed to do so again. Under "Chapter 13" this prohibition doesn't apply as long as you have repaid at least 70 percent of your debts.

OTHER SERVICES OF COMMERCIAL BANKS

Commercial banks offer three basic services to their customers: lending, saving, and checking. The first has already been treated in this chapter, and savings will be covered in Chapter 16. What remains, then, is a brief overview of checking and other less important banking services. While checking accounts are being offered now by savings and loan associations and mutual savings banks, the vast majority of these accounts are still the province of commercial banks. Therefore, this section will deal almost exclusively with checking services as offered by commercial banks.

How a Checking System Works

In a checking system, cash is rarely actually transferred from one bank to another. Most commonly, check transactions are a series of bookkeeping entries. That is, the bank upon which a check is written reduces its customer's account by the amount of the check, while the bank to which the deposit is made increases its depositor's account by a like amount.

When both the check writer (payer) and check receiver/depositor (payee) have accounts at the same bank, this process occurs quickly, generally the same day. When both the payer's and payee's banks are served by the same regional check clearinghouse, the process usually takes one or two days. When there is a substantial distance between the subject banks, then the Federal Reserve System comes into the picture. Among its many functions and responsibilities, it provides and administers a nationwide network within which most of our private banking organizations can interact with each other.

Let us assume Bill Trow writes a check against his account at a Cincinnati, Ohio, bank to purchase certain items from a mail-order house in San Francisco. Here's how the process works.

1. Bill mails his check to San Francisco.
2. The mail-order house receives the check and deposits it in its checking account at a local bank.
3. The bank, receiving this check, deposits it with the regional Federal Reserve bank, in this case also located in San Francisco (SFFRB).
4. The SFFRB sends the check to the regional FRB located in Cincinnati (CFRB).
5. The CFRB debits the account of Bill Trow's commercial bank by the amount of his check.
6. Bill's bank debits his actual account by the amount of his check.
7. The CFRB credits the SFFRB with a like amount.
8. The SFFRB credits the mail-order house's commercial bank.
9. The mail-order house's commercial bank deposits the credit in the mail-order house's actual account.

Depending on circumstances, this process can take anywhere from two days to two weeks.

Choosing a Checking Account and a Bank

Several different types of checking accounts are available at most banks (Table 11-5). You should take the time to learn what the alternatives are in order to choose an account that best meets your needs at the lowest cost. For example, do you need an account just for yourself or a joint account with your spouse or business associate? Also, is an interest-bearing NOW (negotiable order of withdrawal) account more appropriate for you than a noninterest-bearing, traditional checking account? NOW accounts generally pay 5¼ to 5½ percent interest on account balances, allow banking by mail, provide monthly statements, and do not charge for checks written as do regular checking accounts. However, if your account balance falls below a prescribed level, various charges will be levied, more than offsetting any interest earned, or else interest will be forfeited. Obviously, the method the bank uses to determine when this minimum balance is reached (average daily versus lowest balance) is important.

The three "C's" apply when considering where to open a checking account: cost, convenience, and courtesy. After you have decided which type of account best fits your circumstances, you need to analyze the costs. Make sure you understand what minimum balance, if any, is required; how it is calculated (average daily or lowest balance); and what charges are levied for bounced checks (those you have written or those written by others to you), stop-payment orders, and the purchase of blank checks. Banks offer numerous services, but not all banks charge for them in the same way. Therefore, be sure you understand the alternatives and the costs before signing up.

Convenience should also be considered. Many people use their checking accounts frequently. If you need to do much of your banking in person, there might not be any savings in driving across town just to bank where free checking accounts are available.

Finally, as a customer you are entitled to courtesy. You may also need personal attention from time to time in handling your account. While the value of such treatment cannot readily be measured in dollars and cents, it should not be overlooked when considering where to open your checking account.

Blank and Restricted Endorsements

Two types of endorsements are used most often: blank and restricted. The former requires only your signature on the back of a check payable to you. With this endorsement, the check becomes cashable by anyone; therefore, never blank endorse a check until the moment you are ready to cash it.

The restricted endorsement specifies that a check can be cashed only by a certain individual (e.g., "pay to the order of Bill Trow only") or can be deposited only to a certain account (e.g., "for deposit only to savings account #4763-254-11762"). As such, it makes the check much less vulnerable to misuse if the check is lost or stolen.

TABLE 11-5

Comparison of Types of Checking Accounts

	Activity Plan ("Special")	Minimum Balance Plan	Free Checking Plan	NOW Plan[a]	Package Plan	Analysis Plan
Charges						
Monthly maintenance	$1 to $5	None[b]	None	None[b]	$2 to $5[c]	Yes[d]
Transactions	10¢ to 25¢ per check written	None[b]	None	None[b]	None	For each deposit and check[d]
Monthly balance	No minimum	Account's minimum balance determined as lowest daily balance during month or as average daily balance	No minimum	$50 to $2,000	No minimum	Credit based on average monthly balance
Frequency of statements	2 to 3 months	Monthly	Monthly	Monthly	Monthly	Monthly
Availability[e]	CB	CB	CB, SL, CU	CB, SL, CU	CB, SL	CB
Comment	Good when few checks written each month	Average daily balance method more favorable to customer	Uncommon; offered by new or existing organizations to attract new customers	Pays 5 percent interest	Generally worthwhile only to persons who use banking services extensively	Good for large personal or commercial account

[a]Negotiable order of withdrawal plan.

[b]If the minimum balance is not maintained, charges will be incurred.

[c]This charge may entitle the customer also to a safe-deposit box, traveler's checks, a bank credit card, a check courtesy cashing card, and the like. Some of these items are often offered free to bank customers, apart from the package plan.

[d]Varies with account size and activity.

[e]CB = commercial bank; SL = savings and loan association; CU = credit union.

1001	$ 31.47
May 7 19 83	
TO ABC Hardware	
Garden tools	

	DOLLARS	CENTS
BAL. FOR'D	400	00
DEPOSITS	217	00
"		
TOTAL	617	00
THIS CHECK	31	47
OTHER DEDUCTIONS		
BAL. FOR'D	585	53

NAME_____

ACCOUNT NO._____

19___

PAY TO THE
ORDER OF_____ $_____

SAMPLE

_____ DOLLARS

FREEDOM BANK
1604 K Street, NW
Washington, DC 20006

1001

90-3534
1211

MEMO_____

⑆:⑈1211353461⑈:

DELUXE CHECK PRINTERS • RJ-1

FIGURE 11-1
An example of check stub method of keeping a running balance.

How to Balance Your Checkbook

The first phase of balancing your checkbook involves keeping a "running balance." This balance can be kept either on the check stubs (Fig. 11-1) that are attached by perforated edge to the left-hand side of each check or via a ledger system (Fig. 11-2) provided with your checkbook. When you open your account, you enter the initial deposit on the stub to the left of your next unused check or in your checkbook ledger. As each check is written, enter also its number (probably preprinted on the stub), the date, amount, payee, and purpose. After each entry (whether deposit made or check written), calculate the remaining balance—adding deposits and subtracting debits. In addition, subtract any service or miscellaneous charges (as for overdrafts, printed checks, account maintenance, a safe-deposit box) as they occur. Most checkbooks provide for such entries on the check stubs or in the ledger. You may prefer to keep a cushion of $25 to $50 in your account each month to absorb these unannounced

PLEASE BE SURE TO **DEDUCT** ANY PER CHECK CHARGES OR SERVICE CHARGES THAT MAY APPLY TO YOUR ACCOUNT

CHECK NO	DATE	CHECKS ISSUED TO OR DESCRIPTION OF DEPOSIT	(-) AMOUNT OF CHECK	√ T	(-) CHECK FEE (IF ANY)	(+) AMOUNT OF DEPOSIT	BALANCE	
	4/27	Opening deposit				400 00	400	00
	5/1	Weekly paycheck				217	217	00
							617	00
1001	5/7	ABC Hardware	31 47				31	47
		Garden tools					585	53

FIGURE 11-2
A sample checkbook ledger for keeping a running balance. Note column for checking off tax deductible expenses.

| ACCOUNT NUMBER |
| 276-54-3076 |

DISPOSITION CODE	NUMBER OF ENCLOSURES	PAGE NO.
	7	1

TERENCE T. CATE
109 MIDDLETON AVE.
NORTH PARK, MI

CHECKING ACCOUNT ACTIVITY (SEE REVERSE SIDE OF STATEMENT FOR IMPORTANT INFORMATION)

CHECKS AND OTHER DEBITS		DEPOSITS AND OTHER CREDITS		LOW BALANCE	AVERAGE BALANCE	SERVICE CHARGE	BEGINNING BALANCE
NO.	AMOUNT	NO.	AMOUNT				
7	750 58	4	868 00	400 42	661 83	00	400 00

TRANSACTION DESCRIPTION	AMOUNT	DATE	TRANSACTION DESCRIPTION	AMOUNT	DATE	RUNNING BALANCE	DATE
1001 CK	31 47	5 09				617 00	5 02
1002 CK	115 00	5 14				802 53	5 09
1003 CK	72 12	5 16				687 53	5 14
1004 CK	12 53	5 19				832 41	5 16
1005 CK	312 46	5 21				819 88	5 19
1006 CK	107 00	5 21				400 42	5 21
1007 CK	100 00	5 29				617 42	5 23
02 DP	217 00	5 02				517 42	5 29
03 DP	217 00	5 09					
04 DP	217 00	5 16					
05 DP	217 00	5 23					
						517 42	
						ENDING BALANCE	

charges until your bank statement arrives; you can then deal with them as part of check reconciliation.

FIGURE 11-3
A sample monthly bank statement.

Check reconciliation, the second phase of balancing your checkbook, involves checking your record keeping against that done by the bank as shown on the statement the bank sends you. This statement is usually monthly, bimonthly, or quarterly. An example of a simplified monthly bank statement is shown in Figure 11-3. To reconcile the bank statement with your checkbook, use the following procedure:

1. Sort the checks into either chronological or numerical order.
2. Check the accuracy of each check and their sum with the corresponding amounts on the bank statement and on the check stubs or checkbook ledger.
3. Check the accuracy of each deposit and their sum with the corresponding amounts on the bank statement and on the check stubs or checkbook ledger.
4. Check the bank statement's arithmetic.

   a. Add the deposit total to the beginning balance.
   b. Subtract from this amount the checks written and any service or miscellaneous charges.
   c. This new amount should equal the bank statement's ending balance. If it does not, and you have double-checked the accuracy of your own computations, you should call your bank. Find out who handles this type of question and bring up the discrepancy you have noted. In most cases, mistakes are easily corrected. Some banks have instituted the practice of not discussing a customer's account over the phone to ensure that the customer's privacy is not breached by a caller posing as a customer. In this instance, you will have to have your questions handled at the bank.

You may have written some checks since the closing date on the bank statement. To reconcile the statement with your checking account's current state of affairs, use the form provided on the back of the bank statement (Fig. 11-4).

The degree of accuracy you use in keeping your checkbook balanced will depend on several factors such as how prone you are to overdrawing your checking account, how large a cushion you can afford to leave in your checking account, how concerned you are about bank accounting errors occurring at your expense, and how much you enjoy mathematical precision.

Avoiding Overdrafts

An overdraft occurs whenever there are insufficient funds in an account to cover a check written on the account. In other words, the check bounces.

Probably the expense of overdrafts (usually $6 to $8 a check) and the poor credit rating that can result from recurrent bounced checks are the greatest incentive to keeping your checkbook records up-to-date and balanced to the penny. Suppose you write a check that overdraws your checking account by $70, and the bank charges you $6 for the overdraft, which lasts three days before you are informed of it; this $6 charge represents an annual interest rate of 1,032 percent ($6/$70 = 8.6\% \times 360/3$ days). That alone should be adequate motivation to avoid overdrafts. Frequent recurrences of bounced checks may impair your ability to obtain credit because a prospective lender would regard you as having difficulty keeping your personal financial affairs in order and therefore as a poor credit risk.

Have you ever made a deposit to your account and soon thereafter written a check against the supposed new balance and wondered why the check bounced? Some banks have a policy of not crediting a checking account with a deposit until the day after the deposit is made, and yet they debit a checking account for any checks written the day they are received. Therefore, if you both deposit and withdraw funds by check from your bank on the same day, your account record may

STATEMENT RECONCILIATION			
STATEMENT BALANCE		$ 517	42
ADD-	DEPOSITS MADE BUT NOT SHOWN ON THIS STATEMENT	217	00
	TOTAL	$ 734	42
SUBTRACT-	CHECKS OUTSTANDING	50	70
TOTAL-	SHOULD AGREE WITH YOUR CHECK BOOK BALANCE	$ 683	72

CHECKS OUTSTANDING			
CHECK NUMBER		AMOUNT	
8	6/1	32	50
9	6/3	12	11
10	6/4	5	09

TOTAL-	ENTER IN THE SPACE PROVIDED ABOVE	$ 50	70

FIGURE 11-4
Sample form for reconciling deposits made and checks written since closing date for bank statement.

show insufficient funds to cover your check even though the bank was in possession of your deposit. The check could also bounce if the bank upon which the check is written that you deposit in your account is a significant distance away; before the deposit is "cleared" for entry into your account, your bank must contact the other bank and receive authorization to credit the amount for deposit in your account.

In general, checkbook records that are kept up-to-date and balanced to the penny present the least risk of an overdraft. Depending on the size of the cushion you can afford to carry in your checking account, you will want to note any service or miscellaneous charges in particular, if you are concerned about lowering your risk of being overdrawn.

Other Types of Checks

In addition to the checks you use as part of your checking account, from time to time you may also need traveler's, cashier's, and certified checks.

Traveler's checks are used primarily by people while away from home. Issued by major financial institutions (usually in $10, $20, $50, and $100 denominations), these checks are accepted by a wide range of restaurants, hotels, retailers, airlines, and the like. Upon purchasing traveler's checks from your bank or savings and loan, you should sign each check. Your signature on the checks minimizes the chance that someone else can cash them if they are lost or stolen.

Each check has a serial number printed on it. When you purchase your checks, you will also receive a small ledger-like page on which to record the serial number and use of each check. You should keep this ledger separate from the checks; therefore, if your checks are lost or stolen, you can immediately notify your bank or savings and loan which checks not to order payment on (i.e., those serial numbers that remained unused at the time of the theft or loss).

When you are ready to cash a traveler's check, you should date and sign it again where indicated, in the presence of the payee. On occasion, the payee will require you to put its name on the check, although most organizations have stamps for this purpose.

The cost to buy traveler's checks is usually 1 percent of the amount of traveler's checks you purchase. Depending upon the type of acount and amount of business you do with your bank or savings and loan, this fee may be waived. Additionally, your bank or savings and loan and the issuing financial institution will be earning interest on the money used to purchase your traveler's checks as long as you do not use them.

A *cashier's check* can be purchased from your savings and loan or bank. It is a check issued by the financial institution itself and so will be accepted by payees in some instances where your personal check might not be readily accepted (often where the amount of the check is quite large). The cost of a cashier's check is its amount plus a small service fee, which can be waived in certain instances (e.g., you are an important customer).

A *certified check* is your personal check with your bank's or savings and loan's certification stamped on it indicating that the amount of the check has been deducted from your account and is available to the payee immediately.

Other Bank Services

Banks offer safe-deposit boxes—private, relatively safe places for keeping valuable papers, jewelry, and the like. Occasionally thieves have broken into safe-deposit vaults. The bank cannot indemnify you against such losses because, if these boxes are to remain private, the bank has no way to verify what was actually in your box before a robbery occurred. You can, however, extend your property insurance to cover items in your safe-deposit box. Some savings associations also offer safe-deposit boxes to their customers.

Most mutual savings banks and savings and loans will execute money orders for their depositors against their savings accounts. Certain of these organizations will also write checks upon request against depositors' accounts or make regular monthly disbursements to cover regularly recurring bills such as mortgage payments and loan payments.

Banks often have trust departments whose principal responsibility is to act as an impersonal professional third party in the administration and investment management of customers' trusts. A more detailed discussion of trusts and the responsibilities of trustees may be found in Chapter 22.

Automation in Banking

Banks have been very active in automating their industry. For example, automatic tellers dispense cash, transfer funds from one account to another, pay regularly recurring bills such as for home loans, and accept deposits—all at the direction of the customer. These machines are being increasingly accepted by banking customers, particularly younger ones, who frequently are comfortable dealing with new technologies.

In order to interact with an automatic teller, you must have a plastic ID card that is imprinted (in most cases) with a special magnetic strip on one side and multiple-digit personal access code, both issued by your bank or savings and loan. To use the teller, you must insert your card in the appropriate slot and punch in your personal access code on the accompanying keyboard. If you do not complete all access steps properly, the teller will refuse to acknowledge your transaction orders. If you fail on several attempts, the computer that operates this terminal may freeze your automatic account on the possibility that it is not you fumbling through the access steps but someone trying to gain unauthorized access to your account. If this freezing occurs, you must go to your bank or savings and loan to straighten matters out.

Obviously, it is very important to safeguard against unauthorized access to your account when an automatic teller is involved. Therefore, never allow others a view of the display screen or key pad while you are inputting your access code or creating transactions; use only ATMs that are in safe areas and well lit at night; keep your access code secret; and never use such common numbers as telephone number, street address, or Social security number as all or part of your access code.

Here are some more examples of automation in banking:

- Computer terminals at many retail stores allow verification of a customer's credit at the time of a purchase, thus reducing the possibility of extending credit to nonpaying customers or of accepting fraudulent checks.
- Computer symbols on checks facilitate check clearance where this process has been automated, such as at regional clearinghouses.
- Many employers have an arrangement with their banks whereby employees can have their paychecks deposited directly to their personal checking accounts.
- The federal government has developed a system to deposit Social Security checks directly in the checking or savings accounts of recipients. This procedure should help stop the thefts that retired people are prey to just after cashing their retirement checks.

Despite these and many other technological innovations in banking, customers have not completely welcomed this trend. Therefore, automatic technology in banking has not proceeded as rapidly as many people originally thought it would. Probably bank customers are afraid that, with impersonal banking techniques, (1) their financial privacy will be easier to violate, (2) computational errors (such as misbillings by computer) will be harder to catch and correct, and (3) thieves with technical backgrounds will be able to rob banks more easily. Automatic technology in banking will probably not reach its full potential until the banking industry has developed adequate safeguards against these problems.

CONCLUSION

Borrowing is a means of increasing your immediate purchasing power. However, if you pay too much for the use of someone else's money or use it unwisely, borrowing can result in unnecessary drains on your financial resources. To ensure that this does not occur, use the measurement devices suggested in this chapter to determine what effect using consumer loans will have on your financial resources. Once you have done your homework, you will be prepared to check various sources of consumer loans and shop for the best deal.

Banks offer a variety of other services besides the use of depositors' money. The most important of these other services is a checking account. Make sure you evaluate the available banks for the best combination of cost, courtesy, and convenience. Once you have picked your bank, make sure you maintain your checkbook records so that overdrafts do not occur.

VOCABULARY

amortization	discounted interest
annual percentage rate (APR)	effective cost
balance outstanding	finance charge
bankruptcy	interest
blank endorsement	loan endorsement
carrying cost	maturity
cashier's check	prepayment penalty
certified check	principal
collateral	restricted endorsement
commercial bank	secured loan
Consumer Credit Protection Act	security
creditor	traveler's check
credit union	unsecured loan

QUESTIONS

1. Examine the validity of arguments used both for and against borrowing. Can it be morally right or wrong? Does it allow a person to live beyond his or her means? Can it lead to financial problems and, if so, how? Is it worth the cost and risks? Are you in favor of borrowing money? Do your reasons have a financial basis?
2. How do the two federal government college loan programs discussed in this chapter differ from each other?
3. Which source of consumer loans offers the most borrowing opportunities to the borrower with a good credit rating? Why?

4. What is the difference between a secured and an unsecured loan?
5. How do income level and position in the life cycle affect the use of borrowed money?
6. How does inflation affect the cost of borrowing?
7. When are there no tax savings associated with the cost of borrowing?
8. In what ways does borrowing resemble a forced savings plan?
9. How can you identify a disreputable lending source?
10. When shopping for a loan, what types of information should you collect?
11. What are the three things you should consider when deciding where to open a checking account?
12. While on vacation, a tourist writes a check to buy a souvenir in a retail store. Describe how the check cashing procedure works in this situation where the two banks involved are located in different parts of the country.

CASE PROBLEMS

1. Your best friend has come to you for advice about obtaining a loan. He needs at least $3,000 to purchase kitchen and laundry appliances, and his family's budget will allow them to make monthly repayments of $125. He has already been out shopping in the money markets. His findings are given in Table 11-6. Based on this information, which alternative is most appropriate for your friend?
2. Another friend supplies you with the following information.

- Eight months ago she borrowed $2,000 at 18 percent APR for 15 months.
- She cannot remember what her monthly payment is, but she knows she has made eight of them.
- She wants to repay the balance outstanding on the loan right now.

Your friend asks you to figure out what her monthly payment level is and how much she will need to resolve the debt in full at this time.

TABLE 11-6

Comparison of Four Consumer Loans

Source	Amount of Loan	Security	Annual Finance Charge	Payback Terms
Commercial bank A	$3,000	None	11%[a] (interest added on)	90-day note[b]
Commercial bank B	$3,500	Purchased goods	10%[a] (interest added on)	3-year amortized note
Consumer finance company	$3,200	None	18%[c] (interest discounted)	Equal monthly installments over 4 years
Credit union	$4,000	Purchased goods	9%[a] (interest added on)	Amortized over 5 years

[a]Effective rate of interest.

[b]This note is to be paid back at the end of the term in a lump sum plus interest; it may be renewed for three 90-day periods.

[c]Stated rate of interest.

3. Edna and Edmund Flander opened a checking account and had the following activity in this account during the first month.

Opening deposit	$900.00
Check 1001	12.72
Check 1002	777.43
Deposit 1	347.50
Check 1003	432.12
Check 1004	112.10
Deposit 2	400.00
Check 1005	342.15
Check 1006	9.67
Deposit 3	347.50
Check 1007	287.30
Check 1008	415.06

a. How many times did the Flanders overdraw their account during the first month, assuming that the payees cashed the checks promptly upon receiving them?
b. What was the negative balance each time?
c. If $6 was charged for each overdraft, what is the final balance in this account?
d. What might the Flanders be doing to cause this problem?

RECOMMENDED READING

ON BORROWING

"The Bill Collector Always Rings Twice." *Consumer Reports*, February 1977.
   Discusses various bill collector techniques.

"How Lenders Size You Up." *Changing Times*, January 1978, pp. 37–39.
   Discusses a credit rating system used by lenders.

Kaufman, Daniel. *How to Get out of Debt without Despair and without a Lawyer.* Los Angeles: Pinnacle Books, 1981.
   Discusses ways to solve debt problems other than by declaring bankruptcy.

"The New Rules about Bankruptcy." *Changing Times*, May 1979, pp. 31–32.
   Describes changes in the bankruptcy laws implemented late in 1978.

"Using What You Have to Borrow More." *Changing Times*, February 1979, pp. 37–38.
   Points up various sources of collateral for loans.

ON BANKING

"The Holdup on Deposited Checks." *Consumer Reports*, February 1981, p. 100.
   Discusses how check clearing procedures work to a financial institution's benefit, not yours.

"Automatic Banking Can Cause You Trouble." *Changing Times*, June 1981, pp. 26-28.
   Discusses the various electronic funds transfer activities that are *not* covered by the federal Electronic Funds Transfer Act.

CHUCK AND NANCY ANDERSON

Computing the Cost of Immediate Enjoyment

Last year, to buy a car, the Andersons took out a monthly payment installment loan of $4,000 at an effective rate of 18 percent, with add-on interest, for three years. Rather than borrow the money, they might have set aside a certain amount in their budget each month so that after three years they could purchase the car for cash.

Questions

1. Use the APR formula to determine the total dollar cost the Andersons must bear for paying for their car with a loan.
2. What is the amount of each monthly payment (assuming level payments) that they must make on their car loan?
3. How much would they have had to invest in a 5 percent savings account at the end of each year for the three previous years in order to have $4,000 to pay for their car last year? (Use Compound Interest Table B in the appendix to find the factor for three years at 5 percent.)
4. How much would the Andersons have had to set aside in their budget each month for those three years to allow for this investment?
5. Would this monthly amount represent a savings or an increased expense over what the Andersons are paying each month in loan repayments? How much?
6. What are the two ways the Andersons could compute the cost of immediate enjoyment of the car?

12

Borrowing: Consumer Credit

This chapter will deal with the second type of lending: where the lender and seller are the same party. There are two types of lending that occur between the retailer and the consumer: open-ended credit and installment credit. Both are included here under the term *consumer credit*.

This chapter discusses how consumer credit works and how you can use it effectively. Being aware of what types of consumer credit there are and the ways in which you are protected by law should help you get the most out of income that is directed toward the use of consumer credit. We will also compare the costs of paying cash for a car, financing it, and leasing it.

HOW CONSUMER CREDIT WORKS

When you obtain credit, you obtain the use of someone else's money for a certain period of time, but no money changes hands. In exchange for the use of this money, you pay a fee called a *finance charge* (Chapter 11). However, as a sales incentive to customers, this fee may be omitted if the debt is paid off within a certain period, usually 30 days. For example, if you buy $15 worth of gasoline on credit, the oil company lends you the amount you need for the purchase at no extra cost (except that the company may charge generally higher prices in order to cover the cost of this service), and you agree to pay it back when you are billed.

With longer-term credit, there is always a finance charge. For example, if you purchase a $200 dishwasher on a 10-month installment credit plan, you might pay $22 a month for a total of $220. The extra $20 represents the charge for the use of the appliance dealer's money over the 10-month period. If you borrow the same $200 on a 20-month plan, you might have to pay $12 a month—a total of $240. Since you borrowed the money for a longer time, you had to pay $20 more in charges. In the end, your dishwasher cost you $40 more than if you had paid cash. As with consumer loans, the longer the payback period you choose for your debt, the more the total interest costs will be. Also, the higher the interest rate charged, the more the total interest cost will be.

OPEN-ENDED CREDIT

Charge accounts and credit cards are convenient, open-ended forms of consumer credit. Once you have qualified, you agree to pay for all items purchased on credit within a certain number of days either after you receive your bill or, sometimes, after you make your purchase.

A non-card charge account is usually offered by an individual merchant for use at that store only. Credit cards are usually issued by manufacturers such as oil companies, for use at local dealers or outlets. Credit cards may also be issued by banks or certain credit organizations to be used at affiliated places of business. Aside from the difference in scope, credit card accounts and charge accounts without cards serve many of the same purposes for consumers.

Open-ended consumer credit is an expense for the creditor because of bookkeeping, billing, collection, insurance, and bad debt losses. These costs generally cause prices to be higher for all customers who shop at a store that offers this type of credit. The cost of this service, however, should be distinguished from interest, which is the cost of using someone else's money.

Computing the Outstanding Balance

The Consumer Credit Protection Act requires that issuers of open-ended credit disclose the period of time that may elapse before finance charges will be levied on outstanding balances (usually 25 or 30 days). They must also identify the method they use to determine what the outstanding balance is.

There are three ways to compute the outstanding balance on open-ended credit:

1. *Previous balance method.* In this process credit charges are calculated on the outstanding balance at the end of the previous month. Therefore, any payments you might have made during the current month will not go to reduce the balance on which the credit charge is levied at the end of the month. When a consumer habitually makes a number of purchases on credit and then pays off the accumulated debt over several months, the ultimate credit costs can be substantial, if the previous balance method is used. Although this method is probably the most common, some states have made it illegal

2. *Adjusted balance method.* In this case, payments made and credits received during the current month are deducted from the outstanding balance. This method is the most advantageous for the borrowers.

3. *Average daily balance method.* Here the average daily balance outstanding is calculated by summing the balances for each day of the current month and dividing by the number of days in the month. The earlier in the month payments are made to reduce the balance, the lower the average daily balance will be. Check to see whether the creditor adds new purchases to your balance without the benefit of a 25-day grace period. If so, purchases made earlier in the month

tend to increase the average. Waiving the grace period for new purchases may also be practiced with the adjusted balance method.

How Much Open-Ended Credit Should You Use and for What?

There is a danger in open-ended credit that you will lose control of your expenditures. This loss of control would undermine the purpose of budgeting. You should use this form of spending only within the limits of your budget categories. To keep track of charge account or credit card purchases, enter them on your budget as they are made, not when the bill arrives monthly. In this manner, you will be able to stop or reduce spending in certain categories when your monthly charges approach your monthly budgeted amounts.

Items purchased with credit cards and charge accounts usually are consumables, items that are quickly used up. By using this form of consumer credit to buy lower priced, frequently purchased items such as food, gasoline, and entertainment, you can avoid having to carry a lot of cash. If you agree, however, that borrowing should be used only to accumulate assets, you should pay your charge account and credit card bills promptly to avoid the finance charge. The fact that the finance charge on this type of borrowing is commonly 18 to 24 percent annually should be all the motivation you need to pay these bills quickly. Do not let the convenience of charge accounts and credit cards cause you to lose control of your finances.

Types of Charge Accounts and Credit Cards

There are many types of charge accounts and credit cards (Table 12-1). Among the most common are 30-day accounts, budget charge accounts, option charge accounts, revolving charge accounts, bank credit card accounts, and national credit cards.

30-day accounts   Debts incurred on a 30-day account must be paid within 30 days. There is no charge for the convenience of having such an account except as might be reflected in generally higher prices. A means of identification such as a card may be required before credit is extended. One example of a 30-day account is the monthly telephone bill.

budget charge accounts   If you have a budget charge account, you are required to pay only a specified portion of your bill within the first 30 days. Although the remaining portion is usually paid regularly over a maximum of 12 months, you may pay off the balance earlier. Fees or interest charges of 1.5 to 2 percent a month (18 to 24 percent a year) on the unpaid balance are commonly levied after the first month. This type of account is frequently offered by retailers such as department stores.

option charge accounts   With option charge accounts, you may pay all or part of the billed amount within 30 days at no charge. Any remaining amount is generally paid over three to six months. There is a usual fee of 1.5 to 2 percent a month (18 to 24 percent annually) on the unpaid balance. You may be required to pay a fixed

TABLE 12-1

Types of Charge Accounts and Credit Cards

Type	Effective Cost	Conditions of Payment	Maximum Credit Limit	Maximum Payment Period
30-day account	No charge for use of service	Debts must be resolved within 30 days of receipt of bill.	At individual creditor's discretion	30 days
Budget charge account	1.5-2% monthly (18-24% annually) on the unpaid balance	Only a specific portion of the bill must be paid within 30 days (at no charge).	Set by creditor for each account	3 to 12 months
Option charge account	1.5-2% monthly (18-24% annually) on the unpaid balance	Consumer has the option of paying all or part of the debt within 30 days (at no charge).	At individual creditor's discretion	3 to 6 months
Revolving charge account	Refers to a feature of some budget and option charge accounts			
Bank credit card accounts	1.5-2% monthly (18-24% annually) on the unpaid balance up to $1,000; lower rates for larger amounts	No charge for debts resolved within 25 days of the billing date. Commonly a fixed amount or percentage of debt outstanding is required to be paid monthly.	Set by creditor for each account	Determined by conditions of payments and maximum credit limit
National credit cards	1.5-2% monthly (18-24% annually) on unpaid balance	No charge for debts resolved within 30 days of receipt of bill.	At discretion of credit card issuer	At discretion of credit card issuer

dollar minimum or a fixed percentage of the bill outstanding each month. Many oil company credit cards are of this type, although they often allow 55 days before finance charges are levied.

revolving charge accounts Revolving charge account is a name that can be applied to both budget and option accounts. The name simply emphasizes that you can continue to charge purchases on such an account (up to specified limits) without first paying off the old debts.

bank credit card accounts Two notable examples of bank credit card accounts are Visa and MasterCard. If you use either of these cards, you may make purchases at numerous locations and receive one monthly statement that covers all of your purchases. Retailers who participate in this program pay the bank a small percentage of what they sell to customers using the cards. In return, the bank assumes the burden of credit investigation, credit collection, and the risk of bad debts. Certain stores may levy a customer service charge for people using this program or they may pass this expense on to all customers through higher prices. This charge or increase would be more likely where such programs do not appreciably increase the merchant's sales volume.

Usually no finance charges are levied if the total bill is paid within 25 days of the billing date. A minimum monthly payment of $10, or 5 percent of your bill if the total exceeds $10, is commonly required. Hence, your total debt may never be entirely paid off. Finance charges of 1.5 to 2 percent a month (18 to 24 percent annually) generally are levied on the outstanding balance up to $1,000. Above that amount the finance charge often is progressively reduced (1.2 percent, 1 percent, 0.7 percent, and so on). This type of credit often has a maximum limit based on the credit rating of each card user. The balance outstanding on the account must never exceed your limit.

national credit cards National credit cards are issued by private credit organizations such as Diners Club, American Express, and Carte Blanche. They are similar to bank credit cards with the following exceptions. First, their credit qualifications are more rigid. Therefore, once you are accepted, your maximum credit limit may be higher. Second, the cards may not be accepted by as wide a range of outlets as are available under bank programs.

The Increasing Cost of Open-Ended Credit

In the spring of 1980, President Carter's administration imposed credit controls briefly to slow the then explosive growth of credit use. Various credit card issuers (banks, major retailers, and credit organizations) were allowed to apply new charges to their services. Shortly thereafter, governmental credit controls were abandoned, but the additional charges have remained.

1. Most banks (generally via Visa and MasterCard) and some major retailers added *annual fees* ranging from $10 to $20, paralleling a practice that travel and entertainment cards have followed for years.

2. Alternatively, *transaction charges* of 10¢ to 20¢ have been instituted.
3. Usury laws, which set maximum interest rate levels on loans, have been either raised (to 24 percent in some states) or eliminated, particularly for loans of less than $500 to $1,000.
4. Some major credit card issuers have dropped the practice of allowing a 25-day grace period on new purchases before interest charges are levied, if there is an existing outstanding balance on the customer's account.

Obviously, there are strategies you can adopt to minimize these new charges. Reducing the number of credit cards you use could have two benefits. Annual fees for certain cards, if no longer used, would be avoided. If you tend to have aggregate credit card balances in excess of $2,000 on which you are paying interest, by using only one or two cards you will be able to take advantage of the lower interest rate charges that apply as your balance outstanding goes above $1,000 to $2,000. Also, cards that charge annual fees only would be preferred if you use your cards frequently. Alternatively, if you are an infrequent user, then cards that have transaction charges only may be for you.

INSTALLMENT CREDIT AND THE PURCHASE AGREEMENT

With installment credit, the retailer requires that periodic payments be made so that he or she can predict cash inflow. Whereas credit cards and charge accounts are used for buying general merchandise, installment credit usually is limited to purchases of higher-priced consumer durables such as appliances. The items purchased are used as collateral. Unlike open-ended credit, installment credit involves a down payment; interest charges begin immediately; there is a rigid schedule of payments; and if you pay off the debt ahead of schedule, you may be charged a prepayment penalty.

Installment credit involves a purchase agreement that may be written either by the creditor or by a bank or major finance company. The purchase agreement may include several components: sales contract, note, and credit life and/or disability insurance policy. The creditor selects the type of purchase agreement and includes those components that offer him or her the greatest protection. As a consumer, you have little or no say in this matter. Therefore, make sure you read, understand, and are willing to accept all conditions specified in the documents associated with this agreement before you sign it. If you are not willing to accept all of them, shop elsewhere. A sample purchase agreement is shown in Figure 12-1.

Sales Contract

The sales contract is one of the most common and significant components of any purchase agreement. This document is designed to protect the creditor against defaults on payments. The content and form of sales contracts is usually specified by state statute. The content commonly required includes the names and signatures of buyer and seller, the date of the transaction, address (residence or business) of buyer and seller, an adequate description of the goods subject to the contract, and services to be rendered. In regard to form, the document usually must be in writing (8-point

**DISCLOSURE STATEMENT
CREDIT SALE OF VEHICLE**

SELLER NAME AND ADDRESS _____

The following disclosures are made pursuant to the Consumer Credit Protection Act by the Seller named herein (herein called Seller) to the Buyer(s) named herein (herein collectively called Buyer) in connection with the proposed credit sale of the vehicle together with equipment (herein called Vehicle) described below:

BUYER NAME(S) AND ADDRESS _____

New-Used	Year-Model I.D.	Make	Body Type	Serial or Engine No.	Key No.

Equipped With: ☐ Automatic Transmission ☐ 3-4 Speed Trans. ☐ Radio ☐ Stereo ☐ Power Steering ☐ Power Brakes ☐ Power Windows ☐ Power Seats ☐ Air-Conditioning   Color ____

Other Equipment: _____

1. **CASH PRICE** (including sales tax only) $_____
2. **DOWNPAYMENT**
   CASH DOWNPAYMENT $_____
   TRADE-IN $_____
   Describe: _____
   TOTAL DOWNPAYMENT $_____
3. **UNPAID BALANCE OF CASH PRICE** (1 less 2) $_____
4. OTHER CHARGES INCLUDED IN AMOUNT FINANCED (Item 7) AND NOT PART OF FINANCE CHARGE (Item 8)
   (a) Official Fees
   License $_____
   Certificate of Title *$_____
   Registration $_____
   (b) Insurance Premiums
   Credit Life $_____
   Credit Disability $_____
   Property $_____
   Liability $_____
   Total $_____
5. **UNPAID BALANCE** (3 plus 4) $_____
6. **PREPAID FINANCE CHARGE** $_____
7. **AMOUNT FINANCED** $_____
8. AMOUNTS INCLUDED IN FINANCE CHARGE
   (a) Time Price Differential $_____
   (b) Trailer Coach VSI (Conversion and Embezzlement) Insurance Premium $_____
   FINANCE CHARGE $_____

9. **ANNUAL PERCENTAGE RATE** _____%
10. **TOTAL OF PAYMENTS** $_____
    Payable in_____payments as follows [Note: Identify any payment more than twice the amount of a regular equal payment as "Balloon Payment"]: _____equal successive payments of $_____each on the_____day of _____commencing_____, 19___,
    _____
    _____
    _____
    _____
    _____
    _____, and a Balloon Payment of $_____on_____, 19____.
    Any Balloon Payment shown above will not be refinanced.
11. **DEFERRED PAYMENT PRICE** (1, 4 plus 8) $_____
12. **DELINQUENCY CHARGE:** A delinquency charge is payable on any payment in default for ten days or more in an amount equal to 5 % of such payment.
13. **PREPAYMENT BEFORE MATURITY:** Buyer may prepay the indebtedness in full at any time prior to maturity and obtain a refund credit of the unearned portion of the time price differential (Finance Charge), after first deducting therefrom $25.00, computed under the "Rule of 78's", provided, however, that no refund of less than $1.00 shall be made.
14. **SECURITY:** Indebtedness is to be secured by a conditional sale contract covering the Vehicle, and by an assignment of fire, theft, collision and comprehensive insurance policies thereon as required by Seller.

INSURANCE

ANY PROPERTY INSURANCE (meaning insurance against loss or damage to property) OR LIABILITY INSURANCE (meaning insurance against liability arising out of the ownership or use of property) TO BE WRITTEN IN CONNECTION WITH THE SALE MAY BE OBTAINED BY BUYER THROUGH ANY PERSON OF HIS CHOICE, provided, however, that Seller may, for reasonable cause, refuse to accept an insurer; on any such insurance which is required by Seller. Such insurance may ☐ not be obtained from or through Seller ☐ be obtained through Seller at the estimated cost indicated:

INSURANCE COVERAGE	DEDUCTIBLE OR LIMITS	TERM IN MONTHS	ESTIMATED PREMIUM
Fire and Theft, ACV			
Comprehensive			
Combined Additional			
Collision			
Bodily Injury			
Property Damage			
Medical			

[Applicable if credit insurance may be written] CREDIT LIFE AND CREDIT DISABILITY INSURANCE ARE NOT REQUIRED IN CONNECTION WITH THE SALE. No charge is to be made for such insurance and none is to be provided unless Buyer is to be insured thereunder signs and dates the statement below. If obtained through Seller, the cost of credit life insurance will be $_____ and of credit disability insurance will be $_____for the term of the credit.

I desire credit ☐ life and ☐ disability insurance.

_____   _____
(DATE)   (SIGNATURE)

* IMPORTANT NOTE: ASTERISK DENOTES THAT THE AMOUNT INDICATED IS AN ESTIMATE.

Buyer acknowledges reading and receiving a duplicate of this Disclosure Statement and that he has not entered into any agreement with Seller for the above credit sale. THIS IS NOT AN OFFER OR AN AGREEMENT TO SELL, OR TO PROVIDE INSURANCE.

_____   _____   _____
(DATE)   (BUYER)   (BUYER)

BBA-TL (CS)-1 (7-69)   ORIGINAL (BANK'S COPY)   DUPLICATE (BUYER'S COPY)   TRIPLICATE (SELLER'S COPY)

FIGURE 12-1
Sample purchase agreement on an installment contract for a car.

type) with no large blank areas and must represent the entire agreement between buyer and seller. A copy of the contract must be delivered to the buyer either upon delivery of the goods or shortly thereafter if so agreed. Other items may be required depending on the state. You should make sure which ones are specified in any contract you sign. These other items include cash sales price; amount of down payment; the difference between the down payment and the cash sales price; amount, cost, and type of insurance required; amount and type of official (local government) fees; balance owed (usually the sum of the previous three items); finance charges as an aggregate amount (in addition to the computations of annual amounts required by truth in lending); amount, number, and frequency of payments (amount will equal the sum of the balance owed and finance charges divided by the number of payments); and some indication of how much more the merchandise bought on credit will cost than if paid for in cash.

two types of sales contracts   There are many types of sales contracts, of which we will discuss the two most common ones: the installment purchase agreement and the financing lease.

The *installment purchase agreement* is the type of agreement you would probably sign if you purchased a new automobile on credit. You may obtain immediate use of the automobile and the title of ownership also passes to you at once, subject to a security interest (a lien against your title) held by the seller. Notice of the security interest is filed with the appropriate local government agency. By doing this, the seller can effectively prevent you from using the automobile as collateral for other loans or installment purchases. If you fail to meet the payment schedule as specified in the purchase agreement, the automobile probably will be repossessed by the seller and resold in order to satisfy the unpaid balance of your purchase agreement. Only if the seller is successful in reselling the automobile for an amount large enough to cover your unpaid balance, as well as the costs of repossession and resale (storage costs, collection fees, attorney's fees, and the like) can you expect to receive back any of the funds you have paid. If the resale proceeds are not sufficient to cover the amount owed to the creditor plus the repossession and resale costs, you may be required to pay the difference.

The *financing lease* is becoming more and more common for installment sales, particularly retail sales of automobiles and furniture. A financing lease typically provides that title and ownership of the leased item do not pass from lessor (seller) to lessee (user) until all lease rentals have been made, at which time the lessee may exercise an option to purchase the item for a nominal sum. It is expected from the outset that the lessee will keep and use the leased item for its useful life. A true lease, on the other hand, typically contemplates use for a fixed period at a fixed rental and then return of the leased item to the lessor, who may thereafter repeat this process several times. If as lessee you default under a financing lease, you will probably be in as poor a position as if you had signed an installment purchase agreement (repossession and possible liability for the unpaid balance remaining after resale). Default under a true lease, however, will generally result in the lessee's being liable for the unexpired rental term, less any re-rental amounts that the lessor has collected from other lessees in that period.

oppressive clauses   These may be part of either of the above types of contracts. They are used to put the borrower at a legal disadvantage in relation to the lender. Although recent legislation in some states has made such practices more difficult for the creditor to justify, they still exist. Here are some to watch out for.

- *Wage assignment* (wage garnishment), whereby you assign to the creditor the right to attach a part of your wages in the event you default on your payments.
- *Confession of judgment*, whereby you waive your right to an attorney or to judicial processes, thus allowing the creditor to make an admission of debt for you with legal authorities when default occurs.
- *Repossession*, whereby you allow the creditor to take back the purchased goods if you fail to make your payments.
- *Add-on clause*, whereby you allow the creditor to repossess items you have already purchased from him or her and paid for, if you default on your payments for additional items.
- *Acceleration clause*, whereby the outstanding balance of payments becomes immediately due if you miss one (or more) payments.
- *Balloon clause*, whereby the payment schedule is structured in such a way that the final payment is substantially larger than the previous payments.

finance charges   These charges are a very important component of the sales contract. It is good to have the creditor itemize them so that you know exactly what you are paying for. Basically, finance charges consist of interest and carrying costs (bookkeeping, credit investigations, allowance for bad debts, credit life and/or disability insurance, and the like). In order to determine whether the annual percentage rate (APR) the creditor quotes you is accurate, use the formula given in Chapter 11.

It is important to know how much more an installment credit contract will cost you than if you paid cash. When you feel that the former is prohibitively expensive, you can plan for the purchase of the items for which the money was needed and avoid using consumer credit altogether.

The Note

The note represents your written promise to resolve the debt you assumed through your purchase. In many instances, a security agreement is given as security for the note. The note specifies the amounts of your payments and when they are to be paid. Some notes and security agreements enable the creditor, in the event of default on payments, to repossess not only the purchased goods but also enough additional property to cover the balance outstanding or to take legal action to obtain that amount if the proceeds from resale do not cover repossession and resale costs and the balance outstanding. There are three general types of notes with which you may be confronted:

- The *demand note* has no maturity date. Usually the creditor retains the right to call in the note and receive full payment of the balance due whenever he or she desires.

- The *time note* has a specified date of maturity. It gives the borrower a definite idea of when the final payments are due, as opposed to the demand note, which leaves the borrower at the mercy of the creditor. Therefore, the time note is probably more attractive to a borrower.
- The *cognovit note* allows the creditor to repossess, without going through legal channels, the goods purchased by a borrower who has defaulted on the payments. Obviously, this is the least attractive type of note for a borrower because it offers the least protection.

Credit Life and Disability Insurance

Occasionally a creditor will *require* a borrower to purchase term life insurance and possibly disability insurance to cover the outstanding balance on installment credit purchases. If this is done, the cost of such coverage *must* be included in the finance charge. Otherwise, accepting such coverage is voluntary. Such insurance will pay off the unpaid balance if the borrower dies or becomes disabled.

Credit insurance costs represent a potential area of abuse since the creditor receives sales commissions, ranging from 25 to 50 percent of the premium on a policy he or she sells, from the insurance company. The creditor may be motivated to use policies that have the highest premiums. Recognizing this, all states except Alaska (as of February 1979) have passed laws setting maximum prices for credit insurance that range from 40¢ to $1 per $100 of coverage. If your creditor requires that you have credit insurance but offers only expensive coverage, obtain coverage elsewhere. A local insurance broker with a substantial business should be a less expensive source of coverage, or you might consider increasing the amount of coverage on your existing life or disability policies.

On car purchase contracts, auto insurance may also be required.

CONSIDERATIONS WHEN SHOPPING FOR CREDIT

1. Do you want to use consumer credit to pay many bills with a single check or to purchase an expensive item?
2. What type of credit can best be used to meet your requirements? If you want to buy gasoline, an oil company credit card would be appropriate. If you need a new appliance, then installment credit may be the answer. Once you know what type of credit you are looking for, you can begin to investigate the alternatives available.
3. How much additional money will it cost you to use consumer credit? As we have seen, some forms of open-ended credit charge you nothing if you pay off the balance within 30 days. If you do not, you may be charged on the unpaid balance at a rate of 1.5 to 2 percent a month. With installment credit you must consider not only the finance charges but also the possibility of a prepayment penalty.
4. Can you afford to pay the total amount represented by the price of the item to be purchased plus the credit costs?
5. What is the best schedule of payments offered? Remember that the longer the payback period, the more the total charges will be.

6. Can you meet the scheduled payments without straining your income unnecessarily? If your family had an emergency, such as a big dental bill, might your credit purchases have to be repossessed?
7. What is the reputation of the creditor you are considering borrowing from? Information about a creditor often may be found by contacting local credit counseling services.

Credit Counseling Services

If you are having credit problems that require more than the above analysis, perhaps you should look for professional assistance. Several sources of advice are available. These include credit bureaus, credit unions, creditors, and family counseling services. These organizations may be able to help you to accept some budgetary discipline and/or intercede on your behalf with creditors who may be exceeding their legal bounds in attempting to gain debt repayment from you.

Credit bureaus serve as a link between creditors and people seeking credit. Their primary purpose is to gather information about the credit worthiness of applicants and provide it for creditors who are conducting investigations. Many credit bureaus, however, offer advice concerning both how to regain or retain a good credit rating and what a reasonable credit limit may be in a particular case. Credit unions often emphasize educating their members about consumer credit. Some of the larger ones employ full-time credit counselors. Of course, you must be a member of a credit union to avail yourself of this service. Some creditors offer counseling services, but the quality of advice varies from creditor to creditor. Family counseling services are likely to offer helpful, objective advice; these community-sponsored organizations may have licensed financial counselors.

CONSUMER CREDIT LEGISLATION

Since 1969, four federal laws of major importance to the consumer have been approved and put into effect. One limits the consumer's liability for unauthorized use of his or her credit cards. Another regulates more strictly the practices of credit bureaus. A third is aimed at eliminating discrimination in lending, and the last one has struck down the holder in due course doctrine, among other things.

Protection against Lost or Stolen Credit Cards

Liability of credit card holders for unauthorized use of their credit cards was greatly restricted in 1971 by the federal government. As a result, you may be held liable only for up to $50 worth of unauthorized use of your lost, stolen, or misplaced cards. (Some states have even freed the consumer of any liability for unauthorized use of a credit card following notification to the creditor that the card was lost.) Issuers may hold you liable for this $50 only if:

• They provided a self-addressed form to be used to notify them of the loss, theft, or disappearance of your card.

- You accepted the card originally.
- They adequately informed you of your potential liability.
- The unauthorized use in question occurred before you notified the issuer of your card's loss, theft, or disappearance.

Because of the negligible amount of your potential liability, assuming you are able to notify the issuer quickly of a lost credit card, credit card insurance would not be a very compelling necessity. Probably the best way to notify a credit card issuer of a lost card is by telegram. Issuers prefer to be notified in writing rather than by phone. Therefore, when accepting a credit card, you should make sure you know where to send a telegram and then keep this address on file. The telegram should contain your name and card number.

Fair Credit Reporting Act

Credit bureaus sell information about the credit worthiness of consumers. The bureaus' customers are usually insurance companies, prospective employers, government agencies, creditors, and mailing list companies. A credit reporting system is an effective means of identifying poor credit risks in advance, and it makes it easy for most individuals with the right qualifications to obtain credit. In some instances, however, a good credit risk receives a poor rating because of misinformation. The chances of this occurring are greater than you might think, because of the methods by which credit bureaus collect information about a credit applicant.

Three information sources are commonly used by credit bureaus:

1. *Credit applications.* Each time you apply for credit, a copy of the application probably goes to the local credit bureau. Because of this, it behooves you to fill out a credit application accurately. Misleading information would have an adverse effect on the credit bureau's opinion of your integrity.
2. *Public records.* Credit bureaus employ individuals to check court cases, judgments, and so on to glean information about consumers. By their own admission, the degree of accurate research and confirmation used by these investigators is often inadequate.
3. *Hearsay reports.* An investigator queries the consumer's neighbors, friends, and acquaintances about the person's morals, private life, reputation, and such. The accuracy of this information is highly vulnerable to human error, bias, and poor judgment.

The Fair Credit Reporting Act, which went into effect April 25, 1971, attempts, among other things, to discourage credit bureaus from dispensing erroneous information about private citizens. If you have been rejected for credit, the prospective creditor must give you the name and address of the credit bureau that supplied the information causing your application to be rejected. This credit bureau must then disclose to you upon request the following:

- The nature and substance of all information contained in your file (although they do not have to show you the actual file).
- Names of creditors who have received reports on you in the last six months.

- Names of potential employers who have received reports on you in the last two years.
- All sources of information in your file except investigative hearsay reports.

If you prove any of the information to be erroneous, inaccurate, or unverifiable, the credit bureau must promptly delete it and send notice of such deletion to creditors of the past six months and to potential employers of the last two years. If you and the credit bureau dispute the validity of certain information, you have the right to include in your file a 100-word refutation of that information. This refutation will also be sent to recent potential creditors and employers. The credit bureau may not charge you for any of their services in revealing the contents of your file in this case or for correcting false information.

If you have not been rejected for credit but want to see your file at the local credit bureau, these rights still hold. The only difference is that you may be charged a reasonable fee, which probably will not exceed $25 since the Federal Trade Commission has taken action against charges in excess of this amount.

Adverse information more than seven years old may not be sent out—with the exception that information about bankruptcies has a 14-year limitation. Also, there is no limitation on the age of adverse information sent out for underwriter reports where the amount of proposed life insurance coverage is $50,000 or more, or for employer reports where the proposed salary is $20,000 or more.

You may sue a credit bureau for false information that results from a malicious or willful intent to injure and for violations of the new law.

Equal Credit Opportunity Act

This set of laws, which went into effect in October 1975, deals mainly with the prevention of discrimination by lenders on the basis of the sex or marital status of the prospective borrower. Among its provisions are the following:

- A lender considering an application from a woman for credit or a loan must give the woman's financial circumstances the same weight as would be given a man of similar circumstances; the lender must consider regular alimony and child support payments as income.
- No inquiries about the sex or marital status of a prospective borrower may be made by a lender.
- An account must be carried in the name requested by the applicant.
- A lender must consider the credit history of the family when reviewing a request for credit by either spouse.
- An explanation, preferably in writing, must be given for a denial of credit.

Should discrimination occur, lenders may be sued for up to $10,000. If you feel you have been unjustly discriminated against and want to pursue a legal remedy, you should contact the local office of the Federal Trade Commission.

Fair Credit Billing Act

Like the Equal Credit Opportunity Act, this legislation went into effect in October 1975. There are four areas you should be aware of here.

holder in due course doctrine   This doctrine required the consumer to continue making payments to a third party creditor even though the items purchased from a merchandiser proved to be faulty. A third party creditor could come into the credit arrangement in either of two ways: the outlet that sold you certain goods could arrange credit for you with a third party creditor, or the outlet could originally extend credit to you and subsequently sell your credit contract to an organization that would in turn become your creditor. If the merchandiser went out of business or no longer held your credit contract, there was little to be gained by seeking recourse against the third party creditor for faulty merchandise.

Now all that is changed. For purchases in excess of $50 made within your state or 100 miles of your residence (whichever is farther), you may refuse to continue paying for items that are faulty until your complaint is remedied. In instances where the merchandiser is owned or operated by the creditor, or the third party creditor solicited you for the merchandiser's products by advertisement, these geographic limitations do not apply.

This new law does not apply, however, to purchases made on a credit card or in instances where the consumer has independently arranged for financing.

The effect of this law is to place the lender at risk for faulty goods or services offered by an unrelated merchant. Presumably, lenders must either be more careful about selecting the products or services they finance, or they must increase their finance charges to cover such potential losses.

billing errors and complaints   The creditor must acknowledge receipt of your complaint within 30 days and has an additional 90 days to resolve the dispute. During this four-month period, the creditor cannot send you dunning letters or issue an unfavorable report on you to a credit bureau without notifying you and notifying the bureau that certain bills are in dispute. If the creditor fails to honor this schedule, you may keep any disputed amounts up to $50, or may sue for $100 damages plus legal fees.

billing procedures   Bills must be mailed at least 14 days before payments are due. Notices of credits or actual refunds must be sent in the billing period that they occur, thus avoiding the possibility of having an unknown refund "gather dust" at a store infrequently used. The bills themselves must contain an address of where complaints are handled and must remind you semiannually of your rights under this bill.

price discounts   Retailers can voluntarily give price discounts of up to 5 percent to cash-paying customers. These customers can thus avoid being charged the costs a merchandiser incurs in extending credit. Previously, some third party creditors prevented outlets from offering this discount to their customers. If cash discounting is done, it must be publicly acknowledged, so that all customers know it is available.

AUTO LEASING

The basic principle of auto leasing is that you (as lessee) agree to pay a monthly fee for a set period of time in exchange for the use of a car. At the end of that period, either the car or an equivalent dollar amount must be returned to the lessor. There are many ways of leasing cars and many types of leases, but the basic procedure is as follows.

Initially, you and the lessor negotiate the current value of the car (purchase price) and the residual value (projected trade-in value). The lessor determines the amount he or she is lending you by subtracting the residual value from the current value. The term *lending* is used here because the lessor purchases the car and lends it to you in return for lease payments. Your lease payments will include a charge (somewhat like interest) for the use of the lessor's money (in the form of the leased car).

When you turn in the car at the end of the lease term (usually two or three years), the car's trade-in value must equal the initially projected residual value. If the car's trade-in value exceeds this amount, you will receive the excess amount. If it is less, you must make up the difference. Should you disagree with the lessor's appraised value of the car, you have the option of finding another person (car dealer or private individual) who will pay you more for it. In this case, you return to the lessor an amount of cash equal to the residual value. The lessor must receive remuneration equal to the residual value in the form of the leased car, the leased car plus cash, or just cash.

An Example

The example (shown in Table 12-2) entails many of the financial considerations necessary in deciding whether to pay cash for a car, finance it, or lease it. In each of these alternatives the total amount that must be paid for the car is $8,500 ($8,000 purchase price plus $500 sales tax). If the car is bought with cash, the initial expenditure totals $8,500. The trade-in value after three years is $3,000, making the total cost of the car $5,500.

If the car is financed, the initial outlay is $2,100, which consists of a 20 percent down payment ($1,600) and $500 in sales tax. Subsequent outlays involve 36

TABLE 12-2

Costs of Paying Cash for a Car, Financing It, and Leasing It

Costs and Adjustments	Paying Cash	Financing @20%	Leasing @20%
Initial outlay	$8,500	$ 2,100	$ 394
Subsequent outlays		8,570	6,698
TOTAL	8,500	10,670	7,092
Trade-in value	3,000	3,000	
TOTAL COST	5,500	7,670	7,092
Inflation adjustment		428	334
Tax savings		543	
TOTAL SAVINGS		971	334
Net Cost	$5,500	$ 6,699	$6,758

monthly payments of $238 each, or $8,570 in total payments on a $6,400 loan. Taking into consideration the car's trade-in value, the total cost is $7,670 ($2,100 + $8,570 − $3,000). The inflation adjustment is computed as follows:

.05 × $1,430 (the average of the first year's payments)	=	$ 71
.10 × $1,430 (the average of the second year's payments)	=	143
.15 × $1,430 (the average of the third year's payments)	=	214
Total inflation adjustment		$428

The tax savings of $543 are based on $2,170 in credit costs ($8,570 paid back on $6,400 borrowed) times 25 percent marginal tax rate. The tax savings and the inflation adjustment amounts are subtracted from the total cost of the car for a net cost of $6,699 ($7,670 − $543 − $428).

If the car is leased, the initial outlay is made up of two months' payments of $197 each (roughly $186 plus $11 sales tax). There is a subsequent outlay of 34 monthly payments of $197 each. The trade-in value ($3,000) is assumed to be equal to the projected residual value. The inflation adjustment is as follows:

.05 × $1,083 (the average of the first year's 11 payments)	=	$ 54
.10 × $1,182 (the average of the second year's 12 payments)	=	118
.15 × $1,083 (the average of the third year's 11 payments)	=	162
Total inflation adjustment		$334

Since no tax deduction is allowed for interest charges on a lease, the net cost is $6,758 ((36 × $197) − $334).

Even after tax savings and inflation are taken into account, in this example the cash purchase of a car costs less than either short-term (three years or less) financing or leasing arrangements, where the terms are the same. Because their costs are generally high (20 percent a year or more), financing and leasing also are not attractive as investment strategies. Instead, they are usually an unnecessary drain on your income.

CONCLUSION

You should use consumer credit responsibly and effectively. First decide how much consumer credit you can afford and what you want to use it for. Then look for the most attractive source of credit. Several laws offer you safeguards in the area of consumer credit. Make sure that you are given full benefit of these laws in all your credit dealings.

VOCABULARY

acceleration clause

balloon clause

charge account

consumer credit

credit bureau

credit card

Equal Credit Opportunity Act

Fair Credit Billing Act

Fair Credit Reporting Act

installment credit

leasing

note

open-ended credit

oppressive clauses

purchase agreement

repossession

sales contract

trade-in value

QUESTIONS

1. What are the six oppressive clauses that may be found in sales contracts?
2. What are four typical items in the finance charge levied by a creditor?
3. Why is credit life and/or disability insurance a potential area of abuse from the consumer's point of view?
4. How are bank-issued credit cards different from those issued by national credit companies?
5. Under what financial circumstances can you justify using open-ended credit?
6. What is your liability for unauthorized use of a credit card that you lost or was stolen from you?
7. What is a credit bureau required to do if you ask to see information from your file? When must you pay for this service? What is a reasonable fee?
8. What are the four main areas of consideration in the Fair Credit Billing Act?
9. What is the best method of computing outstanding balances on credit accounts from the consumer's viewpoint?

CASE PROBLEMS

1. Credit bureaus generally make it relatively easy for people whose finances are sound to obtain credit. They also enable creditors to avoid extending credit to individuals who probably would not be able to repay a debt. In order to make these judgments, credit bureaus must investigate people's financial circumstances and personal character. Certain of these activities are often considered an invasion of a prospective borrower's privacy. Furthermore, the methods credit bureaus use to gather information can result in the inclusion of inaccurate data in a person's file.

   What is your position concerning credit bureaus? Which types of data, if any, do you think are valid for credit bureaus to gather? How would you improve their research efforts without violating personal privacy? What stand should the government take in this matter?
2. Because of the elimination of the holder in due course doctrine, the consumer has some recourse against a third party creditor when shoddy merchandise is involved. What is a hidden cost in this benefit? How is it likely to be handled?

RECOMMENDED READING

"Beat the Rising Cost of Credit Cards." *Changing Times*, December 1980, pp. 60–63.
  A good discussion of the increased costs associated with credit card usage.

"Compare the Big Name Credit Cards." *Changing Times*, August 1978, pp. 37–40.
  Discusses the services, costs, and benefits of the major credit cards.

"Credit Insurance: The Quiet Overcharge." *Consumer Reports*, July 1979, pp. 415–17.
  A very good treatment of some potential abuses in consumer credit.

"Credit Rules That Give Women a Fair Shake." *Changing Times*, May 1977, pp. 13–15.
  Discusses women's rights in regard to credit.

"How to Shop for Credit." *Consumer Reports*, March 1975, pp. 171–78.
  Discusses various cost considerations in different forms of credit.

"New Rights When You Buy on Time." *Consumer Reports*. May 1976, p. 302.
  Discusses impact of elimination of holder in due course doctrine.

What Truth in Lending Means to You. Board of Governors of the Federal Reserve System,
Washington, DC 20551.
  A good explanatory pamphlet.

CHUCK AND NANCY ANDERSON

Analyzing Their Debt Structure

Chuck and Nancy agree that borrowing money is most effective when it is used to purchase assets. They also think that they should borrow money only at rates lower than those they can achieve on their investment portfolio. Table 12-3 compares their debt costs and their portfolio's return on investment—based on a combined (federal and state) marginal tax bracket of 25 percent and a rise in inflation of 5 percent a year.

Question

Which loans would you advise the Andersons to pay off?

TABLE 12-3

Comparison of the Andersons' Debt Costs and Investment Return

Debts	Gross Rate	Tax Effect	Effect of Inflation	Net Rate
Home	9%	−2.25%	−5%	1.75%
Car	14	−3.5	−5	5.5
Furniture	15	−3.75	−5	6.25
Margin account	10	−2.5	−5	2.5
Investment return	9	−1.5[a]	−5	2.5

[a] Reflects taxes on long-term capital gains.

13

Automobiles and Major Appliances

An important component of the strategy "getting the most out of your income" is to be a wise consumer of the big ticket items, such as automobiles and major appliances. Generally, this text focuses on financial management principles (such as the methods of financing auto and appliance purchases discussed in the preceding two chapters) rather than on the complementary topics of consumerism and buymanship. However, we believe that the purchase and operating costs of automobiles and major appliances affect the budget so much that a discussion of them rounds out the body of knowledge we call personal money management.

THE BUYING PROCESS

In general, the buying principles summarized here apply to everything from automobiles and housing to television sets, blue jeans, and breakfast cereal.

Step I: Know Your Needs for a Product

What is the motivation behind your proposed purchase? No decision is purely practical; there is an emotional side as well. Even the person who shuns high performance or luxury cars in favor of an economical subcompact is often gaining ego satisfaction from a public display that says "environmental and energy concerns are the smart way in my culture."

In general, what is the estimated total cost of your proposed purchase—initial purchase and operating costs? Would you rather spend some of that money elsewhere in your budget? Is there an alternative way to meet your need so that you can save some money—initially or over the long haul? Would a used one, for example, save you money? Sometimes you can save a considerable sum on nearly new products, such as a demonstrator, a floor model, or a discontinued model.

Step 2: Select the Product That Meets Your Needs

Consider price, function, features, operating and repair costs, and warranty coverage of particular brands and models. A *warranty* is a contract that specifies what the manufacturer will and will not assure regarding the product's reliability once you buy it. Your choice of a dealer or store for your purchase may affect the warranty coverage, as well as the repair costs. It might not be wise, for example, to buy a car that can't be easily serviced nearby.

As we shall see, some of these criteria are more important than others, depending on the product under consideration.

Step 3: The Purchase Itself

Shop around and be patient. Some times of the year may be better than others to buy certain items, such as clothes and household goods in the post-Christmas sales. Just before Christmas is probably the worst time to obtain a low price on anything, except during some recession years when retailers have held sales to spur poor sales.

Salespeople often try to sell customers a higher priced model than they had originally intended to purchase. If you are tempted by such a "trading up" offer, you should take the time to consider whether you really want to buy those extra features; after all, you could spend the money on something else. If necessary, leave the store while you consider the alternatives.

An important procedure on products such as cars and stereo sets is to negotiate with the dealer to obtain a price that is often significantly lower than the listed, or "sticker," price.

Finally, you will have several choices for paying for such a purchase: cash, credit cards, installment loans, bank loans, and leasing. As discussed in Chapters 11 and 12, it is easiest on your budget in the long run if you pay cash or use a short-term payment method on which the retailer charges no interest. This promotional gimmick is better than paying cash, because your funds can continue to earn interest for perhaps a couple of extra months; however, you may be paying for this privilege in a higher price for the product. If you do have to borrow or buy on credit, it pays to shop around for the best terms, as you learned in Chapter 12.

Step 4: Once You Own It

Repair and operating costs are often so large that a little effort in controlling them can be financially worthwhile.

AUTOMOBILES

Only housing and food require a greater portion of your budget than does transportation.

Step 1: Know Your Needs for a Car

motivation   Although the basic rationale for owning an automobile is to provide personal, flexible transportation, many other factors complicate the decision. Would your status in your peer group be best enhanced by a luxury car or an old beat-up

KNOW YOUR NEEDS

"anti-luxury" car? Some people enjoy driving particular types of vehicles such as a four-wheel drive truck, a sports car, or a high performance car. How much are you willing to allocate out of your budget to meet such needs?

From a practical point of view, you should buy only as much car as will satisfy your normal daily needs. It makes no financial sense to drive a large recreational vehicle to work each day just so you can take it camping three times a year. It would be cheaper to commute in a compact car and rent the RV when you wanted it.

cost The purchase price of an automobile is only part of the total cost picture. How much will it cost to operate?

You will need to consider both variable costs (gas and oil, maintenance, tires) and fixed costs (insurance, tax, license, registration, depreciation) as well as the number of miles you are likely to drive each year. Figure 13-1 presents an example of the

Variable Costs	Average per mile
Gas and oil[a]	6.27¢
Maintenance	1.18
Tires	.72
Total	8.17¢[b]

Fixed Costs	Average per year
Comprehensive insurance ($100 deductible)	$ 76.00
Collision insurance ($250 deductible)	180.00
Property damage and liability insurance ($100/300/25)	254.00
Property tax, license, registration	88.00
Depreciation[c]	1,287.00
Total (or $5.16 per day)[b]	$1,885.00

Total for Moderate Driver	
10,000 miles @ 8.17¢	$ 817.00
Fixed costs	1,885.00
Annual Total (or 27.0¢ per mile or $225 per month)	$2,702.00[d]

Total for Active Driver	
20,000 miles @ 8.17¢	$1,634.00
Fixed costs	$1,885.00
5,000 miles extra depreciation @ $44 per thousand	220.00
Total (or 18.7¢ per mile or $312 per month)	$3,739.00[d]

Source: American Automobile Association, *Your Driving Costs* (Falls Church, Va: AAA, 1981).

[a] In 1981 gasoline cost approximately $1.30 a gallon.

[b] For air conditioning, add 0.15¢ per mile and 20¢ per day.

[c] Average of each of first four years for up to 15,000 miles of driving per year. Four years is the usual length of time that most people hold on to a car, though this may change with the increase in new car prices.

[d] Does not include highway and bridge tolls, parking fees, or finance charge on an installment loan.

FIGURE 13-1
National average costs for a 1981 four-door sedan (6-cylinder engine, automatic transmission, power steering, power brakes).

data that can be obtained from the American Automobile Association on the costs for particular types of new cars. This information can give you a general idea of how much you can expect to spend on a car.

One of the biggest expense items is the depreciation cost, which is the difference between what you pay for the car and what it is worth when you sell it. Generally, most of the depreciation is due to the age of the car, not its level of use. As a result, if you drive a car, say, only 6,000 miles a year, it would probably pay you to keep it for 15 years since it offers better transportation value than the used resale price would indicate. In inflationary times, however, used car prices can increase if inflation decreases the value of money at a faster rate than the car itself ages.

Some foreign cars have increased in value due to their popularity; their value increased even faster in the 1970s when the value of the dollar was declining relative to foreign currencies. It is difficult to say whether these trends will continue. The dollar in fact rose in value in 1981.

Finally, it is commonly known that full-size cars depreciate faster than compacts. However, much of this can be offset by the fact that you can negotiate a better price discount on the purchase of a big car than you can on a small car.

What alternatives might you consider for meeting your transportation needs or lowering the cost of buying or operating a new car?

1. Use public transportation. A two-income family that can get along with one car if one worker uses public transportation can save $100 or more each month, depending on the fare for the bus, train, or subway.
2. Buy a used car or a dealer's demonstrator.
3. Buy a mo-ped. For $200 (used) to $1,000, you can get a vehicle delivering 100 miles per gallon of gas. Of course, they are somewhat dangerous, though probably not as dangerous as a high-powered motorcycle.
4. Carpool with friends. You can share the cost of someone else's car and not have to pay the whole cost yourself.
5. Live closer to work. As Table 13-1 shows, a 20-mile one-way commute will cost

TABLE 13-1

Comparison of Monthly Costs by Type of Car, Region, and Amount of Driving
(includes cost of installment loan)[a]

Commute Each Way (miles)	Other + Driving (miles)	Small Towns and Rural Areas		Large Metropolitan Areas	
		Subcompact (4 cylinder)	*Standard (8 cylinder)*	*Subcompact (4 cylinder)*	*Standard (8 cylinder)*
5	3,000	$170[b]	$236[b]	$213[b]	$283[b]
5	8,000	$194	$272	$244	$331
20	8,000	$247[c]	$348[c]	$307[c]	$422[c]

Source: Data derived from American Automobile Association, *Your Driving Costs* (Falls Church, Va.: AAA, 1981).

[a] Interest expense on four-year, 15 percent loan, assuming 20 percent down payment.

[b] Additional savings in insurance may be available for low total annual mileage.

[c] Includes annually $114 extra depreciation for 2,600 miles over 15,000, plus $110 to $160 additional insurance costs for long commute vs. the short commute, as well as the variable cost differences of gas, oil, maintenance, and tires.

SELECT THE CAR THAT
MEETS YOUR NEEDS

$53 to $91 more a month than a 5-mile one-way commute (with 8,000 miles of other driving). A shorter commute might also mean that you could ride a bicycle to work or walk, at least at some times of the year.

Step 2: Select the Car That Meets Your Needs

This step involves considerable time in getting out to see and price the cars that approximate what you need. As you see different cars, continue to evaluate your decisions about your needs.

price   The asking price can be used to make comparisons, but the final cost will be subject to negotiation with the dealer.

function and appearance   You can probably best determine a car's reliability, safety, and the like by consulting the broad-based surveys such as are conducted by *Consumer Reports* or *Road and Track*. These sources are more likely to be representative of the car than a sampling of one or two friends, who may have had an unusually positive or negative experience with a particular car. However, when analyzing the surveys and studies, decide for yourself which factors are the important ones. You may come to a different overall conclusion for your purposes than did the magazine, which has its own way of weighting the criteria.

Use the mileage ratings supplied by the Environmental Protection Agency only as a basis for comparing one car to another. The government tests are performed under laboratory conditions and are probably superior to what you can do under actual driving conditions. Independent road tests such as in *Consumer Reports* or car magazines offer more reliable data and many cars can be compared in one publication. Also, beware the data offered by your friends; their egos will usually cause them to overstate the gas mileage they are actually getting in their car.

features   Extra features can be very appealing, and basic ones (such as power steering on a heavy car) can even enhance the resale value. Find out from the dealer's used car handbook how much each option you're considering is likely to be worth when you trade the car in. A general rule of thumb is that the more options you load into a car, the more chances there are for things to go wrong and need potentially expensive repair. Choose option packages that go naturally together (such as air conditioning and tinted glass).

JUST ONE MORE
WINTER...

operating and repair costs   What can you do to reduce the costs of operating a car so that they fit more easily into your budget?

1. Buy the smallest, least expensive car that will satisfy your needs. As Table 13-2 shows, it can cost from $69 to $113 more a month in total cost to own a standard-size car than a subcompact, depending on where you live.
2. Buy a used car.
3. Hold subcompacts or compacts only four to six years or 60,000 to 80,000 miles, whichever comes first. Beyond that, the repair costs are more than the deprecia-

TABLE 13-2

Comparison of Fixed, Variable, and Monthly Costs by Type of Car and Region

Type of New Car	Small Towns and Rural Areas			Large Metropolitan Areas		
	Annual Fixed Cost[a]	Variable Cost per Mile	Monthly Cost[b]	Annual Fixed Cost[a]	Variable Cost per Mile	Monthly Cost[b]
Subcompact (4 cylinder)	$1,737	$ .057	$192	$2,354	$ .074	$258
Compact (6 cylinder)	2,040	.068	227	2,431	.088	276
Intermediate (6 cylinder)	2,234	.074	248	2,693	.098	306
Standard (8 cylinder)	2,782	.088	305	2,782	.114	327

Source: Data derived from American Automobile Association, *Your Driving Costs* (Falls Church, Va.: AAA, 1981).

[a]Figures assume insurance rates based on pleasure use only (less than 10 miles to work, no youthful driver, finance charges at 15 percent on purchase, and depreciation based on trade-in after four years.

[b]Assumes total usage of 10,000 miles per year.

tion costs of a new car.[*] Of course, some makes of car have better repair records than others, as tabulated in *Consumer Reports*. For full-size cars, the repair costs on an old car are no more than the depreciation costs of a new car.

warranty   New cars offer the best warranty. Be sure to read it.

In recent years manufacturers have begun offering extended warranty packages as an extra cost option. Although we are generally skeptical of the value of service contracts, these packages may be of value for two reasons. First, the auto makers are offering them to counteract a poor-quality image and aid the sale of their cars, not to make a big profit on the warranty contracts themselves. Second, because these contracts cover major cost items rather than routine maintenance, they are not especially expensive, usually costing from $200 to $500 for plans covering from three to six years.

Most really expensive repairs occur after the warranty period. Should they occur in the first few years after purchase, you may not need the protection of a warranty to avoid the expense of these repairs. Your state may have an *implied warranty* law that requires the manufacturer to cover items normally expected to last a long time, such as the engine block, drive train, and chassis, even if they are not expressly covered by a written warranty. Check with your state attorney general's office or office of consumer protection to find out whether your state has such a law and, if so, how to make such a claim.

[*]L. L. Liston and C. A. Aiken, *Cost of Operating an Automobile* (Washington, D.C.: U.S. Department of Transportation, 1976).

Used cars may have a very limited warranty if purchased from a dealer. The best reliability protection for a used car is to have it (both engine and chassis) examined by a reputable mechanic before you purchase it.

Step 3: The Purchase Itself

Some people say that the best time to buy a car is late in the model season, typically between August and October. Other people recommend buying a car early in the model year because then you have use of the car for a full year before the next year's model begins the depreciation cycle. Also, should you wish to order a car to your specifications, you must do so before the factories shut down for model changeover, usually in late summer; the dealer has no inventory carrying costs on a made-to-order car and can therefore deliver a good price in any season (subject to the availability of cars).

Negotiating a final price can be emotionally trying. Americans are typically not comfortable with the process, partly out of inexperience, yet the car salesperson does it for a living.

It helps to know the facts before you start. You should know four things.

- *Dealer's cost.* From your library or news store, obtain a copy of *Edmond's New Car Prices,* Car/Puter's *New Car Yearbook,* an April edition of *Consumer Reports,* or similar publications. These compile the dealer's cost of both the basic car and optional equipment. Basic car costs are typically 15 to 24 percent below the sticker prices, and options run 24 to 26 percent below sticker. You can also write or call Car/Puter (1603 Bushwick Avenue, Brooklyn, NY 11207), who will send you, for a small fee, a printout of the basic cost of any car plus specific options.
- *Wholesale cost of your car.* If you are going to trade your car in, have a dealer show you the price of your car in the *Kelley Blue Book* or *Official Used Car Guide.* This is what dealers would probably pay to have the car on their sales lot. Of course, you could sell it for more on your own if you choose to try to earn the retail markup yourself.
- *Dealer's markup.* Dealers need to cover their sales commissions, overhead costs, and interest costs on carrying their inventory as well as make a profit. The *minimum* margin over dealer cost that most dealers will accept is $100 to $500, typically $300 to $500.
- *Competitive situation.* Dealers who are selling a certain popular type of car faster than they can obtain the cars from the factory have little incentive to reduce the price below the sticker price. At such times you may have to choose between paying the price, buying a different type of car, or waiting perhaps many months for the supply to equal the demand.

In summary then, barring competitive complications, you should be able to get a car for the following price:

Dealer's cost of car and options
Less: wholesale price of your trade-in
Plus: dealer's markup
_____
Net price (plus sales tax and registration)

If the dealer won't come close to meeting that price, leave. The dealer may call you back in an attempt to recover the sale, or you can try another dealer. Quotas and selling strategies may vary from dealer to dealer.

When buying a used car, your choices in makes, colors, and options will be limited to what is available at any given time. Check not only with used car lots, but also owners, who usually advertise in the papers. To make sure you're not buying someone else's problems, it makes sense to pay a trusted mechanic to look over your proposed purchase; you will get a limited warranty at the time of purchase (none from a private individual). An often effective negotiating ploy is to convey only as much cash as you are willing to pay for a used car; many a seller has been motivated by the sight of cash to bring the price down and close the sale.

Step 4: Once You Own a Car

There are three important aspects to controlling the operating cost of a car once you own it.

1. *Get full value from the warranty.* On any warranty problem, first see the dealer. Once you are certain that the dealer is unable or unwilling to correct the problem, ask the dealer to arrange a meeting with the manufacturer's representative in your area. This strategy should resolve 99 percent of all problems. Occasionally, you may have to call or write the public relations department of the manufacturer's home office, or contact the local consumer complaint coordinating office listed in the phone book.
2. *Reduce repair and operating costs.* Part of this is a result of how you drive. If you avoid fast starts and stops and hard cornering, you can lower your expenses for gas, tires, brake repairs, and the like. Another aspect is locating a service facility that will satisfactorily make, at reasonable cost, only those repairs that are necessary. Your friends are the best source of advice for your area. Also check with the local Better Business Bureau to see how many complaints it has received on a particular repair shop and how well those complaints were handled. Finally, you may wish to take a course at your local community college or adult education school to learn to do much of the routine maintenance and repair work yourself. At labor rates of $10 to $29 an hour, the savings can be considerable.
3. *Minimize the depreciation cost.* If you take care of your car, it should take longer before expensive repairs are needed and you should get a better price on resale. Park it under a roof when you can, keep it waxed, perform the preventive maintenance work as recommended, and avoid abusing the car by the way you drive or where you drive it.

MAJOR HOME APPLIANCES

These typically are high-priced items, often with high operating costs for energy use and repairs. They also have a fairly long useful life. So, to avoid being stuck with an appliance that is not only expensive but also not right for you, make the purchase carefully.

Thoughts for Apartment Renters

If you are an apartment renter, you may think you have little need right now for the information in this section. However, you may buy a television, or rent an apartment without a refrigerator. In addition, many of the money management principles discussed in this text can be applied to other furniture or major items you might buy. For example, you may find that a furnished apartment costs $40 a month more than an unfurnished one. If you shop the used furniture stores and the newspaper want ads, you can probably furnish the apartment, in a couple of weekends' effort, with good quality, slightly used furniture for less than the extra year's rent of $480; from then on you own the furniture and can continue to save on your rent bill.

Step 1: Know Your Needs for an Appliance

motivation   Eventually you may decide to own numerous appliances to get your daily chores accomplished more conveniently. However, you probably can't afford them all at once, and so you will have to set priorities. You'll probably first want at least a range and refrigerator/freezer but perhaps also a clothes washer and dryer, television, and stereo. Realize, however, that these long-lived assets have a very low resale value on the used market.

If you're not sure what refrigerator, for example, you'll want for the next 15 years or so (their average life), perhaps it would be wiser to buy a used one for $50 that suits your needs today, and defer spending $300 to $500 on a new one until you're more certain of your future needs. You may have a bigger family, a different house with more space for it, or a more productive garden requiring storage space at the peak season. Otherwise, if you buy a new $300 refrigerator now and it turns out not to meet your needs three years from now and you sell it, you may well get only $80 for it used.

If you want to wash and dry clothes, what are the trade-offs between owning your own washer and dryer and going to the laundromat? Don't forget the variable cost of driving to the laundromat. What would you do with the extra time if you had your own machines?

cost   The total cost of an appliance is more than just its purchase price. There are three other cost items to consider: operating cost, depreciation, and lost interest that could have been earned. The latter cost becomes even greater if you *pay* interest by buying on credit. The final decision may be a matter of personal choice, but at least you should have this cost information in order to weigh intelligently the budget trade-offs. As Figure 13-2 shows, for example, the annual cost to own an average upright freezer is $136; this cost should be compared with the savings that can be gained by buying foods on sale, in bulk, or at seasonal low prices and the convenience of preparing foods in advance and reducing the frequency of shopping trips.

Some similar high energy-consuming appliances are room air conditioners (which consume about $68 of electricity for 1,000 hours of operation each year), manual defrost refrigerator/freezers ($38 to $59), and automatic defrost refrigerator/freezers ($97 to $177). These figures all assume a cost of 8¢ per kilowatt-hour

Operating cost		
Electricity (8¢/kwh)		$75[a]
Repairs (estimated)		5
Depreciation (useful life of 15-20 years)		
$500 cost ÷ 20 years		25
Interest lost on cash purchase		
$500 x 9%	45	
Less income taxes at 30% on interest	−14	
Net after-tax interest		31
Total Annual Cost		$136

[a]According to the Pacific Gas and Electric Company (*Guide to Energy Usage*, June 1981), upright manual defrost freezers cost $57 to $89, and upright automatic defrost freezers cost around $148, based on a cost of 8¢ per kilowatt-hour.

FIGURE 13-2
Estimating the operating cost, depreciation, and lost interest on an upright freezer.

(kwh). To determine the rate in your area, divide a monthly electric bill by the number of kilowatt-hours used. Currently, the Federal Trade Commission (FTC) requires that major appliances (air conditioners, washers, freezers, refrigerators, furnaces, and water heaters) carry a label showing the estimated yearly operating cost based on national average electric rates.

Step 2: Select the Appliance That Meets Your Needs

price Because of the long useful life of most appliances, it is often wise to consider spending a little more for the quality and function that you know you will be happy with for a long time. Of course, your budget limitations may dictate otherwise.

function, appearance, features, operating and repair costs Let's say you want to be able to freeze food. Would a large freezer compartment in a refrigerator/freezer be adequate? If you want a separate freezer, do you want the easy accessibility of an upright model, with its higher operating cost (because the cold air pours out onto the floor every time you open the door), or do you want a more efficient chest-type freezer (where the heavier cold air stays trapped within the freezer when the lid is lifted)?

A good source of information on the quality and usability of various products can be found in recent issues of monthly magazines such as *Consumer Reports, Money,* and *Changing Times.* As we cautioned with automobiles, however, do not blindly buy the top-rated brands or models; the specific reasons for the top rating may not be as important to you as some other set of criteria.

Table 13-3 suggests the relative *financial* importance of certain groups of criteria for various types of appliances. For example, a refrigerator usually requires very little repair service and has only moderate price variation from brand to brand.

TABLE 13-3

Financial Importance of Criteria When Shopping for Appliances

Appliance	Service	Price	Design Features	Operating Costs
Air conditioner	Yes	Moderate	Moderate	Yes
Television	Yes	Yes	Yes	No
Range	No	Yes	Yes	No
Refrigerator	No	Moderate	Yes	Yes
Freezer	No	Moderate	Moderate	Yes
Dishwasher	Moderate	Moderate	Yes	Moderate
Clothes washer	Yes	Moderate	Moderate	No
Dryer	Moderate	Moderate	Moderate	Moderate

However, refrigerator design features such as shape and location of storage areas or manual or automatic defrost vary considerably; operating costs also vary widely depending on insulation, size, and defrost features. Conversely, television sets usually require several expensive repairs over their life and vary widely in price and design features. However, operating costs for solid state sets are probably no more than $1 per month for electricity even if the TV is used every day.

warranty Where you buy the appliance is important for the price the store may offer, but perhaps more important for appliances that require frequent servicing is the store's service department. Do they offer warranties in addition to the manufacturer's? Resolving warranty claims locally can be more satisfactory than dealing with a distant factory authorized repair center. Does a local merchant have more repair experience with the product line than with the slightly cheaper line at the department store that has no service department (though many do)? Have your friends or co-workers had good or bad experience with the service department? Do they get things repaired properly the first time and at a fair price? Has the firm been in business in the area for a long time and does it look successful? This success wouldn't occur if many customers were dissatisfied with the merchandise and service. Again, a check with the Better Business Bureau can offer some help, especially if you are new to the community.

Step 3: The Purchase Itself

Shop around before making the final choice. Take advantage of sales that occur at "slow" times of the year when most people are not very motivated to buy certain items:

Television	July, August
Air conditioner	September, October
Other appliances	January, February, October

An advertised "sale," however, at one store may not be as good a deal as another store's regular price. The language used to describe a sale is not of consequence. What matters is the price you pay. Also, some local dealers will negotiate the price (especially in stereo equipment) in order to make the sale.

Step 4: Once You Own It

The key here is to make the product serve out its full useful life with a minimum of service calls. First of all, use the appliance only as described in the owner's manual; it will last longer if you follow the operating and cleaning instructions. Second, before having the service representative come (at a *minimum* fee of perhaps $25), see whether there is a simple remedy to the problem. Is something jammed? Are you sure the appliance cord is plugged into a live outlet? Have you checked the owner's manual for the basic repair solutions suggested? It is surprising how many repair calls are a result of abuse, improper operations and connections, or just ignorance.

Service contracts are often heavily promoted as a panacea for repair problems. However, because such contracts entail sales costs and commission costs, and sellers of service contracts expect to profit from them, you are almost certainly better off to pay for repairs only when needed. Put half the monthly cost of the service contract into a special repair fund, and you will probably have enough to cover all future service costs. Also, do not be misled by apparently low service contract fees in the early years. As the appliance ages and needs more repair, the cost of the contract will probably greatly increase at each annual renewal.

If you have a service complaint, first give the firm who did the repairs a chance to solve the problem. They probably do not want a dissatisfied customer giving them bad word-of-mouth publicity. If necessary, see the manager or owner. If all else fails, file a report with the Better Business Bureau. Even if that doesn't get the problem corrected, at least future customers who check with the BBB can be steered away from facing the same problem themselves.

When you want to trade in a still functioning appliance, advertise in the local want ads. You'll probably be surprised at how easy it is to obtain much more than a dealer would allow on a trade-in.

CONCLUSION

In any major consumer purchase, consider these four important steps.

1. Determine what you really need to buy and why you feel that way. Consider both the rational and emotional aspects of the decision. Both are important.
2. Carefully select the brand and model that best meets your needs.
3. Shop around for the best price and service package you can locate. Be prepared to negotiate. Do not let the salesperson talk you up from your intended purchase; first leave the store and give the matter careful consideration.
4. Once you own it, take care of it and work hard at keeping the repair and operating costs down.

VOCABULARY

depreciation
fixed costs
implied warranty
service contract
variable costs
warranty

QUESTIONS

1. Why does it help to distinguish between fixed costs and variable costs in automobile ownership?
2. Would you purchase an appliance with below-average reliability if it had a good two-year warranty? Why or why not?
3. Which is the most financially desirable alternative—selling a used car or appliance yourself or trading it in on a new one?
4. Describe two things you can do to help negotiate a low price for a new car.
5. What should you do if you have a warranty problem on an automobile?
6. What should you do if you have a service complaint on an appliance?
7. How might you reduce the number of service calls on your appliances?
8. Would you advise your friends to follow the recommendations in magazines such as *Consumer Reports*? Why or why not?
9. Which criterion would you rate most important when buying a dishwasher: service, design features, price, or operating costs?
10. A local discount store just advertised its "home appliance clearance sale of the decade." How would you decide whether the claim was valid? What other considerations would you have besides price?

CASE PROBLEM

Matt Ahlquist bought a new Cutlass Supreme two-door coupe, fully equipped, in 1981 for $9,500 and planned to keep it six years. Typical depreciation on this model over that period would be about 55 percent (based on historical experience, including the effect of inflation). What could Matt expect to sell the car for in 1987? What would be Matt's depreciation cost per mile if he drove the car 12,000 miles a year? What might happen to the resale price if consumer prices in general rose, over those six years, a total of 30 percent more than the rate of inflation in the 1970s?

RECOMMENDED READING

ON AUTOMOBILES

American Automobile Association. *Your Driving Costs*. Falls Church, Va.: AAA, annual editions.

> Provides up-to-date figures for estimating the cost of buying and operating four classes of vehicles. Check your library, local AAA office, or write 8111 Gatehouse Road, Falls Church, Virginia 22042.

Consumer Reports. This magazine publishes an auto issue every April. The 1981 edition covered these topics: which cars do best in crashes; financing a car at sky-high rates; how options boost car prices; the 1981 cars—list price vs. dealer cost; how CU tests and rates cars; CU judges the 1981 cars (95 models); body dimensions; mechanical specifications; frequency of repair records 1975–80; good bets in used cars.

Garretson, K. "New Cars: How to Get the Best Deal in Today's Market." *Better Homes and Gardens*, June 1980, p. 79.
> An update of some successful bargaining methods.

Gregory, F. M. "25 Ways to Avoid a Lemon." *Motor Trend*, October 1980, p. 79.
> Some factors that can increase the chances that the car buyer will enjoy the ownership of the car.

Road and Track. This monthly magazine specializes in thorough analyses of automobiles from the car buff's point of view, which may be somewhat different from the viewpoint of consumer magazines such as *Consumer Reports*.

"Saving Way to Sell a Car." *Changing Times*, December 1978.
> Some tips on handling the sale yourself instead of trading it in.

Sutton, Remar. *Don't Get Taken Every Time: The Insider's Guide to Buying Your Next Car.* New York: Viking, 1982.
> Having worked as an auto dealer, the author analyzes a fictional but typical car-selling operation and advises prospective car buyers on how to avoid being taken.

"The Trouble with Auto Warranties." *Consumer Reports*, October 1979.
> A thorough discussion of contractual warranties and implied warranties.

Ullman, Joseph E. "Cost of Owning and Operating Autos and Vans, 1979." Washington, D.C.: U.S. Department of Transportation, 1979.
> Excellent tables showing the cost components of owning and operating different sizes of automobiles.

ON APPLIANCES

Booklets. Call the customer service office of your electric and gas utility company for useful free booklets on selecting appliances.

Israel, B., "How to Shop for the Right Appliance." *Working Woman*, May 1981, p. 18.
> Some updated thoughts on coping with the widening array of choices in home appliances.

"Major Appliance Buymanship." *Better Homes and Gardens*, September 1978.
> As is customary with personal money management articles in this magazine, sound common sense guidelines are offered.

GENERAL

Consumer Reports. In addition to the monthly magazine, annual buying guides offer useful analyses for comparing appliances.

Lang, Larry A. *Strategy for Personal Finance.* 2d ed. New York: McGraw-Hill, 1981.
> Chapter 11 (on automobiles) and Chapter 12 (on appliances) offer charts of shopping features to consider.

14

Housing

Your decisions about housing are among the most important you make as manager of your family's financial resources. They usually do not need to be made very often, but the size of the dollar investment required gives them special significance. If a hasty decision is made, the results may sap your income unnecessarily.

YOUR PERSONAL CIRCUMSTANCES

Where you are in your financial life cycle, your choice of work, and your lifestyle will dictate in large part what type of housing you look for. If you intend to occupy a particular residence for only a short time (less than two years), then renting might be appropriate. This situation could occur for people with careers in the military, for example. Generally, the longer your intended residency, the more financially appropriate is buying a home. Also, the more substantial your financial resources, the more likely that you will be able to afford a home and benefit from the U.S. tax laws that heavily favor homeowners.

The number of times you have previously made a housing decision can determine what activities and alternatives you pursue. For example, almost everyone selecting a first place to live chooses a rental alternative. First-time home buyers probably will have to consider moving their personal belongings. However, this change is much less complicated than for the existing homeowner, who, in addition to moving, must deal with selling the current home. This transaction often involves making cosmetic repairs and improvements and deciding whether or not to help the prospective buyer by lending part of the purchase price (to be discussed later). Family size is another factor. A family of seven rarely seeks a one-bedroom apartment, while singles generally avoid four-bedroom suburban houses.

TO RENT OR TO OWN

If you are a young person not yet ready to settle down in one place, a single adult, a couple without children, a holder of a job that requires frequent transfers, or an elderly person uninterested in the responsibilities of home maintenance, then renting may be appropriate for you. You may, however, find home ownership intrinsically more attractive than renting, regardless of personal circumstances. Nevertheless, you should be aware of the advantages and disadvantages of both options.

Advantages and Disadvantages of Renting

Renting has several advantages. Initially, it involves no major capital outlay, such as a down payment. Despite the time constraints of a lease, changing accommodations is probably less expensive for a renter than for a homeowner. Some rental complexes offer swimming pools, game rooms, and health clubs. As a homeowner, you would be hard pressed to duplicate these benefits as conveniently and economically on your own. Furthermore, rental units come in smaller sizes (e.g., studios and one-bedroom, one-bath units) than do most homes. The responsibilities for gardening, maintenance, and repair of rental units usually rest with the management.

The disadvantages of renting can be both financial and personal. As a renter, your entire rent payment is an expense item. You are building up no asset value. Also, you do not have the tax deductions for mortgage interest and property taxes that the homeowner has. You have little protection beyond the term of the lease against rent increases caused by inflation. If you rent an apartment of poor design and construction, your privacy may be sacrificed more than if you owned your own home. You also have the burden of maintaining good relations with your landlord, as discussed later in this chapter.

Advantages and Disadvantages of Owning

Many of the advantages of home ownership cannot be expressed in dollars and cents, but rather in the feelings of permanence and security, pride and responsibility that can come with owning a home.

From a financial viewpoint, once you have negotiated your mortgage, the amount of your loan payments should remain constant unless you utilize one of the new alternative mortgage instruments (AMIs), which will be discussed later in this chapter. If you rent, you cannot be as certain that your rental payments will remain constant after your lease has expired. This greater predictability of payments when buying a home makes it easier for you to project your housing expenditures. Furthermore, your mortgage payments represent a form of savings. With each payment, you own an increased percentage of your home. In addition, it is often less expensive over the long run to own rather than to rent.

The disadvantages that may offset these advantages are not many, but should be recognized. In many instances, owning a home for a very short time can be more expensive than renting. Furthermore, a down payment is required as a minimum investment. This outlay could sap your financial resources and leave you vulnerable in financial emergencies. Once you have purchased a home, your ability to move without great cost is severely reduced. For this reason, of course, you should buy a house only after careful planning, thought, and searching.

Comparing Costs

The costs of renting and buying are difficult to compare because the value (e.g., an apartment in the city) you receive for your rent or lease payment can be quite different from the value (e.g., a four-bedroom home in the suburbs) you receive for your mortgage payment. The costs of home ownership are also more numerous than just the mortgage payment. The only effective cost comparison must be made between renting a house and buying a house or between renting an apartment and buying a similar condominium unit.

In establishing the amount of the rent payment, landlords attempt to receive enough money to cover property taxes, maintenance, obsolescence, mortgage payment, a return on their investment plus a vacancy allowance and management costs. The costs of owning a home include all these expenses except the last two, since a vacant home does not deprive the owner of usual income and a homeowner does not have to engage a manager.

A cost you incur as a homeowner but not as a renter is the cost of selling your home when you move. This cost is made up of expenses such as real estate commission, termite inspection, title clearance, and advertising. It is a one-time expense that must be spread over several years of ownership before owning a home is more economical than renting one. Assume, for example, that your selling costs are $2,000. Spread over two years of ownership, this would add $1,000 annually to the cost of owning. If you owned your home for eight years, however, this additional cost of owning would average only $250 a year. The longer you own your home, the less the cost (measured as an average annual expense) of selling it.

Maintenance costs tend to run higher in a rented home than in an owned home, where a sense of responsibility and pride of ownership tend both to minimize the cost of upkeep and to keep things in continual good repair. Costs unique to renting, such as the vacancy allowance and management fees, gradually build up and make renting more expensive than owning a home after about three to five years. One factor that can hasten the profitability of home ownership is rapid appreciation in the value of the property. When this occurs, owning may become more economical than renting in two years or less.

an example   To show how paying off a mortgage and taking deductions for mortgage interest and property taxes make owning a home less costly than renting it, we will use the example of a house that is bought with a $20,000 down payment and annual mortgage payments of $6,000 ($5,400 interest, $600 principal). Let us assume that property taxes are $1,000 and maintenance and repairs cost $500, making the basic cost of the property $7,500 a year. Table 14-1 shows that for one year the net cost of buying a house is $2,000 less than the net cost of renting that same house. Of course, because of closing costs and selling costs (both of which will be discussed

TABLE 14-1

Comparison of Costs for Renting and Owning a Home

	Renter			*Owner*	
$7,500	Basic cost		$7,500	Basic cost	
+ 800	Landlord profit		−1,600[a]	Tax savings on $5,400 interest and $1,000 property taxes as excess itemized deductions	
8,300	Rent/year		$5,900	After-tax cost of ownership	
−1,000	5 percent earned after tax on $20,000 not put out in down payment		− 600	Reduction of balance due on mortgage	
$7,300	Net cost		$5,300	Net cost	

[a]Calculated for a 25 percent tax bracket ($6,400 reduction in taxable income).

later in this chapter), an early sale can distort the expense figures in favor of renting unless significant price appreciation has occurred.

effects of inflation It is often said that home ownership is profitable because a house appreciates in value. If, however, all housing prices have risen equally because of inflation, any supposed profit on the sale of your old home will be lost because of the increased cost of your next home. Only by purchasing a smaller, less expensive house will you be able to retain some of the proceeds from your first sale. If your second home is similar to your first, logically it should cost you as much as your old one cost the person who bought it from you. A more valuable, larger home should cost you more than you received from the sale of your old home.

The most likely way to profit from an increase in value is to sell at a time when your property has appreciated faster than most on the housing market. Another way to benefit from escalating housing prices might be as follows. Suppose you bought your first home 10 years ago for $10,000 down and a $30,000 mortgage, on which $20,000 remains to be paid. If you sell the house now for $90,000, you have $70,000 to put as a down payment on another home. If your financial ability to assume larger mortgage payments has also increased, you conceivably could buy a home in the $100,000 to $150,000 price range. Deflated or declining housing values are similarly affected by the extent of price depreciation that has occurred and by the cost of the house you buy with the proceeds from the sale of another house.

Inflation and deflation affect rent and mortgage payments in that, during periods of inflation (or deflation), rents can be expected to rise (or fall) while mortgage payments remain fixed. Therefore, inflation favors the home buyer while deflation favors the renter.

SELECTING YOUR HOME

Once you have an accurate understanding of your needs and whether renting or buying is for you, it is time to consider selecting your home.

Location

There is a maxim in the real estate business that it is better to buy a modestly attractive home in a very attractive neighborhood than the most attractive and expensive home in a less attractive neighborhood. Another maxim states that the three rules of real estate are "location, location, and location." In other words, the best value for your home investment dollar occurs in middle-range houses in good neighborhoods. While these insights would not have become folk wisdom had they not contained some truth, they are by no means universally true. You should first consider your specific needs and financial resources and then consider general guidelines.

What sort of location are you looking for? Do you want the closeness of nature in the country or the cultural variety of the city? (Tony and Angela Minelli, for example, prefer country living and have both a German shepherd and a kitten. They want to consider only suburban or rural locations so that they and their pets will have freedom of movement and open space.) You should also consider the proximity and adequacy of public transportation, shopping facilities, recreational and medical facilities, schools and churches, and fire and police facilities. If you work, do you want to live close enough to your job that you can walk or ride a bike to work, or is easy access by car or public transportation a primary concern?

In addition to generally determining whether you buy or rent, often the place to settle—whether rural or urban or somewhere in between—is dictated by your choice of work, position in the financial life cycle, and lifestyle. If you are highly competitive and live for your time-consuming, travel-laden career, then a large city with its high-powered salaries and job opportunities may be for you. If your material goals are lower and you yearn for simplicity and tranquility, then a country setting may be your choice.

Once you have determined the characteristics of location that appeal to you, you should investigate the areas that offer these qualities. This search may take time but, if done properly, can result in the selection of a well-situated home. One very important aspect of this search is getting an approximation of the cost of living in each seriously considered location. For major metropolitan areas, this information is often published and can be found at major libraries. The U.S. League of Savings and Loan Associations annually publishes these data for 28 major cities. For smaller communities, you probably will have to visit them to do your own research. A simple comparison can be made by gathering information on four standard, but major cost groups: housing (including upkeep, insurance, and property taxes if buying), food, recreation/entertainment, and transportation. Once you have gathered these data, you can use them in combination with the intangible inputs that you picked up while doing your research (such as the appeal of the people you met and the scenery, degree of crowding, or ease of movement).

A certain location may now offer many of the qualities you seek in a neighborhood and a community, but maybe not for long. Urban use patterns are constantly changing. You should try to ensure that this process will not adversely affect the quality of your chosen location. For example, check the highway department's 10-year plan to make sure that a freeway is not planned to pass near the location you like.

Although strict zoning laws and building codes do not protect against all adverse changes, they control them somewhat. Look into the quality of these controls and the degree to which they are enforced. Officials of the local planning agency where you are considering moving can probably tell you about the zoning laws and possible changes in them. Talk with people such as home contractors. Because they must comply with the building codes, they should be able to offer you some insight into the quality of construction being undertaken in your chosen area.

The final concern is how many other people are also looking at your "ideal location" or will be doing so in the future. A check with local officials and population growth trends published by the Bureau of the Census will help you here.

Your Housing Alternatives

What characteristics of a home are most appropriate for your needs? Because Tony and Angela plan to have children soon, they want to find a three-bedroom, two-bath house. When you determine your housing needs, make sure you consider not only your present needs, but your future needs as well.

Deciding what age home to rent or buy is another important consideration. Your choice of location may restrict the availability of new or old residences. Older homes, for example, are located almost exclusively in the older sections of a community, whereas newer homes may be found in almost any section. Be sure to compare the costs for both a new and an old residence. A new apartment, for example, is likely to be more expensive than an old apartment since the former offers more amenities such as dishwashers, air conditioning, and recreational facilities. A new house is usually easier to sell in the short term and easier to finance than an old house. The minimum down payment is smaller and the mortgage maturity is longer. As such, buying a new home may impose less of a financial strain on you.

An older home does have advantages, however. Generally you can obtain a larger older house for the same cost as a smaller new house, although certain facilities such as the garage may be inadequate. Older homes may also have more landscaping and interior decorating than new homes. Property taxes can often be lower as well. Probably the most attractive aspects of an older home or apartment are its uniqueness and character. These qualities are not always available in new, mass-produced houses or apartments. Unlike new apartments, there are few large complexes of old apartment units.

In reality, your alternatives for a suitable residence are more varied than just a conventional house or apartment. We will discuss not only houses, but also manufactured homes (formerly known as mobile homes), cooperative apartments, and apartments/condominiums (basically the same type of unit although the former is generally rented and the latter owned).

the conventional house and lot When evaluating a lot, you will want to check the size and adequacy of yards and gardens; driveway access to and from the street; sewage facilities; noise from freeways, airports, railroads, or factories; and drainage (to ensure safety of the house and garage in the event of flooding).

Checking the condition of a house is not always as easy. If it is a new house, you need an estimate of how well the house will hold up for the period you plan to occupy it. Obviously, if you plan to buy rather than rent, your evaluation should be more thorough and more careful. With an older home, the question of durability has already been partly answered. What should concern you here is how much longer the various elements of the house will hold up before costly repairs are needed. If you are planning to rent, it is important to find out who will be responsible for making these repairs.

Probably the best way to evaluate the condition of a house is to engage the services of a professional house inspector. By hiring an impartial builder, architect, or home appraiser (often for as little as $50 to $100) you can receive a good assessment of your prospective home's condition. What you must be concerned with, however, is the quality of this assessment. You can judge the completeness of a professional inspection by comparing it with the items checked in Figure 14-1. An appraisal that covers these items should be fairly complete. If not, perhaps you should find a more competent inspector. In all cases where you are buying, make sure a termite inspection is made. In some states, this is required by law.

With termite inspection reports it is often extremely difficult to tell whether the problems discovered are real threats to the condition of your future home or are merely business-generating activities for the inspector, who may hope to make the corrections himself. If the seller is required and willing to pay for all recommended corrections, you have no problem. But if the seller objects to portions or all of the report and is not legally compelled to accept it, you may need to find a disinterested but qualified professional to evaluate the report. A seasoned builder, particularly one who has had extensive experience remodeling older homes (termites rarely occur in new homes), might be of help. At a minimum, deal only with termite control firms that have a good reputation with local lenders and realtors.

In recent years, with the costs of home ownership rising at a rapid rate, many people have been seeking to buy living accommodations other than the traditional house and lot. In many cases, these alternatives are attractive because they do not require a substantial outlay of money to purchase the land itself.

the manufactured home Until the early 1980s, these units were known as "mobile homes," a step up from their earlier days when they were known as "trailers," hauled behind the ubiquitous automobile. Since these units commonly have 1,000 to 2,000 square feet of space and only 4 percent are ever moved, the term "manufactured home" seems more accurate now than "mobile home."

More has been happening with this form of housing than just a name change. Financing has switched in many instances from installment-type loans to more advantageous mortgages. Interest rates and down payments can be lower and the maturity longer, particularly if you purchase the underlying lot and agree not to move the unit. Construction quality is much higher since the Department of Housing and Urban Development set standards in 1976. Manufactured homes often look like conventional homes, instead of like aluminum boxes as did older mobile homes. Also, these units are now being taxed as real estate rather than as vehicles; therefore, the tax revenues go to the municipality rather than to the state. This change explains in part why zoning has become more favorable to manufactured home developments in recent years. Finally, as manufactured homes are being viewed and used

Part of House	Structural Soundness	Waterproof	Weatherproof	Durability	Safety	Operational Effectiveness	Product Guarantee	Adequacy of Layout
Basement and foundation	✓	✓		✓				✓
Ceilings	✓	✓		✓				
Exterior siding	✓	✓	✓	✓				
Fireplaces and chimneys	✓	✓	✓	✓	✓	✓	✓	✓
Floors	✓	✓		✓				
General floor plan					✓			
Kitchen		✓	✓	✓	✓	✓	✓	✓
Painted surfaces		✓	✓	✓		✓		
Plumbing		✓	✓	✓	✓	✓	✓	✓
Roof	✓	✓	✓	✓	✓	✓	✓	✓
Temperature control mechanism					✓	✓	✓	✓
Walls	✓	✓	✓	✓	✓	✓	✓	✓
Wiring		✓	✓		✓	✓	✓	✓

FIGURE 14-1
Items that should be checked in a house inspection.

more like houses than vehicles, they have also been retaining their values, rather than depreciating as they used to.

Manufactured homes resemble good-sized apartments or small houses. Two 14-by-75-feet manufactured homes can be combined to provide 2,000 square feet of living space. Prices range from $15,000 to $50,000. Triple wides and quadruple wides run over 3,000 square feet and cost over $75,000. People with transient lifestyles such as college students, project engineers, construction workers, and military personnel find this form of housing quite convenient. Both young marrieds and retired persons who need low-cost housing, with some built-in furnishings, requiring minimum upkeep may find the manufactured home an attractive alternative. This form of housing can also serve very effectively as a recreational second home.

In selecting a manufactured home, your first consideration should be not the home itself, but where you're going to live. There are different levels of quality of manufactured home developments. The quality of a manufactured home development can be assessed by consulting Woodall's rating scheme. You should choose your development with as much care as you would choose a neighborhood when buying a home, perhaps more, since the small lots mean close neighbors and many developments have recreational centers offering regular community activities. If you intend to rent the "pad" and the home, you should check the terms of your lease to see what rental protection you can expect; the terms will probably be similar to those in apartment leases (to be discussed later in this chapter).

cooperative apartments   Membership in this housing alternative involves purchasing an ownership share proportionate to the living space you occupy in the entire dwelling complex. For example, if your apartment contains 5 percent of the living space of the entire building, then you can purchase a 5 percent ownership share. Your right to the apartment is secured by a proprietary lease that lasts as long as you live.

As a member of the cooperative, you are subject to a monthly charge to cover maintenance, upkeep, debt retirement, taxes, insurance, and an emergency fund. In many instances, the costs of living in a cooperative apartment are less than renting because members of the cooperative, as owners, need not make a profit on their investment. Your equity buildup could also be advantageous if you are in a quality building that is well located.

Before signing your membership contract, make sure you are satisfied with the conditions of ownership. Otherwise, you may be adversely affected by policy decisions made by management and approved by a majority of shareholders. For example, a plan to accelerate the payment of the mortgage would increase your assessment. There might also be restrictive policies concerning features such as subletting, entertaining, and resale.

apartments/condominiums   Unlike cooperatives, with this housing alternative you rent or purchase a specific unit in a building of units, which can range in total from two to 200. For your rent or purchase price you gain, in addition to your living quarters, a proportionate interest in common areas such as lobbies, corridors, and grounds. Consequently, apartments or condominiums are often attractive to the person who does not want the responsibility of caring for a yard. Also, the higher density land use, construction savings due to common walls, and the like make apartments/condominiums lower cost alternatives to renting or owning a separate home and yard. Assessments for taxes, exterior building maintenance, gardening, and so on are usually determined according to the circumstances of the specific accommodations and whether you rent or own.

Before you decide to rent or buy, you will want to satisfy yourself that your neighbors are responsible tenants or homeowners and that the current quality and ongoing maintenance of all common facilities meets your standards. The kind of neighbors you have will influence the condition of the common areas. After all, the availability and relatively low expense of these areas are two of the principal attractions of this form of living. When shopping for a condominium unit, watch for several danger signs:

1. Sales programs for new projects may, to entice purchasers, underestimate the maintenance costs. Try to get accurate estimates, perhaps by checking their costs against those for similar, already occupied projects. If you are buying into an older project, this should be less of a problem.
2. Developers of a new project sometimes retain control over certain aspects of the complex (and thereby continue to obtain revenue from it) through ground leases or management contracts. You will want to ensure that the developers cannot arbitrarily increase their fees and must justify them through competitive market forces; for example, if they do not submit the lowest bid for a management contract, the owners association can give the contract to the bidder who did.
3. Be wary of having to pay extra for use of the recreational facilities and therefore being exposed to arbitrary increases in the cost of using them.

Upon purchase, you will be required to sign certain documents, two of which are very common. The *declaration of ownership* establishes your membership in the owners association, describes the complex (individually owned versus commonly owned areas), and lists the basic requirements and responsibilities of membership. The *owners association bylaws* deal with the specific details of the operation of the complex.

Your Price Range

Once you have done some thinking about your needs and the available alternatives, it is time to think about the costs involved.

the costs of renting　How much can you afford to pay in rent for an apartment or house? A rough estimate can be made quickly by figuring out what 25 percent of your after-tax income is. The amount arrived at by this procedure should be taken not as an absolute upper limit on your rental expenditure, but as a guide to help you narrow your search realistically. Chances are that if you are willing to pay approximately one week's salary in rent a month, you will be able to find suitable accommodations and yet have enough money for other expenses.

the costs of buying   What you can afford to pay for a home must be accurately identified. If you have a firm idea of what you can afford, you will be better prepared to negotiate a price with the seller and to control your emotions and, thus, to avoid buying a home that is completely outside your price range.

Traditionally, the annual recurring costs of home ownership, including mortgage payments, usually amounted to 10 percent of the face value of the house. On the basis of national averages, this amount was also likely to equal 25 percent of the annual after-tax income of the homeowner. From these figures, it might seem reasonable to purchase a home valued at no more than two and one-half times your annual after-tax income.

In recent years, lenders have been willing to lend larger amounts to home buyers because of rising home prices and incomes. Buyers were also willing to buy homes that exceeded their immediate needs because of the price appreciation potential and because mortgage interest rates were generally lower than inflation rates and were tax deductible to boot. Thus, it was not uncommon for the annual recurring costs to exceed 35 percent of a homeowner's after-tax income! Now that (1) housing prices have ceased their relentless climb, (2) the rate on mortgages has become a variable, and (3) the federal income tax rates have been reduced (as of 1981), it seems unlikely that devoting such a large percentage of income to housing expenses can be justified in the future.

Rather than simply using income as a means of finding an appropriate range of purchase prices, determine what you can afford by analyzing separately the various costs involved. Here you should make a distinction between those costs that occur only once and those that recur annually. The most significant *one-time cost*, of course, is the down payment. This represents the amount of cash you pay the seller to obtain use of the home. Other one-time costs are the *closing costs*, expenses that complete the sales transaction. Fees may be charged for credit reports; a conditional Federal Housing Administration (FHA) commitment to insure the mortgage; title search, examination, and insurance; loan origination; legal work including document preparation and recording plus an attorney's time; escrow duties; and property survey. (The Consumer Protection Act requires that these expenses not be considered part of the finance charge on a mortgage.) Local practices and negotiations usually determine whether the buyer or the seller covers these costs. As a buyer you may pay from $200 to over $2,000 for closing costs. The sooner you know the number and amounts of these fees, the better prepared you will be to negotiate their payment with the seller.

To determine how much you can realistically afford to pay in one-time costs, you should consult your balance sheet. The amount should not be so large as to undermine the stability of your financial resources. Nevertheless, there are several reasons why you may want to make this amount as large as possible.

- The more cash you pay initially, the smaller the loan you need. By minimizing the loan amount, you also minimize your total interest costs.
- A larger down payment may preclude the need for a second mortgage, which can be very expensive.
- Often when a substantial down payment (25 percent of the purchase price) is

made, the interest rate on the accompanying mortgage is 0.5 percent lower than if only a minimum down payment is made.
• A larger down payment increases your chances of getting a mortgage.

Under some circumstances it may be best for you to make as small a down payment as possible and place your excess funds in an investment program. Generally, this is advisable only when the after-tax return on your investment consistently exceeds the after-tax costs of borrowing (i.e., interest) on your mortgage.

To determine how much you can afford to pay out in *annual recurring costs*, you should begin by identifying what these costs will be. Your real estate agent could be very helpful here. Generally these costs fall into five categories: loan repayments (both interest and principal), insurance (most likely property and liability), utilities (gas, electricity, water, and garbage disposal), maintenance, and property taxes.

Next, consult your income statement or budget to determine how much you have been paying for housing. These old costs, of course, would not be added to the new costs. If you find that the annual recurring costs associated with a purchase are greater than what you have been paying, you may choose to look for a less expensive house or to postpone the purchase until you can more reasonably afford it. Or you can reassess your budget limits and cut down in some categories so that more money can be used in the housing category. For example, the interest paid on a mortgage and property taxes are excess itemized deductions from adjusted gross income. The result can be a reduction in your income taxes. Therefore, you may not have to budget as much money to this category as you did before. This would leave more funds for housing expenditures.

You might also go back to your balance sheet to see whether a larger down payment is possible. If so, the loan size could be reduced. An alternative to decreasing the loan size, however, is extending the payment period. Either approach can result in lower payments, although the latter approach will increase the total amount of interest paid in the long run. (We will discuss the down payment and mortgage in more detail later in this chapter.)

sharing the costs People have been sharing the costs of rental units for years. Because leases commonly run for only one year, the potential financial harm if one or more of the "rent sharers" renege on their financial obligation is not great.

The increase in home purchase costs and the rise in single-member households has led to another type of cost sharing—*copurchasing*. Because the costs of home ownership are substantial, it is very important that a legal agreement be worked out, with legal assistance, among the copurchasers. At a minimum, this agreement should specify how legal title to the property will be held (rely on legal advice here), what happens when one or more of the copurchasers default for a month or longer on their share of the mortgage payment and/or operating expenses, and what will be done with the interest of a copurchaser who wants to sell out in cases of incompatibility, job relocation, and the like.

You should exercise great care in selecting one or more people with whom to share the cost of a home purchase. Aside from the legal considerations mentioned above, the potential emotional strain of later untangling the relationship makes a compelling case for proceeding judiciously.

RENTING

Before deciding to rent, you should know what your signature on a rental agreement or a lease may require of you, and what your options are if your apartment house undergoes a "condo conversion."

Rental or Lease Agreement

A rental agreement usually proceeds on a month-to-month basis, and the rent can be raised monthly (although this would rarely occur); a lease agreement covers a longer period—one or more years, for example—during which the rent payment usually remains fixed. With a rental agreement, payment of each month's rent is often assumed to mean that you as renter are continuing to accept the terms of the written agreement you entered into before you moved in. Leases are renegotiated at the expiration of the lease period.

There is no standard rental or lease form used in all instances. Therefore, you cannot assume that all clauses in your favor are automatically included. Furthermore, such agreements are legal documents designed to protect the lessor (landlord), just as the sales contract (Chapter 12) is designed to protect the creditor. Several vague or ambiguous clauses might appear innocuous but in reality put you at a considerable disadvantage compared with your landlord. Therefore, make sure you understand the entire agreement and are willing to accept the terms before signing it. If you are confused or want some clauses deleted or altered and receive an unsympathetic response from your prospective landlord, look elsewhere for living accommodations or seek out legal assistance.

It is very important that you satisfy yourself as to the condition of the unit to be rented or leased before you sign an agreement. Often this can best be done by jointly touring the apartment or house with the prospective landlord. If you find unacceptable living conditions (such as leaky faucets or cracking plaster), you should have the landlord correct these before you sign the agreement. Deteriorating conditions that arise while you are a tenant should quickly be brought to the landlord's attention. Your options if the landlord refuses to make corrections will be discussed after we look more closely at terms likely to be included in a rental agreement or a lease.

rent Rent is usually paid on a monthly basis. Make sure the amount due and the date on which it is due (e.g., first day of each month) are stated. Occasionally the landlord will require that you prepay not only the first month's rent but also the last month's, in case you move before the agreement has expired. There may also be a 5 percent penalty for late rent payments.

deposit A deposit may be required in lieu of, or in addition to, the prepayment of the last month's rent. This amount is reserved by the landlord to repair and refurbish the apartment or house when you vacate. If you have maintained it reasonably well, a portion or all of this amount may be returned to you at the end of the agreement. (If there is any damage to the premises before you move in, be sure the details are noted in writing on the agreement before you sign, lest your deposit be used to cover its repair.) However, a cleaning charge will probably be assessed against your deposit, regardless of the condition in which you leave the house or apartment. Final judgment on any amounts to be returned usually rests with the landlord, but substantial disagreement can often be reconciled satisfactorily in a small claims court.

terms   Rental agreements run from month to month. Lease terms are commonly one year, although some may run as long as five years. This aspect can make a lease financially attractive for you since it means that your monthly payments will remain fixed for a certain time. The lease should also state what happens when it expires: whether it becomes renewable on a month-to-month basis; whether you may renew for an additional term at a renegotiated rental rate; or whether it is automatically extended if you fail to inform the landlord of your intention to leave.

expenses   In addition to the rent, the agreement should state who pays for utilities, repairs, replacements, insurance, and so on.

restrictions   Make sure the agreement enumerates the landlord's policy on overnight guests; children; pets; use of piano, radio, television, and the like; subleasing; and alterations made by the tenant. These are generally reasonable conditions required by landlords to protect the quality of their investment.

Tenant-Landlord Relations

Tenants are occasionally faced with the vexing problem of motivating their landlords to make repairs needed to maintain adequate living conditions in their dwelling units. The withholding of rent has gained popularity as a strategy for obtaining such repairs. However, this strategy is in conflict with the traditional legal view of the tenant-landlord relationship. According to that view, the landlord, in exchange for the tenant's rent, conveyed only possession of a dwelling for a stated period of time. It was up to the tenant to maintain the rented premises in good repair. Forcible entry detainer (FED) statutes allowed the landlord to evict a nonpaying tenant (regardless of the unit's condition) by proving only ownership of the premises, an existing lease, and the tenant's failure to pay the required rent. In addition, many states allowed the landlord to seize the tenant's personal property and sell it to pay the rent owed.

Proponents of tenants' rights have argued that the traditional legal notions of the tenant-landlord relationship arose in a simpler, slower-paced time when a lease usually involved a single-unit dwelling and when it was more reasonable to assume that a tenant would be available to make repairs and would be capable of making them. They have pointed out that in this faster-paced age of specialized employment and multi-unit, technically complex rental facilities, the tenant no longer can be expected to have the time, skills, and equipment necessary to personally make repairs.

In recent years, courts have begun to improve the legal position of tenants.

1. An implied warranty of habitability has evolved in most states. That is, landlords have been held to be in violation of public policy when their rental units do not conform to local building and housing codes. In such situations, tenants generally have been given the right to void the lease and move, to make their own repairs and deduct the cost (usually up to a certain limit within a specified period of time) from rent payments, or to pay a reduced rent on the grounds that the value of the leased premises has been reduced due to improper maintenance.
2. Under the FED statutes, the landlord could obtain a summary ruling against the nonpaying tenant without having to answer to the court for failure to maintain livable quarters. But some courts have held that such statutes unconstitutionally deny tenants their day in court because the statutes prevent tenants from proving how a landlord has failed to live up to obligations in the lease agreement.
3. In certain circumstances, it has been held to be an unconstitutional violation of a tenant's right of free speech under the First Amendment to evict a tenant at the end of the lease term in retaliation for the tenant's earlier actions in pressuring the landlord to make needed repairs.
4. In some instances, landlords have been denied the right to seize and sell the personal possessions of nonpaying tenants in order to pay the rent owed.

Legislatures also have improved the tenant's legal position. In at least 16 states, the Uniform Residential Landlord and Tenant Act has been adopted establishing an explicit warranty of habitability and providing numerous remedies for tenants to force landlords to improve and repair unsatisfactory premises. The laws of some states go beyond the act in providing tenants with legal remedies, but in many states adoption of the act would be constructive.

Dealing with Condo Conversions

More and more tenants are finding that their rental unit has become part of a condominium conversion project. When this happens, the owner of an apartment complex sells some or all of the rental units to the tenants or other purchasers. The benefits to you as the renter-now-buyer are essentially those of home ownership discussed earlier in this chapter. The risks are that you may pay too much for your unit or settle on an inappropriate form of home ownership, because the prospect of the conversion caused you to act too fast. Here are some suggestions on how to deal with this experience.

First, decide whether now is an appropriate time in your financial life cycle to be considering home ownership. If it is not, begin looking for another acceptable rental unit. If now is a good time to consider buying, you will want to go through many of the considerations cited earlier in this chapter. Chief among these would be making sure that this rental-unit-to-be-converted really fits your needs as a home. If it does not, look elsewhere. You should at least widen your search to satisfy yourself that the price being asked for your unit is competitive.

Second, investigate the legal rights and responsibilities you might have that are unique to condominium conversions. Some municipalities have enacted laws that give tenants certain rights and protections during a condominium conversion. You will also want to consider whether you are prepared to accept the responsibilities of co-ownership found in condominiums. At a minimum, if you are seriously considering buying, you should engage an attorney to assist you.

No matter what, do not allow the mere fact of a conversion project to force you into buying a home. This action should be taken only when you judge it to be appropriate for you.

BUYING YOUR HOME

Whether or not you are buying a home for the first time, it is very important to devote full attention to each aspect of buying a home. The important role a home plays in our lives and the magnitude of the costs dictate this involvement.

Begin by choosing a *real estate broker* to help you make the proper purchase. Reputable brokers will be licensed by the state in which they work. In some states, a brokerage license is granted only after the prospective real estate broker has a specified number of years of experience and has passed a state-administered battery of qualifying exams. Licenses to operate as a *real estate agent* may or may not require successful performance on qualifying exams and/or sponsorship by a licensed, practicing real estate broker. Because of the more exacting training and licensing requirements, it is generally preferable to deal with brokers. In either case, you should make sure that the broker is active in the area where you wish to purchase.

Guard against brokers who use high-pressure sales techniques, are inexperienced, have obviously overpriced listings, or have mostly listings that are offered by several real estate agencies. An "exclusive" listing is initially offered by only one broker, generally because he or she is known to offer excellent services that enhance the possibilities of a sale. If you are suspicious of a broker, check out his or her reputation with local lending sources, the Better Business Bureau, and the local board of real estate brokers.

A good broker will want to know what you are looking for and what you can afford. Discuss your housing needs and financial situation. With this information, he or she can search for the best available house for you. This task will be easier for the broker than for you because this person knows what is for sale in your chosen location. You can expect 10 days or two weeks of attention from your broker; if after this time you have not demonstrated a serious intent to buy, the broker will probably turn his or her attention to other customers. Although not expecting you to buy a house within this time, the broker does want some assurance that you are not still trying to decide in general whether to buy a house and that you have some definite ideas about the type of house you are looking for.

Asking Price vs. Counteroffer

Karen and Sparky Bern went house-hunting without first discussing what they were prepared to pay for a home or finding out how the process of negotiating a home purchase works. The second home their realtor showed them was just what Karen was looking for. Sensing the importance of this house to his wife but concerned that the asking price was too high, Sparky immediately began negotiating with the seller.

He tried intimidating the seller into lowering the price dramatically. The longer the seller resisted Sparky's overtures, the more heavy-handed Sparky became. That evening the Berns found themselves back in their old home, negotiations for the new house irretrievably severed, and barely speaking to each other.

In general, the prices set by sellers (usually in collaboration with their realtors) are higher than they will sell for. They expect to be haggled down. Often this premium is 10 percent. Under such circumstances, you make a counteroffer perhaps 15 to 20 percent below the seller's asking price (also called list or offering price). Your counteroffer and accompanying terms are generally contained in a purchase contract, much like the one shown in Figure 14-2. Your realtor takes your offer to the seller and his or her realtor. It is very unlikely that the seller will be willing to accept your first counteroffer. The seller usually counters your offer again by changing price and terms to suit him or her and returns the purchase contract to you for your acceptance or further negotiations. At some point, a deal is struck or negotiations are broken off.

Unless you enjoy bargaining (which many Americans don't), you probably would prefer to avoid this aspect of home buying. During the process of offer and counteroffer the emotional stress can be substantial, because buying a home can be so important to prospective buyers. However, with a little forethought and restraint you can save yourself a substantial amount of money and emerge from the home-buying experience with your self-esteem intact. To make the negotiating process as successful as possible, we recommend the following steps:

1. Determine to what degree you are operating in a buyer's market or in a seller's market. In some very popular areas, the buyer is at a disadvantage because the demand for housing far exceeds the supply. Or you may be at a disadvantage if your circumstances dictate that you buy a home quickly. However, when homes have gone unsold for months or when there are circumstances such as a death, divorce, or job transfer in the seller's family, the buyer will have an advantage. Knowing the circumstances under which you are operating will give you some indication of the risks you can take during the negotiating.
2. Set your limits in advance regarding price, down payment, financing terms, and the like and stick to them. Having these limits will prevent you from being manipulated into accepting, for emotional reasons, terms that your better judgment would have you avoid for financial reasons.
3. Prepare for the negotiations by making sure your offer is reasonable. To determine what your prospective house is worth in the current market, find out what a similar house in the neighborhood recently sold for and what the selling price is for similar homes in similar locations nearby. Also, ask a real estate lender for an appraisal of the home. Some sophisticated realtors in metropolitan areas maintain this type of information via computer. Be sure to check to see whether your realtor can offer this service.
4. Know what aspects of the deal you are willing to compromise on. Although negotiating is basically competitive, allowing the other side to influence the deal often results in a successful transaction for both parties. So be flexible in those aspects of the deal where you can afford to be.

REAL ESTATE PURCHASE CONTRACT AND RECEIPT FOR DEPOSIT

CALIFORNIA REAL ESTATE ASSOCIATION STANDARD FORM

THIS IS MORE THAN A RECEIPT FOR MONEY. IT MAY BE A LEGALLY BINDING CONTRACT. READ IT CAREFULLY.

....California................................19...........

Received from..

....herein called Buyer,

the sum of ....Dollars ($.............................)

evidenced by cash ☐, personal check ☐, cashier's check ☐, or ....

as deposit on account of purchase price of ....Dollars ($.....................)

for the purchase of property, situated in.........................County of................................., California, described as follows:

....
....
....
....

Buyer will deposit in escrow with...

the balance of purchase price as follows:...

....
....
....
....

1. Title is to be free of liens, encumbrances, easements, restrictions, rights and conditions of record or known to Seller, other than the following:.................

....
....
....

Seller shall furnish to Buyer at.....................................expense a standard California Land Title Association policy insuring title in Buyer subject only to liens, encumbrances, easements, restrictions, rights and conditions of record as set forth above. If Seller fails to deliver title as herein provided, Buyer at his option may terminate this agreement and any deposit shall thereupon be returned to him.

2. Property taxes, premiums on insurance acceptable to Buyer, rents, interest, and.....................(Insert in blank any other items of income or expense to be prorated) shall be prorated as of (1) the date of recordation of deed or (2)..............................(Strike (1) if (2) is used). The amount of any bond or assessment which is a lien shall be paid / assumed (Strike one) by.....................Seller shall pay cost of revenue stamps on deed.

3. Possession shall be delivered to Buyer (Strike inapplicable alternatives) (a) on close of escrow, or (b) not later than..............days after closing escrow, or (c)..........

4. Escrow instructions signed by Buyer and Seller shall be delivered to the escrow holder within.............days from the Seller's acceptance hereof and shall provide for closing within..............days from the opening of escrow, subject to written extensions signed by Buyer and Seller.

5. Unless otherwise designated in the escrow instructions of Buyer, title shall vest as follows:.....................

....
....

[THE MANNER OF TAKING TITLE MAY HAVE SIGNIFICANT LEGAL AND TAX CONSEQUENCES. THEREFORE, GIVE THIS MATTER SERIOUS CONSIDERATION.]

6. If the improvements on the property are destroyed or materially damaged prior to close of escrow, then, on demand by Buyer, any deposit made by Buyer shall be returned to him and this contract thereupon shall terminate.

7. If Buyer fails to complete said purchase as herein provided by reason of any default of Buyer, Seller shall be released from his obligation to sell the property to Buyer and may proceed against Buyer upon any claim or remedy which he may have in law or equity; provided, however, that by placing their initials here ( ) Buyer ( ) Seller and Seller agree that it would be impractical or extremely difficult to fix actual damages in case of Buyer's default, that the amount of the deposit is a reasonable estimate of the damages, and that Seller shall retain the deposit as his sole right to damages.

8. Buyer's signature hereon constitutes an offer to Seller to purchase the real estate described above. Unless acceptance hereof is signed by Seller and the signed copy delivered to Buyer, either in person or by mail to the address shown below, within.....................days hereof, this offer shall be deemed revoked and the deposit shall be returned to Buyer.

9. Other terms and conditions: (Set forth any terms and conditions of a factual nature applicable to this sale, such as financing, prior sale of other property, the matter of structural pest control inspection, repairs and personal property to be included in sale.)

....
....
....
....

10. Time is of the essence of this contract.

Real Estate Broker...By...

Address..Telephone...

The undersigned Buyer offers and agrees to buy the above described property on the terms and conditions above stated and acknowledges receipt of a copy hereof.

Dated:...

Address...

Telephone...Buyer...

ACCEPTANCE

The undersigned Seller accepts the foregoing offer and agrees to sell the property described thereon on the terms and conditions therein set forth.
The undersigned Seller has employed the Broker above named and for Broker's services agrees to pay Broker, as a commission, the sum of.....................

.................................Dollars ($) payable as follows: (a) On recordation of the deed or other evidence of title, or (b) if completion of sale is prevented by default of Seller, upon Seller's default, or (c) if completion of sale is prevented by default of Buyer, only if and when Seller collects the damages from Buyer, by suit or otherwise, and then in an amount not to exceed one half that portion of the damages collected after first deducting title and escrow expenses and the expenses of collection, if any.

The undersigned acknowledges receipt of a copy hereof and authorizes Broker to deliver a signed copy of it to Buyer.

Dated:...

Address:...

Telephone:...Seller...

Broker consents to the foregoing.

Dated:...Broker...

A REAL ESTATE BROKER IS THE PERSON QUALIFIED TO ADVISE ON REAL ESTATE. IF YOU DESIRE LEGAL ADVICE CONSULT YOUR ATTORNEY.

THIS STANDARDIZED DOCUMENT FOR USE IN SIMPLE TRANSACTIONS HAS BEEN APPROVED BY THE CALIFORNIA REAL ESTATE ASSOCIATION AND THE STATE BAR OF CALIFORNIA IN FORM ONLY. NO REPRESENTATION IS MADE AS TO THE LEGAL VALIDITY OF ANY PROVISION OR THE ADEQUACY OF ANY PROVISION IN ANY SPECIFIC TRANSACTION. IT SHOULD NOT BE USED IN COMPLEX TRANSACTIONS OR WITH EXTENSIVE RIDERS OR ADDITIONS.

Copyright 1967 by California Real Estate Association

FORM NCR-D

FIGURE 14-2
Sample purchase
contract.

5. As you get closer to reaching an agreement, it becomes emotionally more compelling to compromise your position unduly. Usually this takes the form of a willingness to accede to the seller's price. The rationale goes, "Well, we're within 5 percent of each other, so I'll give in rather than risk having the seller reject my next offer and have the deal fall through." It is better to translate this 5 percent into actual dollars; it could amount to $3,000 or more. Recognizing that some portion of the amount saved by further negotiating represents several months of groceries or even take-home pay might stiffen your resolve to see the negotiations through to a more advantageous conclusion.

6. Bear in mind that, as with most of us, there are probably several houses that will more than adequately meet your needs. Think of a house as being like a streetcar—there will be another one along any time now. If you can remain somewhat detached in this way, you can resist being forced into accepting disadvantageous terms and, if the deal falls through, the disappointment will be more bearable.

7. Consider the seller's emotional involvement. Just as the pressure mounts on you, it often does on the seller as well. The seller might be more willing to compromise than he or she lets on and is probably anxious to avoid losing the sale.

Deposit

After the purchase price has been settled, you will put up a deposit. Often called "earnest money," this deposit is evidence of your intention to buy and may be applied toward the down payment. If you change your mind and decide not to buy a house on which you have made a deposit, you may have to forfeit the money.

By mutual agreement between you and the seller, the deposit is sent to an *escrow agent*. Such an individual or organization acts as an impartial third party who guards all involved monies until the purchase agreement has been completed. With the deposit, you send instructions to the escrow agent to hold this money until you authorize its release to the seller.

Purchase Contract

A purchase contract is signed by you and the seller when the deposit is made. In some areas, this contract is confusingly termed a "deposit receipt." It is not a receipt, but a contract specifying all the conditions you and the seller have arrived at through negotiations and agreed to meet before the transaction is completed. You can cancel the contract and thus obtain a refund of your deposit only if one or more of the terms in the agreement are not met. Therefore, be sure that you are satisfied with all points and "escape clauses" in the contract before you sign. Provisions appropriate to your particular situation can be included only at your request. Here is a partial list of the provisions that should be included in a purchase contract:

- Purchase price
- Prohibition against raising the purchase price
- Specification of amount of down payment and minimum acceptable financing
- Date on which seller is required to deliver property

- Hour and day of closing the sale
- Delineation of builder's and/or seller's responsibility to complete plans and specifications after you move in
- Prohibition of liability to you for seller's unpaid claims (such as property taxes up to the time of the new owner's occupancy)
- Agreement about who pays title search and insurance costs
- Total number of square feet in structure and in lot
- Mutual escape clauses, if any (to specify conditions under which buyer or seller may break contract)
- Any appliances, carpets, drapery, or other personal property to be included
- Seller's agreement to maintain premises and to insure premises for an amount equal to the purchase price until the transaction is closed
- Satisfactory passing of a house inspection
- Disclosure of all existing easements (public or private) and zoning restrictions
- Evidence that the property is not subject to any current or future condemnation proceedings

Figure 14-2 gives an example of a deposit receipt that might be used in simple transactions. Note the suggestion at the bottom of the form to consult an attorney. It is imperative that all important aspects of the purchase be included in the contract before you sign it. The assistance of a good attorney will be invaluable here.

Deed and Title

A deed is a legal document used to transfer or convey title (ownership interest) to property from one party (grantor) to another (grantee). Of course, there may be more than one grantor or grantee. Title can sometimes be difficult to determine legally. For example, a previous owner of a piece of property may have put a restriction on its use by retaining mineral rights or specifying that no building over two stories may be built on it. After several transfers of property, this restriction may have been temporarily lost and may not appear in the title until too late.

Several devices have been developed to offer title protection.

- A title *abstract* offers a history of the ownership of a piece of property.
- A *certificate of title* gives an attorney's opinion as to the condition of the title of a piece of property. This includes a description of limiting restrictions placed on the title by past owners. Such a certificate often is used when the title abstract is lost or unavailable.
- *Title insurance* covers you against loss of your equity in the property if a flaw in the title is discovered later. Certain firms dealing solely in this type of insurance sell title insurance to cover the amount of the purchase price. These companies, of course, conduct a title search before they write their policy. In some states, title insurance companies also serve as escrow agents.

Table 14-2 offers examples of the costs of title insurance at various home sales prices for northern California. Rates vary for other regions of the country. Whether you or the seller pays for this insurance and how much is charged are usually determined by local real estate practices.

TABLE 14-2

Sample Costs for Title Insurance and Escrow Services for California

Insurance Amount	Title Insurance[a]	Escrow Services[a]
$ 40,000	$234	$130
50,000	266	145
60,000	299	160
70,000	331	175
80,000	364	190
90,000	396	205
100,000	428	220

[a]Basic rates taken from *Partial Schedule of Title Insurance Premium and Escrow Fees in California*, Transamerica Title Insurance Co., 1981 (latest edition).

Once the purchase transaction has been completed, title is passed to the new owner. When mortgages are involved, title to the property is generally used as security. To be valid, a deed must be in writing and include date, identification of grantor and grantee, consideration clause, signatures of witnesses, and signature of grantor. It must also be delivered to the grantee, and title conveyance should be registered at the county recorder's office immediately after the sale.

There are several types of deeds. The safest type to have is a *warranty deed* since it guarantees that the title is conveyed free of any encumbrances—even those that may have been placed by prior parties. A *special warranty deed* guarantees only that the grantor has not placed any encumbrances on the title. A *quitclaim deed* extinguishes the grantor's title but does not transfer property or make any guarantee about the title. This type of deed is generally used when a grantor, such as an heir, gives up any claim he or she may have to property, thus removing doubt about the completeness of the grantee's claim. A *deed of bargain and sale* generally lacks the full title warranty coverage offered by the warranty deed but does carry with it an assertion that the grantor has an ownership interest in the property being transferred.

An attorney should be able to advise you on how the title to your new home should best be held and make sure this asset is included in your will if necessary. (See Chapter 22 for a discussion of titles and wills.)

Down Payment

The down payment represents the initial amount of cash you put up to buy the property. How large should it be? Part of your concern should be to ensure that, in addition to the down payment, you will have enough cash to cover the expenses of moving, closing costs, and any initial remodeling or refurnishing that may be required to make the house more livable. These considerations may make a lower down payment and a larger mortgage preferable, especially if the borrowing costs on a mortgage would be less than those on a loan to cover the cost of home improvements or furnishings.

Financing

With the dramatic rise in the cost of housing that occurred during the 1970s and early 1980s, buyers increasingly had to search for "creative" forms of financing in order to make their home purchase. At the same time, lenders showed little enthusiasm for continuing to offer home mortgages at fixed interest rates during a period of rising interest rates. As a consequence, today's home financing alternatives are much more varied than they once were.

the mortgage   This is the security offered by a borrower to a lender to obtain the loan necessary to buy a house. As in installment credit transactions, title to the property is conveyed to the lender. In the event of payment defaults, the lender may repossess the house and sell it to regain his investment. The interest rate on mortgage loans can vary according to market conditions, practices of the institution granting the loan, and changing conditions in the general economy.

As we discussed in Chapter 11, amortization allows you to pay off a debt by making periodic payments of equal amounts. Each payment is used to pay the interest due, and then any remaining portion of the payment is used to reduce the amount of principal outstanding. Over time the amount of interest due decreases because the principal is continually being reduced.

types of mortgages   As stated above, mortgage alternatives today are quite varied. They include the conventional mortgage, variable rate mortgage (VRM), flexible payment mortgage, renegotiable rate mortgage (RRM), and second mortgage.

Conventional mortgage

The *conventional mortgage* involves a transaction solely between you and the lender. There is no government participation in terms of loan guarantees or insurance. Occasionally, these loans may be insured by a private loan insurance organization.

Typically, conventional mortgages are amortized, use the fixed payment plan, and mature in 25 years or more. The size of the loan usually ranges from 60 to 90 percent of the appraised (not market) value of the property. For example, if the lender's appraiser sets the value of the property at 80 percent of the market value, your loan at 60 to 90 percent of the appraised value would be for only 48 to 72 percent of the market value. Therefore, a sizable down payment of from 28 to 52 percent of the purchase price may be required.

Variable rate mortgage

The *variable rate mortgage* (VRM) allows for changes in the interest rate charged on the loan as interest rates change in the financial markets. To avoid capricious actions by lenders, government regulations dictate how rates may be changed. For savings and loan associations, the Federal Home Loan Bank Board will allow mortgage rates to be pegged monthly to the movement of any public index of interest rates that can be verified by borrowers and not controlled by lenders. For commercial banks, the Comptroller of the Currency will allow mortgage rates to be raised or lowered 1 percent every six months in accord with the movement of three specified indexes of interest rates. In general, variable rate mortgages favor the lender because they do not protect the borrower as much as fixed rate mortgages do during periods of rising rates. Also, even with prepayment penalties, borrowers of fixed rate mortgages can take advantage of significantly falling rates by refinancing their mortgages at a lower rate.

There are a few factors, however, that may make a VRM attractive to you.

1. Lenders often write variable rate mortgages from a quarter of 1 percent to 1 percent (in rare instances) below the rate they are currently charging on fixed rate mortgages. Thus, until rates are raised on such VRMs due to generally rising interest rates, your interest costs could be less with this alternative.
2. VRMs generally do not have prepayment penalties.
3. Many VRMs can be assumed by another borrower, the person who buys your home.

The advantages of VRMs for borrowers generally occur in the first two to four years of the mortgage because that is when (1) the interest savings over fixed rate mortgages are most likely to occur, (2) fixed rate mortgages most commonly have prepayment penalties, and (3) the assumption of your mortgage would be most attractive to a prospective buyer of your home. Therefore, VRMs make the most sense if you intend to own your home only for a short time.

Flexible payment mortgage

The *flexible payment mortgage* allows the level of payments to be tailored to suit the borrower's circumstances. Young homeowners might benefit by making payments that are lower in the early years and rise as their income does. Older homeowners might want higher payments during their remaining working years and lower payments when retired. Of the flexible payment plans available, the graduated payment mortgage (GPM), in which the payments increase over time, seems to be the most popular.

Flexible payment mortgages can be insured by public or private sources. The Department of Housing and Urban Development and the Federal Housing Administration will insure five different plans, each featuring payments that increase at a certain rate over a specified period of years and then fixed payments thereafter.

Period of Increasing Payments (years)	Annual Increase (percentage)
5	2.5
5	5.0
5	7.5
10	2.0
10	3.0

A variation on the GPM is the *flexible loan insurance plan* (*FLIP*), whereby certain private insurers back graduated payment mortgages under the following arrangement. In addition to the down payment, the buyer deposits in a savings account a specified amount, say 50 percent of the down payment. This amount plus earned interest is paid out monthly over five years, for example, to pay a portion of each month's mortgage payment. Thus, the payments that must come out of the borrower's income are smaller in the early years. Once the savings account is depleted, the borrower pays the full amount each month. Keep in mind that the early lower payments always result in the total interest cost being greater than on a standard mortgage of level payments. Also, each payment should cover the interest due for that period to avoid "negative amortization," or paying interest on unpaid interest.

Renegotiable rate mortgage

The *renegotiable rate mortgage* (*RRM*) is really a series of three- to five-year loans at a fixed interest rate, secured by a long-term mortgage. The lender may renegotiate the interest rate at the end of each three-, four-, or five-year loan period. However, because of the long-term mortgage, the borrower is assured that the lender will renegotiate a new loan as each period ends. This feature protects the borrower from the prospect of not receiving new funds during "tight money" periods.

Second mortgage

The *second mortgage* is commonly used if the down payment is small and the original lending source is not willing to write a mortgage for the balance of the purchase price. Second mortgages are generally more expensive (have a higher interest rate) than first mortgages since the house cannot be used as security. Therefore, they offer lenders more speculative investment returns. Such loans are now written by banks, savings and loan associations, and credit unions as well as consumer finance companies.

The second mortgage is sometimes written by the seller. A seller would be motivated to do this if it expedited a sale at a price to his or her liking. Be careful, however, that the seller's willingness to take back a second mortgage does not mean you will pay an unnecessarily high price for the home. As homeowners' equities have increased with home values and as the original mortgage balance has been paid down, second mortgages have become viable for more and more homeowners. They are using them to obtain funds for home improvement, college education, debt consolidation, and the like.

Rates range from 12 to 24 percent, depending on money market conditions, with maturities generally from five to 10 years. Seconds usually do not have points (see definition in later section) upon origination, but do have certain origination fees. They usually do not have prepayment penalties, but may have penalties of 5 percent for late monthly payments.

FHA loan insurance   This type of loan is insured up to certain limits by the Federal Housing Administration (FHA), a division of the U.S. Department of Housing and Urban Development. The FHA was established by Congress in 1934 to provide mortgage and home improvement loan insurance to private lenders. It does not make loans; it only insures them.

If you have FHA insurance, lenders generally do not require as large a down payment as would be necessary with a conventional loan. To qualify for insurance protection, the FHA requires that a 3 percent down payment be made on the first $25,000 of appraised value and closing costs, and 5 percent on the balance over $25,000 up to a maximum ranging from $67,500 to $90,000, depending on geographic region involved.

FHA offers insurance on many types of loans, including those for property improvements, home purchase and improvements, second home purchases, multifamily dwelling financing, and low-income housing rehabilitation. For information on the types of loans that qualify for FHA insurance, contact the local FHA office or talk to a mortgage loan officer at a bank or savings and loan association.

Veterans Administration loan guarantee   The main purpose of this loan program is to ensure that a veteran will be able to obtain a loan to finance a home at reasonable interest rates. The Veterans Administration (VA) does not make loans. It offers a guarantee against loss to lending institutions and private lenders. The VA appraises property and offers a guarantee of no more than 60 percent of the appraised value of the home, with a maximum guarantee of $27,500. Originally, the loan guarantee dollar maximum was $4,000; it has been raised several times.

To be eligible for a VA mortgage loan guarantee, the amount of the loan must not exceed the VA's appraised value of the home, the loan must have an interest rate that does not exceed current government standards, and the buyer must have served at least 90 days of active duty if a World War II, Korean War, or Vietnam War veteran (all others are 181 days) and been discharged for reasons other than dishonorable unless service-incurred injuries resulted in an earlier discharge. This guarantee is available to qualified veterans more than once, if their previously guaranteed loan has been paid off and they have disposed of the property.

A bill in effect since December 1974 altered the GI Home Loan Law, which provides for VA mortgage loans. A provision of this bill includes "manufactured" homes as an alternative for obtaining a financing guarantee. In this case, the guarantee is for 50 percent of the loan value up to a maximum loan of $20,000.

If you are a World War II or Korean War veteran with unused guarantee benefits, you might want to take advantage of this provision by financing a manufactured home as a retirement residence. If you are a younger veteran, you may initially use your benefits to finance a manufactured home. Once it is paid for, you may use this benefit to buy a regular home. The reverse sequence of financing may also be used.

There is also a provision that entitles severely disabled veterans to a residence specially adapted to their disability. The VA will contribute half of the purchase price of such a residence up to a dollar maximum of $32,500. One often misunderstood fact is that veterans are liable to the VA for any loan losses until the VA releases them from this responsibility.

points This is a term applied to a practice in the real estate mortgage market. This practice has developed because the federal government dictates the maximum interest levels for FHA and VA mortgages rather than allowing these rates to be determined by money market forces. If the rate on conventional mortgages is greater than the regulated rate on FHA/VA mortgages, lenders would find the former type of mortgage a more attractive investment instrument. Consequently, funds for FHA/VA mortgages would dry up.

To compensate for the lower yield from a government regulated mortgage, the lender generally requires that a lump-sum fee be paid at the start of the loan. The method of determining the amount of this fee is called *points*. One point equals 1 percent of the amount borrowed. Generally, two points are charged for each quarter of 1 percent difference between the rate available on conventional mortgages and the ceiling rate on FHA/VA mortgages. For example, let us assume that the conventional mortgage rate is 12 percent and the ceiling rate on government backed mortgages is 11 percent. On a loan of $20,000, one point is equal to $200. Hence, eight points, or $1,600, will be charged on a government regulated mortgage since there are four quarters between the 12 percent conventionals and the 11 percent governmentals.

In addition, a fee called a *loan origination fee* or a *front-end load* may be charged on either conventional or governmental mortgage loans. It is also expressed in points and ranges from one to four points.

repayment period (maturity) Allowing for money market conditions and the age and condition of the house you buy, you have a choice of mortgage maturity periods ranging, generally, from 10 to 30 years. The total amount of interest you pay on a loan is determined by both the interest rate and the length of the repayment period. The longer you take to repay the loan, the smaller your monthly payments are and the more expensive the house you can buy with the same income. However, the longer the repayment period, the slower the reduction in principal, making the interest on the principal greater in total. As a result, a 20-year mortgage requires monthly payments that are more than half the amount of monthly payments on a 10-year mortgage (Table 14-3).

Why, then, might a wise money manager take out a mortgage loan that has a longer maturity than necessary? There are two possible reasons. First, taking a shorter mortgage might mean eliminating budgeted monthly savings and investment dollars. It may be more important to build up an emergency cash reserve than to keep interest costs down. Second, a longer mortgage maturity is attractive if the amount saved by not taking a short maturity is invested at a higher rate of return than the interest on the mortgage. (Chapters 15 through 20 will discuss rates of return on various types of investments.)

- The period should not be so short as to necessitate large annual payments that put an undue financial burden on your budget.
- The period should not be so long that large aggregate interest costs are incurred—unless you can, and will, invest the extra money at a higher rate than you are paying on the mortgage.

TABLE 14-3

Sample Payments for Standard Mortgage
A. Monthly Payments

Mortgage Amount	8% Mortgage			9% Mortgage		
	10-Year Maturity	20-Year Maturity	30-Year Maturity	10-Year Maturity	20-Year Maturity	30-Year Maturity
$20,000	$ 243	$ 159	$ 147	$ 253	$ 180	$ 161
$30,000	364	251	220	380	270	241
$40,000	485	335	294	507	360	322

B. Total Interest and Principal over Life of Mortgage

$20,000	$29,160	$38,160	$ 52,920	$30,360	$43,200	$ 57,960
$30,000	43,680	60,240	79,200	45,600	64,800	86,760
$40,000	58,200	80,400	105,840	60,840	86,400	115,920

You should be certain that there will be no penalty for prepayment if you later want to refinance the mortgage at a lower interest rate. You should also make sure that there is no clause that allows the lender arbitrarily to call back the loan or accelerate the payments.

Sources of Mortgage Loans

Savings and loan associations are the most prominent source of mortgage money. Mutual savings banks, credit unons, and private lenders also participate in this market. Mortgages written by commercial banks usually call for large down payments and short-term maturities. Occasionally, life insurance companies write mortgages on expensive homes.

In addition to traditional commercial sources of home mortgages, there are several other alternatives for obtaining home financing. You may be able to obtain a first mortgage from the home's current owner. Often called a "purchase money" mortgage, its terms are similar to those of a conventional mortgage from a commercial source. Owners usually do not charge points or a loan origination fee, especially if the loan makes it easier for them to sell the house and the mortgage represents an attractive investment for them.

The seller may be willing to take back a second mortgage if your down payment and first mortgage do not fully cover the purchase price. Or you may be able to persuade the seller to deposit an amount equal to the second mortgage with the commercial lender granting the first mortgage. This deposit would encourage the commercial lender to increase the size of the first mortgage to cover the entire difference between the purchase price and the down payment.

For example, assume that you make a $12,000 down payment on a $70,000 house but cannot find a commercial lender willing to offer more than a $50,000 first mortgage. If the seller places the $8,000 difference in escrow, the lender might be encouraged to increase the first mortgage to $58,000. The seller may be willing to do this to expedite the sale of the home and to earn interest on the $8,000. The difficulty is in finding a seller with $8,000.

Finally, you may be able to assume an existing mortgage. This arrangement would be most attractive to you if the interest rate on the assumable mortgage is less than that available from lenders and the balance outstanding is still substantial. For example, a $10,000 mortgage on a $50,000 house would not be a good one to take over since it would require a down payment and probably a second mortgage totaling $40,000. Some recent mortgages have been written to discourage assuming or transferring an existing mortgage. If you are seriously considering taking either of these actions, we recommend that you seek legal assistance.

BUILDING A HOME

If you choose to build a home rather than buy an existing one, you must decide early on what your role in the process will be. It can range from doing everything yourself to hiring outside professionals to do it all for you. How qualified are you to accomplish certain tasks—especially those associated with the architectural, supervisory, and construction phases of building a home? How much time can you devote to the project? Being honest with yourself in answering these questions is extremely important. If you are too busy or inexperienced to do effectively the portions of the homebuilding that you decide to take on, you may be disappointed with the results and may have to pay someone else to do the work after all.

The following discussion of the major tasks to be accomplished when building a home represents just the tip of the iceberg. We recommend that you give the decision to build a home much thought and research before embarking on such a project. With the exception of the portions on location, much of the following discussion is also applicable to adding space to your existing house.

Location

Picking and purchasing a lot is fairly straightforward and something you will no doubt want to participate in yourself. The basic considerations involved in location selection and purchase negotiation are similar to those discussed earlier in this chapter for buying a house. You will probably want to involve several professionals: a real estate broker to facilitate your selection and an expert such as a soils engineer to determine whether your proposed building site is sound.

It is absolutely necessary to find out from the local planning commission, before you buy a lot, whether there are zoning or building restrictions that might prevent you from building your dream house. You might also put a condition in the purchase contract requiring the approval of preliminary building plans by the local housing authorities. Finally, you should be prepared to pay cash for your lot; few loan sources lend money to individuals for house lots.

A Plan for a House

Ask local builders, lenders, and realtors to recommend architects proficient in home design. You will need to interview several in order to gain a perspective for evaluating the abilities of each one. In particular, you will be looking for at least the following three qualities:

1. Creative imagination. Some architects have none at all and some operate exclusively at the frontiers of design. By viewing an architect's recent works, you should get some idea whether the person's level of creativity meets your needs.
2. Knowledge of the "nuts and bolts" of home construction—the ability to translate ideas into reality. An architect should be able to specify materials that will bring the cost of construction within your price range without unduly sacrificing construction quality. Unfortunately, not all architects are equally strong in both the creative and technical areas. You may want to pick an imaginative architect and rely on your contractor for technical support.
3. Understanding of your wishes and willingness to design a house you are comfortable with. There are numerous cases where architects have disregarded client wishes in the name of creative license, and prospective home builders have had to pay for plans they did not want and start over with another architect.

As an alternative to paying the high cost of an architect and running the risk of design errors, you should consider buying a stock plan. These are available through builders (they may have several catalogs of plans to choose from) or through advertisements for plan catalogs in newspapers or home magazines. Ordering and using a set of such plans could save you several thousand dollars. The primary disadvantages are that (1) you lose the chance to indulge your creative urge to build a one-of-a-kind home and (2) you do not have the architect of the plan available to act as a supervisor to make sure the contractor follows the specifications accurately.

Whether you choose an architect or a stock plan, you will probably be involved in many little decisions that will seem quite important, such as the selection of plumbing fixtures, doorknobs, electric fixtures, paint colors, carpets, and drapes. Be prepared for many hours of searching through catalogs and stores, for frustrations due to out-of-stock items, and for a possible strain on your family's relationships from the pressures of arguing over the choices and deciding.

Supervision

The role of the general contractor is frequently the one that individuals decide to provide for themselves. In doing so, they avoid the general contractor's overhead and profit markup on materials and services used during the construction phase. The primary disadvantage of doing it yourself is that generally you have less leverage than a contractor might have in getting the subcontractors to do the work well and on time. The general contractor's function usually involves:

- Selecting subcontractors to accomplish various tasks based on their submitted bids. The lowest bid may not be accepted because of some question about the bidder's ability to perform the job well, without substantial delays.
- Knowing when to do what. For example, the floors should not be finished until all other heavy interior work has been done.
- Supervising the pace and quality of work.

If you wish to use a contractor, referrals can be made by realtors, lenders, and architects. Once you have interviewed several and identified two or three you approve of, have them submit bids based on the architect's plans and specifications. Your architect, if you have one, can help you evaluate the bids and make your selection.

Financing

This phase you will definitely have to participate in yourself. Before you get your permanent mortgage, you must obtain the "interim financing" to pay for the cost of construction of your home. Again, the procedures discussed in Chapter 11 for shopping for loans apply. Look particularly for points charged, the manner in which funds are to be dispensed by the lender to cover bills, and whether you must agree to obtain your home mortgage (once construction is completed) from the same lender. The lender might require that the interest rate on the eventual home mortgage be set at the prevailing rate at the time the construction loan is written. Should mortgage rates fall during the construction period, you will be assuming a mortgage loan at an above-market rate. Lenders often make this requirement if they think mortgage rates will drop soon.

Construction

There are a myriad of tasks involved in this phase: carpentry, wiring, plumbing, masonry, painting, and the like. Unless you have the ability and time to perform all or most of these tasks, it is crucial that you pick qualified people to perform them and to purchase materials economically. General contractors and architects may well earn their fees by making these decisions for you, saving you time and energy as well as the expense of inexperience.

SELLING YOUR HOME

Most of this chapter is devoted to the considerations involved in buying a home. Knowing how to sell one is also important.

Preparation

As when buying a home, you should probably engage the services of a good realtor. His or her experience in the legal, financial, and sales aspects of this transaction and frequent contact with numerous potential buyers will generally make this individual worth the 5 to 7 percent commission.

Before you put your home up for sale, you should clean it and make inexpensive but significant repairs. You might, for example, replace a damaged screen door, but you would probably not have new electrical wiring installed. Engage a qualified real estate appraiser if you find it difficult to establish an appropriate selling price. A good realtor should be able to offer this advice, too.

Transition

While you are selling your current home, you will probably also be looking for a new one. It is very important that you accomplish the sale effectively, or else you might find yourself with two homes and two sets of monthly mortgage payments. How firm you are about not lowering the asking price on your current home will depend in part on how much you need some money in order to culminate your new home purchase.

Becoming a Mortgage Lender

A prospective buyer might ask you to provide a second mortgage—the difference between the selling price and the combined down payment and first mortgage—or even to provide all of the financing. In lending circles, financing some or all of the sale is known as "taking back paper," which can be much different from "taking money" for your home sale.

The buyer might ask you to do this because he or she cannot qualify for enough conventional financing to buy your home. In this case, if you agree to make the loan, you will be taking a big risk. Since private transactions like this rarely feature an interest rate above commercial rates, you are essentially accepting a risk (that the buyer might default on the loan) without the benefit of an appropriately higher return.

However, even if the buyer does not default, you could still lose a considerable amount. Let's see how. Assume you are prepared to sell your home for $80,000. The buyer asks you to lend $60,000 at 10 percent for five years so that the person can "swing the deal now and refinance later with a conventional mortgage when rates have retreated from their current lofty heights of 14 percent." The first thing to understand is that those lofty rates represent an opportunity for you. If you accept the prospective buyer's proposition, you can expect to earn only 10 percent on $60,000 for five years, or $30,000 in total interest. If you decline this offer and wait for a buyer who qualifies for conventional financing, you can reinvest the $60,000 immediately upon receipt from the buyer. If you invest in mortgages, government bonds, or corporate bonds, you can earn 14 percent interest, for a total $42,000 (assuming no reinvestment of your interest) after five years. The $12,000 difference in interest earned can be viewed as your reducing the price of your house by $12,000. The problem is that you do not get the benefits of reduced commission and closing costs and capital gains taxes because, on paper, your home has still sold for $80,000.

Another disadvantage of choosing this approach is that you must start behaving like a mortgage lender. For example, in the loan origination phase you will have to do credit checks to evaluate the credit worthiness of your buyer and engage legal counsel to draft a loan agreement full of clauses designed to protect you, particularly in the event of default. You will also have to "service" the loan, i.e., collect the monthly payment. Collecting may entail headaches if the buyer is chronically late and must be monitored closely to make the payments.

Finally, assume you get fed up and decide to sell the loan to another investor. If the stated interest rate on the loan is below market rates, you will have to discount the face amount of your loan to the new lender. Suppose your loan of $60,000 has three years to run at 10 percent and market rates are now 12 percent. The difference in interest earned on $60,000 for three years at 10 percent ($18,000) and that earned at 12 percent ($21,600) would be $3,600. To make up this difference, the loan would have to be discounted to around $56,000. The actual discounting process is complicated because the buyer will take into account the time value of money; i.e., interest payments today are worth more than a bonus (the $4,000 difference between $60,000 and $56,000) at payoff three years later. On top of this, you will probably have to employ a mortgage broker, whose commission can easily exceed 10 percent of the loan amount (or another $5,600), to help you complete the transaction.

All in all, there is a lot to be said for not becoming your own mortgage lender under such circumstances.

A SECOND HOME

Because of increased affluence and the deterioration of the urban environment, more and more Americans want land in the country—somewhere to build a weekend home. If this ever becomes one of your goals, you should know how to reach that goal without incurring unnecessary expenses.

If you are shopping for country property in order to build a cabin or second home (not for investment, which is highly speculative and requires a complicated analysis), we recommend that you buy a lot from an individual rather than a developer. Otherwise, you could spend more money than necessary. Before buying a lot, use the following guidelines to minimize both expense and frustration.

1. Visit the property. It may be swampy or undesirable in some other equally important way. While you are there, check with other realtors to compare prices on similar lots.
2. Find out what your utilities, sewer or septic tank, water well, and the like will cost so that you know in advance whether you can afford them.
3. Get bids on the potential building cost.
4. Visit the assessor's office to determine what the property taxes will be after the purchase. They may go up a significant amount.
5. Check with the state commissioner's office to see what protection, if any, you have under state laws. In California, for example, buyers can change their mind without cause and without penalty up to 14 days after signing a contract with a developer. The law also provides that subdivisions of more than 50 lots cannot be sold unless the state real estate commissioner has issued a report on the project and the report has been issued to the prospective buyer.

CONCLUSION

The decisions you make about housing represent substantial investments. Therefore, make your decisions only after extensive investigation—not only of several housing alternatives but also of various financial arrangements and choices. Once this process has been accomplished, you should be able to make a housing decision that will reflect your needs and avoid unnecessary drains on your income.

VOCABULARY

alternative mortgage instruments (AMIs)

closing costs

condo conversion

condominium

cooperative apartment

copurchasing

counteroffer

deed

Department of Housing and
Urban Development (HUD)

deposit

down payment

equity

escrow

Federal Housing Authority (FHA)

landlord

lease agreement

manufactured home

mortgage

offering price

real estate agent

real estate broker

selling costs

tenant rights

title

Veterans Administration (VA)

QUESTIONS

1. What costs are exclusive to renting? To home ownership? Explain how they differ.
2. Under what circumstances can increased value in your home be of economic value to you?
3. When you buy a home, what services will an attorney perform? A house inspector? Realtor? Why is it important to obtain each of these services?
4. How do you determine whether a realtor is competent and honest?
5. Under what circumstances would you need a second mortgage?
6. What is the primary difference between FHA and VA mortgages?
7. Describe why points exist and how they work.
8. Why is the deposit receipt, or purchase agreement, important?
9. What is the purpose of title insurance?
10. Describe the pitfalls of "taking back paper" when you sell your home.
11. What is the difference between a VRM and a GPM?

CASE PROBLEMS

1. Terry and Andrea Carr are both 25. They have been married for three years and have a one-year-old son. Terry's monthly salary is $1,500, of which he actually brings home $1,200. The Carrs also have $41,000 in assets consisting of $12,300 in a money market fund, $16,200 in a mutual fund earning 10 percent a year, $4,500 in two cars, and $8,000 in personal property. Their liabilities amount to $6,000—$4,500 for an education loan and $1,500 for a car loan. Their net worth is $35,000.

   The Carrs have been shopping for a home and are seriously considering two prospects, as shown in Table 14-4. To make up the $15,000 difference between the purchase price of the house and the first mortgage on it, they can either pay all cash or pay $10,000 cash and assume from the seller a second mortgage of $5,000 at 10 percent amortized over five years ($106 a month). The difference of $10,000 between the purchase price of the condominium and the first mortgage on it can be made up entirely with a cash down payment. The Carrs also have the option of assuming a $3,000 second mortgage at 10 percent for five years ($64 a month). The Carrs realize that, irrespective of which housing prospect they choose, they will have to purchase an additional $2,500 in furniture, drapes, carpets, and appliances. Property taxes, mainte-

TABLE 14-4

Comparison of Two Housing Prospects

Description	Selling Price	Mortgage	Finance Charge	Payback Terms	Closing Costs
Three-bedroom, two-bath home	$55,000	$40,000	9.5%	$399/month for 25 years	$800
Two-bedroom, one-and-one-half bath condominium	45,000	35,000	10	$338/month for 20 years	$600

nance costs, and insurance are expected to average $90 a month for the house and $70 a month for the condominium.

Which housing prospect and which financing option seem most appropriate for the Carrs? Give your reasons for your choice and for discarding the other alternatives. What additional information would you need to make a better decision?

2. John and Marsha Dowdrey recently came across a house for sale that they found most attractive. It was priced at $65,000. Their initial offer was for $60,000. The seller countered with an offer of $64,750. What interpretation should they make of the seller's action and how should they react? What information about the seller would it be helpful to have before proceeding further?

RECOMMENDED READING

"Are These New Low-Payment Mortgages Worthwhile?" *Consumer Reports*, January 1979.
> Discusses VRMs and graduated payment mortgages.

"Cutting Real Estate Commissions." *Consumer Reports*, September 1980, pp. 572–73.
> Discusses the historical reasons for fixed real estate commissions and some things to do about them.

"Dealing and Wheeling in Mobile Homes." *Money*, March 1980, pp. 54–56.
> A good discussion of recent improvements in manufactured homes.

Hess, Nancy R. *The Home Buyer's Guide*. Englewood Cliffs, N. J.: Prentice-Hall, 1981.
> A thorough guide to buying or building a home in just 200 pages of text. Some of the financial aspects covered may become dated.

"How to Read a Lease." *Consumer Reports*, October 1974, pp. 707–11
> A very comprehensive treatment of some of the more onerous clauses in lease forms from the tenant's perspective.

Scher, Les. *Finding and Buying Your Place in the Country*. New York: Macmillan Publishing Co., 1974.
> Still the best comprehensive work on the subject. Written by an attorney/consumer advocate, it gives you the details you should know to avoid getting burned.

Settlement Costs and You: A Guide for Homeowners. U.S. Department of Housing and Urban Development, June 1976.
> A very detailed treatment of the costs and considerations of the settlement procedure for buying a home.

"Should You Take Back a Mortgage When You Sell?" *Changing Times*, April 1981, pp. 53–55.

> Discusses the attractions and pitfalls of becoming your own mortgage lender.

"Should You Take on a Second Mortgage?" *Better Homes and Gardens*, March 1979, pp. 17–18.

> Discusses the uses and misuses of second mortgages.

"When Renters Get Together." *Changing Times*, April 1981, pp. 18–20.

> A good brief discussion of tenants' rights and remedies.

"Your Building Is Going Condo. Should You Buy?" *Changing Times*, March 1981, pp. 60–62.

> An excellent discussion of this issue.

CHUCK AND NANCY ANDERSON

Buying a New Home

The Andersons have outgrown their house. Because of their increased skills and actions as money managers, they decide that they can afford to buy a new home. After much searching, they find a brand new house they can buy for $100,000. They can sell their present home for $85,000 with selling expenses of $5,100. It has a mortgage of $43,500. Their best mortgage offer on the new house is $75,000 at 13 percent for 30 years with monthly payments of $830. Closing costs plus initial furnishing and landscaping costs on the new home will amount to $10,000.

Questions

1. What factors should the Andersons take into account when looking for a new home?
2. What information would you need to determine whether the Andersons are financially justified in buying another house?
3. How will taxes and inflation affect the rate the Andersons must pay on their new mortgage?
4. How are the costs of property taxes, utilities, property insurance, repairs, and gardening at the new house likely to compare with those at the old house?

IV

Increasing
Your
Income

Liquidity . . . maturity . . . straddle . . . proxy . . . no par . . . OTC . . . To most people, these terms are part of a complex language spoken only by sophisticated investors. Often there is more than one term to describe the same thing. Not only are the terms confusing, but also the concepts they represent are unfamiliar. Therefore, most people find it hard to develop expertise in making investments. You should learn enough about various types of investments in Chapters 15 through 20, so that you can begin to overcome these difficulties.

Unit II dealt with the strategy for protecting what you have. There you learned how to protect your financial resources against calamities by developing meaningful insurance programs at the lowest cost. In Unit III, the strategy for getting the most out of your income was developed. You learned how to eliminate unnecessary drains on financial resources. As a result of applying what you learned in those two units, you should have more money to invest.

In Unit IV the strategy for increasing your total gross income will be treated. Chapter 15 presents the basic concepts and principles of investing. The five chapters after that treat specific investment alternatives: fixed dollar investments, stocks and bonds, mutual funds, and real estate. When you have completed this unit, you should understand fundamental investment concepts as well as specific investment alternatives. You should also be able to decide intelligently which investment goals are appropriate for you and to identify accurately the investments that represent realistic strategies for achieving these goals.

15

Investment Principles

It is possible to have a six-figure net worth without having a rich aunt who names you in her will. Because of compounding on your investment, you could invest $10,000 today at an average return of 12 percent a year and have $170,000 in 25 years. Or you could invest $2,000 each year at 10 percent for 25 years and have $196,600. People have become rich using relatively small stakes and ordinary investment media such as the stock market and real estate. One such person put $10,000 down on a $42,000 piece of land in 1963 and sold it in 1972 for $400,000! Of course, he was extraordinarily fortunate; the return on his investment was approximately 80 percent annually.

You might argue that even 12 percent is a high rate of return over a 25-year period, one that can be achieved only with considerable luck. Perhaps, but let us examine opportunities for such profit. If in 1960 you had randomly selected a broadly diversified portfolio on the New York Stock Exchange, reinvested all dividends, and sold the stocks for cash in 1968, you would have achieved a 15.6 percent compound return! Of course, you would need a fair amount of wisdom and luck to achieve such good timing. After selling the stocks, you might have been able to take further advantage of the economic situation by buying real estate if you had known that real estate is a good hedge against above-average inflation. Indeed, some real estate values rose in excess of 15 percent a year from 1968 through 1980. A very simple method for achieving a 25-year 15 percent annual return in mid-1981 would have been to buy a good quality corporate bond maturing in 2006, put it away in a safe-deposit box, and collect the interest payments until it was redeemed in 2006. (It is worth noting that, depending on one's particular tax situation, perhaps 20 to 50 percent of these investment returns would have gone to federal and state governments.)

Although these profits are possible, most American families do not make such investments. Instead, most people spend nearly everything they earn. If they build up any balance sheet assets, these assets are typically in the form of their home equity, a small savings account, and maybe some cash value in their life insurance. We do not believe, however, that this typical pattern should cause you to set low goals. Rather, the above-average income typically earned by a college graduate, combined with the skills discussed in this unit, can help you achieve above-average investment objectives.

BUT I DON'T HAVE ANY MONEY TO INVEST

Before you can learn how to use investment alternatives to full advantage, you must have something to invest. If you have trouble saving money, you may be able to use one or more of the following six techniques to avoid overspending.

Budget Your Savings

The budget techniques outlined in Chapter 4 are probably the surest and most sophisticated means of regularly saving the amounts you need. If you have not given budgeting a try yet, go back and review that chapter. There is nothing better to help solve family financial woes than a good budgeting program.

Have Someone Else Help You

If even a flexible budget seems too constraining for you, you may at least be able to authorize your employer to withhold a certain percentage from your paycheck each month to be invested in the credit union, savings bonds, or company stock, if available. Because of the low yield on savings plans or savings bonds, you should periodically transfer your accumulations to a better investment medium. Or you may buy a cash value insurance policy and have the insurance company force you to save through regular premium notices (a very low return on investment). You may overwithhold on your income taxes, and receive a refund each April to be invested or spent as your savings plan dictates. Remember, however, that the government pays no interest on withheld taxes! You could also consider one of the mutual fund savings accumulation plans discussed in Chapter 19.

Don't Pass Up the IRA

As of 1982, anyone with a job can put up to $2,000 into an individual retirement account (IRA) and deduct the amount from taxable income. If you are in, say, a 25 percent tax bracket and you put $2,000 into an IRA, you save $500 in income taxes. In effect, you have put $1,500 away toward retirement and Uncle Sam has put in $500. With these kinds of matching grants, your savings can grow even faster.

Of course, during your first 10 or 15 working years, you may find it hard to put much money into an IRA when there are so many financial demands involved in buying a house and appliances, starting a family, or whatever. Perhaps you could start the IRA habit with just $500 a year until you can put in more later. The worst that can happen is that you may have to withdraw the money early (anytime before age 59½) and pay a 10 percent penalty tax (as well as add any withdrawals to your regular taxable income for the year).

Spend Greenbacks Only

Many people save pennies until they have a jar full and then use them to make an addition to their savings account. It works, but it is a very slow way to save money. A more effective method is to put all loose change in a jar at the end of each day. In fact, if you never use change to help pay for purchases but accumulate it all in a jar, you may be able to put $50 a month in your savings account! Some couples save as much as $75 each month by spending only greenbacks. Their paper money is their spending budget; their change is their savings budget.

Try a Frugality Month

A crash savings program can help you save money quickly. The key to this program's success is to ask yourself a question before you spend money for any reason: "Do I really need to make this purchase?" You will be surprised how often the answer is no, and how rapidly your savings can mount. A period of frugality may also be beneficial in the long run. Once you become used to spartan living, you can add back only half of your previous expenses and perhaps discover that the other half really constituted unnecessary luxuries (such as a cafeteria lunch instead of a brown bag lunch). Your savings can then continue to grow.

Take Advantage of Windfalls

Everyone periodically discovers windfalls in his or her budget. Perhaps you are buying a car on the installment plan. After you make your last payment, continue writing a check for the same amount each month, but use it to increase your savings and investments. Next time you buy a car, you can pay cash for it and have money left over. Or perhaps you have received a $100 monthly raise. Last month you managed to get by on the previous paycheck; do it again this month and bank the raise. The general rule is: *Do not let windfalls disappear into your daily expenses.*

RISK AND CERTAINTY

In Unit II we discussed risks that can be covered by insurance. Now we will talk about investment risks, which generally are not insurable.

Risk is defined as the possibility that the actual return on an investment will be different from what you expected. In the absence of risk, there is certainty, or complete and perfect information about the future. The more information you have about what will happen in the future (i.e., the more certainty), the less the potential risk that something will give you a smaller return than you expected or perhaps even cause you a loss. The measure of this relationship between risk and certainty is often termed the *degree of risk exposure*. That is, the degree of risk is simply a function of the amount of knowledge you have about future events. Although the relationship between risk and amount of knowledge is shown in a linear fashion in Figure 15-1, the line may be curved for different situations. The main idea, however, is that the more you know about the future, the less risk you must take.

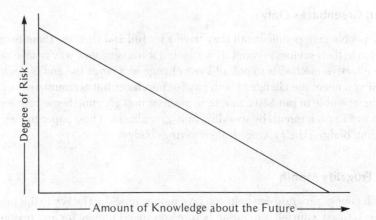

Relation of Risk and Certainty to Investments

If you invest in a U.S. savings bond, you can be certain that your principal and interest are guaranteed as fully as possible. You have virtually eliminated risk from your investment. (You have eliminated all risk in dollars, but not in real, inflation-adjusted terms, as we shall see later.) If you invest in a growth common stock, there is a chance that you will make a 20 percent annual gain, considerably more than you would make on a savings bond. However, there is also a chance that the price of the stock will decline and you will lose money. If you invest in a small mining company, you might quadruple your money if the company strikes a big ore body. Conversely, the company may go bankrupt—and you could lose your entire investment.

The higher the rate of return in an investment, the greater the risk assumed by an investor. This concept is graphed in Figure 15-2. A high degree of risk, however, does not necessarily indicate an expected high return. For example, a high risk investment such as a hamburger stand may offer a return no higher than that of an insured savings deposit.

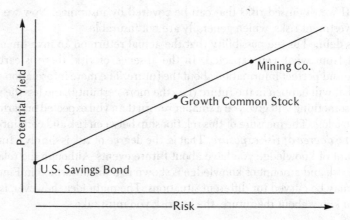

The Components of Risk

To gain a better understanding of the meaning of risk, it is useful to consider its components, both those related to the investments themselves and those related to investors. As we proceed through the strategy of increasing your income, we will discuss these aspects of risk (and how to minimize or control them) as they pertain to each investment medium: fixed dollar investments, stocks, bonds, mutual funds, and real estate.

investment-related risks Of the many possible classifications of investment-related risks, we will consider six:

- *Inflation risk:* the reduced purchasing power brought on by the accelerating depreciation of currencies. For example, a savings bond would be undesirable during a period where the rate of inflation becomes higher each year, because the holder of the bond would be paid back principal and interest worth less than the dollars originally deposited. Stable rates of inflation, such as occurred in the 1950s and early 1960s, are not a risk because interest rate levels at the time you make the investment take such inflation into account. It is the unexpected, increasing rate of inflation such as we had in the 1970s that results in the reduction in value of certain investments—particularly savings accounts, insurance policies, bonds, and, to a lesser extent, common stocks.
- *Deflation risk:* the reduction in asset value as the general price level declines because of a severe recession or because of a contraction of the money supply by the federal government. For example, real estate declined dramatically in value from 1926 to 1933. It also showed a modest decline in 1981 that carried into 1982.
- *Business risk:* the possibility that adverse events could reduce or destroy an investment's ability to generate the returns originally expected of it. For example, a competitor of Xerox Corporation could discover a new method of copying for significantly less money, thus impairing Xerox's ability to compete.
- *Interest rate risk:* the decline in market value that occurs as the general level of interest rates on new, similar investments rises. For example, if you purchase a bond° at par value (usually $1,000) with an interest rate of 10 percent, the current market value of that bond will decline if interest rates on subsequently issued bonds go above 10 percent. (Who would pay you the full $1,000 for a 10 percent bond, if they could buy a 12 percent interest bond for the same $1,000?)
- *Market volatility risk:* the relative volatility of the various asset markets. For example, over a year's time, one would normally expect greater fluctuations upward or downward in the prices of common stocks than in the prices of residential real estate.

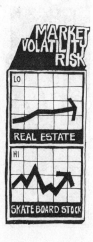

- *Illiquidity risk:* the loss in capital value you would incur in selling a particular investment in a hurry. For example, selling 100 shares of a large company's stock is usually possible at the going price, and you could get your money within a week. There is no penalty for selling quickly; although the market price may not be what

---

°A bond is an investment whereby you loan money to a corporation or government, which agrees to repay the amount at a predetermined date years in the future and meanwhile makes regular interest payments. See Chapter 17 for a more complete discussion of bonds.

you would like to get (it may even be less than you paid), you will receive the full current market price. However, if you were to sell a piece of real estate, you might have to wait months to find a buyer willing to pay the market price for that property and then wait several more weeks for the transaction to be completed. Had you wanted your money quickly, you might have had to reduce the price to below market to attract buyers. This reduced price is a measure of the illiquidity risk. Real estate has a very real illiquidity risk.

At various times in the economic cycle, some of these risks have greater impact on investments than others. For example, in a recession, business risk and illiquidity risk are more significant than inflation risk. Conversely, in a boom, inflation risk and interest rate risk may be more important than business and illiquidity risks.

Market volatility risk can be reduced by diversifying your portfolio over several different investment markets that don't necessarily move together. For example, you might invest in stocks and real estate, which fluctuate differently, and also invest in savings certificates, which have no market volatility risk at all.

You should not necessarily give these six components equal consideration in your investment decisions. Look at the economic circumstances, appraise what risks are most important during the phase over which you will be investing, and judge an investment based on your appraisal of the relative risks.

The relative impact of these six components of risk on various investment media is shown in Table 15-1. As you study each chapter in this unit, this table will become more meaningful to you; be sure to refer to it as you proceed. Of course, you should not merely focus on the risks of an investment but also view them in light of their potential returns. These will be discussed at greater length later in the chapter when the discussion revolves around Table 15-5, another valuable exhibit to refer to as you study this unit.

investor-related risk   There is a *psychological risk* that one may be unable to control one's emotions when investing. A classic example of this type of risk is the tendency of many stock market investors to become discouraged and depressed when stock prices are low and sell their stocks—and to become excited about investing when prices have had a long period of increase and therefore buy stocks at very high prices. Another example is the tendency to become so convinced that one type of investment just can't miss that people put all of their money into it. In 1980, many people became convinced that inflation would continue to get worse and that gold at $800 an ounce was sure to go to $2,000 or more; by early 1982, gold had dropped to $340, as new government economic policies began to slow the pace of inflation.

You Can Reduce Risk

There are basically two ways to reduce risk: through knowledge and through proper diversification, which entails diversification both *among* investment media and *within* each medium. Of course, it is nearly impossible to diversify away such broad-based risks as war, political changes, or crop failures.

TABLE 15-1

Six Components of Investment Risk

Investment Medium	Inflation Risk	Deflation Risk	Business Risk	Interest Rate Risk	Market Volatility Risk	Illiquidity Risk
Savings Accounts and Money Market Funds	Moderate	d	Very low	Very low	Very low	Very low
Insurance and Annuities	Moderate	d	Low	Very low	Very low	Low
Bonds Investment grade Speculative	High High	d Moderate[a]	Low High[a]	High High	Moderate High	Low Moderate
Common Stocks	High	High	Moderate[a]	High	High[a]	Low
Common Stock Mutual Funds	High	High	Low	High	High	Low
Your Home	b	Moderate[c]	Very low	Low	Low	Moderate
Real Estate Your own	b	Moderate-high[c]	Moderate-high[a]	Moderate	Moderate	Moderate
Syndicates	b	Moderate-high[c]	Moderate-high[a]	Moderate	Moderate	High

[a] Risk may be reduced through diversification among several different investments.

[b] Because these investments increase in value because of inflation, they offer an offset to the inflation risks on the other investments.

[c] The risk increases as the size of the mortgage payments increases relative to income.

[d] Because fixed dollar investments and bonds become worth more in terms of purchasing power, they offer an offset to the deflation risks of other investments.

knowledge   Why are some people generally successful in the stock market while others fail every time? We believe that it is largely because these people have more than average knowledge about, and expertise in, their investment. They consciously strive to be very good at their kind of investing. They have learned much from their own experience and from history and are therefore better prepared to anticipate and understand the future. One very effective way to reduce risk in any investment medium is to gain as much knowledge and expertise concerning that medium as is possible. Studying this unit on investing is a good first step toward increasing your knowledge.

diversification among investment media   This type of diversification has the greatest effect on reducing inflation risk and deflation risk. Look at the inflation risk column in Table 15-1. If you held nothing but investment grade bonds during a period of rising inflation rates, that risk would severely reduce the value of your holdings. However, if you also owned some real estate, that real estate would probably increase enough in value to offset your losses in bonds. Conversely, you would not want to put all of your money in real estate, because as you can see from the deflation risk column, you might find your investments wiped out during a deflationary period, whereas good bonds would probably appreciate as interest rates declined. Further, the dollar return from your bonds would be worth more to you as prices in general declined.

Proper diversification is often a function of one's goals and one's emotional needs either to increase risk (gamble) or to control risk. However, you should seriously examine your reasons for allocating your investment portfolio much differently from the following broad guidelines:

- Fixed dollar investments   5–20% (minimum two months' take-home pay)
- Bonds (investment grade)   10–35%
- Common stocks or common stock mutual funds   20–50%
- Real estate, including your home (include only the equity investment, i.e., market value minus the mortgage balance due)   20–50%

To provide a diversified portfolio for a generally inflationary period such as that since 1945, you should hold more in stocks and real estate. During potentially deflationary periods, your portfolio should emphasize quality bonds and fixed dollar investments. While marked deflation has not been seen for many years, it could happen again. During the 1930s, owners of real estate and common stock saw their investments dwindle in value to a fraction of their purchase price, as deflation reduced corporate profits and dividends and reduced rents available from real estate because of the tenants' declining incomes. Deflationary pressures were again beginning to be felt in 1981 and 1982, perhaps more this time in real estate than in the stock market. In 1929–32, the Dow Jones averages dropped 90 percent from top to bottom!

diversification within investment medium   This type of diversification can significantly reduce business risk, particularly in the last two groups above. For example, many investors concentrated their holdings in oil company stocks during the 1970s' energy crisis, but the attractiveness of the oil business as an investment diminished when legislation was passed to increase taxes on oil companies and when both oil companies and foreign governments—in their rush to get their share of oil profits—ended up producing an oil glut and declining prices. In 1981, oil company common stocks declined in price an average of 50 percent. These investors would have been more successful had they diversified their holdings in several different economic sectors. We will discuss this kind of diversification at greater length as we consider each investment topic in this unit.

INCOME AND GROWTH

The basic concept behind a financial investment is that you commit money today in the expectation of a return in the future. This return may be received both as *income from the principal* and as *growth of the principal*. Income from the principal may be obtained as interest, dividends, or rent payments. Growth of the principal is obtained as price appreciation (capital gains on property that is sold for more than was originally paid for it). For example, you may purchase 100 shares of a growth stock at $60 a share for a total cost of $6,000. (We will ignore commissions in this example.) If during the year the company pays dividends totaling $1.40 on each share, your income from the principal would be $140 for the year. If you sold the shares at the end of the year for $70 a share, you would have a profit of $10 a share and your return due to the growth of the principal would be $1,000 (capital gain). Your total return (income plus growth) would then be $1,140.

Types of Investment Income

In order to understand the investment concepts introduced in later chapters, you should be thoroughly familiar with the various terms describing types of investment income: interest, dividend, rent, capital gain, and retirement payments.

interest   The payment you receive for allowing someone to use your money is called interest. For example, banks or savings and loan associations use the money you deposit with them to invest for their own gain. They in turn use some of the income from their investments to pay you interest for the use of your money. This interest is usually expressed in terms of an annual percentage rate.

dividend   A dividend is a distribution of corporate profits to shareholders. For example, if a major company makes $10,000,000 after taxes in an average year, it might pay stockholders $6,000,000 in dividends. In this way, dividends represent income to the person who owns stock in the company. A company that has one or more unprofitable years or that needs to retain cash for growth may not pay any dividends. Corporate dividends are not assured. They depend both on the level of profits and on the way the company's management uses them. In the example above, the company decided to retain $4,000,000 of its profits for corporate growth.

rent   Rent is the payment you receive for allowing someone to use your property. Rental agreements usually run from month to month. Lease payments are the same as rent, but leases involve agreements that bind both parties for the duration of the contract, usually at least a year.

capital gain   A capital gain is income that you receive when you sell property or securities at a price above the total of what you paid for them plus commissions and selling costs. If you do not make a profit on a sale of property or securities, you have a capital loss, even though you may have received rent or dividends.

retirement payments   Retirement payments such as Social Security, pensions, life insurance benefits, and annuities represent a return of an original investment. Only to the extent that such payments include investment return above the original cost is there any investment income.

Compound Yield

Compound yield occurs when investment income—whether interest, dividends, or capital gains—is reinvested with the principal. For example, if you were to receive the interest from your savings account by check each quarter and not reinvest it, you would receive *simple interest*, not compound interest. If you were to leave the interest on deposit and get interest on interest, you would have compound interest, or a compound yield. Similarly, other types of income must be reinvested, rather than spent, if they are to achieve a compound yield. In the case of a common stock, the dividends received or capital gains realized should be reinvested in stock to achieve a compound yield on the investment.

We have included compound interest tables in the appendix to this book. You should learn how to use these tables, since they will help you both to understand the chapters in this unit and to make sound investment decisions.

lump-sum investment Compound interest Table A illustrates the value of $1 invested at various yields for up to 30 years. For example, assume that you invest $100 in a savings account with an annual yield of 6 percent. If you let the interest compound, in 10 years your $100 investment will be worth $180. If you request that the interest be paid to you each year, you will receive only $6 annual interest (simple interest) and in 10 years your total investment will have brought you $160 ($100 + (10 × $6)). Another $20 could be earned, however, because of the compounding effect of interest on interest. Over longer periods of time, the actual dollar amounts that can be earned by compounding become more significant. Over 30 years, for example, $100 compounded at 6 percent would be worth $570, as opposed to the $280 it would be worth with simple interest ($100 + (30 × $6)).

Assume that you invest $1,000 for 20 years in a mutual fund with an average rate of return of 10 percent a year. You could take your profits in cash, so that there would be only the original $1,000 in the fund at the end of each year. You would receive an average of $100 simple return each year, and in 20 years the total amount received would be $3,000 ($1,000 + (20 × $100)). Or you could leave your investment income in the fund to be reinvested in additional shares. In 20 years the $1,000 would be worth $6,700. This amount is more than twice what would have been achieved through a simple return. Table 15-2 demonstrates how annual compound-

TABLE 15-2

Value of a $1,000 Investment

Years	Return on Investment (compounded annually)	
	5%	10%
0	$1,000	$ 1,000
10	1,629	2,594
20	2,653	6,727
30	4,322	17,449
40	7,040	45,259

ing affects the size of an investment, both over increasing periods of time and at higher rates of return.

15 · INVESTMENT
PRINCIPLES

annual investment   The second compound interest table, Table B (appendix), illustrates the value of investing $1 each year at various compound interest rates and for various lengths of time. For example, if you invested $100 a year in a 5 percent savings account, after 15 years you would have accumulated $2,160.

INVESTMENT ALTERNATIVES

As we will see in Chapters 16 through 20, there are many investments from which to choose: fixed dollar investments (such as savings accounts), stocks and bonds, mutual funds, and real estate. There are, however, basically only two ways to invest money: an investor can either lend money at interest or own part of an income-producing asset.

Lending

There are four ways in which the average investor can lend money and receive interest:

- Lend money through a savings account to a bank, a savings and loan association, or a credit union.
- Buy government or corporate bonds and thereby lend money to the government or to a business.
- Buy mortgages (usually second mortgages or second deeds of trust) and thereby lend money to a homeowner.
- Lend money to a life insurance company by buying cash value life insurance.

Owning

There are several ways investors can obtain ownership of an asset in the hope of gaining a return on their money. They can buy common stock in a corporation; preferred stock in a corporation; mutual funds of common stocks, which are an indirect means of investing in stocks; a partnership share in a small business; a share in an investment syndicate (usually involved in real estate); the deed to a piece of real estate; or personal property such as stamps, coins, and art works.

Effect of Inflation on Lending and Owning

As you can see from Table 15-3, if you had put $2,000 in your mattress in 1940, it would buy only $286 worth of 1940 goods in 1981 (compared to $2,000 worth of goods in 1940). If you wanted your money to be worth as much in 1981 as it was 41 years ago, you would have had to average about 5 percent annual compound return on your money after taxes; this is because inflation, as measured by the consumer price index, has averaged 4.9 percent (compounded) over the last four decades.

TABLE 15-3

Purchasing Power of the U.S. Dollar Since 1940

(1967 = $1.00)

Year	Value of the Dollar via Consumer Price Index	Approximate Annual Percentage Rate of Inflation
1940-44	$2.38 (1940)	4.0%[a]
1945-49	1.85 (1945)	4.7[a]
1950	1.39	5.1
1951	1.28	8.0
1952	1.26	2.2
1953	1.25	0.8
1954	1.24	0.0
1955	1.25	0.0
1956	1.23	1.5
1957	1.19	3.5
1958	1.16	2.7
1959	1.14	0.8
1960	1.13	1.5
1961	1.12	1.1
1962	1.10	1.1
1963	1.09	1.3
1964	1.08	1.6
1965	1.06	1.8
1966	1.03	3.0
1967	1.00	2.3
1968	.96	4.6
1969	.91	6.0
1970	.86	5.5
1971	.82	3.4
1972	.80	3.3
1973	.75	6.2
1974	.68	11.1
1975	.62	9.1
1976	.58	5.8
1977	.54	6.4
1978	.49	9.0
1979	.42	13.3
1980	.37	12.4
1981	.34	10.4

Source: U.S. Department of Labor, Bureau of Labor Statistics, *Handbook of Labor Statistics 1975*, Bulletin 1865, p. 313; and *Economic Indicators*, January 1982.

[a] Annual average over five-year period.

Let us compare the effects of inflation on lending and owning. Assume that you buy equal amounts of a car manufacturer's bonds and common stock and hold them 15 years. If in that time, the company does not grow in size and inflation causes the dollar to buy half as much as it does today, the sales volume of autos, the cost of wages, and so on will be double that of today. The increased costs and their effect on

TABLE 15-4

Comparison of Common Stock and Bonds during a Period of General Inflation

Value of the Dollar	Today	In 15 Years
Amount needed to buy one car	$9,000	$18,000
The Company		
Autos sold	2,000,000	2,000,000
Price per car	$9,000	$18,000
Total sales	$18,000,000,000	$36,000,000,000
Labor and materials	$17,000,000,000	$34,000,000,000
Net profit	$ 1,000,000,000	$ 2,000,000,000[a]
Bonds		
Redemption value	$10,000	$10,000
Annual interest	$800	$800
Common Stock		
Average market value	$10,000	$20,000
Dividends paid	$400	$800

[a] It takes twice as many dollars to achieve the same profit level since the dollar is worth half as much as before.

the value of your stocks and bonds are hypothetically projected in Table 15-4. You can see from this example that in terms of purchasing power, stocks give you a chance to break even, since the dividends paid by the company, the profitability of the company, and therefore the market value of the stock tend to rise with inflation. Bonds, however, have a fixed value. During inflation you lose purchasing power on them.

If 15 years ago you bought a house for $30,000, today you could probably sell it for $90,000, even if you have made no permanent improvements in it. If you sell it, you will have only enough money to buy another house like it, but at least you will not have lost money. If 15 years ago you had put $30,000 in a mattress, today you could buy only one-third as much house as you could have bought then.

During periods of deflation (price decreases), such as the one the United States experienced in the late 1920s and the depression of the 1930s, cash (lending) increases in value, whereas real estate and common stocks (owning) fare poorly. Deflation seems to occur less frequently than inflation, as Figure 15-3 shows. Historically, periods of deflation in the United States have occurred from 1815 to 1843, from 1865 to 1896, and from 1921 to 1933. One might speculate that the cycle will be repeated again in the 1980s, but, of course, no one can know for sure.

CHARACTERISTICS OF INVESTMENT TYPES

All types of investments share certain characteristics in varying degrees. The seven most relevant characteristics that investors use to differentiate the alternatives available to them are overall degree of risk, average annual compound yield, liquidity,

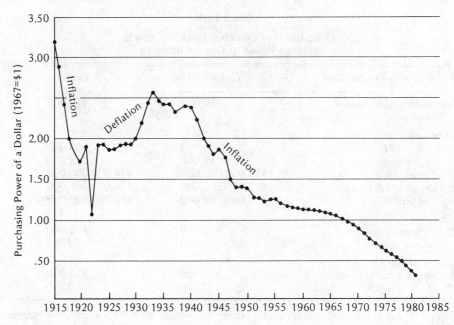

FIGURE 15-3
Trends in the purchasing
power of the U.S. dollar
since 1915.

Source: Data taken from U.S. Department of Labor, Bureau of Labor Statistics, *Handbook of Labor Statistics 1975*, Bulletin 1865, p. 313, and *Economic Indicators*, January 1982.

personal investment management required, maturity, protection against inflation, and tax aspects. Table 15-5 compares these characteristics for the investment media to be discussed in Chapters 16 through 20. You should refer to this figure as you read this unit and become better acquainted with these media.

Overall Degree of Risk

The degree of risk involved in an investment is affected by the six factors discussed earlier. In Table 15-5 we have, by way of simplification, assigned a general overall risk level to each investment medium. However, this simplified risk level does not mean that you should concentrate all of your money in the investment that offers the most comfortable risk and return for you. As we discussed earlier, diversification is all-important if you want to avoid disastrous declines in the real value of your portfolio.

Average Annual Compound Yield

The average annual compound yield is an average of the specific annual returns over a period of years. The yearly fluctuations you might expect in investment returns from various media will be explained in Chapters 16 through 20.

TABLE 15-5

Seven Characteristics of Investments

Investment Medium	Overall Degree of Risk	Average Annual Compound Yield[a]	Liquidity (average time before conversion to cash)	Personal Investment Management Required	Maturity	Protection against Inflation	Tax Aspects
Savings Accounts and Money Market Funds	Low	3-10%	1 day (up to 90 days for some accounts)	None	90 days to 10 years, depending on medium	Almost none	Income taxes on interest (some are tax deferred)
Life Insurance and Annuities	Low	3-9%	2 to 3 weeks	None	10 years to life, depending on medium	None	Income taxes deferred to maturity
Common Stocks	Moderate to high	0-16%	1 week or more	Generally moderate to substantial	May be sold at any time	Variable, but generally good	Income taxes on dividends over $100 a year per person; capital gains taxes on sale
Corporate Bonds (high quality)	Moderate	3-14%	1 week or more	Very little	Up to 30 years	None	Income taxes on interest; capital gains taxes on sale
Municipal Bonds (high quality)	Moderate	2-9%	1 week or more	Very little	Up to 30 years	None	Interest is tax-free; capital gains taxes on sale
Mutual Funds	Generally moderate (high in some funds)	0-14%	1 to 2 weeks	Very little	May be sold at any time	Variable, but generally good	Income taxes on dividends; capital gains taxes on sale
Real Estate (other than residence)	Moderate to high	5-25%	2 months to 2 years	Generally moderate to substantial	Depends on specific investment	Generally good	Some income sheltered by depreciation; capital gains taxes on sale
Real Estate Syndicate Shares	Generally high	0-25%	Depends on specific investment	Very little	Depends on specific investment	Generally good	Same as above

[a]Range over last 30 years, for any five-year period, as estimated by the authors.

LIQUIDITY

Liquidity

In Table 15-5 the column headed "liquidity" describes the ease with which an investment can be converted into cash. Liquidity does not mean that you can always get back all of your original investment when you want it. Liquidity does mean that you can readily convert the current value of an investment into cash.

This characteristic can be important to investors who are likely to need money in a hurry for emergencies. For example, you can always readily convert your common stock to cash, if you accept the current market price. The same is not necessarily true of real estate.

Personal Investment Management Required

The amount of personal investment management required can be important to people who are busy or do not want to spend time watching over their investments. For example, it takes quite a bit of time to manage an apartment house or to play the stock market for short-term gains. If you do not want to spend the time, you can invest in a real estate syndicate or a mutual fund in which professionals do the investment management for you.

Maturity

The maturity of an investment usually refers to the dates on which certain types of investments may be redeemed at face value. In this section of the text, however, we shall use the term to mean the minimum amount of time you must wait before you can realize the rate of return you expected when you made the investment. For example, you cannot buy a government savings bond today, sell it next week, and expect to be paid interest. You normally must hold the bond for at least six months.

Protection against Inflation

The degree of protection against inflation can often be an important consideration in making investments. Because of the long-term effect of inflation, owning stocks (because of rising earnings and dividends) or real estate (because of rising rents) usually offers a chance to stay even with inflation, or perhaps even profit from it, whereas lending money through savings accounts, bonds, and life insurance offers a chance to stay even with inflation only in the infrequent occurrence where the after-tax interest yield is equal to the rate of inflation. This is because lending guarantees only a certain number of dollars—not what those dollars will buy. Owning guarantees a percentage share of ownership that will increase in dollar value during prolonged periods of inflation, provided that intrinsic value does not decline (i.e., the corporation becomes less profitable or the real estate deteriorates).

Tax Aspects

The higher the tax bracket an investor is in, the more important the tax aspects of an investment. A person in a 50 percent tax bracket might welcome the chance to invest for long-term capital gains and pay taxes on only 40 percent of the gain (for an equivalent tax rate of 20 percent on the entire gain instead of the 50 percent rate that applies to other investment income). The interest on municipal bonds is tax-free. Table 15-6 summarizes the income tax effect on the returns from four types of investments.

Real estate depreciation is another way to reduce the effect of taxes on income. (This topic will be discussed in Chapter 20.) U.S. government savings bonds require no payment of taxes on the interest until you cash them in, and you may be in a lower tax bracket by that time. These and other tax considerations will be discussed in the following chapters.

Appropriateness for IRA or Keogh Plans

Because of the peculiar tax aspects of IRA and Keogh plans, some kinds of investments are more appropriate for these plans than others. While investments are in the IRA or Keogh plan, the income is tax sheltered; but when it is distributed out of the plan, it is *all* taxed as ordinary income. Thus, there is no incentive in taking big capital gains risks, because there is no capital gains tax advantage. For this reason, we recommend investing in bonds or high-yield stocks. The plans sponsored by banks, savings and loans, or money market mutual funds offer too low a yield for such a long-term investment objective. Growth stocks and real estate should be owned outside an IRA. Bonds or high-yield stocks can be bought via a brokerage house plan (for larger IRA accounts—over $10,000 to $20,000—which can justify the fees) or via a bond or income stock mutual fund (see Chapter 19).

ESTABLISHING INVESTMENT GOALS

Before making investments, you should think about why you want to invest and establish your investment goals. If you have a reason for investing, the chances that your efforts will result in the necessary financial resources are greatly improved.

Types of Investment Goals

People may have several reasons for saving and investing money. They may wish to have emergency money in case they are disabled. They may wish to build up funds

TABLE 15-6

Effect of Federal Income Tax on Return from Four Types of Investments
(Assumes federal income tax law as of January 1982)

Investor's Marginal Tax Rate	8% Interest on Savings Account	Interest on 12% Corporate Bond	8% Interest on Municipal Bond	10% Long-Term Capital Gain
0%	8.0%	12.0%	8.0%	10.0%
30	5.6	8.4	8.0	8.8
50	4.0	6.0	8.0	8.0

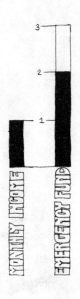

for a down payment on a house, for a summer vacation, or for retirement income. These goals can be classified as follows:

Type I	Having an emergency fund of two to three months' take-home pay
Type II-A	Reaching specific goals of major importance
-B	Reaching specific goals of minor importance
Type III-A	Having a basic retirement income
-B	Having extra retirement money for travel and other such goals
Type IV	Building an estate

Once classified, these investment goals can be ranked in order of importance. The type I goal is usually considered first, since it is very important to any family. The type IV goal is of little importance until the family has satisfied the first three types of goals. Thus, the importance of the goal types is generally in the order in which they are listed above.

This order may change, however. As you get older, having money for retirement and building an estate become more important, since your type I goal and many of your type II goals will have been satisfied. Also, as your investments accumulate, these early goals are likely to lose their importance for you. Eventually, as you acquire substantial funds, you may no longer be concerned about meeting any of the goals except building an estate for your heirs. At any one time your hierarchy of goals reflects both your stage in the life cycle and the status of your financial resources.

If you can separate your investment goals into these types, it will be much easier for you to know how much you will need at different times in your life and to enjoy the things you really want from your resources. Also, if you classify your goals, you will be better able to use the 11-step procedure (presented later in this chapter), in which you identify basic investment strategies.

An Example

At the age of 20, Richard Keller had only one investment goal: to build up at least $4,000 to cover the costs of setting up a household (type II-A goal) before he married Deborah Levinson. Since this was a must goal for him, he did not want to risk his savings trying to get a high return. Therefore, he put $2,000 each year into a savings account and married Debbie two years later.

As soon as they were married, Rich and Debbie decided to put away $2,000 as emergency money (type I). Since they wanted to make sure that the dollars would be available when they needed them, they kept the money in an insured savings investment yielding 8 percent a year.

Their next important goal was a down payment for a house (type II-A), and they decided to try to build up $15,000 for this purpose. Since they had no specified date at which they had to have a house, they decided to try for a higher investment return (and thus assume greater investment risks) and attempt to build up the money as soon as possible. If they failed, the consequence would be a longer wait for

their own home. Since Rich knew little about investing at this time, he invested $300 a month in a voluntary accumulation plan (Chapter 19) in a mutual fund. Within three years they had accumulated $13,000, when a drop in the stock market reduced the value to $11,000. At this point, they decided not to risk this money any further (since they were not too far from their goal), and so they put it in their savings account.

Two years later, at the age of 27, Rich and Debbie had $18,000 in their savings—and a new baby. Because of the baby, they decided that $6,000 should now be their emergency reserve. They did not want to take on the financial risks of home ownership without an emergency cushion. Since this left only $12,000 for the house down payment, they decided to put that money back into a mutual fund to try to build it up again. Four years and some luck later, they finally reached their house down payment goal (now costing $20,000) and made a down payment on an $80,000 home. They had used up all of their type II-A funds, but the value of these funds was now reflected in their equity in their new home.

As their next goal, Rich and Debbie wanted to start building up money for their child's college education (type II-A). This proceeded slowly at first, because they had to furnish their home. They finally built up an extra $4,000 in their savings account and began to think about the college fund when Rich's company had financial trouble and Rich was laid off. $3,000 of this money went to pay the mortgage and the bills before he found another job. The Kellers still had their $6,000 emergency fund to draw on if their financial situation had worsened. Two years later, they had the $4,000 saved up again. At age 36, Rich knew that their child would not be starting college for 8 years. Thus, he had time to take some risk and seek a higher rate of return. In addition, he had to allow for the higher educational costs that inflation might bring.

By now he had learned something about investing in the stock market and had made friends with a good broker. If he could make 12 percent a year on this first $4,000, it would be worth $10,000 in 8 years (see compound interest Table A). He wanted at least that much. He made additional investments during the following years and had accumulated $25,000 a year before their child would start college. He put $15,000 of this amount in their 8 percent account to make sure that at least that much would be available for initial college expenses. Once they had satisfied their type I and major type II goals, they could begin to think about type II-B and type III goals, such as building up a little retirement money to buy a cabin on a lake. They also wanted to have enough extra income to travel. These goals were less crucial and lay further in the future, and so they were willing to make high yield investments.

Since Rich and Debbie paid for much of their child's education on a "pay as you go" basis, there was still $7,000 left in the college fund after graduation. They decided to put $2,000 into starting an IRA account and $5,000 into a real estate syndicate. This syndicate investment offered a possible 10 to 20 percent return a year, depending on its success. In addition, it offered some tax shelter because of depreciation. The tax aspects of investments were becoming more of a concern, since Rich and Debbie were now in a higher tax bracket. From this perspective, the Kellers should have started their IRA plan sooner, because Uncle Sam would have helped add to their investments by virtue of the tax savings.

As the years passed, Rich and Debbie bought their cabin on a lake (type II-B goal), built up $66,000 worth of stocks and mutual funds for additional retirement income purposes (type III-A goal), and built up $23,000 in real estate investments for an around-the-world cruise (type III-B goal). With these resources, the Kellers could allow their emergency reserves to dwindle to $2,000, as they no longer needed to consider type I investments. Now that they had achieved their type I, II, and III goals, they could either spend their income as they pleased, or build an estate for their heirs (type IV goal).

As we look over Rich and Debbie's first 35 years of investing, several points are worth noting:

1. Because they planned ahead for the goals they wanted to reach, they improved their chances of getting many of the things they wanted.
2. By thinking about their goals in order of importance, they avoided confusing them and the timing of their investments to reach them.
3. This clear planning allowed them to assume higher risk investments with higher potential returns for long-term and low-priority goals, without jeopardizing the family's financial stability.

Because they had done these three things, they had plenty of resources with which to enjoy their later working and retirement years. And in the interim, they had accumulated enough money to buy a home, send a child to college, buy a cabin for use as a second home, and take summer vacations. Results such as these show the importance of careful investment planning.

11-STEP PROCEDURE FOR PLANNING INVESTMENTS AND ACHIEVING GOALS

You have learned some fundamental investment concepts, as well as how your hierarchy of investment goals may change—especially if you make more money. You should now be ready to learn the 11-step procedure for planning your investments and achieving your goals. If you never use such a procedure, you would have to be lucky to achieve your goals in the face of inflation, taxes, and the desire to spend your money today.

In Figure 15-4 you will find the worksheet that Chuck and Nancy Anderson used for this 11-step procedure. The blank spaces are part of the case problem at the end of this chapter.

Instructions

1 *Look at your balance sheet and enter the total amount of your investment assets, less a reserve for emergencies (type I goal) in the blank under column G showing the amount of money on hand.* Investment assets include all assets except personal property, home, and automobile.

The Andersons reviewed the investment assets they initially had on their balance sheet: $1,200 in a savings account, $1,500 in savings bonds, $5,600 (net of margin loan balance) in stocks, $1,400 in mutual funds, $4,800 in cash value

NAME(S) *Chuck and Nancy Anderson*

DATE *March 1983 Assumed average after-tax return 8%*

WORKSHEET FOR PLANNING INVESTMENTS AND ACHIEVING GOALS

A	B	C	D	E	F1	F2	G	H
					Return Factor from Table		Lump-Sum Investment[a]	Annual Investment[b]
Goal	Amount Needed	Years	Inflation Factor[a]	Adjusted Amount Needed (B X D)	A[a]	B[b]	(E ÷ F1) $20,700	(E ÷ F2) $4,400
Jim's college	$10,000[c]	10	(8%)2.2	$22,200	2.2		$10,000	
Amount remaining							10,700	
Melissa's college	10,000[c]	13	(8%)					
Amount remaining								
Furniture and carpets	4,000	3	(6%)					
Amount remaining								
Replace car	4,000	4	(6%) 1.3	5,200		4.5		$1,156
Amount remaining								
Motorboat	6,000	15	(6%)					
Amount remaining								
Retirement	(To be computed in Chapter 21)	30	(6%)	(To be computed in Chapter 21)			5,000	
Amount remaining								

[a] Refer to compound interest Table A.
[b] Refer to compound interest Table B.
[c] $2,000 minimum for each year. Additional annual college expenses are to be covered out of current income at that time.

life insurance, and $36,400 (after subtracting commissions and mortgage loan balance) in equity from the sale of their home. From this total of $50,900 they subtracted the outlays they had already made with this money: down payment on the new house ($20,000), moving costs and closing costs on the new house ($2,000), auto loan balance paid off ($2,900), furniture loan balance paid off ($2,300), and emergency fund set aside ($3,000). These uses amounted to $30,200, leaving them with $20,700 for investment goals.

FIGURE 15-4
Sample worksheet for planning investments and achieving goals.

2 *Look at your income statement and budget plan and estimate the amount you will have available each year for investment toward goals.* Enter this amount in the blank under column H showing the amount of money available.

The Andersons reviewed again their income statement as a result of their revised financial programs and arrived at a projected annual cash surplus of $4,400.

3 *Decide which goals are important to you and your family and enter them in column A.* List them in order of your family's current priority of goals, starting with the most important goal.

Deciding which goals are really important is a step that too many people pass over lightly. If you do not sit down with your family and do some serious thinking about goals, several problems may arise. First, you may not adequately consider the emergency fund before you begin your investment program. Second, you may forget about a goal until it is too late to achieve the dollar amount required. Third, you may fail to understand the importance of the goal and therefore choose an inappropriate investment strategy for achieving it.

The Andersons decided that their goals, in order of importance, are college educations for the children, furniture and carpets for the new house, a new car to replace Nancy's, a motorboat, and retirement income.

4 *Estimate the amount of money needed (in today's dollars) to satisfy each goal, and enter the sums in the appropriate blanks of column B.* Do not try to estimate the retirement sums needed; they will be discussed in Chapter 21.

The Andersons estimated what each of their goals would cost: $10,000 for each of the children's college educations (any additional college expenses would be paid for out of the family's annual income during the college years), $4,000 for furniture and carpets, $4,000 net on trade-in of a car, and $6,000 for a motorboat. (The amount needed for retirement will be computed in Chapter 21.)

5 *Enter in column C the number of years you have to achieve each goal.*

The Andersons predicted that it would be 10 years until they would need the money for Jim's college education, 13 years until they would need it for Melissa's, three years until they would buy the furniture and carpets, four years until they would replace the car, 15 years until they would buy a motorboat, and 30 years until they would retire.

6 *Estimate the rate at which inflation will probably affect your goal amount and select the appropriate factor from compound interest Table A.* While inflation has averaged about 5 percent since 1940, it has ranged from 0 to 13 percent. Of course, not all costs rise at the same rate. For example, college tuitions have risen more than three times as fast as the price of automobiles. To keep abreast of price trends and outlooks for specific items, you should read the appropriate articles in the various news media.

The Andersons decided that a 6 percent rate would be appropriate for all their goals except the children's college education, which would probably increase at a rate of 8 percent. According to compound interest Table A, the inflation factor for 8 percent over 10 years (length of time until money is needed for Jim's college education) is 2.2; the factor for 6 percent over four years (length of time until money is needed to replace Nancy's car) is 1.3.

7 *Multiply the inflation factor times the original amount needed to arrive at your adjusted amount needed (column E).*

The Andersons' first goal of $10,000 would cost $22,000 (2.2 × $10,000) in 10 years at an 8 percent inflation rate; their fourth goal of $4,000 would cost $5,200 (1.3 × $4,000).

8 *Decide how diversified your investment portfolio will be.* Unless you have nothing but ear-marked savings accounts, it is difficult to conceive ahead of time which investment will be drawn down or sold to achieve which goal. Those decisions will be easier to make at the time you need the money. Meanwhile, you should simply select a general investment strategy. We offer the following three choices.

	Estimated Average
General Strategy	*Compound Return after Tax*
A. Fixed dollar investments only	6%
B. "A" plus stocks, bonds, mutual funds	7½%
C. "A" and "B" plus real estate	8%

All three choices assume reasonably diversified portfolios and the selection of investments that offer the highest potential returns consistent with good quality (i.e., not high risk).

You might choose strategy "A" if you had only a limited amount of money, did not want to take the time and effort to improve your rate of return, or did not want to assume the price volatility risks of strategies "B" or "C." "B" and "C" help offset the pure inflation risk of "A," but require that you assume other risks that will make your investments move up and down unpredictably. Strategy "B" requires a portfolio of probably $5,000 to $10,000 minimum, as you will learn in later chapters, while "C" requires $15,000 to $20,000 minimum. The Andersons chose strategy "C." You will be better able to make your choice once you have completed your study of this unit.

9 *If you plan to use a lump-sum investment to satisfy a given goal, select the appropriate factor from compound interest Table A, and enter it in column F1.* For example, for 10 years at 8 percent, the factor would be 2.2. Divide this factor into your adjusted need (column E) to arrive at the necessary lump sum. Enter this investment amount in column G and subtract it from the amount above it on your sheet of calculations (as in Figure 15-4) to arrive at the lump-sum amount remaining for other purposes. Of course, this process is only an initial estimate. Each year you can redo this procedure to see whether you are above or below your target and make adjustments.

The Andersons divided the $22,200 they would need for their son's college education by 2.2 and learned that if they invest a lump sum now to achieve their first goal in 10 years, they would have to invest $10,000.

10 *If you plan to use an annual investment of a regular amount, select the appropriate factor from compound interest Table B, and enter it in column F2.* Continue this procedure as in step 9.

The Andersons thought that they would make an annual investment toward replacing the car and therefore divided $5,200 by 4.5 and got $1,156 as the amount they would have to invest each year.

11 *If you run out of investment funds (columns G and H) before your top priority goals are satisfied (and this will likely be the case if you are young), you have four alternatives: rearrange your budget to free up more money for investment purposes; select a higher yield investment strategy; reduce the dollar amount for some goals; and increase the length of time allowed to achieve certain goals.* A variation on this last alternative is to wait until one goal is achieved; then any annual funds that were set aside for it can now be set aside for the next goal. For example, the Andersons can begin to save for the motorboat once they have bought the furniture and carpets. After you have made one or more of these adjustments, go over the procedure again to see whether your revised plan will be successful in achieving your important goals.

Do not be dismayed if, as a young family, you discover that none of the options in step 11 enables you to achieve all of your top priority goals. You may yet have a fifth option. This extra option is that your family income or assets may increase in several ways. As your career progresses, you may qualify for promotional raises in pay, which may give you extra income for achieving goals. Or the family may add a second income source if the homemaker goes to work outside the home, perhaps when the children start school. This whole second income could be used for investment purposes.

There is always the possibility that gifts or inheritances may increase your income. However, these should not be counted on, but should be considered windfalls and only allocated when actually received. As one or more of these items in the fifth option occurs, you can reapply the 11-step procedure.

CONCLUSION

There are several important concepts that you should understand before you leave this chapter. First, higher potential yields are usually associated with higher risk investments. Take time to understand how various risks affect investments you might be interested in as well as to analyze your own tolerance for risk. Second, compound rates of return can make small regular investments grow into sizable sums. Be sure you know how to use the compound interest tables at the end of the book. Use them to help you formulate reasonable investment strategies. Third, know how to apply the 11-step procedure for planning investments and achieving goals. Fourth, refer to Table 15-5 before you make any major investment decisions, in order to be sure that you select an investment medium appropriate for your goal.

VOCABULARY

compound interest	interest
compound yield	liquidity
deflation	maturity
diversification	principal
dividend	rate of return
equity	rent
growth of the principal	risk
income from the principal	simple interest
inflation	yield

QUESTIONS

1. What would a $5,000 savings account with a 6 percent annual interest rate be worth in 12 years? What would $5,000 be worth in 12 years if it were invested in a real estate syndicate with an average annual rate of return of 12 percent?
2. If you save $50 each month to invest at the end of each year in U.S. savings bonds that have a 7 percent return, how much will you have in 10 years before taxes?
3. What is meant by *investment risk*? What are its components? What can you do to reduce risk?
4. If the price of automobiles keeps rising at an annual rate of 5 percent, what will a $7,000 automobile cost in 20 years?
5. How much would you have to invest each year in a 7 percent savings account in order to have $20,000 (already adjusted for inflation) for a house down payment in five years?
6. From an investment point of view, why is lending less desirable than owning during long periods of inflation?
7. Assume that you have $2,000 to invest toward a major goal. To achieve this goal, you need $3,200 (allowing for inflation) in five years. According to compound interest Table A, you would have to get an average annual rate of return of 10 percent. However, because of the importance of the goal, you are unwilling to take such a high risk. Describe, in numerical detail, four alternative strategies for using a 6 percent investment strategy to solve this problem.

CASE PROBLEM

Mike and Mary Todd were recently married. They are both working, and so they have money to put toward their five financial goals: an emergency reserve ($3,000); a trip to the Caribbean in two years ($2,500); a home in four years ($16,000 down plus $4,000 for basic furnishings); a child in five years ($2,200 initial medical costs); and a camper trailer in seven years ($2,000).

They plan to use a savings account and mutual fund strategy to achieve their goals. They have $5,800 in savings, and they expect to save $600 a month.

1. What inflation percentage do you think would be appropriate for each goal? Why?
2. What is the resulting adjusted amount needed for each goal?
3. What must the Todds invest toward each goal in order to be able to achieve it if the investments do well?

4. Can they satisfy all their goals with their present resources? If not, how can they revise their plans? (Base your answer on numerical computations as much as possible.)
5. If Mary were to quit her job when they start their family, what effect would this have on their overall strategy?

RECOMMENDED READING

"Investment Safety Special Report." *Money*, January 1982, pp. 36–59.
    A series of articles providing an interesting overview of such things as risk, strategies for investing, and defending against possible savings and loan failures.

CHUCK AND NANCY ANDERSON

Planning Investments and Achieving Goals

You have seen how Chuck and Nancy used the 11-step procedure to compute both the lump sum they must invest for their son's college education and the annual investment they must make to replace Nancy's car. Carry out the computations for their other goals except retirement. Assume that the Andersons make a lump-sum investment for Melissa's college and annual investments for the furniture and carpets and motorboat.

Investment certificate . . . savings and loan account . . . savings bond . . . credit union share . . . passbook savings account . . . club account . . . savings certificate . . . money market mutual fund . . . fixed annuities—these are all forms of fixed dollar investments, or time deposits. They require that money be deposited for a specific period of time in order to earn an investment return.

More people use fixed dollar investments than any other investment instrument. Despite the widespread use of time deposits, however, people continue to be confused by the ever-growing number of alternatives available.

INTEREST RATES

The interest rate on your time deposit determines the rate of return on your investment. Interest rates can be confusing, unless a few common terms are understood.

Nominal Interest Rate and Effective Interest Rate

The *nominal interest rate* is the stated rate of interest. For example, a 6 percent passbook account has a nominal interest rate of 6 percent. The *effective interest rate* is the rate you actually receive on your invested savings.

The amount of your effective interest rate depends upon how your interest is compounded. If your interest is compounded annually, your effective rate is equal to the nominal rate. If it is compounded in any term shorter than a year, your effective rate is higher than the stated rate. Obviously, the highest effective rate would be interest compounded daily, although the difference is not great. For example, a nominal 6 percent annual rate is actually worth 6.14 percent when compounded quarterly, and 6.18 percent when compounded daily. Therefore, if other factors such as stated rate, security, and convenience are about the same, you should deposit your savings with the institution offering the shortest compounding period and, therefore, the highest effective rate.

an example Assume that Gene wants to invest $10,000 in a time deposit. He should first consider the stated, or nominal, interest rate. For example, he might invest his $10,000 in a 6 percent 90-day account and pass up a chance for more interest income from an 8 percent investment certificate. (Both the savings account and the certificate are equally safe.) In the first year it would make a difference of $200 ($800 – $600). In succeeding years, this effect would be magnified by compounding, as Table 16-1 shows. Gene would get $3,681 more interest over 10 years by investing his money at 8 percent than at 6 percent. (As you proceed through this unit on investing, you might question whether Gene should invest his whole $10,000 for such a long time at only 8 percent.)

The second feature Gene should consider is how often interest is compounded. Suppose that he has his choice of two savings institutions: one offering 6 percent compounded annually and one offering 6 percent compounded quarterly. Table 16-2 shows what he would receive the first year both if the interest on his investment were compounded annually and if it were compounded quarterly. The extra $13.63 that he would receive with quarterly compounding represents the interest paid each

TABLE 16-1

Comparison of Interest Rates
($10,000 investment, compounded annually)

Years	6%	8%
1	$ 600	$ 800
2	1,236	1,664
3	1,910	2,597
4	2,625	3,605
5	3,382	4,693
10	7,908	11,589

TABLE 16-2

Comparison of Annual and Quarterly Compounding
($10,000 investment)

| Quarter | 6% Interest | |
	Annual Compounding	Quarterly Compounding
First	$150	$150.00
Second	150	152.25
Third	150	154.53
Fourth	150	156.85
Total	$600	$613.63

quarter on the interest received in previous quarters. Therefore, he would be better off choosing the institution offering quarterly compounding.

Computing Interest

Even though an institution may pay interest on sums held the full quarter, the actual interest paid can vary depending on the method of computation used: FIFO (first in, first out), LIFO (last in, first out), daily interest, or low balance.

Table 16-3 shows the quarterly interest (5 percent annual rate) paid using each of these methods except low balance. If you deposit $1,000 at the beginning of a quarter, another $1,000 halfway through, and withdraw $1,000 just before the end of the quarter, the FIFO method assumes that the $1,000 you withdrew is the first $1,000 you deposited. If interest is paid only on sums held the full quarter, you would receive no interest that quarter, even though you had at least $1,000 on deposit the whole time. The LIFO method assumes that the $1,000 you withdrew was the second (or last) money you deposited, and so you would receive full interest on the initial $1,000 deposited. The difference at a 5 percent rate would be $12.50 more interest than that computed by the FIFO method. In any given quarter, the LIFO method can mean a difference of 50 percent or more over the FIFO method, depending on your deposit and withdrawal patterns in that quarter.

Daily interest always yields the highest return and has no complications. Not only does daily interest yield a higher return, but also you do not have to leave your money in the account for the full quarter to get interest. You must keep your account open, however, to the end of the quarter, which usually means maintaining some minimum balance. Interest is paid from the day of deposit to the day of withdrawal.

The low balance method pays interest on the lowest balance in your account during the quarter, regardless of how much was deposited. To compare this method of computing interest with the others, you would have to know the pattern of deposits and withdrawals. This method can, however, yield about as low a return as the FIFO method does.

TABLE 16-3

Comparison of Three Methods of Computing Interest

Week	Transaction	Method of Computing Interest		
		FIFO	LIFO	Daily
1	Deposit	+ $1,000[a]	+ $1,000	+ $1,000
5	Deposit	+ 1,000	+ 1,000[a]	+ 1,000[a]
8	Withdrawal	− 1,000	− 1,000	− 1,000
13 balance		1,000	1,000	1,000
Interest paid[b]		$0.00	$12.50	$15.62

[a]Withdrawn in week 8.
[b]5 percent annual rate.

Ask at savings institutions in your area to find out what method each uses in calculating interest. Then you will be able to choose among those that compute interest daily. If none do, consider those that use the LIFO method.

APPROPRIATENESS OF TIME DEPOSITS AS AN INVESTMENT

Before you decide that time deposits are right for you, you should consider your reasons for using them and their advantages and disadvantages compared to other forms of investments.

Reasons for Using Time Deposits

There are four major reasons why people invest their money in time deposits: for use in emergencies, for special goals, as a safe investment, and as a temporary investment.

emergency fund   Having an emergency source of funds is one of the prime motives for investing in time deposits. The dollar amount of such an investment is guaranteed. If you have an emergency, the total amount you invested will be there since most time deposits are not subject to market fluctuations. In addition, you can readily withdraw the funds in an emergency. That is, they are liquid assets, as accessible as your cash or checking account.

special goals   The advantages inherent in accumulating funds for special goals provide another motive for the use of time deposits. These goals may include a house down payment, Christmas holiday expenses, vacation funds, a college education, or a new car. For example, if you can regularly save the money you will need to buy a new car instead of financing it, you can add $500 or $600 to your purchasing power. These extra dollars are made up of saved finance charges and interest income earned on your savings.

safe investment   A safe investment with reasonably assured income is the only reason many people need for saving money in time deposits. They may have no definite reason for the investment when they make it. However, you should have a reason for each financial decision you make, including how to save money. You should use a savings account for your investment program because it is the best alternative for a given financial goal, not simply because it is convenient or because you are most familiar with that method.

temporary investment   You may wish to use a savings account to accumulate funds for another investment. Or you may wish to put your stock market profits temporarily in a savings account where they will earn interest while the market goes through a period of declining prices. Or you may wish to use a savings account to receive interest automatically from a certificate account where the interest cannot be left to compound. Or you may have achieved one of your investment goals a year or two ahead of time and wish to preserve your gain by liquidating your investment and putting the proceeds in a savings account until you spend them.

Advantages of Time Deposits

Time deposits experience no price fluctuations such as those experienced by investments in the stock market or real estate. Your savings dollar is, in effect, guaranteed.

Furthermore, in banks and many savings institutions, federal government agencies insure each account (in a different name) for up to $100,000. The $100,000 limit applies to the total of all types of accounts under the same name held by any one commercial bank, savings and loan association, or federally chartered credit union. Similar accounts in the same name in separate branches of the same institution do not qualify for separate insurance limits. Nearly all commercial bank deposits are insured by the Federal Deposit Insurance Corporation (FDIC). Almost three-fourths of all savings and loan associations (holding 96 percent of savings and loan assets) are insured by the Federal Savings and Loan Insurance Corporation (FSLIC). The other savings and loan associations are covered either by similar state insurance plans (Massachusetts, Ohio, Maryland) or not at all. The value of U.S. savings bonds is also fully insured by the federal government.

Another advantage of time deposits is that investment income is generally assured. The interest on most types of savings accounts is legally guaranteed at the stated value. That is, your deposit with the bank represents a legal debt, upon which the bank must pay interest as promised. However, the extent of the bank's responsibility may be subject to two considerations. First, there may be a certain minimum balance (from $5 to $200) on which no interest is paid or a fee may be charged because the cost of opening a small account does not make it worthwhile for the bank. Second, if there is excessive withdrawal activity, the bank may impose an interest penalty or a flat fee per withdrawal to compensate for the extra bookkeeping. Check with your bank to find out their ground rules. On other savings investments, such as money market mutual funds, the payment of interest is still a contractual obligation, although the rate varies daily with the rates available in the money market and with the quality and maturity of the investments purchased by the fund.

There are no transaction costs such as brokerage fees or commissions involved in opening and closing a savings account. You may withdraw your funds immediately whenever they are needed, provided it is a business day. This feature makes savings investments appropriate for emergency funds. However, under certain circumstances the federal government can require 14-day notice for withdrawing funds from a federally insured bank or savings and loan. This provision is designed to provide a cooling off period in the event there is a run on the banks. A bank or savings institution would use the time to reduce the amount of new loans or mortgages being written so that inflowing loan or mortgage repayments could cover excessive deposit withdrawals. Instead of using this right, however, savings and loan associations usually turn to the Federal Home Loan Bank and banks turn to the Federal Reserve Bank to borrow funds (up to certain limits) whenever their withdrawals exceed their unloaned deposits. The right of notice before withdrawal of funds is also rarely exercised by mutual savings banks.

A final advantage of time deposits is that they offer convenient alternatives. You may deal face-to-face with your local institution; you may use a payroll deduction plan; or you may deal with them through the mail.

Disadvantages of Time Deposits

Although there are only two disadvantages, each can have a significant impact, depending on your situation. First, you are likely to get a lower rate of return with time deposits than with higher risk investments such as stocks, bonds, mutual funds, or real estate syndicates. Second, because time deposits are a fixed dollar value investment, they offer poor protection against inflation. A 6 percent passbook might give you an after-tax return of 3 to 5 percent.

Since 1945, according to the consumer price index, inflation has reduced the value of the dollar by an average of almost 5 percent a year. During the high inflation years of 1974, 1979, and 1980 (1981 was "only" 8.9 percent), prices advanced at more than 10 percent, resulting in a 5 to 7 percent or greater net loss in the purchasing power of savings, not counting the loss due to income taxes! There is little margin for a reasonable rate of return on a time deposit investment. An example of the resulting purchasing power of your savings is shown in Table 16-4.

ACCOUNTS AT YOUR LOCAL INSTITUTION

Most people place their savings with a nearby bank, savings and loan, mutual savings bank, or credit union. They offer many types of accounts, with varying maturities, interest rates, flexibilities, and sizes. They also now offer checking accounts that pay interest (called "NOW" accounts) with certain qualifying requirements (see Chapter 11). The security of your investment depends on the institution and the insurance available on your account.

The popularity of these institutions probably lies more in tradition, convenience, and ready understanding than in their strict investment merit. Depending on the prevailing level of interest rates in general, a money market mutual fund (discussed later in this chapter) may offer a better combination of yield and flexibility, though they do not offer federal agency insurance.

It does pay to shop around and compare the alternatives, at least once a year, in order to keep your fixed dollar money working for you as effectively as possible. This section will give you some background on what comparisons to look for.

TABLE 16-4
Savings Accounts after Taxes and Modest Inflation

Items in Computation	Percentage Amounts	Dollar Amounts
Amount invested	100%	$2,000
Annual yield	6	120
Income taxes[a]	−1.5	− 30
After-tax yield	4.5	90
Loss due to 4% average inflation	−4.0	− 80
Net gain in purchasing power of your savings	0.5%	$ 10

[a] Assume 30 percent income tax bracket.

The Differences between Banks, Savings and Loans, and Mutual Savings Banks

As Congress passes new legislation and new regulations are handed down by the Federal Reserve Board or Federal Home Loan Bank Board, the differences between the various types of institutions become ever more blurred.

Commercial banks (your local full-service banks) offer a complete line of lending, regulated in an effort to preserve their financial integrity and avoid the difficulties and closures that occurred in the depression of the 1930s. Accounts are insured up to $100,000 by the Federal Deposit Insurance Corporation.

Savings and loan associations are designed to stimulate the home building industry by accumulating savings and investing them primarily in residential real estate mortgages. There are two types of savings and loan organizations: mutual and corporate. The mutual is the more widespread form. The savings account holders are the owners of the organization and are known legally as share owners. In a mutual savings and loan company you usually have one vote (for members of the board of directors) for each $100 deposited. Corporate savings and loan companies issue stock just as other corporations do. They are located primarily in California, Ohio, and Texas. Many corporate savings and loan companies pay interest instead of dividends.

Dividends paid out of profits by savings and loan associations are not guaranteed. In any given quarter, a savings and loan association may reduce the dividend payment because of profitability problems (although this reduction occurs very rarely). At a bank, the depositor is a creditor and the interest is legally guaranteed, whether or not the bank makes a profit. If a savings and loan association pays interest instead of a dividend, the interest is guaranteed.

Your account's value is insured for up to $100,000 by the Federal Savings and Loan Insurance Corporation. Savings and loans are also federally regulated, but their relatively fixed asset structure (mostly long-term mortgages) results in a periodically less flexible, stable financial condition than is possible with a well-run commercial bank. In 1981, for example, over 200 smaller savings and loans (out of 4,213) went out of business generally by being merged into other savings and loans.

Mutual savings banks are located primarily in the eastern United States, but there are a few in the Northwest. Founded for the convenience and benefit of savers, they are organized as mutual associations with no capital stock. Dividends are paid out of earnings, but at an established rate, as banks and savings and loan associations do. The rate is somewhat higher than for banks since the dividends are not guaranteed. The principal and accumulated dividends, however, are generally insured by the federal government up to $100,000 for accounts in one name. There are limits on the total amount that may be invested in a mutual savings bank by one person. These vary according to state regulations.

Types of Accounts Offered

As of early 1982, these institutions were allowed to offer a certain list of types of accounts, defined by maturity, yield, minimum size, and interest penalty for early withdrawal. Table 16-5 lists the basic rate regulations in effect at that time. Because

TABLE 16-5

Maximum Interest Rates Allowed at Federally Insured Institutions

Type of Deposit	Commercial Banks	Savings & Loans and Mutual Savings Banks
Daily passbook savings and club accounts	5¼%	5½%
NOW accounts (checking)	5¼	5¼
Fixed-ceiling time account (partial list)		
90 days to 1 year	5¾	6
2½ to 4 years	6½	6¾
6 to 8 years	7½	7¾
IRA to Keogh plans	8	8
Special variable-rate accounts (rate fixed for term of deposit)		
6-month money market	Usually pegged at ¼-½% above current 6-month Treasury bill rate	
2½ years or more	Usually pegged at ¼-½% above the average 2½-year Treasury security yield	
Deposits over $100,000	No limit	No limit

Source: *Federal Reserve Bulletin,* April 1982, p. A9.

savings and loans and mutual savings banks cannot offer as complete a range of financial services, they are generally allowed to offer a ¼ percent higher yield than on similar accounts at commerical banks.

daily passbook savings accounts   These accounts may or may not have a savings passbook, since most institutions have their operations computerized. Your quarterly statement from the bank lists the latest interest credited and is all you need to prove how much money you have on deposit. The primary advantage of passbook accounts is that they offer the greatest flexibility in account size and deposit or withdrawal activity. Lately, however, in an effort to control costs, many banks have begun to charge fees for small accounts (under $100 or $200) or accounts with excessive withdrawal activity (more than three times per quarter). In addition to such penalties, there is the universal "penalty" of generally having to accept the lowest interest rate available among all the fixed dollar investment alternatives.

negotiable order of withdrawal (NOW) accounts   These accounts are now allowed by the federal government at any bank, mutual savings bank, or savings and loan that chooses to offer them. These are, in effect, interest-paying checking accounts. The interest rates are set at very low ceilings (see Table 16-5) and, should you fall below the bank's minimum or average balance requirements, you may incur a fee.

club accounts These are special types of accounts developed to draw or keep customers and to boost deposits, while enabling customers to budget their savings for a specific goal, such as Christmas gifts or a vacation. These accounts help you acquire a regular (monthly or semimonthly) savings habit. The bank may even furnish a coupon book to help you make your deposits on schedule. Sometimes, however, there is little or no interest paid on such accounts because of the extra bookkeeping and the small balances involved. Even if the bank offers its regular rate, you may not receive the interest unless you keep your money on deposit for the required period. Of course, once you have effectively set your budget in operation, you should not need such an account. If you do need the coupons of a club type of account to help you save, make your own coupon book for deposits to your regular passbook account rather than risk losing interest in a club account.

fixed-ceiling time accounts Also called certificate accounts, CDs, or time accounts, these accounts offer higher interest rates for those savers willing to tie up their money for a fixed period of time, ranging from 90 days to eight years, depending on the account chosen. The certificate or passbook you get when you open the account specifies the amount deposited, the interest rate to be paid to maturity, the maturity date (the date you can withdraw the funds), and the penalty you would incur for early withdrawal of the funds. Interest may be left to accumulate and compound in the account or may be paid quarterly, depending on the option chosen at the time you open the account.

Penalties typically range from three to six months' interest on the prematurely withdrawn sums. Incurring this penalty may be justified if you have an emergency or if you want to switch your funds to a higher yielding alternative. Compare the penalty with the extra return over the life of the new investment to see whether the switch is justified. Generally, you should not commit the funds for longer than you are likely to keep them invested.

special variable-rate accounts These accounts are becoming increasingly common as the money markets become more volatile. The interest rates offered vary each week or each month with the rates available on U.S. Treasury bills or notes (see Chapter 17), and are limited typically to ¼ or ½ percent above those rates. Once you make the investment, however, the initial rate is guaranteed, or fixed, for the life of the account (typically three or six months or two and one-half years).

large investment certificates These so-called jumbo certificates are for amounts in excess of $100,000 and are not federally regulated. The terms and rates are individually negotiated. In high-cost money times such as 1981, rates went over 15 percent on relatively short-term certificates.

Ownership and Insurance of Accounts

Among the various types of accounts you may open at any savings institution, the most common are an individual account, a joint tenancy account, a tenancy in common account, a trustee account, a minor's account, and a fiduciary account.

(Since each account bears a different name or set of names, each would qualify for separate $100,000 insurance limits.) An *individual account* has one owner. A *joint tenancy account* is one to which each owner has access. A *tenancy in common account* requires that both owners sign any withdrawal slip before it will be honored.

A *trustee account* may be owned by an adult for his or her child; the child cannot withdraw money without the adult's signature, but the adult, as owner, must pay taxes on the interest income. A *minor's account* may be opened with permission of the parent when the child is old enough to sign her or his name. Unlike a trustee account, the minor is the owner and must pay taxes, if any, on the interest. Another type of account that may be provided for children under your state's laws is a *"Uniform Gift to Minors Act" account* (custodian account), wherein an adult can retain control until the age of majority, but the account funds cannot be taken back into the custodian's name without also reassigning all past interest income from the minor's tax returns to the custodian's return.

A *fiduciary account* may be opened in the name of an estate by an executor or in the name of a minor child or incompetent person by his or her guardian.

Thrift Institutions

Thrift institutions are similar to small loan companies in that their primary purpose is to make small personal loans. Some of these institutions may be known as thrift and loan associations. Unless they specifically display the FSLIC or FDIC seals, which guarantee that deposits are insured, your savings dollars are probably not insured. The security of your investment is therefore dependent on the history, integrity, and business expertise of the owners and managers of these organizations. Because of this lower security (higher risk), such institutions may offer dividends or interest at higher rates than on insured deposits.

Credit Unions

The purpose of credit unions is to provide low-cost consumer loans to members, who are individuals with a common interest such as having the same place of employment. The credit union pools the savings of its members for lending purposes. Members elect the board of directors to operate the credit union on a one-person, one-vote basis.

You can invest in a credit union by purchasing shares, generally in $5 amounts. Most credit unions will immediately repurchase your shares at your request. Others may require a waiting period. Your maximum investment may be restricted to $5,000 or $10,000 if the credit union is small. By enforcing a ceiling on individual investments, they avoid potential large withdrawals.

advantages of credit unions   Employee-related credit unions often have payroll deduction plans for savings investment. Such a plan helps develop a thrift habit for people who could not save without this service.

Dividend rates range from those of regular bank accounts on up. The actual dividend rate paid depends on the earnings of the credit union, after provision for expenses and a bad-debt reserve.

In addition to payroll savings plans and a high dividend yield, most credit unions offer free term life insurance protection, matching $1 of insurance for each $1 deposited up to a maximum of $1,000 or $2,000. Thus, a $2,000 deposit could yield $4,000 to your beneficiary if you died. After age 55, a declining scale applies for such coverage. Most credit unions also offer free loan protection insurance, which pays off any outstanding debt to the credit union in the event of your death or disability.

As already mentioned in Chapters 11 and 12, credit unions offer low-cost consumer loans to members with collateral; up to $2,000 in unsecured loans may be taken out at a slightly higher rate; and financial counseling services may also be offered.

disadvantages of credit unions Since your credit union is managed by your associates, a portion of your financial affairs is not strictly private. Lack of safety may be another disadvantage. The security of your investment depends largely on whether the credit union has a federal or state charter. On January 1, 1971, federally chartered credit unions began to automatically offer federal deposit insurance; however, this automatic feature expired on January 3, 1974, for credit unions that failed to meet federal government financial qualifications. The federal deposit insurance is available for state-chartered credit unions, provided they apply for it and qualify. So far, only a few credit unions have done so, because of the costs of joining the program.

If you are depositing savings in a noninsured credit union, you are relying on its management ability to protect your funds. However, in some states, the rules of the charter and the periodic checks by state examiners have caused the record of noninsured credit unions to be quite good.

U.S. GOVERNMENT SAVINGS BONDS

The U.S. savings bond is the smallest of the three major methods of financing the federal government. The other two are tax receipts and Treasury bonds (Chapter 17).

Series E and Series H

Until January 1980 there were two types of savings bonds sold: Series E and Series H. Series E bonds were sold at three-fourths of face value to yield a 6 percent annual average rate if held to maturity (five years). Interest accumulated with the bond until you cashed it in for its face value. If you cashed it in before the maturity date, you got less than face value and your yield might be 5 percent or less because of graduated interest yields. Bonds ranged in size from $25 to $1,000 face amount.

Series H bonds were current income bonds. You bought the bond at its face value in $500 multiples: average interest of 6 percent was paid to you by check twice yearly until the bond matured in 10 years. As with Series E bonds, interest was less than 6 percent in the early years but later rose above that point to make the 10-year average yield 6 percent. The maximum annual purchase of Series H was $10,000 per person. Yields have periodically been increased on these bonds, so that investors continuing to hold them now receive 8 percent.

Series EE and Series HH

In January 1980, the Treasury replaced the Series E and H bonds with two new series, EE and HH, because administrative costs had risen over the years. The new bonds are expected to save the federal government $20 million a year. The new Series EE bonds have an issue price of 50 percent of the face value (rather than 75 percent on the Series E bonds) in minimum denominations of $50, and a maturity of 9 years. If you hold them beyond maturity, the bond will grow in value at the then correct rate of interest. The new Series EE bonds are redeemable after six months and have a maximum annual purchase limitation of $15,000 per individual.

The new Series HH bonds will pay a steady 7½ percent interest rate rather than a graduated scale beginning at some lower level. The new Series HH bonds, when purchased for cash—rather than in exchange for other bonds—will be subject to an interest penalty if redeemed before maturity. The maturity of Series HH bonds is 10 years. The minimum denomination for Series HH is $500, but the maximum annual purchase limitation was raised to $20,000. Holders of Series E and EE are allowed to exchange these bonds in multiples of $500 for Series HH bonds.

Advantages and Disadvantages of Investing in Savings Bonds

U.S. savings bonds are a safe investment because the principal is fully insured and the interest is fully guaranteed by the federal government. The bonds can be replaced easily if they are lost, stolen, or destroyed. They are also conveniently available through payroll savings plans at many companies or through banks.

There are certain tax advantages in that no local or state income taxes are charged on the interest; you can defer the federal income tax on Series E and EE bonds until you cash them in; and you can exchange your Series E or EE bonds for Series HH bonds on a tax-free basis and pay taxes only on the interest from the HH bonds, thus deferring your taxes even further. If you die before cashing them in, the interest will become taxable income to your heirs.

One of the disadvantages of investing in savings bonds is that you generally receive a somewhat lower rate of return than for some of the other time deposit investments. Also, the long maturity period results in some loss of flexibility in planning and managing your cash resources.

MONEY MARKET MUTUAL FUNDS

Perhaps the best combination of good interest returns and flexibility can be found in the relatively new concept of money market mutual funds. First begun in late 1971, there are now about 100 such funds, with nearly $200 billion in combined assets, a sum rivaling the deposits in bank savings accounts. Table 16-6 shows the growth of these funds since 1974.

Essentially, money market mutual funds are pools of money that are invested in such media as bank certificates of deposit and U.S. government securities. The funds are managed by private corporations that charge a fee of one-half of 1 percent a year for their services. The actual investments are held by a commercial bank in a custodial account. Investors simply mail in their deposit and receive a statement of

TABLE 16-6

Trends in Money Market Funds

Calendar Year End	Number of Reporting Funds	Number of Shareholder Accounts	Total Assets (billions)
1974	15	103,800	$ 1.7
1975	36	208,800	3.7
1976	48	180,700	3.7
1977	50	177,500	3.9
1978	61	467,800	10.9
1979	76	2,307,900	45.2
1980	96	4,745,600	74.4
1981		10,000,000[a]	182.0[a]

Source: Investment Company Institute, *1981 Mutual Fund Fact Book* (Washington, D.C.: Investment Company Institute, 1981), p. 11.
[a]*Donoghue's Money Fund Report,* January 1982.

their interest in the fund. (For a more complete description of the mechanics of a mutual fund, see Chapter 19.)

There is generally no commission charge for making such investments; the interest is paid to you after the fund's management has collected its fee. The minimum initial investment is generally restricted to amounts of $500 or more.

Distinguishing Features

Three features distinguish money market mutual funds from other time deposit alternatives: variable interest, a lack of federal deposit insurance, and the flexibility to write checks against your balance. The interest paid by such funds depends on the interest received on the fund's investments. Since the investments are generally short-term (maturing in less than one year), the interest rate is continually changing; it has ranged from under 5 percent to over 15 percent. Table 16-7 illustrates how these yields have varied in recent years. Because of this varying interest, actual interest is credited on a daily basis (daily compounding), although the fund may record it on your statement only once a month. The current yields on major money market funds are reported weekly in the *Wall Street Journal* and other major newspapers.

Although money market fund accounts are not covered by the FDIC's $100,000 insurance, the investments are generally considered quite secure. To the extent the fund holds U.S. government securities, there is no risk of loss. Bank certificates of deposit and corporate "commercial paper" investments are subject to the risk of bankruptcy by the issuing bank or corporations. However, most money market funds restrict their investments to issues of the largest and most financially strong institutions, and they diversify their holdings among 20 to 50 different banks and corporations. Since you can generally be assured that your deposits will be returned

Table 16-7

Typical Yield Range on Money Market Funds*

Year	Approximate Yield Range
1973	5¼-8¾%
1974	7-8¾
1975	5¼-7
1976	4½-5½
1977	4½-6¼
1978	6¼-9¼
1979	9-12
1980	7-15½
1981	11-16¼

Source: Council of Economic Advisors, *Economic Indicators* (Washington, D.C.: U.S. Government Printing Office, January 1982), p. 30.

*Estimated from yields offered by three-month U.S. Treasury bills, which reflect general interest rate conditions in the economy.

to you, plus interest, we do consider these funds as a comparable alternative to the more common forms of time deposit investments discussed earlier. If you are concerned about this issue, you might check the investment publications (often available in the library) that rank the funds according to their quality (lack of risk).

One of the most interesting features of money market funds is the ability to write checks against your fund investment. You may write a check one day, mail it the next, have the payee cash it several days later, and have it clear the money market fund's custodian bank perhaps two days after that. Meanwhile you have had your money earning interest on that amount for at least five days longer than if you had withdrawn your money from a conventional savings account to write the check. Typically, there is no charge for writing such checks, although there may be a fee for opening the checking account. (If you do not want the checking account feature, you can use the more normal forms of funds withdrawal by either mail or telephone.) Usually these checking accounts are useful only for large expenditures, because there may be minimum check limits of around $500.

Tax-Free Money Market Funds

In the past few years, a new breed of money market funds has been developed which invests in tax-free municipal bonds and notes (see Chapter 17). Interest rates are lower, but, typically, if you are in a 30 to 35 percent tax bracket or higher, your returns on these funds are higher than the after-tax yields on taxable money market funds.

Where to Find These Funds

Most major stock brokerage firms now offer a money market fund affiliated with their company. These give the active investor a convenient place to park the funds that are between investments. Further, a number of these give you a check register printout at the end of each month, a VISA card, and other services. There are also a great number of money market funds available to anyone with the $300 to $3,000 minimum capital available to open such an account. (Once it is open, you may draw the account down to some lower minimum level before the fund will close your account.)

To locate all such funds, you can look at newspaper ads or consult such references as *Donoghue's Money Fund Directory*, available at bookstores and libraries. This service, from P & S Publications, Inc. (Box 540, Holliston, MA 01746), lists all funds, showing their address, phone number, average annual yield, types of investments they hold, total assets, minimum balances required, checking account services, fees, and the like.

How Not to Do It

Betty was concerned about inflation rates skyrocketing and their effect on her emergency reserve. She figured that her 5¾ percent bank savings account was losing 1¾ percent to income taxes (she was in the 30 percent marginal tax bracket) and 8 percent to inflation (if inflation continued at 8 percent a year) for a net *decrease* in purchasing power of 4 percent. She went to her local bank branch to discuss this problem and was informed of various certificate accounts that paid 6½ to 8 percent if a minimum of $1,000 was kept on deposit for 2½ years or longer. These accounts didn't seem to help much and greatly hampered her flexibility, so she walked across the street to another bank. This savings account officer recognized her need and recommended the six-month variable rate certificate, which guaranteed 9¼ percent for the next six months' term. Even though this type of account at times might pay much lower rates, it also often paid very high rates when inflation was running at high rates. This fact, plus the six-month flexibility and federal insurance made this a much better alternative for her emergency funds, and this is what she did.

If Betty believes that inflation will continue to increase, she certainly should not "lock in" a yield for a long period of time. Instead she should keep her investments as liquid and as short-term as possible so that as inflation pushes interest rates up, she can put her money into higher-interest-bearing instruments. In a rising inflation scenario, probably the best alternative Betty should consider is a money market fund, yielding around 9 percent currently. Because money market funds invest in a market basket of high-yielding, short-term maturity instruments, this yield will rise and fall as interest rates change; but they should, over time, rise with inflation. Of course, if Betty believed that inflation was not going to get worse, she probably should select the guaranteed 8 percent for six years and lock up that rate while it is still available.

ANNUITIES

An annuity is an investment program that provides monthly income for life. When you buy an annuity, you make an investment; there is no insurance coverage attached unless you request some. A company pension is one form of annuity; Social Security is another. In both cases, during your working years you build up a lifetime retirement income through an investment program. You can supplement these incomes with other annuities, which are usually purchased from insurance companies.

Fixed or Variable

In selecting an annuity investment, you generally have two major alternatives: the fixed annuity and the variable annuity. Your *fixed annuity* choices are identical to the settlement options (lump sum, interest income, installment, and annuity—as discussed in Chapter 9) on your life insurance, except that you can buy a fixed annuity without having to buy insurance protection as well. The payment schedule for fixed annuities can be projected and paid at a fixed rate. Only if the company's return continues to increase from one year to the next will the payments grow.

A *variable annuity* offers the same payment options except interest income, and the payment amounts vary from year to year according to the company's investment management results and stock market price fluctuations. Variable annuity funds are invested in common stocks, whereas fixed annuity funds are invested in mortgages and bonds. Variable annuities will be covered in more detail in Chapter 18.

Maturity Date

The maturity date of an annuity is the date selected by the contract holder for monthly payments to begin. The *accumulation period* is the time before the maturity date, when the interest on fixed annuities accumulates either on the lump-sum payment or on the installments as they are being paid. If you die before the maturity date, the funds accumulated up to that time are paid to your designated beneficiary, just as they would be with any other investment.

The *distribution period* begins on the maturity date. At this time, whichever settlement option you have chosen goes into effect and cannot be changed. If you have chosen an annuity without refund and you die, the insurance company keeps the rest of the money. (Of course, you have been receiving the highest monthly benefit available.)

Also, on the maturity date and sometimes at other dates specified by the company, you have the option of withdrawing your investment in a lump sum rather than taking the monthly income payments from an installment or annuity option. You must carefully decide before the maturity date which settlement option you want for the rest of your life.

Endorsements Sometimes Offered on Annuities

Many companies offer a choice of two extra endorsements (at additional cost) on an annuity purchase. The first is the disability waiver of premium endorsement, which calls for the company to finish paying your premiums in the event that you become disabled. In effect, this is a convenient way to add to your disability coverage. Costs of this protection vary from company to company. The second is the addition of term life insurance. In effect, the latter converts your annuity into an endowment insurance policy: when considering it, you should ask yourself whether you need this type of coverage.

Advantages of Buying an Annuity

Some of the advantages of an annuity are similar to those for cash value life insurance: forced savings and tax deferral. People regard premium notices as bills, even though an insurance company cannot demand payment. If a premium is not paid, the contract lapses, leaving the holder with an annuity program worth only a portion of the cash value that would be present at maturity. To start such a program again, the investor would probably have to purchase a new annuity contract.

With annuities, you can build your investment on a tax-deferred basis during your working years. Taxes on fixed annuities are deferred until you begin taking out the principal and interest in monthly payments—probably in your retirement years when you will be in a lower tax bracket. Upon maturity, annuities are subject to ordinary income taxes on the same basis as other investments: total proceeds minus total costs equal taxable profits. However, the taxes are prorated over your expected lifetime for any of the lifetime annuity options or over the specified term for an installment annuity.

Some people, such as the employees of nonprofit health, educational, or welfare institutions, qualify for the tax-sheltered annuities under section 403.B of the Internal Revenue Code of the federal government. The distinguishing feature of a tax-sheltered annuity is that it can be purchased by having your employer reduce your pay by the amount of the investment (generally limited to a maximum of 16 percent of your pay), thereby avoiding the payment of income taxes on that money in the year it is received. However, when you receive any payments from the annuity program, the entire amount is taxable for federal income tax purposes. The advantage is that you are earning income on money that would otherwise have been lost to taxes before you could invest it.

Disadvantages of Annuities

Fixed annuities offer a lower yield than most other equally safe investments. (Of course, the other investments would not offer the guaranteed life payment provision, which can take away much of the need for financial worry during retirement years.) Also, fixed annuities offer no protection against inflation; the fixed monthly income will buy less and less each year during periods of inflation.

With a variable annuity, you cannot change investments from one insurance company to another without liquidating the annuity and paying ordinary income tax on any gains should your variable annuity investment managers do poorly.

Purchasing an Annuity

The only application requirement for purchasing an annuity is proof of age, such as a birth certificate. The older you are when monthly income payments begin, the higher will be your monthly income per premium dollar paid. No medical examination is required since annuities offer no death benefit. If you were to die before the maturity date, all your beneficiary would generally get would be a return of premiums paid to date.

Annuities are generally purchased from an insurance company under one of two plans. First, you may make a lump-sum investment, either with cash or with the settlement options of your life insurance policy. Annuities are available at the lowest possible cost through settlement options since they involve no sales commissions. Second, you may purchase an annuity with a series of installments (or premiums) much as you would purchase life insurance. Table 16-8 gives typical annual premium rates per $100 monthly income for life (with 10 years certain and continuous option) starting at age 65.

Since the value of a fixed annuity will not change after you buy it, you need not consider whether it is better to buy one with a lump-sum purchase at retirement or to begin much earlier by purchasing one with annual premiums. With variable annuities, however, the method of purchase is an important decision. You must consider both the flexibility you would have with a variable annuity and the short investment performance records of companies offering them. There may be better investment returns available elsewhere if you are willing to work for higher yields and accept the accompanying higher risks and thus prepare to buy a variable annuity later with a lump sum. Since many life insurance companies have only recently entered the field of variable annuities, it may be difficult to compare their records and select a superior program, but you should select a variable annuity program much as you would select a mutual fund (see Chapter 19).

In some states you can buy an annuity that is part variable, part fixed. During the accumulation period your funds are invested in stocks, but during the distribution period your monthly payments remain fixed. Be careful not to buy this type of annuity if you are really looking for a variable annuity.

TABLE 16-8

Annual Premium per $100 of Monthly Annuity Beginning at Age 65 for Men

Payments	Initial Age				
	30	35	40	45	50
Guaranteed @ 3½%					
Annual	$226	$293	$388	$534	$782
Semiannual	115	149	198	272	399
Quarterly	59	76	101	139	203
Guaranteed @ 12%					
Annual	18	33	59	110	213
Semiannual	9	17	30	56	109
Quarterly	5	9	15	29	55

CONCLUSION

If you are looking for security and an assured return on your savings, time deposits may be a proper investment for you. You should keep in mind, however, that they offer little protection against inflation unless you invest in a variable rate certificate and are in a low tax bracket. Even then, there is little real profit after you subtract the effect of inflation on your purchasing power. Before you decide to use time deposits as your major investment, examine the other opportunities outlined in the remainder of this unit.

If you do decide to put some of your money (especially your emergency money or your accumulations for short-term goals) in time deposits, be sure you select time deposits that offer the most appropriate liquidity, flexibility and maturity, the greatest degree of security or insurance, a short compounding period, LIFO or daily interest (not FIFO or low balance), and the highest possible interest rate consistent with the foregoing considerations and your objectives. Buying an annuity may only be advantageous because it encourages a regular savings habit and defers income taxes.

Once you have satisfied these considerations, you can be confident that you are getting the most out of your time deposit investments.

VOCABULARY

annuity	LIFO
accumulation period	low balance
certificate of deposit	money market fund
daily interest	nominal interest rate
distribution period	passbook savings account
effective interest rate	tax-free money fund
FDIC	thrift institution
FIFO	time deposit
fixed annuity	U.S. savings bond
FSLIC	variable annuity

QUESTIONS

1. What are the four major reasons for having a savings account as part of your savings and investment program? Give examples of each.
2. What are the principal differences between a savings account program offered by a bank and one offered by a savings and loan? Which, if any, are of significance to you as an investor?
3. If all local savings institutions offered the same stated rate of interest, but different methods of computing and compounding interest, what would be the optimum situation for your savings?
4. Assuming both paid the same stated yield, U.S. savings bonds would be preferable to passbook accounts under what circumstances?
5. What combination of features distinguish money market mutual funds from other time deposit alternatives?

6. Under what circumstances may a credit union be the most advantageous place for a savings account? What are the key factors you should consider before opening an account with one?

7. Assume that you have a $10,000 savings account that earned 6.2 percent last year. Inflation was at the rate of 3.4 percent as measured by the consumer price index. Your tax bracket is 32 percent, combined state and federal. What was your net gain in real purchasing power for the year?

8. Henry is 52 years old and is in a 40 percent tax bracket. Which of the following low-risk investments would assure him of the greatest lump sum at age 65 if he invested the same amount in each: a 6 percent savings account, U.S. savings bonds bought through payroll deductions, or a 13-year fixed annuity accumulation?

9. What is the significance of the maturity date with any type of annuity program?

10. What is probably the biggest disadvantage of fixed annuity investment programs?

CASE PROBLEMS

1. Allison is a sophomore at State University. The bank where she has her checking account offers free accounts to students who maintain a minimum $100 monthly balance. Her account rarely goes below $300 and she uses it mostly to make payments on her car. The bank also offers 5 percent passbook savings accounts, computed on a LIFO basis, and 5.5 percent bonus accounts on funds held the full 90-day quarter. The savings and loan association nearby offers 5.5 percent passbook accounts, with interest from the date of deposit to the date of withdrawal, and 6.75 percent on one-year certificates of deposit.

   Allison's parents pay for her expenses during the summer when she lives with them as well as her tuition and room and board at the university. (Her mom sends her $1,000 check for her tuition and room and board about three weeks early each quarter to make sure she receives it in time.) Allison is responsible for all other expenses. To cover these, she earns $400 (take-home pay) a month for two and one-half months' work during the summer and $120 (take-home pay) a month on a part-time job at school. Her summer savings usually are exhausted by the following June.

   In what ways, if any, could Allison make use of a savings account? Does she need an emergency fund? Why or why not? If Allison were to put money aside in a time deposit, should she use an account at the bank, an account at the savings and loan, or U.S. savings bonds? What, approximately, is the maximum amount of dollars that Allison could earn each year in interest (before taxes) if she took advantage of several opportunities peculiar to her situation?

2. Paul's checking account has a $300 minimum balance requirement, which he regularly violates, and it costs him an average of $2 a month in check charges. However, if his balance stayed above $300 continuously, there would be no charges. Should he leave his $1,000 emergency fund entirely in his 6 percent (compounded annually) savings account, or keep $700 in savings and put $300 in his checking account? If he is in a 30 percent tax bracket, what is the dollar difference between the two alternatives for the next year?

RECOMMENDED READING

1982 Credit Union National Association Yearbook. CUNA, P.O. Box 431, Madison, WI 53701.

   An annual update of credit union statistics, regulations, and services.

1982 Savings and Loan Fact Book. United States Savings and Loan League, 221 North La Salle Street, Chicago, IL 60601.

Goodman, Jordan E. "Pumping Up Earnings in Your Checking Account." *Money*, January 1982, pp. 105–11.

> A new link between some money market funds and banks lets your cash flow to the best yields, with only a $2,500 minimum balance.

CHUCK AND NANCY ANDERSON

Selecting Their Savings Investments

Chuck and Nancy have $2,200 set aside in an emergency fund, and they need to put $533 a year in a savings investment that earns at least 5.5 percent in order to save for the car they plan to buy four years from now. They are trying to decide on the best type of savings investment for each of these, and so they gathered information on the minimum balance, maturity, stated annual rate, compounding interval, and safety of the following savings investments: passbook and bonus accounts at a bank, passbook and bonus accounts and certificates of deposit at a savings and loan, an account with the credit union where Nancy works (they also offer payroll deduction plans), and U.S. Series EE savings bonds. This information is presented in Table 16-9.

Questions

1. Which of these savings investments would be best for the Andersons' emergency fund? Under what circumstances would one alternative be better than another?
2. Which of these savings investments would be best for the new car savings fund? Why? Under what circumstances would the credit union be the best alternative?

TABLE 16-9

Comparison of Several Time Deposits

Type of Investment	Minimum Balance	Maturity	Stated Annual Rate	Compounding Interval	U.S. Government Insured
Bank					
Passbook	$ 100	90 days	5.0 %	Quarterly	Yes
Bonus	2,000	1 year	5.5	Quarterly	Yes
Savings and Loan					
Passbook	1	1 day	5.5	Daily	Yes
Bonus	2,000	1 year	5.75	Daily	Yes
Certificate	5,000	2 years	6.5	Daily	Yes
Credit Union	10	90 days	6.0	Quarterly	No
Series EE U.S. savings bonds	25	5 years	6.0	Annually	Yes

17

Stocks and Bonds

"September. This is one of the peculiarly dangerous months to speculate in stocks. Others are October, November, December, January, February, March, April, May, June, July, and August." Sam Clemens was one of America's unluckiest investors, and his attitude is typical of many people today who either are afraid to invest in the stock market or have done so once or twice and lost money.

The key word in the quotation is *speculate*. Speculation is an extreme form of risk taking—investing in the face of total uncertainty. Those who buy stock on "hot tips" or on chance discoveries by fly-by-night companies are more likely to agree with Sam Clemens than are those who take a businesslike approach to investing in the stock market.

You might imagine that only the professional invests in the stock market. This is not true. Of the nearly 30 million Americans who owned stock in 1980, 43 percent had annual household incomes of less than $25,000, 49 percent were under 45 years old, and 57 percent had stock portfolios worth less than $5,000. There are still millions of new, small investors getting into the stock market.[*]

If you had bought a broadly diversified portfolio of common stock in 1926, you would have realized a 9 percent average annual compound rate of return up to 1960.[†] This period includes the crash of 1929 and the depression years of the 1930s and excludes the boom years of the 1960s. During much of the 1960s the market would have yielded an average rate of return close to 15 percent.

Granted, in the 1970s, common stocks offered returns below that available in savings accounts. However, a longer term view of the stock market indicates that it has always gone through extraordinarily good periods (the 1960s)

---

[*] *New York Stock Exchange Share Ownership 1980* (New York: New York Stock Exchange, 1981), pp. 3, 7.

[†] Lawrence Fisher and James H. Lorie, "Rates of Return of Investments in Common Stock," *Journal of Business* (July 1968).

and extraordinarily poor periods (the 1970s). On balance, these periods average out to an 8 to 9 percent return (depending on the academic study one reads), while interest on savings accounts averaged 4 to 5 percent.

Some stocks go up and down with the market; others are doomed to prolonged downtrends; still others continue to grow year after year. Bonds are a different sort of investment. For the long-term investor, this investment can seem more like a savings account. For the trader, short-term price fluctuations in bonds can be just as unpredictable as stocks. The yield on bonds is generally only two or three percentage points, at most, above savings accounts. This is less than the long-run potential of common stocks, but bonds do offer less risk than stocks.

Chapters 17 and 18 should enable you to distinguish among the various types of stocks and bonds and gain some insight into why their prices move as they do. In addition, these chapters will help you understand the basic concepts involved in stock market investments, thereby enabling you to avoid making bad investments because of ignorance. Much of what separates success from failure in the stock market is knowledge and cool-headedness. You, too, can invest successfully in the stock market, if you equip yourself with the proper tools.

OPPORTUNITIES IN THE SECURITIES MARKETS: A GENERAL CLASSIFICATION

There are several types of securities: common stock, preferred stock, bonds, convertible bonds, and convertible preferred stock. These types may be compared according to their potential for capital gain or loss, the income they provide, their right to corporate income, the voting rights an owner may be entitled to, and the order of their claims on corporate assets if a company is liquidated. Table 17-1 shows how these types of securities compare on the basis of these characteristics. You may want to refer to this figure as we treat each type of security in more detail.

COMMON STOCK

Common stock represents an ownership interest in a corporation. If you own 10 percent of a corporation's stock, you own 10 percent of the corporation. As owner, you are called a shareholder or stockholder. All corporations have at least one shareholder, and many corporations have thousands of shareholders. A corporation must have stockholders with a monetary interest in it before a bank will loan it money or it can sell bonds to the public.

From a Stockholder's Point of View

For the stockholder, a publicly traded common stock provides an opportunity to own part of a profit-making enterprise that may or may not yield current income through dividend payments. It also offers a chance for capital gains income through price appreciation of the stock.

TABLE 17-1

Comparison of Types of Securities

Security	Right to Corporate Income	Voting Rights	Current Income	Capital Gain/Loss Potential	Priority of Claim to Assets (if company is liquidated)[a]
Common stock	Yes	Yes	Dividends although not guaranteed	Yes	3
Preferred stock	Only to limit of fixed dividend	Generally none	Dividends usually paid if company is profitable	Same as for bonds	2
Bonds	None	None	Interest assured as long as company remains financially sound	Only if interest rates change or company's credit rating changes	1
Convertible bonds	(Same as for bonds until converted to common stock by investor. Security is lower since convertible bonds are generally subordinated to other bonds in their priority of claim to assets.)				
Convertible preferred stock	(Same as for preferred stock until converted to common stock by investor)				

[a]The higher the rank (e.g., 1), the lower the degree of risk of a total loss.

corporate income   All profits, after bond interest and preferred stock dividends, are used to benefit the holders of common stock in one way or another. Any dividends paid out of such profits must go to them. Profits not paid out in dividends are normally reinvested in the company to foster its growth. Owners of common stock benefit in both cases because they get either the dividend income or, because of reinvestment, the prospect of greater income and security from a larger business. Common stocks with strong prospects of future earnings are usually of greater value to investors than stocks with poor prospects. The right to corporate income, current and/or future, is the only sound financial reason that investors should have for buying common stock.

It is interesting to put corporate profits into the perspective of the economy as a whole. As you can see in Table 17-2, corporate profits represented a declining share of national income throughout the 1950s and 1960s; this was also the case for small businesses (proprietors). The 1970s saw corporate profits hold at about 10 percent of the national income. As a consequence, there was generally less incentive for investors to put their money to work in corporations. In addition, Congress increased capital gains taxes from 1969 through 1978. Both the declining profit shares and the increased tax burden are probably reflected in the fact that the stock market showed no real growth in prices between the mid-1960s and 1981. What implications this has for future growth in jobs and in profits for investors remains to be seen, but the outlook is not clearly optimistic. On the other hand, perhaps this is merely a cyclical phenomenon that will sometime revert to the growth years of the 1940s and 1950s. Perhaps the 1978 and 1981 reductions in maximum income and capital gains tax rates will be enough to generate new capital investment and growing profits and, eventually, turn the market around.

control of the company   Stockholders may vote to elect the board of directors. The number of votes each stockholder has is proportionate to the number of shares he or she owns. The board of directors, in turn, both makes the major policy decisions and selects the principal operating officers of the company. The stockholders elect the board of directors at the company's annual meeting. A stockholder who cannot attend the meeting may vote by using the proxy that is supplied with the announcement of the meeting's place, date, and time. In reality, the average shareholder has relatively insignificant voting strength compared to that of officers or founders who hold large blocks of the company's stock.

claim to corporate assets   If the company is liquidated, holders of common stock will receive only whatever remains after all debt obligations and preferred stock claims have been met.

From the Company's Point of View

For the company issuing a publicly traded common stock, the proceeds from the sale of stock provide funds for working capital, growth, acquisitions, or debt payments. The stock price also provides an established valuation of the company for borrowing purposes, mergers, and the like.

TABLE 17-2

The Changing Share of National Income

| Year | Total National Income (billions) | Percentage Share of National Income | | | | | | | Consumer Price Index |
		Compensation of Employees	Corporate Profits	Proprietors (Small Businesses) Farm	Proprietors (Small Businesses) Non-Farm	Rental Income of Persons	Net Interest Income	
1950	$ 241	64.1%	15.6%		15.5%	3.9%	0.8%	71.6
1955	331	67.8	14.2		12.6	4.2	1.2	80.2
1960	414	71.0	12.0		11.2	3.8	2.0	88.7
1965	566	70.0	13.6	2.2%	7.8%	3.0	3.3	94.5
1970	798	76.3	8.3	1.7	6.4	2.3	4.7	116.3
1975	1,239	75.1	8.9	2.1	5.2	1.8	6.8	161.2
76	1,379	75.1	10.0	1.4	5.1	1.7	6.3	170.5
77	1,546	74.5	10.6	1.3	5.2	1.7	6.5	181.5
78	1,745	74.5	10.6	1.5	5.2	1.6	6.6	195.4
79	1,963	74.4	10.0	1.6	5.1	1.6	7.3	217.4
1980	2,121	75.2	8.6	1.1	5.0	1.5	8.5	246.8
81	2,344	75.6	8.1	0.9	4.8	1.4	9.2	272.4
10-year dollar increase	+169%	+172%	+127%	+47%	+107%	+66%	+362%	+124%
31-year dollar increase	+873%	+1051%	+403%	n.a.	n.a.	+257%	+10,316%	+280%

Source: *Economic Indicators,* Council of Economic Advisors, U.S. Government Printing Office, various editions.

An Example: ABZ Corporation

To show you how and why stocks are issued, how dividends and retained earnings are used by a company, and how stock is traded between investors, we will use the example of a fictitious company. The ABZ Corporation was founded for the purpose of manufacturing small pleasure boats. Since the company needed $1 million to set up a plant and begin producing and marketing boats, it issued 100,000 shares of stock at $10 each.

Several years later, the company became profitable and earned $100,000 after taxes. For each $10 share of stock owned in the company a stockholder had the right to $1 of the earnings ($100,000 ÷ 100,000 shares). Future earnings were projected to reach $3 or $4 a share in 5 to 10 years. Because the company was still rapidly growing, however, it needed to retain its earnings in order to finance the expansion of its production facilities and its sales force. Therefore, the board of directors declared no dividends. The stockholders had to forgo their possible $1 a share in exchange for the prospect of greater earnings in the future.

Soon the company was making more money, had brighter eanings prospects, and was basically financially sound. It gained the attention of other investors. Many of them wanted to buy stock in the company, but ABZ Corporation had no need to raise funds by issuing more stock at this time. Hence, others could buy stock only from the original investors, some of whom agreed to sell their shares for $15 more than they had paid because they wanted compensation for the loss of future dividends. They chose to take their income as a capital gain of $15 a share.

Over the next few years, the stock continued to be sold from one person to another at prices ranging from $18 to $46 a share, depending on the current price mutually agreed upon by buyers and sellers. The price was based on the company's earnings, its prospects, and the effect of those prospects on the attitudes of both buyers and sellers. Eventually the company was making $500,000 a year after taxes and did not need all of its earnings for expansion purposes. As a result, the board of directors declared a dividend of $200,000 for that year ($2 for each of the 100,000 shares). The directors decided to pay the dividend in cash payments of 50% per share each quarter.

Several years later, ABZ Corporation decided to expand its operations into the manufacture of travel trailers, water skis, and, eventually, snow skis. However, in order to do this, it needed considerably more financing than could be obtained by retaining earnings or borrowing money. Therefore, it decided to issue more stock. This time the company sold 100,000 more shares at $50 each and raised $5,000,000. The company could get more than $10 a share on this second stock offering because it had become an established enterprise. Many of the people who purchased this new stock were already stockholders in the company; others were buying ABZ stock for the first time. After that sale there were 200,000 shares of ABZ stock outstanding.

The company became more and more successful. Annual sales were up to $24 million. The price of the stock went up to around $80 a share. However, it was difficult to buy or sell the stock efficiently because there was no central place where buyers and sellers could meet to trade it. Instead, a broker searched by phone to match buyers and sellers. In addition, the price varied substantially from person to person.

In order to eliminate this problem, the ABZ Corporation worked to meet the requirements for membership on the American Stock Exchange (Chapter 18) and finally got its stock listed on that exchange. From then on, its price was regularly established at a central location according to the supply and demand generated by the sellers and buyers of ABZ stock. Anyone could buy stock in the ABZ Corporation and hope that it would continue to grow, earn more money each year, and eventually pay higher dividends. Even if the company never again needs to issue new stock, it should continue to be possible to buy ABZ stock from owners willing to sell their shares, provided the price is right.

The Concept of Total Return

When investing in common stocks, some investors look only at the dividend yield. Others ignore dividends and try to estimate how much the price of the stock will go up. Such investors fail to consider the total return on the proposed investment: *both the dividend yield and the potential capital gains.*

The dividend yield on a common stock is expressed as a percentage computed by dividing the dollar amount of the annual dividend by the current market price. For example, if ABZ stock is paying a $2 annual dividend per share and the stock is selling for $100 per share, the current dividend yield is 2 percent. An investment in ABZ stock will yield 2 percent a year based on the current dividend alone.

Table 17-3 shows that yields fluctuate from year to year. However, these fluctuations are due less to changes in dividend payments than to more rapid changes in stock prices.

The capital gain potential of a common stock is entirely different from its dividend yield and depends on many factors. Suppose that you purchased 10 shares of ABZ stock for a total cost of $1,040 including commissions (($100 × 10 shares) + $40 commission). One year later you sold the stock for $119 a share, and the commission was $50. Your total proceeds from the sale were $1,140 (($119 × 10) − $50). Your net capital gain was $100 ($1,140 − $1,040), or $10 a share. Therefore, on your original purchase price of $100 a share you made a $10 profit, or a 10 percent capital gain yield. Your total return on the ABZ stock investment would be 12 percent (2% dividend yield + 10% capital gain yield). If you had realized a 10 percent capital loss on the sale of the stock, your total return would have been a minus 8 percent (2% − 10%).

To obtain a compounding effect on your total return, you must reinvest the dividends, though not necessarily in the same stock. However, many corporations do allow you to have your cash dividends automatically reinvested in additional full and fractional shares of their stock.

Some Terms You Should Understand

earnings per share (EPS) This is the mathematical result of dividing the total after-tax earnings of the company by its total number of shares outstanding (in the hands of investors). For example, if after several more years the ABZ Corporation earns $3,400,000 after taxes, and there are 1,000,000 shares of its stock outstanding,

TABLE 17-3

Dividend Data on All Dividend-Paying Common Stocks
Listed on the New York Stock Exchange (1929-1977)

Year	Median Dividend Yield	Total Cash Payments (billions)	Year	Median Dividend Yield	Total Cash Payments (billions)
1929	n.a.	$ 2.71	1966	4.1%	$16.15
1930	n.a.	2.67	1967	3.2	16.87
1935	n.a.	1.34	1968	2.6	18.12
1940	6.1%	2.10	1969	3.6	19.40
1945	3.6	2.28	1970	3.7	19.78
1950	6.7	5.40	1971	3.2	20.26
1955	4.6	7.49	1972	3.0	21.49
1960	4.2	9.87	1973	5.0	23.63
1961	3.3	10.43	1974	7.4	25.66
1962	3.8	11.20	1975	5.0	26.90
1963	3.6	12.10	1976	4.0	30.61
1964	3.3	13.55	1977	4.5	36.27
1965	3.2	15.30			

Source: *New York Stock Exchange 1978 Fact Book*, p. 76.

the earnings per share for that year are $3.40 ($3,400,000 ÷ 1,000,000). This figure is usually computed by the company when it issues its earnings reports.

P/E ratio (P/E multiple)   This is the ratio of the price of a stock to its earnings per share. For example, if the ABZ stock that offers $3.40 in annual earnings per share sells for $34 a share, it has a P/E ratio of 10 ($34 ÷ $3.40). The normal P/E range for the stocks in the Dow Jones averages (Table 17-4) is from about 10 to 18. However, high growth stocks such as Apple Computer may have a P/E ratio as high as 40 to 60 or more, since investors expect the earnings per share to continue to grow at substantial rates in future years. For example, a stock selling for $100 might have current earnings of $2 a share for a P/E multiple of 50. However, in a few years the company might be earning $5 a share and that price of $100 would then be only 20 times earnings. (The phrase "20 times earnings" means the same as "a P/E ratio of 20.")

The P/E ratio is one of the key figures that an investor examines in determining the worth of a potential investment. A decline in price does not necessarily mean that a stock is a good buy. The earnings might have declined even more. It is the ratio of price to earnings in combination with the outlook for future earnings that investors should analyze. For example, the price may drop from $30 to $20, but if the earnings have dropped from $3 a share to $1, the P/E ratio will actually have risen from 10 to 20! If the expectation is for earnings to recover, a P/E of 20 may be acceptable; if not, the stock may be overpriced.

par value   In the past this term was used to signify the level below which a company would not offer its shares to the public. However, it was often misunderstood to be a continued minimum price level guaranteed by the company. The figure is of no significance to the investor, and most new stock is simply issued on a no par (zero par value) or a low par (usually $2) basis.

cash dividends   These are simply a distribution of the company's earnings to its stockholders, in cash. The board of directors usually declares dividends on a quarterly basis (the quarters may end in months other than March, June, September, and December). Also, if it has had an especially good year, a company may occasionally declare special or bonus dividends in addition to the regular dividend. Or it may

TABLE 17-4

Dow Jones Industrial Averages

Year	Price Index at Year End	Approximate P/E Ratio at Year End	Approximate Annual Cash Dividend Yield	Year	Price Index at Year End	Approximate P/E Ratio at Year End	Approximate Annual Cash Dividend Yield
1929	$248	12.5	4.9%	1960	$ 616	19.1	3.3%
32	60	d	7.7	61	731	22.9	2.9
37	121	10.5	7.3	62	652	17.9	3.4
38	155	25.8	3.1	63	763	18.5	3.0
39	150	16.5	4.0	64	874	18.8	2.9
1940	131	12.0	5.4	1965	969	18.1	2.9
41	111	9.5	6.8	66	786	13.6	3.8
42	119	12.9	5.4	67	905	16.8	3.3
43	136	14.0	4.6	68	941	16.3	3.3
44	152	15.1	4.3	69	800	14.0	4.2
1945	193	18.3	3.5	1970	839	16.1	3.7
46	177	13.0	4.2	71	889	16.9	3.5
47	181	9.6	5.1	72	1,020	15.2	3.2
48	177	7.7	5.9	73	851	9.9	4.2
49	200	8.5	5.9	74	616	6.2	6.1
1950	235	7.7	6.6	1975	852	11.3	4.4
51	269	10.1	5.7	76	1,005	10.4	4.1
52	292	11.8	5.2	77	831	9.3	5.5
53	281	10.3	5.4	78	805	7.7	6.0
54	404	14.4	4.2	79	839	6.8	6.0
1955	488	13.7	3.8	1980	964	8.7	5.6
56	499	15.0	4.0	81	875	7.1	6.3
57	436	12.1	4.7				
58	584	20.9	3.3				
59	679	19.8	2.9				

d = deficit earnings for the year

simply raise the level of the regular dividend, if the board of directors expects the higher level of earnings to continue. The term *dividend yield* refers to cash dividend divided by current price.

stock dividends   These represent the issue of new stock certificates, not cash, on a basis proportional to the number of shares each investor owns. For example, if the board of directors declares a 10 percent stock dividend, each stockholder will receive one free share of stock for every 10 shares he holds at the time. An investor who owns an odd number of shares will usually have the option of paying the extra amount for a whole share or receiving cash for a partial dividend share.

Many investors think that stock dividends represent an increase in the value of their holdings. In reality, even though there may be a temporary rise in the price of the stock because of a stock dividend, there is no permanent benefit from such a distribution because the price of all shares normally goes down by the amount of that dividend within a few days. For example, assume that you own 10 shares of ABZ stock selling for $100 a share before a stock dividend and that the earnings per share are $5. After a 10 percent stock dividend you would own 11 shares. Table 17-5 shows that both before and after the stock dividend you hold $1,000 worth of ABZ stock. There is no gain for you. In essence, the same pie has merely been divided into more pieces.

It may seem that if the cash dividend rate is kept the same, you will receive an extra share's worth of dividends. For example, if the old stock paid a $2 annual dividend per share, you would have received $20 in dividends a year. If the dividend rate per share remains unchanged after the stock dividend, you will receive $22 a year on your 11 shares. But do not construe this as an effect of the stock dividend. In effect, the directors simply raised the cash dividend payout by 10 percent to each stockholder. The directors might just as well have raised the cash dividend on the old stock to $2.20 and not offered the 10 percent stock dividend.

TABLE 17-5

Comparison of Value of Stocks Before and After Stock Dividend

Items in Computation	Before 10% Stock Dividend	After 10% Stock Dividend
Number of shares outstanding	1,000,000	1,100,000
ABZ Corp. after-tax profits	$5,000,000	$5,000,000
Earnings per share	$5	$4.55[a]
Normal average P/E ratio	20	20
P/E ratio times earnings per share	$100	$91[a]
Value of 10 shares	$1,000 (10 X $100)	$1,000[a] (11 X $91)

[a]Figures not exact because of rounding.

stock splits   For the investor, these seem the same as stock dividends, except on a bigger scale, and this bigger scale can make a difference. (There are technical differences between stock splits and stock dividends, but the discussion of these is more appropriate to a corporate finance text.) A 100 percent stock dividend, in which the investor receives one new share for each share held, is equivalent to a two-for-one stock split. In either case, the investor has twice as many shares as before the declaration. On such a split, the company will also usually split the cash dividend. For example, on a two-for-one split a dividend of 50¢ per share would become 25¢ per share.

Stock splits often have real value to the investor. The split may broaden the market by making more shares available and may also bring the price down enough so that it falls into what is generally considered the popular trading range—$30 to $60 a share. These changes can arouse greater investor interest in the stock and permanently improve the P/E ratio for that stock.

book value   This is the dollar value of a company's assets minus its liabilities. It is comparable to a person's net worth on his or her balance sheet. This valuation for a company is generally of significance only if its assets are to be sold and its debts paid off—in other words, if the company is to be liquidated.

The *book value per share* is the book value of the company divided by the number of shares outstanding. To the investor, the book value per share is seldom a relevant consideration. A company may have a high book value; but if it is making very little profit, it would have little value as an investment, unless it is likely to earn more in the future. Occasionally other companies want to purchase those assets by making a public offer to buy the stock at an attractive price. In such cases, a high book value company would be of interest to the investor who wished to speculate on such a possibility.

Investor's Classification of Common Stocks

Although it is difficult to classify every stock, certain groups of stocks have characteristics that are useful to keep in mind when you are reviewing a particular stock for a proposed investment. We will use five categories: growth stocks, second-tier growth stocks, mature growth stocks, cyclical stocks, and special situations. As you read this section, refer to Table 17-6 for some typical examples of each category.

Sometimes you will hear stocks classified by other terms such as "blue chip," "defensive," "income," or "speculative." Some of these terms may be synonyms for those discussed here; others will overlap more than one category. Generally, you must learn how the user is defining a term; then you can better understand the stock in question and reclassify it into one of the five categories used here.

growth stocks   These are the stocks of corporations that are leaders in their industry and that have experienced several consecutive years of above-average growth in earnings (10 percent a year or better) and are expected to continue to do so in the future. Because of their growth history, such companies usually have annual sales volumes ranging up from $1 billion. These stocks usually sell at high P/E

TABLE 17-6

Sample Stocks for Each Investor Category
(Based on market judgments in 1982)

Stock	Approximate P/E Ratio[a]	Dividend Yield[b]	Annual Sales (billions)	5-Year EPS Growth[c]
Growth Stocks				
Procter & Gamble	10.3	5.0%	$11.4	+12%
Eastman Kodak	8.8	5.0	10.6	+10
McDonald's	9.0	1.7	2.5	+22
Merck	16.0	3.3	2.9	+12
IBM	10.9	5.5	28.3	+12
Second-Tier Growth				
Betz Laboratories	16.8	2.4	0.3	+22
Crum & Forster	4.8	5.5	1.6	+31[e]
Wetterau, Inc.	10.9	7.7	1.9	+ 9
Church's Fried Chicken	7.7	3.1	0.4	+36
National Semiconductor	8.3	0.0	1.1	+20
Mature Growth				
Dart & Kraft	8.3	7.3	10.2	+11[e]
American Telephone	6.5	9.5	57.2	+10[e]
Wells Fargo	4.7	7.6	3.1	+16[e]
Sears Roebuck	7.7	8.4	27.5	+ 6
Pacific Power & Light	6.4	12.9	1.3	+ 2
Cyclical Stocks				
Boise Cascade	7.3	6.7	3.2	+14[g]
General Motors	35.0[d]	6.8	63.0	g, f
National Gypsum	5.4	7.4	0.9	+20[g]
U.S. Steel	1.9	8.5	14.1	g, f
Dow Chemical	7.1	8.6	11.9	+ 8[g]
Special Situations				
A.M.F. Corporation	7.0	6.4	1.3	+ 4
Greyhound	4.8	8.1	4.8	+ 6
SCM Corp.	3.6	9.5	1.9	+12
Dataproducts	15.8	1.6	0.3	+15
CULBRO	10.6	2.7	0.4	f

[a] Based on February 17, 1982, prices and 1981 actual or estimated earnings per share.

[b] Based on February 17, 1982, prices and current dividend amount.

[c] Compound annual rate.

[d] Much lower than normal because of poor industry auto sales worldwide.

[e] Reflects an abnormally good five-year period for this company.

[f] Reflects an abnormally poor five-year period for this company.

[g] EPS growth varies considerably depending on whether the company is coming down from an earnings peak or rising from a trough.

multiples because investors are looking forward to higher expected earnings in the future, generally over the next three to five years. Because these corporations are growing rapidly, their stocks offer a relatively low dividend. The companies usually pay out less than 25 percent of their earnings in dividends; the rest is retained for growth.

second-tier growth stocks   Many corporations with excellent growth records find their stock priced lower (on a P/E basis) than the "top-tier" growth stocks described above. This lower ranking is usually due to lack of general investor awareness about, and acceptance of, the company. Perhaps it does business in only one region of the country, or is not one of the largest in its industry, or is still too small to be considered one of the major American businesses, regardless of its industry. Such companies sometimes have a higher dividend yield than growth companies, not because they pay out a higher proportion of their earnings in dividends, but because the stock has a lower P/E ratio.

mature growth stocks   These are the stocks of large companies that have demonstrated consistent earnings. These companies usually have long-term growth potential and are fairly stable because of their above-average size (generally several billion dollars or more in annual sales). However, smaller companies may fall into this category because their earnings growth is regulated, as is that of electric utilities. Although mature growth companies may demonstrate fairly consistent earnings growth, this growth usually averages less than 8 percent a year.

Because these companies generally pay out about half of their earnings in dividends, and offer less exciting growth potential than the first two categories of stocks, mature growth stocks tend to sell at lower P/E ratios and to have above-average dividend yields. These characteristics make such stocks relatively attractive to conservative investors who are looking for a good level of current income. They are also known as "defensive stocks."

cyclical stocks   These follow the ups and downs of cycles such as the general business cycle, in which the up phases are called *expansions* and the down phases *recessions*. Companies whose earnings follow these cycles are commonly found in industry groups such as automobiles, steel, copper, paper, textiles, and heavy machinery. When the economy appears to be entering a recession, cyclical stocks tend to fall somewhat in price, and vice versa. Many investors invest in such stocks whenever they expect an upward movement in a cycle to occur. Since the stock price cycles, however, run in advance of the actual profit cycles, smart investors should look ahead at least 12 months to make a profit on trading cyclical stocks. In fact, such stocks tend to sell at high P/Es when the earnings are down, and at low P/Es when the earnings are up, because investors tend to anticipate the next turn in the company's fortunes.

special situations   In this group fall all the companies whose stocks don't fit any of the other categories. A special situation may arise out of one or more of several factors: the company is too young; it is too small; it is having unusual business problems; its recent earnings have deviated greatly from its historic pattern; or the stock is highly speculative. The latter may occur, for example, when an oil company that has been losing money suddenly strikes a new oil field. Investors would bid up the price of such a stock in speculation about the size of the field and the effect its discovery might have on the company's future earnings.

Factors Determining the Price of a Stock

The major determinant of the price of a common stock is the law of supply and
demand. If there are more investors who wish to buy ABZ stock than there are
stockholders who wish to sell it, the supply and demand for ABZ stock is out of
balance. If such an imbalance occurs when the price of ABZ is $20 a share, for
example, the price may have to rise to $25 before enough of those who hold the stock
can be induced to sell it. As the price goes higher, the number of people who wish to
buy the stock decreases, and so, at some level, there is a temporary balance in the
supply of and the demand for a stock. Of course, this point varies from day to day as
the company's prospects for growth and profitability change and investors respond
to these changes, and as the mood of investors varies.

How do investors decide when $20 is a good buy or when $25 is too expensive?
The fundamental reason for investing in common stock should be to obtain the right
to corporate earnings. Therefore, many investors view the price of a stock in relation
to its earnings per share, and the law of supply and demand often tends to revolve
around a stock's P/E ratio and what investors think of that ratio. If they feel it is low,
they will buy and drive it up, and vice versa. Most investors think in terms not only
of current earnings per share, but also of the forecasted level of future earnings
(hence the high P/E ratio on growth stocks). If a company has no current earnings,
there is no current P/E ratio and the price of the stock is based on some expected
future earnings.

A wide array of factors affect the P/E ratio. They are often divided into two
classes: fundamental and technical. Fundamental factors basically affect the company and its earnings. Technical factors affect only the actual trading of the stock.

fundamental factors   Investors who analyze fundamental factors generally first
ask the question: "What is the current situation of the company, and what is the
outlook for its sales and earnings per share (EPS)?" If the answer is "above-average
growth in earnings," they will tend to project rising earnings per share and stock
prices into future years and be willing to pay higher current P/E ratios to buy such
stocks (Fig. 17-1a). If the company is growing more slowly but has very stable

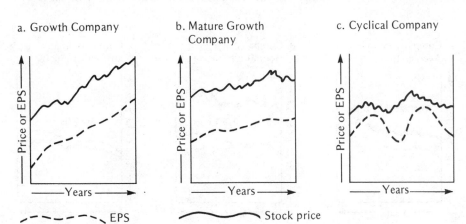

a. Growth Company

b. Mature Growth
   Company

c. Cyclical Company

FIGURE 17-1
How type of company
affects stock prices.

earnings year after year, they may be willing to pay a modest P/E ratio simply for the stability of such stocks (Fig. 17-1b). If the stock is cyclical, the P/E ratio is often based on average earnings over the long run. Hence, the prices of cyclical stocks tend to anticipate profit trends by six months or more and to vary less than do the earnings (Fig. 17-1c).

Another factor that must be considered is the general business prospects for the industry in which the company is involved. The charts in Figure 17-2 illustrate three different possible situations for companies with similar earnings characteristics. The brighter the outlook for the industry, the more investors will be willing to pay in terms of P/E ratio. In fact, this effect often carries over to the stocks of companies that have not yet themselves been able to cash in on a current industry boom. For example, during the 1970s the stock of companies involved in computers, semiconductors, or genetic engineering often sold for high P/E ratios, even though the company had yet to prove its management expertise or its ability to make a good profit. Conversely, if the industry outlook is gloomy, even a well-managed company's stock may be dragged down in price by a general negative reaction to the industry as a whole on the part of investors. For example, in the mid-1970s, congressional activities to regulate and raise taxes on the oil companies tended to reduce the P/E ratios on all such stocks.

An especially significant factor that concerns mature growth companies is the dividend yield. For example, although a company growing at 7 percent a year in earnings per share may not seem to be a particularly attractive investment, that growth rate becomes a potential 15 percent total return over the long run when a current 8 percent dividend yield is added to the average capital gains potential. Thus, if the general level of interest rates in the economy tends to rise, these stocks tend to decline in price to bring the dividend yield in line. Conversely, as interest rates fall (as they did in 1975), such stocks tend to rise in price, as investors shift money out of other investments into high yielding stocks, thereby driving the price back up (and the yield back down, more in line with other interest rates).

technical factors An analysis of technical factors takes into account prevailing market forces as evidenced by volume of shares traded, number of stocks that rose in

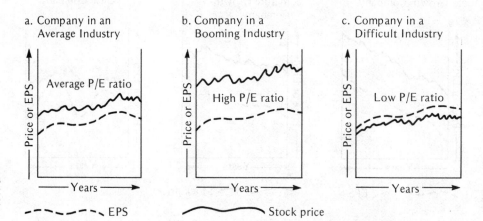

a. Company in an Average Industry

b. Company in a Booming Industry

c. Company in a Difficult Industry

FIGURE 17-2
How business prospects for an industry affect stock prices within that industry.

price compared to those that declined, ratio of short sales to other sales, and many other statistics. Such technical items really belong in the realm of the professional market analyst or the expert stock trader. Their analysis involves too much time and expertise for the average investor. However, a brief discussion of the philosophy behind such analysis should help you both to understand the behavior of the stock market and to time the purchase and sale of your investments.

Investor psychology often plays an important role in temporarily overpricing or underpricing a stock. For example, when ABZ Corporation decided to enter the travel trailer business, it attracted many more investors than before. As people began to buy in and the stock began rising, people became more and more enthusiastic about buying the stock. Temporarily, this enthusiasm drove the price and the P/E ratio well above any foreseeable trend in earnings per share. As enthusiasm reached a fever pitch, the more sophisticated and cool-headed investors began to take their profits; the resultant selling eventually outweighed the buying and the price began to retreat to a more reasonable level. Just the opposite effect often occurs near the bottom of a long price decline. Figure 17-3 illustrates how psychological overreactions typically result in unreasonably wide price swings for a stock. Smart investors try to take advantage of such peaks and valleys by timing their purchases and sales accordingly.

The general market trend also affects the price of a stock. When sell orders exceed buy orders for the market as a whole, prices drop. If investor disenchantment or lack of enthusiasm continues, we have a declining market—a bear market. In such a psychological environment, only a few stocks can sustain uptrends in price, but some stocks will drop less than others. The same kinds of overall price trends can be found in up markets (bull markets) as well. A more complete discussion of bull and bear markets is to be found in the next chapter.

How Appropriate Is a Common Stock for You?

There are several advantages and disadvantages in investing in common stocks. If you first acquire the knowledge and skills discussed in both this chapter and the following one, you should know exactly what benefits you might expect, as well as

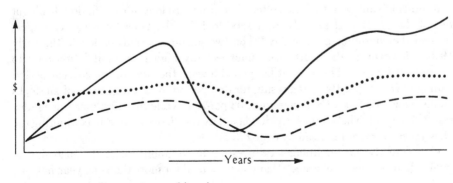

```
··············· Average reasonable price
─────────────── Actual price
─ ─ ─ ─ ─ ─ ─ Earnings per share
```

FIGURE 17-3
How investor reactions
affect stock prices.

TABLE 17-7

Comparisons of Historic Returns
(Total return at annual compound rates)

Period	Common Stocks	Long-Term Corporate Bonds	90-Day U.S. Treasury Bills[a]
1926-78	+ 8.9%[b]	+ 4.0%[b]	+ 2.5%[b]
1974	−28.2%[c]	+ 3.1%[b]	8.0%
1975	+39.8[c]	+14.6[b]	5.8
1976	+23.2[c]	+18.6[b]	5.0
1977	− 7.8[c]	+ 1.7[b]	5.3
1978	+ 5.9[c]	+ 0.1[b]	7.2
1979	+18.4[c]		10.0
1980	+30.8[c]		11.5
1981	− 5.0[c]		14.1
1974-81 (compound annual return)	+ 7.8%[c]		+ 8.7%

[a] This return is approximately what a money market mutual fund or a variable rate savings account would have returned in these periods.

[b] Roger G. Ibbotson, and Rex A. Sinquefield, "Stocks, Bonds, Bills and Inflation: Updates," *Financial Analysts Journal*, July-August 1979.

[c] Equal to change in S&P 500 stock index plus dividends.

what problems you might encounter, before you decide whether to invest in the stock market at all or how much to invest.

advantages   Common stocks offer a high potential total return on your investment. Over time, you should expect an average annual rate of return in excess of those available from bonds or fixed dollar investments, if past trends continue. (See Table 17-7.) The 1974–81 period was unusually poor for stocks relative to fixed dollar investments. Common stocks also offer the chance for unusually big gains. For example, if you had bought K-Mart or McDonald's stock in 1963, by 1975 you could have increased your investment 25 times.

Another advantage is that they offer a hedge against long-term inflation. In all but two of the 51 25-year periods from 1900 to 1976, the Dow Jones stocks outperformed the consumer price index.° The two laggard periods ended in the early 1950s. However, in the short term, unexpectedly high rates of inflation tend to depress stock prices. This is what happened toward the close of the 25-year period ending in December 1981; as a result, for that period the average price of all stocks on the New York Stock Exchange rose 203 percent, while the consumer price index rose 234 percent. The average dividend paid by the 30 stocks used in computing the Dow Jones averages has risen by over 175 percent.

There are also tax advantages to investing in common stocks. If you realize a capital gain on the sale of a stock that you have held for more than one year, only 40

° "In Spite of What You've Heard, Stocks Have Been a Perfect Long-Term Inflation Hedge," *Journal of Portfolio Management* (Winter 1977), p. 73.

percent of the gain is included in your gross income. Also, the first $100 ($200 on a joint return if the stock is jointly owned) of dividends can be received tax-free. Further, since 1981, taxes payable on dividends of up to $750 per year from public utility companies may be deferred if you reinvest the dividend income in additional shares of that company or another qualified public utility. One of the important reasons why Congress has put such tax advantages into law is to induce people to invest in corporations, thereby providing the capital needed for a fast growing economy for both wage earner and investor.

disadvantages In exchange for the higher potential return offered by common stocks, you must accept a greater degree of risk, particularly market volatility risk. In exchange for the chance for really big gains, there is also the chance for really big losses. The stock market often goes through significant periods of general price declines, as, for example, when the outlook for the economy changed in early 1969 and 1970, again in 1973 and 1974, and again in 1981 and 1982. Stock prices generally fell in amounts ranging from 25 to 60 percent, depending on the type of stock. Sometimes individual stocks have disastrous results, regardless of the overall stock market pattern. If, for example, you had bought stock in Brunswick Corporation at its high of $74 in 1961 and held it, you would have held a stock worth as little as $6 a share in 1966. It has since risen well above that low point, though it is nowhere near $74. For other examples, Memorex Corporation stock dropped 70 percent during a period of a few months in 1970, and Intel declined over 50 percent in 1981, in line with other semiconductor stocks.

In addition to the market volatility risk are the important inflation and interest rate risks. During periods of unexpectedly high rates of inflation such as we had in 1973 and 1974 and again in 1979 through 1981, interest rates on money market funds, Treasury bills, bonds, and mortgages tend to go higher to help offset the loss in purchasing power due to inflation. As the general level of interest rates increases, common stock dividends (including future expected dividend increases) become relatively less attractive to investors, who can achieve high yields without taking the extra risk of common stock investments. As a consequence, common stock prices decline to the point where P/E ratios and dividend yields do become competitive with other investments. Thus, while stocks do offer a good hedge against stable, long-term inflation, unexpectedly high levels of inflation can have a disastrous effect on stock prices.

Common stocks offer a lower current income than might be obtained with other investments. Although some slower growing stocks offer a dividend yield of up to 10 percent or more, the average stock with growth potential has a dividend yield ranging from 0 to 5 percent. Therefore, the common stock investor often sacrifices current dividend income for the prospect of longer term capital gains income.

Common stock investments require the constant attention of active investors. (You may elect just to buy quality stocks, put them away, and hold them for the long term.) Active investors must keep abreast of general business news, as well as specific news about companies whose stock they own or plan to own. They must watch over their portfolios either to avoid big losses through price erosion or to take their gains after a stock has appreciated. Of course, if your account is big enough, you can get your broker or an investment adviser to take care of much of it and make decisions

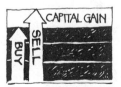

for you. However, hiring a professional does not necessarily ensure any better results than those you might obtain on your own.

Stock market investing requires a certain amount of experience and expertise before you can expect that, more often than not, your investments will be successful. However, this does not mean that you must begin investing before you really know how. You can do considerable research and simulated investing on paper before you actually begin to invest. Even then, there is much that you cannot learn about your reaction to market conditions until you have actually been investing for several years. Perhaps the most important technique for avoiding serious losses is the diversified portfolio management approach discussed in the next chapter.

What Is the Right Price?

Stock market investing involves personal judgment. Whenever you buy or sell a stock, there is always someone on the other side of the transaction who feels differently about that stock! Always be sure, however, that you are investing in stocks for the right to corporate income and for no other reason. For example, consider a company whose earnings per share are growing at the rapid rate of 20 percent a year. If the current EPS is 50%, it is difficult to justify paying $100 for this growth stock since, at that rate, the projected EPS for three years from now is only 85%. You would still be paying over 100 times future earnings for this high growth stock!

If you follow the precept of getting value for your investment, you will minimize your chances of behaving like many investors whose enthusiasm causes them to buy when stocks are high and whose depression causes them to sell when stocks are low. This is no way to make money in the stock market. One rational approach to getting value for your investment in the stock market is to determine the right price for a given stock. To do this, compute the average P/E ratio for that stock (or for its industry group) over the past 5 or 10 years. This method results in an average right price for the stock over a period of time—provided that there has been no change in the fundamental character of the company during that time.

You should also determine the typical high and low ends of the P/E ratio range over the past decade so that you can plan to buy the stock at below-average prices (within, say, 25 percent of the low end of the P/E ratio range) and sell the stock at above-average prices—provided that the long-term fundamental outlook for the corporation's profits remains good. Such buying and selling opportunities occur for most stocks every two to five years. Two to five years can seem like an eternity when you're living with the market each day, but patience is usually rewarded.

Many other methods of securities management have been successfully applied. Further guidelines on investing in the stock market will be discussed in the next chapter.

PREFERRED STOCK

Like common stock, preferred stock represents an ownership interest in a corporation, but to a different degree. Holders of preferred stock do not generally participate in the profit growth of a company but do receive a high fixed dividend yield.

Fixed Dividend Payment

This dividend must be paid before dividends can be paid on common stock. Preferred stock dividends may be paid only if there are earnings or profits, but interest on bonds must be paid in any case.

The fixed dividend means that the value of your investment depends on current interest rates. If general interest rates are rising, the price of preferred stock will fall in order to keep the dividend yield in line with other interest rates available to investors. Conversely, if interest rates are falling, the price of preferred stock will go up. For example, if you hold a preferred stock that was issued at $100 and pays an $8 dividend and comparable interest rates fall to 6 percent, the price of the stock may go up to $133. However, the price may not go that high because the preferred stock may have a call feature whereby the company reserves the right to buy back outstanding preferred stock at its original issue price plus a premium of, say, 5 percent. A company will want to do this in the hope of issuing a new preferred stock with a lower dividend rate or selling bonds at a lower rate of interest.

Some companies issue two classes of preferred stock: *first preferred* and *second preferred*. Dividends are paid on the former before they are paid on the latter. In exchange for this preference, the dividend rate on first preferred may be somewhat lower than on second preferred.

A preferred stock may or may not have a *cumulative dividend* provision, which assures the stockholder that all dividends will be paid. A company that offers this provision and has no profits for a few years will keep track of the missed dividends and try to pay them off as soon as it regains profitability. However, some companies get so far behind in their dividends that they must negotiate a smaller settlement with their preferred stockholders.

If a preferred stock has a participating provision, or *bonus dividend,* the holders may receive a percentage of corporate earnings over a certain amount. This changes the stock into a hybrid of preferred and common stock.

Prior Claim to Corporate Assets

If a company goes bankrupt or is liquidated, the preferred stockholders must receive the full value of their shares before money can be paid to the holders of common stock. Of course, all corporate debts, including bonds, must be paid off before even the holders of preferred stock get any money.

No Voting Rights

Preferred stocks generally offer no voting rights, except in specific situations. For example, a preferred stock may allow its holders to vote if the dividend goes unpaid for a certain number of years.

A Questionable Investment

In summary, preferred stocks have much of the business and market risks associated with common stocks, yet offer none of the growth potential through participation in corporate profits. They also have the interest rate risk associated with bonds that causes prices to fluctuate, yet do not offer the security that bondholders have in the form of a known redemption value at maturity. (See the bond discussion following.) Preferred stocks simply have the risks of both types of investments, without offering the benefits of either.

BONDS (LONG-TERM DEBT)

Bonds may be issued by corporations or by federal, state, or local governments to raise capital for various investment purposes.

Corporate Bonds

Bonds are an important source of long-term debt financing for corporations since banks generally do not like to loan money for longer than a few years. Corporate bonds usually have maturities ranging from 20 to 30 years, although some are as short as five years. They offer a fixed dollar amount of interest and pay back the principal on the maturity date. They are usually issued in face amounts of $1,000 each, but bond prices are quoted in terms of percentage of face value. A quote of 87, for example, means that the bond is selling for $870.

types of corporate bonds The *mortgage bond* and the *collateral trust bond* are generally the most secure types because they have specific real estate assets (such as buildings) or other specified assets pledged as collateral. A *debenture* (ordinary bond) is a promissory note. In this most common form of bond, the corporation simply promises to pay off its debt and, if it does not, the debenture holder has a right to all assets not pledged to mortgage or collateral trust bonds. A *subordinated debenture* is also a promissory note, but it has relatively low security (unless the corporation is financially strong) since holders of such bonds can claim assets only after other creditors and bonds and bank debts have been paid off. Generally, the security of a bond is indicated by its financial rating according to either Standard and Poor's or Moody's (Table 17-8). The lower the degree of security, the higher the bond's interest yield.

fixed interest payment By law, interest must be paid on corporate bonds whether or not a profit is made. Some of the older bonds are coupon bonds, which require the bond holder to clip off a coupon and send it to the company in order to collect the interest. Registered bonds pay you interest without your having to send in coupons. There is potential for capital gains on bonds if general interest rates decline, if the company's financial rating improves, or if you purchase a high quality bond that sells for less than face value, but is within a few years of maturity.

factors affecting bond prices The prices of corporate bonds change from day to day just as stock prices do. *As general interest rates in the economy rise, the market prices of bonds decline, and vice versa.* This is because the dollar payout is fixed for the life of the bond. For example, if a 30-year maturity, $1,000 corporate bond is

TABLE 17-8

Bond Ratings

Meaning of Rating	Moody's	Standard and Poor's	
Investment quality	Aaa	AAA	
	Aa	AA	
	A	A	
	Baa	BBB	
		BB	
Speculative	Ba	B	
	B	CCC	
	Caa	CC	
	Ca	C	
Already in default	C	DDD	(Depends on prospects
		DD	for cash return on
		D	liquidation)

purchased for $1,000 and bears a stated interest rate of 8 percent, the company will pay the holder $80 in interest every year. If general money market interest rates rise to 12 percent for comparable debt issues, the market price of the bond will drop to about $667 ($80 ÷ 12% = $667). However, if you hold the bond to maturity, you will collect the original $1,000 you invested, and in the meantime you will receive $80 a year. (Preferred stocks do not have this certainty of future redemption value, since they have no redemption date but may remain outstanding indefinitely.) Conversely, if interest rates fall, the price of the bond will rise, and you may wish to sell it through the bond market and take your profit in capital gains, rather than take the $80 a year. In these ways, investing in long-term bonds can be something like investing in the stock market.

Several factors affect bond prices relative to other bonds. The investment quality (or credit rating of the company) is very important. Standard and Poor's and Moody's publish bond ratings (Table 17-8) based on the chances that companies will not be able to repay amounts borrowed on bonds (risk of default). The higher the rating, the greater the safety. The lower the investment quality, of course, the higher must be the yield on the bond to justify the assumption of greater risk by investors. An investor may have to wait 20 years to redeem a bond at maturity and, by then, a weak company may have gone out of business. The closer the bond is to its maturity date, the smaller will be the difference between the market price and the face (redemption) value of the bond. (Face value is also called *par value*, a term that should not be confused with the par value of stocks.)

There may be a *call feature*, which allows the company to repurchase the bond at a set price (usually slightly above par) after a specific date (usually 5 or 10 years after issue). Because investors, via the call feature, may find their bonds called in before maturity, there is often a slightly higher yield, the closer the call date is to the present. In fact, the very presence of a call price can keep the market price from going above that point even if interest rates drop, since there is the possibility that the company may call the bond for redemption at that price.

determining the effective yield on bonds   Although you can ask your broker to compute a bond yield for you (using rate computation charts), it is useful to understand the procedure yourself. If a bond is selling at par, or maturity value (usually $1,000), the effective yield is simply the annual interest yield. For example, on a bond selling for $1,000 (quoted at 100) and paying $120 interest a year, the effective yield to maturity is 12 percent.

Bonds selling at a discount from par value require a three-step procedure for computing their yield. Let us take a hypothetical example of an ABZ bond selling for $900 (quoted at 90), paying $45 annual interest, and maturing in four years. (At maturity, the company will redeem the bond for the full $1,000.)

1. Compute the effective current interest yield by dividing the annual interest by the current price.

$$\frac{\$45}{\$900} = 5\% \text{ effective interest yield}$$

2. Compute the effective capital gains yield by dividing the maturity value by the current price to get a factor that will be used in conjunction with compound interest Table A.

$$\frac{\$1,000}{\$900} = 1.11$$

Since the $900 is a lump-sum investment, compound interest Table A can be used to find the percentage equivalent of the factor 1.11 for four years. This percentage equivalent, or the effective capital gains yield, is approximately 2.75 percent.

3. Add the results of steps 1 and 2. The total effective rate of return for this ABZ bond is 7.75 percent. This yield is slightly better than a 7.75 percent savings account after tax since 60 percent of the $100 capital gain is tax-free. Of course, the risk is slightly higher; but bonds rated A, Aa, or Aaa have never gone bankrupt while holding those ratings. Thus, to be certain of avoiding a default, you should switch out of any bond whose rating is downgraded to BBB or Baa or lower.

advantages and disadvantages of corporate bonds   For the investor who has a financial goal to achieve within three or four years or who is conservative but wants higher yields than those offered by savings accounts, and wants to lock in higher interest rates than might be available later should interest rates on money market funds decline, corporate bonds are a good answer. There are five major advantages investors seek when buying corporate bonds: diversification of a common stock and/ or real estate portfolio (spreading of risk); guaranteed return of principal if held to maturity; assured income through fixed interest payments; security, especially if the bond is issued by a substantial company; and a hedge against a possible serious recession or depression. When interest rates fall, quality bonds appreciate in price, thereby helping to offset losses incurred in stocks or real estate. Bonds also offer a low cost of purchase (the standard broker's fee is $5 per $1,000 bond).

There are two disadvantages to keep in mind before you decide to invest in bonds. First, small changes in interest rates can produce large fluctuations in the value of your principal, especially on bonds with maturities 10 to 20 years away. Second, bonds are not a hedge against inflation, since inflation causes all costs to rise, including interest rates (at least temporarily), thus forcing bond prices down. Besides, the face value of bonds cannot grow with inflation.

U.S. Government Securities

The United States government finances most of the federal budget deficits, as well as its working capital needs, through the issue of Treasury bills (T-Bills), notes, and bonds. (These are different from U.S. savings bonds.) Notes and bonds are similar to corporate bonds, and pay semiannual interest via coupons. On Treasury bills interest is paid by issuing them at a discount from their redemption value; no actual interest payments are made. As with Series E savings bonds, this discount produces an interest yield when the bond is held to maturity, at which time the government redeems it at face value. New issues of bills are sold weekly to the highest bidder, while notes and bonds are offered irregularly. They are bought by individuals and investment houses, who may or may not resell them on the open market to other investors. Table 17-9 shows the basic differences in maturities and minimum face amounts for the three types of securities.

The market price of these securities varies, of course, with general market conditions, just as the market price on corporate bonds does. (The listings are in a separate section of the newspaper financial pages.) The closer the securities are to maturity, the closer the market price is to its redemption value. The primary advantage of federal securities is their safety and ready salability. As a result, they also offer the lowest current yields available on bond-type investments.

Municipal Bonds

State and municipal governments and special districts such as school or irrigation districts issue bonds to help finance their operations. These may be bought at a discount and accrue interest, or they may be bought at face value and pay interest.

TABLE 17-9
Basic Features of U.S. Government Securities

Type of Government Security	Maturity	Minimum Face Amount
Treasury bills	3 to 6 months	$10,000 (sometimes $1,000)
Treasury notes	1 to 5 years	$1,000
Treasury bonds	More than 5 years	$1,000

The primary advantage of municipal bonds is that the interest is exempt from federal income taxes. They may also be exempt from state income taxes in the state in which they are issued. They are generally more appropriate than corporate bonds for investors in the 35 percent tax bracket and up. For example, to a married couple reporting $35,200 to $45,800 taxable income (33 percent tax bracket), an 8 percent municipal is as desirable as a corporate bond offering a 12 percent interest yield. Although municipal bond interest is tax-free, capital gains on the sale of a bond are taxable.

Invest only in *general obligation bonds* that are rated A or better by Moody's or Standard and Poor's. Such bonds are backed by the full faith, credit, and unlimited taxing power of a financially sound municipality, county, or state. *Revenue bonds* have limited taxing ability (e.g., tolls from toll roads) and usually do not offer the safety of general obligation bonds.

We recommend state bonds over city bonds. In the depression of the 30s, only one state (Arkansas) defaulted on its bonds, while over 4,500 local governments failed to meet their obligations. Most of these defaults did not involve major cities. Of course, this does not mean that major cities are immune to financial problems. In 1975, New York City was, at the last minute, saved from bankruptcy only by means of federally guaranteed loans. If you are a resident of a state that has income taxes, you may want to buy only bonds issued by your state or one of its governmental subdivisions to avoid paying state income taxes on the bonds. This tax must be paid on out-of-state bonds.

Since marketability of some bonds is a problem and therefore reduces liquidity, we recommend buying only well-known, actively traded issues.

Guidelines for Investing in Bonds

Investors in high tax brackets who are seeking tax advantages should consider municipal bonds, since their interest is tax-free. Investors in more moderate tax brackets who want maximum marketability should consider U.S. government bonds or major corporate bonds.

You should always buy corporate bonds issued by stable companies rather than assume a greater risk on your investment just to obtain a slightly higher interest payment. Bank trust departments usually stick to bonds rated Baa (Moody's), BBB (Standard and Poor's), or better to assure quality. To be really safe, you should restrict your selection to those rated AA or better. Of course, the higher the rating, the lower the total return.

If you want to avoid extreme price fluctuations in your corporate bond investments, restrict yourself to bonds with a maturity of five years or less. Such investments are much like time deposits, but with a slightly higher after-tax yield. If you get longer term bonds, try to buy bonds that were issued some time ago when interest rates were lower, and yet have 10 to 20 years remaining to maturity. Thus, you will be able to buy the bonds at a discount from face value. By avoiding the purchase of bonds at or near face value, you will also avoid the risk that interest rates might fall and the bonds be called back (redeemed) by the issuer, thereby preventing you from realizing a capital gain. With discount bonds, when interest rates fall, the price simply rises closer to the face value earlier than it would have under the normal progression to the maturity date.

You should shop around for brokerage houses offering the lowest commissions on bond transactions. Some houses charge significantly higher fees than others for buying and selling bonds.

CONVERTIBLE BONDS AND CONVERTIBLE PREFERRED STOCKS

Convertible securities allow the investor to convert his or her holdings into a fixed number of shares of common stock. Such investments offer the investor some of the security of a preferred stock or a bond and some of the capital gains potential of common stock. However, in exchange for these features, there is usually a lower dividend or interest rate.

Nearly all convertibles have a call feature, which gives the company the right to redeem the securities on or after a stated date in exchange for a stated amount in cash, usually a few points above the issued price. The company would want to exercise this feature and force conversion to reduce the amount of money it has to pay in interest. The possibility of a call increases as the price of the common stock rises above the conversion price.

Convertible bonds are like regular bonds, except for the conversion feature. Therefore, convertible bond prices tend to be related more to the price of the common stock than to the interest yield, unless the stock price has fallen so far that there is little hope of profitable conversion in the foreseeable future.

Assume that you have bought a convertible preferred for $100 that pays a $9 dividend and may be converted into 10 shares of the company's common stock at any time. The common stock is currently selling for $8 a share. If the price of the common goes to $12, the price of your preferred will go to $120 and you can make the conversion at no loss to you. If the price of the common stock falls to $5 a share, the price of the preferred may not drop to $50 a share unless comparable preferred stocks are also yielding 18 percent ($9 ÷ $50).

Convertible securities may seem to offer the best of both worlds. However, you should ask yourself two questions when considering such investments. First, how sound is the issuing corporation? The quality rating is just as important for investors in convertibles as it is for investors in straight bonds and preferreds. Second, what are the prospects for the common stock? Since you would probably consider buying a convertible for its appreciation prospects, this is a very important question. Why buy the convertible bond of a company whose earnings outlook is poor? If the prospects for the common stock are very good, you may pay a large speculative premium for the conversion privilege. That is, the price of the bond may be 20 or 30 percent higher than the total current price of the number of converted shares. In such a case you may be better off investing in the common stock only.

CONCLUSION

There are three basic types of investments you can make in the securities markets: you can buy common stock, preferred stock, or bonds. You can also sometimes purchase convertible bonds and convertible preferred stock, which you may subsequently convert into a fixed number of shares of common stock.

The basic reason for investing in common stock is to obtain the rights to corporate income. The more money the company earns, the more income you receive from your common stock investment as dividends or capital gains. The price of the common stock depends to a great degree upon the earnings history and earnings prospects of the company. Therefore, the price-to-earnings ratio (P/E ratio) is commonly used by investors to determine whether a stock is overpriced or underpriced.

Some important advantages of investing in common stocks include possible above-average return on investments, long-term hedge against inflation, and capital gains taxes at 40 percent of the ordinary income tax rate. Major disadvantages are possible above-average loss on your investment and the amount of investment management required.

Most common stocks can be classified into the following categories: growth, second-tier growth, mature growth, cyclical, and special situation. The amount of each type of stock in which you invest depends on your investment objectives. You should understand the differences between the various classifications, and know how to identify the type of stock investment you wish to make.

Bonds have fixed interest rates. They can be of value to you if you want some conservative diversification, want to protect your net worth against the consequences of a serious recession or depression, or have a very important goal to achieve within a few years and do not want to lose money. To minimize price fluctuations due to interest rate changes, consider bonds that mature in five years or less, or else buy longer term bonds selling at a discount from face value. In any case, buy only quality issues.

VOCABULARY

book value	mortgage bond
bond	municipal bond
call feature	par value (of a bond)
collateral trust bond	par value (of a stock)
common stock	P/E ratio
convertible bond	preferred stock
convertible preferred stock	proxy
coupon bond	second-tier growth stock
cyclical stock	special situation stock
debenture	stock dividend
dividend (cash)	stock split
dividend yield	subordinated debenture
earnings per share (EPS)	Treasury bill
growth stock	Treasury bond
mature growth stock	

QUESTIONS

1. What is the most important right held by the common stock investor?
2. What is the primary reason why corporations issue common stock?
3. Explain the difference between a cash dividend, a stock dividend, and a stock split. Which is the most attractive to an investor?
4. ABZ common stock is selling for $90 a share. The cash dividend is $1.80. The EPS are $4 for the most recent 12-month period and are projected to be $4.50 for the next 12 months. The par value is $10; the book value is $45. There are 2,000,000 shares outstanding.

   a. What is the current P/E ratio on ABZ common?
   b. How many dollars after taxes is the company expected to earn next year?
   c. What is the current dividend yield?
   d. If ABZ stock were split 3 for 1, what would be the current EPS?
   e. At first glance, would you call this a mature growth stock or a growth stock?

5. Assume that you purchased 10 shares of XYZ common stock for $100 a share, held it for one year, and then sold it at $108. During that year you received $26 in cash dividends and a 10 percent stock dividend. Your commissions for both buying and selling totaled $25. What is your total percentage rate of return before taxes for the year?
6. What might be the difference between a growth stock whose EPS are growing at an average of 10 percent a year and ABZ Corporation stock, whose earnings are growing at a similar rate?
7. Why should an investor analyze both the fundamental outlook for a company and its P/E ratio before buying or selling a common stock?
8. When are corporate bonds an appropriate investment?
9. The QQZ Corporation bond (Aa rated) is selling for $850 and matures in five years. The annual interest payment is $30. What is the total average yield to maturity?

CASE PROBLEM

The case at the end of Chapter 18 is intended to cover the concepts in both Chapters 17 and 18.

RECOMMENDED READING

Please see listing at the end of Chapter 18.

CHUCK AND NANCY ANDERSON
Using Long-Term Stock Charts

Chuck and Nancy want you to help them select the best three or four stocks out of six through which they might reach their goal of buying a motorboat 14 years from now. (Keep in mind Chuck's moderately aggressive, growth-oriented stance regarding stocks.) Use the long-term charts showing trends for the prices and earnings of six common stocks (Fig. 17-4) to answer the questions.

The long-term stock charts are constructed on a logarithmic grid, and so a percentage change at a low price shows up the same size as an equal percentage change at a high price. Also, whenever the price and EPS lines are at the same point, the P/E ratio is 15. When the price is above the EPS, the P/E ratio is greater than 15, and vice versa. As a result, you can visualize from these charts the changes in P/E ratio values over the past decade. Of course, these changes may be due to a variety of factors such as overall market conditions and fundamental outlook for the company.

QUESTIONS

1. What is the P/E ratio and dividend yield (in round figures) for each stock at the end of 1972? What is the P/E ratio and dividend yield (in round figures) for each stock at the latest date on the charts?
2. Which company, in spite of its past rapid growth, now appears to be having operating difficulties? How can you tell? What are the earnings per share now? What are they at the high? What is the stock's price now? What was it at its high?
3. Which company appears to be the most typical cyclical company? Why? What are the high and low earnings per share on the chart? What are the high and low prices per share?
4. General interest rates rose significantly in 1974 and in 1979–81 because of inflation. The price of which stock appears to be related more to interest rates than to the stock's past P/E ratios? What is the current dividend yield on this stock? Would you call this a mature growth stock?
5. Which stock warrants further study of industry and corporate prospects because it seems fully priced relative to its past P/E range and the recent earnings trend looks unpromising?
6. Which two stocks appear to be reasonably priced growth stocks?
7. Now that you have made a superficial screening of these stocks, which three or four in this group do you believe might be appropriate for Chuck and Nancy? Why? Why do you exclude the others?

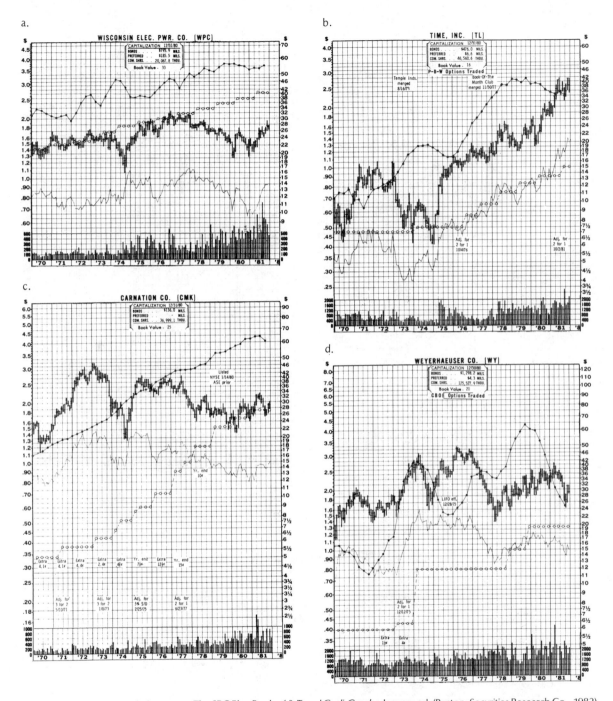

Source: Securities Research Company, *The SRC Blue Book of 3-Trend Cycli-Graphs,* January ed. (Boston: Securities Research Co., 1982). This book may be available at a broker's office or a library, or it may be subscribed to (Securities Research Company, a Division of United Business Service Company, 208 Newbury Street, Boston, Massachusetts 02116) for $59 a year (quarterly editions).

FIGURE 17-4
Trends in prices and earnings for six common stocks.

f.

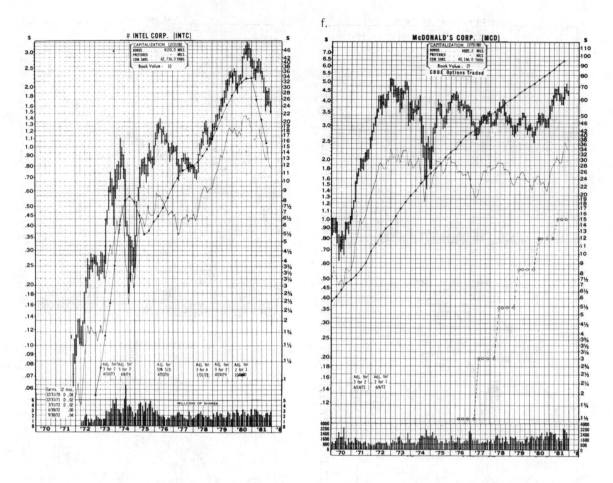

Earnings per share for most recent 12 months. (Read values from left-hand scale.)

Dividend rate per share for most recent 12 months. (Read values from left-hand scale.)

Monthly price range per share of stock. The crossbar on each vertical range bar indicates closing price for the month. (Read values from right-hand scale.)

FIGURE 17-4   (*continued*)

18

Buying and Selling Stocks and Bonds

Now that you understand common stock, preferred stock, and bonds, you are about halfway to understanding the fundamentals of stock market investing. You must still learn how to buy and sell these securities on the various markets. You will need to be able to use stock price tables and market averages both to help you decide on an investment before you make it and to follow its progress afterward. You will also need to know what to look for when choosing a stockbroker. Finally, you must be able to put all this knowledge together in the effective management of a stock portfolio.

SECURITIES MARKETS

As you recall from the ABZ Corporation example (Chapter 17), common stocks are first sold by a company to the public. After this initial sale, the stocks are sold back and forth among investors. The original sale by the company involves the use of primary markets to distribute the shares to the investor public. The second type of sale, stock trading among investors, involves the use of secondary markets. Secondary markets include organized exchanges as well as over-the-counter markets. Figure 18-1 shows how stocks or bonds move in each of these types of markets.

Primary Markets

Investment bankers handle all the transactions of the primary markets. They may work for stock brokerage houses that deal with the public or for organizations that specialize in investment banking. Investment banking primarily involves raising money for corporations. This task is called *underwriting*.

To demonstrate how underwriting works, let us return to the example of the ABZ Corporation. Assume that the company did not have the time and contacts required to sell the 100,000 shares in the initial offering. Therefore,

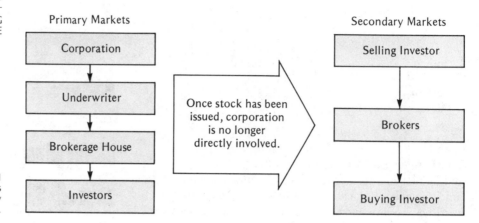

FIGURE 18-1
Flow of stocks and bonds
on primary and secondary
markets.

they engaged Funstun Brothers & Query, a fictitious investment banking house, to handle this task. In the judgment of Reginald I. Query, the appropriate price at which to offer the stock to the public should be $10 per share. Next, the company and the investment bankers had to agree on a discounted price that would determine the net proceeds per share to the company—that is, the price the investment banker would pay ABZ Corporation for each share of stock. Generally, the greater the risk that the underwriters will not be able to sell all of the issue, the larger the discount they want. Funstun Brothers & Query arrived at a discounted price of $8.50 for the ABZ stock.

The investment banking house then purchased the 100,000 shares from ABZ Corporation for $850,000. The investment banker made a public announcement in the financial journals that the primary offering of 100,000 shares of ABZ Corporation common stock at $10 per share would occur on a certain date. If all 100,000 shares are sold at $10 each, the proceeds to Funstun Brothers & Query would be $150,000 ($1,000,000 − $850,000).

Funstun Brothers & Query may sell portions of the stock to many different brokerage houses, usually at a discount. (For example, the other brokerage houses may pay $9.50 a share to Funstun Brothers & Query and keep the 50¢ difference as their commission for selling the stock to the public.) The brokerage houses then distribute the shares to their various branches. Thus, each branch may have only a few hundred or a few thousand shares to sell. Before the day when shares go on sale, the brokers at the branch offices contact some of their preferred customers (those who have accounts that generate substantial commissions). If any shares are left after these first contacts, the general public may buy them on a first-come, first-served basis. However, as a general rule, if the preferred investors do not buy all of a primary offering, it probably is not a good investment. Ideally, before buying, everyone should examine the *prospectus* that must be issued by the company in accordance with government regulations. This publication describes the characteristics of the stock and the company.

rights The bylaws of some companies require that any new offerings of common stocks (or bonds) be first offered to existing shareholders. They are considered to have a preemptive right to maintain their proportionate ownership in the company if they so desire. Let us return to the example of ABZ Corporation, in which each of 100 stockholders initially held 1,000 shares. Each investor held 1 percent of the company. If the company wished to issue 10,000 new shares, it could have issued stock purchase rights to the existing shareholders at the rate of one right for each 10 shares of stock already owned. That is, each right would allow a stockholder to purchase one share of the new issue. A stockholder who exercised this option and purchased 100 shares would own 1,100 shares of stock—exactly 1 percent of the 110,000 shares outstanding, the same proportion of the company that the stockholder owned before the second issue.

A right is issued as a certificate to the stockholder. A stockholder who does not wish to purchase the extra stock (or does not have the money to do so) may sell the right to someone else. These rights are traded on the same stock exchange as the parent company's stock and are valued at the price spread between the regular stock and the new issue stock. For example, if ABZ stock sold for $10 a share, and the new issue was set at $9 a share, the price spread would be $1. The rights would be traded at $1 each. When the term of the rights expires (usually in about a month), any unsold shares are sold to the general public, still at the issue price of $9. However, as long as the investment is a good one, the chances of acquiring these few remaining $9 shares are very slim.

warrants Warrants are functionally the same as rights to the investor trading in them. However, there are four possible technical differences between rights and warrants. First, rights are issued to finance an immediate and specific corporate need, whereas warrants are issued for both present and future financing needs. Second, rights generally involve a shorter option period than do warrants. Third, the new issue price exercisable by the right is generally below the current market price of the stock, whereas the new issue price exercisable by the warrant is generally above or at the current market price of the stock. Fourth, the new issue price exercisable by the right is fixed, whereas the new issue price exercisable by the warrant may vary.

Secondary Markets

Secondary markets are simply forums where investors can buy and sell securities among themselves. For little known companies, or companies whose stock is infrequently traded, this market may be nothing more than a single brokerage house that matches buy and sell orders for its customers. This is the rudimentary form of the over-the-counter (OTC) market. The more active OTC stocks have their prices quoted on a central computer for nationally competitive trading among investors at different brokerage houses.

For actively traded securities of well-established companies, organized secondary markets such as the New York Stock Exchange enable buyers and sellers to complete their transactions via brokers and telephones at a central location. Exchange specialists match orders to buy at a certain price with orders to sell at a certain price. No sale occurs until there is a match. Therefore, if there is very little trading activity in a stock, a transaction request will be recorded on a specialist's books to await a counter-transaction request, which may not come for several hours or even days. Normally, your broker can have a buy or sell order transacted within a few minutes if you are willing to accept the current market price. He or she simply telephones the order to the brokerage company's trader in New York; that person contacts the company's broker on the floor of the exchange, who takes the order to the specialist coordinating transactions in that stock. As soon as the trade is made, the floor broker returns the phone call and explains the details of the transaction. Figure 18-2 shows the movement of such a transaction.

organized exchanges Each of the organized exchanges has a central trading floor. In order for a company to have its stock traded on an organized exchange, it must meet certain requirements (Table 18-1). These requirements ensure that the exchange will not get a bad reputation by selling stocks issued by fly-by-night companies. A company's stock may be delisted if it fails to meet the exchange's listing requirements at any time. The most stringent listing requirements are those of the New York Stock Exchange, followed by the American Stock Exchange.

The *New York Stock Exchange* (NYSE) was founded in 1792 as a federation of about a dozen securities traders. Today, it is the largest stock exchange in the world. Ninety percent of the market value of all publicly owned stocks in the United States is listed on this exchange, and U.S. stocks account for half the world's market value of stocks. There are about 1,500 companies listed on the NYSE. They are, by and large, the industrial giants of America, accounting for over 60 percent of our country's total output of goods and services and offering over 2,100 different stocks and 2,300 different bonds. (Bonds are listed on the New York Bond Exchange.)

Only members of the NYSE are permitted to transact trades on the floor of the exchange. Membership in the exchange is limited to regulated stock brokerage

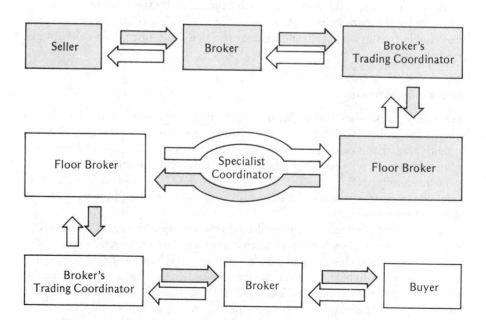

FIGURE 18-2
Flow of orders on an
organized exchange.

houses and other highly qualified individuals who are able to purchase a seat on the exchange at the going price, which has ranged in recent years from $35,000 to $300,000 depending on such things as market conditions.

The board of governors for the exchange sets up the principles, practices, and code of ethics for exchange members. (The board must abide by the rulings of the U.S. Securities and Exchange Commission and cooperate in its investigations.) The governors also set up the requirements a company must meet in order to have its stock listed on the exchange. In addition to the basic requirements about shareholders, shares, valuation, earnings, and net assets (Table 18-1), the company's character, stability, quality of markets, degree of national (as opposed to local) interest, and the like must all be approved by the board of governors before they will grant listing on the exchange.

The *American Stock Exchange*, also located in New York City, is the second largest stock exchange in the world. However, it accounts for an average of 10 percent of the dollar volume of shares traded on registered exchanges in the United States. The NYSE accounts for about 80 percent and all other exchanges combined account for the remaining 10 percent. The American Stock Exchange was unof-

TABLE 18-1

Requirements for Listing Companies on the Four Major Exchanges

Requirement	Exchange			
	New York	*American*	*Pacific*	*NASDAQ*
Shareholders				
Total number		1,200	750	300
Minimum number holding at least 100 shares each	2,000	800		
Shares				
Total number outstanding			250,000	
Number held by public (as opposed to company officers and their families)	1,000,000	400,000		100,000
Valuation				
Total market value of shares outstanding	$16,000,000 (in public ownership)	$3,000,000	$1,000,000	
Minimum price per share		$5	$2	
Earnings				
Before income taxes	$ 2,500,000	$ 750,000		
After income taxes		$ 400,000	$ 100,000	
Net Assets	$16,000,000	$4,000,000	$1,000,000	$1,000,000

ficially begun in 1849 on a corner of Wall Street by a group of dealers in unlisted securities. This street corner soon became a regular trading spot known as the Outdoor Curb Exchange. In 1921, the renamed New York Curb Exchange moved to an indoor location. Although the name was finally changed to the American Stock Exchange (ASE or Amex) in 1953, it is still referred to by many investors as "the Curb." Today, the American Stock Exchange has over 1,300 listed stocks and over 190 listed bonds. Their requirements for membership and stock listings (Table 18-1) are somewhat less stringent than those of the NYSE.

The *Pacific Coast Stock Exchange* (PCSE) is one of several regional stock exchanges in the United States. It has trading floors in Los Angeles and San Francisco. Many of its listed stocks are also listed on the NYSE or Amex. The PCSE is usually open two hours longer than are the major exchanges in order to generate extra volume from late trading after the New York City exchanges close for the day. Listing requirements (Table 18-1) are less rigorous for this exchange.

The *Midwest Stock Exchange* is the other major regional exchange in the United States. Its trading floor is located in Chicago.

There are other stock exchanges throughout North America, but most of these do a fairly small amount of trading compared to the NYSE and Amex. If you are interested in trading special types of stocks, one of the smaller exchanges may merit consideration. For example, most Canadian mining stocks can be bought on the Toronto or Montreal exchanges.

over-the-counter markets (OTC)   The over-the-counter market is not an organized central stock exchange. It is the mechanism by which brokers negotiate trades between each other for the benefit of their clients. For example, if you had wanted to buy ABZ stock before it was listed on the American Stock Exchange, your broker would have had to call other brokers to find one who represented an ABZ shareholder willing to sell some ABZ stock for the price you were willing to pay.

OTC stocks consist of all those publicly traded stocks that are not listed on one of the organized stock exchanges. Some of these stocks are traded as actively as many of the listed stocks. Certain brokers specialize in making a market in one or more of these active stocks: they clear so many trades per day that they have a good idea of what the going market price is and can build a reputation among other brokers as market-makers in these OTC stocks. Brokers who make markets in a stock actually keep an inventory of it on hand so that they can readily sell stock or buy it back at the going prices.

Two prices are always quoted for OTC stocks: the bid price and the asked price. The *bid price* is the price at which a broker would be willing to buy a stock from you—the price the broker is willing to bid for your stock. The *asked price* is higher and is the price at which a broker would be willing to sell a stock to you—the price the broker is asking for the stock. The difference between the two current prices ("the spread") is part of the broker's commission. A standard brokerage commission will also be charged if the firm is not a market-maker in that issue.

Current prices of OTC stocks are sometimes difficult to obtain. Local newspapers usually list only the prices for the OTC stocks of companies likely to interest local readers because of their location, type, and so forth. The *Wall Street Journal* has the most extensive daily listing of OTC prices. As an alternative, you can call your broker to get the latest prices. If the stock is very small and only infrequently traded, even your broker may have trouble getting a firm quote.

On over 3,000 OTC stocks, however, your broker can obtain for you the best quotes through the National Association of Securities Dealers automated quotation system (NASDAQ). In operation since 1971, this system involves a central computer with live terminals at the member brokerage firms. These houses regularly supply to the central computer their current quotes on OTC stocks in which they make a market. With everybody's quotes out in the open, the OTC market for NASDAQ stocks behaves much like the organized exchanges.

Regulation of the Securities Markets

The fraud, manipulation, and concealed information of the 1920s brought about the passage of the Securities Exchange Acts of 1933 and 1934. These acts created the Securities Exchange Commission (SEC) to administer the regulations of the organized securities exchanges. Because of the activities of the SEC, small investors can avail themselves of a complete and current disclosure of information and thus are much less likely to be abused by swindlers or by unethical big investors and brokers. The following is a list of the SEC's powers.

- To regulate and register the exchanges
  To register all securities listed on an exchange
- To regulate investment advisers and all dealers and brokers who are members of an organized exchange
- To require that audited and reasonably current financial reports be filed and that most of this information be made available in reports to the stockholders
- To require that the trading of stock holdings by officers and directors be disclosed
- To require that proxies and proxy statements be mailed to all stockholders so that they can vote in absentia at annual meetings
- To regulate and review all advertising by brokers and by companies (in their prospectuses), thereby eliminating false promises and exaggerated claims
- To control credit on both broker-to-client and broker-to-broker loans by setting margin requirements (minimums are set by the Federal Reserve Board) and requiring that all finance charges on margin accounts be disclosed to holders at least every three months
- To prohibit all forms of stock price manipulation

The state governments have also set up organizations to regulate the issue of new stocks by both new and established corporations. Such regulations may, for example, prevent the sale of stock in financially shaky corporations to uninformed investors.

The National Association of Securities Dealers (NASD) regulates the over-the-counter markets and NASDAQ. This self-regulatory body works to preserve the integrity of the OTC market by monitoring the ethics of brokers who deal in OTC stocks.

The exchanges themselves have set up governing bodies to police their activities and maintain their public integrity.

SOURCES OF INVESTMENT INFORMATION

Even though most investors lack the time and the contacts necessary to conduct their own in-depth research on a particular investment opportunity, such research is necessary before one can make intelligent investment decisions. In addition, an investor must be able to get a perspective on the general economy and make comparisons between one industry and another.

Investor demand for a way to overcome this handicap has fostered the development of daily, weekly, monthly, quarterly, and annual publications that offer insights into specific companies and industries and into business conditions in general. In fact, there are so many publications to choose from (including numerous "Get Rich Quick" paperbacks) that we have compiled a list (presented at the end of this chapter) of the more commonly used and generally available publications. Some of the materials may be bought at the local newsstand or bookstore, some are available at libraries, and some may be used at stockbroker offices.

If you are a novice in stock market investments, perhaps you should first read some of the publications that offer general information about investing in the stock market. Other sources on the list can help you keep abreast of general business news and learn about specific stocks and bonds. You should always consult the latter sources before you make a final investment decision. Do not rely on hearsay; do your own research to make sure that your information is complete and correct.

Information on Stocks and the Stock Market in the Newspapers

Nearly every major newspaper in the country lists the daily prices of stocks on the major stock exchanges. In addition to the prices of individual stocks, the newspapers report on the general trend of market prices by giving market indices such as the Dow Jones averages, Standard and Poor's averages, the New York Stock Exchange index, and the American Stock Exchange index. Investors follow these averages to acquire a feel for general market trends, for aid in timing their purchases and sales, and to have a means of measuring their investment performance.

listings of individual stocks   The individual stock listings can be easily understood through the following example (Fig. 18-3). Your local paper may omit some of the items to save space. The first two columns in the stock listing give the high and low prices of the stock for the latest 52-week period. If a split or a stock dividend of 25 percent or more has been paid, this range is shown for the new stock only. In Figure 18-3, Mill House common stock has sold for as high as 94½ and as low as 60¼ a share in the past year. The next entry is the name of the stock, in this case Mill

FIGURE 18-3
Individual stock listing.

52 Weeks High	52 Weeks Low	Stocks	Div.	Yld. %	P/E Ratio	Sales in 100s	High	Low	Close	Net Chg.
94½	60¼	M Hse	2.60	3.4	13	481	76¼	74	76	+1¼

House common stock. An entry for a preferred stock might be written, for example, "M Hse pf," and this should be read "Mill House preferred stock."

Under the "div." heading and printed right after the name of the stock is the current annual dividend paid. The current annual dividend amount is based on the amount of the last quarterly or semiannual declaration. Therefore, if a company has been paying a dividend of 20¢ per share each quarter, the rate listed in the table would be 80¢, the annual rate. If that company raised the regular quarterly rate to 25¢ at the next director's meeting, the rate in the table would be changed to $1 as soon as the first payment was made at the new rate. In this case, Mill House common pays a dividend of $2.60 per share a year, although you may receive it in quarterly amounts. If a stock dividend is also regularly paid, a footnote will notify you of that.

The next column calculates the cash dividend yield on that day's price. The next column indicates the stock's P/E ratio computed using today's price and the earnings per share for the most recently reported 12-month period. In this case, Mill House is selling at 13 times earnings.

The next column, sales in 100s, reports the actual number of shares of stock that changed hands during the day. In this case, there were 48,100 shares of Mill House stock traded that day. The next three columns report various significant prices at which Mill House stock was traded during the day: the highest price at which it was traded (high); the lowest price (low); and the price at which the last sale was made before the exchange was closed (close). In this case, Mill House stock was traded during the day at prices ranging from $74 to $76.25 per share.

The last column, "net chg.," reports the difference between today's closing price and yesterday's closing price. In this case, the figure of 1¼ indicates that today's closing price of $76 is $1.25 higher than yesterday's close, which must have been $74.75.

Although the stock price tables in the newspaper give most of the basic, current data about a security, there are many qualifying remarks for which there is no room in the actual tables. Therefore, there are always explanatory notes, or footnotes, at the end of the listings. Since these notes are not always easily understood, we have explained them more fully in Figure 18-4. Footnotes "a" through "x" apply to special or extra dividends or payments that are not regular. The other footnotes usually refer to factors other than dividends.

Dow Jones averages   The Dow Jones averages are not actual dollar averages of current market prices; they are instead an index value of the average price of a specific group of stocks. Many investors use these indices as general indicators of market trends. The Dow Jones Company computes price indices for 30 industrial stocks, 20 transportation stocks, 15 utility stocks, and a composite of all 65 of the stocks. These stocks are hand-picked to represent a cross section of the market leaders, not all stocks on the New York Stock Exchange (which are used in computing the NYSE index). Substitutions are made from time to time in the list of stocks used in the averages in order to ensure that the list represents the personal interest of a broad spectrum of the investing public. Sometimes such substitution decisions have a major effect on the averages. For example, in 1939 the Dow Jones Company decided to remove International Business Machines from the list of Dow z   **Sales in full**   Some stocks are sold in 10- or 25-share round lots instead of the usual 100-share round lots. In this case, the figures given are the total actual sales for the day; you do not have to add the usual double zero to the sales figure.

a   **Also extra or extras**   The company paid an extra dividend, over and above the regular rate, sometime in the past year.

b   **Annual rate plus stock dividend**   In addition to the regular cash dividend, the company paid a stock dividend.

c   **Liquidating dividend**   This is the amount of money being paid to stockholders as a consequence of the liquidation of all or part of the company.

d   **Indicates a new 52-week low**   The closing price is the lowest price recorded for that stock in the past 52 weeks.

e   **Declared or paid in preceding 12 months**   The dollar amount paid in the preceding 12 months. The dividend rate for this year is still uncertain.

i   **Declared or paid after stock dividend or split up**   The total amount paid since a recent stock dividend or stock split.

j   **Paid this year, dividend omitted, deferred, or no action taken last meeting**   Although the company has paid a dividend in the amount printed, for some reason there was no positive action taken on continuing the preceding dividend rate.

k   **Declared or paid this year, an accumulative issue with dividends in arrears**   A cumulative preferred stock that still owes back dividends, even though it has so far this year paid the amount stated under "div" in the listing.

n   **A new issue**   This is a newly issued common stock that has yet to establish a dividend pattern. The 52-week high and low range begins with the start of trading.

r   **Declared or paid in preceding 12 months plus stock dividend**   The cash amount paid to stockholders in preceding 12 months, along with a stock dividend. So far this year, no dividend has been declared.

s   **Stock split or stock dividend amounting to 25 percent or more since January 1, 19XX**   The 52-week high and low range and dividend begin with the date of the split or stock dividend and do not cover the full 52-week period.

FIGURE 18-4
Explanations of
footnotes found in
stock price tables.

industrials. If IBM had been left on the list, the peak of the average in 1968 would have been over 1500 instead of at 998! The 65 stocks currently used in the averages are listed every Monday in the *Wall Street Journal*. The movements of the actual indices are charted daily by the *Journal* and sometimes by local papers, too.

t   Paid in stock in preceding 12 months, estimated cash value on ex-dividend or ex-distribution date   The amount of the stock dividend expressed in dollars. For example, if a 10 percent stock dividend is payable in a few months and the stock generally sells for around $10, the estimated value of the stock dividend (in dollars) is claimed to be $1. There have been no cash dividends declared so far this year.

u   Indicates a new 52-week high   The closing price is the highest price recorded by that stock in the past 52 weeks.

Cld   Called   The issue, perhaps a convertible preferred, has been called by the company and will soon be delisted, as the security will no longer exist.

x   Ex-dividend or ex-rights   All persons who own the securities on this date will receive the current dividend payment. If you buy the security after this date, you must wait until the next dividend payment. Theoretically, the stock would decline in price by the amount of the dividend on that date; this is indicated in the net change figure for that security. For example, if a stock is paying a $1 quarterly dividend and the previous day's closing price for the stock was $105, the net change column would show +1 if the stock closed at $105 the day it went ex-dividend.

Similarly, in order to claim the rights currently being distributed to all stockholders, you must have owned the security on that day.

y   Ex-dividend and sales in full   A combination of the z and x footnotes.

x-dis   Ex-distribution   Similar to the x footnote, except that in this case the note refers to stock dividends.

xw   Without warrants   This stock is being traded without the warrants that were issued in conjunction with the stock. The former stockholder apparently retained ownership in the warrants when he sold the stock.

ww   With warrants   The opposite of xw.

wd   When distributed   Similar to when issued.

wi   When issued   A security has not yet been issued, but rights to the stock have. Therefore, investors are essentially trading the rights at this time, before the stock itself is actually issued.

vj   In bankruptcy or receivership or being reorganized under the Bankruptcy Act, or securities assumed by such companies   If you buy this stock, you may only be buying assets in the process of liquidation, not those of an income-producing corporation.

FIGURE 18-4
(*continued*)

The Dow Jones averages are sometimes criticized because they measure the price changes of a few stocks rather than the general market. However, these averages do often follow the general trend of the markets, and they are part of the everyday language of stock market investors.

Standard and Poor's averages Standard and Poor's computes indices for 400 industrial stocks, 40 financial stocks, 40 utilities, and 20 transportation stocks, and all 500 stocks taken together. The Standard and Poor's index, like the Dow, hand-picks stocks from the NYSE to use in their sample, but it is generally regarded as a better measure of the overall trend of the market because it uses a greater number of stocks. The relative effect of each stock on the index is weighted by the total market value of the outstanding stock of the company. For example, as of December 31, 1981, IBM accounted for 3.9 percent of the S&P 500, even though the average stock would only be 0.2 percent of the index. Standard and Poor's averages are reported daily in the *Wall Street Journal* and are sometimes charted daily in the financial sections of local newspapers.

New York Stock Exchange index This index records the average price and net change of all common stocks listed on the New York Stock Exchange. As with the S&P indices, each stock is weighted by market value. The computation of this index was made possible by the use of high-speed computers. It is widely used because of the precision with which it measures the price movement of the general market. In addition to the general (composite) common stock index, the exchange publishes indices for industrial, transportation, finance, and utility stocks.

American Stock Exchange index This index is similar to the NYSE index. It is the only index of any significance publicly published for ASE stocks. Because it measures the price activity of the smaller companies, it is often followed by analysts who are looking for signs of excessive speculation or severe pessimism as signals of major market tops or bottoms.

Other Indices

The only generally available unweighted indices are those published by professional advisory services, such as *Value Line* or the *Indicator Digest* (see the list of readings at the end of the chapter for a description).

BROKERS AND BROKERAGE HOUSES

Brokers are licensed to buy and sell securities for clients as well as for themselves. These securities include common stocks (both listed and unlisted), preferred stocks, bonds, mutual fund shares, annuity contracts, real estate syndications, oil drilling programs, and other investment programs. Other terms commonly used in place of the word *broker* include *registered representative*, and *account executive*. The brokers of nearly all major public brokerage houses go through a training and apprenticeship period and must pass federal and/or state examinations before they become licensed as full-fledged brokers.

Brokerage houses are the companies that stockbrokers represent. Some brokerage houses are partnerships; others are corporations. Some are local; others have regional or nationwide networks of branch offices.

Types of Brokerage Houses

Most investors are familiar with *general brokerage houses*. Some of these houses require a minimum-sized account, but most welcome even small investors (persons who spend maybe a few hundred dollars on stocks each year) and offer nearly all of their services to them. Firms registered with the New York Stock Exchange generally offer the widest range of services.

Specialty brokerage houses usually deal only with persons who have substantial accounts, generally ranging from $50,000 to $100,000 and up. These houses offer personal consultation and special portfolio research and management as a regular service. The general houses may perform such services as well, but only on a selective basis.

Brokerage House Regulations and Ethics

In general, brokerage houses do their best to stay within the law and to maintain a high standard of ethics. This, of course, helps them maintain the good public reputation that keeps them in business.

All brokerage houses that are members of organized exchanges (and most are) are regulated by the SEC. One of the most significant regulations, as far as the investor is concerned, is the prohibition of untrue or overstated advertising. The houses must clearly state what is fact and what is opinion with regard to any investment recommendations they make.

In addition to the regulations, there are certain ethics common to most houses. First, the names and financial circumstances of all customers are to be kept in strict confidence. Second, brokers should not try to persuade you to make a stock transaction that you really do not want to make. Third, all orders are executed faithfully for you by your broker. If he or she makes a mistake, it will be corrected at no cost to you.

Brokerage Commissions and Other Fees

Brokers receive a commission on every buy-and-sell transaction they make. There used to be a system of fixed commissions, but it was abolished by order of the SEC as of May 1, 1975. Now brokers must be prepared to negotiate a fee on each transaction, although they generally stick to their published rates on small trades in inactive accounts. For stocks traded on the NYSE or Amex, most member firms charge commissions generally ranging from 1 percent (on large transactions) to 6 percent (on very small transactions).

Because of the way commissions are graduated, it generally makes economic sense to buy or sell at least $1,000 worth of stock per trade. This keeps your percentage cost per transaction under 4 percent. If your transaction is not in 100-share multiples, there is an additional charge of 12½¢ per share. This is known as the odd lot commission.

One way to reduce your commissions is to do business with one of the so-called "discount houses." These firms charge reduced rates on transactions because they do

not offer other brokerage services such as market advice and the like. See Table 18-2 for sample rate schedules.

For stocks changing hands in New York State (any stock traded on the NYSE or Amex), there is a small tax amounting to about one-half of 1 percent of the value of the sale (less for non–New York residents). Certain other states may also charge such a tax. Another fee is the federal registration fee on securities. This relatively insignificant charge is levied against the registration of the stock in your name when you buy it.

Typical Brokerage House Services

In addition to the trading service for which a commission is charged, many houses offer extra free services designed to encourage investors to do business with them. Others charge separately for such services. Most of these services involve supplying information. Many brokerage houses send monthly statements of your account balance, dividends received, and the like. Written analyses of individual stocks and special industry reports are often printed by brokerage houses and are available upon request. Sometimes your broker will mail them to you if he or she thinks you might be interested. If there is urgent news about a stock, some houses print newswire bulletins for distribution by brokers to their clients who hold that stock. Stock price quotations are supplied over the telephone at your request.

Some brokerage houses also have available in their offices ticker tape, newswire, quote board, and telequote machines for their customers' use. If your broker has a telequote machine available for clients to use, find out how to use it. A general reference library is often available to the clients of a brokerage house (and sometimes even to passersby). Such a library will usually contain Standard and Poor's stock sheets, house publications, copies of the *Wall Street Journal*, *Barron's*, and similar publications.

You can get the house's recommendations regarding a certain stock upon inquiry. Most houses have a full-time staff of research analysts who continually review stocks and make recommendations about whether you should buy, sell, or hold a given security. Of course, this is only their opinion and you may choose to do differently.

TABLE 18-2

Sample 1982 Stock Brokerage Commissions

Transaction	A Major Wall Street Firm in 1982[a]		A Major Discount Broker in 1982	
Share price	*$10*	*$50*	*$10*	*$50*
100 shares	$ 36.00	$ 92.00	$ 30.00	$ 66.00
200 shares	$ 72.02	$175.28	$ 42.00	$ 87.00
500 shares	$140.96	$371.21	$ 66.00	$132.00
1,000 shares	$251.23	$572.18	$ 87.00	$207.00

[a]The broker will often discount from this stated "retail" rate for large trades (over $10,000 or so) or for active accounts (over $500 annual commissions).

Safe-keeping of your securities is another useful service offered by most houses. A brokerage house that holds securities in its safe for a client is said to hold them "in street name." This service is usually convenient and safe for the clients.

If the broker holds your securities in street name, you do not have to keep track of the certificates, sign them over when you sell them, transfer them in and out of your own safe-deposit box, and so on. It is easier to compound your investment by reinvesting all of your dividends. The dividends are paid to your account, not sent to you by check, and so you avoid spending dividend payments on daily expenses. However, you must request that any credit balances in your account because of dividends or sale of stock be either sent to you by check or invested in the brokerage house's money market fund. Otherwise your funds will be held in your brokerage account and not receive interest.

The house keeps securities in its vault, and they are insured by the federal government through the Securities Investor Protection Corporation (SIPC). This corporation provides up to $500,000 insurance ($100,000 for cash not currently invested in securities) per account in case of brokerage house failure. Some houses purchase additional insurance to cover larger accounts. For accounts larger than the amounts covered by the insurance, however, there is the risk that if the brokerage house goes bankrupt, the investors will lose much of their investment.

This type of insurance provides only for the return of your actual securities, not for the return of their dollar value at the time of the house's failure. Furthermore, it may take weeks or months to clear up the accounts of bankrupt houses; hence, your stocks may be tied up and may decline in price while you are unable to sell them. These and other problems with SIPC are causing Congress to study possible improvements in the law.° If you keep your stocks yourself, however, and you lose the certificates, you will have to replace them at a penalty. (To be sure of relatively easy replacement of lost certificates, you should record the transfer agent's address and the certificate numbers in a location separate from the actual certificates.)

Brokerage House Research

Most brokerage houses do not consistently excel in all areas of their investment research because of three practices. First, each researcher may be assigned to research a certain industry group. While this may make the researcher a specialist in that group, it also may cause him or her to recommend purchasing the best stocks in that industry when, in comparison with other industries, none of these stocks is currently a good buy. Second, most brokerage houses do not research all industries. Third, many brokerage houses that handle the primary offering of a stock and are committed to its success recommend it even when it has become overpriced.

Within brokerage houses or research organizations there are people who turn out high-quality research, in spite of these three practices.

Identifying reliable and experienced researchers is a difficult job even for professional investment managers. It can probably be accomplished only by doing your own reading of research reports, investigating, and interviewing. If you find a

---

° "Confused Muir Liquidation Raises Doubts about Investor Protection," *Wall Street Journal*, February 2, 1982, p. 25.

person whose research you would like to have and this person works for a pure research organization, you may have to pay a subscription fee. If the person does research for a brokerage house, you may have to open an account there. The larger your account, the more leverage you have in obtaining good research very quickly.

Selecting a Broker and Opening an Account

Your relationship with your broker is very important. You should select your broker and brokerage house as carefully as you would select a doctor or a lawyer. Talk to your banker and your friends, read the ads and brochures, and talk to representatives in several different houses before you select the person and the house that you feel best suits your objectives and your situation.

It is important when choosing a particular broker within a brokerage house that his or her investment attitude be similar to yours. Since brokers trade in the market for themselves as well as for their clients, they know more about the stocks and trading techniques that suit their own goals than about those attractive to someone with a different investment philosophy. If you wish to invest for long-term growth, make sure you do not select a broker who is interested in trading for short-term gains, and vice versa. If, after you have been with a broker for a while, you find that he or she does not suit your needs, you may request a change or even transfer your account to another house. (Your new broker will handle this transfer for you.)

One way to distinguish the broker who is interested only in generating commissions from the broker interested in providing a good long-term service is to ask this question early in your initial interview: "What stocks do you recommend for making money in the market?" Brokers who begin immediately to explain their favorite stocks may well be primarily securities salespeople. If a broker responds by asking about your objectives and your financial situation, you can be more certain that he or she will endeavor to give responsible advice.

Once you have decided on a broker, it is simple to open an account. You fill out a few forms, and you are ready for your first stock purchase. At first you may rely heavily on your broker's recommendations and advice, especially once he or she understands your investment objectives. Of course, as time goes on, you should acquire more and more expertise in the market and be able to do much of your own decision making.

THE CONDITION OF THE MARKET: BULLS AND BEARS

When the stock market is in an uptrend, as measured by the stock market averages, investors refer to it as a *bull market*. If the market is in a downtrend, it is referred to as a *bear market*. Among the factors that can initiate a bull market are investor optimism that the economy will improve over the next six months or so, and economically stimulating government actions—such as a tax cut or reduction in interest rates. Of course, to maintain a bull market for a long time there must be continued economic growth (as measured by the quarterly gross national product), continued government actions that are not intended to restrain the economy, and, most important, continued growth in corporate profits.

Bear markets are usually initiated by one or more of the following factors: widespread pessimism among investors, an unexpectedly high rate of inflation, or perceived negative government acts such as tax increases or widening federal budget deficits. Any minor decline (correction) in stock market prices can grow into a major bear market if the following occur: the GNP growth rate slows to well below normal; the government continues to work on restraining an unusually difficult siege of inflation; or, especially, corporate profits go into a period of decline. There have been times (1966, for example) when pessimism about the future of the stock market has actually brought about bear markets, even though the economy did not slow down. Bear markets are usually short-lived. Over the long run, stock prices have generally tended to rise, as Figure 18-5 shows.

Regardless of the condition of the general market, investors can be bullish about certain well-selected stocks. For example, Procter & Gamble stock rose 29 percent in 1969, when the NYSE index dropped about 15 percent (a bear market). The converse can also be true. In the bull market of 1965 (up 15 percent), General Portland Cement stock dropped 37 percent because of considerable overcapacity in the cement industry.

Trading Techniques for the Long-Term Investor

The basic trading technique with regard to bull markets or growth stocks is simply to buy long—to buy a stock and hold it for price appreciation. With regard to bear markets or stocks with poor prospects, however, this technique is not very successful. Many long-term investors simply wait out short-term price erosion (decline), which may happen even to stocks with good prospects. You must be aware of both bull and bear market trends in order to time your trades to best advantage. You would want to buy stock whenever the market or an individual stock has undergone a sustained bearish trend, because the stock would probably be relatively cheap (provided that you have reason to believe that the stock will rise again). Conversely, you would want to sell a stock and take your profits in cash whenever the market has sustained a long bullish trend and a bear market seems imminent. Later, you could use those cash profits (which were not affected by the bear market) and reinvest them in the same, or different, stocks at a much lower price.

When you ask your broker to buy or sell a stock, you will in all likelihood give him or her either a market order, a limit order, or a stop order. Any of these orders can be used with odd lots (fewer than 100 shares of stock) or round lots (multiples of 100 shares). For the investor who does not have time to follow every turn of the market, dollar cost averaging is a useful investment technique.

market order A market order is an order to your broker to buy or sell a stock for you at the best price he or she can obtain at that time. Since you probably know what the current price of a stock is before you buy (or sell) it, you simply tell your broker to buy (or sell) as many shares of the stock as you want at the market. Your broker will attempt to complete the order for you within a few minutes after you place it with him or her.

limit order A limit order is an order to buy (or sell) a stock at the best possible price, but not above (or below) a specified limit price. For example, you might tell your broker to buy 100 shares of ABZ stock at a price of $18 per share or lower—a "limit" of $18. He or she would immediately forward this order to the specialist on the floor of the exchange. If the price dropped to 17⅞, your order may be activated. If there were other limit orders on the specialist's books ahead of yours, they might buy up all ABZ stock offered at that low price before your order could be executed. In that case supply and demand would force the market price back above 18, and

The New York Stock Exchange Common Stock Index:
Annual Data for the Years Beginning with 1939

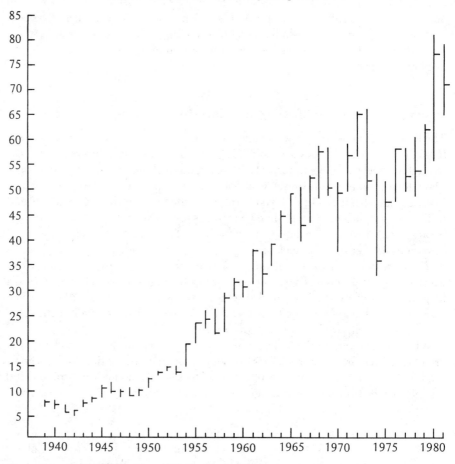

Source: *New York Stock Exchange 1981 Fact Book.*

Note: The vertical lines for each year plot the extent of the high and low readings for the index. The horizontal tick marks the closing price of the index for the year. For example, in 1965 the market closed at 50. During 1966 the average price of all stocks plunged to as low as about 37 (bear market), but eventually closed that year at about 43. The index was not calculated for the years prior to 1939. It was set at 50.0 on December 31, 1965.

FIGURE 18-5
General rise in stock prices shown by annual data.

you would have missed your opportunity to have your limit order executed. If you really thought that ABZ stock represented a good investment opportunity, your limit order might have been unwise; it cost you the chance to buy ABZ stock simply because you wanted to save 25¢ per share. Later, if the stock sold for $29 per share, your unwillingness to pay a little over $18 per share would probably seem foolish.

However, when the market for a given stock is undergoing rapid and extreme price fluctuations a limit order can make sense. Limit orders, unlike market orders, prevent you from buying a stock at a price higher than desired and give you a chance for a good price on your purchase without sitting by the ticker tape waiting for the time when exactly the right price is available. Another time when limit orders are useful is when the stock is so infrequently traded (e.g., a small OTC stock) that you are unsure what the market price might be until your order is executed. In such instances, a limit order can prevent unpleasant surprises.

stop order   A stop order, also called a "stop-loss order," is an order to sell stock *at the market* (i.e., at the next possible transaction) when it reaches or goes below a certain price. The stop order is useful if you become nervous about a stock you own and want to make sure that your loss is no greater than a certain amount, in case the stock really goes into a nose dive.

Assume, for example, that you purchased ABZ stock at $18 per share. Since that time there has been some discouraging news about the company's earnings, and the price of the stock has gradually dropped to $14 per share. You are unsure whether or not the next earnings report will indicate a resumption in the earnings growth of the company, and you decide not to sell until you can see the report. As time goes on, you become a little more nervous about the prospects for the stock and decide that you do not want to take a loss of more than 33 percent. Therefore, you give your broker a stop order on ABZ stock at $12. This means that if the stock goes to $12 or lower, the floor specialist will sell it at the best price he or she can get for you.

The next report from the company indicates that the earnings decline will be a long-term problem. The price of the stock drops rapidly to $12, and your order goes into effect. However, by the time the specialist on the exchange matches your order to a buy order, the price of the stock is $11.50. Over the next six months the price of ABZ stock ranges between $6 and $9 per share and the stop-loss order has proved its usefulness to you. This order would have been especially useful if the stock had dropped all the way to $9 per share in one day. You might not have learned of the price drop until you read about it in the papers the next day, when it would have been too late to sell the stock at a higher price.

Of course, that $11.50 price you sold for could also have been the low point for the stock—a point at which you might not have sold if the stop order had not been in effect. For example, you may have been following ABZ stock and had news, as its price neared $11.50, that caused you to feel that the stock would not go much lower. In that case, you would not have decided to sell; but, if you had had a stop order in, you would have had no choice. If you had not placed the stop order, however, or if you had removed it in time, you would have still been holding the stock when the price turned around. You can see that limit orders and stop orders should not be used indiscriminately.

odd lot transaction   All trading on the organized exchanges occurs in round lots. If you want to buy or sell 263 shares of ABZ stock, for example, 200 shares would be treated as a round lot and sold in a direct floor trade. Your order on the other 63 shares would be handled separately by your firm's rules or by an odd lot broker. If an odd lot broker gets your order, he checks the very next price for a round lot trade in that stock on the floor. Then, he completes the transaction out of his own inventory at that price, plus a small commission. If your order is a buy order, and the broker does not have sufficient inventory of that stock, he will buy a round lot for himself at the next floor trade and resell part of that lot to you.

The commission you pay the odd lot broker is collected both when you buy and when you sell stock in odd lots. This fee amounts to an extra one-eighth of a point per share. For example, if you have your broker order 15 shares of ABZ stock for you and the next price on the ticker tape is $19, your statement from your broker would show a purchase price of 19⅛ per share. In addition to the odd lot commission, you would also pay the regular commission to your broker.

dollar cost averaging   Dollar cost averaging simply involves investing the same *fixed dollar amount* in the *same stock* at *regular intervals* over a *long period of time*. All four of these variables must be observed for this investment method to succeed. The principle is that fewer shares are bought when the price is high than when the price is low.

Assume that you select ABZ Corporation and decide to buy as many shares as you can with $500 every six months for five years. The results of this program are shown in Table 18-3. As you can see, the $6,916 value of the portfolio after five years represents a total return, on paper, of about 39.8 percent. Of course, you might claim that that was an easy accomplishment, regardless of the technique used, since the

TABLE 18-3
Results of Investing $500 Every Six Months for Five Years

Year	Price[a]	Shares	Cost	Total Shares	Total Value	Cumulative Total Cost
1	$10	50	$500	50	$ 500	$ 500
	12	41	492	91	1,092	992
2	7	71	497	162	1,134	1,489
	6	83	498	245	1,470	1,987
3	9	55	495	300	2,700	2,482
	13	38	494	338	4,394	2,976
4	15	33	495	371	5,565	3,471
	10	50	500	421	4,210	3,971
5	13	38	494	459	5,967	4,465
	14	35	490	494	6,916	4,955

Note: $4,955 ÷ 494 = $10.03 average price paid per share.
[a]Commissions included.

price of the stock advanced from $10 to $14 a share over that period—a rise of 40 percent.

To see whether another method would have been as effective, let us assume that you bought 50 shares every six months. As Table 18-4 shows, the $1,550 paper profits resulting from this method amount to only a 28.4 percent gain on an investment that is $495 larger than that for the dollar cost averaging method. With the fixed number of shares method, you bought 50 shares each time, no matter how high the price. With the fixed dollar amount method, you bought fewer shares when they were high priced, more shares when they were low priced. Therefore, the average price paid per share using the fixed amount method was $10.03, compared with $10.90 using the other method. Dollar cost averaging gave you a profit even when the stock was worth only $9 a share (in the third year). The other technique, however, showed a loss. There would be an even greater contrast if the two programs were carried out for a longer time and for ever-increasing stock prices.

Trading Techniques for the Trader

The trader (short-term investor) likes to try to make money in both bull and bear markets. In order to take full advantage of bear market opportunities, traders try to anticipate the beginning stages of a market downtrend. They look at the leading general economic indicators computed by various federal agencies because the stock market often begins a downturn several months before an economic recession is really in evidence. They also observe the mood of Wall Street. General attitudes about the future course of the market often are printed in the *Wall Street Journal*, *Forbes*, and the like. Among the trading techniques traders use are short sales, margin buying, and puts and calls.

TABLE 18-4
Results of Buying 50 Shares Every Six Months for Five Years

Year	Price[a]	Shares	Cost	Total Shares	Total Value	Cumulative Total Cost
1	$10	50	$500	50	$ 500	$ 500
	12	50	600	100	1,200	1,100
2	7	50	350	150	1,050	1,450
	6	50	300	200	1,200	1,750
3	9	50	450	250	2,050	2,200
	13	50	650	300	3,900	2,850
4	15	50	750	350	5,250	3,600
	10	50	500	400	4,000	4,100
5	13	50	650	450	5,850	4,750
	14	50	700	500	7,000	5,450

Note: $5,450 ÷ 500 = $10.90 average price paid per share.
[a]Commissions included.

selling short A short sale is the opposite of the usual stock market transaction. When you sell short, you sell the stock and later buy it back, hopefully at a lower price. To do this, you borrow the stock from your broker. Then you sell that stock at the market. Later, you buy the stock back at the market and return to your broker the number of shares that you previously borrowed. Only listed stocks can be sold short.

Perhaps an example will help you understand short selling and how a trader can profit from such a transaction. Assume that the common stock of the ABZ Corporation has risen in price from $18 to $33 in the past six months because of continued investor enthusiasm about growth in the company's profitability. However, you believe that the company will suffer because of a newly emerging competitor and an impending recession. Therefore, you feel that the stock could easily drop back down to $18, and you decide to sell it short.

You telephone your broker and ask him or her to sell 100 shares of ABZ for you at the current price of $30. Your broker loans you the shares, if available, to make the sale and then completes the transaction for you. (These shares are borrowed from an investor who is holding them in his margin account. The only cost of borrowing them is that you must pay the owner any dividends they would normally earn.) The broker will also require you to put up a cash deposit equal to no less than the Federal Reserve Board's current margin requirements on the value of the borrowed stock. For example, if the current margin requirements are 80 percent, the broker will require a cash deposit of $2,400 ($3,000 × 0.80). If, a few months later, ABZ stock is selling for around $19, you can buy back those 100 shares you sold and make a sizable profit on the deal. If those 100 shares cost you $1,900, and your commissions both ways amounted to $100, you would have made $1,000 ($3,000 − $2,000) on your short sale. In the event that the stock does not drop in price, but rises instead, you could lose money. In fact, you might later decide that your losses had run far enough and buy back the 100 shares at, perhaps, $41 each, returning them to your broker at a loss of $1,200 ($1,100 loss plus $100 in commissions).

With short selling you are going against the long-term uptrend of the stock market. It is possible to lose more money on a bad short sale than on a bad decision when you are buying long. If that $30 stock rose to a price of $70, you would lose $40 a share on a short sale—more than the stock was worth when you initiated the deal. If you bought the stock long at $30, the most you could lose would be the $30 you invested if the company went broke.

Furthermore, your broker could require you to increase your cash margin deposit if the price of ABZ stock went very far above the original $30 price. If you did not have the extra reserve cash, you would have to use the cash in your account to buy back the stock right away to cover your short position and pay off your debt to the broker. You can see that selling short has greater risks and requires more expertise than buying long.

buying stocks with borrowed money Borrowing money from your broker to buy stock is called *buying on margin*. Your broker will loan you up to 60 percent of the face value of the stock you intend to purchase, depending on the current requirements of the Federal Reserve Board. In addition, you would pay interest on the loan from your broker at about the lowest possible rate, usually about 0.5 to 1 percent above the rate the brokerage house must pay to the bank (usually close to the prime rate).

In order to open a margin account, you must make at least a $2,000 cash down payment and agree to let your shares be loaned to short sellers. Otherwise, the down payment must be at least equal to the current margin requirements set by the Federal Reserve Board. For example, if the requirements were set at 70 percent, and you wished to buy 100 shares of a $40 stock, you would have to put up a $2,800 down payment ($4,000 $\times$ 0.70). Your broker would lend you the rest of the money ($1,200) at his or her current annual interest charge. This technique lets you buy more stock than you otherwise could with the same amount of money, thereby raising your potential return or loss on your investment. However, your potential return is reduced and your loss is exaggerated because of the interest you must pay on the margin loan, regardless of whether the stock goes up or down. You can purchase only a limited number of over-the-counter stocks on margin.

Assume that you have $7,000 to invest in one stock for one year. Rather than invest only your own money, you decide to buy on margin when the margin requirements are set at 70 percent. This means that on a $10,000 stock purchase (100 shares at $100 a share) you can borrow $3,000. One year later you sell the stock at $140 a share. As Table 18-5 shows, buying on margin has increased your rate of return by 13.7 percentage points over what it would have been if you had invested only your $7,000. If, however, you had sold the stock at $60 a share, your rate of loss would

TABLE 18-5

Comparison of a Profit and a Loss
When Buying on Margin and Without Margin

Transaction	Without Margin	With 70% Margin
Original purchase ($100/share)		
Number of shares	70	100
Dollar amount	$7,000	$10,000
Loan from broker		$ 3,000
Profit ($140/share sale price)		
Dollar receipts	$9,800	$14,000
Interest (8%) on loan		$ 240
Original cost	$7,000	$10,000
Net profit (before commissions)	$2,800	$ 3,760
Rate of return on $7,000	40%	53.7%
Loss ($60/share sale price)		
Dollar receipts	$4,200	$ 6,000
Interest (8%) on loan		$ 240
Original cost	$7,000	$10,000
Net loss (before commissions)	($2,800)	($ 4,240)
Rate of loss on $7,000	(40%)	(60.6%)

have been 20.6 percentage points greater than if you had not used borrowed money. Because of the possibility of greater loss, margin buying is generally used only by sophisticated market traders who are willing to take such risks.

You will be required to put up extra money if the stock price falls to the point where your equity (total share value minus the amount of the loan) is 25 percent or less of the total market value of your shares. For example, if that $100 stock dropped to $40 a share, the total value of the 100 shares would be $4,000. If you were to sell the stock at this time, you would have only $1,000 left after you paid back the $3,000 loaned by your broker. This $1,000 is exactly 25 percent of the current value of the stock ($4,000). If the stock's price were to drop any further, your broker would call for more margin (more cash on deposit).

using puts and calls   An investor who buys a put buys the *right to sell*, within a given period of time at the price specified in the contract, 100 shares of a specified stock to the person who wrote the put. A call is the *right to buy*—from the person who wrote the call—100 shares of a stock at a stated price. Investors can buy calls on many listed stocks through their brokers via one of the exchanges that specialize in this business, principally the Chicago Board of Options Exchange (CBOE) and American Stock Exchange. Puts are currently handled individually through dealers in this business.

For example, you may buy a 30-day call costing $200 that gives you the option of buying stock for $30 a share, its current price. If the stock rises to $35 within that time, you would want to exercise your call option and take your profit. You could buy the 100 shares for $30 each, or a total cost of $3,000. You would then sell those 100 shares on the market for $35 each, or $3,500 total. The $500 gain, minus the $200 cost of the call, gives you a net profit of $300. On the $200 investment, this gives you a return of 150 percent in one month! Of course, if the stock had not gone above $32 (your break-even price is $30 + ($200 ÷ 100)), you could not have exercised your call profitably, and you would have realized up to a 100 percent loss on your $200 investment.

Sometimes speculators buy both a put and a call on the same stock. If the price goes up or down, they can take advantage of it. This is called a *straddle*. Of course, if both options are bought, a $500 gain will be cut by $400 ($200 for each option), and the investor's profit will be only 25 percent on the $400 investment. If the stock did not go up or down, the investor would show a 100 percent loss on the whole $400. These examples show why buying puts and calls is appropriate only for risk-oriented investors.

Many conservative investors have come to use call options as a way of increasing their current income from a stock and reducing their risk. By selling a call option on a stock they already own (called *hedging*), they obtain the cash from the sale of the option to help offset any possible decline in the stock price. Of course, if the price of the stock goes above the call price, the stock will be called away (purchased by the option holder) and the investor will lose any potential appreciation above what was received by the call price plus the cash from sale of the option.

Puts and calls may be used for purposes other than speculation. For example, you may buy a put on a stock to protect your paper profit in it if you wish to delay the cash profits until the next taxable year. For a more complete discussion of such concepts, refer to one of the basic texts listed at the end of this chapter or to one of the booklets published by the exchanges dealing in options.

charts and mechanical rules   Over the years, successful traders have attempted to ascribe their skill to some special charting technique they have developed, such as the Dow theory, various forms of point and figure charts, or trendline analysis; or they have claimed success through applying rigid trading rules such as "sell whenever a stock drops more than 15 percent or rises more than 50 percent." When put into actual practice, or when simulated on a computer using historical data, it is generally found that such techniques rarely have enough margin of success over a buy-and-hold strategy to pay for even the commission costs of the trading that is involved. In fact, in the very short run, the market behaves in a *random walk* fashion. That is, very recent moves in a stock are very poor predictors of the next price moves in that stock. Obviously, successful traders must also rely on special insights or luck to support their success, rather than on mathematical models or mechanical rules.

THE EFFICIENT MARKET THEORY

The random walk hypothesis has developed into a full-fledged theory of the *efficient market*. It has become increasingly accepted, at least in academic circles, that no one can consistently outperform the stock market averages. In fact, the conclusion is that an investor would be better off with a buy-and-hold philosophy than to try to beat the market by trading in and out; traders, on the average, typically fall short of the market averages by the amount of the commissions they incur.

The theoretical basis for this conclusion is that the stock market is completely efficient; that is, at any point, the buyers and sellers of a stock have taken into account all the present knowledge, as well as future possibilities, about a company and the market, and, therefore, the company's stock price accurately reflects its present worth. As new knowledge of possibilities emerges, the market forces quickly bring about a change in price to reflect this new information. Therefore, one has no reasonable hope of beating the market, except by luck.

Institutions vs. Private Individuals

Efficient market theory studies have been based on historical observations of large, professionally managed pools of money, such as mutual funds and bank managed trust funds. This is because these are the only groups that have publicly available performance results for nearly all the members of the group.

The managers of institutional investment funds have certain constraints on their management. For one, they work with such large amounts of money that they must generally restrict themselves to the several hundred largest listed corporations. Smaller companies' stocks do not have sufficient trading volume to allow large funds to acquire a meaningful position (not even 1 percent of the portfolio) without upsetting the normal supply/demand balance for the stock, thereby bidding up the

price of that stock by their own activities; a similar problem would occur when selling the stock. A second constraint, also brought on by large size, is the inability to create a significant cash position as an offset to bear markets. Whenever institutional managers perceive a bear market in the offing, many of them will, of course, perceive it at about the same time. As they all rush to sell stock, there are no buyers of comparable size to absorb the downward price pressure that is created by the selling. As a consequence, by the time an institutional manager has achieved a cash position equal to 5 or 10 percent of the institution's portfolio, the bear market has usually nearly run its course; the opposite effect will then plague the professional fund manager who tries to beat the competition at the beginning of a bull market. Because these people have so much money to manage, they, in effect, have *become* the market; how, then, can any of them hope to *beat* the market, except by sometimes being a little luckier than other institutional managers?

Private individuals, or small professional managers, on the other hand, do not have such constraints on their flexibility. In our opinion, investors who have the entire universe of listed and OTC stocks to work with, and who have the ability to liquidate nearly all of their holdings within a week's time, need only reasonable experience, judgment, and foresight to have a fair shot at outperforming the stock market averages. This superior performance is particularly likely if the investor is trying to take advantage of the major price cycles lasting months and years. Traders looking to make money from daily or weekly price swings are likely to find that the random walk nature of the market has averaged out their performance to equal the market, less commissions, over the long term.

Beta

Some institutional managers appear to have significantly outperformed others over a considerable number of years. However, upon analysis, it has been found that such apparently superior performance is generally the result of assuming either above-average risk during bull markets or below-average risk during bear markets. Here, risk is defined as *market volatility*, or *beta*. Beta measures the relative price increase in a single stock compared to an increase in the stock market as a whole (or a decline in the stock in a declining market).

The market, generally described by the Standard and Poor's index of 500 stocks, is assigned a beta of 1.0. Recently General Motors stock was calculated to have a beta of 0.9. This means that if on any one day there is a 1 percent increase or decrease in the S&P 500, you might expect General Motors to be up or down nine-tenths of 1 percent (on the average). Its volatility is 10 percent less than that of the market. The movement of any single stock may deviate significantly from that predicted by its beta and you may not think this concept has much value. However, for a well-diversified portfolio, the beta for the entire portfolio (weighted by the percentage amount in each stock) is a reasonably good predictor of overall volatility, or risk. Thus, portfolios of high beta stocks do better than those of low beta stocks in bull markets, and vice versa in bear markets.

For a more in-depth discussion of the efficient market theory we refer you to the references at the end of this chapter or to other recent investments texts.

MANAGING YOUR PORTFOLIO

The most important objective for studying Chapters 17 and 18 is to be able to construct and manage a portfolio of common stocks that both satisfies your investment objective and is consistent with your tolerance for risk. There are two important considerations here. One, how much money do you put into common stocks? A conservative investor who has modest long-term goals might put only 20 percent of his net worth into common stocks; a more aggressive investor who has high goals and is willing to accept the risk might invest 50 percent of his net worth in common stocks. Go back to the 11-step procedure in Chapter 15 and ask yourself where you fit on such a spectrum. The second consideration, then, is which common stocks do you buy. This is the subject of this section of the chapter.

Select Your Risk Level

The first step in constructing a portfolio is to determine what market volatility risk, or beta, is appropriate for you. If you have high objectives for your portfolio, and you won't be too upset if your portfolio drops 30 percent in value because the market is off by 20 percent or so, then you should buy a portfolio of stocks with an average beta of around 1.3 or 1.4. (Your broker, or publications such as *Value Line*, can supply you with the necessary historical beta figures.) If you want a portfolio that might do only a little better than the market, and with a little more risk than the market (which is defined as a beta of 1.0), select a lower average beta of around 1.1 or 1.2. For the conservative investor, betas of 0.8 to 1.0 are feasible.

Earlier we mentioned that historical betas are poor predictors of relative market volatility for an individual stock. Future events and circumstances surrounding any one stock can create more or less volatility in its price than it has shown in the past. But for a well-diversified portfolio of stocks, these variances offset each other and average out so that the historical beta *is* a good indication of future relative volatility. The key here is the definition of *well-diversified*. Ideally, to build a 1.0 beta portfolio, one must buy some of every listed stock in the proportion the total market value of its shares bears to the total value of the entire stock market. Of course, this approach is impractical for all but the largest institutional investors. However, there are some rules that have been found to be of significant value in creating a stock portfolio that will generally perform in line with its expected relation to the overall market. The essence of these rules is to approximate the diversification of a major market index, and thereby have your portfolio behave in much the same way.

Diversify by Stock Category

Every portfolio should have at least some portion of its total invested in each of the five categories of stocks discussed in Chapter 17. The amounts will vary with personal preference, judgment, and objectives. For example, an aggressive risk taker might concentrate more money in growth, second-tier growth, and special situation stocks. A conservative investor looking for income might concentrate more in the cyclical and mature growth stocks.

The key is to avoid overconcentration in one area to the total neglect of the others. In the early 1970s, for example, this is exactly what the banks and mutual funds failed to do. Their favorable experience with the stock markets of the 1960s caused them to overemphasize growth stocks, to the neglect of cyclical and mature growth stocks. As a consequence, when the bear market of 1973–74 hit, many of these portfolios fared much worse than the market as a whole.

Diversify by Economic Sector

Nine economic sectors can be identified in which every portfolio should have some representation. These are listed in Table 18-6, along with the approximate proportions in each area in the S&P 500.

To construct this table, each of the 500 stocks in the S&P index was assigned to one of the economic sectors. Where companies have operations in more than one sector, they were placed in the sector where their largest amount of business activity was conducted. By this process, it was determined that, for example, of the total 1981 year-end market value of the S&P 500, 3.2 percent was represented by the total market value of the corporations whose major business activity was in distribution. As you can see, this proportion was down from 5.2 percent in 1975. This means that distribution stocks over those three years fared relatively worse than the S&P index. Conversely, energy stocks performed relatively better (perhaps rebounding from their depressed levels of 1974–1975). Because each economic sector can deviate for a time from the national economic and stock market trends, it is wise to diversify your portfolio according to these percentages if you want your portfolio's performance to approximate that of the S&P 500. You may want to overweight or underweight your portfolio in one area in an attempt to outperform the market. This is

TABLE 18-6

Approximate Diversification of the Stock Market by Economic Sector

Economic Sector (and major examples)	Total Market Value of Stocks in Category as a Percent of S&P 500 Market Value
	1/2/82
Nonconsumer Manufacturing (chemicals, steel, computers)	16.0%
Energy (oil, gas, coal)	23.7
Consumer Manufacturing (food, recreation, autos)	12.5
Services (hotels, restaurants, telephone utilities)	10.6
Health and Education (drugs, publishing)	7.9
Finance (banks, insurance companies, savings and loans)	6.2
Distribution (retailing, wholesaling)	3.2
High Technology	12.5
Transportation (airlines, railroad, truck, bus)	2.1
Resources, natural (copper, aluminum, gold)	1.0
Utilities	4.3

fine as long as you recognize that a wrong guess means that you will *under*perform the averages!

This market diversification strategy does not necessarily mean you must have at least nine stocks in your portfolio with the relative investment in each according to the proportions in Table 18-6. Many stocks do not belong entirely in one group or another. For example, Santa Fe Industries is about two-thirds in transportation (railroad and trucking) and one-third in energy (oil production). Sears Roebuck is nearly half involved in the finance area (Allstate Insurance, Coldwell Banker, and Dean Witter). IT&T is involved a bit in nearly every area.

The principal reason for diversification by economic sector is to reduce the business risk in your portfolio. Business cycles, congressional actions, or international disputes can have a broad effect over all the companies in any one sector, and it would indeed be unfortunate to have your portfolio concentrated in that sector. Or, you may find you have missed the peak in a given sector. Many managers who continued to believe in an energy shortage throughout 1981 found that their portfolios fell faster than the market, as oil company stocks fell by 30 to 50 percent.

Buy and Hold?

If you do not believe you have the time or expertise to follow the market and try to sell near the tops and buy near the lows, perhaps it is best just to buy and hold for long-term investment objectives such as retirement. On the other hand, if this area does interest you, you should study some of the general market books listed at the end of this chapter and give it a try. Of course, you will probably never want to be entirely out of the market (that is, have 100 percent of your stock market portfolio in cash), because no one is *ever* 100 percent sure of predicting a bear market!

Learning from Mistakes

The Sullivans, a 50-year-old couple, inherited a modest sum that they decided to invest for extra retirement income and to pass on to their children, who had all struck out on their own by this time. They did not need the money for the foreseeable future, and the stock market seemed like a reasonable place to invest in 1972. They hired an investment counselor who recommended generally low-to-moderate-risk stocks. 1973 and 1974 were bear market years, and, even though the Sullivans' portfolio was one-third in cash and was faring better than the market averages, they were losing sleep worrying about all the bad news (Watergate, oil shortages, inflation) and felt the stock market might decline indefinitely. In spite of strong advice to the contrary, the Sullivans closed their account with the advisor in September 1974 (two weeks before the market bottomed out), sold all their stocks, and put the money into savings.

In mid-1978, with four good years in the market to give them renewed encouragement, the Sullivans returned to the investment advisor to reopen their account. He asked them whether they could stomach another bear market, and they wisely answered no. They stayed in their fixed dollar investments, and finally did something right. They recognized that, if they continued to invest at market tops and sell

out in a panic at market bottoms, they would see their portfolio soon shrink to insignificance!

GUIDELINES FOR STOCK MARKET INVESTORS

Carefully study these ten guidelines for investing in the stock market. Investors who follow such rules usually do much better over the long run in their securities investments. Take the list to your stock broker sometime. He or she should be able to tell you of several experiences confirming each of the guidelines.

1. *Investigate before you invest.* This time-honored Wall Street maxim is the best preventive for the plague of the "hot tip." At a minimum, you should consult an S&P sheet (Figure 18-6) for the basic history and outlook for the company and its stock. Often, what you may think is inside information is already public knowledge on the S&P sheet.
2. *Avoid buying high and selling low.* This may seem obvious, but too many investors let their emotions tell them to buy when the stock is riding high and the news is good and to sell when the stock is overly depressed and the economy is already in bad shape.
3. *Do not buy too many different stocks.* The average investor does not have time to watch over a portfolio of more than 10 to 20 different stocks. If you want broader diversification, buy a mutual fund.
4. *Begin with quality.* There are too many special kinds of risks for the average beginning investor to deal with when investing in small company, over-the-counter stocks. Start with listed stocks or major OTC stocks.
5. *Diversify.* You will be taking too much risk and relying too much on luck to concentrate on a single stock category or a single economic sector. Your crystal ball just can't be that good.
6. *Do not be afraid to take a loss.* If your stock is down, and its prospects for recovery are poor, sell it and put the proceeds into something that has a good outlook. Don't be "locked in."
7. *Do not sell just for tax-loss write-offs.* If your stock is down, but the prospects for a recovery seem good, keep it!
8. *Wait for the right deal.* If you think stocks are currently high priced and you cannot find a suitable investment, keep your money in a savings account and wait for lower prices. That was a winning strategy in 1968 and 1973.
9. *Accumulate dividends for reinvestment.* This will enable you to achieve the full effect of compounding on your investment dollars (as long as you do not need the current income of the dividends).
10. *Do not use short selling, buying on margin, or puts and calls*—unless you really know what you are doing. That generally means having a full-time commitment or hiring good professional management.

CONCLUSION

This chapter has presented a general overview of the securities markets, sources of information, brokerage houses, and trading techniques. Even if you have time only to buy long, you should at least understand the basic types of orders you can place with your broker, as well as the effects of bull and bear markets. Most importantly, you should be able to construct a diversified portfolio to meet your needs.

VOCABULARY

Amex	limit order
asked price	margin buying
at the market	NYSE
bear market	odd lot
beta	over-the-counter (OTC)
bid price	primary offering
broker	prospectus
bull market	put
buy long	right
call	round lot
commission	SEC
diversification	secondary offering
dollar cost averaging	short sale
Dow Jones averages	specialist
economic sector	stop order
efficient market theory	underwrite
investment banker	warrant

QUESTIONS

1. How is the issuing corporation involved in a primary offering of its stock? How is it involved in the sale of its stock in the secondary market?
2. Why does the average over-the-counter stock have a greater chance of going broke than the average American Stock Exchange stock?
3. What is the most important factor to consider in selecting a broker? Why?
4. Recently ABZ stock has been fluctuating weekly between $31 and $39 a share. If you believe that the stock is a good buy, but do not wish to pay more than $3,300 for 100 shares (before commissions), what order would you give your broker? What would he or she do with the order? What is your risk in using such an order?
5. Compare the usefulness of the Dow Jones averages with that of the New York Stock Exchange index.
6. What qualifications should an investor have before engaging in such activities as selling short or buying on margin? Under what circumstances would it make sense to sell short? To buy on margin?
7. One should always use a stop order at 10 to 20 percent below current market price. Comment on this statement.
8. Assume that your 100 shares of ABZ stock are worth $50 a share, and you paid $100 a share for them 14 months ago. Your marginal tax rate is 40 percent. You believe that the stock has an excellent chance to recover to at least $70 a share during the next six months. Should you sell for the tax write-off or hold the stock? What would be the after-tax dollar loss between selling now and selling at $70 in six months?

General Motors 978

NYSE Symbol GM   Put & Call Options on CBOE

Price	Range	P-E Ratio	Dividend	Yield	S&P Ranking
Aug. 26'82	1982				
47⁷/₈	49¹/₂–34	50	¹2.40	⁵5.0%	B

Summary

This giant, financially sound company accounts for well over half of all the automobiles assembled in the U.S. A deficit was incurred in 1980 for the first time since 1921, and the quarterly dividend rate was reduced. However, a modest profit was reported for 1981, further progress is likely for 1982, and strong earnings improvement appears attainable over the longer term.

Current Outlook

Earnings for 1982 are expected to rise to about $3.75 a share from 1981's $1.07, despite an unfavorable first-half comparison.

The current $0.60 quarterly dividend rate seems likely to hold, although it was not earned in 1980 or 1981, and capital expenditures are expected to average an exceptionally heavy $8 billion annually in the five years through 1984.

Industrywide passenger car and truck assemblies should recover in 1982's second half, but for 1982 are likely to be somewhat below 1981's depressed level. However, earnings will benefit from high average selling prices, a richer product mix, reduced product conversion expenses, major efficiency improvements, and a stock-for-bonds exchange. Better foreign volume also is anticipated.

Sales (Billion $)

Quarter:	1982	1981	1980	1979
Mar.	14.72	15.72	15.71	17.90
Jun.	17.14	18.02	13.79	18.98
Sep.		13.41	12.03	13.31
Dec.		15.55	16.20	16.12
		62.70	57.73	66.31

Sales for 1982's first half declined 5.6%, year to year, on a 12.1% decrease in factory unit sales of cars and trucks. Results were hurt by the lower unit volume and 88% higher interest expense. After a $20.5 million tax credit versus taxes at 50.0%, and a 105% gain in earnings of nonconsolidated affiliates, net income was down 2.4%, to $2.23 a share from $2.35. Foreign exchange translation activity added $1.08 and $0.64 a share to earnings in the respective halves.

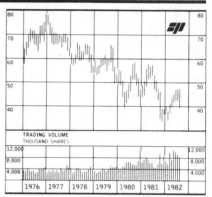

Common Share Earnings ($)

Quarter:	1982	1981	1980	1979
Mar.	0.41	0.63	0.52	4.39
Jun.	1.82	1.72	d1.43	4.13
Sep.		d1.59	d1.95	0.06
Dec.		0.31	0.21	1.46
		1.07	d2.65	10.04

Important Developments

May '82—GM exchanged 1,100,000 shares and $44 million cash for about $140 million principal amount of 8⁵/₈% debentures due 2005 at a gain of about $49 million ($0.16 a share).

Apr. '82—Members of the United Auto Workers Union approved a 2¹/₂-year agreement with GM that has been estimated to save it $2-$3 billion from what labor costs would have been under the old contract.

Next earnings report due in late October.

Per Share Data ($)

Yr. End Dec. 31	1981	1980	1979	1978	1977	1976	1975	1974	1973	1972
Book Value	57.43	59.22	65.30	60.56	54.16	49.18	44.55	42.65	42.86	39.71
Earnings	1.07	d2.65	10.04	12.24	11.62	10.08	4.32	3.27	8.34	7.51
Dividends	2.40	2.95	5.30	6.00	6.80	5.55	2.40	3.40	5.25	4.45
Payout Ratio	224%	NM	53%	49%	58%	55%	55%	104%	63%	59%
Prices—High	58	58⁷/₈	65⁷/₈	66⁷/₈	78¹/₂	78⁷/₈	59¹/₈	55¹/₂	84⁵/₈	84³/₄
Low	33⁷/₈	39¹/₂	49³/₈	53³/₄	61¹/₈	57³/₄	31¹/₄	28⁷/₈	44⁷/₈	71¹/₄
P/E Ratio—	54–32	NM	7–5	5–4	7–5	8–6	14–7	17–9	10–5	11–9

Data as orig. reptd. 1. Rate indicated by latest quarterly. NM-Not Meaningful. d-Deficit.

Standard NYSE Stock Reports   September 2, 1982   Standard & Poor's Corp.
Vol. 49/No. 170/Sec. 8   Copyright © 1982 Standard & Poor's Corp. All Rights Reserved   25 Broadway, NY, NY 10004

FIGURE 18-6
Sample Standard and Poor's Stock Report. The format is similar for all stocks listed. S & P sheets are updated periodically and gathered in a loose-leaf binder.

978

General Motors Corporation

Income Data (Million $)

Year Ended Dec. 31	Revs.	Oper. Inc.	% Oper. Inc. of Revs.	Cap. Exp.	Depr.	Int. Exp.	Net Bef. Taxes	Eff. Tax Rate	Net Inc.	% Net Inc. of Revs.
1981	62,699	4,798	7.7%	9,741	4,406	995	2 210	NM	333	0.5%
1980	57,729	2,992	5.2%	7,762	4,178	532	2 d1,148	NM	d763	NM
1979	66,311	7,853	11.8%	5,387	3,187	368	2 5,076	43.0%	2,893	4.4%
1978	63,221	9,521	15.1%	4,564	3,036	356	2 6,596	46.8%	3,508	5.5%
1977	54,961	8,369	15.2%	3,647	2,387	282	2 6,272	46.8%	3,338	6.1%
1976	47,181	7,257	15.4%	2,307	2,243	284	2 5,471	46.9%	2,903	6.2%
1975	35,725	4,475	12.5%	2,236	2,093	294	2 2,371	47.2%	1,253	3.5%
1974	31,550	3,267	10.4%	2,554	1,711	163	2 1,677	43.4%	950	3.0%
1973	35,798	6,250	17.5%	2,104	1,990	105	2 4,513	46.9%	2,398	6.7%
1972	30,435	5,841	19.2%	1,839	1,793	75	2 4,223	48.8%	2,163	7.1%

Balance Sheet Data (Million $)

Dec. 31	Cash	Current Assets	Current Liab.	Ratio	Total Assets	Ret. on Assets	Long Term Debt	Common Equity	Total Cap.	% LT Debt of Cap.	Ret. on Equity
1981	1,321	13,716	12,555	1.1	38,991	0.9%	4,044	17,438	21,765	18.6%	1.8%
1980	3,715	15,421	12,273	1.3	34,581	NM	2,058	17,531	20,825	9.9%	NM
1979	2,986	16,557	9,868	1.7	32,216	9.1%	880	18,896	20,711	4.2%	15.8%
1978	4,055	18,000	10,051	1.8	30,598	12.3%	979	17,286	19,163	5.1%	21.3%
1977	3,240	15,957	8,327	1.9	26,658	13.1%	1,068	15,483	17,308	6.2%	22.5%
1976	4,625	15,473	7,916	2.0	24,442	12.6%	1,070	14,102	15,927	6.7%	21.5%
1975	3,383	12,840	6,445	2.0	21,665	5.9%	1,223	12,799	14,547	8.4%	9.9%
1974	1,338	11,645	6,103	1.9	20,468	4.7%	877	12,247	13,596	6.4%	7.6%
1973	3,046	12,167	5,970	2.0	20,297	12.4%	757	12,283	13,502	5.6%	20.1%
1972	2,947	10,559	4,974	2.1	18,273	11.9%	791	11,399	12,644	6.3%	19.6%

Data as orig. reptd. **1.** Reflects accounting change. **2.** Incl. equity in earns. of nonconsol. subs. NM-Not Meaningful. d-Deficit.

Business Summary

This giant car and truck producer derived its sales and net income in 1981 as follows:

	Sales	Profits
Automotive products	93%	−20%
Nonautomotive products	7%	120%

In 1981 the U.S. accounted for 208% of total net income, Canada for a loss of 10% and overseas for a loss of 98%.

Various models of the Chevrolet, Buick, Cadillac, Oldsmobile, and Pontiac divisions accounted for 44.5% of total new U.S. car registrations (including foreign-built cars) in 1981, versus 46.4% in 1980. Comparable figures for Chevrolet and GMC trucks are 37.1% in both years. GM has about 10,650 U.S. car dealers. Worldwide factory sales of cars and trucks in 1981 were 6,762,000 units, down 4.8% from 7,101,000 in 1980. Factory sales in the U.S. in 1981 were 3,894,000 cars and 717,000 trucks.

Nonautomotive products include diesel and aircraft engines and locomotives. Earnings of unconsolidated GMAC (vehicle financing and insur-ance) in 1981 rose 58%, to $365.2 million.

Employees: 662,000.

Dividend Data

Dividends have been paid since 1915. A dividend reinvestment plan is available.

Amt. of Divd. $	Date Decl.	Ex-divd. Date	Stock of Record	Payment Date
0.60	Nov. 2	Nov. 5	Nov. 12	Dec. 10'81
0.60	Feb. 1	Feb. 5	Feb. 11	Mar. 10'82
0.60	May 3	May 7	May 13	Jun. 10'82
0.60	Aug. 2	Aug. 6	Aug. 12	Sep. 10'82

Next dividend meeting: early Nov. '82.

Capitalization

Long Term Debt: $4,409,300,000.

$5 Cum. Preferred Stock: 1,835,644 shs. (no par); redeemable at $120.

$3.75 Cum. Preferred Stock: 1,000,000 shs. (no par); redeemable at $100.

Common Stock: 308,000,000 shs. ($1.66⅔ par). Institutions hold about 31%. Shareholders: 1,138,000.

Office—3044 W. Grand Blvd., Detroit, Mich. 48202. Tel—(313) 556-5000 Chrmn & CEO—R. B. Smith. Pres—F. J. McDonald. Secy—C. M. Conklin. Treas & Investor Contact—C. F. Jones (212) 486-5000. Dirs—A. L. Armstrong, C. B. Cleary, J. T. Connor, J. D. deButts, J. H. Evans, W. A. Fallon, C. T. Fisher III, M. L. Goldberger, R. S. Hatfield, R. H. Herzog, J. Horan, R. R. Jensen, H. H. Kehrl, F. J. McDonald, W. E. McLaughlin, T. A. Murphy, E. C. Patterson, E. T. Pratt, Jr., G. P. Shultz, J. G. Smale, F. A. Smith, J. S. Smith, R. B. Smith, L. H. Sullivan, C. H. Townes. Transfer Agents—Company's Offices—767 Fifth Ave., NYC; 3044 W. Grand Blvd., Detroit, Mich. Registrar—Chase Manhattan Bank, NYC. Incorporated in Delaware in 1916.

Information has been obtained from sources believed to be reliable, but its accuracy and completeness are not guaranteed. D.W.B.

FIGURE 18-6
(continued)

9. What advantage does dollar cost averaging have for investors who tend to become emotionally involved in their stock holdings? What possible disadvantage is there for such investors?
10. Where could you find out quickly and easily the corporate history and P/E ratio ranges for a listed stock?
11. What does *beta* mean with regard to common stocks? When is it useful?
12. What does it mean to have a diversified stock portfolio?

CASE PROBLEM

This case is designed to utilize what you have learned from Chapters 17 and 18. Assume that your father inherited a $64,900 portfolio of common stocks. Because he knew little about the stock market and wanted to provide a good educational experience for you, he asked you to evaluate the portfolio and advise him on when to buy and sell the stocks. Your father's investment objective is to obtain long-term growth of capital for his retirement without taking speculative risks. On the other hand, he is not going to worry about interim ups and downs in his portfolio. He has no requirement for current income from the stocks, and so any dividends he receives can be reinvested in the market. As compensation to you, he plans to pay you 1 percent of the total market value of the portfolio each December 31. You will be performing this job in your spare time.

Table 18-7 shows the stocks he inherited. Establish your plans by answering the following questions.

1. What is the percentage amount of each holding currently?
2. What is the current P/E ratio and dividend yield for each of the stocks?
3. How would you classify each stock by stock category?
4. What are the major flaws in diversification by economic sector in this portfolio?
5. Assume you wanted 15 stocks in your final portfolio. What kinds of stocks not already in the portfolio would you buy? Which ones in the portfolio would make good candidates for selling? Why?
6. What average beta probably makes the most sense for your father? Why?
7. Would it ever make sense to hold cash temporarily in the portfolio?
8. What kind of brokerage house and individual broker should you select to help you with this account?
9. What sources would you consult before making your final decisions about what stocks to buy?
10. Under what circumstances might you want to use limit orders or stop orders for this portfolio?
11. Are there circumstances under which you would use margin buying or short selling for this portfolio?

RECOMMENDED READING

GENERAL INFORMATION ABOUT INVESTING IN THE BOND AND STOCK MARKETS

Dougall, Herbert E., and Corrigan, Francis J. *Investments*. 10th ed. Englewood Cliffs, N.J.: Prentice-Hall, 1978.
Excellent comprehensive coverage of the entire field of securities investments.

Engel, Louis, and Wyckoff, Peter. *How to Buy Stocks*. 6th ed. New York: Bantam, 1977.

TABLE 18-7

Facts about Stocks in the Case Problem Portfolio

| Number of Shares | Issue | Current State | | | | Average Annual EPS Growth (past 5 years) | Five-Year P/E Range | Economic Sector[a] |
		Price	EPS	Dividends per Share	Total Sales for Company (millions)			
900	Mutual Life	$ 5	$ .10	$ 0	$ 5.0	+ 8%	20—60	F
500	First Insurance	10	.80	.30	200.0	+10	9—16	F
300	Busy Stores	80	4.00	.80	565.0	+12	11—30	D
300	State Airlines	11	.50	.10	290.0	+ 8	15—22	T
200	Major Oil	12	1.30	.60	600.0	+10	8—18	E
200	State Savings	10	.50	.05	3.5	+11	15—30	F
200	Dyno-research	8	.04	0.00	1.5	+10	180—300	HT
100	Bolt Textiles	60	4.00	2.50	15.0	− 2	6—21	CM
100	City Bank	36	3.00	1.00	450.0	+10	10—16	F
100	Major Steel	25	2.60	1.10	800.0	+40	6—20	NM
100	Z. Gas & Electric	25	2.00	1.30	263.0	+ 8	9—16	U
50	Q. Gas & Electric	18	1.50	1.00	180.0	+ 4	9—14	U
20	N.Y. Mfg.	210	7.00	2.00	394.0	+12	18—42	CM
10	Multitron	240	2.40	.10	32.0	+15	30—105	HT

[a]Abbreviations taken from initial letters of categories shown in Table 18-6: finance, distribution, transportation, energy, high technology, nonconsumer manufacturing, consumer manufacturing, utilities.

This popular book is written simply, but covers every important aspect of stock market investing. It is almost a must for anyone beginning a stock market investment program.

"Instant-Everything Accounts for Investors." *Changing Times*, January 1982.
A review of (1) the things you get with a Merrill Lynch cash management account and (2) some of the competitor firms' accounts with similar features.

"Investment Clubs Are Coming Back." *Changing Times*, April 1981, pp. 46–49.
An article of particular interest for the beginning investor wishing to learn from fellow investors.

Little, Jeffrey B., and Rhodes, Lucien. *Understanding Wall Street*. 6th ed. Cockeysville, Md.: Liberty Publishing Co., 1980.
A comprehensive and easy-to-read guide to stocks and bonds.

Reddig, William. "Investment: The Clubs Come Back." *Money*, September 1981, pp. 123–28.
A good discussion of how investment clubs help people learn about the market and what it takes to set one up and run it.

Rosenberg, Claude N., Jr. *Stock Market Primer*. New York: Warner Books, Inc., 1981.
A readable book that offers common sense rules for the nonprofessional investor, now proven in its fifth edition since 1962.

"Safe Strategies for Small Investors." *Changing Times*, November 1978.
Several conservative approaches to investing for the investor who has little to invest.

Sivy, Michael. "Bonds Unbound." *Money*, August 1981, pp. 55–59.
This article goes beyond the moderate risk strategies discussed in this text by briefly covering all the different types of bonds available to the investor.

"Stock Market Basics for Beginners." *Changing Times*, June 1981, pp. 41–46.
A good overview of the key things you should know to get started as an investor in the stock market.

Williams, Jonathan. "When Brokers Go Broke." *Money*, January 1982, pp. 57–59.
Steps you can take to protect yourself, written by a researcher at John Muir & Co. whose job ended August 17, 1981, when the company went bankrupt.

UNITED STATES ECONOMY, THE STOCK EXCHANGES, AND SPECIFIC INDUSTRIES

Barron's National Business and Financial Weekly.
This weekly tabloid offers information written expressly with the investor's viewpoint in mind.

Brokerage house special reports.
Your broker may occasionally have available special industry or general economic reports that have been prepared by his or her company.

Business Week.
The "Business Outlook" section (two-page weekly summary) in this magazine is very useful for the busy investor. This magazine also has frequent reports on various industries.

Financial sections in major daily newspapers.
Papers such as the *New York Times, Chicago Tribune*, and *Los Angeles Times* have especially good business and financial sections.

Forbes Magazine.
This magazine offers interesting market commentaries and industry and company reports.

Indicator Digest.
Twenty-four issues per year offer market timing information through the use of technical indicators.

New York Stock Exchange Fact Book. Published annually by the NYSE.
This book is crammed with historical facts about the exchange, sales volumes, prices, dividend yields, numbers of shareholders, and so on. A similar publication is published by the American Stock Exchange.

Standard and Poor's Outlook.
This publication offers market analyses.

U.S. News and World Report.
This weekly magazine has coverage of political trends that affect businesspeople and investors.

Value Line Investment Survey.
This weekly advisory service often runs special analyses of industry groups.

Wall Street Journal.
This daily newspaper is the last word in news for the serious investor. The "Outlook" column in the Monday edition gives in-depth analyses of various aspects of the general economy. The column "Keeping Abreast of the Market" offers useful analyses of the stock market. The paper also provides daily market averages and the like.

SPECIFIC STOCKS
Companies themselves.

A company publishes a certain amount of information for the benefit of its stockholders and prospective investors. Such publications include the annual report and quarterly reports, which show the company's income statement and balance sheet. Also, whenever the company issues new stock, it must publish a prospectus describing the new stock and the company.

Moody's Handbook. Published annually.

This publication provides special survey updates as well as good summary information concerning most major industries.

Standard and Poor's Stock Guide. Published monthly.

This excellent summary of almost all publicly traded stocks provides much of the basic information that an investor needs before making an in-depth survey of a stock. This information includes prices, dividends, P/E ratios, earnings, and the Standard and Poor's ranking from A through C on the stability and growth of earnings and dividends. It is generally available from your broker.

Value Line Investment Survey.

This weekly advisory service gives excellent, up-to-date statistical summaries on individual stocks.

CHUCK AND NANCY ANDERSON

Their Securities Trading Account

As we saw in Chapter 15, Chuck and Nancy selected common stocks as the investment medium for their low-priority goal—the motorboat. They favored mutual funds for their other goals because of their limited time and expertise.

The Andersons have a margin account and have borrowed $1,500 from their broker. Although they sometimes ask him for his opinion, they usually find a couple of hours once or twice a month for research and stock selection on their own, and then they plan the timing of purchases and sales.

Questions

1. Should the Andersons maintain the loan in their margin account? Why or why not?
2. Should they do any short selling? Why or why not?
3. Should the Andersons try mostly for long-term or short-term trading gains? Why do you think so?
4. Should they invest in two to four stocks or five to seven stocks at the beginning of their boat investment program? Why do you think so?

19

Mutual Funds and Other Professional Management

The fifth-floor staff at the Automatic Tractor Company often talked about the stock market during their lunch hour. One of them, Bernie, was regarded as the expert, since he had achieved a 15 to 20 percent return each of the three years that he had been active in the stock market. Although Bernie spent a lot of time researching and investing in the market, he was frustrated that he currently had only about $3,000 for investment purposes and had to pay so much in commissions on small trades.

One noon hour, Kathy and Tony were talking with Bernie about the market. Neither Kathy nor Tony had ever been much involved in investing. As Tony put it: "I just don't have time to fool with all those charts, pamphlets, and notebooks that you spend so much time on, Bernie. Besides, I'd rather invest for long-term gains, but I have only enough to buy stock in one or two companies. And, if either of those stocks turned out to be a lemon—brother! I just can't live with that kind of risk."

"Well, then," Kathy interjected, "what we need to do is pool our money somehow and pay Bernie some percentage of the assets to manage the money for us. Then we would have three advantages. One, we'd have our expert taking care of the investment chores and responsibilities. Two, we could minimize our commission costs by buying bigger blocks of stock. And three, we would have enough money to buy several different stocks and, if one turned out to be a real loser, we wouldn't get hurt so badly because our risk would be spread."

"That's a great idea!" exclaimed Bernie and Tony. With that, the three of them wrote up an agreement and tried to get other fifth-floor staffers to join their Fifth-Floor Mutual Investment Fund.

Ten people joined the group. Each invested $1,000 and received 100 $10 shares in return. At the end of one year, Bernie's efforts showed some real success. The fund had achieved a 14 percent growth in portfolio value. The original $10,000 was now worth $11,400. So the unit asset value per share had risen from $10 to $11.40. The stocks owned by the fund also earned dividends amounting to $274. After Bernie's fee of 1 percent ($114) of the portfolio value was subtracted, $160 in dividends was distributed to the 10 fund shareholders—$16 each. The Fifth-Floor Mutual Investment Fund was indeed proud of its first year's record.

WHAT ARE MUTUAL FUNDS?

The concept of a mutual fund is fairly simple. An investment company sells its mutual fund shares to individual investors, pools the dollars gained from the sale of such shares, and—depending on its investment objective—invests them in common stocks and publicly held companies, in preferred stocks, or in corporate and government bonds. The company continues to buy and sell investments on a regular basis as it finds appropriate opportunities to do so.

The mutual fund industry began as a public business in this country in the early 1920s, but its main development came after World War II (see Table 19-1). Today, there are more than 600 mutual funds with assets ranging from a few million dollars to over a billion dollars. All these mutual funds together control over $50 billion in

TABLE 19-1

Growth of Mutual Funds
(Excluding money market funds)[a]

Calendar Year End	Number of Reporting Funds	Number of Shareholder Accounts	Total Assets (billions)
1940	68	296,056	$ .4
1950	98	938,651	2.5
1960	161	4,897,600	17.0
1970	361	10,690,312	47.6
71	392	10,900,952	55.0
72	410	10,635,287	59.8
73	421	10,330,862	46.5
74	416	9,970,400	34.1
75	390	9,712,500	42.2
76	404	8,879,400	47.6
77	427	8,515,100	45.0
78	444	8,190,600	45.0
79	446	7,482,200	49.0
1980	458	7,212,000	58.4
81	n.a.	7,193,100[b]	51.6[b]

Source: Investment Company Institute, *1981 Mutual Fund Fact Book* (Washington, D.C.: Investment Company Institute, 1981), p. 11.

[a]For money market fund data, see Table 16-6.

[b]Investment Company Institute release for period ending 9/30/81.

TABLE 19-2

Assets of Major Institutions and Financial Intermediaries
(billions of dollars)

Savings Institutions	1970	1974	1977	1980
Commercial Banks	$576.7	$919.6	$1,145.4	$1,576.6
Credit Unions	17.9	32.0	54.1	71.7
Mutual Savings Banks	79.0	109.6	147.2	171.8
Savings and Loan Associations	176.2	295.5	459.2	629.7
Life Insurance Companies	207.3	263.3	350.5	477.3
Bank Administered Trusts	292.2	325.3	502.7	503.0a
Mutual Funds				
Closed end	6.1	9.0	7.4	7.8
Open endb	47.7	35.8	48.5	134.8
Pension Funds				
Private	104.7	111.7	181.6	225.2a
Government (book value)	123.7	176.5	221.9	n.a.

Source: Investment Company Institute, *1981 Mutual Fund Fact Book* (Washington, D.C.: Investment Company Institute, 1981), p. 64.

a Figure shown is for 1979. 1980 not available.

b Includes money market funds.

total assets. Out of every $30 worth of stock on the New York Stock Exchange, $1 is held by mutual funds.° Of course, as you can see from Table 19-2, mutual funds are still a relatively small factor in the investment marketplace, compared to bank trusts, pension funds, and other such institutional investors.

There are over seven million shareholder accounts outstanding, the average size of which is about $7,000.

An Investment Company Grows: Fifth-Floor Mutual Investment Fund

Once the news of the success of the Fifth-Floor Mutual Investment Fund spread around the office, many people who had been skeptical of the fund wanted to invest with it. The 10 original investors held a meeting to decide what to do.

Tony was the first to speak as Bernie opened the floor for discussion. "I think we ought to let well enough alone. We have 1,000 shares outstanding and this seems to be about right. Let's not let a good thing get out of hand! Only if somebody wants to leave the fund should anyone else be allowed in. The newcomer can buy the shares from the person who is leaving."

Kathy felt differently. "I don't see anything wrong with bigger size. The more the merrier! Besides, one of the current shareholders might want to increase his investment in the fund. Why not print share certificates for anyone who wants to buy them?" Bernie then said, "Also, we ought to provide a way for someone to leave the fund. Calvin is to be transferred to West Lockport in a month, and he ought to be

° Investment Company Institute, *Mutual Fund Fact Book* (Washington, D.C.: Investment Company Institute, 1981), p.16.

able to sell his shares back to the fund—rather than have to find someone else to buy them. He should be able to cash in his shares and collect the net asset value per share as of that date."

The 10 members voted in favor of the last two proposals.

Types of Investment Companies

There are two basic types of investment companies: closed end and open end. Neither of these allows the stockholder to participate in stock voting rights. The fund management votes as it sees fit the common stock shares that the fund holds. However, the mutual fund shareholder does have voting rights on some fund business, such as fund share splits. Both types of investment companies customarily take their management fees as a percentage of net assets. A single group of managers may manage more than one investment company; such groups are known as families of funds. All publicly held investment companies are regulated by the SEC. Table 19-3 summarizes the differences between closed-end and open-end companies, as will be discussed next.

closed-end companies   These companies issue a fixed number of shares that are traded like common stocks either on organized exchanges or over the counter. The cost of buying and selling such shares is the standard broker's commission for stock transactions. Closed-end companies account for less than 10 percent of total investment company assets. In our example of the Fifth-Floor Mutual Investment Fund, the fund would have become a closed-end company if the fund holders had decided not to issue any new shares.

open-end companies   These companies (popularly called mutual funds, although the term really applies to both types) continually sell and redeem their shares to meet investor demand, with no limit on the total number to be sold. The

TABLE 19-3

Comparison of Closed-End and Open-End Companies

Characteristic	Closed-End Fund	Open-End Fund
Number of shares issued	Fixed	Variable
New share offerings	Once	Continuous
Price	Varies with supply and demand; may be above or below NAV	Net asset value (NAV) plus sales charge, if any
From whom bought	From another shareholder in the same way as common stocks	From the company either directly or through a broker or salesperson
To whom sold	To another investor in the same way as common stocks	Redeemed by the company at NAV

price is equal to the *net asset value (NAV)* per share of the fund. This value is computed at the end of each business day, when liabilities are subtracted from the market value of the fund's assets, and the resulting figure is divided by the number of shares outstanding. For example, at the end of a business day a fund might have net assets consisting of $98,000,000 in common stock, $4,000,000 in cash holdings, and $500,000 in cash from the sale of new shares that day. From this total of $102,500,000 the fund subtracts its liabilities and bills due, which might amount to $300,000. This leaves $102,200,000 in net assets. If the fund had 9,950,000 fund shares outstanding yesterday and sold 50,000 new shares today, the total shares outstanding would be 10,000,000. Therefore, the net asset value per share at the close of business that day would be $10.22 ($102,200,000 ÷ 10,000,000). This would be the price at which shares would be redeemed by the fund the next day (the bid price). In our example of the Fifth-Floor Mutual Investment Fund, the fund holders' decision to issue new shares caused the fund to become an open-end company.

A sales charge, called a *load*, may be added when the fund sells its shares. *Load funds* (those with a sales charge) sell their shares through regular stockbrokers and/or salespeople employed by one or more investment companies. Sales commissions are charged only on purchases you make; you can sell your shares back to the company without charge. The bid price of a load fund share is its net asset value; the asked price is equal to the net asset value plus the sales commission. A listing may read, for example, "N Fund $11.12–$12.15." You could buy shares that day at $12.15 each and sell them back at $11.12 each (the net asset value). Commissions usually average 7.5 to 8.5 percent of the net asset price of the stock. For sizable purchases (around $25,000 or more) the commission rate is usually reduced. Some of these funds can be purchased through payroll deduction plans. Under these circumstances the load charge is often 1 to 3 percent.

No-load funds charge no sales commissions because there are no salespeople. Shares are bought and sold directly from the company, either through the mail or over the phone. The bid and asked prices quoted in the newspaper are the same and, therefore, equal to the net asset value. However, a few no-load funds charge a 1 or 2 percent commission to redeem shares.

The sales commission should not be the deciding factor in buying a load or no-load fund. It is not wise to buy a no-load fund simply to save the sales charge. A poorly managed no-load fund may yield a poorer return on your investment than a well-managed load fund. Always check a fund's past record to get an idea of its management quality. However, everything else being equal, you should avoid the 8 percent commission of a load fund.

MUTUAL FUNDS CLASSIFIED BY PORTFOLIO AND INVESTMENT OBJECTIVE

Depending on its objectives, a mutual fund's investment holdings (portfolio) may include primarily common stocks, or bonds, or preferred stocks, or even mutual funds; or it may include both stocks and bonds. Those funds that concentrate on common stocks may specialize in particular stock types such as high dividend or growth stocks or those relating to certain industries. The investment company's prospectus outlines the objectives of the fund.

TABLE 19-4

Types of Mutual Funds

Type of Fund	Type of Portfolio	Investment Objectives
Diversified Common Stock	Income-growth	Income primary; long-term growth secondary
	Growth stock	Long-term growth with some income
	Speculative stock	Aggressive growth; high appreciation potential
	Specially selected stocks	Unusual price appreciation
	Specialization in an industry or related industries	Varies
	International securities	Varies
Bond	Corporate and government bonds	Safe and relatively stable rate of return
	Tax-exempt state and municipal bonds	Safe and relatively stable tax-free income
Mutual Fund	Selected mutual funds	Wide diversification; long-term growth
Balanced (bond-stock)	Common and preferred stocks; corporate and government bonds	Relatively safe fixed return from bonds; chance for growth through capital gains from stock investment
Money Market (See Chapter 16)	Bank certificates of deposit, short-term government bonds, and the like	Relatively safe return; interest income varying with current available rates

Table 19-4 shows how the portfolio typically relates to the investment objectives for each type of fund. This classification scheme is one of several. Each of the fund information services listed at the end of this chapter has its own system. The key point to keep in mind is that you should read the prospectus to see how any particular mutual fund defines its investment objectives.

Diversified Common Stock Funds

These are one of the most popular types of mutual funds. By and large, the best long-term capital gains records are found in growth funds. Figure 19-1 shows a typical portfolio for a growth fund: risks are spread over a variety of growth stocks. A few funds are so completely diversfied that they call themselves *index funds*; that is, their performance is designed to parallel closely one of the popular market indices. Many of the funds that invest in speculative stocks (the so-called "go-go" funds and hedge funds) often use trading techniques such as short selling, margin buying, and puts and calls. The record of most funds using these techniques does not indicate superior results, although they are more volatile.

Number of Shares	Market Value	Number of Shares	Market Value
Airlines (1.3%)		Petroleum (12%)	
150,000 American	$1,200,000	75,000 Exxon	$ 6,000,000
47,000 Delta	1,400,000	22,000 Halliburton	3,000,000
	$2,600,000	200,000 Standard Oil (Indiana)	8,000,000
		60,000 Phillips	3,000,000
Aerospace (1.5%)		174,000 Texaco	4,000,000
83,000 Boeing	$2,000,000		$24,000,000
66,000 Cessna	1,000,000		
	$3,000,000	Cosmetics (2.3%)	
		100,000 Avon Products	$4,600,000
Amusement and Recreation (4%)			$4,600,000
110,000 Walt Disney	$5,000,000		
18,000 Holiday Inns	2,000,000	Drugs (9.4%)	
11,000 Milton Bradley	1,000,000	150,000 Becton-Dickinson	$ 6,000,000
	$8,000,000	64,000 Merck	5,000,000
		85,000 Syntex	3,000,000
Chemicals (3%)		52,000 Johnson & Johnson	4,800,000
30,000 Dow	$3,000,000		$18,800,000
40,000 Hercules	1,000,000		
30,000 Monsanto	2,000,000	Electronics (9.5%)	
	$6,000,000	170,000 AMP	$ 5,000,000
		400,000 Sony	4,000,000
Financial Services (5.5%)		80,000 General Electric	4,000,000
60,000 J.P. Morgan	$ 3,000,000	50,000 Texas Instruments	5,000,000
170,000 Franklin Life	3,000,000	25,000 Motorola	1,000,000
70,000 Connecticut General	3,000,000		$19,000,000
110,000 NLT	2,000,000		
	$11,000,000	Photographic Products (5.5%)	
		80,000 Eastman Kodak	$ 8,000,000
Food Products (6%)		80,000 Polaroid	3,000,000
100,000 Annheuser-Busch	$ 4,000,000		$11,000,000
210,000 Beatrice Foods	5,000,000		
100,000 General Foods	3,000,000	Public Utilities (4%)	
	$12,000,000	54,000 Florida Power & Light	$2,000,000
		170,000 Continental Telephone	2,000,000
Housing (4.5%)		130,000 Houston Industries	3,000,000
150,000 Ryan Homes	$3,000,000	90,000 Sierra Pacific Power	1,000,000
160,000 Skyline Corp.	2,400,000		$8,000,000
90,000 Weyerhauser	3,600,000		
	$9,000,000	Miscellaneous (10.0%)	
		88,000 Phelps Dodge	$ 3,000,000
Machinery (2%)		50,000 Hewlett-Packard	5,000,000
100,000 Black & Decker	$2,200,000	20,000 Ford Motor	1,000,000
70,000 Clark Equipment	1,800,000	142,000 H & R Block	2,000,000
	$4,000,000	90,000 Minnesota Mining	
		& Manufacturing	5,500,000
Merchandising (4.5%)		16,000 Pinkerton's	500,000
70,000 Sears	$5,000,000	100,000 Santa Fe Industries	3,000,000
250,000 Lucky Stores	4,000,000		$20,000,000
	$9,000,000		
		Cash and Equivalents (5.5%)	
Office Equipment (9.5%)		Corporate bonds	$ 5,000,000
10,000 Burroughs	$ 1,000,000	Certificates of deposit	3,000,000
80,000 IBM	16,000,000	Net cash	3,000,000
40,000 Xerox	2,000,000		$11,000,000
	$19,000,000		
		TOTAL ASSETS (100%)	$200,000,000

Note: Figures rounded for convenience.

FIGURE 19-1
Sample portfolio for a growth-oriented fund.

A relatively new breed of mutual funds are those that specialize in investing in the stocks of companies listed on foreign stock exchanges, such as London, Tokyo, Paris, or Hong Kong. At times, there are better opportunities and economic growth in other countries than in the United States. These foreign markets also give better diversification, since they generally do not all move in unison. Some funds focus on certain countries whereas others take a broader view.

Bond Funds

Bond funds offer the small investor the opportunity to invest in a diversified portfolio of corporate or municipal bonds, depending on the fund's stated objective. In order to offer the high income yields (after fund expenses) sought by investors in such funds, the portfolio often includes lesser rated (A and BBB) issues than was recommended in Chapter 17. In addition, the funds usually invest only in par bonds, which offer greater downside risks and less upside potential than is provided by bonds selling at a discount from par, whenever interest rates change. In an attempt to increase the rate of return to the investor, bond funds engage in considerable buying and selling of bonds, always trying to sell bonds with lower yields in order to buy ones with higher yields. Many studies suggest that such trading usually covers the transaction costs, but is of little net value to the investor, except for short periods of time when one fund happens to be luckier than another.

unit trusts   These are fixed portfolios of bonds specializing in either corporate or municipals. Usually assembled by large brokerage houses, they are offered in units to their investor clients, priced to yield currently competitive interest rates. No new bonds are added to the trust and none are sold. When a bond matures, the proceeds are distributed to the investors. Eventually the trust liquidates itself.

The sales charge on a unit trust is typically 3 to 4½ percent, but there is no annual management fee and annual operating expenses are less than 0.2 percent. Thus, over time these trusts may have lower expenses than a no-load mutual fund in bonds. These are probably a good way for a small investor to get a diversified portfolio of bonds. However, these are par bonds and do not fully offer the advantages of discount bonds as discussed in Chapter 17.

Mutual Fund Funds

This breed of mutual fund spreads its risk over the many stocks of many mutual funds. Such a fund is allowed to charge only 1 to 3 percent load commission. Otherwise, the investor might have to pay an 8 percent load plus a 1 percent management fee on top of the 4 to 5 percent commission paid by the fund when it buys the shares of other mutual funds. In general, the multilayered fee structure tends to argue against owning this type of fund.

Balanced Funds

With balanced funds, the proportion of money invested in bonds and stocks varies. When stocks become high-priced, the fund may gradually transfer its investment into bonds (vice versa when stocks have experienced a long decline in price). The bonds offer protection against recessions, and the stocks offer some protection against inflation. Although risk is thus minimized, so is the chance for above-average investment return. However, for the investor with only a few thousand dollars who wants a diversified portfolio of *both* stocks and bonds, this is an attractive alternative.

Money Market Funds

Since money market funds are really more similar to a savings account than to a mutual fund, they have already been discussed in Chapter 16.

SPECIAL FEATURES OF OPEN-END MUTUAL FUNDS

All funds in the mutual fund listings in your newspaper are of the open-end variety. You may buy and sell shares at net asset value from the company at any time. There may or may not be a sales commission, depending on whether it is a load or no-load fund.

If you buy into an open-end mutual fund on an irregular basis, the minimum purchase each time may range from $100 to $1,000. Most funds allow you to purchase a straight dollar amount, regardless of the price per share. For example, if you buy $300 worth of a fund (after commissions) whose net asset value is $22 per share, your account would be credited with 300/22, or 13.636 shares. If you wish to buy a mutual fund in smaller amounts than their normal minimum investments, you may use their savings accumulation plan.

Savings Accumulation Plan

With a savings accumulation plan you agree to invest fixed amounts at regular intervals. Monthly or quarterly investment minimums generally range from $25 to $100. Such an investment method follows the principle of dollar cost averaging. Also, the notice you receive helps foster a program of regular savings and investment.

The plans offered include contractual and voluntary accumulation plans. Under a *contractual accumulation plan*, the investor agrees to invest a specified amount over a specified number of years—for example, $10,000 over 10 years; commissions are paid on the shares only as they are purchased; there is no penalty for not making a payment. Contractual plans are offered only by load funds.

The *voluntary accumulation plan* (offered by all mutual funds) has no fixed total dollar amount or number of years of payments. The investor simply invests a certain minimum amount on specified dates, usually monthly or quarterly, when a reminder comes from the company. If you do not maintain a regular investment habit, eventually the company will remove you from the plan, however, and put you on a normal (irregular purchase) account; on such an account, your minimum required investment per payment will probably be higher.

Automatic Reinvestment Plan

Automatic reinvestment plans are offered by mutual funds to enable investors to reinvest their earnings at no extra commission, thereby automatically compounding their investment. This plan may be for just dividends or for both dividends and capital gains distributions. Most voluntary plans require automatic reinvestment of dividends and capital gains distributions into fund shares at no extra sales commission.

Dividends represent the dividends and interest received by the fund from its investments, less management fees and operating costs. These dividends are taxed as a part of your ordinary gross income, whether they are reinvested or not. The dividends may be reinvested automatically in whole and fractional shares of the fund at no extra charge if you so request or if required by your voluntary plan.

Capital gains distributions represent the capital gains that the fund has realized through the profitable sale of some of its stock holdings. Such distributions may also be reinvested automatically in whole and fractional shares of the fund at no extra charge.

Table 19-5 shows the results of investing $10,000 in 1954 in a fictitious mutual fund that seeks long-term growth by investing in a diversified portfolio of common

TABLE 19-5

Value of Investment Alternatives as of December 1981
(Based on $10,000 initial investment in 1954)

Investment Alternative	Value of Shares at Net Asset Value	Not Reinvested		Total Value	Compound Annual Return
		Dividends	Capital Gains Distributions		
Mutual Fund Dividends and capital gains taken in cash	$ 46,200	$17,700	$14,200	$ 78,100	7.9%
Capital gains reinvested	76,100	26,800		102,900	9.0
Capital gains and dividends reinvested	118,800			118,800	9.6
Common Stocks (dividends taken in cash)				133,600[a]	10.1
Savings Account (dividends left to compound)				44,550[b]	5.7

Note: No adjustments have been made for taxes on dividends, interest, or capital gains.

[a] Assumes a total return equal to the NYSE composite index plus dividends equal to the median dividend yield.

[b] Assumes an average annual interest rate available in the United States on passbook savings from 1954 through 1978, and on money market fund yields from 1979 through 1981.

stocks. This fund represents a composite of several large funds with above-average performance. Some funds have done better; many have done worse. Nevertheless, at the end of 1981, the value of the original shares was $46,200 and the cumulative value of the reinvested capital gains distributions was $29,900, for a total share asset value of $76,100, plus $26,800 in dividends.

What would have happened to the $10,000 investment if both dividends and capital gains distributions had been reinvested? What would have happened if the $10,000 had been invested in average common stocks or in a savings account and money market funds? Table 19-5 shows how compounding affects the total return from the mutual fund investment when greater and greater portions of the investment income are reinvested. The value of the savings account and money market funds would be much lower than that for any of the other investments. The stock investment should be compared solely with the mutual fund plan that reinvests both capital gains and dividends. In this case, the mutual fund underperformed the stock market by about $14,800. This difference probably reflects either the management fee or the fund's management expertise or both.

Systematic Withdrawal Plans

All open-end mutual funds offer one or more types of systematic withdrawal plans provided you have at least $10,000 worth of shares when you start the plan. These plans allow you to draw income from your investment as you need it, leaving the rest invested in the fund. You simply authorize the fund to send a regular check until you authorize a change or until the money runs out. There often are four types of plans offered:

1. *Fixed dollar amount plan.* The investment company pays you a fixed amount each month or quarter, as you designate. There is usually a minimum withdrawal of $50 a period. Each payment is mailed directly to you. The company redeems only enough shares to meet the payment.
2. *Fixed number of shares plan.* The payments vary, depending on the current asset value of the shares. The monthly or quarterly minimum is usually $50. Under this plan, you avoid excessive depletion of your investment during periods of low stock prices. You have to be willing to accept lower monthly payments, but in periods of high stock prices, your payments are higher. Of course, you own only a fixed number of shares (plus those from any automatic reinvestment plans) and eventually your fund will run out.
3. *Percentage of asset growth plan.* This plan assures that your investment will never be depleted. For example, say you authorize 80 percent of the asset growth to be paid to you each quarter. If there is no growth in that quarter, you get no payment.
4. *Dividends and capital gains distributions plan.* The principal is not touched, but is allowed to accumulate toward your estate or other goals. Only dividends and capital gains distributions are sent to you. Such a plan offers a good chance to stay ahead of inflation. In 1954, for example, typical total dividends from a $10,000 investment were $380. By 1981 your annual dividend income would have been $1,900 and your original $10,000 investment would still have grown

to $46,200. In addition, you would have received an irregular capital gains distribution.

None of these plans is permanent. At any time you can choose a different option or take out all the money. Your choice of a plan depends on how much other income you have, how much you want to leave to your heirs, and how long you want your mutual fund income to last. If you have an investment in a diversified growth stock fund and you want it to yield regular payments for at least 10 years, you should withdraw no more than $140 a year per $1,000 invested. If you want your funds to last at least 20 years, then you should take out no more than $95 a year per $1,000 invested. These guidelines assume an average rate of return of 7 percent. This return is intentionally set low in case the early years are declining ones. Should this happen, a high rate of withdrawals, combined with the reduced market value, would leave the investor with too small a base on which to earn a return in future years.

Insurance against Loss

Since 1969, it has been possible to get insurance against loss of value in several of the mutual funds. Under such plans, you can buy insured shares, guaranteeing that at the end of 10, 12.5, or 15 years (terms selected by the fund) you will suffer no dollar loss on your investment. This insurance usually costs about 6 percent of the total investment, spread over the term of the coverage. Shares must be held the full term of the plan, and all dividends and capital gains distributions must be reinvested. If you quit the plan early, you have no more insurance, and you owe no more payments.

In our opinion, such plans merely serve to help sell fund shares during bear-market periods. They are not worth losing investment flexibility for 10 to 15 years. After all, there have been very few instances when any claims would have been paid had such a program been in force, and those losses would have been small.

IRA and KEOGH

Approved retirement plans are offered by most open-end mutual funds, and these are probably the best place to put a relatively small (less than $10,000 or $20,000) IRA or Keogh plan.

Although banks and savings and loans charge no fee for their IRAs, they offer only fixed dollar investment programs, which have rather low interest rates—barely above the inflation rate—when averaged over the years. Brokerage house plans offer flexibility in investing, but their minimum fee schedules make them unattractive until a plan is larger.

A mutual fund family (i.e., a group of funds with different objectives but handled by the same management firm) offers a flexible investment program and relatively low cost. The extra charge levied by management for providing the IRA or Keogh legal structure is usually only about $5 a year. You can switch your money from fund to fund, or spread it over different funds, with just a phone call. For no-load funds there is usually no fee for such transfers.

Select mutual fund families that offer a broad choice of objectives and have a history of good performance. Among the choices, we recommend the high-income, lower-risk alternatives—money market fund, bond fund, or income-oriented stock fund—since distributions from your IRA or Keogh will be taxed as ordinary income, regardless of the nature of your investment profit. Your capital gains risk should be taken in your personal investments, outside the IRA or Keogh, where you can be rewarded for taking that risk through the favorable capital gains tax.

To learn more about the details of these IRAs and how easy they are to use, write to one or more of the following better no-load fund families for their information kit.

Fidelity, 82 Devonshire St., Boston, MA 02109
Neuberger & Berman, 342 Madison Ave., New York, NY 10173
T. Rowe Price, 100 East Pratt Street, Baltimore, MD 21202
Value Line, 711 Third Ave., New York, NY 10017

Most other mutual funds also offer IRA and Keogh programs, and so your choice is not limited to those above.

A CLOSER LOOK AT CLOSED-END FUNDS

The market price of the shares of closed-end funds is generally different from the net asset value. Since closed-end funds issue a fixed number of shares, investors may place a special value on the prospects of the fund or of the market or on the dividend yield. As with common stocks, the law of supply and demand determines the market price. While most closed-end shares sell at a discount from their net asset value, a few sometimes sell at a premium above this value. You may purchase a closed-end fund through your broker just as you would purchase a common stock.

Advantages of Closed-End Funds

If you buy a closed-end fund at a discount, you will probably sell it at a discount. However, there may be an advantage to this. The amount of the dividend is generally related to the net asset value. When you can buy a closed-end fund at an amount below net asset value, your effective yield may be higher than it would be on an open-end fund purchased at the same price. This is because the cash dividend yield on the closed-end fund is computed on a smaller per-share price.

Another possible advantage is related to the restriction on the total number of shares outstanding. When an open-end fund is very successful, many new investors may buy shares, hoping to take advantage of the success. This phenomenon may easily triple the size of the assets of a smaller fund in less than a year. The fund may temporarily become too unwieldy for the existing management and go into a slump or be unable to sustain its previous growth rate. Closed-end funds, however, have only one means of growth in the size of their total assets: the increase in value of the investments held by these funds. This growth is distinctly different from increasing the size of total assets by selling more shares. Thus, a closed-end fund avoids the problem of becoming too large too quickly.

Disadvantages of Closed-End Funds

No savings accumulation plan is provided by closed-end funds. Also, to reinvest the dividends you receive, you must pay the regular broker's commission, and there is no systematic withdrawal plan.

TAX ASPECTS OF MUTUAL FUNDS

The investment company, if it is highly specialized and nondiversified, receives the same tax treatment as any other corporation. Diversified investment companies (which include most closed-end and open-end funds) pay no federal income taxes, provided certain restrictions are met. In other words, the profits from your investment in a mutual fund flow directly to you: you are the only one who must pay taxes.

Each year, the mutual fund shareholder must pay ordinary income taxes on dividends received, and capital gains taxes on capital gains distributions and on gains resulting from the sale of fund shares held for more than one year. These dividends qualify for the $100 federal income tax dividend exclusion ($200 on a joint return), but only if they are from a common stock mutual fund. Some states, such as California, treat capital gains distributions as ordinary income for state income tax purposes.

HOW DO MUTUAL FUNDS RATE AS AN INVESTMENT?

Mutual funds provide a way for the small investor to invest in a broadly diversified portfolio of stocks and/or bonds, depending on the mutual fund that is selected. As we discussed in Chapter 15, diversification is vital to minimizing the risks involved in investing. An investment in a mutual fund may be spread over 40 to 100 stocks. You could not do this on your own because of the time and effort involved in managing a large portfolio. With mutual funds, professionals do the worrying about when and what to buy and sell. Only if you become discontented with their results must you consider changing your investment.

Professional management, however, does not assure good results. Although individual managers range from poor to excellent, the average mutual fund manager does no better and no worse than the market in general over the long term. In many cases, superior performance seems to be due to nothing more than luck. Some of the stock funds at the top of the list for one 10-year period may find themselves near the bottom in another 10-year period.

Mutual fund returns are, on the average, a reflection of the performance of the stock or bond markets that they invest in. As we saw in Chapters 17 and 18, stocks and bonds are volatile investments that go through cycles. The 1969–78 period was particularly poor for common stock investments, but other periods were generally profitable. Table 19-6 shows how these trends affected mutual fund results.

Short-term fluctuations must be expected. Like common stocks or long-term bonds, mutual funds are a long-term investment. If you invest for a short time only, you may have to sell during bear market conditions. So the primary dangers to be aware of when investing in mutual funds are selecting a poorly managed mutual

TABLE 19-6

Average Common Stock Mutual Fund Results for Five-Year Periods Since 1950
(All distributions reinvested)

Period	Liquidating Value of $10,000 Initial Investment	Period	Liquidating Value of $10,000 Initial Investment
1950-54	$21,241	1965-69	$13,555
1951-55	20,492	1966-70	11,119[a]
1952-56	19,155	1967-71	13,764
1953-57	15,396	1968-72	12,040[a]
1954-58	21,299	1969-73	8,448[a]
1955-59	16,394	1970-74	7,317[a]
1956-60	14,135	1971-75[b]	11,029[a]
1957-61	16,372	1972-76[b]	11,937[a]
1958-62	16,156	1973-77[b]	9,265[a]
1959-63	13,716	1974-78[b]	11,554[a]
1960-64	14,167	1975-79[b]	19,050
1961-65	16,137	1976-80[b]	17,815
1962-66	12,234[a]	1977-81[b]	13,704
1963-67	17,676		
1964-68	17,451		

Source: Adapted from *FundScope*, ed. Allen Silver (Los Angeles: May 1972, p. 106 and May 1975, p. 38.)

[a] Investing $10,000 in a 6 percent savings account (compounded daily) would result in $13,510 in five years.

[b] Figures for periods ending after 1974 are calculated assuming the total return on the S&P 500 minus 1 percent a year, to approximate actual mutual fund performance.

fund and investing for only a short period of time during which the stock market declines. In either case, you could lose money.

Bear in mind that professional management has its costs too. One study showed that even the average common stock funds tended to perform 0.5 to 1 percent worse per year than the stock market averages.° This difference is probably due to the management fee.

Mutual funds offer several features besides diversification and professional management that may be advantageous. You can fairly easily match your goals with the investment because the fund is required to show you a prospectus before you buy and the prospectus states the fund's goals in plain language. An accumulation plan can help you develop a regular savings habit. A systematic withdrawal plan can help you avoid quick dissipation of your investment. There is also the advantage of capital gains tax rates.

GUIDELINES FOR BUYING A MUTUAL FUND

The following points of consideration should help you choose between the hundreds of mutual funds available.

1. *Investment goals.* The investment goals of the fund should match your own.

_____
°William F. Sharpe, "Mutual Fund Performance," *Journal of Business* (January 1966), pp. 119–35.

Before you invest, examine the fund's prospectus to find out the objectives of the fund's management.

2. *Closed-end versus open-end.* Do you want the size restrictions of a closed-end fund? Would you prefer to have the various accumulation, reinvestment, and withdrawal plans available with open-end funds? (Remember, with closed-end funds you will also have the cost of standard brokerage commissions and the problems of a market price that may fluctuate slightly more than the asset value of the stocks held by the fund.)

3. *Sales commission.* This charge can range from nothing (for a no-load fund) to 8.5 percent of the amount of each purchase. The management fees, which may range from 0.5 to 1 percent a year for most funds, are of little consequence in fund comparisons.

4. *Past record.* Mutual funds are continually starting up. Generally, the younger the fund, the less experienced the management and the shorter the record that you have to look at. One year in a bull market would not be representative. However, if a new fund is simply a new addition to an old family, you may have an excellent blend of experience and flexibility.

Most prospectuses give the full details of a fund's record; be sure to check for any recent changes in top management personnel. In addition, the information sources listed at the end of this chapter can be useful in comparing the records of several funds.

You may wish to avoid the risk of relatively poor performance by investing in an index fund. Vanguard is one company that offers such a fund.

5. *Size.* You should probably not invest in small mutual funds (less than $25 million in assets) if they have recently performed exceptionally well. Such a record usually attracts a flood of investor dollars and, almost overnight, the fund grows to a major size. The management that was expert at investing a small flexible fund is suddenly in a very different situation, and the results can be disastrous. For example, the O'Neil Fund was the number one fund in 1967, with a growth rate of 115.6 percent and total net assets of $9.2 million. In 1968, a great influx of new investor dollars made the fund five times larger (total net assets of $48.7 million), and O'Neil wound up near the bottom of mutual fund ratings with a gain of only 3.8 percent in the bull market of 1968.

A fund may gradually grow in size with age, since an open-end fund usually continues to acquire new shareholders. Table 19-7 may help you decide what size mutual fund (diversified common stock) to buy, assuming that size correlates with experience and age.

If you have decided to purchase a closed-end fund, see your stockbroker both for information about the company and to purchase the shares. For open-end load funds, contact your broker or respond to an advertisement in the newspaper. Your broker may be an authorized and commissioned representative for the fund you wish to buy. Otherwise, a fund salesperson will call on you. In either case you should realize that both the broker and the fund salesperson will want to make a sale and take a commission.

With open-end no-load funds, you must write to the company for information and a prospectus. All dealings will be directly with the company. You can get

TABLE 19-7

Characteristics of Mutual Funds Based on Size

Range of Fund's Net Assets (approximate)	Possible Characteristics
Less than $50 million	Low experience or security (unless new fund in old family) Generally high price fluctuations Flexibility to take advantage of opportunities or to sell stocks and hold cash in bear markets Possible aggressive growth
$50-$300 million	Blend of experience, stability, and flexibility Possible above-average growth
Over $300 million	Security, stability, and experience Limited flexibility to buy stocks of smaller companies or to sell stocks and hold cash in bear markets Fund growth may approximate that of the general market

addresses from ads in the newspaper, from your broker, and from other information sources. Here is a list of some major no-load funds with good records. The funds stressing long-term growth and those stressing performance were selected on the basis of their returns for 1974 through 1980, which included both bear and bull markets.

Corporate bond funds

Dreyfus A Bonds Plus, 767 Fifth Ave., New York, NY 10153
Fidelity Corporate Bond Fund, 82 Devonshire St., Boston, MA 02109
Vanguard Fixed Income Securities Fund, P.O. Box 1100, Valley Forge, PA 19482

Municipal bond funds (varying maturities)

Dreyfus Tax Exempt Bond Fund, 767 Fifth Ave., New York, NY 10153
Fidelity Municipal Bond Fund, 82 Devonshire St., Boston, MA 02109
Nuveen Municipal Bond Fund, 115 S. LaSalle St., Chicago, IL 60603
Price Tax-Free Income Fund, 100 East Pratt St., Baltimore, MD 21202
Scudder Managed Municipal Bonds, 175 Federal St., Boston, MA 02110
Vanguard Municipal Bond Fund, P.O. Box 1100, Valley Forge, PA 19482

Balanced funds

Dodge & Cox Balanced Fund, One Post St., San Francisco, CA 94104
Safeco Income Fund, Safeco Plaza, Seattle, WA 98185
Selected American Shares, 111 W. Washington St., Chicago, IL 60602
Unified Mutual Shares, 207 Guaranty Bldg., Indianapolis, IN 46204
Wellington Fund, P.O. Box 1100, Valley Forge, PA 19482

Funds stressing long-term growth or growth and income

Constellation Growth Fund, 331 Madison Ave., New York, NY 10017
Dreyfus Number Nine Fund, 767 Fifth Ave., New York, NY 10153
Hartwell Growth Fund, 50 Rockefeller Plaza, New York, NY 10020
Lexington Growth Fund, P.O. Box 1515, Englewood Cliffs, NJ 07632
Partner's Fund, 342 Madison Ave., New York, NY 10173
Pennsylvania Mutual Fund, 127 John St., 19th Floor, New York, NY 10038
Safeco Growth Fund, Safeco Plaza, Seattle, WA 98185
Scudder Development Fund, 345 Park Ave., New York, NY 10022
Sherman, Dean Fund, 120 Broadway, New York, NY 10271
Twentieth Century Growth Investors, P.O. Box 200, Kansas City, MO 64141
Twentieth Century Select Investors, P.O. Box 200, Kansas City, MO 64141
Weingarten Equity Fund, 331 Madison Ave., New York, NY 10017
Windsor Fund, P.O. Box 1100, Valley Forge, PA 19482

Funds stressing performance (often highly volatile)

Acorn Fund, 120 S. LaSalle St., Chicago, IL 60603
Evergreen Fund, 550 Mamaroneck Ave., Harrison, NY 10528
44 Wall Street Fund, 150 Broadway, New York, NY 10038
Lindner Fund, 200 S. Bemiston, St. Louis, MO 63105
Loomis-Sayles Capital Development Fund, 225 Franklin St., Boston, MA 02110
Mathers Fund, 125 S. Wacker Drive, Chicago, IL 60606
Mutual Shares Corp., 26 Broadway, New York, NY 10004
Sequoia Fund, 540 Madison Ave., New York, NY 10022

Funds that invest abroad:

G. T. Pacific Fund, 601 Montgomery St., Suite 1400, San Francisco, CA 94111
Rowe Price International Fund, 100 E. Pratt St., Baltimore, MD 21202
Scudder International Fund, 345 Park Ave. at 51st Street, New York, NY 10154
Transatlantic Fund, c/o Kleinwort Benson International Investment, Ltd., 100 Wall St., New York, NY 10005

OTHER SOURCES OF PROFESSIONAL SECURITIES MANAGEMENT

Depending on your individual circumstances, you may choose from the following sources of professional management, in addition to the mutual funds and unit trusts of the chapter discussion to this point.

Variable Annuities

A variable annuity is a securities investment program offered by a life insurance company. (Fixed annuities, also offered by life insurance companies, were discussed in Chapter 16.) The special feature of annuities is the guaranteed lifetime income they provide through various settlement options (Chapter 9). In a variable annuity, the payment amounts vary from year to year depending on the performance of the stock and bond portfolio behind the annuity contract.

The special advantages of an annuity are the regular premium investment plan (forced savings) and the deferral of income taxes on investment returns until benefits are paid out. The disadvantages are inflexibility and the taxation of all profits at ordinary income tax rates (even if the profit is due to capital gains). If the management performs poorly, you cannot change from one variable annuity to another (unless they're offered by the same insurance company) without paying taxes on all profits accumulated to that point. As with a mutual fund, you should select a variable annuity by shopping around, looking for the best performance record.

The oldest variable annuity program is the College Retirement Equities Fund (CREF), begun in 1952. CREF is available to college professors. Table 19-8 shows the annuity payout amounts for each unit held for a professor retiring at age 65. From 1952 to 1981, the payout rate increased 259 percent, while the cost of living rose 225 percent—not bad when compared to a fixed annuity's payout, which would have increased only a token amount, if at all.

Bank Trust Departments

Banks provide individual investment management through their affiliated trust departments. In addition, they may act as trustee (see Chapter 22 for information about trusts and trustees) and custodian of your cash and securities in their vaults. Most of them charge a separate fee for each function. Total fees for all three generally run from 0.5 percent to 1.5 percent annually, often depending on the size

TABLE 19-8

Payments per Unit for Person Retiring at Age 65
under the College Retirement Equities Fund (CREF)

Year	Unit Value	Year	Unit Value	Year	Unit Value
1952	$10.00	1962	$26.13	1972	$35.74
53	9.46	63	22.68	73	31.58
54	10.74	64	26.48	74	26.21
1955	14.11	1965	28.21	1975	21.84
56	18.51	66	30.43	76	26.24
57	16.88	67	31.92	77	24.80
58	16.71	68	29.90	78	23.28
59	22.03	69	32.50	79	27.28
1960	22.18	1970	28.91	1980	26.27
61	26.25	71	30.64	81	35.86

Source: Teachers Insurance and Annuity Association/College Retirement Equities Fund, *Annual Report*, various issues through 1981 (New York, 1981), p. 7.

Note: For example, a retiree age 65 in 1960 would have received $22.18 per unit that year, $26.25 the next, $26.13 the next, and so on.

of the account. Small accounts must often pay the fee set for the minimum account size (usually $100,000).

The investment management may be handled on the basis of an individually managed portfolio, or you may simply own a portion of the bank's commingled fund, much as you would own an interest in a mutual fund.

Each officer in a trust department typically has a large number of accounts, and so it is difficult for such officers to be particularly responsive to individual needs on any but their largest accounts. The investment management style tends to be conservative—sticking to bonds, and growth, cyclical, and mature growth stocks. If a bank is written into someone's will or trust as trustee (as is often the case), it is nearly impossible for the beneficiaries of the account to change managements should they become dissatisfied.

Investment Advisors

In 1982 there were over 3,800 investment advisory firms registered with the SEC. Many of these offer individualized management of investment accounts. Others simply offer newsletter advisory services by mail. There is tremendous variation in the size of the firms, the minimum size account they will accept, the quality of their services, and the depth and breadth of individual counseling they offer.

As a result, the selection of an investment advisor requires careful research on your part. Meet with several firms to learn by comparison. Examine their performance record. Avoid firms with conflicts of interest. Do they, for example, benefit directly from each commission incurred on making a trade in your account? Get referrals from attorneys, accountants, brokers, bankers, or friends you have confidence in.

Profit Sharing Plans

Your employer may have a savings program or profit sharing program, where the ultimate return to you depends on the performance of the investments in the program. Sometimes you may have a choice of investment vehicles. Consider these a part of your overall investment portfolio and diversify accordingly (Chapter 15). The management of the plan may be entrusted by the company's officers to a mutual fund company, a life insurance company, a bank trust department, or a registered investment advisor.

CONCLUSION

Mutual funds and other professional managements provide average investors with a way to invest in bonds or the stock market without either risking money on just a few securities or spending a lot of time watching over their investments. In exchange for this, the investor must pay an annual fee of about 1 percent of the value of the assets. The only task left to the investor is to choose an appropriate fund, a task that we hope this chapter has made less burdensome.

VOCABULARY

balanced fund	open-end fund
capital gains distribution	prospectus
closed-end fund	redemption value
contractual savings plan	registered investment advisor
investment company	savings accumulation plan
load	systematic withdrawal plan
load fund	unit trust
net asset value (NAV)	variable annuity
no-load fund	voluntary accumulation plan

QUESTIONS

1. What is the difference, if any, in commissions and management fees charged by load funds and no-load funds?
2. Describe the kind of investor for whom mutual funds are an appropriate investment.
3. Why may your stockbroker not be an appropriate source of information regarding the selection of mutual funds? What would be a good source?
4. What special advantages do mutual funds have over individual stock market investments? Describe at least four.
5. Which professionally managed securities alternative might be appropriate for a woman about to retire who didn't want to worry about running out of money if she lives another 30 years?
6. How might the size of a mutual fund be a factor in your investment decision?
7. What is the most important factor in selecting a mutual fund?
8. Why are closed-end investment companies much like common stocks?
9. Why might it be better to invest in a mutual fund that was consistently above average over the past decade than in a new fund that was the leading growth performer last year?

CASE PROBLEM

Two months ago Jay graduated from college and started a well-paying job. Since as a student he had become accustomed to living on a part-time income, he was able to save about $200 a month from his salary. His job and his personal life kept him busy, and so he decided to keep his investments simple by selecting a mutual fund. Having neither dependents nor high-priority investment objectives as yet, he was willing to take a certain amount of risk in exchange for a potentially high return.

In order to find a good aggressive growth mutual fund, Jay read the prospectuses on eight mutual funds that were recommended by a business professor of his. Table 19-9 shows how these funds compare in objective, age, size, and performance history.

1. What is the average compound return for each of these funds since its inception? Does Jay's professor seem to have selected an above-average group of funds?
2. Which of these funds appears to be most appropriate for Jay in objective, size, and management performance? Give several reasons for your choice.
3. If Jay wanted to look at other funds and make a quick comparison of performance over comparable time periods, what should he do?

TABLE 19-9

Comparison of Eight Mutual Funds (Fictitious)

Management Company	Investment Growth Objective	Age (years)	Size (millions)	Performance History			
				Year 1	Year 2	Year 3	Year 3 Value of $10,000 Investment[a]
1. Smith & Co.	Long term	20	$400	Down	Up	Down	$105,000
2. Black & Co.	Aggressive	10	520	Down	Up	Up	29,000
3. Black & Co.	Aggressive	2	45	—	Up	Even	15,000
4. J. Jones, Inc.	Long term	20	460	Even	Up	Up	137,000
5. J. Jones, Inc.	Aggressive	3	105	Down	Up	Up	16,000
6. W.W. Wilson	Aggressive	2	20	—	Up	UP	16,000
7. P. Green Co.	Long term	18	90	Down	Up	Even	79,000
8. P. Green Co.	Long term	4	60	Even	Up	Up	15,000

[a] Invested at fund's inception; all dividends and capital gains distributions reinvested.

4. What would you recommend to Jay if the fund you selected had a $1,000 minimum investment requirement, with a $50 monthly minimum thereafter, while the other funds required an initial minimum of $400? (Assume that Jay has saved $400 from his salary for his first two months' work.)

RECOMMENDED READING

The following sources should help you compare and select mutual funds. Most are expensive, but they are available at major libraries and brokerage houses.

Forbes (60 Fifth Avenue, New York, NY 10011)
> This business magazine is published twice a month and costs $15 a year. Each year the mid-August issue (available individually for $1.50) presents a survey of fund performance and rates mutual funds according to its own evaluation system.

Mutual Funds Almanac (William E. Donoghue, Box 540, Holliston, MA 01746)
> An inexpensive way ($25) to compare 10-year performance histories of over 600 funds.

Investment Companies (Wiesenberger Services, One New York Plaza, New York, NY 10004).
> This annual publication also provides quarterly supplements on leading funds. This book is a large and complete reference source, now in its forty-first edition. It gives general information about mutual funds and provides facts and figures on individual funds.

Johnson's Investment Company Charts (246 Homewood Ave., Buffalo, NY 14217)
> This annual publication with quarterly updates presents readily comparable data on mutual funds through graphs that show the results of a $10,000 investment made over several different time periods.

United Mutual Fund Selector (United Business Service Company, 210 Newbury St., Boston, MA 02116)

A semimonthly advisory letter ($65 a year) that recommends a supervised list of mutual funds; it also gives information on the industry and specific funds.

SPECIFIC ARTICLES

"Investment Funds That Specialize." *Changing Times*, January 1979, pp. 15–18.

A listing, by industry group, of the mutual funds offering more narrow objectives or different geographic emphasis than the typical diversified common stock fund offers.

Kessler, Jeffrey. "Should You Buy a Foreign Fund?" *Financial World*, September 1, 1981, pp. 26–29.

A summary and critique of 17 American-managed mutual funds that invest abroad.

Runde, Robert. "IRAs: The Switch-Fund Solution." *Money*, March 1982, pp. 85–91.

Argues for investing your IRA money in one of the top "families" of mutual funds.

"Taxes and Your Mutual Fund." *Changing Times*, September 1981, pp. 56–58.

A review of the special tax rules that apply to this kind of investment.

CHUCK AND NANCY ANDERSON

Computing the Effective Return on a Mutual Fund

Chuck and Nancy have decided that mutual funds are an appropriate investment for some of their goals. Now they must decide which funds to invest in. After reading several prospectuses, they decided that Growth Fund and Dynamic Fund have objectives that match theirs. Each is fairly large, offers a voluntary accumulation plan, and is under the same management as when it started. On closer inspection of the prospectuses for these two funds, Chuck and Nancy find the following statements:

(Growth Fund) Assume a $10,000 investment in March 1968. If all dividends and capital gains were received as cash, the value of your shares today would be $21,370. If only capital gains were reinvested, the value of your shares would be $39,625. If both dividends and capital gains were reinvested, your $10,000 investment would have grown to $48,512 as of March 31, 1982.

(Dynamic Fund) Assume a $10,000 investment in June 1965. If all dividends and capital gains were received as cash, the value of your shares today would be $34,420. If only capital gains were reinvested, the value of your shares would be $48,122. If both dividends and capital gains were reinvested, your $10,000 investment would have grown to $53,260 as of June 30, 1982.

Questions

1. Which figure in these quotes is the appropriate one to compare for each fund?
2. What is the effective compound rate of return for each fund?
3. Which fund should Chuck and Nancy select?
4. If they read the prospectus of a third fund, the Dynagrowth Fund, founded in 1976, would they probably be able to make a fair comparison of the three funds? Why or why not?
5. What source could they use if they needed information that would help them compare funds with widely disparate founding dates?

20

Real Estate

"Real estate never wears out; it never goes out of style."

"Money in land isn't spent—it's saved."

"The supply of land is fixed; you can't manufacture more of it. Yet the demand inevitably grows with the population."

"You don't wait to invest in real estate; you invest and then wait."

Nearly everyone hears such ideas at some time and seriously considers investing in real estate. Fortunes have been made in real estate because of these simple premises; but thousands of unsophisticated real estate investors have lost money because they were unaware of the risks involved or how to avoid them.

This chapter will deal with several phases of real estate investing: investing in trust deeds and investing in professional trusts and syndicates. Investing in and managing real estate on your own will be mentioned only briefly, since a fully useful discussion would require another complete text, at the very least.

HIGH INTEREST ON YOUR MONEY: MORTGAGES AND DEEDS OF TRUST

Mortgages and deeds of trust are two slightly different legal mechanisms for borrowing money against a piece of real estate. Unlike a mortgage, a deed of trust is held by an independent party (trustee) until the debt is paid off. Usage of one or the other varies from state to state.

First mortgages, or first deeds of trust (commonly known as *firsts*), have first claim against a property in the event of a default in loan payments; second mortgages, or second deeds of trust (*seconds*), have claim to the equity remaining after the first holder's claim has been settled. For example, a $60,000 home may have a $48,000 first and a $6,000 second; the owner of the home has only $6,000 of his or her own money in the property. The rest is borrowed from the first and second lender.

In the event of a default on either loan, the lenders would begin foreclosure proceedings. That is, they would go through the state legal process to put the home up for a quick sale in order to recoup their loans. If there were any money left after the first and second lenders had been paid off and the legal expenses paid, it would go to the homeowner. (Often such legal expenses can run as high as 5 to 10 percent of the sale price of the property.)

First Mortgages (or First Deeds of Trust)

Firsts are usually issued by banks, savings and loan associations, and similar institutional investors. However, sometimes such investments are available to private investors through mortgage pools. For example, a bank, having run out of loanable funds and unable to satisfy its customers' demands for mortgage loans, may pool several mortgages and offer investment shares in the pool to the public for perhaps $5,000 each. Such shares may carry interest rates one or two percentage points above those allowed on federally insured deposits. In this case, your insurance is the security offered by the mortgages or deeds of trust themselves. Since such loans usually amount to no more than 70 or 80 percent of the market value of the property, they are usually considered fairly safe investments.

Second Mortgages (or Second Deeds of Trust)

A second mortgage is usually issued to finance the portion of the purchase price on a piece of property that is not covered by the down payment and the first mortgage. In the event of default, a second has a claim to the property but only after the balance on the first has been settled. Hence, there is less protection for the investor in second mortgages. In exchange for this higher risk, seconds usually offer a return that is several percentage points above the rates on firsts. For an investment of $3,000 to $5,000, for example, the investor in recent years has received 10 to 20 percent or higher in interest income, depending on market conditions and on the usury limits in the state.

In general, second trust deeds are used by borrowers to reduce the down payment on the purchase of a home, to provide capital to start a business or for some other investment, or to consolidate higher interest cost debts into one lower cost package. Terms are flexible, with maturities ranging from 3 to 10 years.

advantages of seconds for the investor   Both second mortgages and second deeds of trust are advantageous because they offer high interest yields. Since the lender who originates the loan retains the front-end points, the return available to the investor who purchases the loan is the annual interest. The investor also usually shares in the prepayment penalties, and sometimes there are late payment penalties.

The regular income, generally monthly or quarterly, from seconds is especially attractive to retired persons or others seeking to supplement their ordinary income. And, finally, there are no management duties required of the investor if the deed is handled by a full-service loan broker.

disadvantages of seconds for the investor   People do lose money in seconds, even though they are secured by supposedly sound real estate value. In periods of excessive speculation, inflated property values can disappear almost overnight. In 1929, Southern California homes fell in price over 50 percent in just six months. Not only did most second-mortgage investors get wiped out, but also many first-mortgage lenders lost money. For example, if a $20,000 home had a 75 percent first mortgage, or $15,000, and it fell in price to $10,000, it no longer made sense for the owner to stay in the house and keep paying on the $15,000 mortgage. The chances of a recurrence of such a situation become more plausible the longer the real estate speculation that gathered momentum in the late 1970s continues. In 1982 as this is being written, mortgage foreclosures are already reaching record post–World War II levels.

Even in stable economic times, an overeager loan broker may write a loan that has inadequate security behind it. A common rule of thumb is to lend an amount equal to no more than half of the available equity (market price less the balance due on the first mortgage). However, if a $50,000 home with a $40,000 first mortgage is appraised by an eager lender at $60,000, he could justify a $10,000 second loan, a risky investment on a home worth $50,000 *before* selling costs. If you have to foreclose, you may find that you cannot sell the house for enough to pay off the first and the broker's fee and still recover your investment, particularly if you are in a market where it is hard to sell houses anyway. In order to minimize this possibility, you should deal only with reputable loan brokers, who will make their loans based on a conservative appraisal. This is your best guarantee of investment security. In normal times, foreclosures generally occur on only about 3 percent of all loans.

There is a long holding period generally required on seconds—three to five years. Of course, if it is an amortized loan with no balloon payment, you will get your money back earlier because of installments. It is also possible to sell seconds that are several years old but not yet at maturity through loan brokers to other investors if you need the funds early. However, such a sale may require a discount from the face value.

There is no inflation protection with seconds, because the face value and the interest rate remain the same, regardless of how the cost of living changes. Of course, when compared with other interest-bearing investments, the high yields on seconds represent a favorable return more often than not.

This investment is not for conservative investors. If you feel uneasy about foreclosures or would worry if a payment came a few weeks late, perhaps for your own peace of mind you would be better off taking a lower rate of return on short to intermediate maturity, top-quality municipal or corporate bonds.

sources of seconds   The primary source of seconds for the investor is a loan broker. He appraises the property, makes the loan, and collects the points as his fee. He will then sell the loan certificate to the investor, who collects the interest and principal payments. The broker makes collections and provides other services such as managing delinquent loans or initiating foreclosure proceedings.

In selecting the proper loan broker, you should examine his foreclosure and loss record. Some large and/or well-managed firms have yet to lose money for their clients. You should also look for the following features in the loans he writes: request for notices of default and sale, penalty on late payments, and prepayment penalties.

The *request for notices of default and sale* requires second and first lenders to let each other know when a loan is in default. In effect, foreclosure by one lender without the knowledge of the other is prohibited. As a result, the first lender will generally go to the second lender for his monthly payments rather than foreclose and sell at a low bid (enough only for the first mortgage) and wipe out the second lender's security.

A small *penalty on late payments*—usually 10 percent of the monthly amount—may be levied. This penalty increases the likelihood that payments will be made on time. If borrowers frequently pay late, however, even a 10 percent interest yield may become a 13 to 16 percent total annual yield. In addition, when loans are paid off early, there may be a small *prepayment penalty*—usually four to six months' interest on the outstanding debt—to compensate the lender for the trouble of getting his money reinvested. This penalty often provides an extra margin of profit for the lender.

OWNING THE PROPERTY, NOT JUST THE MORTGAGE

If you have several thousand dollars that you know will not be needed for several years and are willing to take the time to learn about selecting and managing real estate, you may wish to consider investing in real estate on your own. If you do not feel competent to select and manage your own real estate but still want to take advantage of such investments, you should consider investing in real estate investment trusts, companies, or syndicates (limited partnerships).

Houses, Duplexes, and Triplexes

When most people think of investing in real estate on their own, they think of buying another home and renting it out, or they buy a duplex or triplex, live in one unit, and rent out the other(s).

advantages of such investments   Generally, the prime attraction of such investments is their price-appreciation potential. In this century homes have appreciated about as fast as common stocks, on average, though at a much higher rate in the 1970s. There are also benefits from paying down the mortgage and tax advantages of depreciation deductions.

disadvantages of such investments   In most cases, the demand for such properties results in high prices relative to the income to be generated; prices are generally in excess of seven to eight times the gross annual rents obtainable, which is the level at which buying a property would make economic sense. Because of this disproportion, large mortgage payments are required, and there is little chance for current income.

Consider the following example of a duplex where each unit rents for $500 a month.

Price at eight times gross annual income $12,000	$96,000
Mortgage obtained at 60 percent of market price	$58,000
Monthly mortgage payment on $58,000 at 12 percent for 30 years	$597

This mortgage payment of $597 a month is 60 percent of the rental income, compared to 50 percent for apartment buildings of around 100 or more units. With taxes and expenses normally at 40 to 50 percent of rental income, there is little, if any, net spendable income from the duplex. Obviously, this higher-priced property requires mortgage payments that are too high relative to the income. Of course, inflation may allow you to raise your rents over time, while the mortgage payments remain constant, thereby generating future net income.

In the late 1970s, investors became convinced that rental rates and property values would continue to increase indefinitely. Prices on small income properties have therefore gone as high as 10 to 15 times gross annual rents, but there is not enough income to cover operating expenses and the very high mortgage payments resulting from such high prices. The investor must continue to invest funds in the property to cover the negative cash flow. The investor is then in the uneasy position of needing inflation in rents and price appreciation of the property *just to break even!*

an example of a single-family home investment   Assume you purchased an $80,000 house with a $25,000 down payment and a 30-year, 12 percent first mortgage. You rent the house for $650 a month and keep it rented year-round except for an average of 18 days (a typical 5 percent vacancy allowance). Even though you perform the simpler repairs yourself, the maintenance costs average $800 a year. (When one figures in the occasional costs of a new roof, repainting, broken water pipes, or worn-out water heater, it is not abnormal to find the annual maintenance and repair costs running at ¼ to 2 percent of the value of the home.) The tenant takes care of the gardening and pays for the utilities.

Figure 20-1 presents the mathematics of determining the total first-year return as the sum of the cash income, tax savings, and the reduction of the mortgage principal. This total return of $398 is equal to about 1.6 percent on your $25,000 investment. Of course, this return will vary from one situation to another, and from one year to the next. Also, this return calculation does not take into account any possible appreciation in value or resale or any capital gains taxes payable on resale. (Note that when you figure the taxable capital gain, the total annual depreciation deductions directly reduce your purchase cost basis in the property.)

This sample analysis should help you do your own financial analysis if this type of investment appeals to you. Be sure to go through the same procedures for buying a home that are discussed in Chapter 14, with one additional step: determine how much rent you will be able to charge *before* you purchase the property.

Real Estate Investment Trust (REIT)

A real estate investment trust is an unincorporated association that invests in mortgages (a mortgage trust) or real property (an equity trust).

Cash income analysis	
Gross scheduled rent	$7,800
Less: 5% vacancy	−390
Rental income received	7,410
Less: property taxes	−900
Less: insurance	−400
Less: repairs and maintenance	−800
Net operating income	5,310
Less: mortgage payments	−6,790
Net cash income	−1,480
First full-year tax benefits	
Net operating income	5,310
Less: interest on mortgage[a]	−6,570
Less: depreciation[b]	−4,267
Taxable income	−5,527
Taxes saved, assuming a 30% tax bracket	1,658
Summary of first-year return on investment	
Net cash income	−1,480
Tax savings	1,658
Reduction of mortgage principal	220
TOTAL FIRST-YEAR RETURN	$398

[a] As the mortgage balance is reduced, the interest portion of the mortgage payment becomes smaller. See Chapter 11 on amortized mortgages.

[b] "Depreciation" as used here is an "allowable tax deduction" not necessarily related to the physical deterioration of the property. In this case, a 15-year useful life is allowed, and we will use straight line depreciation. Assuming that 20 percent of the purchase cost is for the land ($16,000 in the land, leaving $64,000 in the depreciable building), this allows $4,267 in annual depreciation deductions ($64,000 ÷ 15 years).

FIGURE 20-1
First-year return analysis
for single-family home.

Investment trusts are a direct result of the Real Estate Investment Trust Act of 1960, which was designed to provide an opportunity for small investors to invest in real estate. They are exempted from corporate income taxes provided they conform to certain rules. Among the rules are that at least 90 percent of a trust's income must be distributed to the shareholders; the trust must have at least 100 shareholders; three-fourths of its income and assets must be related to real estate investments, either ownership or mortgages; capital gains income is limited to 30 percent of its gross income (to minimize wild stock or land speculation that might offer more risk to shareholders than they expected when they made their investment); a trust cannot directly manage any property it owns (to prevent the investor from being victimized by unethical trustees who may extract many different, and often hidden, management fees).

The income received by REIT stockholders is taxed only to them, not to the trust, and they pay capital gains rates on the capital gains portion of this income. Other portions of the income may be tax-free because of depreciation shelter provisions in the tax law regarding equity trusts.

Investment trusts spread their risk over many different properties. Mortgage trusts, for example, do not necessarily invest their funds in first and second mortgages. Many of the mortgages are construction loans to builders at high rates of interest (12 to 24 percent annually) for short periods of time.

short-term mortgage trusts Some trusts concentrate on making short-term construction loans because of the high returns that are possible. During the early 1970s, such trusts paid dividends equal to 9 to 10 percent of the original issue price of the shares (high for that era). However, during 1974 and 1975, several things happened to place these trusts in serious trouble. Much of the money loaned by these short-term trusts had been borrowed from banks at interest rates that varied with, and were higher than, the prime bank lending rate. As the prime rate rose (to as high as 12 percent in 1974), mortgages that had their interest rate fixed, either by contract or by state usury laws, generated net losses to the REIT lenders; high interest rates, along with high construction costs, resulted in losses on many projects, forcing developers out of business. Thus many REIT loans were foreclosed against unfinished projects. Compounding all these problems was the fact that the earlier "easy money" had caused many REITs to borrow heavily from banks and not be critical of the quality of the construction mortgages they issued. As a result, most short-term mortgage trusts have paid no dividends since 1975, a number failed to survive, and some are still struggling to regain a reasonable level of profitability. The average share price of REITs fell from $62 in early 1974 to $18 in 1975. By October 1981 they had climbed back only to $38.50.*

The sad fact is that most REITs formed were of this short-term type, because they offered the most attractive returns to investors during the '60s and the early '70s and the easiest fees to the trust managers. It bears repeating that where there are high returns, there are also high risks!

long-term mortgage trusts Other REITs concentrate on investing in longer term mortgages in which the interest returns are more modest, but so are the risks. The properties have completed construction. Also, the REITs could not borrow from banks to issue such mortgages because of the higher cost of bank loans. Their situation is better. Many of these trusts also are partly equity trusts.

equity trusts These concentrate on owning the properties, not just on making mortgage loans. To date, these trusts have not taken such great risks and have a better record. In fact, one of the oldest, Real Estate Investment Trust of America, has paid dividends every year since 1887. Of course, the long-term success of such trusts depends on the ability and foresight of the REIT manager. In summary, equity trusts may not offer the high current dividends sometimes paid by mortgage REITs, but they can offer lower risks (especially if the properties are not heavily mortgaged) and a potential for price appreciation if the properties in the trust increase in value. Because of depreciation deductions, the dividends may be partially or fully sheltered from income taxes. Many trusts do not distribute the sheltered income but reinvest it in additional property.

---

*The REIT Report, National Association of Real Estate Investment Trusts, Washington, D.C., December 1981, p. 7.

buying REITs   There are over 100 investment trusts whose shares are traded on the open market just like common stock. Since they are traded like stocks, their value is usually not equal to the asset value of the holdings but fluctuates with changing market conditions. In recent years, most trusts have sold for less than their asset value. To answer this problem, several new trusts have been formed with the stated objective of liquidating their portfolio of properties within 10 years and returning the proceeds to the investor. This limited-life concept assures the investor of receiving the full real estate value eventually, even if the market price of the shares falls below the value of the real estate (appraised annually) in the meantime.

Many trusts are listed on major stock exchanges. To minimize investment risks in the highly competitive REIT industry, stick with the major listed trusts that have had reasonably good operating results. Your stockbroker can identify most of them for you. In addition, he or she may have reports on REITs in general. You should evaluate REITs much as you would common stocks.

Real Estate Investment Company

A real estate investment company is similar to a trust except that it must pay a corporate income tax. Therefore, you can be taxed twice on the same real estate income—first at the corporate level and then at the individual level when any income such as dividends is distributed. The advantage in this sort of company is that it can retain its earnings and grow faster than a trust can; investors thus benefit from the capital growth of their shares. This type of investment is simply another common stock investment.

Limited Partnerships: The Real Estate Syndicate

A real estate investment syndicate is a group of people (partnership) joined together under one management (general partner) to buy and manage property—usually a single piece of property, but sometimes as many as 10 or 20 pieces. Most syndicates are limited partnerships, in which nonmanaging investors (limited partners) assume a risk up to the limit of their original investment (as little as $3,000). Syndicate shares are usually sold in multiples of $500 or $1,000.

Two forms of syndicates are offered in many states: single property and blind pool. The single property syndicator simply purchases, for a small percentage sum, an option to buy one apartment house, mobile home park, office building, or other property, and then offers shares in the project to prospective investors in order to raise the rest of the money needed to close the deal. With the blind pool type of investment, the syndicator first raises several million dollars or more (based only on the strength of his reputation as a syndicator) and then decides on purchases of several properties in different areas, thus diversifying the investors' risk.

In a single property syndicate, a group of 30 investors might decide to purchase a $1,000,000 apartment complex by putting $300,000 down (an average of $10,000 each). A blind pool would involve more properties and require more money from a greater number of limited partners. The syndicate management, usually a real estate brokerage or finance firm, would take a small percentage of the income as its fee and distribute the rest of the income to the investors. The management usually takes fees for other services, such as property management, as well.

total yield   Investors in real estate syndicates should look at four aspects of return on the investment in order to get the true picture of their anticipated total yield: cash flow distribution, equity buildup, price appreciation, and tax shelter benefits.

The *cash flow distribution* is the actual cash distributed to all investors out of the cash income (rental revenues) of the property. For example, an annual operating statement might look like this for an apartment building:

Rent revenues (at 95 percent occupancy)		$480,000
Operating and management expenses	$186,000	
Mortgage payment	225,000	
Reserve for repairs (5 percent)	24,000	
Partnership expense	10,000	
Total	445,000	
Cash flow to partners		$ 35,000

If the investors had invested $600,000, this cash flow would amount to 5.8 percent a year. Because of the depreciation provisions of the tax law, most, if not all, of that distribution is tax-free to investors. Annual cash flow generally ranges from 4 to 8 percent of an investment each year for average properties under normal conditions. On the one hand, in hard economic times or with poor management, the cash flow may be zero or negative. On the other, if a property is purchased cheaply during difficult economic situations, or if inflation pushes rents up substantially, later cash flow rates may rise to over 20 percent annually!

The *equity buildup* is the amount by which the investor's equity investment grows each year as mortgage balances are reduced by the monthly payments made from revenues. Such equity buildup can add 1 to 5 percent each year to the total return, provided the property does not decline in price. If at least part of the mortgage loan is paid off, the eventual sale of the property should result in more cash to the investor.

Price appreciation may occur if the property is bought for a good price, well maintained, and well managed for growing profits. Negotiating a good purchase price for the investor and upgrading the property's value are difficult jobs that not all syndicators do well. If they are done well, however, an annual price appreciation of 3 to 5 percent is not uncommon (but by no means guaranteed). Of course, if the property does not generate a higher level of income, there will probably be little price appreciation, since investment property is typically sold on its fundamental investment income merits.

Tax shelter benefits are also available. During the first few years, there may be excess tax shelter benefits (depreciation losses) over and above the cash flow amounts, which you can deduct from your gross income, whether or not you itemize your other deductions, and thereby reduce your income taxes.

potential risks   There are four broad categories of risk that you should be aware of before investing in a real estate syndicate.

1. *Will there be price appreciation or depreciation?* This problem can often be minimized by making sure you are not paying too much for the property. (You must realize that the syndicator is probably taking a commission related to the dollar amount of the purchase price.) In general, there are two guidelines for estimating the right price. One is the gross income multiplier (GM), and the other is the capitalization rate (cap rate).

   The *gross income multiplier* is computed by dividing the total price (all monies paid to close the deal, including mortgages) by the projected gross rents. For example, a $1,200,000 purchase projecting rent revenues—gross income—of $200,000 (assuming no vacancies) would have a GM of 6. Such a figure may or may not be good, depending on the local rate. Check with several local realtors to determine the average GM for the area. Generally, it is very difficult to show positive cash flow with a GM in excess of 7.

   The *capitalization rate* is derived by dividing the net operating income (after expenses but before depreciation and loan payments) by the total purchase price. For example, a $1,000,000 property with net income of $100,000 would have a cap rate of 10 percent cash yield each year, as long as the building was 95 percent full. The minimum acceptable cap rate for any income property should be approximately equal to current long-term mortgage interest rates or higher, depending on the risk involved. Inflationary expectations of the 1978–81 period caused investors to be willing to buy properties at a 6 to 10 percent cap rate when mortgage rates ran 12 to 17 percent. This disparity indicated negative cash flow, a need for seller financing below market rates, and a generally fragile speculative environment for real estate investors.

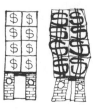

2. *Will the building stay fully rented at the proposed rents?* Although you cannot know the future for a building that is new, you can at least check with a few realtors to see whether the proposed rents are realistic for that type of property. Check also to see whether there are unusual vacancy problems in similar properties around town. For an existing building, check the syndicators' projections by asking the present manager what the rent is and how many units are vacant. An investment may be highly speculative because a property has a small down payment and a sizable mortgage. The mortgage payments may be so high that the property could tolerate only a slight vacancy problem before foreclosure would be likely. Generally, total mortgage payments should not exceed 45 to 50 percent of gross income.

3. *Will the IRS challenge your right to some of the proposed tax deductions?* Syndicators sometimes try to squeeze more than the last drop of tax loss out of a property. Check with a tax attorney or CPA to see whether your proposed investment may have trouble getting by the IRS. You should be especially suspicious of any syndicator who promises more than a 50 percent write-off in the first two years of your original investment (e.g., over $5,000 in tax losses on a $10,000 investment).

4. *Will the general partner stay solvent and stand behind the investment?* If the general partner goes bankrupt, property management often declines in quality or becomes nonexistent while the limited partners try to decide whom to sue and whom to get for a new manager. The consequences often result in default on the properties and foreclosure by the lender. Therefore, you should seek out estab-

lished general partners who have a strong balance sheet (positive net worth with a good proportion of liquid assets) and a history of profitability. Established general partners have been known to stand behind a property that was having temporary financial difficulty by waiving their management fee and/or extending low-interest loans to the partnership. A financially weak general partner could not do this.

advantages of a syndicate investment   The major advantages that attract investors to real estate syndicates are high total yield, no management required of the investor, and economies of scale. It is not uncommon for total after-tax, compound return on an investment in a real estate syndicate to range between 8 and 15 percent a year (20 to 30 percent in the 1975–1981 boom), depending on the investor's tax bracket, the syndicator's expertise, and local real estate conditions. Furthermore, in order to retain limited partner status (and, therefore, limited liability status), the investor is not allowed to participate in management functions except to vote on sale of property, amendment of the partnership agreement, disbandment of the partnership and replacement of the general partner/manager. Economies of scale—such as management overhead, advertising, grounds maintenance, and supplies and equipment purchasing—begin to occur with apartment houses of about 100 or more units. An investor with only $5,000 could not obtain these economies on his own but could via a syndicate. In addition, blind pools offer diversification over several large properties, something that would be even more impossible for the small investor. However, the usual advantages of real estate investing (tax benefits and price appreciation, for example) are available to investors just as if they were investing on their own.

disadvantages of a syndicate investment   As with all real estate investments, the investor should consider syndicates as a long-term investment. It usually takes at least six or seven years before the interest and depreciation deductions decline to the point at which it may be advantageous to sell or trade because the cash flow is no longer tax sheltered. Also, the high transaction (brokerage and the like) costs involved in selling and buying real estate generally make short holding periods uneconomical. Selling your share to someone else at a profit before the actual building is sold is difficult, if not impossible, no matter what the syndicator says, and this holding period could be a disadvantage for some investors. There are some companies or individuals that will offer to buy your shares, but they will almost always offer 25 to 30 percent less than what they appraise the real estate to be worth. Because of the lack of liquidity, an investor should never invest more than 40 to 50 percent of his investment dollars either in real estate syndicates or in speculative real estate on his own.

Another disadvantage of investing in real estate syndicates is the many risks associated with them. As we stated in Chapter 15, high potential yields on an investment usually indicate high risks. In this case, your investment could suffer from too many vacancies and, therefore, have insufficient cash to meet the mortgage payments. Or the syndicator may have paid so much for the property that

PICKING A WINNER

there will be a loss when it is sold. Of course, proven management can minimize these risks.

The $2,500 to $10,000 minimum investment required may be a disadvantage if you do not have that much money for a long-term investment. In that case, you should consider REITs (trusts) instead of syndications. Or maybe you have that much money but do not meet minimum state financial qualifications. In California, for example, you must have $20,000 in gross income and $20,000 in assets—not including your home, household furnishings, or auto—in order to invest in a regulated syndicate offering. For single-property syndicates, the requirements are stiffer. These regulations are designed to screen out unsophisticated investors. Even if you are willing to invest without meeting the qualifications, the syndicator will prevent you from signing if he finds out that your financial situation does not qualify. He does not want to risk losing his license from the state.

locating and making the syndicate investment   To locate real estate syndicates, you can search the ads on the financial pages of the newspaper (many such firms hold seminars on real estate that are really only sales promotions to solicit syndicate investors); ask large local real estate brokerage firms whether they put together syndicates; and consult several stockbrokers in order to review several different programs. Different brokerage houses will sponsor, or underwrite, different syndicators' offerings.

Before making a final decision on a syndicate investment, you should do three things. First, check with the local Better Business Bureau, Chamber of Commerce, and real estate boards to make sure that the management's practices are fair and honest. Second, if it is a private offering (not registered with the state or SEC), check with your attorney as to the legality of the syndicate's partnership agreement and with your CPA as to the tax structure. Third, apply to the proposed investment the 14 points for evaluation outlined below. This analysis could take you several hours, but it might also keep you out of one of the many bad deals being offered. Better yet, if a qualified independent advisor who knows real estate is located in your area, be willing to pay for his or her opinion.

1. *Ignore the tax shelter gimmicks.* Depending on the nature of the property and the front-end management fees and how small the down payment is, your first two years' tax write-offs could range from 5 to 100 percent of your original investment. Look past these tax shelter gimmicks to see whether you are getting an investment that is sound on its own merits. Tax shelter selling is often a cover-up for an otherwise bad deal that a syndicator is trying to push for his own gain. This is very likely to be the case when write-offs greater than 50 percent are promised, especially near year-end.

2. *Look at the syndicator's record.* Does the firm have at least several years of experience in real estate syndicates? If not, are the principal officers experienced in real estate, particularly the financial and managerial aspects, or have they been involved in real estate merely as brokers? Brokers know how to sell properties, not necessarily how to manage them or structure financial agreements.

3. *Look for public deals only.* Registration of a syndicate with the state commission or SEC discourages outright fraud. Although many private deals offer above-average potential for friends of the syndicator or small groups of large investors, all too often they are loaded with excessive and hidden fees for the syndicator.

4. *Determine whether the price for the property is fair.* The simplest way to do this is to apply the gross income multiplier, a figure similar to the stock market P/E ratio. If your figure is too high compared to local gross income multipliers, the syndicator is apparently too anxious to put together a deal. Look for a syndicator offering properties with better value. In general, any property priced at more than seven times annual gross income is probably too expensive. Better yet, if you have realistic projections to work with, check the price via cap rate analysis.

5. *Evaluate the financing.* The proposed project should have at least a 20 to 35 percent down payment, and the total annual debt service (principal and interest) should not exceed 45 to 50 percent of the project's gross income. Also, note when the second mortgage balloon payment is due. Is the maturity at least three to five years away? Do not count on being able to refinance the second at favorable terms until the first mortgage balance has been paid down by several years of payments and management has had time to increase the operating income.

6. *Find out whether the partnership has any reserves.* Roughly 5 percent of the partners' total contributed capital should be set aside in a reserve fund for such normal things as new air conditioners, water heaters, and roofs. If the property has been run down, start-up reserves for refurbishment should be even larger. If the reserves are inadequate, you can probably bet that the cash flow projections will not be achieved. Also, 2 to 5 percent of the gross income should be set aside each year as additional reserves.

7. *Be wary of appreciation factors.* To boost their yield projections, some syndicators automatically plug in an annual price appreciation factor of 5 to 10 percent. Appreciation is not automatic. It can be achieved only if the building is worth more upon resale (income has grown faster than expenses); only at that time can you know what the price will be. Compare your alternatives without the appreciation factors.

8. *Consider the vacancy allowances.* You might think that a syndicator who plugs in a 2 percent vacancy allowance is being conservative. On the contrary, 2 percent is the minimum economic vacancy on normal tenant turnover rate. A 5 percent rate is more realistic. It is preferable to compare the projected rate with current vacancy rates in that project as well as those in the surrounding area. A local realtor can often help you here.

9. *Consider whether the syndicate is diversified or one building only.* An investor in a diversified syndicate can take advantage of the spreading of some overhead costs and the spreading of risks even if he has only $5,000 or $10,000 to invest. Since in this case he is buying the syndicator's management expertise, however, he is unable to evaluate the individual properties. Diversified syndicates usually buy properties only as they raise the funds—over a period of 6 to 12 months. Of

course, if the syndicator's record is good, diversified syndicates may be a wise investment.

10. *Make sure your liability is limited.* Check to see whether there is a clause providing for assessments if additional money is needed. If so, be sure that it is limited to an amount you can afford, or else you may have to forfeit profits. Also, be sure you are investing only as a limited partner and not as a general partner or a participant in a joint venture, in which cases your liability would be unlimited.

11. *Look for potential conflicts of interest.* Avoid investments where, according to the prospectus, the partnership may purchase a property from the syndicator or from one of his subsidiaries. He may be making a substantial markup over cost. Also, be careful if insurance, repair, or other services can be provided by the syndicator's firm without requiring competitive bids.

12. *Look up what the syndicator gets.* Typical fees can include up to 6 percent real estate brokerage commissions on property purchases and sales (generally limited to a maximum of 18 percent of the investor's cash investment); 3 to 6 percent of rentals for on-site property management; 5 to 10 percent of net cash flow for partnership management; and 10 to 20 percent of resale profits, usually payable only after the limited partners receive a 100 percent payback of their investment. Try to avoid syndicates that take more than this, especially if there are sales commission charges on the syndicate shares of 8 or 9 percent paid by the investor in addition to the real estate brokerage commissions or if the syndicator takes more than 6 percent of the gross income for combined property and partnership management fees. Excessive fees serve only to reduce your potential return. For a comparison of syndicate fees to those a private investor might incur, refer to Table 20-1.

13. *Avoid government subsidized projects.* These investments generally offer substantial tax losses, but little or no cash flow and no resale value, because they are overpriced, highly leveraged, and closely regulated by government agencies. In fact, if the project should be sold or go into foreclosure, there would probably be substantial recapture of earlier tax savings, even if the project generated no cash to pay such taxes! The risk of foreclosure is generally higher with such projects than with conventionally financed projects.

14. *Look for in-house property management.* Only syndicators themselves have the motivation to do the difficult tasks to make the property generate cash flow and increase in value. The only way to do this is to raise rents when vacancies are low, and to control expenses such as by turning off the pool water heater earlier in the autumn. Independent property managers, on the other hand, do not have an ownership interest, and generally try to "keep the property quiet" by doing exactly the opposite.

CONCLUSION

Second deeds of trust, when properly screened and managed by professionals, can offer relatively secure fixed income and high yield. They are especially appropriate

TABLE 20-1

Comparison of Fees for Real Estate
Limited Partner and for Individual Investor

Type of Fee	Real Estate Limited Partner	Investing in Real Estate on Your Own
Underwriting fees (paid to brokerage industry for raising capital)	0 to 8% of investment	Not applicable
Partnership formation costs (such as legal, printing)	2 to 5% of investment	Not applicable
Property acquisition fee (real estate brokerage)	8 to 18% of cash investment (typically at higher end)	Ranges from legal costs only on a sale by owner to 30% of investment if there is 6% brokerage fee on purchase price and you put 20% down
Property management fee	5 to 6% of gross rental income	3½ to 6% of gross rental income
Partnership management fee	Typically 10% of net cash flow paid to investor plus accounting and printing costs	Generally accounting costs only plus personal supervision of property management, resale, refinancing, or refurbishing decisions
Property resale fee (real estate brokerage)	Typically half of acquisition fee	Typically 3 to 6% of property sale price
Subordinated incentive fee	10 to 15% of net profit after investor receives 100% of his capital plus 6 to 8% per year cumulative thereon	Not applicable

for persons who are in low tax brackets and do not seek additional long-term capital gains. As such, they can be considered a substitute (though illiquid and with a higher default risk) for a portion of the bond holdings in a diversified portfolio.

Equity investments in carefully selected, professionally managed real estate trusts or syndicates can provide high yield with tax advantages through depreciation deductions and with a hedge against inflation. This chapter should in no way be construed as offering insights into real estate analysis, acquisition, and management on your own.

VOCABULARY

capitalization rate
cash flow distribution
deed of trust
depreciation
equity buildup
equity trust
foreclosure

general partner
gross income multiplier (GM)
limited partner
mortgage trust
real estate syndicate
real estate investment trust (REIT)

QUESTIONS

1. What risks must you assume in exchange for the high yields offered by second deeds of trust?
2. What are the income tax consequences of investing in second deeds?
3. What is the primary risk in second trust deeds?
4. What is the difference between a short-term mortgage REIT, a long-term mortgage REIT, and an equity REIT?
5. Under what circumstances would an equity REIT be a more appropriate investment than a real estate syndicate?
6. Compare blind pool and single property syndicates.
7. As a syndicate investor, what three types of financial items should you keep a record of if you wish to compute your total return on your investment?
8. Name three potential risks that you face when you invest in real estate limited partnerships.
9. What is the primary reason for investing in single-family homes or duplexes?

CASE PROBLEM

In June, Barb and Ken Winkelmann graduated from college, and in August each started a well-paying job. They had no investments but wanted to start some, and so by the next June they had accumulated $5,000 to use in this way. They expected that by the end of the year they would have $7,000 to $8,000 in addition to their emergency fund. Since they had that much money for investments and their $20,000 joint taxable income would be taxed in a combined state and federal marginal tax bracket of 30 percent, they decided to consider investing in real estate. This investment might provide them with not only long-term growth and a hedge against inflation but also tax savings. Table 20-2 compares the five alternatives they had to choose from.

1. Which of these five alternatives would probably be best for the Winkelmanns? Why? What is a major reason for not selecting each of the other four? (Give one reason for each alternative.)
2. What will be the tax effect this year if the Winkelmanns invest $5,000 in a real estate syndicate?
3. Should they invest $2,000, $5,000, or $8,000 in the alternative you have selected for them? Why?
4. Should they consider investments other than those related to real estate? Why or why not?

TABLE 20-2

Characteristics of Various Types of Real Estate Investments

Investment	Projected Income Yield	Minimum Investment Amount	Income Tax Aspects
Second deeds of trust	10% (interest)	$2,000	Interest fully taxable
Long-term mortgage trust (REIT)	9 (dividend)	$20 per share	Dividend fully taxable; long-term capital gains taxed at one-half
Equity trust (REIT)	8 (dividend)	$20 per share	75% of dividend tax-free; remainder as in mortgage trust
Single property syndicate	6 (cash flow)	$5,000	Cash flow tax-free in early years; 40% of initial investment tax deductible in year committed
Blind pool syndicate	6 (cash flow)	$5,000	Same as single property syndicate

RECOMMENDED READING

Greenebaum, Mary. "Searching for Bargains among the REITs." *Fortune*, March 12, 1979, pp. 153–156.

> Investors were so cautious after the bad experience of 1974–75 that the sound REITs were still undervalued in the stock market in early 1979.

Hoagland, Henry E., and Stone, Leo D. *Real Estate Finance*. 6th ed. Homewood, Ill.: Richard D. Irwin, 1977.

> A good text for the student wishing to learn more about real estate investing.

Rudoff, Arnold G. *Limited Partners Letter*. A monthly publication available for $197 per year from Prologue Press, 1225 Crane Street, Menlo Park, CA 94025.

> This service keeps investors up to date on investment, tax, and legal matters relating to real estate and other kinds of syndications.

"Ten Costly Mistakes Real Estate Investors Make." *Changing Times*, October 1981, pp. 60–62.

> How to avoid following the conventional wisdom (such as "negative cash flow means good tax shelter") when it's wrong.

CHUCK AND NANCY ANDERSON

Their Real Estate Investment Program

As part of Chuck and Nancy's investment plan, they allotted $5,000 to investing in real estate as a long-term program of building up funds for their retirement.

Questions

1. Which of the three real estate investment types—second trust deeds, mortgage REITs, or equity REITs and syndicates—seems most appropriate for the Andersons? Why? Why would you reject the other alternatives?
2. If you selected second trust deeds, check the Yellow Pages for local mortgage brokers and ask them about investments available in your region.
3. If Chuck and Nancy were choosing only between REITs and syndicates, which should they probably select? Is liquidity (with accompanying price fluctuations) an important consideration for the Andersons? If they were to select an REIT, should it be a mortgage or an equity trust? Why? If they selected a syndicate, would a single property or blind pool type be more appropriate? Why?

V

Planning For Retirement and Estate Transfer

Perhaps, back in the first chapter of this book you established as one of your financial goals being able to enjoy a comfortable retirement. Since then you have learned how to protect your resources, how to get the most out of your income, and how to increase your income. In Chapter 21 you will learn how to use these strategies to prepare for retirement.

By using the skills and strategies you have learned in this book, you will probably not only assure having an enjoyable retirement but also build an estate. It does not matter whether your estate is large or small. Having worked to assemble your financial resources, you should take precautions to see that they are not dissipated through senseless investments and undue taxation after your death. Chapter 22 is presented to help you avoid these problems.

21

Achieving Your Largest Financial Goal: Retirement

Retirement is eagerly anticipated by many people as a time for leisure and relaxation after a long span of productive years. It is a time to enjoy grandchildren and to pursue the interests and hobbies there was never time for when working. The major effect of stopping working is the loss of income generated by that activity. Therefore, it is very important that you ensure the presence of various financial resources upon retirement to "take up the slack."

To maximize your financial well-being during retirement, you must consider (1) how much you will need in financial resources to provide for your retirement and (2) the financial means available to achieve these goals, including what you can expect from the federal government, your employer, and programs you can use to supplement payments from these sources.

THE IMPORTANCE OF PLANNING

Advance planning is your best guarantee that you will be able to afford retirement. As we discussed in Chapter 15, retirement is a type III goal. Once you have put your investment programs into effect and are achieving your type II goals, it is time to turn your attention to retirement planning. We recommend that you begin your planning and investing at least 20 years before you expect to retire. These years of preparation should give you enough time to reach your financial retirement goals—and allow for the effects of inflation as well. Hand-in-hand with advance planning goes frequent plan assessment. Then, if circumstances change or your strategies do not turn out as expected, you can adapt your plans as necessary.

How Not to Do It

Marvin Pierce was 59 years old and had been working continuously for 40 years. As he approached age 60, he began to consider taking early retirement at age 62. However, the Pierces had maintained a lifestyle that consumed most of what he brought home. His wife persuaded him to meet with a financial counselor to analyze the wisdom of early retirement. Marvin came home from his meeting very discouraged. The counselor's analysis indicated that as a result of maintaining a high lifestyle relative to their income, the Pierces had acquired few investments (aside from Social Security and a pension) with which to fund their retirement. As a consequence, Marvin would have to continue working to age 70.

Your Planning Perspective

There are several things to consider before you begin the actual planning process.

life cycle stage at retirement   You must identify fairly accurately what your position in the life cycle will be at that time. It seems reasonable to assume, for example, that most people will have neither dependent children nor dependent parents to support if they retire rather late in their own lives. The younger you retire, however, the more likely these possibilities become.

For example, John and Martha Shipstead are both 45 and are considering retiring in five years. At that time, their youngest child will be entering college and both of Mrs. Shipstead's parents (whom the Shipsteads are supporting) will be 70 years old. Obviously, when planning his own retirement, John must make allowances for the expenses of these dependents.

If you are married, it is best to assume that both you and your spouse will be living when you retire. If you are single and marriage seems unlikely, your life cycle considerations are going to be different.

living longer   The average lifespan has been slowly increasing for years. Table 21-1 shows the most recent projections. In all likelihood, 30 years from now people will be living even longer. Therefore, be conservative and assume a long retirement period when you plan.

tax assumptions   It is commonly asserted that when people retire their taxes drop because they are no longer earning a living. True, Social Security benefits are not

TABLE 21-1

Average Future Lifetime in the United States

Age	Average Remaining Lifetime (Years)	
	Male	*Female*
50	25	31
55	21	26
60	17	22
65	14	18
70	11	15
75	9	11

Source: U.S. Department of Health, Education, and Welfare, 1977 data.

taxed and there is a retirement income credit. Nevertheless, if you intend to maintain your current lifestyle after retiring, you will probably have to rely to some extent on taxable sources of income. For example, suppose you invest $3,000 a year for 30 years in a tax-deferred retirement plan. At an 8 percent annual return, this investment will be worth $339,000. If you withdraw 8 percent annually from this fund after retiring, you will have at least $27,000 of taxable income. It is not difficult to see why taxes could remain relatively high even during one's retirement.

investment flexibility   The ideal achievement horizon for financing your retirement, 20 to 30 years, is a long time. Dramatic changes will occur in the personal financial environment during that period. Therefore, it is important that you select investment strategies that are not "carved in stone."

retirement goals   At a minimum, you will want to be assured that you will always have the basic necessities: food, shelter, clothing, and health care. Your first point of planning should be to ensure that these needs will be fulfilled. Only after you have satisfactorily provided for them should you consider your other retirement goals, such as traveling, pursuing hobbies and interests, spending time with your family and grandchildren, and increasing the size of your financial estate. Achieving these goals can transform retirement from merely a secure existence into an enjoyable experience.

The Basic Strategies

Your basic investment strategies will shift dramatically upon retirement. While you are working, you will probably focus on capital appreciation over the long term and take advantage of the various tax-deferred investment options. Once retired, however, you will probably emphasize income generation. If you are aware beforehand of the need for this change in investment approach, you are more likely to make this transition successfully. Later in this chapter, we will provide more details on what to emphasize in each phase and how to make the transition.

COMPUTING YOUR TOTAL RETIREMENT NEEDS

The further away from retirement you are, the more difficult it is to estimate what it will cost. Nevertheless, the earlier you begin planning and estimating the costs, the easier it will be to adjust for changes in living expense needs or in projected income as your retirement draws nearer. To compute your total financial needs for retirement, use the following procedure. Figure 21-1 shows how the Shipsteads used it to determine their retirement needs. Completion of this procedure should give you a reasonably accurate estimate of what your retirement will cost, and you will then be ready to consider how to finance it.

Instructions

1 *Age at Retirement. Decide at what age you plan to retire.*
   John and Martha Shipstead decide to defer their retirement to age 65, when they will probably have no dependents.

NAME(S) _John and Martha Shipstead_

DATE _March 1983_

RETIREMENT LIVING EXPENSE NEEDS

1 Age at Retirement

Husband	65
Wife	65

2 Basic Living Expenses

	Month	Year
Housing		
Utilities	$ 75	$ 900
Repairs		
Insurance		
Taxes		
Other		
Rent or mortgage payments	500	6,000
Food	250	3,000
Clothing, personal care		
Him		500
Her		800
Gifts, contributions		500
Transportation		
Gas	50	600
Repairs	20	240
Licenses	10	120
Insurance	20	240
Auto payments or purchase	100	1,200

Medical	
Doctor	300
Dentist	120
Medicines	120
Insurance	160
Taxes (personal income)	1,000
TOTAL	15,800

3 Recurrent Extra Expenses

Gardening	300
Travel	1,000
Other _entertainment_	500
TOTAL	1,800

4 Total Annual Living Expenses	$ 17,600
5 Expected Number of Years of Retirement	20
6 Total Living Expenses during Retirement	$ 352,000
7 One-Time Costs	$ 11,000
8 Total Funds Needed at Retirement	$ 363,000
9 Years to Retirement	20
10 Inflation Factor	2.6
11 Total Inflated Living Expenses at Retirement	$ 943,800

FIGURE 21-1
Sample computation of retirement living expense needs.

2 *Basic Living Expenses. Consider what your lifestyle during retirement is likely to be and how much it will cost.* Your basic living expenses for food, housing, clothing, and health care will be prescribed by your lifestyle.

To get an idea how much your retirement lifestyle is going to cost, consult your budget records. They should indicate what it is costing to maintain your present lifestyle. If your current lifestyle is substantially different from what you envision for retirement, this difference should be taken into consideration in your projections. For example, at present you may need a larger home than you will after retirement. Therefore, housing expenses will be considerably less in those later years. If you do plan to continue living in your present home, make sure that your mortgage is paid off in advance so that mortgage payments do not drain your retirement income. Also, current living expenses may include the expenses of dependent children or parents. These might not be a consideration when you retire. Review Medicare benefits and costs (Chapter 8) to make sure that your health insurance program will not duplicate the coverage offered by Medicare and that your retirement health needs will be adequately covered. Note that the medical insurance portion of Medicare is optional and can be applied for by age 65 if it is desired. Under Medicare the federal government pays half the premium, thus offering very low-cost protection. Be sure to take these changes in your living expenses into account when developing your cost estimates.

On the basis of their current expenses, the Shipsteads estimated what their basic living expenses would be during retirement. They also took into consideration that they would probably be living near New York and that their lifestyle would probably require a high level of budget expenditures. They expect to pay off the mortgage on their home, sell it, and move to an apartment. Of course, if the Shipsteads were to decide not to sell their home, they would not include $500 a month rental cost in the living expense estimates for their retirement years, but would include enough to cover property taxes, insurance, and upkeep. A major expense will probably be maintaining a car. They expect to receive Medicare benefits and so are not allotting much for health care except possibly supplemental health insurance.

3 *Recurrent Extra Expenses. Determine how much you are likely to spend each year fulfilling retirement goals other than meeting basic needs.*

The Shipsteads want to pursue their interest in gardening and also have money each year to visit their children and grandchildren at Christmas and during the summer. The annual cost of these two recurring expenses and entertainment comes to $1,800.

4 *Total Annual Living Expenses. Add the totals for annual basic living expenses (step 2) and your annual recurrent extra expenses (step 3).*

The Shipsteads have a total of $17,600 in annual living expenses.

5 *Expected Number of Years of Retirement. Use the estimates in Table 21-1 to determine how many years your retirement is likely to last.* In the table find your average life expectancy upon reaching retirement. If there is reason to believe that you or your spouse will live longer than average (due to good health and/or the experience of other members of the family), add an appropriate estimate to the longest figure. To be conservative, do not use a shorter estimate than that given in the table.

John Shipstead can expect to live approximately 14 years after he retires, and Martha about 18 years. To be conservative, they estimated that their retirement will last about 20 years (two years longer than her expected remaining lifetime).

6 *Total Living Expenses during Retirement. Multiply your total annual living expenses (step 4) by your expected number of years of retirement (step 5).*

The Shipsteads estimate that their total living expenses during retirement will be $352,000.

7 *One-Time Costs. Add the lump-sum cost of reaching goals that can be expected to occur only once or twice.*

The Shipsteads want to have $11,000 for an around-the-world cruise sometime during their retirement.

8 *Total Funds Needed at Retirement. Add your total one-time costs (step 7) to your total living expenses during retirement (step 6).*

The Shipsteads have a total of $363,000 that they will need at retirement.

9 *Years to Retirement. Subtract your age now from your age at retirement.*

Since the Shipsteads are both now 45 and plan to retire when they are 65, it will be 20 years before they retire.

10 *Inflation Factor. Use compound interest Table A to find the inflation factor that accords with both the most likely annual rate of inflation and the number of years from now until you retire.* Since World War II, inflation has averaged roughly 5 percent a year.

The Shipsteads find that for a 5 percent annual rate of inflation and the 20 years until they retire, the inflation factor is 2.6.

11 *Total Inflated Living Expenses at Retirement. Multiply the inflation factor (step 10) times your total funds needed at retirement (step 8).* This will indicate how much money you will need upon retirement to offset the effect of inflation up to that time. Although inflation will continue to affect your cost of living during retirement, the investments made for retirement purposes should continue to grow and to offer higher income during those years. For example, assume that you need $20,000 in investments to begin retirement and will spend $1,500 of that amount each year. At the end of the first year, that principal would amount to only $18,500. However, if the money is in a 10 percent savings certificate, the principal plus interest would be worth at least $20,425. (The $1,925 represents 10 percent on an average balance of $19,250 in the account for that year.) That extra amount is more than would be needed to offset a 5 percent rate of inflation. The effect of inflation after retirement has begun is important only if all your investment money is tied up in a fixed annuity such as a pension plan that offers only fixed monthly payments for life. The important thing is to prepare properly before your retirement by selecting investments with an inflationary hedge.

The Shipsteads figure that they will need $943,800 to cover living expenses after they retire.

"PACKAGED" SOURCES OF RETIREMENT INCOME

Very few people must depend solely on investment programs developed through their own initiative to provide for their retirement years. Some of the most common programs offered by other sources are Social Security (the federal government) and pension funds (employers). Nevertheless, in recent years there has been a dramatic increase in do-it-yourself alternatives.

Social Security

When earnings stop or are reduced because the worker retires, dies, or becomes disabled, monthly cash benefits are paid out of a pool of Social Security contributions made by employees, employers, and self-employed people. Four types of payments are made: disability payments, Medicare, survivor's benefits, and retirement payments.

eligibility for retirement benefits Retirement benefits are generally available to individuals when they reach age 65. Benefits at a reduced level may be available as early as age 62. There are several special considerations concerning divorcees, nonworking spouses, and certain dependents. Contact your local Social Security office if you feel you might be eligible under any of these special circumstances.

Recipients of Social Security retirement benefits who also work are still entitled to their usual benefits if they are (1) under 65 and earn no more than $4,440 a year or (2) 65 to 72 and earn no more than $6,000 a year. Above these amounts $1 of benefits is forfeited for each $2 earned, with the following exceptions:

1. If you elect to continue working at 65, you may earn $6,000 that year (no more than $500 in each month of that year) before the 2-for-1 forfeiture begins.
2. If you are 70 or older, the forfeiture procedure is not applied.

There are loopholes in this regulation. First, not all income is considered earnings for Social Security purposes. Among excludable items are private pension payments; dividends from stocks; rents and royalties; profits on securities transactions; and interest on savings deposits. Second, you may collect full benefits for any year in which you earn less than the income limitations discussed in the previous paragraph. Your payments may be reduced or stop when a marriage or divorce changes your status, when your children grow out of being qualified dependents, or when you die.

Benefit payments are not automatic. An application must be filed before they can begin. We recommend that you get in touch with the local Social Security office within the six months before you retire.

the future of Social Security For several years now there has been increasing concern about the ability of the Social Security system to pay benefits to retirees exclusively from the tax revenues it receives. This problem is projected to occur

intermittently during the early 1980s and then reappear much more dramatically early in the twenty-first century.

Let us consider how our national attitude toward Social Security has evolved since the program's inception in 1935. Originally, the concept of *equity* alone prevailed. People thought that each retiree had a right to receive benefits based on contributions made to the system in the form of employee and employer taxes. This attitude still exists very strongly today. In the 1960s and early 1970s the concept of *adequacy* arose: the system should pay benefits based on the recipient's need. The system does this in several ways: (1) it pays recipients at least a minimum benefit level (irrespective of contribution level); (2) the benefits paid to a low income earner are a higher percentage of his or her preretirement earnings than are those paid to a higher income earner; and (3) it makes additional payments to recipients who have dependent spouses or children.

In the late 1970s and early 1980s a third concept, *affordability*, surfaced. Many people have become concerned about the system's long-term financial viability for several reasons. First, people are living longer and this trend is expected to continue because of advances in medicine and health care. Thus, the average amount of benefits paid per recipient is increasing. Second, people are retiring earlier, further increasing the average amount of benefits received. Third, benefits, which are raised in concert with the consumer price index, have risen in recent years much faster than the taxes that fund these benefits. Although Social Security taxes are a percentage of wages, which tend to increase with overall economic growth, inflation has been outstripping this growth for several years. Finally, the ratio of people paying taxes into the system to people receiving benefits is changing dramatically. Currently there are about three people working and paying taxes for each retired Social Security recipient. By 2010, this ratio is projected to drop to 2:1 as the people born between World War II and 1965 retire.

There is no simple, painless (economically or politically) solution. Possibilities are to raise Social Security taxes even higher, fund benefit deficits from other government revenues, lower benefits, allow benefits not to increase faster than tax receipts grow, or move the normal retirement age up to 68 from 65.

Evaluating Employer-Sponsored Plans

You will want to pay close attention to the quality of an employer's retirement plan since its soundness and other features could have a major impact on your financial circumstances during retirement. Commonly employers offer one or more of three programs: a pension plan, a deferred profit-sharing plan, or a thrift and savings plan. Here are the major issues to scrutinize.

type of contribution   Pension plans commonly employ one of two methods. The "defined contribution" plan fixes the amount of the annual contribution to the fund. The amount of retirement benefits this accumulation of contributions will provide depends on (1) how successfully this fund is managed by the investment managers before retirement and (2) prevailing economic experience, principally economic growth and inflation. The "defined benefit" plan fixes the level of benefits to be paid relative to income earned. The employer is then required to ensure that contributions are made to fund these benefit levels. Obviously, the second method is more attractive to you as an employee, particularly if the benefit-to-be-paid calculation is made during your years of highest earnings, which commonly occur just before retirement.

Pension funds may be financed in two ways. "Pay-as-you-go" financing involves no advance buildup of funds. The organization involved merely draws checks on its bank account as benefits come due. This type of pension fund financing offers its members or beneficiaries no assurance that benefits would continue if the organization were dissolved or went out of business.

The second form of financing involves advance funding. With this method, organizations contribute funds annually to a managed investment fund. These contributions will be made to cover benefits earned but not yet payable, benefits currently being earned, or a combination of both. With this form of financing, the faster the funds are contributed, the more secure future benefits are—as long as the funds are not mismanaged. As the benefits earned become payable, disbursements are made from the pension fund. Obviously, the latter form of financing is more attractive to you as a future pension beneficiary.

Contributions to finance a pension plan can be obtained through three methods. First, the sponsoring organization might provide all the funds. Second, the organization's members or employees might be required to provide part of the funds. Third, the members or employees might have the option of voluntarily providing additional funds. In the latter case, a person who contributes voluntarily usually receives additional benefits in proportion to his or her contributions.

Management of pension funds that use advance funding can be conducted by two types of management groups—an insurance company or a trustee. In the first case, as funds are contributed they are turned over to an insurance company and used to buy either cash value life insurance or deferred annuities. If cash value insurance is bought and you die before retirement, your survivors receive a death benefit; if you live to retirement, the cash value life insurance may be converted into an annuity payment program. If deferred annuities are purchased with the contributed funds, you receive an annuity upon retirement. To provide death coverage during your working years, term insurance can be carried on you, in effect converting your deferred annuity program into a cash value insurance program.

In the second case, the fund is managed by a trustee, which might be a bank or a group of the organization's executives. The funds may be invested in annuities, preferred stocks, bonds, or another investment medium depending on the policies of the fund's trustee. This is the most common form of pension fund management. When you retire, money is withdrawn from the fund either to purchase an annuity for you or to provide you with regular benefits. These programs are often supplemented with some form of life insurance.

Deferred profit-sharing plans make contributions only out of company profits. This approach aligns the economic self-interest of employees (for retirement income) with that of shareholders (for return on investment) around the importance of profitability.

Thrift-and-savings plans involve employers matching employees' contributions by a preestablished ratio—for example, 1 to 4 with the combined contribution not to exceed, say, 15 percent of an employee's earnings.

membership The Employees Retirement Income Security Act (ERISA), passed by Congress in 1974, placed the maximum waiting period for eligibility for membership in a retirement program at one full year of employment for employees 25 and older. Find out how long you must be a member of an organization before you are eligible for its retirement fund program. Some programs offer eligibility from the beginning of service or employment. Others require a minimum period of service or employment or a minimum age level (often 25) before admitting someone to the program. Also find out how old you can be and still be admitted to a pension fund program. Do not wait too long to join or you may be left out.

Some programs require that members belong for a certain length of time before they are eligible to receive benefits. Check the program's required retirement age to make sure that there are enough years of employment before retirement to make you eligible for retirement payments. In some instances, organizations allow you to continue your membership or employment past the required retirement age so that you can be eligible for retirement benefits.

retirement date Programs usually specify the date on which an employee may retire—June 1 of the year in which he or she turns 65, for example. Many retirement funds make reduced retirement payments to employees who retire before this date. Be sure to consider these stipulations when making your retirement plans.

If you leave a company before retirement, the amount of pension payments you can look forward to will depend on the pension fund's rules and the circumstances under which you leave. At a very minimum, any amount that you have contributed to the fund, plus interest, should be returned to you. You also might have the option of leaving your contributions in the program to provide a future retirement benefit.

If you are *vested* with, or given, rights to retirement benefits based on contributions made by your employer, you will receive partial benefits based on those contributions even if you leave the company before retirement. Usually, to receive this right, you must leave any contributions you have made in the fund. The more progressive programs often vest you with an interest in retirement payment rights that increases in proportion to the length of time you participate in their program. Most of them require that you either work for a certain number of years or until you reach a certain age (or both) before the vesting procedure is completed. For example, you might become vested with a 50 percent right to benefits after five years in the program. Each succeeding year, you would be vested with an additional 10 percent. After 10 years, you would be 100 percent vested. This means that, whether you left the company before retirement or not, you would be entitled to a full retirement benefit based on the company's contributions. Regardless of what vesting schedule a company uses, according to ERISA an employee must be fully vested with his or her benefits after 15 years of full membership in the program. In addition, faster vesting is mandated by ERISA in certain circumstances.

receiving retirement benefits Payments may be taken in any of several forms, depending upon the options offered by the organization. A common option is *straight life annuity.* However, there are several variations on this basic form. A *refund annuity* will provide a smaller monthly payment so that a lump-sum payment may be made to your beneficiary upon your death. A *certain and continuous*

annuity makes monthly payments for life or for a specified period of time, whichever is greater. Should you die before this period expires, the payments will be
continued to a designated beneficiary to the end of the period. If, for example, you
were to choose a life annuity 10 years certain that paid $500 a month, you would
receive this amount each month no matter how long you lived; but if you lived, say,
only six years into retirement (or any period short of 10 years), your beneficiary
would receive $500 a month for the remaining four years (or however long to the
end of the 10-year term). The *joint-and-survivorship annuity* pays an annuity to
you and to another person. Upon the death of one of the annuitants, the remaining
portion is paid in annuities to the survivor. A *Social Security annuity* is designed for
individuals who retire before they are eligible for Social Security retirement benefits. In this instance, you would receive large monthly payments until you begin to
receive Social Security benefits, at which time your annuity payments would be
reduced.

tax treatment of retirement payments   Social Security, railroad retirement, and
veterans' pension benefits are tax-free. Military retirement benefits and lump-sum
distributions of Keogh plan funds (to be discussed later in this chapter) are all fully
taxable. If you belong to a retirement program to which you make contributions
during your working years, part of your benefit payments will be tax-free. This
portion represents a return of your original contribution. For example, if your
contributions equaled 25 percent of the value of your benefits, then theoretically 25
percent of each benefit payment would be tax-free. In practice, the computation
required by the IRS to determine the tax-free portion may be much more complex.

The *retirement income credit* represents a tax break, liberalized by the Tax
Reform Act of 1976, for taxpayers 65 and older. If your retirement income comes
mainly from dividends, interest, rent, taxable pensions, and the like, this credit can
benefit you. You can receive a credit for 15 percent of taxable income up to (1)
$2,500 for single persons or for married couples where only one spouse is 65 or older
and (2) $3,750 for married couples filing jointly ($1,875 if filing separately) where
both spouses are 65 or older. These base amounts are reduced by (1) Social Security
benefits and other exempt income received and (2) one-half of adjusted gross income in excess of $7,500 for single persons and $10,000 for married persons filing
joint returns ($5,000 if filing separately). The credit may not exceed the tax other-
wise due for the year.

ERISA   As mentioned earlier, in 1974 Congress passed the Employees Retirement
Income Security Act. The basic thrust of this legislation was to set minimum levels of
acceptability for private retirement plans. For example, the act improved the
chances that benefits would not be lost entirely if an organization went bankrupt
and became unable to make future benefit payments. The Pension Benefit Guaranty
Corporation was established to provide workers of bankrupt or defunct organizations with benefits up to certain levels that these workers would otherwise have been
entitled to. This corporation's funds come from compulsory insurance premiums
paid by organizations with retirement benefit programs.

provisions for   In addition to the considerations just discussed, you will want to
ascertain how your employer's retirement program handles:

- interrupted service—Will you forfeit any future benefits or will you be allowed to continue accruing benefits once you return to work?
- inflation protection—Do your retirement plan's investment managers pursue investment strategies that provide a hedge against inflation (particularly important in defined contribution plans)? Can you look forward to your retirement payments increasing to offset inflation?
- early retirement—What reduction in annual benefits occurs if you choose to retire before the normal retirement date? How early can you retire and still receive benefits?
- death payments—What will be paid to your designated beneficiaries from your retirement plan if you die before retirement?
- working past normal retirement—Will you accrue additional benefits by working past the normal retirement date or not?

lump-sum distribution Whether to take a lump-sum distribution of your accrued retirement benefits in an employer-sponsored plan is a very important decision. Your options as to what to do with the funds include IRAs and Keogh plans, which will be discussed in the next section. Certain considerations relevant to this decision will be treated here.

Historically, most retirees have accepted one of the annuity payment options discussed earlier in this chapter. In recent years, taking the money with you if you leave your employer well before normal retirement age has become increasingly popular. Your main options are three: outright distribution, IRA rollover, or Keogh plan rollover.

You would want to accept an outright distribution if you had an immediate need for the money without investment restrictions (e.g., you are starting your own business). Under these circumstances, the distribution would be subject to tax via a 10-year averaging method according to IRS regulations. This alternative is often favored by individuals who can look forward to being in continuously high tax brackets, even after retirement.

If you do not have an immediate need for the funds (e.g., they are targeted to help fund your retirement beginning sometime after age 59½), then the tax deferral aspects of an IRA rollover (must be accomplished within 60 days of distribution) or a Keogh plan rollover (you must have self-employment income to qualify for such a plan) may be appropriate. Because there will be a relatively large amount of money involved in such a distribution, we strongly recommend that you seek qualified tax counsel before proceeding.

Do-It-Yourself Retirement Plans

As discussed earlier, the vexing economic conditions of recent years (fluctuating economic growth and investment returns in an environment of rising prices) have caused many people to become less sanguine about the financial aspects of their upcoming retirement. With the ability of the Social Security system to continue to pay increasing benefits in question, and with some employer-sponsored retirement plans also under financial strain, individuals have increasingly realized that they must take independent action to deal with these circumstances. The most common strategies are establishing tax-advantaged individual retirement or Keogh plans or using professional corporations.

individual retirement plans   These plans were improved by the Economic Recovery Tax Act of 1981. There are three different plans available: the individual retirement account (IRA), the individual retirement annuity, and the special retirement bond issued by the federal government. The first of these offers the most opportunity for financial well-being.

An IRA can be established for an individual who receives compensation in the form of wages, salaries, professional fees, personal service income, and the like. The plan can be established by the employee, by an employer for employees' benefit, or by a labor union for its members' benefit. Individuals are no longer restricted from establishing IRAs if they are also covered by an employer's IRS qualified retirement plan. Annual contributions can amount to 100 percent of compensation up to $2,000. These contributions are deductible from gross income. Therefore, it is not necessary to take deductions from adjusted gross income to avail yourself of the IRA deductions. If both spouses work, the annual contribution and deduction against gross income for each is $2,000, for a total of $4,000. If only one spouse works, a plan may be established that allows an additional annual contribution/deduction of $250, for a total of $2250.

To be valid, the annual contribution must be deposited into a government-approved custodial or trustee account. Examples of organizations that offer approved accounts are commercial banks, savings and loan associations, insurance companies, securities companies, federally insured credit unions, and mutual funds, among others. Voluntary employee contributions to a regular employer-qualified retirement plan that has this feature are also possible.

Probably one of the most attractive aspects of an IRA is that you may direct the investment strategy as you see fit. The best strategies probably involve high-yield instruments such as CDs, money market instruments or funds, corporate bonds or funds, high dividend paying stocks or funds, insurance annuities, or income-oriented real estate limited partnerships. These instruments are preferable because taxes on the IRA's earnings are deferred until you begin taking retirement distributions—between ages 59½ and 70½. Strategies that do not make much sense are investments in tax-exempt securities (since the yield on normally taxed bonds is deferred for IRA investments) or investments that only stress capital appreciation (since any realized capital gains will be taxed as ordinary income when distributions commence). Investment strategies that are not allowed include trading on margin and purchasing life insurance contracts or collectibles.

Individual retirement annuities (which allow investments only in joint and survivor or endowment annuities) and federal retirement bonds are less attractive than individual retirement accounts (IRAs) because of the lack of investment flexibility.

Simplified employee pensions are a form of IRA that allow for direct contributions by the employer. The annual amount that may be contributed by the employer and deducted by the employee is 15 percent of the employee's compensation, up to a dollar maximum of $15,000. Even if your employer makes such a contribution to your IRA, you can still make your own annual contribution/deduction to the same IRA of 100 percent of compensation, up to a dollar maximum of $2,000. Because of the attractiveness of simplified employee pension plans, we strongly recommend that you consult your employer's benefits coordinator and your tax advisor to see whether such a plan can be put into effect for you.

Keogh plans   These allow self-employed individuals to set up their own retirement funds. The act applies to professional people such as lawyers, doctors, artists, accountants, and architects as well as farmers, business partners, and sole proprietors of their own businesses. All these people receive income that is not subject to withholding for income tax purposes. Generally, any income of this nature may be diverted in part to a retirement fund.

For such a fund to fall under the guidelines of this act, it must fulfill the following qualifications. First, as with IRAs, the retirement benefits to be derived from the fund cannot be initiated before the individual is 59½ years old and they must be initiated before the age of 70½. Second, if the person setting up the plan has employees, he or she must also set up retirement funds for all full-time employees who have worked for that individual at least three years. In this case, the employer must make the same percentage of salary contribution for each qualified employee as for himself or herself. Third, contributions to the retirement plan must be invested in an approved manner. Eligible investment plans include trusts administered by a bank or trust company, annuities and endowment life insurance, and mutual funds. Most mutual funds and insurance companies have plans that have received official approval from appropriate government agencies. If a trust arrangement is desired because of specific considerations not covered by the more generalized plans, official sanction is required before the plan may be put into effect.

There are two tax advantages to such plans. First, plan contributions of up to 15 percent of earned income gained from self-employment (up to a dollar maximum of $15,000) may be deducted from annual gross income for federal income tax purposes. Alternatively, 100 percent of the first $750 of self-employed earned income may be deducted if the total income is less than $15,000. (For taxable years beginning with 1984, these dollar and percentage limitations are eliminated, and contributions to a Keogh plan with respect to any individual will be subject to the dollar and percentage limitations generally applicable to retirement plans, i.e., $30,000 and 25 percent of earned income less planned contributions.) Second, income earned from the fund, plus any capital appreciation that occurs, is not subject to federal taxation until the retirement benefits have begun to be paid. The tax rate that applies during retirement years will probably be less than the rate that would have applied during the working years when the fund was growing. When similar treatment is accorded by state income tax regulations, the value of these two tax advantages is increased.

salary reduction   As mentioned in Chapter 10, in 1982 the IRS issued regulations that enable employers to set up salary reduction plans. Under this alternative, you can elect to have your employer reduce your salary by as much as 10 percent or more (the amount depends on how much else you are already deducting for retirement programs) and contribute this amount to an employer-sponsored thrift or savings plan. Such a program may have advantages for you: (1) any amount contributed by your employer is currently not taxable to you; (2) income earned on these contributions is not subject to tax while they are building up; and (3) there is a special 10-year averaging calculation that applies if you withdraw your accumulated contributions and earnings in a lump-sum distribution upon quitting work. Alternatively, upon leaving your employer, you can roll over your accumulated contributions and earnings into an IRA account or into your next employer's plan (if one exists). While still employed, you can get at these funds without paying a penalty if there are certain hardship circumstances as approved by your employer. You can participate in a salary reduction plan without forfeiting your opportunity to contribute to your own IRA.

There may be several disadvantages to these programs: (1) you are subject to the investment results of the employer-sponsored program; (2) the level of your contribution may be limited by the amount of participation by employees at other income levels; and (3) employers may be reluctant to establish these programs because of their complex, nondiscriminatory, bureaucratic regulations.

professional corporations   These organizations are available only to individuals who must be licensed to pursue their professions, such as physicians, dentists, engineers, and architects. The tax benefits that are in part responsible for the attractiveness of such vehicles include the opportunity to purchase medical, disability, and life insurance by the corporation for the professional with pretax dollars. Also, a qualified retirement plan is possible. This plan allows the buildup of retirement funds through annual tax-free contributions by the corporation, often in excess of what would be available to the unincorporated self-employed professional through an IRA or Keogh plan.

ACHIEVING YOUR RETIREMENT GOALS

Earlier in this chapter, you used a procedure to determine what amount of financial resources you need to achieve your retirement goals. In this section, we will present a procedure that allows you to determine what you can expect in the way of contributions from Social Security, employer-sponsored retirement plans, and do-it-yourself plans. In addition, we will outline the types of investment strategies that make sense for self-directed retirement plans and any other assets you might bring to bear to achieve your retirement goals. We will also distinguish between appropriate investment strategies before and after retirement.

Calculating Your Financial Resources

This procedure is illustrated with financial data for the Shipsteads (Fig. 21-2).

Instructions

1 *Age at Retirement. Decide the age at which you plan to retire.* This age may affect the amount of Social Security benefits as well as your retirement payments.

  The Shipsteads still plan to retire at age 65.

2 *Monthly Social Security Benefits. Use the Social Security addendum in the appendix to determine these.* Estimating your retirement benefits in terms of

NAME(S) _John and Martha Shipstead_

DATE _March 1983_

RETIREMENT INVESTMENT NEEDS

1 *Age at Retirement*

Husband	65
Wife	65

2 *Monthly Social Security Benefits*

Worker at 65	$ 400
Spouse at 65	200
TOTAL	600

3 *Annual Income from Social Security* — $ 7,200

4 *Inflation Factor* — 2.6

5 *Inflated Annual Income from Social Security* — $ 18,720

6 *Annual Pension Benefits*

Worker	$ 6,000
Spouse	2,000
TOTAL	$ 8,000

7 *Total Estimated Annual Income from Social Security and Pension* — $ 26,720

8 *Expected Number of Years of Retirement* — 20

9 *Total Estimated Retirement Income from Social Security and Pension* — $534,400

10 *Total Inflated Living Expenses* — $819,000

11 *Investment Needed at Retirement* — $284,600

12 *Expected Value of IRA at Retirement*

Annual contributions	
Worker	$ 2,000
Spouse	250
Total	$ 2,250
Number of contributions	20
Annual growth rate assumption	10%
Appreciation factor	57.3
Value at retirement ($2,250 x 57.3)	$128,900

13 *Profit from Sale of Home* (after taxes and selling costs) — $145,000

Current market value of home	$ 75,000
Inflation factor	2.19
Market value at reitrement	$164,200

14 *Adjusted Total Investment Needed at Retirement* — $ 10,700

15 *Investment Strategy Needed*

Amount to be invested yearly	$ 1,250
After-tax interest	5%

FIGURE 21-2
Sample computation of
retirement investment
needs.

monthly payments is a somewhat inaccurate procedure. To be completely accurate, you would have to wait until you retired and applied for benefits. At that time, the Social Security Administration would make the computations for you. Nevertheless, attempt to estimate what these benefits will be. Without some idea of the amounts involved, projections concerning Social Security's contributions to your retirement goals will be useless.

The Shipsteads estimated that at age 65 he would be eligible to receive $400 a month in Social Security benefits and she would be eligible to receive $200—a total of $600.

3 *Annual Income from Social Security. Multiply the total monthly Social Security benefits (step 2) by 12.*

The Shipsteads can expect to receive $7,200 from Social Security in yearly retirement payments.

4 *Inflation Factor. Use the figure derived in step 10 of the procedure for computing retirement needs.* (We have assumed that Social Security benefits will roughly increase with the rate of inflation in the general economy.)

The Shipsteads find that, for a 5 percent annual rate of inflation and the 20 years until they retire, the inflation factor is 2.6.

5 *Inflated Annual Income from Social Security. Multiply annual income from Social Security (step 3) by the appropriate inflation factor (step 4).*

The inflated value of the Shipsteads' annual Social Security benefits is $18,720.

6 *Annual Pension Benefits. Find out the method used by your employer to compute pension benefits and use it to compute yours.* The amount of your pension benefits depends upon your organization's computation method. One method adds a specific dollar amount to your monthly retirement payment for each year of eligible membership or employment completed. A second method adds a dollar amount to your monthly retirement payment based on a fixed percentage of your annual wage or salary. A third method computes a fixed percentage of your average annual earnings over the duration of your membership or employment and pays this amount to you. These three basic methods offer fixed monthly payments during retirement. However, some pension funds may try to offset the effect of inflation by investing part of their funds in variable annuities, thereby increasing the size of monthly retirement payments as the cost of living increases.

The Shipsteads' employers use the third method of computing pension benefits, as shown in Table 21-2. The Shipsteads have no assurance that their pension plan will be able to offset the effect of inflation.

7 *Total Estimated Annual Income from Social Security and Pension. Add inflated annual income from Social Security (step 5) and total annual retirement benefits (step 6).*

The Shipsteads expect to have a total annual income of $26,720.

8 *Expected Number of Years of Retirement. Use the figure derived in step 5 of*

TABLE 21-2

One Method of Computing Pension Benefits

Pension Recipient	Length of Employment to Age 65	Average Annual Salary	Pension Payment Factor	Annual Value of Pension
Mr. Shipstead	30 years	$16,700	30%	$5,000
Mrs. Shipstead	15 years	$13,300	15%	$2,000

the procedure for computing retirement needs. You need not be concerned that you might live well beyond your estimate. Your Social Security and pension benefits will continue; and, with careful planning, your investments should continue to grow faster than the rate of inflation and thus provide funds for those later years.

The Shipsteads expect their retirement to last 20 years.

9 *Total Estimated Retirement Income from Social Security and Pension. Multiply total estimated annual income from Social Security and pension (step 7) by the expected number of years of retirement (step 8).*

The Shipsteads expect to have a total income of $534,400.

10 *Total Inflated Living Expenses. Insert the figure derived in your earlier computations of retirement living expense needs (Fig. 21-1).*

The Shipsteads will need $819,000 at retirement.

11 *Investment Needed at Retirement. Subtract total inflated living expenses (step 10) from total estimated retirement income (step 9).*

The Shipsteads will need $284,600 at retirement.

12 *Expected Value of IRA at Retirement.* This calculation involves several steps. First, determine the annual contribution you anticipate making to the IRA. Then determine the number of annual contributions—how many years between now and retirement you anticipate contributing to your IRA. Next you must make an assumption about how much your IRA (yield and appreciation) will grow each year tax-free. Then turn to compound interest Table B in the appendix and determine the future value of a regular annual contribution to your IRA. Multiply this factor times the annual IRA contribution to reach the value of your IRA at retirement.

The Shipsteads expect to contribute the full $2,000 for him and $250 for her, as a nonworking spouse. They plan to do this each year until retirement—a total of 20 years. The Shipsteads decide to assume a 10 percent rate of growth, realizing that they may have to lower this rate if their IRA turns out not to perform this well. They find that the factor for 10 percent a year for 20 years is 57.3. Their IRA value turns out to be $128,900 (rounded off).

13 *Profit from Sale of Home. Multiply the current market value of your home by an appropriate appreciation factor to determine market value at retirement and then subtract probable taxes and selling costs.* If you do not plan to sell your house or if for some reason you think a profit would not result from the sale, you cannot count on this financial resource to reduce the amount that must be invested in preparation for retirement.

The market value of the Shipsteads' home is $75,000. To be conservative, they assume that their home will appreciate in value about 4 percent a year between now and retirement. According to compound interest Table A, the factor for 4 percent for 20 years is 2.19. At this rate, the house and property would be worth $164,200 ($75,000 × 2.19) when they retire. They estimate that $145,000 would be left after all taxes and selling costs have been paid.

14 *Adjusted Total Investment Needed at Retirement. Subtract your IRA value at retirement (step 12) and profit from sale of home (step 13) from total investment needed at retirement (step 11).*

The $128,900 IRA value and the $145,000 received from the sale of the Shipsteads' home would result in an adjusted total investment need of only $10,700.

15 *Investment Strategy Needed. Use compound interest Table B to determine how much you must invest each year until you retire and at what rate of return in order to reach the figure derived in step 14.*

To reach $10,700 the Shipsteads need to invest approximately $325 a year ($27 a month) for the next 20 years, averaging 5 percent after taxes.

Retirement Investment Strategies

If you have calculated your retirement living expense needs (as in Figure 21-1) and your retirement investment needs (as in Figure 21-2), you may have found (like the Shipsteads) that Social Security, your IRA program, and the sale of your home can fulfill almost all of your inflation-adjusted needs. Still, you may have to rely on investments to meet your remaining retirement needs. In general, select investment programs that allow you the flexibility to change strategies as the investment environment changes—not only in the years before retirement, but afterward as well. It is not uncommon for people to life 15 to 20 years after retiring.

before retirement Investment strategies for IRAs and Keogh plans were discussed earlier in this chapter. Investments that do not offer the tax advantages of IRAs and Keogh plans—e.g., discount bonds (tax-exempt issues, if appropriate), growth stocks, and real estate—should be evaluated for their capital appreciation potential. Diversify your total preretirement portfolio, bearing in mind the following percentages: cash equivalents, 5 to 10 percent; bonds, 15 to 25 percent; stocks (both domestic and international), 35 to 45 percent; and real estate, 30 to 40 percent.

after retirement The single most important change from the prior period is to switch from focusing on capital appreciation to focusing on income generation. This is already the emphasis you have been placing on investment strategies for your IRA or Keogh; no change need occur in these plans, since the income they earn continues to be tax-advantaged in retirement (only your withdrawals are taxed).

With regard to diversification, cash equivalents should be raised to 10 to 15 percent, bonds raised to 30 to 40 percent, stocks lowered to 25 to 35 percent, and real estate lowered to 20 to 30 percent. Thus, income and liquidity will be increased. More specifically:

- Bonds selected should have higher coupons at the expense of lower yield-to-maturities.
- Stocks should have higher dividend payout ratios. (See Chapters 17 and 18 for more specific guidance.)
- Real estate should be income-oriented, mature properties (e.g., REITs) with less emphasis on tax shelter and appreciation prospects.

Buy annuities only if you are not inclined to manage a disciplined investment and withdrawal program yourself. As mentioned in Chapter 16, annuities do not offer competitive yields and their payout basis assumes an unrealistically long life expectancy.

There is a significant tax break attached to selling your home when you retire. The tax law provides a once-in-a-lifetime exclusion for persons 55 and older on $125,000 of the gain ($62,500 on a separate return of a married taxpayer) realized on the sale of a home. To be eligible, you must have occupied your home as your principal place of residence at least three of the five years preceding the sale. You may need to consult a tax authority to determine the application of this law to your circumstances.

Once you have sold your home, there are numerous things that can be done with the money. You might make an investment that will provide a monthly payment to cover the expense of renting an apartment and possibly a portion of other living expenses. You might buy a manufactured home or a membership in a retirement community with part of the proceeds. The remaining proceeds might then be invested to help provide for monthly living expenses (including the rental of a manufactured-home site).

Alternatively, you might consider obtaining a reverse amortized mortgage during the later years of your retirement. This mortgage allows you to be paid a monthly amount by a mortgage lending organization (e.g., commercial bank, savings and loan) based on your house's equity. Then when you sell your house, the proceeds will be used first to pay off the accumulated amount of these monthly payments and accrued interest. Any remaining proceeds will go to you or your heirs after estate and inheritance taxes. This strategy should be used as a last resort, however. We recommend that you convert your liquid assets to retirement support payments first. An example would be an annuitization of your mutual fund investments, as discussed in Chapter 19.

CONCLUSION

The key to a successful and pleasant retirement is to plan for it in advance. In this chapter, we have provided a framework to guide your planning. We have also indicated what you might expect from the more common retirement programs and what you can do for yourself. With this background, you must take the initiative in planning for and achieving your retirement goals.

VOCABULARY

deferred profit sharing	professional corporations
Employees Retirement Income Security Act (ERISA)	Social Security retirement benefits
	retirement income credit
individual retirement account (IRA)	reverse amortized mortgage
Keogh plan	vesting
pension fund	

QUESTIONS

1. Why do retired individuals with incomes below $6,000 seldom need to pay any personal income taxes?
2. How would you compute the effect of 5 percent annual inflation for 25 years on a $10,000 current living standard?
3. Under what circumstances is it possible to work during retirement and not forfeit Social Security retirement benefits?
4. How does vesting work in relation to pension plan benefits? Why is it important to consider this retirement income source?
5. What are the tax advantages of selling your home after you reach age 55?
6. Why are fixed annuities a poor hedge against inflation? What types of investments offer an effective hedge?
7. What is the most important consideration for a successful retirement as far as financial resources are concerned?
8. What is the purpose of the retirement income credit? What is the dollar maximum of this credit available to retired individuals?
9. What are the different contribution maximums under Keogh and IRA?

CASE PROBLEM

Jim and Janet Meyers are both 65. They are in good health and have jobs that allow them to work to age 70. They are eligible for combined Social Security retirement benefits of $4,800 annually, and from pensions they can expect to receive an additional $2,000 a year. They also receive an average of 6 percent a year from the $50,000 they have in bank savings accounts and good-quality corporate bonds. They estimate that their annual retirement needs will cost $10,000, but realize that inflation is likely to increase this amount by 5 percent each of the 20 years that they expect to live.

1. If they were both to retire today, is there enough in their investment portfolio (earning 3 percent a year after inflation) to make up the difference between the $6,800 they would receive annually from Social Security and pensions and the $10,000 they need to cover their annual retirement living expenses?
2. Will they probably have to pay income taxes on their investment income?
3. How would their retirement planning be affected if they were to retire at age 70? How would their income situation change?

RECOMMENDED READING

"Choosing a Place to Live When You Retire." *Changing Times*, May 1979, pp. 33–36. Good discussion of topic; plus it contains a valuable list of other materials on the subject.

"Do-It-Yourself Pensions." *Money*, March 1981, pp. 64–68.
Overview of IRAs, Keoghs.

"Getting a Hunk of Cash from a Retirement Fund?" *Changing Times*, October 1981, pp. 48–55.
Good discussion of the options, considerations when confronting the receipt of a lump-sum retirement distribution.

"Know the Pension Plan *Before* You Start the Job." *Changing Times*, January 1981, pp. 47–50.

U.S. Department of Health, Education, and Welfare. *Your Social Security.* SSA–79–10035, January 1982 (updated annually).
A complete treatment of Social Security in lay terms.

"Will You Ever Collect a Pension?" *Consumer Reports*, March 1982, pp. 124–130.
Thoughtful discussion of major issues affecting pension programs.

"Your Stake in the Fight over Social Security." *Consumer Reports*, September 1981, pp. 503–510.
Excellent and thorough treatment of the issues involved in rectifying the ills of this program.

CHUCK AND NANCY ANDERSON

Planning for Retirement

Although retirement is 30 years away for Chuck and Nancy, they feel it is necessary to begin planning for it now. By the time they reach age 65, their children will be grown and self-supporting. Therefore, the Andersons will have no dependents to support. They have made a careful analysis of their current living expense patterns and have thought a lot about the hobbies and interests they wish to pursue during retirement. They estimate that, in current dollars, they will need $18,000 annually to achieve their desired retirement lifestyle.

Now they must figure out the total amount they can expect to receive from Social Security in retirement benefits and from the pension fund where Chuck works. They estimate that Chuck's annual retirement benefit from Social Security will be $6,600. Chuck's conservative estimate of what he can expect from his firm's pension fund upon retirement is $8,000 a year. The Andersons feel that it is reasonable to expect Social Security benefits to rise with inflation, but they doubt that this will happen with the pension benefits.

Questions

1. How long can the Andersons reasonably expect to live after reaching age 65?
2. What would be an appropriate inflation factor for them to use for the next 30 years?
3. What aggregate amount will Chuck and Nancy need upon retiring?
4. What is the annual amount represented by Social Security (with the inflation adjustment) and pension fund benefits?
5. What is the aggregate value of these retirement income sources?
6. Does this exceed or fall short of the Andersons' total retirement living expense needs?
7. What investment strategies would help Chuck and Nancy make up any difference there might be?

22

Transferring Your Estate

For a family, the financial implications of the death of their breadwinner can be twofold. They will probably lose not only part or all of their earning power, but also their primary money manager. In Chapter 9 you determined what your family's income needs would be if you, as breadwinner, were to die. In reading this book, you have since learned how to obtain life insurance and income-producing assets to fulfill these needs. Now that the problem of finding sources of adequate income has been dealt with, it is time to consider the problems that might arise if another family member has to take over management of your financial resources.

The transfer of an estate is not automatic. Nor can there be any assurance that the transfer of management responsibilities will be smooth and efficient unless certain steps have been taken while the primary breadwinner and money manager is still alive. The first step is to make sure that you and your family know exactly what your financial resources are. Many people have only a vague idea about what assets they own, how much their assets are worth, or even where they are. The second step is to keep the family members apprised of your money management activities. Too often family estates are quickly wasted because the heirs have little knowledge or ability concerning the management of these assets. The third step—a very important one—is to keep accurate, up-to-date records of your family's financial activities.

This chapter deals with many of the legal and financial considerations that will affect a family's financial resources upon the death of their head-of-household. Read it now, even though death may seem remote. It is never too early to lay the foundation for a smooth transfer of your estate—assets such as cash, personal property, life insurance policies, marketable securities, savings, real estate (including your home), and ownership interests in ongoing businesses. We will discuss first the legal aspects of transferring an estate and then the financial aspects of such a transfer,

including ways to reduce the cost of the probate fees and taxes. In so doing we will take note of the sweeping changes made in gift and estate taxation by the Economic Recovery Tax Act (ERTA) of 1981.

LEGAL ASPECTS OF ESTATE TRANSFER

To transfer your estate means to transfer to another (or others) those assets in which you have the legal rights of ownership, or title. If the legal right of ownership of a portion or all of your family's assets is vested in you, then you must make arrangements for the transfer of these rights according to your wishes upon your death. The most common means of accomplishing this is to make a will. In the absence of a valid will declaring how your estate should be settled, the state in which you are a legal resident will normally settle it.

Ownership Rights

There is an important distinction to understand about property rights; it is the difference between *source* and *form*. There are essentially two sources, or derivations, of property rights: separate property and community property. The sources of property rights vary according to state statute. These statutes may be roughly divided into community property and noncommunity property statutes. There are only eight states with community property laws. They are Arizona, California, Idaho, Louisiana, Nevada, New Mexico, Texas, and Washington. The other states have no community laws as such.

Property rights in a community state are derived from two sources. *Community property* represents that property earned by a husband and wife during their marriage, irrespective of which one is the breadwinner. *Separate property* represents that property which was acquired by an individual prior to marriage or which the individual specifically inherited or received via gift during the marriage.

Title to property in noncommunity states is derived solely as separate property. However, these states have passed specific laws that generally create the same end result for title to property earned by the joint efforts of a married couple. What this means is that one spouse has a marital right to a portion of property acquired by the other spouse during marriage.

The *forms of title* are basically (1) separate property, (2) community property, and (3) joint ownership. The important thing to note is that the form in which you hold title does not necessarily have to parallel its source. For example, separately derived property might be held as community property or in some form of joint ownership. Where this occurs, there are usually important tax and legal considerations. We recommend that you seek legal advice before deciding what form of title in which to hold any substantial portion of your assets.

Joint ownership can take the form of joint tenancy, tenancy by the entirety, or tenancy in common. In *joint tenancy*, there may be two or more owners, each of whom owns a percentage, but not a specific piece, of the property. Each may dispose of his or her share without the permission of the other owner(s). Upon the death of one owner, that person's share passes to the surviving owner(s). *Tenancy by the entirety* is available only to husbands and wives, neither of whom can dispose of the share without the permission of the other (while both are living). Upon the death of one spouse, entire ownership of the property becomes vested in the surviving spouse. *Tenancy in common* may have two or more owners, each of whom may dispose of his or her share without the permission of the other owners. Upon the death of one owner, that person's share goes to his or her heirs, who may not necessarily be the other owner or owners.

Your Will

A will is a written, legal document that expresses the manner in which you desire to have your estate disposed of upon your death. In most states, anyone of sound mind and legal age (18 or 21) can make one. The following elements are essential to a will: opening recitation, disposition clauses, administration clauses, testamonium clause, and attestation clause. The opening recitation usually describes you, your place of residence, any previous will(s) to be revoked, and the procedure to be followed for settling the debts of your estate and resolving funeral expenses. The disposition clauses indicate what elements of your estate are to be distributed and to whom. The administration clauses indicate how the instructions of your will are to be carried out. The testamonium clause contains your signature of approval. The attestation clause contains a recitation of the circumstances under which the signing of the will was witnessed and the signatures of the witnesses.

Before writing your will, discuss possible instructions with your spouse and maybe with other members of your family. Determine just what you want to accomplish in your will. A will can be used to designate your choice of an executor; to itemize what property is to be distributed, to whom, and in what manner; to create trusts (legal contracts whereby you deposit certain assets with a trustee who will control and manage them); and to designate guardians for children who are minors.

choosing an executor   An *executor* (*executrix*) is charged with the responsibility of administering the disposition of your estate. This person or organization should be trustworthy, responsible, and capable of handling the administrative matters related to the *probate process* (that process which attempts to settle your estate according to your wishes). If you choose a friend, you will ensure that a personal interest will be taken in the disposition of your estate. (In this case, an alternative executor should be named in case your designated executor dies before you do or while your will is in probate.) If you are not sure how capable a friend would be of administering your estate, you might choose a professional trust company as executor. This organization will probably still be in business when you die, although they may take little or no personal interest in the disposition of your estate. Some people try to gain the best features of both alternatives by appointing a personal friend and a professional trust company as coexecutors.

distributing your property   If you want to eliminate a possible source of family quarrels after your death, you should try to distribute your property evenly among family members of equal status. For example, if you are married and have children (setting estate tax-saving strategies aside for the moment), you may want your spouse to receive the largest percentage of your property; however, the remaining property might most wisely be distributed equally among your children. Be sure you correctly identify each beneficiary by using his or her complete name and current address. You should also state whether inheritance taxes are to be paid initially out of your estate or individually by each beneficiary. The former method may be preferable, since it may facilitate disposition of the estate. For example, it might be difficult for a beneficiary to pay estate taxes on a house without having to sell it.

You should include instructions about the disposition of your estate if you and your primary beneficiary were to die simultaneously—as in an automobile accident, for example. You should also take precautions to avoid an excessively long and expensive probate on your property if your primary beneficiary were to die shortly after you do. To accomplish this, many people include a conditional survival clause in their wills. This clause states that beneficiaries must survive the deceased by a certain period of time, say 120 days, to qualify as heirs. (For estate tax purposes, conditional survival is limited by law to six months or less.)

creating trusts   As grantor, or *trustor*, you may deposit certain assets with a *trustee* who will be responsible for the control and management of these assets. The individuals who are to receive the income from the management of these assets are known as *beneficiaries*. Those who are to receive the assets in the trust upon its termination are known as *remaindermen*. For example, Lee Fong owns $100,000 worth of securities, which pay annual dividends of $6,000. He put these securities in a trust with directions that the annual dividends are to be paid to his son Lou and the securities are to become the property of Lee's grandchildren when the trust agreement expires. Lou is the beneficiary and Mr. Fong's grandchildren are the remaindermen.

A trustee has two primary duties: (1) to preserve the principal and invest it so that the beneficiaries receive a reasonable return and (2) to carry out the fiduciary responsibility prudently and in good faith at all times. If your beneficiaries are dissatisfied with your trustee's performance, they may petition the appropriate state court for a change in the trust agreement, a change of trustees, or similar help.

Therefore, the trustees charged with the responsibility of managing the assets you put in trust must be chosen very carefully. You can select either individuals—such as friends, relatives, or associates—or professional trust companies. An individual whom you know well and respect for his or her integrity will probably take a personal interest in managing your trust for the sake of your beneficiaries. A professional trust company, however, can offer investment competence and management continuity for the life of the trust as well as integrity. If your heirs have shown a tendency to squander your financial resources or if you fear that the management of your estate will be too difficult for them after your death, the prospects offered by the professional investment management of a trust may be quite attractive.

You would be well-advised to make the trust agreement as flexible as possible. First, you should ensure that your trustee is given the ability to deal effectively with changing economic and business conditions, changing styles of prudent investing, and changing statutes governing trust administration. (For example, it might be unwise to restrict your trustee to fixed principal investments, which would probably not be appropriate during times of inflation.) Second, you could provide a power of appointment as a legal means whereby a surviving beneficiary would be given the power to determine how the income and proceeds of the trust shall be distributed upon his or her death. This provision would eliminate the possibility that you might leave out deserving beneficiaries (often unborn grandchildren).

writing your will   Once you have done this background work on your will, you will be ready to engage the services of an attorney to help you write it. It is a good idea to have your spouse meet your attorney so that he or she will feel comfortable when dealing with your attorney after your death. You should discuss with your attorney any bequests you have in mind so that he or she can advise you on whether they are legally defensible. Most states have homestead laws that prevent you from disinheriting your spouse and that protect your heirs against creditors. To a certain extent, they also set limits on the duration of trusts. Your attorney should also be invaluable in helping you to write your will according to the accepted wording in your state. By using words whose meanings have been clearly established, a potential source of confusion can be avoided.

Revising your will is as important as its initial writing. Changes in your will should be made as the laws governing estate taxation change, the composition of your estate changes, and/or the number of beneficiaries increases or decreases. Most revisions can be made by means of a *codicil*, a legal instrument that enables you to revise your will without completely rewriting it. If you move your principal residence to another state, be sure your will is valid in the new state.

The best place of safekeeping for your will is probably with your attorney or in your safe-deposit box. A copy of your will should be kept in your general file at home.

how not to do it   Mildred Moore took care of the family finances for herself and her sister, Margaret. They shared a home together and had done so for 40 years. Each had appointed the other as executrix of her will. When Milly died, the Moores' family attorney asked Margaret to reconstruct various financial transactions and inventory Milly's holdings such as savings accounts and stocks. Because Margaret had never taken any interest in either hers or her sister's finances and because Milly had made no effort to keep Margaret informed of what she was doing or how her records were kept, Margaret was at a loss. Therefore, the attorney was forced to do all this himself. His fees for settling the estate amounted to twice what they would have been had Margaret been able and inclined to fulfill more responsibilities as an executrix.

Letter of Last Instructions

Often the letter of last instructions is a more appropriate place than your will for instructions concerning the details of your burial. This document should also indicate where all your records, as well as your will, are located. This letter is normally kept at home where it will be readily available in time of need. Be sure your executor knows where it is located.

The Probate Process

Before your will can be put into effect, a determination must be made as to its authenticity and legality. First and most important, your will should be in writing. Second, your signature must appear in ink immediately after the last sentence. It is preferable that you sign your will with exactly the same name as that appearing in the body of the will. Third, there usually must be at least two witnesses who have signed your will. It is never advisable to have your spouse or any prospective beneficiaries witness your will. By performing this function, they will probably invalidate their claims to your estate. The best witnesses are individuals of legal age but younger than yourself, who are not your heirs, and who could testify in court when the will is probated.

Once the appropriate state court has satisfied itself as to the legality and authenticity of your will, it will direct a qualified executor (usually the one appointed in the will) to administer the settlement of your estate. This direction is provided through the issuance of what are termed *letters testamentary*. When this point is reached, the primary burden of responsibility for the estate will be shifted to the executor. This person or organization must, however, keep detailed records of all transactions and periodically report to the court officials.

duties of the executor   The executor must first assemble and preserve all the deeds and certificates of ownership to property in which you had an interest upon death, as well as all records of outstanding debts. This job will be much easier if you have kept complete and orderly records of your financial affairs.

The executor must also safeguard and manage your financial interests. This can be a very demanding task, particularly if you had an extensive investment portfolio. For example, rents might have to be collected, securities managed, life insurance proceeds collected, and small businesses operated. While you are alive and as your investments become more extensive and complex, you should ensure that professional investment management will be retained or continued during the probating of your estate.

Resolving claims by creditors against your estate is another task for your executor. You may have owed $8,000 for an around-the-world trip completed shortly before your death. This would be an enforceable claim that would have to be resolved before your estate could be distributed to your heirs. Creditors are usually notified through a legal announcement in the newspapers that they must submit their claims within four to nine months from the beginning date of the settlement period. Any claims that are submitted after this time are usually declared invalid.

Payment of taxes is yet another duty of your executor. This person or organization must see to it that a final income tax return and payment is filed for you as well as a tax return for the income earned by your estate between the time of your death and the final distribution of its assets to your heirs. Taxes based on the final value of your estate must also be paid. These taxes come in two forms: estate taxes and inheritance taxes. The federal government and some states levy an *estate tax on the transfer of property*. This tax is based on the taxable value of your entire estate and is paid by the estate. States commonly levy an *inheritance tax on the right to receive property*. This tax is based on the value of property received by each heir and can be paid

either out of the estate or by the heir—whichever way you have designated in your will.

The last duties of the executor are the distribution of your estate according to your will and a final accounting to the probate authorities.

Partially Bypassing the Probate Process

You may use gifts, joint ownership, or trusts to have certain pieces of property in your estate bypass the probate process. This does not mean, however, that you may necessarily avoid the entire process.

gifts   The most obvious and easy way to have part of your estate bypass the probate process is to give it away before your death. In this way, you will reduce both the size of your estate and possibly the amount of estate taxes that will have to be paid. Of course, any gifts you make may be subject to the federal gift tax. To make the transfer valid, you must divest yourself of all ownership interests in the property given away. Many people find it emotionally difficult to relinquish control of their hard-earned financial resources.

joint ownership   When you die, all property held as joint tenancy automatically goes to the surviving joint owner(s), usually your spouse, without having to go through probate. Property held as tenancy by the entirety would also pass automatically to your spouse. Since this transfer cannot be affected by your will, the property passes outside the probate process. Therefore, a certain degree of the expense and effort associated with the probate process is avoided. Property held as tenancy in common goes to the deceased joint owner's designated heirs. Therefore, it is included in the deceased's estate and must pass through probate.

The advantanges of joint ownership lie chiefly in the time- and cost-saving features related to probate. In addition, a jointly owned home is protected against the claims of creditors in some states. The disadvantages are several. First, no one joint owner has complete control. Second, selling the property can pose a problem. Under one form of joint ownership, one owner can sell his or her share without obtaining the approval of the other owner(s). Under another form, one owner cannot sell his or her share without obtaining the approval of the other owner(s). Third, joint ownership does not offer the flexibility to adjust to changing circumstances that a will does (through revision). Fourth, some states allow jointly owned property to be seized to satisfy claims against one of the joint owners of that property.

trusts   There are two primary forms of trusts. The first is termed a *living* (or intervivos) trust because it is put into effect during the lifetime of the trustor. The second is termed a *testamentary* trust because it is set up in the trustor's will and does not go into effect until his or her death.

There are three categories of living trusts: revocable, irrevocable, and a hybrid of the two called reversionary or short-term. In the *revocable trust* the trust agreement may be canceled by the trustor at any time. The assets transferred to the trust are still considered part of the trustor's estate. Life insurance trusts are one of the most

popular forms of revocable trusts. They are usually recommended, however, only where substantial amounts of life insurance are involved. Proceeds from the trust are paid to the beneficiaries as an annuity, which may include a return on investment or a return of part of the principal plus an investment return. The most significant advantage of a living revocable trust is that all assets in the trust pass outside probate. In addition, this type of trust can be coordinated very effectively with any testamentary trust provisions.

In the *irrevocable trust*, the trust agreement can never be canceled once it has been put into effect. Because of the complete loss of control over the assets involved, this type of trust is used mostly as a protection against senility, investment incompetence, or mental instability, but it can also be a convenient way to reduce the size of one's taxable estate.

The *reversionary* (or short-term) *trust* is a hybrid of the revocable and the irrevocable trust. It must be irrevocable for more than 10 years or until the occurrence of an event specified in the trust agreement, such as the death of the income beneficiary. This event must not normally be expected to occur within a 10-year period. (Life expectancy forecasts are relevant to this consideration.) The income from such a trust must be accumulated for the benefit of, or distributed to, a beneficiary other than the trustor. This type of trust represents a gift of income, not principal, as the principal returns to the trustor upon termination of the trust agreement. Therefore, estate taxes are not avoided. A gift tax on a partial value of the assets put into trust will be levied. There are definite income tax advantages in such trusts. For example, a taxpayer in a high income tax bracket may transfer income to a taxpayer in a lower tax bracket by placing certain income-producing assets in a reversionary trust. The effect is to reduce the total amount of taxes paid and so increase the total amount of income retained.

The attractive feature of a testamentary trust is that during his or her lifetime, the trustor does not have to relinquish control of the property to be put in trust, and yet the beneficiaries will be protected from unscrupulous individuals or their own investment incompetence after his or her death. However, these trusts do not avoid the federal estate tax.

The period for which all but charitable trusts (which may continue indefinitely) are allowed to remain in effect is determined by state law. The most common maximum period allowed ends 21 years and nine months after the death of all living individuals named specifically in the trust agreement. This makes it possible for grandchildren not born when the trust was created to be included as beneficiaries and remaindermen.

Intestacy

The absence of a valid will declaring how your estate should be settled upon your death is termed *intestacy*. The state in which you are a legal resident will normally settle your estate if you die intestate. The guidelines for this type of settlement are set down in state law. Since they are designed for general situations, you have little assurance that considerations unique to your estate will be taken into account or that your estate will be disposed of according to your wishes or in the best interests of your survivors. For example, Mr. J. B. Jones died leaving no known living relatives and no will. He had long been very interested and active in the Boy Scouts and had intended to leave his estate for the benefit of this organization. Because he never made a will, his wishes were not fulfilled, and his property went to the state in which he resided.

FINANCIAL ASPECTS OF ESTATE TRANSFER

There are essentially two types of costs of estate transfer with which you should be concerned: (1) probate and administrative fees and (2) taxes. The fees include court costs, accountant's fees, appraisal fees, legal fees, and executor's fees and expenses. They are generally levied as a percentage of the gross estate, less debts. (The percentage for particular estate sizes is determined in many cases by statute and may bear little or no correlation to the cost of services rendered to probate an estate. In recent years, however, more members of the legal profession have adopted the practice of merely charging their regular hourly rate for probating estates.) On an estate of $100,000 the fees might be over $8,000. This expense should not be taken lightly. Any of the means you can use to bypass the probate process should help save some of this expense.

The second type of expense is taxes, which may be both federal estate taxes and federal gift taxes. Before the 1976 Tax Reform Act, federal gift and estate taxes were computed independently of each other, except for certain gifts made within three years of death. The Tax Reform Act of 1976 unified the gift and estate taxes into a single system for taxing all transfers from one person to another during a lifetime or at death. Although there is now a unified system for transfer taxes, transfers during life are still described as subject to a gift tax and transfers at death are still referred to as subject to an estate tax. The new system of taxation is more easily understood by examining the gift tax first.

Federal Gift Tax

This tax is imposed on the transfer of property from one person to another when no payment or consideration is received in return. The amount of the tax is based on the value of the property transferred, the person to whom it is transferred, and the amount of prior taxable gifts. Taxable gifts are computed by subtracting from the value of all gifts made the annual exclusion and the marital and charitable deductions.

annual exclusion   Every year you and your spouse are each allowed to exclude from federal gift taxation the first $10,000 worth of gifts that you make to each donee for that year. Conceivably, if you had five children, you could give $50,000 away tax-free each year by giving each child no more than $10,000 worth of gifts. In addition, your spouse could also give away $10,000 each year tax-free to the same five children. If you and your spouse give away property in which each of you own half interest, then the exclusion limit for each donee would be $20,000 (the sum of the $10,000 exclusions available to you and your spouse).

You should be aware that methods of calculating state gift taxes can vary from state to state.

deductions The *marital deduction* permits you to deduct from your total gifts a portion of your property (whether separate or community property) given to your spouse, no matter how large such a gift might be.

In addition, all charitable contributions are deductible from your total gifts, no matter how large such contributions might be. (However, for income tax purposes, charitable contributions may be deducted from your income only up to a limited percentage of your adjusted gross income each year.)

cumulative structure of gift tax Taxable gifts are the total of all gifts made by you during the current period less the annual exclusion and appropriate deductions. The tentative gift tax is computed on the sum of all taxable gifts made by you in the current period and during your lifetime in all previous periods (including those periods before 1977) using the schedule set forth in Table 22-1. The tentative gift tax is then credited for gift taxes paid or payable in previous years. The result is that each new gift is taxed in a higher bracket than the gifts made in previous periods.

unified credit After the gift tax is computed you are also allowed to apply against the tax a credit described as the unified credit. The unified credit is being phased in over a six-year period as follows:

Period in which gift made	Amount of credit
1982	$ 62,800
1983	79,300
1984	96,300
1985	121,800
1986	155,800
1987 and after	192,800

example An example will illustrate the computation of the gift tax. Prior to 1977, J. Paul Wetherhill, a widower, had made taxable gifts of $100,000. In July 1984 he made a $160,000 gift outright to his son. Mr. Wetherhill's 1984 gift tax is computed as follows:

Pre-1977 taxable gifts		$100,000
July 1984 gift	160,000	
Less: annual exclusion	(10,000)	150,000
TOTAL TAXABLE GIFTS		$250,000
Tax on total taxable gifts of $250,000 (from Table 22-1)		$70,800
Less: tax payable on pre-1977 gifts (from Table 22-1)		(23,800)
Net tax		$47,000
Less: unified credit (available between 12/31/83 and 1/1/85)		(96,300)
Net Gift Tax due for 1984 gifts		None

TABLE 22-1

Unified Federal Estate and Gift Tax Rates

Taxable Estate or Gift Over (1)	But Not Over (2)	Tax on (1)	Rate on Excess (1)
		1983	
0	$ 10,000	0	18
$ 10,000	20,000	$ 1,800	20
20,000	40,000	3,800	22
40,000	60,000	8,200	24
60,000	80,000	13,000	26
80,000	100,000	18,200	28
100,000	150,000	23,800	30
150,000	250,000	38,800	32
250,000	500,000	70,800	34
500,000	750,000	155,800	37
750,000	1,000,000	248,300	39
1,000,000	1,250,000	345,800	41
1,250,000	1,500,000	448,300	43
1,500,000	2,000,000	555,800	45
2,000,000	2,500,000	780,800	49
2,500,000	3,000,000	1,025,800	53
3,000,000	3,500,000	1,290,800	57
3,500,000	—	1,575,800	60
		1984	
0	$ 10,000	0	18
$ 10,000	20,000	$ 1,800	20
20,000	40,000	3,800	22
40,000	60,000	8,200	24
60,000	80,000	13,000	26
80,000	100,000	18,200	28
100,000	150,000	23,800	30
150,000	250,000	38,800	32
250,000	500,000	70,800	34
500,000	750,000	155,800	37
750,000	1,000,000	248,300	39
1,000,000	1,250,000	345,800	41
1,250,000	1,500,000	448,300	43
1,500,000	2,000,000	555,800	45
2,000,000	2,500,000	780,800	49
2,500,000	3,000,000	1,025,800	53
3,000,000	—	1,290,800	55
		1985 and Thereafter	
0	$ 10,000	0	18
$ 10,000	20,000	$ 1,800	20
20,000	40,000	3,800	22
40,000	60,000	8,200	24
60,000	80,000	13,000	26
80,000	100,000	18,200	28
100,000	150,000	23,800	30
150,000	250,000	38,800	32
250,000	500,000	70,800	34
500,000	750,000	155,800	37
750,000	1,000,000	248,300	39
1,000,000	1,250,000	345,800	41
1,250,000	1,500,000	448,300	43
1,500,000	2,000,000	555,800	45
2,000,000	2,500,000	780,800	49
2,500,000	—	1,025,800	50

gift tax returns The filing of a gift tax return and the payment of the tax are due by April 15 of the calendar year following the year in which the taxable gift was made.

Federal Estate Tax

Since the Tax Reform Act of 1976 the federal estate tax is computed as if your estate were one last gift. The computation is made in four steps:

1. Compute your gross estate.
2. Compute your taxable estate by subtracting the appropriate marital, charitable, and other deductions from your gross estate.
3. Add your taxable estate to the total of all your prior lifetime taxable gifts made after 1976. Compute the estate tax on that sum, using the unified gift and estate tax rates shown in Table 22-1 for the appropriate year.
4. Subtract credit for all gift taxes paid on gifts made after 1976 and certain other credits.

gross estate Your *gross estate* includes both your separate property and one-half the value of all community property in which you had an ownership interest upon your death. Either of these might include the following assets:

- Cash
- Personal property
- Real estate
- Stocks and bonds
- Promissory notes receivable
- Business and partnership interests
- Certain annuities
- Joint ownership interest (one-half of joint interest between spouses or to the extent of the contributions of the decedent in other instances)
- Transferred property on which certain ownership rights were retained by the transferor (such as reversionary or revocable trusts)
- Life insurance where the deceased retained any of the ownership rights
- Certain powers of appointment
- Certain gifts made prior to death

Although this list is not complete, it does include some of the major items. We recommend that you consult a tax authority if you have questions about specific treatment of these items or about items not listed here.

ordinary and charitable deductions Certain ordinary deductions are subtracted from your gross estate to arrive at your *taxable estate*. There are five major categories of expenses that qualify as deductions against your gross estate for tax purposes: (1) funeral expenses paid by the estate; (2) administrative expenses incurred in the collection of the estate's assets, the payment of its debts, and the distribution of the estate to its beneficiaries; (3) expenses incurred in the administration of the estate's assets not subject to the probate process (for example, trusts and joint ownership interests); (4) enforceable claims (debts, mortgages, and taxes) against the estate; and (5) losses occurring during the administration of the estate to the extent that they are not covered by insurance.

In addition, a deduction is allowed for any property passing to a qualified charitable organization, such as corporations operating exclusively for charitable, educational, literary, religious, or scientific purposes, and any congressionally approved veteran's organization.

marital deduction   Your estate is allowed a *marital deduction* for the value of certain property passing to your spouse.

The marital deduction is not allowed in certain instances. If, for example, property deducted from your estate in this manner would not be subject to taxation in your spouse's estate upon his or her death, then the marital deduction would not be allowed. For example, a husband might leave $100,000 worth of stocks in trust for his wife and his son with the income to go to his wife (as needed in the trustee's discretion) for the rest of her life and the remainder to his son on the wife's death. Since this $100,000 bequest never becomes part of the wife's estate—even though she may receive some of the income—the husband cannot include this amount in any marital deduction computation for his estate.

The Economic Recovery Tax Act of 1981, however, created a special form of trust that qualifies for the marital deduction. Called the qualified terminable interest property (q-tip) trust, this instrument must distribute all of the trust's income to the spouse, and no other individual can be a beneficiary of this trust during the spouse's life. This trust allows the decedent to benefit the surviving spouse and to avoid federal estate taxes. The property is subject to federal estate tax when the surviving spouse dies, however.

computation of tax   Your gross estate less all appropriate deductions equals your taxable estate. The *tentative estate tax* is computed by adding your taxable estate to the value of all taxable gifts made after 1976 and then finding the tax due on that sum from the schedule in Table 22-1. The tentative estate tax is then credited with the amount of gift taxes paid on gifts made after 1976 to obtain the *gross estate tax* due.

unified and other credits   Once the gross estate tax is computed, a number of *credits* may be applied against it to reduce the amount actually due. The first and most important credit is the unified credit, which was phased in over six years as follows:

Period in which decedent died	*Amount of credit*
1982	$ 62,800
1983	79,300
1984	96,300
1985	121,800
1986	155,800
1987 and after	192,800

In addition, your estate receives a credit for (1) state death taxes imposed up to certain limits, (2) federal estate taxes imposed on property received by you from someone who died within 10 years of you, and (3) certain foreign death taxes imposed on your estate.

The *net estate tax* due is your gross estate tax less the appropriate credits.

example   An extension of the J. Paul Wetherhill example above will illustrate the computation of the estate tax. Assume Mr. Wetherhill died in 1985 with a gross estate of $325,000. Against this are deducted ordinary expenses (funeral costs of $5,000, estate administration expenses of $30,000, and debts of $65,000) of $100,000. He also has a qualified charitable bequest of $25,000. Since Mr. Wetherhill is a widower, there is no marital deduction involved. Therefore, his taxable estate is $200,000. The federal estate tax would be computed as follows:

Taxable estate	$200,000	
Post-1976 taxable gifts	150,000	(see page 548)
TOTAL	$350,000	
Tentative tax on $350,000	$104,800	(from Table 22-1)
Less: post-1976 gift tax paid	0	(see page 548)
Gross Estate Tax	$104,800	
Less: unified credit for 1985	$121,800	(see page 548)
Less: credit for state death taxes	Not applicable because no federal estate tax will be due	
Net Estate Tax	0	

estate tax return filing   The estate tax return must be filed within nine months of the date of death if the decedent's gross estate exceeds a certain sum. That sum was phased in as follows:

Year of death	Amount of gross estate requiring a return
1982	$225,000
1983	275,000
1984	325,000
1985	400,000
1986	500,000
1987 and after	600,000

The estate tax is paid at the time of filing unless an extension of time is obtained.

Effect of Gifts, Joint Ownership, and Trusts on Taxes

Now we will look at what the tax treatment would most likely be for each means of bypassing probate. Any tax savings would be in addition to savings from reduced probate and administrative fees.

gifts   The tax advantage of transferring your estate by making gifts is that the gift's recipient is likely to pay less in income taxes on the income from the gift than the donor would have had to pay because the recipient is often in a lower tax bracket. The principal disadvantage of making gifts is that the donor loses both the income-producing value of the gift and any funds used to pay his or her gift tax liability.

If, while still alive, you give away your life insurance policy and all its rights of ownership, your policy will not be considered part of your estate, and you will avoid paying estate taxes on it. If you intend to transfer your policy to your child, it is important that your child pay any subsequent premiums from his or her property. The ownership rights include borrowing against the cash value; owning the policy; changing the beneficiaries; retaining any economic benefit from the policy; using proceeds upon your death for the benefit of your estate; and surrendering and canceling the policy. Although you avoid estate taxation, you subject your policy to the gift tax. The tax will be paid on the existing cash value.

GIVING IT
INSTEAD OF
WILLING IT

joint ownership   The tax considerations here are threefold. First, in the case of property that is held in joint tenancy, when one joint owner dies, for estate tax purposes the IRS treats the entire property as if it were owned by the deceased, except when the joint owners are husband and wife. If you are a joint owner of property that is held in joint tenancy and you want to ensure that the property belonging to the other joint owner(s) is not taxed in your estate, the surviving owner(s) must be able to document that he (they) contributed to the purchase of the subject property. Otherwise, upon your death the entire value of the property might be taxed in your estate; and when the surviving joint owner dies, the entire property may be subject to estate taxation again. When husband and wife are joint tenants, only one-half of the value of the joint property is includable in the estate of the first spouse to die.

Second, joint ownership permits the splitting of income and capital gains among the joint owners proportionate to their interest. This could be beneficial for husbands and wives filing separate income tax returns. Third, a gift tax could be levied if one joint owner pays for the entire property, allowing the other joint owner to acquire an ownership interest without making any contribution. This tax would be assessed on the value of the portion the noncontributing joint owner received.

trusts   There are two possible tax advantages that might be derived from transferring some of your estate through trusts. First, if you are in a high income tax bracket and place certain income-producing assets in a reversionary trust with income going to someone (e.g., a child) who is in a lower tax bracket, that income would be taxed at a lower rate. Second, a trust's ultimate effect on your estate would be to divert, to other persons, income that otherwise might contribute to the size of your estate and therefore increase your estate taxes. Table 22-2 summarizes these tax advantages.

CONCLUSION

There is no substitute for careful and thoughtful planning involving estate transfer. Be sure to include your family in this process. Because of the often complex nature

TABLE 22-2

Effect of Trusts on Taxes

Type of Trust	Gift Tax Incurred	Estate Tax Reduced	Probate Fees Reduced	Control Lost	Income Taxed to
Living					
Revocable	No	No	Yes	No	Grantor
Irrevocable	Yes	Yes	Yes	Yes	Beneficiary or trust
Reversionary	Yes[a]	No	No	Temporarily[b]	Beneficiary[c]
Testamentary	No	No	No	No	

[a] Gift taxes are paid, subject to standard exclusions, on approximately 44 percent of the value of the assets placed in trust for 10 years. For periods longer than this, the percentage will increase.

[b] Must be irrevocable for at least 10 years.

[c] Realized capital gains are taxed to the donor, however.

of these transactions, enlist the assistance of good professionals. They will ensure that the means you use to make the transfer efficient and economical are also in the best interest of you and your survivors.

VOCABULARY

adjusted gross estate (AGE)
annual exclusion
beneficiary
codicil
community property
estate
estate tax
executor (executrix)
gift tax
gross estate (GE)
inheritance tax

intestacy
joint ownership
letter of last instructions
marital deduction
probate process
remaindermen
separate property
trust
trustee
trustor
will

QUESTIONS

1. What types of property may be included in a person's gross estate?
2. What does it mean to die "intestate"? What are its consequences?
3. What can a will be used to accomplish?
4. How does the probate process work? What role does the executor play in this process?
5. What are the two major costs of estate transfer? How do the methods of determining their amount differ?
6. What is the difference between an estate tax and an inheritance tax?
7. How do the three types of living trusts differ in the way they are treated for federal estate tax purposes?
8. What are the three forms of joint ownership and how do they differ from one another?
9. What must you do to ensure that life insurance death benefits are not included in your estate?

CASE PROBLEM

Assume it is 1984, and Whitney Cragge's taxable estate is $150,000. In 1977 he gave away $50,000 in taxable gifts upon which he paid $10,600 in gift taxes. What would be his gross estate tax?

RECOMMENDED READING

"Could a Trust Fund Save You Money?" *Changing Times*, July 1975, pp. 37–40.
    A good discussion of the basics of trusts.

"Maybe Joint Ownership Is Right for You, Maybe Not." *Changing Times*, June 1975, pp. 51–53.
    A good discussion of joint ownership.

Consumer Agency Guide, Social Security Addendum, and Compound Interest Tables

CONSUMER AGENCY GUIDE

The traditional view of the buyer in the marketplace has been *caveat emptor,* "let the buyer beware." However, even broad legislation, business self-regulation, the forces of competition, and the generally high standards of American business have not been enough to protect the consumer completely from being taken advantage of. Over the years, all levels of government have gradually decided that consumers need help making decisions and negotiating in the marketplace. Therefore, the maze of federal, state, and local regulations and consumer agencies has become increasingly complex.

Much of this legislation and regulation has been discussed at length in the appropriate sections of this text (see "consumerism" in the index). This agency guide is offered merely as a reference to help you locate the appropriate source of assistance from among the bureaucratic jumble of possibilities. Industries have also organized associations to aid the consumer, many of which have an excellent record of handling complaints.

If you are a dissatisfied consumer, you should first try to solve the problem with the company involved. If that does not work, contact one of the locally represented agencies specifically designed to deal with the issue. In the white pages of the telephone book under "consumer complaint and protection coordinators," you will find numerous phone numbers for agencies set up to deal with complaints relating to everything from accountants to funeral directors to service stations to veterinarians.

Then, if your complaint is still not resolved, you should probably contact one of the private or federal government agencies listed below. To find out about federal agencies and publications that develop after this text has been published, write to the Consumer Information Center in Pueblo, Colorado, for a free Consumer Information Catalogue, or to the Superintendant of Documents, U.S. Government Printing Office in Washington, D.C., and ask for the latest copy of its *Guide to Federal Consumer Services.* You can also subscribe to the twice-monthly *Consumer News* published by the Office of Consumer Affairs. In addition, most states have set up consumer protection offices, usually listed in your phone book.

Regardless of whom you present your appeal to, provide copies (not originals) of receipts, guarantees, and correspondence. To expedite your request, be specific about product names, purchase dates, prices, serial numbers, places where you have already sought relief, and dates of these attempts.

American Bankers Association
1120 Connecticut Avenue NW
Washington, DC 20036
(202) 467–4000
  For chronically unsolved problems with your bank.

Civil Aeronautics Board
Consumer Assistance Division
Washington, DC 20428
(202) 673–6047
  For complaints against airlines.

Consumer Information Center
Pueblo, CO 81009

Write for free *Consumer Information Catalogue*. In general, a place you can write to for help in unraveling the maze of federal agencies. You can also contact the regional Federal Information Center listed in your phone book under "United States Government" listings.

Consumer Product Safety Commission
Washington, DC 20207
(800) 638–8326

Responds to complaints of unsafe products by removing them from sale; provides information regarding hazards in the use of normally safe products; and develops uniform safety standards that manufacturers must incorporate into the design of their products.

Department of Housing and Urban Development
Office of Fair Housing and Equal Opportunity
Washington, DC 20410
(800) 424–8590

Offers information on home buying and government-insured mortgages.

Department of Housing and Urban Development
Office of Real Estate Practices
Washington, DC 20410
(202) 755–6524

For information about real estate settlement procedures.

Equal Employment Opportunity Commission
Washington, DC 20506
(202) 634–6814

For help if you feel you have been unfairly denied a job because of age, sex, race, or religion.

Federal Aviation Administration
Community and Consumer Liasion Division
APA-400
Department of Transportation
Washington, DC 20590
(202) 426–1960

Regulates and coordinates air safety programs.

Federal Communications Commission
Consumer Assistance Office
Washington, DC 20260
(202) 245–5445

Receives consumer opinions on programming by radio and television and uses them to help decide on renewals of stations' licenses. Also regulates political advertising.

Federal Insurance Administration
Federal Emergency Management Agency
Washington, DC 20472
(800) 424–8872
    For information about flood insurance.

Federal Trade Commission
Bureau of Consumer Credit
Washington, DC 20420
(202) 389–2567
    Works to halt unfair or deceptive practices in advertising and packaging. Also
    regulates warranty policies. Has local offices.

Food and Drug Administration
Consumer Communications
Department of Human Health and Services
5600 Fishers Lane
Rockville, MD 20857
(301) 443–3170
    For information on the labeling, quality, and safety of food (except meats), drugs,
    and cosmetics. Complaints may also be made with a regional FDA office.

Interstate Commerce Commission
Office of Consumer Protection
Washington, DC 20423
(800) 424–9312
    For complaints against railroads, household moving companies, truckers, and
    buses.

Mail Order Action Line
6 East 43rd Street
New York, NY 10018
(212) 689–4977
    For unresolved mail order problems.

Mail Preference Service
Name Removal Program
6 East 43rd Street
New York, NY 10017
(212) 689–4977
    To reduce your unsolicited mail.

Major Appliance Consumer Action Panel (MACAP)
20 N. Wacker Drive
Chicago, IL 60606
(312) 984–5858
    Coordinates unresolved complaints against manufacturers.

National Foundation for Consumer Credit
1819 H Street, NW
Washington, DC 20006
(202) 223–2040
  For credit counseling help.

National Highway Traffic Safety Administration
Department of Transportation
Washington, DC 20590
(800) 424–9393
  Handles automobile safety and recall programs.

National Labor Relations Board
Washington, DC 20570
(202) 254–9430
  Regulates and reviews unfair labor practices.

Office of Consumer Affairs
Department of Commerce
Washington, DC 20230
(202) 377–5001
  Channels consumer complaints to the appropriate agencies.

Pension Benefit Guaranty Corporation
2020 K Street, NW
Washington, DC 20006
(202) 254–4817
  For problems with pension claims.

Securities and Exchange Commission
Office of Consumer Affairs
Washington, DC 20549
(202) 523–3952
  For complaints about securities and brokerage frauds.

U.S. Department of Agriculture
Office of the Consumer Advisor
Washington, DC 20250
(202) 447–3975
  For information on nutrition, gardening, and federal food stamp program. Has
  local offices.

U.S. Postal Services
Chief Postal Inspector
Washington, DC 20260
(202) 245–5445
  For complaints regarding mail fraud, unordered merchandise, and obscenity.

HOW TO QUALIFY FOR SOCIAL SECURITY

To qualify for Social Security benefits, you must meet the length of service requirements; that is, you must have worked for a certain length of time in an occupation covered by Social Security. The type of benefits (retirement, survivors, disability, or Medicare) available to you depends on the number of quarters of credit you have accumulated, i.e., the length of time you have worked. The amount of benefits depends on your average annual earnings during the time you worked.

Nine out of every 10 people who work are covered by Social Security.° The only workers not covered are state and local government employees (including teachers), railroad workers, some household and farm workers, and persons with less than $400 a year in net earnings from self-employment. If you are among these, check with your Social Security Administration office for further details about the rulings.

Quarters of Credit

To receive credits that go to satisfy the length of service requirements, you must earn at least $340 of nonfarm income in a calendar quarter (less in earlier years). If you earn $340 or more during each of four consecutive three-month periods, you accumulate one full year of credit. The minimum service requirement that must be met before any benefits will be paid is one and one-half years (six quarters). Table 1 shows how many years of credit must be accumulated to qualify for various types of retirement, survivors, disability, and Medicare benefits.

Average Annual Earnings and Monthly Benefits

To determine the amount of monthly benefits you may be eligible to receive, you must first determine your average annual earnings (salary plus any bonuses, tips, and personal business income). You can do this by using the following procedure. We have used the example of Chuck Anderson and his family to illustrate this procedure.

Instructions

1 *Find the initial year you must use in figuring the number of years you must count.* If you were born before 1930, start counting with the year 1956. If you were born in the year 1930 or thereafter, begin counting with the year in which you reached your twenty-eighth birthday. At least two years of earnings must be used to figure disability or survivors benefits and at least five years to figure retirement benefits.

   Chuck was born in 1946 and is 37 years old. Since he was born after 1930, he must begin counting with 1974, the year in which he reached age 28.

2 *Subtract this initial year (step 1) from the present year to obtain the number of*

°*Your Social Security Benefits* Social Security Administration, February 1982.

TABLE 1

Length of Service Requirements for Social Security Benefits

Type of Benefits	Payable to	Minimum Years of Work under Social Security
Retirement	You, your wife, child, dependent husband 62 or over	10 years (fully insured status) (If age 62 prior to 1991, you may need only 7½ to 9 years.)
Survivors[a] Full	Widow 60 or over Disabled widow 50-59 Widow if caring for child 18 years or younger Dependent children Dependent widower 62 or over Disabled dependent widower 50-61 Dependent parent at 62	10 years (fully insured status)
Current	Widow caring for child 18 years or younger Dependent children	1½ years of last 3 years before death (currently insured status)
Disability	You and your dependents	If under age 24, you need 1½ years of work in the 3 years prior to disablement. If between ages 24 and 31, you need to work half the time between when you turned 21 and your date of disablement. If age 31 or older, you must have 5 years of credit during the 10 years prior to disablement.
Medicare Hospitalization (automatic benefits)	Anyone 65 or over	If you turned 65 after 1975, you need 10 years of work experience. If you turned 65 before 1975, consult your local Social Security Administration office.
Medical expense (voluntary benefits)	Anyone 65 or over who pays monthly premiums	No prior work under Social Security is required.

Source: U.S. Department of Health and Human Services, 1982.

[a] A lump-sum death benefit no greater than $255 is also granted to dependents of those either fully or currently insured.

years you must count. Both men and women 62 or older would count until the year of their sixty-second birthday.

Chuck must count nine years of earnings (1974 through 1982), since it is now 1983.

3 *List your earnings for all years beginning with 1951.* Do not count more than $3,600 of earnings for any one year 1951 through 1954, $4,200 for any one year 1955 through 1958, $4,800 for any one year 1959 through 1965, $6,600 for any one year 1966 through 1967, $7,800 for any one year 1968 through 1971, $9,000 for the year 1972, $10,800 for 1973, $13,200 for 1974, $14,100 for 1975, $15,300 for 1976, $16,500 for 1977, $17,700 for 1978, $22,900 for 1979, $25,900 for 1980, $29,700 for 1981, $32,400 for 1982.

Chuck listed his earnings through 1982.

4 *Cross off your list the years of lowest earnings until the number remaining is the same as the number derived in step 2.* If the number derived in step 3 is less than that derived in step 2, you will have to include years in which you had no earnings.

Since Chuck need count only the nine years of highest earnings and has earned more and more each year, he counted his earnings only for each year back to and including 1974. Each year he has earned more than the allowable maximum. He was allowed to count only $13,200 for 1974, $14,100 for 1975, and so on.

5 *Total your earnings for all the years remaining on your list and divide by the number of years you were to count (step 2).* The result is your average annual earnings.

Chuck's average earnings were $20,855 ($187,700 ÷ 9).

6 *Use Table 2 to determine the size of retirement benefits you and your dependents can expect from Social Security.* For people who become disabled, the figures are in the same general range. For people retiring after 1983, the figures may be significantly higher. The rules for such calculations are so complex that the Social Security Administration no longer publishes tables of benefits for all situations.

From the table of benefits, Chuck estimated that he and his family (Nancy, Jim, and Melissa) would probably begin receiving in excess of $900 a month if he became disabled or died. However, he must check with the SSA to find out the exact amount, since his average annual earnings are above the amounts reported in the table.

Applying for Social Security Benefits

No benefits begin unless you file a valid claim. To file a claim for benefits, contact your local Social Security Administration office. They will provide the necessary forms. Once your application has been approved, monthly checks will be mailed to you by the U.S. Treasury Department shortly after the close of each month.

TABLE 2

Monthly Amounts of Social Security Retirement Benefits for Workers Who Reach Age 62 in 1979-83

Type of Benefits	Monthly Benefits for Sample Average Yearly Earnings				
	$1,200 or Less	$4,000	$6,000	$8,000	$10,000
Retirement					
Retired worker 65 or older	$156.70	$296.20	$388.20	$482.60	$534.70
Spouse 65 or older	78.40	148.10	194.10	241.30	267.40
Retired worker at 62	125.40	237.00	310.60	386.10	427.80
Spouse at 62, no child	58.80	111.10	145.60	181.00	200.60
Maximum family payment	235.10	506.20	712.10	844.50	935.70

Source: U.S. Department of Health and Human Services, August 1981.

INSTRUCTIONS FOR USE OF COMPOUND INTEREST TABLE A

1. To find the future value of a lump-sum investment after a specific number of years, multiply the amount of the investment by the factor derived as follows: find the line representing the number of years the money will be invested and read across it until you reach the column representing the rate of return you expect to receive on the investment. For example, if you put $1,000 in a 6 percent savings account and allowed the interest to compound for 10 years, the factor would be 1.8 and the total in the account would be $1,800.

2. To find the inflated future cost of a goal after a specific number of years, multiply today's price by the factor derived as follows: find the line representing the number of years within which you want to achieve the goal and read across it until you reach the column representing the expected percentage rate of inflation. For example, if inflation is expected to rise at an average rate of 5 percent a year, a car that cost $8,000 today would sell for $10,400 ($8,000 × 1.3) in five years.

3. To find the lump-sum amount you must invest today to achieve a goal within a specific number of years, divide the inflated future cost of the goal (the second use of Table A) by the factor derived as follows: find the line representing the number of years within which you plan to achieve the goal and read across it until you reach the column representing the rate of return you expect to receive on your investment. For example, if you plan to invest in a mutual fund with an average annual growth (percentage rate of return) of 8 percent so that in five years you will have enough money to buy a car you have calculated will cost $10,400, you would have to invest $6,933 ($10,400 × 1.5).

4. To find the percentage rate of return you need to receive on an initial investment in order to reach a certain goal within a certain length of time, divide the goal amount by the investment amount and use the resulting factor as follows: find the line for the year when the total amount of money will be needed for the goal and read across it until you find the factor you derived, which will be in the column for the appropriate percentage rate of return. For example, if you will need $4,400 in 10 years and you have $2,000 to invest initially, the factor is 2.2 (4,400 × 2,000), and the rate of return you need is 8 percent.

5. To find the number of years required to achieve an investment goal by investing a lump sum at a certain rate of return, divide the goal amount by the investment amount and use the resulting factor as follows: find the column representing the highest rate of return you feel comfortable striving for and read down it until you find the factor you derived, which will be opposite the number of years required to reach the goal. For example, if you have $2,000 to invest at 8 percent to reach an investment goal of $4,400, the factor is 2.2 (4,400 × 2,000), and 10 years will be required to reach the goal.

TABLE A

Compound Interest for Lump-Sum Investments

Length of Invest-ment (years)	Percentage Rate of Return or of Inflation											
	2%	3%	4%	5%	6%	7%	8%	10%	12%	14%	16%	20%
1	1.02	1.03	1.04	1.0	1.1	1.1	1.1	1.1	1.1	1.1	1.2	1.2
2	1.04	1.06	1.08	1.1	1.1	1.1	1.2	1.2	1.2	1.3	1.3	1.4
3	1.06	1.09	1.12	1.2	1.2	1.2	1.3	1.3	1.4	1.5	1.6	1.7
4	1.08	1.12	1.17	1.2	1.3	1.3	1.4	1.5	1.6	1.7	1.8	2.1
5	1.10	1.16	1.22	1.3	1.3	1.4	1.5	1.6	1.8	1.9	2.1	2.5
6	1.13	1.19	1.26	1.3	1.4	1.5	1.6	1.8	2.0	2.2	2.4	3.0
7	1.15	1.23	1.32	1.4	1.5	1.6	1.7	2.0	2.2	2.5	2.8	3.6
8	1.17	1.27	1.37	1.5	1.6	1.7	1.8	2.1	2.5	2.8	3.3	4.3
9	1.20	1.30	1.42	1.6	1.7	1.8	2.0	2.4	2.8	3.2	3.8	5.2
10	1.22	1.34	1.48	1.6	1.8	2.0	2.2	2.6	3.1	3.7	4.4	6.2
11	1.24	1.38	1.54	1.7	1.9	2.1	2.3	2.8	3.5	4.2	5.1	7.4
12	1.27	1.42	1.60	1.8	2.0	2.2	2.5	3.1	3.9	4.8	5.9	8.9
13	1.29	1.47	1.66	1.9	2.1	2.4	2.7	3.4	4.4	5.5	6.9	10.7
14	1.32	1.51	1.73	2.0	2.3	2.6	2.9	3.8	4.9	6.3	8.0	12.8
15	1.34	1.56	1.80	2.1	2.4	2.8	3.2	4.2	5.5	7.1	9.3	15.4
16	1.37	1.60	1.87	2.2	2.5	3.0	3.4	4.6	6.1	8.1	10.7	18.5
17	1.40	1.65	1.95	2.3	2.7	3.2	3.7	5.0	6.8	9.3	12.5	22.2
18	1.43	1.70	2.02	2.4	2.8	3.4	4.0	5.6	7.7	10.5	14.7	26.6
19	1.46	1.75	2.11	2.5	3.0	3.6	4.3	6.1	8.6	12.0	16.7	31.9
20	1.48	1.81	2.19	2.6	3.2	3.9	4.7	6.7	9.6	13.7	19.6	38.3
21	1.52	1.86	2.28	2.8	3.4	4.1	5.0	7.4	10.7	15.6	22.7	46.0
22	1.55	1.91	2.37	2.9	3.6	4.4	5.4	8.1	11.9	17.8	26.4	55.2
23	1.58	1.97	2.46	3.1	3.8	4.7	5.9	8.9	13.4	20.3	30.6	66.2
24	1.61	2.03	2.56	3.2	4.0	5.1	6.3	9.8	15.0	23.1	35.5	79.4
25	1.64	2.09	2.66	3.4	4.3	5.4	6.8	10.8	17.0	26.4	41.2	95.3
26	1.67	2.16	2.77	3.6	4.5	5.8	7.4	11.9	19.2	30.1	47.8	114.0
27	1.71	2.22	2.88	3.7	4.8	6.2	8.0	13.1	21.6	34.3	55.4	137.0
28	1.74	2.29	3.00	3.9	5.1	6.6	8.6	14.4	24.2	39.1	64.2	165.0
29	1.78	2.36	3.12	4.1	5.4	7.1	9.3	15.9	27.1	44.6	74.5	198.0
30	1.81	2.43	3.24	4.3	5.7	7.6	10.1	17.4	30.1	50.8	86.5	237.0

INSTRUCTIONS FOR USE OF COMPOUND INTEREST TABLE B

1. To find the future value of a regular annual investment, multiply the amount of the investment by the factor derived as follows: find the line representing the number of years over which the investment will be made and read across it until you reach the column representing the percentage rate of return you expect to receive. For example, if you invested $1,000 each year for 15 years in a mutual fund with an average annual growth (percentage rate of return) of 8 percent, at the end of that time you would have $27,200 ($1,000 × 27.2).

2. To find the amount of the regular annual investment you must make to achieve a goal within a specified number of years, divide the inflated value of the goal (derived by using compound interest Table A) by the factor derived as follows: find the line representing the number of years within which you plan to achieve the goal and read across it until you reach the column representing the percentage rate of return you can expect to receive on your investment. For example, if you want to make regular annual investments for a period of five years at a rate of 6 percent in order to buy a car that will cost $10,400, the amount of your regular annual investment must be $1,857 ($10,400 × 5.6).

3. To find the percentage rate of return you need in order to achieve a goal by investing a certain amount annually for a certain number of years, divide the goal amount by the investment amount and use the resulting factor as follows: find the line for the total number of years of the investment and read across it until you reach the factor you derived, which will be in the column for the appropriate percentage rate of return. For example, if you invest $1,000 annually in order to have $14,500 in 10 years, the factor is 14.5 (14,500 × 1,000), and the percentage rate of return you need is 8 percent.

4. To find the number of years required to achieve a goal by investing a certain amount annually at a certain rate of return, divide the goal amount by the investment amount and use the resulting factor as follows: find the column representing the percentage rate of return you feel comfortable striving for and read down it until you come to the factor you derived, which will be opposite the number of years required to reach the goal. For example, if you invest $1,000 a year at a rate of 8 percent in order to have $14,500, the factor is 14.5 (14,500 × 1,000), and 10 years will be required to reach the goal.

TABLE B

Compound Interest for Investments Made at the End of Each Year

Number of Years	Percentage Rate of Return										
	3%	4%	5%	6%	7%	8%	10%	12%	14%	16%	20%
1	1.0	1.0	1.0	1.0	1.0	1.0	1.0	1.0	1.0	1.0	1.0
2	2.0	2.0	2.0	2.1	2.1	2.1	2.1	2.1	2.1	2.2	2.2
3	3.1	3.1	3.2	3.2	3.2	3.2	3.3	3.4	3.4	3.5	3.6
4	4.2	4.2	4.3	4.4	4.4	4.5	4.6	4.8	4.9	5.1	5.4
5	5.3	5.4	5.5	5.6	5.8	5.9	6.1	6.4	6.6	6.9	7.4
6	6.5	6.6	6.8	7.0	7.2	7.3	7.7	8.1	8.5	9.0	9.9
7	7.7	7.9	8.1	8.4	8.6	8.9	9.5	10.1	10.7	11.4	12.9
8	8.9	9.2	9.5	9.9	10.2	10.6	11.4	12.3	13.2	14.2	16.5
9	10.2	10.6	11.0	11.5	12.0	12.5	13.6	14.8	16.1	17.5	20.8
10	11.5	12.0	12.6	13.2	13.8	14.5	15.9	17.5	19.3	21.3	26.0
11	12.8	13.5	14.2	15.0	15.8	16.6	18.5	20.6	23.0	25.7	32.2
12	14.2	15.0	15.9	16.9	17.9	19.0	21.4	24.1	27.3	30.8	39.6
13	15.6	16.6	17.7	18.9	20.1	21.5	24.5	28.0	32.1	36.8	48.5
14	17.1	18.3	19.6	21.0	22.6	24.2	28.0	32.4	37.6	43.7	59.2
15	18.6	20.0	21.6	23.3	25.1	27.2	31.8	37.3	43.8	51.6	72.0
16	20.2	21.8	23.6	25.7	27.9	30.3	35.9	42.7	50.9	60.8	87.4
17	21.8	23.7	25.8	28.2	30.8	33.8	40.5	48.9	59.1	71.6	105.9
18	23.4	25.6	28.1	30.9	34.0	37.4	45.6	55.7	68.3	84.0	128.1
19	25.1	27.7	30.5	33.8	37.4	41.4	51.2	63.4	78.9	98.5	154.7
20	26.9	29.8	33.1	36.8	44.0	45.8	57.3	72.0	90.9	115.2	186.7
21	28.7	32.0	35.7	40.0	44.9	50.4	64.0	81.7			
22	30.5	34.2	38.5	43.4	49.0	55.5	71.4	92.5			
23	32.4	36.6	41.4	47.0	53.4	60.9	79.5	104.6			
24	34.4	39.1	44.5	50.8	58.2	66.8	88.5	118.2			
25	36.4	41.6	47.7	54.9	63.2	73.1	98.3	133.3			
26	38.5	44.3	51.1	59.2	68.7	79.9	109.0	150.3			
27	40.7	47.1	54.7	63.7	74.5	87.4	121.0	169.4			
28	42.9	50.0	58.4	68.5	80.7	95.3	134.0	190.7			
29	45.2	53.0	62.3	73.6	87.3	104.0	149.0	214.6			
30	47.6	56.1	66.4	79.0	94.5	113.0	164.0	241.3			

Note: The numbers at the end of the last columns are not supplied because they are not needed for financial planning. It would be unrealistic to expect such high returns over long periods of time.

Glossary

acceleration clause   An oppressive clause often found in installment sales contracts whereby all or part of the outstanding balance of payments becomes immediately due if the borrower defaults on any of the payments.

account executive   See "registered representative."

accumulated cash value   The amount of money to which a policyholder is entitled after discontinuing his or her cash value life insurance. It is made up of portions of life insurance premiums not used to buy protection but held by the insurance company as savings of the insured.

accumulation period   For an annuity, the period of time prior to the maturity date.

accumulation plan   See "savings accumulation plan."

activity plan   A checking account used most appropriately when check writing activity is low.

acts of God   Natural phenomena (such as lightning and floods) that are considered impossible to prevent or control and are usually insurable because they are fortuitous in nature.

actuary   A mathematician who uses probability theory to calculate degrees of risk for use in insurance rate-making.

additional living expenses   The amount of money that an insurance company may pay a policyholder to cover what it costs to live elsewhere while his home is being restored or repaired after some calamity that it is insured against. All homeowner policies contain a provision for additional living expenses.

add-on clause   An oppressive clause often found in installment sales contracts whereby the creditor may repossess items already purchased from him and paid for, if the borrower defaults on payments for additional items.

adjusted balance method   The method of calculating credit charges on open-ended credit account balances whereby the interest charge is applied to the balance remaining at the end of the billing period.

adjusted gross estate   For federal estate tax purposes, the value of the deceased's gross estate passing to the surviving spouse is figured by deducting the deceased's interest in all community property and appropriate amounts of ordinary deductions. This figure is derived solely to calculate the marital deduction.

adjusted gross income   For federal income tax purposes, the amount of an individual's annual income that results from subtracting deductions from gross income.

administrator   A person appointed by a probate court to settle the affairs of an estate whose owner did not leave a valid will.

advertising   The process of making public information concerning the merits and attractiveness of various products and services.

agent   Typically, one who sells and services insurance policies or who sells real estate. In insurance, an exclusive agent usually represents only one company; an independent agent may represent several. In real estate, an agent is usually a salesperson who works for a fully licensed real estate broker. (See also "transfer agent," health/life agent," and "property/ casualty agent.")

all-risk coverage   Insurance protection against all perils or hazards that might jeopardize what is being insured—with the exception of perils that are specifically excluded in the insurance contract.

alternative minimum income tax   An alternate method of calculating federal income tax for those individuals who have special income circumstances that would otherwise result in paying little or no regular income tax. Taxpayers can therefore not benefit significantly from tax shelter investments because of the presence of alternative minimum tax.

alternative mortagage instrument (AMI)   All types of mortgages other than the fixed rate, amoritized mortgage. (See also "graduated payment mortgage," "renegotiable rate mortgage," "reversed amortization mortgage," and "variable mortgage.")

amended tax return   An additional tax return that is filed to correct erroneous information on a tax return already filed or to add subsequently received information to it.

American Stock Exchange (Amex or ASE)   The second largest stock exchange in the world.

amortize   To resolve a debt, usually through periodic payments of equal amounts.

analysis plan   A checking account in which there are monthly maintenance fees plus charges for deposits and checks processed, with credits based on the size of the average monthly balance.

ancillary charges   The charges (although not specifically finance charges) that may arise in an installment sales contract.

annual exclusion   The amount ($10,000 per donee each year) not subject to federal gift taxation by the donor.

annual percentage rate (APR)   Federally approved definition of the annual interest cost of consumer credit.

annual report   A yearly publication by a business (such as a corporation or a mutual fund) depicting its current financial situation, recent financial results, and other relevant information about the company for the preceding year.

annuitant   An individual who receives monthly annuity benefit payments.

annuity   A guaranteed income for life, with payments received at regular intervals; a type of investment offered by insurance companies.

apportionment clause   This clause states that the maximum extended coverage for any peril covered by a fire insurance policy is equal to the ratio of (1) that policy's fire coverage to the total fire coverage on the same property by both that policy and all other policies or (2) the nonfire coverage to the total nonfire coverage on the same property. This clause may be appended to dwelling, dwelling contents, and homeowners insurance policies.

appraisal   An impartial determination of property value.

appraiser   An expert in establishing current market value for property such as a house, jewelry, or antiques, depending on the appraiser's specialty.

appreciation   Increase in the dollar value of an asset over time.

asked price   The price at which a broker is willing to sell a security to a customer. (See also "bid-price.")

asking price   The price on a house set by the seller (usually in collaboration with the realtor). Usually it is set high enough (perhaps 10 percent over what the seller really hopes to get) to allow room to bargain. Also called the list price or offering price.

assets   In financial usage, all forms of property owned by a person or a business. (See also "fixed assets" and "monetary assets.")

asset value   See "net asset value."

assigned risk plan   A state-administered plan that provides auto insurance protection for persons whose driving records prohibit them from obtaining insurance through regular channels.

at the market   A term used to describe orders to buy or sell securities at the best price currently available in the market.

audit   A formal or official examination to verify the accuracy of figures and statements in an account book or on a tax return.

authorized stock   The total number of shares of stock that a company's articles of incorporation allow it to issue; any additional authorization requires the approval of stockholders representing a majority of the stock outstanding.

automatic reinvestment plan   An optional plan offered by most open-end mutual funds whereby an investor instructs the fund to reinvest in additional fund shares all cash dividends and capital gains distributions that otherwise would be sent to the investor by check.

average daily balance method   The method of calculating credit charges on open-ended credit account balances whereby interest is charged on the average daily balance during the billing period.

avoidance   Legal reduction (i.e., by using exclusions and deductions) of the amount of income tax that must be paid. (See "evasion.")

balanced fund   A mutual fund with a portfolio consisting of stocks and bonds and offering prospects for both capital growth and income; the proportion of money invested in stocks or bonds varies according to the condition of the market.

balance outstanding   The amount of unpaid principal on a loan.

balance sheet   A financial form that lists, as of a specific date, the financial assets and liabilities of a person, family, or business and shows the difference between the two (net worth); also known as a statement of financial condition.

balloon payment   A final loan payment that is substantially larger than any previous payments.

bankruptcy   A state of insolvency. State law usually allows a bankrupt person's creditors to have his or her estate, with the exception of property protected by homestead rights, administered for their benefit in settling the person's debts to the fullest extent possible.

basic form   A type of homeowners insurance policy (often called HO-1) that covers property against losses due to perils such as fire, windstorm, explosion, smoke, vandalism, and theft.

bear market   A securities market characterized by generally declining prices over a period of several months.

bearer bond   See "coupon bond."

beneficiary   The recipient of the death benefits of a life insurance policy. (See also "primary beneficiary" and "contingent beneficiary.") Also, the person named in a will or trust agreement to receive the right to property or income from an estate or a trust.

benefits   The amount of money to be paid to an insured or to the insured's beneficiary by an insurer according to the terms of the insurance contract.

bequeath   To give or leave property by means of a will.

bequest   A gift of personal property made while alive. Also, property transferred through a will. (See also "legacy.")

beta   A term describing the price volatility of a common stock, or a portfolio of common stocks, as compared to some accepted market index, typically the S&P 500.

bid price   The price at which a broker is willing to buy a security from a customer. (See also "asked price.")

blank endorsement   The signature alone of the payee on the back of a check, thereby making the check cashable by anyone. (See also "restricted endorsement.")

blanket coverage   Insurance protection provided by a single policy that covers all types of property to the same degree.

blue chip stock   The common stock of large, fairly stable companies that have demonstrated consistent earnings and, usually, have long-term growth potential.

board of directors   A stockholder-elected committee responsible for ensuring that a company is managed according to the best interests of its stockholders.

book value   The dollar value of a company's assets minus its liabilities. Book value per share is the company's book value divided by the number of its common stock shares outstanding.

bond   An interest-bearing certificate of public or private indebtedness.

bonus account   A passbook-type savings account paying .25 to 0.5 percent higher than the rate on a regular passbook account provided that a minimum required balance or a minimum holding period is maintained or that additional specified deposits are made regularly.

broad form   A type of homeowners insurance policy (often called HO-2) that covers property against nearly all perils except landslide, flood, and earthquake.

broker   One who acts as a selling and/or buying middleman for securities, insurance, or real estate. (See also "registered representative.")

bull market   A securities market characterized by generally rising prices over a period of several months.

buyer's market   A market in which demand for a certain product is so low that the buyer has the definite advantage in price negotiations.

buy long   To invest in securities with the hope of selling them at a higher price in the future.

buy on margin   To buy securities with a partial payment and borrow the rest of the required cash from one's brokerage house.

calendar year   The 12-month period beginning January 1 and ending December 31.

call   A purchased option to buy, within a certain period of time at a price that has been agreed upon, 100 shares of a specified stock from the person who wrote the call.

call feature   A clause whereby a corporation reserves the right to buy back outstanding preferred stock or bonds, often at the issue price plus a specified premium.

cancellation   The termination of an insurance contract by either the insurer or the insured according to provisions set down in the contract.

capital   Cash or cash equivalents.

capital asset   For federal income tax purposes, any property other than that used in a trade or business; includes stocks, bonds, residences, personal automobiles, household furnishings, and jewelry.

capital gain   A gain derived from the sale or exchange of a capital asset.

capital gains distribution   A distribution to shareholders of all net capital gains realized by a mutual fund during its business year.

capital gains tax   The tax levied on capital gains made on sales or exchanges of capital assets held for more than one year.

capital improvements   For federal income tax purposes, improvements to a piece of real property that increase its value or materially prolong its useful life. (Expenses that are not capital improvements can be deducted in the year they are paid; deductions for capital improvements must be spread over the expected useful life of the improvement as directed by specific IRS regulations.)

capital loss   A loss incurred on the sale or exchange of a capital asset.

career   The course of a person's working life; a profession or sequence of related jobs.

carrying costs   The part of the finance cost that is charged by most creditors to cover costs incurred by loaning money or extending credit—billing fees, administrative expenses, and bad debt losses.

cash flow   The cash surplus generated from an investment irrespective of the amount of taxable profit involved.

cashier's check   A check drawn by a bank on itself.

cash surrender value   See "accumulated cash value."

cash value   See "accumulated cash value."

cash value life insurance   A type of life insurance policy, such as whole life or endowment, that offers a combination of decreasing term insurance and accumulation of cash savings.

casualty insurance   See "liability insurance."

ceiling rate   The maximum tax rate that may be levied on specified taxable transactions. Also, the maximum interest cost for certain types of consumer credit. Also, the maximum interest rate payable on some types of savings accounts.

certain and continuous annuity   An annuity payout option in which payments are guaranteed to the annuitant for life or to the annuitant's beneficiary for the balance of a specified period of time—often 5, 10, or 20 years—if the annuitant dies within that time.

certificate of deposit (CD)   In normal usage, a time deposit requiring a larger investment and yielding a higher return than a normal savings account.

certificate of title   A document giving an attorney's opinion on the condition of the title to a piece of property and describing the limiting restrictions placed on the title by past owners.

certified check   A check certified to be backed by adequate funds by the bank upon which it is written.

certified public accountant (CPA)   An accountant who has fulfilled local, state, and federal requirements and is therefore allowed to represent himself or herself to the public as a certified accountant.

charge account   A form of consumer credit whereby purchases are financed by the retailer via one of several methods.

charitable trust   A trust whose beneficiary is a qualified charity.

chattel   An item of real or tangible property other than real estate.

check   A written order presented by an individual to a bank to withdraw funds from the individual's account at that bank.

checking account   An individual's bank deposit upon which checks can be written to make withdrawals from this fund.

claim   A policyholder's demand for benefits in accordance with his or her insurance contract or another person's contract.

class A stock   A common stock with income rights but not voting rights.

class B stock   A common stock with both income and voting rights.

clearinghouse   In banking, facilities where checks are processed when the payer's and payee's bank accounts are not at the same bank.

closed-end fund   A mutual fund with a fixed number of shares to be bought and sold, like common stocks, over the counter or through organized exchanges.

closed-end plan   A plan offered by health expense associations whereby the insured is covered for treatment only at specific contracted hospitals. (See also "open-end plan.")

closing costs   The costs of transactions necessary to complete a real estate sale; these include credit reports, title search, and escrow duties.

club account   A special type of savings account developed by banks to enable customers to budget their savings for specific goals such as buying Christmas gifts.

codicil   A legal document used to revise parts of a will without rewriting the entire will.

coexecutor   One of two or more executors of a will.

cognovit note   A written promise to repay a debt, signed by the borrower, allowing a creditor to repossess purchased goods without going through legal channels if the borrower defaults on the payments.

coinsurance clause   For property insurance, a provision requiring the insured to buy insurance coverage for at least 80 percent of the value of the property being insured in order to receive full payment of claims up to the face amount of the policy. For health insurance (usually major medical policies), a provision requiring the insured to share with the insurance company expenses arising from a claim.

collateral   The security provided by a borrower for a creditor's loan in the form of either pledged assets or endorsement by a cosigner; if the debtor defaults on the payments, either the assets may be taken or the cosigner, if there is one, must complete the payments.

collateral trust bond   A corporate bond with specified assets pledged as collateral.

collision coverage   Automobile insurance that pays for collision damage to the insured's automobile regardless of fault.

commercial bank   All institutions (except mutual savings banks) that are commonly referred to as banks.

commission   A fee paid to an agent or employee for transacting some business or performing a service, usually a percentage of the money involved in the transaction.

commodities futures   Contracts for future delivery of economic goods, such as agricultural and mining products, at a predetermined price; these contracts are traded on commodities exchanges.

common stock   Securities representing an ownership interest in a corporation.

community property   Property held jointly by husband and wife; according to community property laws in some states, property accumulated during marriage (except through inheritance or gift) belongs equally to each spouse.

comparative negligence   A newly emerging legal theory that, in many accidents, both parties may be at fault and must share the costs proportionate to their degree of negligence.

compound interest   The interest earned on interest already paid on the invested principal when it is left to accumulate with the principal.

compound yield   The income realized on reinvested income from an investment.

comprehensive coverage   Physical damage coverage that protects an automobile against loss due to every possible peril except collision damage.

comprehensive form   A type of homeowners property insurance policy that is basically all-risk coverage.

condo conversion   The process whereby an apartment building owner obtains legal permits and sells the apartments, one by one, to individuals as condominiums.

condominium   An individually owned home in a multifamily apartment type of structure.

confession of judgment   An oppressive clause often found in installment sales contracts whereby the borrower waives in advance the right to representation by an attorney or to judicial processes if he or she defaults on the payments.

consumer price index (CPI) An economic index prepared by the U.S. Department of Labor to indicate the relative change in the prices of a selected group of consumer goods and services.

contingent beneficiary An individual or entity who receives death proceeds from a life insurance policy if the primary beneficiary dies before receiving the full amount of the proceeds.

contributions For federal income tax purposes, monetary and nonmonetary gifts made to qualified charities but not to private individuals.

contributory negligence In a negligence suit, a defense that the person suing is partly at fault. In the past, this defense, if proven, cleared the defendant of *any* liability for damages. (See also "comparative negligence.")

convertibles Various types of securities that can be exchanged for other forms of securities at a predetermined conversion ratio; convertible bonds and convertible preferred stock often may be converted into common stock.

conveyance A written document by means of which title to real estate is transferred from one individual to another.

corporation A business firm that has been chartered by a state, allowing it to become a legal entity responsible for its own debts and operations. The owners of a corporation are its stockholders.

cosigner An individual with a good credit rating who provides security for another person's loan through his or her endorsement. Also, an individual who signs a note jointly with one or more other borrowers.

coupon bond A debt obligation on which the bond holder collects interest by regularly sending a coupon to the bond issuer, who then makes the interest payment. (See "registered bond.")

coverage provisions The clauses within an insurance contract stating the conditions under which the insurer will make benefit payments, how much they may be, and how long they will continue.

credit bureau An organization owned by local creditors to collect credit information on individuals who utilize credit at the members' establishments (banks, retailers, and others).

credit card A card issued by a creditor as evidence that a consumer is authorized to purchase various goods and services up to predetermined credit limits imposed by the creditor.

credit life insurance A life insurance contract on a borrower in which the death benefit always equals the balance outstanding on his or her debt and which is used to resolve the debt if the borrower dies.

creditor One who extends credit.

credit rating A measure used by credit bureaus to determine an individual's ability or willingness to pay his or her debts; based on the individual's history of resolving debts and his or her current financial position.

credit union An organization composed of members with a common interest who bind together to offer loans to each other at rates lower than they might be able to obtain otherwise.

cumulative dividends Unpaid back dividends that must be paid to holders of preferred stock before any dividends are paid to holders of common stock.

current assets Cash, marketable securities, receivables, and inventories.

current liabilities Accounts payable, unpaid taxes, and other debts due within one year.

custodial gift A gift to a minor child from an adult who retains control over the gift, or grants such control to another adult, until the child reaches majority and can legally accept responsibility for the gift.

cyclical stock A common stock whose fluctuations in price and earnings per share typically show a rough correlation with some other economic cycle—commonly the three-to-five-year cycle of business expansion and recession.

daily interest Interest that is computed daily on the balance of a savings account.

death benefits See "benefits."

death tax Any tax paid because of a death-related occurrence; this tax is usually imposed by states. Examples are inheritance tax, legacy tax, and succession tax.

debenture A corporate bond or debt obligation on which the corporation promises that, if it fails to pay off its debt, the debenture holder has a right to all assets not pledged to mortgage or collateral trust bonds.

decedent A deceased person.

declarations Information given by the insured regarding characteristics such as age, sex, and marital status; these guide the insurance company in rate-making.

decreasing term insurance A type of life insurance whose face amount, or death proceeds payable, decreases each year the policy is in force. As a term policy, it offers no cash value buildup, but simply protection if the insured dies. The face amount may decrease an equal amount each year (uniform decreasing term) or just a small amount during the first few years the policy is in force and an increasingly larger amount in the later years (mortgage term).

deductible clause A provision in a property, auto, or health insurance contract that directs the insured to pay the amount of any loss up to a certain limit above which the insurance company will pay the balance.

deductions Expenditures that, as expressly provided by tax law and/or IRS regulations, can be deducted from gross income, adjusted gross income, or gross estate, when computing taxes. (See also "excess itemized deduction," "marital deduction," and "percentage standard deduction.")

deed A legal document used to transfer title (ownership interest) to property from one party to another.

deed of trust The security offered by a borrower to a lender in order to obtain a loan on real property. The deed is held by an independent third party (trustee) until the debt has been paid.

default Failure to fulfill the conditions of a contract (most commonly, by not making the scheduled payments on a debt).

defensive stock A common stock whose price and earnings per share typically remain relatively constant throughout economic recessions.

deferred income bond A type of bond on which interest income is not payable until several years in the future.

deferred profit sharing A program whereby a company sets aside a small fixed percentage of its profits in a trust fund and each employee is credited with a portion of the fund according to his or her wage or salary level and/or length of employment; often used as a supplement to, or a substitute for, a pension fund.

deflation A decline in the general level of prices.

degree of risk exposure A measure of the total potential monetary loss one might incur. (See also "risk.")

demand deposit   Another term for a checking account.

dependent   For federal income tax purposes, an individual who is recognized as a dependent by law (as are most close relatives and adopted or foster children), derives more than 50 percent of his or her support from a taxpayer, and has a gross annual income lower than the level at which he or she would be required to file a return. A child under 19 or a full-time student (no age limit) may also be considered dependent, no matter what his or her gross income, as long as the other two conditions are met.

deposit   Money pledged to show the sincerity of one's intention to buy. Also, the money a person places in a savings account or checking account.

depreciation   Decline in the dollar value of an asset over time and through use. For tax purposes, the dollar amount of annual depreciation may be computed differently from the actual decline in value.

depression   A time in the economic cycle when growth is at a standstill, and economic activity and employment are at very low levels; often defined as a depression when more than 10 percent of the labor force is unemployed. At such a time, levels of consumer and business demand are so low that, historically, prices and interest rates have declined.

devise   To give real estate (not personal property) through a will.

devisee   A recipient of real estate (not personal property) from a will. (See also "legatee.")

disability, partial   For disability insurance purposes, a condition brought about by an accident or illness that prevents a person from performing all of his or her usual job duties, although he or she may be able to do other types of work or perform a portion of the previous job.

disability, permanent   For disability insurance purposes, a disabled condition that will last for the rest of one's life.

disability, temporary   For disability insurance purposes, a disabled condition that a person can expect to recover from within a certain length of time.

disability, total   For disability insurance purposes, a condition brought about by an accident or illness that prevents a person from working at any job either temporarily or permanently.

disability waiver of premium endorsement   An endorsement stating that the insurance company will pay a policyholder's premiums if he or she becomes disabled and is unable to work.

disclosure statement   A printed document, in standard form and type, citing the various terms and conditions of consumer credit contracts as required by truth in lending.

discounted interest   A deduction from principal for finance charges at the time a loan is made. The remaining amount is repaid through installment payments.

discounted price   The price of a security (usually bonds) that has a market price less than its face value and accrues interest until it reaches its face value.

dismemberment   For insurance purposes, loss, or loss of use, of an arm or leg, part of an arm or leg, or one or both eyes.

disposable personal income   Income available for personal spending after payment of income and Social Security taxes.

distribution period   For an annuity, the period of time following the maturity date during which the annuitant receives regular (usually monthly) payments.

diversification   The principle of reducing risks by spreading your money among several different investment areas.

dividend   A share of profits distributed in cash to stockholders. (See also "stock dividend.")

Also, a share of surplus revenues allocated to the holder of a participating insurance policy; in reality, this is a refund of premium. (See also "nonparticipating policy.")

dividend clause A provision in a participating insurance policy to indicate to the policyholder the various ways in which annual dividends (returns of capital) may be paid: in cash, in credit to reduce premiums, in payments for paid-up additions or term additions, or in deposits left with the insurance company.

dividend yield For stocks, the annual cash dividend divided by the current market price of a security and expressed as a percentage. For savings accounts that pay dividends rather than interest, the same as the effective rate of interest.

dollar cost averaging A method of buying stocks in installments by investing the same fixed dollar amount in the same long-term growth stock at regular intervals over a long period of time, making the average purchase price per share less than the average price of all the transactions.

domicile Legal place of residence.

donee Recipient of a gift.

Dow Jones averages Numerical indicators of the movements of prices of certain groups of securities (utilities, industrials, transportation, and composite) on the NYSE. These averages are computed by Dow Jones Company, a provider of statistical information services.

down payment The initial amount of the purchase price of an item bought on credit that the purchaser pays in cash.

double indemnity A clause in a life or accident insurance policy that pays the insured double the ordinary insurance benefit payments if accidental death or dismemberment occurs in some specified way.

dual purpose fund A mutual fund with two separate classes of shares: those offering only income and those offering potential capital growth only.

earnings per share (EPS) The mathematical result of dividing the total after-tax earnings of a corporation by the total number of its shares outstanding.

economic sector A term used in this text to indicate broad economic categories for purposes of diversifying common stock portfolios.

effective interest cost See "effective rate."

effective rate The percentage figure representing the true cost of credit, based on the average outstanding amount of credit throughout the scheduled life of a credit contract. Also, the real or actual return one receives on an investment. (On a savings account it may be higher than the nominal rate if the interest is compounded more frequently than annually.)

effective yield See second definition of "effective rate."

efficient market theory A theory that, because of the relatively good flow of information, no one person can so manage a portfolio that it consistently outperforms the stock market averages.

election An option whereby the taxpayer may choose among two or more alternatives in certain areas of tax treatment.

emergency cash reserve See "emergency fund."

emergency fund An amount of money placed in a liquid investment medium as a reserve to handle possible financial calamities; also called an emergency cash reserve.

emotions Feelings (such as fear, greed, joy, and sorrow) as opposed to rational thought.

encumbrance A liability or claim placed against property.

endorsement   A change in or an addition to an insurance or annuity contract, made in writing and attached to the policy itself. Also, the signature of a person (cosigner) with a good credit rating who agrees to complete payment on a secured loan if the borrower defaults on the loan. Also, the payee's signature on the back of a check. (See also "blank endorsement" and "restricted endorsement.")

endowment policy   A type of cash value life insurance in which savings accumulate more rapidly than in other types of similar insurance.

Equal Credit Opportunity Act   Set of laws prohibiting sexual or marital discrimination in lending practices.

equity   The amount of one's investment in an ownership position. In regard to real property, it is calculated as the market value minus claims against the property, such as a first mortgage balance.

ERISA   Employees Retirement Income Security Act of 1974, which established minimum federal levels of acceptability for private pension plans.

escape clauses   Clauses inserted in contracts to enable either or both parties to declare the contract null and void if certain conditions are not met.

escrow   A deed, bond, money, or piece of property placed in the safekeeping of a third party until the first and second parties to a transaction have successfully completed it.

estate   One's ownership interest in all forms of property. Also, the financial resources and personal assets left upon death.

estate tax   A tax levied on the transfer of rights to property in an estate.

estimated tax   Amount of income tax (paid in quarterly installments) on current income not subject to withholding.

evasion   Unlawful failure to pay all or part of one's income taxes. (See also "avoidance.")

excess itemized deduction   A deduction against adjusted gross income in excess of the zero bracket amount.

exchange   An organized market for trading securities. Also, the giving or taking of property for remuneration other than money and/or debt obligations.

excludable items   Income items that are not included in gross income for tax purposes.

exclusion   For insurance purposes, a condition under which insurance protection is not provided. Also, for federal income tax purposes, an income item that has no tax liability.

exclusive listing   Real estate offered for sale through only one realtor. (See also "multiple listing.")

exculpatory clause   A clause included in a trust or will absolving trustees and executors of blame for mistakes (usually of omission) that have minor consequences.

ex-dividend   Without dividend. A buyer of a stock with this notation cannot receive the current dividend, but will receive the next declared dividend.

executor (executrix)   The individual appointed in a will and approved by a probate court to administer the disposition of an estate according to directions in the will.

exemption   For income tax purposes, the amount a taxpayer is allowed to deduct—for himself or herself, for each dependent, and for certain special circumstances such as the blindness of a spouse—the total of which is deducted from income to determine taxable income.

expansion   A period of economic growth characterized by increases in employment, productivity, incomes, profits, and general prosperity.

extended coverage   A clause providing protection against additional perils; it is appended to normal fire insurance contracts. (See "apportionment clause.")

face amount   See "face value."

face value   For insurance, the dollar value that expresses coverage limits; it appears on the front of the policy. For a bond, the value at which it can be redeemed at maturity. (See also "par value.")

Fair Credit Billing Act   Set of laws specifying acceptable billing practices for creditors and overturning the holder in due course doctrine.

Fair Credit Reporting Act   Set of laws specifying appropriate credit bureau practices and granting limited consumer access to bureau files.

fair market price   The amount of money a buyer is willing to offer and a seller willing to accept (assuming both are fully informed and act voluntarily and intelligently).

Federal Deposit Insurance Corporation (FDIC)   A government agency insuring savings deposits of Federal Reserve member banks and of other banks that seek their protection.

Federal Housing Administration (FHA)   A division of the U.S. Department of Housing and Urban Development established by Congress to provide mortgage and home improvement loan insurance to private lenders. It insures loans but does not make them.

Federal Insurance Contribution Act (FICA)   An act that combined Social Security old age, survivors, disability, and hospital insurance taxes into a single tax.

Federal Reserve System (FRS)   The federal banking system authorized by the U.S. government. It is controlled by a central board of governors (**Federal Reserve Board**) and has a central bank (**Federal Reserve bank**) in each of 12 districts. It has wide powers in controlling credit and the supply of money and in regulating and supervising its member banks.

Federal Savings and Loan Insurance Corporation (FSLIC)   This organization offers the same deposit insurance programs for savings and loan associations as the FDIC does for banks.

Federal Trade Commission (FTC)   The federal regulatory agency charged with responsibility for policing unfair trade practices.

Federal Unemployment Tax Act (FUTA)   This act created the Social Security unemployment insurance tax.

fiduciary responsibility   The responsibility entrusted to a third party by a first party to be carried out according to the wishes of the first, for the benefit of the second; trust responsibility.

finance charge   The fee, consisting of both interest and charges for carrying costs, that is paid by a borrower for the privilege of using credit.

financial life cycle   The changing financial needs as your age and family circumstances change.

financial responsibility laws   State laws requiring that the operator or owner of a motor vehicle give evidence of ability to pay, by means of either insurance or personal financial assets, claims against him or her arising from the operation of that vehicle. Requirements of these laws differ from state to state but normally apply only to drivers who have had a previous accident requiring them to pay damage or injury claims in excess of certain minimums.

financial lease   A new type of installment sales contract.

"first dollar" coverage   Insurance coverage that begins with the first dollar of expense; 100 percent of all losses are reimbursed.

first-in, first-out (FIFO)   A technique used by savings institutions to compute the interest they owe on the balance in a savings account. (The first money deposited is considered to be the first money withdrawn.)

first mortgage   The senior security (in the form of real property) offered by a borrower to a lender to obtain a loan on a piece of property.

fixed amount option   An annuity payout option in which the monthly benefit level is selected by the annuitant; payments are made by the insurance company to the annuitant or his beneficiary until the principal and accrued interest are exhausted.

fixed annuity   Guaranteed income, received at regular intervals, for which the basic amount of each payment has been fixed in advance; there may be minor variations due to interest rate changes.

fixed assets   Property not easily convertible into cash—i.e., furniture, clothes, cars, and real estate. (See also "monetary assets.")

fixed costs   In any economic analysis, those costs that must be incurred whether or not there are any variable operating costs.

fixed expenses   On a budget or income statement, those expenses (such as monthly rent or mortgage payments) that must be paid at regular intervals and in fairly set amounts.

fixed income investment   A type of investment in which the dividend, interest, or rental income is contractually fixed, either until maturity or in perpetuity.

fixed period option   An annuity payout option in which the annuitant selects the period of time for which he or she wishes to receive benefits; the insurance company computes the monthly benefit amount by calculating the interest expected to accrue over the life of the declining principal balance; also known as the "installment refund option."

flexible payment mortgage   A mortgage in which the level of payments is tailored to the borrower's financial circumstances.

floater   An insurance policy covering property not only while it is in one's home but also wherever it may be transported.

forcible entry detainer statutes   Laws often used by landlords to evict nonpaying tenants.

foreclosure   The legal process by which a lender, in case of a mortgage payment default by the owner of mortgaged property, can force the sale of that property in order to recover the money he lent on it.

Form 1040   The standard federal income tax return form used by individuals to file separate or joint returns.

fortuitous loss   A loss that happens by chance and is, in both its timing and degree, unexpected.

free checking plan   A checking account with no minimum average balance requirements or monthly transaction charges.

front-end load   Commission and other costs deducted from the amount placed in an investment such as mutual funds, real estate syndicates, or oil and gas drilling funds.

full measure plus endorsement   On a property insurance policy, a clause stating that the sum of all the individual coverage limits shall apply as a blanket total coverage for your loss, without regard for the limit on any one category.

general partner   A member of a general partnership or a limited partnership (in which there are also limited partners).

general partnership   A partnership in which each member is fully liable for all partnership debts and has the right to manage the partnership's affairs.

gift tax   The tax levied by federal, state, and foreign governments on the transfer of financial assets as gifts.

glamour stock   Securities that are relatively high priced because of their attractive growth potential, but not necessarily because of their past growth record.

grace period   The length of time an insurance policy remains in force past its expiration date before a premium must be paid. Also, the period of time for reinvestment of a savings certificate before it reverts to the standard savings account.

graduated payment mortgage   A prenegotiated mortgage payment plan whereby monthly payments increase over time.

grantee   One who receives something.

grantor   One who gives something. (See also "trustor.")

gross estate   An individual's net worth plus existing life insurance proceeds and any portion of an annuity that a beneficiary may receive. For federal estate tax purposes, the amount from which deductions are taken to find the amount of one's taxable estate.

gross estate tax   For federal estate tax purposes, the tax computed on the amount of one's taxable estate before the amount allowed for any credits (state death taxes paid or to be paid, the unified credit, certain estate taxes paid on an earlier estate, and foreign death taxes) is subtracted to find the amount of the net estate tax.

gross income   All income in the form of money, property, and services that is not, by law, expressly exempt from tax.

gross national product (GNP)   The total production of the nation in terms of goods and services for an expressed period of time, usually one year, as measured by their current market prices.

group insurance   Insurance (either health, life, auto, liability, or property) written for a specific group of people. A master policy is issued by the insurance company covering the whole group; members of the group are issued joinder agreements that tie them to the master policy. Reduced administration costs and savings due to favorable loss experience for the group as a whole generally make these policies less expensive than individually written policies.

growth stock   The stock of a small to medium-sized company that has experienced several years of above-average growth in earnings and appears likely to continue such growth.

guarantee   A signed promise obtained by a prospective borrower from someone whose credit worthiness is stronger than his or hers to make good a debt obligation if he or she defaults on it.

guaranteed cash value   See "accumulated cash value."

guaranteed renewable provision   A clause (found primarily in annual renewable term life insurance contracts and health insurance contracts) that prohibits the insurance company from refusing to renew coverage for the next coverage period until the insured reaches a certain specified age.

guardian   An individual appointed in a will or by court order to care for minor children or for an incompetent adult.

head-of-household   An individual, not necessarily married, who provides more than 50 percent of the support for at least one qualified dependent.

health expense association   A nonprofit organization that dispenses medical treatment and charges members a monthly, quarterly, or annual fee.

health/life agent   An insurance representative who sells health and life insurance policies.

health maintenance organization (HMO)   An organization created for the purpose of dispensing health care to members who pay an annual fee. These prepaid health care facilities, though privately operated, are funded by the federal government.

hedge   To protect oneself against a potential investment loss by making a counterbalancing transaction.

hedge fund   A mutual fund that invests in speculative stocks and uses many sophisticated trading techniques in an attempt to achieve an above-average return on investment in both bull and bear markets.

heir   One who inherits or is entitled to inherit property.

holographic will   A will written entirely in the handwriting of the individual making it.

homestead laws   Legislative acts passed in most states generally to (1) permit a family head to declare that his house and land are his family's homestead and therefore exempt from the claims of creditors and lawsuits and (2) protect the home for the benefit of his spouse and minor children upon his death.

homestead rights   The rights granted to citizens under homestead laws.

hybrid policy   A type of insurance policy that either combines features of both term and cash value insurance or offers a variable, higher guaranteed cash value.

implied warranty   Some states have implied warranty laws that require manufacturers to cover items normally expected to last a long time, even if they are not expressly covered by a written warranty.

incidents of ownership   See "rights of ownership."

includable items   For federal income tax purposes, items considered as part of gross income.

income averaging   A means whereby taxpayers who experience radical fluctuations in their incomes from year to year are allowed to spread their income evenly over a period of five years and avoid having to pay exceptionally high taxes in high income years.

income before exemptions   For federal income tax purposes, the amount of income remaining after all deductions have been taken.

income splitting   Various techniques used to shift income from an individual in a higher tax bracket to someone in a lower one in order to take advantage of lower tax rates.

income statement   A financial form that serves as a record of all income and expense transactions occurring over a specific period of time, usually one year.

income stock   A common stock whose high dividend yield and historical consistency in meeting its cash dividend payments make it attractive for investors seeking a high rate of steady income from their investment.

indemnity   Security against loss; insurance policies are contracts of indemnity because they ensure that a policyholder will not suffer a financial loss.

index   In economics, a numerical figure that describes relative changes in some quantity. Examples are the consumer price index and the New York Stock Exchange index.

individual retirement account (IRA)   A retirement program for employees, who may or may not be covered under other retirement plans. It enables such individuals to make tax-deferred investments.

inflation A rise in the general level of prices.

inflation guard policy A property insurance policy that automatically raises the coverage limits each year by 8 to 10 percent, supposedly to allow for rising costs.

inflation protection endorsement An addendum to a homeowners policy that places the burden of assigning the correct replacement value to your home (physical structure only) on the insurance company. Such an endorsement ensures that the insurance company will reimburse the policyholder for the actual replacement cost of the structure at the time of loss, regardless of the policy limits on the dwelling.

inheritance tax A tax based on the value of property received by an heir; it can be paid either out of the estate or by the heir.

installment debt A debt resolved in two or more payments made at regular intervals over a period of time.

installment purchase agreement A type of installment sales contract.

insurable risk A potential financial calamity that insurance companies deem profitable to insure; normally, such a risk will not be associated with a possible widespread disaster such as an earthquake, and the amount of the potential loss must be easily measurable.

insuring clause A provision in an insurance contract designating the benefit to be paid and the perils insured against.

interest A charge made for allowing someone else to use one's money, usually a percentage of the amount being used. Specifically, for a borrower, the cost of borrowing money; for an investor, the payment received from a bank or similar institution for lending money to it.

interest adjusted method A method of determining and comparing the cost of life insurance that considers the time value of money.

intestacy Absence of a valid will.

Internal Revenue Service (IRS) The U.S. government agency that directs the collection of federal taxes.

investment company A mutual fund. Also, a real estate investment management company.

investment profit The amount of money an insurance company or other financial institution may earn from the investment of its cash reserves in excess of its investment expenses.

issued stock Capital stock issued in exchange for money, claims to money, or other considerations.

jacket provisions The clauses in an insurance contract that state what the insured must do to qualify for insurance benefits.

joint-and-survivorship annuity An annuity payout option that specifies a certain payout level for two joint annuitants while alive and, usually, a lower payout level for the surviving annuitant after the death of the other.

joint owners Two or more individuals possessing ownership interests in the same property. (See also "joint tenants," "tenants by the entirety," and "tenants in common.")

joint return A method of reporting federal income tax whereby a husband and wife file on the same form.

joint tenants Two or more persons each of whom owns a percentage, but not a specific piece, of some form of property; each may dispose of his or her share without the permission of the other(s). Upon the death of one owner (joint tenant), the surviving owners (joint tenants) assumes full ownership of the assets, regardless of what was specified in the decedent's will.

joint tenants with right of survivorship (JTWROS) Same definition as "joint tenants." The "WROS" is included to help explain the term to a layperson.

joint venture A business agreement between two or more individuals or corporations to set up and operate a jointly owned business enterprise.

Keogh Act The federal Self-Employed Individuals Tax Retirement Act of 1963. It enables self-employed persons to make tax-deferred retirement investments.

landlord The owner of a property offered for rent to tenants.

last in, first out (LIFO) One of the techniques used by banks for computing the interest they owe on the balance in a savings account. (The last money deposited is considered to be the first money withdrawn.)

lease An agreement entered into by lessee and lessor whereby the lessor makes available certain property to the lessee under specific conditions for a rental fee; also known as true lease.

leasehold clause A clause covering a renter for damages to any leasehold improvements he or she may have made. For example, if you have just repainted, at your own expense, an apartment that you rent, you can be reimbursed for that expense if fire or a similar peril destroys the apartment.

legacy A gift of personal (not real) property made in a will. (See also "bequest.")

legatee A recipient of a gift of personal (not real) property made in a will. (See also "devisee.")

letter of last instructions The means by which individuals can give their survivors important information after their death (i.e., the circumstances they arranged for their burial and the whereabouts of their will and personal records). It is not a substitute for a will.

letters testamentary Probate court's certification of the legality of a will and approval of the qualifications of the executor(s).

level term insurance A form of life insurance that has no cash value; the face amount remains level over the entire policy period.

leverage The use of borrowed money to get a higher rate of return provided that the interest rate on the loan is lower than the rate of return on the investment.

liability The extent to which one may be subject to punishment under the law for interference with another person's rights as recognized in the Bill of Rights. Also, an obligation to pay one's current debts—bills, loans, balances due on charge accounts, or mortgages on a home.

liability insurance A form of coverage that protects a policyholder against claims derived from negligence on his or her part.

lien A legal claim to property in the event of payment default.

limited liability The concept under which an investor in certain business arrangements cannot lose more than the amount of the investment.

limited partner A member of a limited partnership.

limited partnership A partnership in which the limited partner members are liable for partnership debts only to the extent of their contributed capital and have limited voting rights to control the partnership affairs. (See "general partnership.")

limited payment life insurance   A form of cash value life insurance that spreads the cost of the policy over a fixed number of years rather than over the entire life of the policy; such a policy is used to restrict premium payments to the policyholder's earning years.

limit order   An order for a broker to buy a stock at the best possible price, provided that it does not exceed a certain amount.

liquid assets   See "monetary assets."

liquidation   The procedure by which a business (often bankrupt) sells its assets, uses the money from the sale to pay off its debts, and distributes what is left to the stockholders.

liquidity   The ease with which an investment can be converted to cash.

listed securities   Stocks or bonds that are traded on an organized exchange.

list price   See "asking price."

load   See "loading charge."

load fund   A mutual fund in which part of the purchase price of a share represents a sales commission.

loading charge   The sales commission plus certain distribution fees imposed on shares in certain mutual funds; also known as load.

loan clause   A provision (found only in cash value life insurance policies) that explains how the policyholder can borrow up to the total accumulated cash values from the policy.

loan endorsement   The signature of someone who is guaranteeing repayment of a loan if the borrower fails to repay the loan.

loan shark   A term for a disreputable source of borrowed money. Such lenders generally charge excessive interest rates and do not comply with government regulations.

long term   For federal income tax purposes, more than one year between buy and sell transactions.

low balance method   A method of computing quarterly interest on a savings account; it applies the percentage rate against the lowest balance in the account for the quarter.

major medical   A term to describe a type of health insurance plan that insures against catastrophic health care situations.

manufactured home   Once called mobile homes, any housing built in a factory and then moved to its site and assembled onto the foundation.

margin account   A stock brokerage account that allows an investor to buy on margin (borrow investment funds from a broker) at the investor's discretion; subject to margin deposit requirements set by the Federal Reserve Board.

marginal tax rate   The highest tax rate at which a portion of one's taxable income is taxed; also called "marginal tax bracket."

margin deposit requirements   Minimum down payment levels, expressed in percentages, for the purchase of stocks and bonds; they are set down by the Federal Reserve Board and changed periodically, depending on FRB policy.

margin loan   A loan from a stock brokerage house, with purchased securities held as collateral.

marital deduction   For federal estate and gift taxation purposes, this deduction allows one to transfer, free of taxation, to one's spouse portions of one's separate property.

marketable securities   Securities that have been cleared by the SEC and/or the appropriate state authority for sale on public securities markets.

market-maker In the over-the-counter markets, a brokerage house that carries an inventory of a certain stock and stands ready to buy or sell that stock at its specified prices.

market value The dollar value one could realize on property if one were to sell it.

mature growth stock The stock of large, stable companies whose earnings growth averages less than about 8 percent a year.

maturity The period of time for which credit, an insurance contract, or a mortgage loan is written. Also, the minimum amount of time one must hold an investment in order to realize the rate of return anticipated when the investment was made.

Medicare A health care reimbursement plan sponsored by the federal government; it is available to people over age 65 and others who receive Social Security disability benefits.

minimum balance plan A checking account in which no charges are levied if certain minimum balances are maintained.

money market The colloquial term for the mechanism whereby lendable funds are traded in the form of short-term bonds or other debt securities.

money market fund A mutual fund that invests in instruments such as bank certificates of deposit and short-term government bonds.

monetary assets All property, owned by a person or a business, that can easily be converted into cash at a readily determinable fair market price such as savings accounts, stocks and bonds, and cash value life insurance; also called liquid assets. (See also "fixed assets.")

mortality table A set of statistics indicating how many people per thousand die at various ages. It can be used to determine one's life expectancy at any age.

mortgage The security offered by a borrower to a lender in order to obtain a loan on real property. (See also "first mortgage" and "second mortgage.")

mortgage bond A debt obligation, issued by a corporation, that has specific real estate assets pledged as collateral.

mortgagee clause A provision in a property insurance contract that defines the obligations and powers of the mortgagee if there is a mortgage outstanding on the insured property.

mortgage term policy See "decreasing term insurance."

multiple line insurance A policy covering more than one type of insurance need (such as liability and property insurance) together in one policy.

multiple listing A mechanism for offering real estate for sale through more than one realtor. (See also "exclusive listing.")

municipal bond A debt obligation issued by a state or local government agency. Such bonds are exempt from federal income taxes.

mutual fund An investment company that uses the proceeds from the public sale of its shares in order to invest in various securities for the benefit of its public shareholders. Also, the popular name for an open-end investment company.

mutual insurance company An insurance company owned by its policyholders. (See also "stock insurance company.")

mutual savings bank An association of savings account holders formed for the purpose of paying out all operating profits to account holders in the form of dividends rather than interest.

National Association of Securities Dealers (NASD) An organization that provides for the self-regulation of securities dealers, particularly those that are not members of an exchange.

negligence For liability insurance purposes, any careless act on the part of the insured for which he or she may be subject to punishment under the law. For federal income tax purposes, intentional disregard of tax regulations but without intent to defraud.

negotiable investment An investment that can be sold.

negotiation The give-and-take process between two or more parties to make a transaction.

net asset value The total value of an investment company's liabilities subtracted from the total of its cash plus the market value of its securities. Also, the listed bid price of a load fund.

net asset value per share The net asset value of an investment company divided by the number of its shares outstanding.

net estate tax The amount resulting from subtracting certain allowable credits (state death taxes paid or to be paid, certain gift taxes, certain gift taxes paid on an earlier estate, the unified credit, and foreign death taxes) from the gross estate tax.

net income Revenues minus expenses, taxes, interest paid, and depreciation.

net income per share See "earnings per share."

net worth The difference between assets and liabilities for a person, family, or business. If the dollar value of assets is greater than that of liabilities, there is a positive net worth. In a business, net worth may also be known as "partnership share" or "owner's equity."

New York Stock Exchange (NYSE) The largest stock exchange in the world.

no fault A method of dealing with auto insurance liability claims that reimburses the claimant up to certain limits regardless of who is at fault.

no-load fund A mutual fund that charges no sales commission on the purchase of its shares because the fund itself buys and sells its shares to the public without salespeople.

nominal rate The rate of interest stated for an investment. See "effective rate."

nonforfeiture option An option that gives a life insurance policyholder who has allowed his or her policy to lapse the right to take the policy's cash value in either cash, extended term insurance, or reduced paid-up life insurance.

nonparticipating policy An insurance contract that pays no dividends.

non-waiver agreement A provision in an insurance policy stating that the insurance company can investigate a claim without invalidating the terms of the contract.

no-par stock A stock issued with no assigned face value.

note A signed promise to resolve a debt.

NOW account A checking account that pays interest, but that can require advance notice of withdrawal.

nuncupative will A will made orally.

occupational disease A disease caused by the nature of one's job.

odd lot A block of shares smaller in number than a round lot, which is the amount (a multiple of 100) usually traded at one time.

offering price See "asking price."

open-ended credit Charge accounts and credit cards.

open-end fund A mutual fund that continually sells and redeems its shares according to investor demand and has no limits on the total number of shares to be bought or sold.

open-end plan A plan offered by health expense associations whereby the insured may receive treatment at any hospital. (See also "closed-end plan.")

oppressive clauses   Conditions set forth in a sales contract that can give a lender an unfair advantage over the borrower in default circumstances.

option   See "put" or "call."

ordinary life   A cash value life insurance policy for which one pays premiums either for life or until the policy is surrendered; also called whole life.

origination fee   A fee (usually 1 to 2 points) often charged by lenders to write loans.

other insurance clause   A clause stating that when more than one insurance company covers the same loss, each pays a share of the expense in proportion to its share of the total insurance coverage for the loss. Also called "pro rata clause" in some types of policies and is one of prorating clauses in disability income policies.

outstanding balance   See "balance outstanding."

overdraft   The excess amount when checks are drawn for more than the balance in a checking account.

overinsurance   Insurance in an amount that exceeds the amount of potential loss.

over-the-counter (OTC)   A means of trading shares of a company not listed on an organized stock exchange.

package plan   A checking account that includes the availability of certain other bank services for a low monthly charge.

package policy   An insurance contract (normally property) that combines several types of coverage. A homeowners policy, for example, combines property coverage with liability and medical coverage. Also, a type of policy that offers a single liability limit and covers more than one residence and one or more automobiles.

paid-up addition   An amount of prepaid cash value life insurance coverage that can be purchased with one policy dividend.

paid-up insurance   Life insurance on which no further premium payments are due.

paper profit   Profit yet to be realized on held securities because no buying or selling transaction has taken place.

par value   The face value assigned and printed on a security certificate. It originally signified the price level below which a company would not offer its shares to the public. Also, the value of a bond at maturity.

participating policy   An insurance policy that returns a portion of the premium, in the form of dividends, to the policyholder at the end of the policy period.

partnership   A legal relationship between two or more individuals acting together as owners of an enterprise. (See also "limited partnership" and "general partnership.")

passbook account   The standard savings account offered by a bank or savings and loan association; it usually offers the lowest interest rates of the various types of available accounts.

Pension Benefit Guaranty Corporation   The organization established by ERISA to guarantee certain levels of benefits of private pension plans for workers.

pension fund   The amount of financial resources set aside to provide income benefits at a future date, usually upon retirement.

personal loss experience   A record of the total amount of money an individual has had to pay because of damage or loss due to perils that have occurred.

P&E ratio   The ratio (expressed as a multiple) of the price of a share of stock to the company's earnings per share.

point In regard to a mortgage loan, an extra service charge initially deducted from it in addition to the regular interest cost; one point is equal to a front-end service charge of 1 percent of the loan amount. In regard to stocks and other securities, a unit used in quoting their price changes. For insurance companies' safe driver plans, values allocated to certain types of auto traffic violations; the number of points a motorist accumulates over a specified period of years is one factor used to determine his or her premium rate.

policy period A specified period of time over which an insurance policy is to remain in effect. It may or may not be renewable for additional periods depending on the terms of the contract.

portfolio The investments held by an individual or by an organization such as a mutual fund. Often narrowly defined to include only stocks and bonds.

power of attorney Written authorization from a person enabling someone else to perform binding legal acts on his or her behalf.

power of appointment A legal means whereby a surviving beneficiary is given the power to determine how the income and proceeds of a trust shall be distributed upon his or her death.

precomputation Procedure by which a borrower receives the principal amount in full and pays back an amount equal to the principal plus finance charges.

preferred risk An individual whose loss experience is good; a situation that has a low degree of risk exposure.

preferred stock A stock featuring a fixed dollar income and, if the company has any earnings, a claim to earnings and assets before the claim of common stock but after that of bonds.

premises A specific location (i.e., land and the buildings thereon) identified in an insurance contract.

premium Money paid for insurance protection or to buy an annuity.

premium payment clause A provision in all insurance contracts stating that premiums may be paid annually, semiannually, quarterly, or monthly.

prepaid interest Interest paid in advance of the due date.

prepayment penalty A fee levied by a lender, on loans paid off before maturity, to reimburse himself for interest lost.

previous balance method The method of calculating credit charges on open-ended credit account balances whereby interest is calculated on the balance outstanding at the beginning of the billing period.

price earnings ratio See "P/E ratio."

primary beneficiary An individual or entity entitled to receive the benefits of an insurance policy or annuity upon the death of the insured. (See also "contingent beneficiary.")

primary offering The sale of previously unissued stock by the issuing company, through investment bankers and brokerage houses, to the investor.

primary market The means whereby new common stock is offered for sale to the public and the net proceeds go to the issuing corporation.

prime rate The lowest loan interest rate charged by all banks at any given time. It is usually available to special customers.

principal The total amount originally invested, including equity and borrowed portions. Also, a major owner of a business enterprise. Also, the face amount of a mortgage loan.

probate process   The judicial procedure for establishing the validity of a will and ensuring that it is fully and properly executed.

professional corporation   A special form of incorporation for doctors, lawyers, accountants, and other professionals.

progressive tax   The system whereby an increasing tax rate is levied on each successive bracket or amount of taxable income. (See also "regressive tax.")

promissory note   A written promise to resolve a debt obligation.

proof of loss   A written statement of a loss submitted as a claim to an insurer.

property/casualty agent   An insurance representative who sells property and casualty insurance policies.

pro rata clause   See "other insurance clause."

prospectus   A publication issued by a company to describe the securities to be offered for public sale and under what conditions they will be offered, as well as the prospects for company performance.

protection period   The length of time over which insurance benefits may be given.

proxy   The means by which stockholders authorize others to exercise their voting rights in their absence, according to their direction.

purchase agreement   A written document between a buyer and seller giving the terms of a sale transaction. It consists of a sales contract, note, and credit life and/or disability insurance policy.

put   A purchased option to sell to the person who wrote the put 100 shares of a specified stock within a certain period of time at the price specified in the contract.

rate-making   Establishing prices of insurance contracts.

rate of return   Measurement of the profitability of invested resources; it is usually expressed as a percentage rate of gain or loss per year on the amount invested; also known as "return on investment" or as the "yield."

real estate investment trust (REIT)   An unincorporated association that invests in real property or mortgages and sells its shares to the general public.

real property   Land and anything permanently fixed thereon.

recession   A period of reduced economic activity during which unemployment rises, productive capacity becomes increasingly idle, and income profitability and general prosperity lag.

reciprocal   An organization offering insurance protection to its members, who pay a proportionate share of any loss that befalls them. Instead of charging premiums based on expected loss, as is typical of insurance companies, reciprocals prorate the actual loss over their members.

refinance a mortgage   To take out a new mortgage on a mortgaged piece of property, often at a lower rate of interest than on the old mortgage, and use the proceeds to pay off the old mortgage.

refund annuity   An annuity payout option that returns to a beneficiary the principal balance remaining at the death of an annuitant.

registered bond   The most commonly issued bond, in which the company automatically mails interest payments to the bond's current owner. (See also "coupon bond.")

regressive tax   A tax that is the same rate regardless of one's level of taxable income. (See also "progressive tax.")

remaindermen   Individuals who are to receive the assets of a trust upon its termination.

renegotiable rate mortgage   A series of three- or five-year mortgages, where the initial fixed rate is renegotiated at each three- or five-year interval.

renewable term insurance   A life insurance policy that has no cash value and may be renewed by the policyholder at the end of the policy period for another policy period of the same duration; a five-year renewable term policy, for example, would have to be renewed every five years.

rent   Payment one receives for allowing someone else to use one's property.

replacement cost   See "replacement value."

replacement cost endorsement   See "inflation protection endorsement."

replacement value   The amount of money that would have to be paid today to replace an object with a new one; this value is acceptable to property insurers only when used to determine the amount of insurance needed for physical structures such as the home. Also called replacement cost.

repossession   Procedure by which a creditor takes back purchased goods when the buyer defaults on the payments.

residual disability insurance   Insurance that pays you if you are disabled according to what you are capable of earning after being disabled as it relates to what you earned before the disability.

restricted endorsement   A statement written by the endorser on the back of a check (usually above his or her signature) to specify to whom the check is payable or to what account it is to be deposited. (See "blank endorsement.")

résumé   A one- or two-page outline summarizing for potential employers a person's biographical data that relate to the job being sought.

retained earnings   Corporate profits that are not paid out in cash dividends, but are reinvested in the company to foster its growth.

retirement income credit   A beneficial federal tax treatment of certain forms of retirement income such as annuities, pensions, interest, rent, and dividends.

reverse amortized mortgage   A monthly payment to the homeowner by a mortgage lender, using the home equity as collateral, where the monthly payment amounts are accumulated as a mortgage against the house, to be repaid when the house is sold.

return on investment   See "rate of return."

rider   An attachment to an insurance policy amending or extending the policy's coverage.

rights   In regard to a piece of property, the ownership interest one has in it (e.g., mineral rights). In regard to securities, negotiable certificates evidencing the privilege given to stockholders to subscribe to a new issue at a predetermined cost that is generally below market price.

rights of ownership   Benefits available to the owner of an asset; also called incidents of ownership.

risk   The possibility of loss now or in the future. With regard to insurable risk, it is the chance of financial loss from perils named in the insurance contract. With regard to investment risk, it is the chance for financial loss due to uncertainty about the future.

round lot   A block of shares, usually in multiples of 100, for trading on the exchanges.

royalties Income, typically on a per unit basis, from the sale of certain rights—usually publishing rights to a book.

rule of 78 The most common method for determining what amount of finance charges should be rebated if a loan is paid off prematurely.

safe-deposit box A private box to which only you and the custodian (commonly a commercial bank or a savings and loan) have keys (both of which must be used to gain entry to the box) in which valuables and important documents are generally kept.

sales charge See "commission."

sales contract The portion of a purchase agreement designed to protect a creditor against defaults on payments.

sales tax A general tax levied (usually by state or local governments) on sales transactions.

savings accumulation plan A means of investing in a mutual fund at regularly scheduled intervals. In a contractual plan with penalty, all commission costs are levied during the initial payment periods. In a voluntary payment plan or a contractual plan without penalty, commission costs, if any, are levied only on the amount of each payment over the entire life of the investment program.

savings bond A savings certificate offered by the U.S. government; it is sold at a certain percentage of its face value and interest accumulates with it for a specified period of time until it can be cashed in for face value. It may also be offered by commercial banks.

schedule A statement of supplementary details appended to Form 1040. Also, a written or printed list, catalog, or inventory, such as that which may be used in an insurance policy.

scheduled floater A type of inland marine property insurance coverage that protects such specific, highly valued items as are described on the face of the policy.

scheduled property Personal property that is described and given an appropriate value, article by article, on the face of an insurance policy rather than lumped together under general property coverage.

secondary distribution The marketing of large blocks of already issued shares of stock in the same manner as new issues are handled; also called secondary offering.

second deed of trust Similar to a second mortgage except that foreclosure proceedings in the event of a borrower's default are easier to initiate and take less time.

second mortgage A loan specifically secured by one's equity in real property, which is subordinated to the equity interests of any first mortgage holder.

second-tier growth stock The stock of a corporation whose earnings growth averages better than 8 percent a year, but, because of its relatively small size for the industry, or other reasons, tends to sell for a relatively low P/E ratio.

secured loan A loan on which title to property is conveyed to the lender as security in the event of default.

Securities Exchange Commission (SEC) The federal agency charged with responsibility for regulating the securities markets and all publicly held investment companies.

Securities Investor Protection Corporation (SIPC) The federal agency that insures a brokerage customer's account for cash and securities held by the firm up to certain limits.

securities market A mechanism for the buying and selling of securities between investors; examples are the over-the-counter markets, New York Stock Exchange, and American Stock Exchange.

security   Property given, deposited, or pledged in a credit agreement to make certain the repayment of a debt. Also, an evidence of debt or of property (as a bond or stock certificate).

security agreement   Synonym for sales contract.

self-employment tax   A form of Social Security tax that is levied on self-employed individuals.

self-insurance   A personal emergency fund used to cover one's own losses instead of buying insurance.

seller's market   A market in which demand for a certain product is so great that the seller has the advantage in price negotiations.

selling costs   The expenses of selling an asset, such as a house; in the determination of capital gains, these may be added to the cost basis of the asset.

separate return   A method of reporting income of one spouse separately from that of the other spouse.

service contract   A written agreement whereby the service company agrees to offer certain specified (or unlimited) repair services for a certain period of time. Such contracts may either be part of the purchase transaction of an auto or appliance or be purchased separately.

settlement options   The ways that a life insurance or annuity policyholder or beneficiary may choose to have policy proceeds paid.

short sale   A trading technique in which an investor borrows shares of a security from a broker in the hope of selling them on the market when the price of the stock is high, buying them back when the price has dropped, and returning them to the broker after having made a profit.

short term   For federal income tax purposes, a period of one year or less between buy and sell transactions.

simple interest   Interest that is calculated only on the original amount of a loan outstanding, not on the average amount outstanding over the term of the loan.

single-limit liability   An auto insurance policy that combines bodily injury liability and property damage liability and pays up to the maximum limit on a per occurrence basis; it does away with the per person limit on bodily injury coverage, thereby expanding the protection offered.

special form   A type of homeowners insurance policy that covers basically all risks to a house but not to personal property.

specialist   One who works on the floor of a stock exchange to coordinate buy and sell transactions in a particular stock.

special plan   See "activity plan."

special situation stock   The stock of a corporation that does not easily fit one of the other classifications: growth, second-tier growth, mature growth, or cyclical.

special warranty deed   A deed guaranteeing that the grantor has not placed any encumbrances on the title.

speculate   To make an investment despite great uncertainty in the hope of achieving a substantial return.

statement of financial condition   See "balance sheet."

stock   Ownership interest (divided into shares) in the assets, earnings, and direction of a corporation.

stock dividend   The issue by a corporation of new stock certificates to current stockholders on a basis proportional to the number of shares each investor owns. These do not represent a distribution of earnings.

stockholder   One who owns part of a corporation as represented by the shares he or she holds.

stock insurance company   An insurance company owned by stockholders. (See also "mutual insurance company.")

stock outstanding   Shares of a company's stock that are held by the public; does not include any issued stock held in the company treasury. (See also "treasury stock.")

stock price tables   Tables in the *Wall Street Journal* and other newspapers that give daily prices and other information on common stocks.

stock right   See the second definition of "rights."

stock split   The division of outstanding shares of stock into a greater number of shares; essentially the same to the investor as a stock dividend except on a larger scale.

stop-loss limit   The maximum amount a policyholder would have to pay for his or her share of medical expenses under a major medical insurance policy.

stop order   An order to one's broker to sell a stock at the market when it reaches or goes below a certain price. Also called a stop-loss order.

stop payment   An order to a bank by a depositor not to honor a certain check written by the depositor.

straddle   A trading technique whereby a speculator buys both a put and a call on the same stock in order to be able to take advantage of any change in the price of that stock on the market.

straight life annuity   An annuity payout option offering the highest monthly payout level. Upon the death of an annuitant, however, any remaining principal balance is claimed by the insurance company; there are no benefits to a beneficiary.

subordinated debenture   A corporate bond that has relatively low security in that holders of such bonds can claim assets only after other creditors and bonds and bank debts have been paid.

surcharge   See "surtax."

surtax   A tax in addition to the normal income tax; it can be either graduated rates for brackets of taxable income or a flat rate; also called surcharge.

syndicate   A combination of individuals or organizations to accomplish an investment goal of mutual interest.

systematic withdrawal plan   A mutual fund payout option whereby an investor may draw regular cash payments from his or her investment by authorizing the fund to send a check for a specified amount at regular intervals until he or she authorizes a change or the money runs out.

taxable estate   For federal estate tax purposes, the amount on which gross estate tax is levied; it consists of the gross estate less ordinary and charitable deductions and any marital deduction.

taxable income   For federal income tax purposes, the amount of income, less exemptions, on which income tax is determined.

tax bracket   For federal income tax purposes, a segment of taxable income that is subject to a certain percentage of taxation (tax rate).

tax court   A court system created by the Constitution to rule on tax disputes.

tax credit   For federal income or estate tax purposes, an amount that may be subtracted directly from one's tax because of special tax law provisions, a previous tax overpayment, or a payment for another type of tax.

tax-deferred investment   An investment on which the payment of income tax owed is postponed.

tax exempt   Not subject to federal and/or state income tax.

tax-free money fund   A money market mutual fund that invests in tax-free instruments such as short-term municipal bonds.

taxpayer identification number   For an individual, the same as his or her Social Security number. For corporations, trusts, or partnerships, this is a specially issued number.

Tax Rate Schedules   A table from which you can calculate your federal income tax if you cannot use the Tax Tables.

tax shelter   An investment that offers certain income tax advantages.

Tax Tables   A table provided by the IRS from which most taxpayers can determine their income tax, once they have calculated their taxable income before exemptions.

tax write-off   An investment loss that can be offset against one's gross income when determining adjusted gross income.

telequote machine   An instrument that provides current market prices and other data for listed securities. It is usually available for investor use in broker offices.

tenants by the entirety   Joint owners of an asset who are husband and wife.

tenants in common   Two or more owners of an asset for which transactions are not legal unless all the owners give their signed permission.

term   The period of time for which an insurance policy is to be in effect.

term insurance   A type of life insurance that offers death benefit protection, but no investment cash value, for the duration of the contract.

termite inspection   Usually conducted before the purchase of a home to determine the physical condition of a house as it pertains to the presence of certain destructive insects, fungi, pests, and organisms.

testator (testatrix)   A person who leaves a will in force at his (her) death.

third-party insurance   Insurance that pays benefits to someone other than the insured (such as liability insurance).

thrift institution   Usually, a savings institution specializing in small personal loans. Savings accounts are not insured by a federal agency.

ticker tape   A continuous and instantaneous teletype printout indicating the price and volume of all transactions that occur on an organized exchange during trading hours.

tight money   Colloquial term used by the financial community to describe the scarcity of loanable funds. This scarcity contributes to high borrowing costs.

time deposit   An investment on which interest is earned according to the length of the investment. The principal is always fixed.

title   Ownership interest in property.

title clearance   Notification that title to a particular asset is free of encumbrances that would lock its sale or use.

title insurance   Coverage against loss of one's equity investment in real property if a flaw in the property's title is found.

title search   Inquiry into the nature of title to a piece of property and the status of any encumbrances on the title.

trader   An investor who takes advantage of short-term (usually daily or weekly) fluctuations in the prices of stocks.

transfer agent   An institution, typically a bank, that is authorized by a corporation to administer and record the transfer of its stocks or bonds between investors. Also handles shareholder recordkeeping for mutual funds, including money market funds.

transfer tax   A tax levied by some states and the federal government on the transfer of securities.

traveler's check   Used by people away from home as a more secure medium of exchange than cash and more readily negotiable than personal checks, these checks are purchased in advance at a financial institution.

Treasury bill   See "Treasury bond."

Treasury bond   A negotiable debt obligation issued by the federal government with a minimum face amount of $1,000 and a maturity greater than five years. Treasury bills and Treasury notes are similar except that they have shorter maturities.

Treasury note   See "Treasury bond."

treasury stock   Corporate stock that was originally issued to the public and has since been reacquired by the corporation to be either canceled or reissued at a later date.

true interest   See the first definition of "effective rate."

trust company   An organization offering professional expertise in trust management and estate administration.

trust   A legal contract for the management and control of certain assets held by one person for the benefit of another.

trustee   An individual or organization legally responsible for managing a trust. Also, the person who holds deeds of trust on properties until they are paid for.

trust fund   Financial resources put in the custody of an individual (trustee) by someone (trustor) for the benefit of someone else (beneficiaries and remaindermen); one person may fill more than one role, depending on the type of trust.

trustor   Individual who provides the assets that are set up in a trust.

umbrella policy   A type of liability insurance contract that extends sizable dollar amounts of coverage over many types of liability exposures, not just one.

underwriter   A person or firm who assumes the risk of selling a stock issue to the public. Also, an insurance agent qualified to write insurance agreements.

uniform decreasing term insurance   See "decreasing term insurance."

universal life policy   Begun in 1981, this type of insurance policy offers term insurance plus a variable investment fund.

unlisted stock   Stocks that are not listed on a national or regional stock exchange.

U.S. savings bond   See "savings bond."

unoccupied   For property insurance purposes, the condition of a building when the contents remain but the tenant is gone. (See also "vacant.")

unsecured loan   A loan on which the only collateral is the signed guarantee of the borrower.

utilities   Stock classification that includes all electricity, gas, telephone, and water companies.

vacancy allowance   The portion of rental fees that is used to offset any loss of revenue due to vacancies.

vacant   For property insurance purposes, the condition of a dwelling when both the contents and the tenants are gone. (See also "unoccupied.")

values   Fundamental concepts of importance (such as success or security) as opposed to interests and attitudes.

variable annuity   A regular lifetime monthly payment, the amount of which varies according to the performance of the securities held in the annuity company's portfolio.

variable costs   In any economic analysis, only those costs that are incurred in the actual operation and vary with the amount or level of operations. (See also "fixed costs.")

variable expenses   Expenses that vary from month to month or year to year and allow a person some control over their amount and timing. (See also "fixed expenses.")

variable mortgage   A mortgage in which either the interest rate or payment schedule can be varied upon the occurrence of certain conditions pre-agreed to by borrower and lender.

vesting   The process whereby an employee receives increasingly greater rights (usually as his or her length of employment increases) to retirement benefits based on contributions made to a retirement fund by his or her employer.

Veterans Administration (VA)   The federal agency charged with administering government-sponsored military veterans programs; one function is to guarantee lenders against losses due to default on VA-approved home mortgages taken out by veterans.

volume   For stock exchange purposes, the total number of shares of all companies traded on an organized exchange during a certain period of time such as an hour, day, or week.

W-2 form   The record received by an employee from his or her employer showing the amount of income earned and the amount withheld from his or her earnings during the year for income and Social Security tax purposes.

wage assignment clause   The means whereby a creditor is granted the right to have a borrower's employer withhold a portion of the borrower's wages if the borrower defaults on payments on a loan or an installment purchase; generally such action must be cleared by court order, but occasionally such a clause may be part of a sales contract. Also known as wage garnishment.

wage-earner plan   A section of the federal bankruptcy statutes that allows you to systematically resolve your debts under court supervision.

waiting period   On a disability income insurance policy, the length of time between the date of disability and the time when income benefits begin.

waiver   The voluntary surrender of a known right, claim, or privilege.

warrant   An instrument issued by a corporation giving to the holder an option to purchase a security at a predetermined price, usually within a specified but long-term period.

warranty   A guarantee, usually written and generally transferable to other owners, of the general reliability and quality of a product. Specifics vary from warranty to warranty. (See also "implied warranty.")

warranty deed   A deed guaranteeing that title to property is conveyed free of encumbrances.

when issued   A term used to describe transactions involving securities that have been authorized for issuance but have not yet been issued and delivered to the public.

whole life   See "ordinary life."

will   A written, legal document through which a person expresses the manner in which his or her estate is to be disposed of upon his or her death.

withholding   For federal income tax and Social Security tax purposes, the procedure whereby an employer pays a specified part of an employee's wages to the government to be applied against these taxes. Also, for federal income tax purposes, the process whereby payers of dividends and interest retain a portion of the recipient's payment and pay it directly to the government to be applied to this tax.

working capital   Investable funds that are not currently tied up in long-term assets; it is equal to current assets minus current liabilities.

yield   See "rate of return."

yield to maturity   The total return (compound annual rate) on a bond held to maturity, including both interest income and capital gain or loss.

zero bracket amount   A deduction of a flat amount against adjusted gross income; available to each individual taxpayer. In recent years, this amount has been built into the Tax Tables.

zoning   Legal ordinances used to restrict the uses to which specific pieces of property may be put.

Index

Personal Money Management